Debates in Medieval Philosophy

Debates in Medieval Philosophy: Essential Readings and Contemporary Responses aims to de-mystify medieval works by offering an illuminating, engaging introduction to the problems that medieval philosophers from Augustine through Ockham wrestled with. Each of the volume's 11 units presents a debate that will enable students to return to the primary texts prepared to think critically and imaginatively about them. Debates include:

- Does Anselm have a hierarchical or a flat conception of free will?
- Is Abelard's ethics conceptually impoverished?
- Does Avicenna teach that we acquire concepts through abstraction or emanation?
- What is Aquinas's purpose in writing the *Summa contra gentiles*?
- How sound are Ockham's criticisms of Scotus's theory of universals and individuation?

The essays newly commissioned for this volume will advance scholarship in medieval metaphysics, ethics, epistemology, logic, and philosophical theology, and in particular they will showcase what is philosophically distinctive and original in medieval philosophy. Students without experience in the history of philosophy will benefit from each unit's clear, sharply written introductions that supply the necessary background to approach the debates intelligently. In addition, the volume's general introduction elucidates the value of studying the history of philosophy through debate, in particular the history of medieval philosophy.

Students will find in these debates models that will train them to formulate their own critical evaluations of a wide range of philosophical texts by thinkers with diverse philosophical commitments.

Jeffrey Hause is Associate Professor of Philosophy at Creighton University.

Key Debates in the History of Philosophy

New students to the history of philosophy risk equating a summary of an important philosopher as the final word on that thinker. Lost in the introductions and primers to the great philosophers are the complexities and range of competing interpretations that result from close readings of the primary texts. Unlike any other undergraduate introduction in this field, **Key Debates in the History of Philosophy** are designed to lead students back to the classic works so that they may better understand what's at stake in these competing viewpoints. Each volume in the series contains 10 to 15 interpretive issues, or sections, with two chapters included in each section. The first chapter is a re-printed well known journal article or book chapter. The second chapter either takes to task or builds upon the argument in the first article and is written by a different scholar especially for the volume. The result is a new kind of introduction, one that enables students to understand philosophy's history as a still-living debate, rather than a string of unearthed truths from the past.

Volumes in the series

Debates in Medieval Philosophy: Essential Readings and Contemporary Responses, edited by Jeffrey Hause

Debates in Modern Philosophy: Essential Readings and Contemporary Responses, edited by Stewart Duncan and Antonia LoLordo

Forthcoming

Debates in Nineteenth Century Philosophy: Essential Readings and Contemporary Responses, edited by Kristin Gjesdal

Debates in Medieval Philosophy

Essential Readings and Contemporary Responses

Edited by Jeffrey Hause

Routledge
Taylor & Francis Group
NEW YORK AND LONDON

First published 2014
by Routledge
711 Third Avenue, New York, NY 10017

and by Routledge
2 Park Square, Milton Park, Abingdon, Oxon, OX14 4RN

Routledge is an imprint of the Taylor & Francis Group, an informa business

Library of Congress Cataloging in Publication Data
Debates in medieval philosophy : essential readings and contemporary responses / [edited by] Jeffrey Hause.—First [edition].
pages cm.—(Key debates in the history of philosophy)
Includes bibilographical references and index.
1. Philosophy, Medieval. I. Hause, Jeffrey, editor of compilation.
B720.D43 2014

ISBN: 978–0–415–50541–3 (hbk)
ISBN: 978–0–415–50542–0 (pbk)

Typeset in Minion
by Swales & Willis Ltd, Exeter, Devon

MIX
Paper from responsible sources
FSC® C013604
FSC www.fsc.org

Printed and bound by CPI Group (UK) Ltd, Croydon, CR0 4YY

Contents

Contributors

E. J. Ashworth is Distinguished Professor Emerita at the University of Waterloo. Her many publications include *Language and Logic in the Post-Medieval Period* (Springer, 1974) and *Les théories de l'analogie du xiie au xvie siècle* (Vrin, 2008).

Deborah Black is Professor of Philosophy and Medieval Studies at the University of Toronto. Her recent work includes "Certitude, Justification, and the Principles of Knowledge in Avicenna's Epistemology" (in *Interpreting Avicenna: Critical Essays*, Cambridge, 2013) and "Avicenna's 'Vague Individual' and its Impact on Medieval Latin Philosophy" (in *Vehicles of Transmission, Translation, and Transformation in Medieval Cultures*, Brepols, 2012). She is author of *Logic and Aristotle's Rhetoric and Poetics in Medieval Arabic Philosophy* (Brill, 1990).

Jeffrey Hause is Associate Professor and Michael W. Barry Chair at Creighton University. He is the author of "Aquinas on Aristotelian Justice: Defender, Destroyer, Subverter, or Surveyor?" (in *Aquinas and the Nicomachean Ethics*, Cambridge, 2013). He is (with Claudia Eisen Murphy) translator of Aquinas's *Disputed Questions on Virtue* (Hackett, 2010), for which he wrote the commentary.

Bonnie Kent is Professor of Philosophy at the University of California, Irvine. In addition to her influential *Virtues of the Will: The Transformation of Ethics in the Late 13th Century* (CUA 1995), Kent has authored "Losable Virtue: Aquinas on Character and Will" (in *Aquinas and the Nicomachean Ethics*, Cambridge, 2013) and "Virtue Theory" (in *The Cambridge History of Medieval Philosophy*, Cambridge, 2010).

Cyrille Michon is Professor of Philosophy at the University of Nantes. Among his many publications are a French translation of the *Summa contra gentiles* books I-II (Flammarion, 1999) and *Prescience et liberté* (PUF, 2004).

Timothy B. Noone is an Ordinary Professor in the School of Philosophy at the Catholic University of America; his philosophical research focuses upon metaphysics and epistemology, particularly within the Franciscan tradition. He is co-editor, with Jorge J.E. Gracia, of *A Companion to Philosophy in the Middle Ages* (2003), co-editor on all five volumes of the recently completed *Opera Philosophica* of John Duns Scotus, and is currently working with the editorial team based at the University of Notre Dame editing Scotus's *Opera Theologica Parisiensia.* He is also a professional harmonica player in a blues and bluegrass band.

JT Paasch is Lecturer for the Bachelor of Arts in Liberal Studies program at Georgetown University. He is the author of *Divine Production in Late Medieval Trinitarian Theology: Henry of Ghent, Duns Scotus, and William Ockham* (Oxford, 2012).

Giorgio Pini is Associate Professor at Fordham University. He has authored multiple influential articles in medieval philosophy, including "Can God Create My Thoughts? Scotus's Case against the Causal Account of Intentionality" (*The Journal of the History of Philosophy*, 2011) and "What Lucifer Wanted: Anselm, Aquinas, and Scotus on the Object of the First Evil Choice" (*Oxford Studies in Medieval Philosophy*, 2013).

T. M. Rudavsky is Professor of Philosophy at The Ohio State University. Her volume *Time Matters: Creation, Time and Cosmology in Medieval Jewish Philosophy* appeared in 2000. She is the editor of three volumes: *Divine Omniscience and Omnipotence in Medieval Philosophy: Islamic, Jewish, and Christian Perspectives* (1984); *Gender and Judaism: Tradition and Transformation* (1995); and *The Cambridge History of Jewish Philosophy: From Antiquity to the Seventeenth Century*, co-edited with Professor Steven Nadler (April 2009). Her most recent book, *Maimonides* (2010) has appeared in the Wiley-Blackwell "Great Minds" series. In addition, she has written numerous articles on medieval Jewish cosmology and philosophical theology.

Ian Wilks is Associate Professor of Philosophy at Acadia University. Among his influential studies of Abelard are "Peter Abelard and his Contemporaries" (in *Handbook of the History of Logic*, Elsevier, 2004), "Abelard on Context and Signification" (*American Catholic Philosophical Quarterly*, 2007), and "Peter Abelard and the Metaphysics of Essential Predication" (*Journal of the History of Philosophy* 1998).

Thomas Williams is Professor of Philosophy at the University of South Florida. In addition to his many articles on the history of philosophy, Williams is editor of *Philosophy in the Middle Ages*, 3rd edition (Hackett, 2010, with Arthur Hyman and James J. Walsh) and co-author of *Anselm* (Great Medieval Thinkers, Oxford, 2009, with Sandra Visser).

Acknowledgments

The editors and publisher would like to thank the following copyright holders for permission to reprint material:

Hasse, Dag, "Avicenna on Abstraction," in Robert Wisnovsky (ed.), Aspects of Avicenna (Princeton: Markus Wiener, 2001), pp. 39–82. By permission of the publisher.

Harvey, Warren Zev, "A Third Approach to Maimonides' Cosmogony-Propheetology Puzzle," Harvard Theological Review 74 (1981): 287–301. By permission of the publisher.

Irwin, Terence, The Development of Ethics: A Historical and Critical Study, Volume 1 (2011). 9000w from pp.7–10, 516–526, 591–593, 597–599. By permission of Oxford University Press.

LaNave, G.F., "Knowing God through and in All Things," Franciscan Studies 67 (2009), 26--299. By permission of the publisher.

Langston, Douglas C., "Scotus on Intuitive Cognition," Synthese 96, 1, 1993, pp. 3–24. By permission of the publisher.

MacDonald, Scott, "Petit Larceny, the Beginning of All Sin: Augustine's Theft of the Pears," Chapter 4 in William E. Mann (ed.), Augustine's Confessions: Critical Essays (Lanham: Rowman and Littlefield, 2006).

Matthews, Gareth, "Wanting Bad Things," Chapter 13 of his Augustine (Malden: Blackwell, 2005). © 2005 Gareth Matthews

McInerny, Ralph, Aquinas and Analogy (Washington, D.C.: The Catholic University of America Press, 1996). By permission of the publisher.

Rogers, Katherin, Anselm on Freedom (Oxford: Oxford University Press, 2008), pp. 55–72.

Sokolowski, Robert, "Intentions and the Will: Aquinas and Abelard," in Sokolowski's *Moral Action: A Phenomenological Study* (Bloomington: Indiana University Press, 1985), pp. 208–214. By permission of the publisher.

Introduction

Debate in Medieval Philosophy

Why study medieval philosophy through debate? Why not single, in-depth essays on representative topics? Or, since this is the *history* of philosophy, why not employ a narrative to explain how key ideas arose, developed, and (at least many of them) came to influence our contemporary way of thinking?

To begin to answer this question, let's consider how students best learn in the classroom. Imagine that you are attending a course on, say, action theory. The professor insists on an unusual pedagogy designed to stimulate student involvement. In this class, there will be no days of straight lecturing; instead, everyone will be required to take a leadership role in class discussion. The professor structures the class so that students have to engage the arguments under discussion with all the tools that philosophy has to offer: There will be no passive learning. Therefore, the professor requires students to take the initiative to come up with their own arguments—or at least to articulate and explain other people's arguments—in a lively classroom setting that will involve everyone in the common project of trying to find plausible answers to the course's main philosophical questions. The course TA and senior undergrads are expected to take leading roles in finding objections and replying to them, but other students must participate as well. Only after the students have finished will the professor speak, and when she sums up the discussion and offers her own views she will also be required to address all the students' concerns.

As intimidating as this class will undoubtedly be (for both the students and the professor), it strikes you as fun and challenging. The topic for this week: Is free will a consequence of rationality? During the last class, students—especially the seniors—presented lively arguments for the positive side. The TA tried to formulate responses on the spot, but today has come up with better ones that he is now trying out on the class. At the last meeting, reading from a prepared note, one student made this argument:

> Humans have free will precisely because they're rational. Rationality is what distinguishes humans from non-human animals, and non-humans act entirely on instinct. A human, by contrast, considers alternative courses of action, assigning each a certain weight depending on how conducive it is to that person's goals, and we choose in keeping with the weight we give the alternatives. Because it's reason that assigns the weights, it's because of reason that we're free.

Another student then blurted (out of turn):

> That makes no sense. On your view, the more rational people are, the less free they are! That's because the more rational people are, the more clearly they see the best alternative and the more effectively they rule out worse alternatives. But if people are so clear-headed that they can't help but see which course of action is best, their acts are necessitated and so not free. So, if you're right, reason isn't the source of freedom—it's the enemy of freedom.

The teaching assistant, taking both student remarks into account, makes this considered reply:

> Reason is neither the source nor the enemy of freedom. It's true that we need reason to offer us alternative courses of action. But reason is in one respect no different from instinct: At the moment when it acts, reason is necessitated to have the thoughts it has. So, reason can't be the source of freedom.

Only after the students have raised their objections and tried out their replies does the professor herself offer an answer to the question.

Student-directed learning, active participation, creative and analytical thinking—this might sound like an innovative, forward-thinking model for a philosophy course. In fact it is, or rather it was, when it was first popularized in the later middle ages. It was called a "disputation," a form that characterized many higher-level courses in the medieval university as well as published works in philosophy, theology, law, and medicine. Just how this sort of exercise evolved is itself a debated matter, but at least one influence on the development of the disputation was the work of the philosopher Peter Abelard, and we do know the value *he* saw in debate. I'll turn to Abelard's own reasons for promoting debate below, although some of the pedagogical benefits of learning through debate should already be clear from the fictionalized example we have just seen. In any case, although we find debate in every period of philosophy, nowhere was it found institutionalized on such a mass scale as in the disputations of the medieval university. So, our learning medieval philosophy through debate already captures some of the spirit of the period.

Debate and Its Alternatives

Even if debate captures some of the spirit of medieval philosophy, that does not by itself show that it is an appropriate form for us to use in the contemporary university. Why study the subject through debate and not some alternative?[1] For example, telling the history of philosophy as a narrative has several advantages. The author of a narrative can explain how certain concepts or methods arose as a response to pressures or problems in the historical milieu. The author can then trace the development of those concepts and methods as successive philosophers refine them and apply them in innovative ways. Finally, we can see how the development of these concepts has come to influence our contemporary way of thinking. Likewise, a volume of longer single essays on key problems has clear advantages as well. Without the constraint of narrow word limits, and without the need to address the issues of its partner essay, the writer of a single essay can develop her thesis more fully, treating her topic in greater depth and more authoritatively. Finally, we might wonder why we should be spending so much time on any form that focuses on the *history* of philosophy when the point of studying philosophy is to *do philosophy* and not just report the ideas of people long dead. We should therefore read and write in the forms that best allow us to grapple with the philosophical problems of our current world (such as books, book chapters, and articles devoted to a philosophical problem of our own day). Historical sources are important chiefly insofar as they inspire us to employ old concepts, distinctions, and arguments to address the concerns of contemporary philosophy. Therefore, according to this line of thought, we should treat the history of philosophy as we do contemporary works: as sources for discussions about the problems we are ourselves grappling with. We are not ancient stoics or medieval monks. Their concerns are not the same as ours; and where they diverge, although learning about them may have a certain historical value, it cannot engage us as philosophers. Insofar as texts from the past can help us to solve *our* problems of philosophy, they are as useful as contemporary writings, and for the same reason.[2]

There is some truth in each of these claims, and that is why each of these alternative approaches is well represented among contemporary thinkers. However, it is important to study the history of philosophy through debate as well, since the debate form in particular helps us to see that studying the history of philosophy really is a way of doing philosophy. As I noted, some people have the impression that the history of philosophy may well be history but is not genuine philosophy. In their view, historians of philosophy report the development of other people's ideas and trace their influence on other philosophers, on politics, on literature, on science, and on popular thought. As valuable as this enterprise is, it is not the practice of philosophy.

Narrative approaches are most often responsible for this distorted understanding of the history of philosophy since they generally spend less time focusing on the detailed problems and arguments that constitute the foundations of so many philosophical discussions. Approaching the history of philosophy through debate requires the more consistent employment of the tools of philosophy.

We might initially be skeptical of this last claim, worrying that the debate form will lead us away from what's important in philosophy to focus instead on exegesis and philological issues. When two contemporary scholars offer opposing interpretations of Anselm on free choice, or Avicenna on abstraction, we may seem to be very far from the loftiest goals of philosophy —the pursuit of wisdom or the good life for human beings—and instead find ourselves bogged down in the most pedantic exercise of textual interpretation. Genuine philosophy engages in such activities as the evaluation of philosophical views as consistent or inconsistent, as consonant or dissonant with pre-philosophical intuitions. Philosophy develops illuminating distinctions to resolve problems that arise through ambiguity or unclarity. It develops taxonomic schemes to reveal the relations among elements in a philosophical system. It examines the explanatory power of competing theories in an attempt to discover which are more plausible. An interpretive debate may be interesting for historical or philological reasons, but it is something other than philosophy.

This objection seriously misunderstands the nature of debates among historians of philosophy, which require scholars to engage in the very same sorts of activities that those working on contemporary problems engage in. It is true that debating the correct interpretation of a philosophical text may call for historical and philological considerations. However, such debates also require scholars to determine which features of a historical figure's work are worth discussing and which are not. If we think, for instance, that Augustine's theft of pears from his neighbor's tree is just an example of excessive guilt over nothing, or an early example of the baneful effects of peer pressure, we would not give it much attention. On the other hand, if the episode teaches us something about the allure of evils and the common structure of all sin, or showcases a radically new account of motivation that explains perverse actions (the two alternatives debated in part I), it is likely to strike philosophers as well worth their attention. Scholars in the history of philosophy do not stop their philosophical practices with identifying worthy topics. Once they have done that, they must next weigh alternative interpretations based partly on consistency with the author's other views, as many of the essays in this volume illustrate (see, for instance, parts IV on Avicenna, V on Maimonides, and X on Scotus). These interpretations will also typically be guided by some version of the principle of charity, which privileges certain readings over others (for instance, those that take the author (a) to be correct rather than incorrect; (b) to have offered valid rather than invalid arguments; or (c) to have said something illuminating rather than something pedestrian). This sort of debate about the history of philosophy is therefore not an activity tangential to philosophy itself. A look at what these historical scholars do shows that they are involved in the same philosophical practices as those who work in contemporary fields, such as determining which views are correct, plausible, instructive, or interesting; evaluating arguments and models; and assessing methodologies for effectiveness.[3]

Although historians of philosophy employ their philosophical skills when they write on historical topics, the motivation for their investigation is not simply to put those skills to use. They could do that on any number of issues—not simply in the currently recognized canon of philosophical topics, but on such arcane matters as alchemy or hermeticism. Few thinkers, however, have the attitude that any topic will do, as long as they can put their philosophical skills to work. A historian of philosophy's inspiration comes chiefly from an interest in the problems of philosophy as they arise in a particular historical milieu. In other words, just as with their colleagues who work in contemporary philosophy, it is philosophical problems that inspire historians of philosophy. Philosophers with interests in virtue or moral psychology often become interested in Aquinas, whose treatments of these topics are rich and illuminating. Likewise, those with a passion for metaphysics often turn to Scotus, a creative problem solver and subtle critic of others' metaphysical positions. Thinking through Scotus and Ockham on universals, as JT Paasch does in chapter 21, is not just a preliminary to doing the "real" work of addressing the problem of universals. Nor is it a treatment of a quaint bit of medieval lore. When Paasch offers his critical analysis of Scotus and Ockham, he is at the same time addressing the problem of universals.

A volume treating topics in the history of philosophy in the single-essay form would of course have many of the advantages I've claimed for a volume of paired essays in debate. In fact, many single essays are written as contributions to ongoing debates. One obvious advantage of a volume that contains multiple contributions to a debate is that it allows those who are not expert in a field to enter more easily into that debate, since readers will have at their fingertips further relevant secondary literature. However, there is another advantage that I'll explain by returning to the example of Peter Abelard. Abelard found that many of the scholars of his era—even scholars of international renown—were content to repackage the views of great thinkers of the past and publish them under their own name. Abelard despised this practice, which he thought was a flight to the comfortable world of custom. To show that custom cannot advance the discipline, Abelard wrote a peculiar work called *Sic et non*, or *Yes and No*. In this work, he assembled a series of important questions that could be answered either yes or no. Under each question, he found authoritative texts that supported the "yes" answer and other authoritative texts that supported the "no" answer. The lesson he meant to teach was that trying to resolve these debated questions by appealing to an authoritative text from the past did not advance the discipline. Instead, scholars had to acknowledge the debate itself, noting the pros and cons of each side. They then had to use their own intelligence to evaluate the arguments for each side and settle on a resolution, or perhaps to re-envision the problem itself in the light of past debate to help make progress toward a resolution. In no case should one simply resort to custom, which was the refuge of minds that were asleep at best or cowardly at worst. Abelard's insight is a salutary reminder of the importance of debate for both newcomers to a field and for seasoned experts. When students new to a field first read a single study of a topic, they commonly find the author's interpretation quite plausible. Over time that reading becomes custom for them, and they treat other interpretations prejudicially, because those interpretations are at odds with the one they are used to. If students immerse themselves in the debate over the interpretation from the start, they will not fall prey to this trap. Debate also helps keep experts in a field from succumbing to lazy and undisciplined interpretations.

Why Debates in *Medieval* Philosophy?

Finally, we should ask why it is important to study debates about *medieval* philosophy in particular. In fact, there are several good reasons. In this period we find the classic statements of certain concepts, problems, or arguments whose complexity and lasting interest warrants debate. That is why this volume contains units that treat the will, a major medieval contribution to action theory and moral psychology (parts I and II). For similar reasons, this volume contains a unit on the problem of universals. Although the medievals were not the first to ask about the nature of universals and particulars, their inquiries into the topic pushed the discussion to new and sophisticated heights that are arguably unrivalled to this day. Therefore, chapter 21 explores the debate on this topic between Duns Scotus and William Ockham, two of the most ingenious contributors to this discussion. In addition, we find in medieval philosophy some sharp, innovative treatments of philosophical problems that can offer us insights for addressing similar problems in contemporary philosophy (such as Maimonides' or Aquinas's treatments of the relationship between revealed religion and philosophy, as we see in parts V and VIII). However, there is one particularly important reason it is important to study debates about medieval philosophy: to put to rest the pervasive idea that what goes by the name of "medieval philosophy" is actually religion or theology. Debate by contemporary scholars on the interpretation of medieval texts brings out the astute, creative, and philosophically rich character of these works, which are not just scriptural exegesis or systematic theology, even when they are rooted in Jewish, Christian, or Islamic scripture.

People commonly assert that there is little or no genuine medieval philosophy in large part because those we classify as medieval philosophers are typically thinkers whose work is defined by its loyalty to divine revelation. That is why Augustine (354–430) is often treated as the first medieval philosopher-theologian (even though he lived in the Roman Empire well before the advent of the middle ages), and Francisco Suarez (1548–1617) is often treated as the last medieval philosopher (even though his life overlapped 21 years with that of Descartes, widely regarded as the first modern philosopher). Augustine and Suarez share the common ideal of holding philosophy to the standard of truth found in the scriptures. Although not all those we call medieval philosophers adhered to this principle—Islamic philosophers in particular often clung to a philosophy independent of revealed religion—it was a common characteristic and one that scholars frequently use to define the era.[4]

Of course, ancient philosophers were often religious as well, as were early modern philosophers. Socrates lists piety among the virtues and thought himself a good and faithful servant of the gods, serving them through the philosophical cross-examinations he conducted in Athens. Plotinus, a 3rd-century neo-Platonist philosopher, was deeply religious and used philosophy to investigate how humans can ascend to the divine realities. Likewise, many modern philosophers devoted their work to theological topics, such as the existence and nature of God and the relationship between God and the world. There were in this period many deeply committed religious believers engaged in the enterprise of exploring the world in the light of their knowledge of God. In fact, a great number of them belonged to the clergy, including Butler, Malebranche, Hutcheson, Berkeley, Price, and Crusius.

However, we can easily see that these are superficial similarities coexisting with deeper differences. In the modern era, the dominant treatment of God and God's relationship with creation was arrived at not through theological systems based on scriptural exegesis, but through philosophy. In the West, the fragmented state of Christianity after the Protestant Reformation left Christians without a central authority or dominant tradition to explain how to interpret the Bible, and the emerging individualism of the age emboldened European Jews and Christians to think through religious truths through philosophy. Among early modern philosophers, Spinoza took the most radical view, asserting that the scriptures were not meant to contribute to human knowledge and so could not be used to check or restrain philosophy at all, but other, less radical, modern philosophers felt free to speculate about God and creation without appeal to Church doctrine or scripture. This "natural religion" was the dominant theological enterprise of the day, not revealed religion. In antiquity, philosophers did not practice religion based on an independent revelation from the gods. For these thinkers, religious thought and practice were themselves generally outgrowths of their philosophy, and the practice of religion was generally philosophical. Socrates reaches his understanding of what service to the gods is by philosophical inquiry, as we learn in the *Apology* and *Euthyphro*. The ancient stoics argue that this world is a cosmos planned by the perfectly rational Zeus, and their philosophical/religious practice is to train themselves to live in accordance with Zeus's plan. But this practice consists in careful self-examination to encourage utterly clear thinking, a refusal to assent to false appearances, and a resistance to being mastered by irrational emotion. Plotinus likewise explains how humans can come to a clearer self-understanding and ascend to the divine realities through the practice of philosophy.

Judaism, Christianity, and Islam did not develop as outgrowths of a philosophical system or movement but grew out of a divine revelation, certain aspects of which were inaccessible to philosophical reflection. Therefore, when ancient Jews and Christians encountered Greek philosophy, it was unclear to them how they ought to approach the discipline. Some of them, such as Justin Martyr, found so much common ground between philosophy and (in his case) Christianity that he saw no serious difficulties in Christians practicing philosophy. Others did not see the matter this way. Tertullian famously asked "What has Athens to do with Jerusalem?" thereby calling into question the relevance of Greek philosophy for Biblical religion. It is not hard to see why an ancient Jew or Christian might worry about the practice of philosophy. The philosophers, after all, had bickered with each other over crucial questions, such as the nature of God, God's concern (or lack of concern) with the world, the immortality of the soul, and the right way to live. If Jews and Christians have God's own word on the matter, why delve into a practice that carries with it such risk of error?

The position that eventually prevailed in Christianity, and one well represented in Judaism and Islam, was that espoused by the 3rd-century Christian thinker Origen. Both Greek philosophy and Christianity were paths to wisdom, Origen admits, but divine revelation puts humans on a surer path to achieve it. Besides, Christianity is the way of Christ, who is Wisdom itself, for he contains in himself the exemplars and plans for the cosmos. Therefore the truest philosophy—the love and pursuit of wisdom—is found in Christianity. Greek philosophy, to be sure, is often correct and salutary, leading its practitioners to a true understanding of the world and a virtuous way of life. However, Origen points out that each philosopher or philosophical school stumbled, some to a lesser extent (such as the Platonists), some to a greater extent (such as the Epicureans, who taught the pernicious doctrine that the gods had no concern for human affairs). Because the scriptures reveal truths we may be certain of, while philosophy sometimes misleads us, the scriptures should serve as a guide, check, and anchor for philosophical reflections. Most philosophically sophisticated Christians before the modern era adopted some variation of Origen's view, but we also find prominent Jewish and Muslim thinkers, such as Saadiah Gaon and al-Ghazali, espousing similar views.

It is because so many thinkers of the medieval period adopted this attitude toward scripture that they are often not regarded as philosophers. What these medievals engaged in, we are told, is the systematic presentation and defense of a doctrine that is itself off limits to rational investigation. In philosophy, however, all teachings are open to rational criticism and evaluation. Even where they moved beyond the presentation of doctrine, they still made use of divine revelation to formulate their arguments. Nevertheless, they did not offer rational criticism of doctrine derived from scripture: Scriptural provenance gave a proposition an unquestionable status, and so at that point rational inquiry came to an end. By contrast, philosophy does not shut off discussion at any point unless there is decisive reason to do so—and that is a matter for philosophy itself to discover or determine. Finally, we are told, this attitude toward scripture kills the spirit of inquiry in philosophy, which is an adventurous openness to whatever reason teaches us. In *The History of Western Philosophy*, Bertrand Russell criticizes Aquinas—and he could just as easily have been lodging the same objection against any number of medievals, such as Anselm—contending:

> There is little of the true philosophic spirit in Aquinas. He does not, like the Platonic Socrates, set out to follow wherever the argument may lead. He is not engaged in an inquiry, the result of which it is impossible to know in advance. Before he begins to philosophize, he already knows the truth; it is declared in the Catholic faith. If he can find apparently rational arguments for some parts of the faith, so much the better: If he cannot, he need only fall back on revelation. The finding of arguments for a conclusion given in advance is not philosophy, but special pleading. I cannot, therefore, feel that he deserves to be put on a level with the best philosophers either of Greece or of modern times.
>
> (Russell 1945, 463)

It is not entirely clear what Russell means when he speaks of following "wherever the argument may lead." The metaphor suggests a mysterious path that we must summon enough courage and endurance to follow if we are to end in the right place, but it is hard to see how following a philosophical argument can be like that. What Russell probably means is that Aquinas closes off certain arguments from the start because he supposedly knows that they are unsound on the basis of divine revelation. It is not that he did not offer justifications for his views; it is rather that he did not remain open to views that could be better justified than the ones he argued for.[5]

The foregoing remarks express two distinct criticisms of medieval philosophy. The first states that much of what we call "medieval philosophy" is not really philosophy at all because it contains arguments whose premises derive from divine revelation and not from rational inquiry. Appeal to divine revelation, where no reasons are forthcoming, stops debate rather than fostering it. Real philosophy must rely on considerations accessible to believers and non-believers alike. The arguments of the medievals may well belong to some other field, such as theology, but they must be excluded from philosophy. The second criticism does not deny that the medievals practiced philosophy and in fact allows that they may well have produced sound and innovative arguments that advanced the discipline. The criticism is that when a prior commitment to revelation sits in judgment of which arguments will find a hearing and which arguments will not, then one is not living up to the vocation of a philosopher. In short, the medievals practiced philosophy, but in a defective way that risked multiple drawbacks, such as lack of innovation and a decreased likelihood of finding the best arguments.

The second argument is the more sophisticated and interesting criticism, so let me address that one first. Anthony Kenny offers a noteworthy and oft-cited dismissal of Russell's evaluation. First, Kenny observes, it does not matter how philosophers arrive at the premises of their arguments. When we evaluate philosophers' arguments, we ask whether those arguments are valid and sound, not what motivated a philosopher to select those particular premises. Moreover, Kenny observes, Aquinas is hardly alone in his project of finding arguments for what he already accepts as true. Many of the great philosophers proceed exactly the same way, such as Descartes, often touted as one of the most innovative philosophers in history, and (Kenny pointedly remarks) Russell himself, who in "*Principia Mathematica* takes hundreds of pages to prove that 1 and 1 make 2."[6] No one disputes that an argument stands as sound or valid on its own, independently of whatever motive a philosopher has in presenting it. But Russell is not objecting to that contention, which is hardly controversial. His concern is that philosophers' motives may well influence the range of considerations, and thus the range of arguments, they are willing to countenance. This is the attitude that would, in Russell's view, bar many medieval philosophers from having a true philosophic spirit.

However, Kenny's second observation may open the way to a defense against Russell's criticism. It is not just the medievals, but any number of other philosophers whose major works consist of arguments for conclusions they accept in advance. In fact, Pierre Hadot contends that ancient philosophy typically proceeds in a similar pattern:

> . . . at least since the time of Socrates, the choice of a way of life has not been located at the end of the process of philosophical activity, like a kind of accessory or appendix. . . Philosophical discourse, then, originates in a choice of life and an existential option—not vice versa. . . This existen-

> tial option, in turn, implies a certain vision of the world, and the task of philosophical discourse will therefore be to reveal and rationally justify this existential option, as well as this representation of the world.
>
> (Hadot 2002, 3)

If we think Russell has lighted on the single necessary condition of the philosophic spirit, we might conclude that, with a few exceptions, no true philosophers appeared on the scene until modernity, and precious few even then. Alternatively, we could dispute that Russell has uncovered the unique touchstone of philosophic spirits and look to see whether there might be other ways of finding admittance into the company of true philosophers.

A full treatment of these issues would require a long and undoubtedly contentious discussion. After all, philosophers have never been able to agree on what counts as philosophy, let alone good philosophy or a true philosophic spirit. I suspect there are many marks of the true philosopher, and the history of philosophy offers us a number of plausible ways of identifying a philosophic spirit besides (and instead of) Russell's. These include but are not limited to (a) having a deep love of truth (or goodness or beauty) that drives one to seek it out and investigate its nature; (b) commitment to a way of life expressing the moral and intellectual virtues; (c) living the examined life in keeping with rational principles; (d) engaging with the world imaginatively and attentively, eschewing self-serving illusion and fantasy; and (e) expressing a habitual curiosity to discover new arguments, distinctions, or concepts that will advance the discipline. If we take these five criteria as marks of a philosophic spirit, then the medievals fare quite well as philosophers. First, many of them developed philosophical systems that were designed to raise the mind to truth, beauty, and goodness, which they typically identified with God (see, for instance, part VI). Most of them taught, and many tried to live out, the ideals in (b) and (c). Augustine's *Confessions* is often interpreted as a paradigm of the examined life (see part I), and Abelard, Maimonides, Bonaventure, and Aquinas all wrote works designed to spur us to examine our lives and turn to virtue.[7] Augustine exemplified (d) not only in his *Confessions*, but in such texts as his famous dismissal of the Greek "fantasy" that we can attain happiness in this life (*City of God* book 19). Likewise, one of Lady Philosophy's tasks in Boethius's *Consolation of Philosophy* is to convince the character Boethius to set aside his self-indulgence so that he can pay genuine attention to his life and situation. Not only the most renowned, but also less famous medieval thinkers, such as John Buridan and Henry of Ghent, exhibited mark (e). In fact, the commitment to scripture that most medievals harbored—the very characteristic that Russell identifies as a constraint on their philosophic spirit—turns out to be a major factor driving their creativity. Many religious doctrines are not easily accommodated by Greek philosophy as it was passed on by the ancients, and so philosophically minded medievals who were committed to Abrahamic religion had to exercise considerable creativity and insight to explain these doctrines, such as the absolute simplicity of God, creation *ex nihilo*, and the Christian doctrines of the Trinity and Incarnation. What they strove for was not an *ad hoc* account that would be applicable only to a single religious doctrine or two, but rather an account that had wide philosophical appeal that would also be applicable to the doctrine under investigation. In other words, rather than appealing to religious doctrine as a way of stopping debate, the medievals often treated it as an inspiration to arrive not just at a theology, but at a better *philosophy*, as we see in medieval discussions of being, causation, virtue, logic, intentionality, and action theory (see, for instance, parts I–III and VII–IX).

In any case, it is clear that some medieval philosophers *did* satisfy even the Russellian condition. For one thing, the medievals took the scriptures to be complex and difficult writings, open to many possible interpretations at multiple levels. Unlike contemporary scripture scholarship, which relies largely on history, archaeology, and social science as guides, medieval scripture scholarship often found its guiding light in philosophy. Therefore, even if medieval thinkers were committed to the scriptures, the right interpretation of those scriptures was often determined by the best philosophical argument. After all, if the truth of philosophy cannot conflict with the truth of revelation (as prominent Jewish, Christian, and Muslim philosophers asserted), then good philosophy should steer people to good interpretations.[8] More importantly, if Russell's charge implies that Aquinas (and the other medievals) did not take alternative arguments or counterarguments seriously or treat them fairly, there are clear counterexamples. As I noted above, classroom disputations, along with their written record, were designed in part to guard against just this sort of academic offense. Philosophers were trained to work in this form so they would treat their opponents responsibly and not as straw men, searching for effective counterarguments and admitting defeat if they could not (as Aquinas famously did when he argued that there was no way philosophy could establish that the world had a beginning, as Christianity taught, rather than being eternal, as Aristotle had argued).

Finally, the assumption that all the medievals thought that scripture was beyond rational questioning is simply false. The 9th century saw a number of skeptical thinkers among Jews and Muslims. For instance, Hiwi al-Balkhi[9] subjected the scriptures to a debunking rational criticism, seeking naturalistic explanations for the supposed miracles reported there. In *A Dialogue between a Philosopher, a Jew, and a Christian*,[10] Peter Abelard depicts a fictional Philosopher who wonders why any sort of revealed law is needed for achieving happiness when the natural law seems sufficient. In any case, the Philosopher asserts, what explains people's religious convictions is not reason, but upbringing; and those who ask the fewest questions are called the strongest in faith. Highly skeptical of these revealed religions (filled with fools and lunatics, in his view), the Philosopher asks the Jew if he has a good *reason* for following the Jewish law. In response, the Jew offers a striking preincarnation of Pascal's Wager, but Abelard leaves it to his readers to determine for themselves whether that response is adequate.

Let me return now to the first criticism, that what we call medieval philosophy is not philosophy at all because its arguments depend on premises derived from revelation and are therefore beyond rational debate. This objection stems from a gross oversimplification of what medieval philosophers actually write, as we can see from every one of the philosophical debates over their views in this volume. *Some* medieval thinkers, in *some* works, constructed *some* arguments with premises drawn from scripture. However, many Jewish, Christian, and Muslim thinkers wrote works of pure philosophy with no premises drawn from the scriptures at all. The Islamic tradition in particular (starting with al-Kindi in the 9th century through Averroes in the 12th) produced philosophy that retained considerable independence from scripture. More interestingly, in unabashedly theological works, medieval thinkers explore, without appeal to revelation, topics we now treat in philosophy, such as the nature of time, causation, modality, the principles of nature, the human mind, action theory, the passions and other emotions, virtue, and political systems. However, because the philosophical study of these topics can have a religious or theological motivation, even theologians in the middle ages contributed widely to these philosophical topics. In short, despite the pre-eminence of theology in the middle ages (especially in the Latin West), philosophy is pervasive. All the debates in this volume, which focus on works of philosophy or on the philosophical elements of theological works, make abundantly clear the contributions of this period to the field we recognize as philosophy.

Notes

1. In this volume, "debate" is used broadly. In some units, you will find contemporary philosophers debating each other about how to interpret a text. In some cases these contemporary philosophers agree on what the alternative interpretations are but opt for different ones (as in part VI on Maimonides), while in other cases they re-envision the possible interpretations (as in part II on free will in Anselm). However, in some units the debate does not take the form of opposition. Sometimes one contemporary commentator builds on the work of another (as in part VI on Bonaventure), while other times the two commentators focus on different elements in the text to illuminate different lines of thought (as in part IX on Aquinas's ethics). Of course, the contemporary commentators are not the only debaters in this volume. Several essays highlight the debates among the medievals themselves (such as part III on Abelard and part XI on Scotus and Ockham).
2. I do not mean to suggest these approaches cannot be mixed.
3. Gisela Striker (1999) succinctly and convincingly explains the philosophical nature of the history of philosophy.
4. See, for instance, Spade (2013).
5. See Graham Oppy (2001) and also Mark T. Nelson (2001).
6. Kenny (2007), 76.

7. See parts III, VI, and IX. For Maimonides, see his works *Eight Chapters* and *Laws concerning Character Traits.*
8. This ideal did not always lead the medievals to the truths they strove to find, since the philosophy they relied on was not always as good as they supposed. For instance, the Jewish and Christian scriptures offer no unambiguous view on slavery or gender equality. The result is that later medieval philosophers (who were never slaves and nearly always men) often turned to their greatest philosophical predecessor, Aristotle, whose arguments in favor of natural slavery and gender inequality made it natural (just in case it wasn't already) for them to take the scriptures as endorsing slavery and the subjugation of women.
9. Most scholars take him to be Jewish, although some have questioned his religious affiliation.
10. A translation can be found in Abelard (1995).

Chronology of Medieval Philosophers

Early Medieval Philosophers Writing in Latin

Augustine (354–430)
Boethius (c.480–525/6)
John Scottus Eriugena (c. 800–c.877)
Anselm of Canterbury (1033–1109)
Peter Abelard (1079–1142)

Philosophers Writing in Arabic or Hebrew

al-Kindi (801–873)
al-Farabi (c.870–950)
Saadiah (882–942)
Avicenna/Ibn Sina (980–1037)
al-Ghazali (1058–1111)
Averroes/Ibn Rushd (1126–1198)
Maimonides (1138–1204)
Gersonides (1288–1344)
Crescas (1340–1410)

Later Philosophers Writing in Latin

Bonaventure (c. 1217–1274)
Albert the Great (1200–1280)
Thomas Aquinas (1224/6–1224)
Henry of Ghent (before 1240–1293)

Duns Scotus (c. 1266–1308)
William Ockham (c. 1287–1387)
John Buridan (before 1300–after 1358)
Francisco Suarez (1548–1617)

Note on the Text

I have altered previously published texts to correct misprints in the originals, to render spelling and punctuation consistent across the volume, and to create uniform reference and bibliographical forms. However, in those few cases where increased uniformity threatened to obscure what the author means to convey, I sacrificed uniformity for the sake of clarity. Deleted material is marked by ellipses (. . .). The few editorial insertions, such as translations of originally untranslated passages, are marked by square brackets.

PART I

Augustine: The Motive for Sin

Editor's Introduction

Reflecting on his youth from the standpoint of middle age, Augustine recalls, in considerable agony, the act that brought him to his moral and spiritual nadir. It was not violence, or villainy, or betrayal of a loved one that saw him fall so low. Rather, he fell to this shameful low by joining a group of teenage hooligans to steal some second-rate pears from a tree and then throwing them to the swine. Among Augustine's purposes in making this astonishing assertion is a philosophical one: He picks a case in which there seems to be no real attraction to the deed, and no real harm done, to draw a vivid illustration of the moral psychology of sin. However, Augustine's subtlety has led his commentators to considerable controversy over just what he means to teach us. What was Augustine's motive? What is philosophically important about it? And why think that acting on it brought him to such moral and spiritual depths?

In his "Petit Larceny, the Beginning of All Sin," Scott MacDonald attempts to untangle these twisted knots. He reminds us that Augustine describes sin as a disordered preference of a lower good to a higher one. For instance, if we seek a good job in a fair way, we do not sin. But if we seek the same job by spreading damaging rumors about our competitors, we seek it by sacrificing the truth and fairness that we should prefer to getting the job. But how does the theft of the pears satisfy this description of sin when Augustine finds nothing attractive whatsoever about the pears? In fact, Augustine believes that what delighted him in the theft was the theft itself or, as he also puts it, the fact that it was forbidden. However, MacDonald explains, the reason Augustine loved what was forbidden is that he was really grasping after freedom and power: the power to follow rules of his own making as he acted in freedom from God's laws. Augustine, then, seeks two genuine goods, but because only God has the real freedom and power to determine things' objective values and thereby create moral laws, Augustine seeks these goods in a disordered way: by trying to do himself what only God can do, a prideful (and futile) imitation of God's genuine excellences. MacDonald suggests that we can find the same structure across the spectrum of sins. Whenever we have a disordered preference of a lesser good to a greater, we arrogate to ourselves what belongs only to God, and therefore we sin from pride. Augustine's examination of the theft of the pears helps him to uncover this structure common to all sin. What makes Augustine's own sin so particularly vile is that he commits the theft in the full knowledge—and relish—of its sinful nature.

Matthews, by contrast, focuses on Augustine's claims that his motive was to do something bad and that there was no reason he did what was bad. In asserting these views, Augustine makes a radical departure from the tradition of Greek philosophy up to his own day, which holds that we want only what we take to be good. Augustine is the first thinker to hold that we can also want something bad without thinking it good in any respect at all. That sort of act will in a sense be unintelligible, since we will not be able to explain it by pointing to something attractive to be gained by it. However, Matthews points out, such perverse and irrational acts are not unfamiliar to us. They conform to patterns of behavior we are all familiar with, such as when people perform irrational and self-destructive acts out of frustration and resentment. If Matthews is right, it is not hard to see why Augustine thinks he sank to moral and spiritual depths in stealing the pears: Because he sought nothing good, his act was an instance of pure evil.

Note on the References

Augustine's *Confessions* is divided into books, chapters, and sections. MacDonald forgoes citing chapters, since the section divisions are shorter and so make it easier to pinpoint the cited text. Matthews includes all three units in his citations. So, when he cites *Confessions* 2.4.9, this refers to book 2, chapter 4, section 9.

De libero arbitrio is the Latin title of a dialogue between Augustine and Evodius on the will. In English, the work is often called *On Free Choice of the Will.*

Further Reading

- William E. Mann (1978). "The Theft of the Pears."
- Robert J. O'Connell (1989). *St. Augustine's Confessions: The Odyssey of the Soul.*
- James Wetzel (2010). *Augustine: A Guide for the Perplexed.*

CHAPTER 1

Petit Larceny, the Beginning of All Sin: Augustine's Theft of the Pears

SCOTT MACDONALD

Augustine might reasonably be accused of having been obsessed with sin both as a theoretical concept and as a personal affliction. As a theoretical concept, sin dominates his thinking. His discovery and articulation of what he took to be the Christian understanding of sin is crucial to his intellectual reconciliation with Catholic Christianity. It is his answer to the problem of the origin of evil: sin—understood as the corrupted free choices of certain of God's good creatures—is the first evil in creation. Evil is therefore not created by God but introduced into creation *de novo* by rational beings acting irrationally. The concept of sin grounds his elaborate two-evils theodicy: all evil is either sin or its consequences. God cannot prevent sin consistent with respecting the rational nature of angels and human beings, and God is morally justified in causing or permitting the evils that are consequent on sin insofar as they are instruments of just punishment and benevolent moral correction and transformation. Augustine's reflections on the nature of sin lead him to his distinctive metaphysical positions on free will and moral responsibility, shape his ethical theory, and give rise to his famously pessimistic view of fallen human nature's ability to do what is good without divine aid. All the major intellectual opponents he faced—Manichaean cosmological dualists, schismatic North African Donatists, and the Pelagians that dogged the last two decades of his life—in Augustine's view fundamentally misunderstood the nature and extent of human sin and its effects on the human psyche.

Perhaps not surprisingly, the theoretical importance the notion of sin has for Augustine's thought is matched, in his reflections on his own life, by the significance he attaches to his own personal sin. In the *Confessions* in particular, it can seem that he focuses on, indeed agonizes over, his own past sins and sinfulness to the point of excess. His confession of his own present sin, in book 10, for example, is relentless not only in length but in detail. His attention throughout the narrative of his life to his struggles with sexual incontinence in particular can seem to border on deviance and, in book 8, to assume a magnitude out of all proportion with reasonable self-assessment. Viewed against this backdrop of searing self-scrutiny the famous story of the theft of the pears, in *Confessions* book 2, can seem—and has in fact seemed to some readers—Augustine's most extreme piece of self-flagellation. He appears to scourge himself mercilessly for what might best be described as a bit of late-night adolescent mischief.[1]

Most commentators agree that there is more to the story of the theft of the pears than this caricature allows. But they have had a hard time agreeing on precisely why Augustine thinks the story is worth relating, what he wants us to take from it, and why he chooses to relate it where he does, in book 2 of the *Confessions*.[2] In this chapter I try to understand what Augustine is up to in the telling of this story.

1. Why Is Augustine Interested in the Theft of the Pears? (book 2, section 9)[3]

Augustine devotes roughly the second half of book 2—the last ten of the book's 18 sections (2.9–18)—to the theft of the pears. All of book 2 is given over to the retailing of Augustine's adolescent sins, sins committed, he tells us, in his sixteenth year while living at home during a break in his schooling. Augustine is now entering young adulthood, and his life is, by his own account, a mess. He is a prodigal son, wandering farther and farther away from God, becoming more and more destitute as he wanders.[4] Augustine wants us to see the sinful state from which his long journey back to God must begin. But he also intends the autobiographical elements to provide a backdrop for important philosophical and theological themes. In particular, he intends reflection on his own sins to yield theoretical understanding of the nature of sin in general.

The first half of the book focuses on his youthful sexual adventures. The difficulty with sexual continence that occupies Augustine's attention throughout the first eight books of the *Confessions* takes root here. Sexual activity has a good purpose and end in God's creation. But unchecked and without regard to their place in the divine order of things, Augustine's desires for sex become wild and uncontrollable. "I boldly thrust out rank, luxuriant growth in various furtive love affairs" (2.1); "A frenzy of lust imposed its rule on me, and I wholeheartedly yielded to it" (2.4); "The thorn-bushes of my lust shot up higher than my head, and no hand was there to root them out" (2.6).[5] As we learn later, in book 8, nothing short of divine grace will be sufficient to bring Augustine's sexual desires under control.

The theoretical point of discussing these youthful indiscretions is clear. Sexual promiscuity is not only a particular kind of sin but also a compelling metaphor for sin generally and illustrative of sin's general characteristics. In Augustine's view, morally significant features of human lives essentially involve human loves, and sin consists in the loving of lesser, created goods in preference to God, the highest and immutable good.[6] Sin, then, is a kind of fornication: giving one's best love inappropriately and unrestrainedly, thereby joining oneself to goods whose value to us is out of all proportion with their real value.[7] We can see Augustine using the metaphor later in book 2 where no actual sexual liaison is in question: "In this way the soul fornicates when it is turned from you and seeks apart from you things which it finds pure and clear only when it returns to you" (2.14).[8] It is easy to see, then, why the sexual adventures come in for extended attention.

It is not as clear why the theft of the pears deserves similar attention. In section 9 of book 2 Augustine turns to the theft of the pears, in this passage:

> Your law, Lord, which clearly punishes theft, has been inscribed on human hearts. Not even wickedness itself can erase it. For what thief is an equinanimous victim of theft even if he is rich and the one who robs him is driven to it by poverty? I wanted to commit theft and I did it, compelled by no need other than a poverty of and scorn for justice and an abundance of wickedness. For I already had plenty of what it was I was stealing, and what I had was far better. Nor did I want to enjoy the thing I was seeking by theft; rather I wanted to enjoy the theft itself and the sin.
>
> There was a pear tree near our vineyard laden with fruit that was appealing in neither appearance nor taste. Late one night, after we had prolonged our revelry in the streets in our pestilential way, our band of no-good youth set off to shake the fruit from the tree and carry it away. We hauled off huge loads, not for our feasts but in order to throw them to the pigs. Even if we ate some of what we took, nevertheless what pleased us was the fact that what we were doing was forbidden.

Of course the theft gives Augustine another example of sin to add to his list: it is another morally bad action, another instance of his violation of the divine ordering of creation, and further evidence of his moral corruption. But these opening lines suggest two other dimensions of the theft that Augustine seems interested in emphasizing. First, he introduces and briefly defends the claim that the divine prohibition of theft has been indelibly inscribed on human hearts. The adolescent Augustine therefore knows that what he is doing is sinful, and he does it anyway. That point is reinforced by his insistence that what pleased him in the act was doing what was forbidden—in order to be pleased by doing what was forbidden he must have *known* at the time that the act was forbidden. The emphasis on antecedent knowledge here distinguishes the theft of the pears from the other sins Augustine has been discussing.

The second feature of the case Augustine calls our attention to here at the start is the motive of the theft. He clearly thinks it strange and especially noteworthy that what attracted him to the act and what pleased him in it was the theft itself, the sin, the doing of what was forbidden. He did not steal because he wanted the pears; he stole because he wanted to steal, to sin, to do what was forbidden. That is not a feature of the other sins Augustine has been discussing in book 2.

So on the basis of what he says in introducing the case, it would be natural to suppose that Augustine adds the theft of the pears to his litany of youthful offenses because these distinguishing marks make it significant to him and his project. Unlike the other sins in book 2, the theft of the pears purports to be a sin committed in full *knowledge* of its being a sin and precisely *because* it is a sin. Never mind that, viewed from an external perspective, the act itself is relatively harmless and perhaps less worrisome than Augustine's sexual improprieties. The peculiar mental state he attributes to himself—his knowledge and motivation—distinguish this case.

Augustine goes on to focus attention on just these features of the case. Here is his initial retrospective assessment of himself:

> Behold my heart, God. Behold my heart which you had mercy on when it was in the depths of the abyss. Behold my heart. It now declares to you what it was seeking there, so that I might be wicked for its own sake (*gratis*) and there would be no cause of my wickedness other than wickedness. It was foul, and I loved it. I loved perishing, I loved my fall—not that for which I was falling, rather I loved my fall itself. My soul was filthy and, not seeking something shamefully but seeking shame, I was casting myself down from your firmament to utter destruction.
>
> (2.9, continuation)

What Augustine is clearly struck by here, and wants us to be struck by, is the depth of the moral perversity in the case. If the external act is no big deal, the heart from which the act springs is foul, and foul precisely in virtue of what it loves and is motivated by—sheer wickedness, the perishing, the shamefulness. To be motivated to act by the prospects of illicit sexual satisfaction is for one's loves to be disordered and misdirected, to seek something shamefully. But the good one seeks is nevertheless recognizable and genuine. By contrast, to be moved to act by the wickedness of an act is for one's loves to be disordered in the extreme, to be directed toward what is in itself not good at all. A heart with loves of that sort is in the very depths of the moral abyss.[9]

What Augustine says later in book 2 confirms this assessment. He tells us that not even the notorious Catiline was so corrupt as to love his crimes simply because they were crimes (2.11). And he says of himself, "What rottenness! What a monstrous life and abyss of death! Could what is not permitted have been pleasing for no other reason than that it was not permitted?" (2.14). And he concludes book 2, "It is foul. I do not want to consider it. I do not want to look at it. . . . I became for myself a region of destitution" (2.18). In the theft of the pears Augustine's prodigality has become dramatic and complete.[10]

The theft of the pears, then, is important to Augustine because it enables him to introduce a particular notion of extreme moral depravity: loving something wicked solely for the sake of the wickedness. That, I think, is the *first* reason for introducing the story. But as the rest of Augustine's extended discussion reveals, there is more attracting his attention than just the depravity of his motive in the case. After having confidently identified the motive and roundly excoriated his adolescent heart for it (in the passages we have just looked at from section 9), he seems, just a bit farther along in the text, to waver: "Wretch that I was, what did I love in you, my theft? . . . I want to know what in the theft gave me delight." (2.12). The question arises not because he thinks his initial account ("what pleased us was the fact that what we were doing was forbidden") involves a mis-remembering of his state of mind at the time, or that he might be wrong about the extent of the wickedness it manifests. His worry seems to be rather that the motive he has attributed to his younger self is impossible, that no one could be moved in that way, that despite his memory of the event, the initial explanation he has given of his theft is in fact unintelligible. This is clearly the main or most explicit problem that Augustine wants the story of the theft to bring out. Nearly all the material in sections 10–18 of book 2 is devoted to articulating and trying to resolve the particular difficulty he has his finger on when he asks this tentative question: "What did I love in you, my theft?" That is the *second* reason Augustine has for introducing the theft of the pears in book 2 of the *Confessions.*

Augustine's handling of that problem is my main concern and I consider it in detail below. But before wandering into that particular thicket I want briefly to suggest a *third* reason Augustine has for including the theft of the pears here in book 2. The theft of the pears gives Augustine the occasion to explain in the context of his own personal pilgrimage the significance of the fall of the first free creatures, angelic and human. There is plenty in the opening paragraphs of the discussion of the theft that invites us to think of the story as analogous to the fall of Adam and Eve in the garden (Genesis 3). Like the adolescent Augustine, Adam and Eve took fruit from a tree. Adam and Eve, too, disobeyed a clear divine prohibition. And they, too, acted crucially in consort—they were a gang of two.[11] There is clear allusion here to the angelic fall, too, in Augustine's casting himself down from the firmament.[12] And there is the unmistakable parallel between the two trees framing salvation history—the tree associated with the fall in the garden and the tree on Golgotha where redemption is wrought—and the two trees framing Augustine's own pilgrimage—the pear tree in this story and the tree in the Milanese garden under which a weeping Augustine finally surrenders to divine grace (in book 8).[13] So we cannot help but be thinking of creation's first sins as we contemplate Augustine and the pears.

So why should the first falls be relevant to Augustine's own story in the *Confessions*? Why should he want to recall them here in book 2? There are no doubt several reasons, but two of them seem to me particularly compelling. First, Augustine intends the story of his own life to represent in microcosm the principles and events that Christianity takes to be fundamental in the larger story of God's creation and redemption of the universe. Insofar as the theft of the pears mirrors the first falls, Augustine is anxious to use it to teach us about those foundational events in Christian history. Second, Augustine believes that the primal sins of Lucifer and Adam and Eve are important not merely because of their temporal priority and causal significance but also because they are in a certain way paradigms. All sins—primal, creation-rending sin, everyday peccadilloes, and everything in between—share a common deep structure, and Augustine thinks that one won't properly understand sin's nature until one sees it. In one obvious sense, Augustine's sins, including the theft of the pears, are not primal: they are preceded by and prepared for by other evils already in creation and in Augustine himself. But in another sense they are: their motives spring ultimately from the same deep wells as the motives of Lucifer and Adam and Eve.[14] Augustine introduces the theft of the pears in book 2 because it allows him to make that important point, as I now proceed to argue.

2. Explaining Motivation (book 2, sections 10–11)

Augustine has identified a motive for his theft of the pears. He puts it in five different ways in the small bit of text we have seen so far, all of which, I think, are meant to convey the same idea:

A. Nor did I want to enjoy the thing I was seeking by theft; rather I wanted to enjoy the theft itself and the sin (*nec ea re volebam frui quam furto appetebam, sed ipso furto et peccato*)

B. Nevertheless what pleased us was the fact that what we were doing was forbidden (*tamen fieret a nobis quod eo liberet quo non liceret*)

C. [My heart now declares to you] what it was seeking there, so that I might be wicked for its own sake and there would be no cause of my wickedness other than wickedness (*quid ibi quaerebat, ut essem gratis malus et malitiae meae causa nulla esset nisi malitia*)

D. It was foul, and I loved it. I loved perishing, I loved my fall—not that for which I was falling, rather I loved my fall itself (*foeda erat, et amavi eam. Amavi perire, amavi defectum meum, non illud ad quod deficiebam, sed defectum meum ipsum amavi*)

E. [My soul was filthy and,] not seeking something shamefully but seeking shame, [I was casting myself down] (*non dedecore aliquid, sed dedecus appetens*)

He repeats some of these variations and adds others as the discussion proceeds. As he understands the case, he performs a certain action, an act of theft, and is motivated to perform that action under that description, that is, just insofar as he takes it to be theft, a crime, something forbidden, something the doing of which will make him wicked and shameful.

It is *that* account of the motivation for his thievery that Augustine finds worrisome, and he spends the next two sections—book 2, sections 10 and 11—building a theoretical framework that will allow him to state the worry clearly. The framework has two main components: what we might think of, respectively, as a subjective and an objective constraint on motivation.

Subjective Constraint on Motivation

Augustine points out that if we are to make sense of a person's voluntary actions, we must understand what in or about those actions moves her to view them favorably, what it is in them that she loves or takes to be worth seeking. His various ways of putting this include saying that we are moved or motivated by what delights us (*delectat*), what pleases us or gives us pleasure (*libet, placet*), what we love (*amare*), or what we want to enjoy (*frui*). It is an assumption of this sort that leads Augustine to ask: "Wretch that I was, what did I *love* in you, my theft? . . . I want to know what in the theft gave me *delight*." (2.12) He supposes that if he is to understand his motivation, he must know the answer to this particular question.

A well known passage in Augustine's commentary on the Sermon on the Mount makes the point a bit more systematically:

> There are three steps by which sin is brought to completion: suggestion, delight (*delectatio*), and consent. A suggestion comes about through memory or a bodily sense (when we see, hear, smell, taste, or touch something). If the enjoyment (*frui*) of this thing delights (*delectaverit*), then if the delight is illicit, one ought to refrain from it. For example, when we are fasting and a desire (*appetitus*) for something to eat arises in us at the sight of food, this occurs only by virtue of delight Nevertheless we do not consent to it, and we restrain it by a command of reason which has control. But if consent were given, the sin would be complete in our heart and known to God—even if the deed fails to occur and [the sin] remains unknown to others.
>
> (*De sermone Domini in monte* 1.34)[15]

Augustine's concern in this passage is to explicate Jesus' claim that a person can violate God's commands—can sin—"in his heart." But the basic account he sketches here applies to voluntary action generally. Whether or not we are fasting, when the sight or smell of food gives rise in us to a desire to eat, the desire is explained or accounted for, on Augustine's view, by our delight at the prospect of eating or enjoying the food. And in general, the thoughts and perceptions that occur to us—what Augustine here calls "suggestions"—lead to desire and ultimately to consent and action only by virtue of their presenting us with something that delights us.[16] It is unclear whether Augustine thinks of the delight and the correlative desire it explains as distinct things, the former causing or giving rise to the latter, or whether he means only to be calling attention to a sort of conceptual truth about desire, namely, that desires, by their very nature, take as their objects things or states of affairs conceived of as in some way delightful. Either way, we can see the point of his identifying delight as crucial for understanding voluntary action: until we know what it is in or about an action that delights the agent, we will not know what motivates her. Being told merely that she *desires* to act in a certain way is uninformative; we need to know why she has that desire, why that action should seem to her desirable.

Augustine's position, then, identifies a subjective constraint on motivation which we might express as follows:

> If an agent *S* voluntarily performs some action (øs), then there must be something, *D*, in or about øing that delights *S* and (for that reason) moves *S* to Ø.

What delights an agent—*D* in this schema—is what motivates her. Sometimes the relevant feature of an action will be something attaching directly to the action itself: acts of virtue are intrinsically valuable, and their intrinsic value can attract us to them. Sometimes the feature that delights will be an object or state of affairs that the action can be expected to bring about or promote, as when one digs in one's garden in order to cultivate a beautiful space.

Objective Constraint on Motivation

Augustine supposes that human beings are designed or constituted to take delight in only a certain range of things. In section 10 of book 2, he offers a brief summary of his views on this matter.[17] Certain bodies have a kind of beauty (*species*) or an appropriate sort of fit (*congruentia, modificatio*) with our bodily senses that causes us to respond with delight to them. Our minds rather than our senses discern and respond to certain other goods such as temporal honor and power, which have a kind of dignity or worth (*decus*), and human friendship, the sweetness of which owes to the unity it secures among different minds. Augustine tells us that all these things have their delights (*habent haec delectationes*) and that this temporal life "has its attractiveness on account of a kind of measure and fittingness of the adornment (*decus*) it possesses where all these earthly beautiful things are concerned" (2.10). His idea seems to be that delight is the result of an appropriate sort of fit or accommodation between an object and the bodily senses or the mind and that, as a consequence, the sorts of objects in which human beings can take delight are the sorts that are fitted or accommodated in the right way to our bodies and minds.

Given that human beings' physical and mental constitution is relevantly determined by their nature, and given that only certain sorts of objects are naturally fitted to the human constitution in the right way, it follows that it is an objective matter—a matter determined by the natures of things—what objects human beings can take delight in. It cannot be that any object whatsoever can be an object of human delight.[18] Hence, Augustine's account of the nature of delight places an objective constraint on the range of objects that can fill that role. For a given case of voluntary action, if we cannot identify an objectively recognizable delight—something with beauty, worth, the sweetness of unity, or in some other way appropriately accommodated to the human body or mind—then we will not have understood the agent's motivation in acting.

Augustine points out that this account of the nature of human delight and the role delight plays in the account of motivation helps us understand not only ordinary, unobjectionable human behavior but also deviant behavior and, in particular, sin. We sin, Augustine believes, not because we are motivated by bad things but because we pursue perfectly natural and appropriate delights inordinately, preferring them and the things in which they reside to higher goods. "Sin is committed for the sake of all these things and other things of this sort when, by virtue of an inclination towards them that is inordinate (since they are the lowest sort of goods), we forsake better and higher goods" (2.10). Augustine's sexual escapades from the first half of book 2 illustrate this account nicely. In his acts of sexual promiscuity Augustine aims at objectively recognizable goods—physical pleasure and intimate communion with another person—but he does so inordinately, preferring those goods to other, higher goods. The genuine goods that motivate sinners—the delights that attract them—make their sinful actions *intelligible*; the disproportionate and disruptive role those motivations play in sinners' lives is what makes their sinful actions *sins*.

Augustine goes on in the next section—section 11—to direct the account he has been developing toward the kind of case he is interested in here, the commission of a crime. It turns out, perhaps unsurprisingly, that criminal acts are just a special case of sin and are subject to the same pattern of explanation:

> And so when there is an inquiry into why (*qua causa*) a certain crime was committed, the charge would not typically be believed unless it is made clear that a desire to obtain one of those goods that we have claimed to be the lowest (or a fear of losing one of them) was possible.

This is just the application of the subjective constraint on motivation. Insofar as it is voluntary, criminal behavior must be motivated by something the criminal himself takes delight in or recognizes as good. Augustine imagines some of the possibilities:

> He committed murder. Why did he do it? He loved the man's wife or his estate, or he wanted to rob him to get money to live on, or he was afraid that he would suffer the loss of something of this sort at the other man's hands. . .

But he is not willing to countenance certain attributions of motive:

> Would anyone commit murder without a reason (*sine causa*), having taken delight in murder itself (*ipso homicidio delectatus*)? Who would believe that?
>
> (2.11)

No one would believe it, Augustine supposes, and the objective constraint on motivation explains why. Murder itself is not the sort of thing that human beings can take delight in. Hence, when someone commits murder, there must be something else, an objectively recognizable delight, that motivates him. Even in the case of the notorious Catiline, who was reputed to have committed his crimes "without reason," Augustine insists that there is in fact a straightforward explanation in terms of motives that fits the general account he has been developing: "Therefore not even Catiline himself loved his crimes; rather he loved something else"—and we might add: "something else which is a recognizable delight"—"which was the reason he committed them."

We are now in position to combine the two components of Augustine's account of motivation, the subjective and objective constraints on motivation:

> If an agent *S* voluntarily performs some action (øs), then there must be something, *D*, in or about øing that delights *S* and (for that reason) moves *S* to ø, where *D* is an objectively recognizable object of delight that is either a feature of øing itself or something *S* intends to bring about or promote by øing.

This schema, I think, articulates the theoretical framework Augustine intends to use in his analysis of the theft of the pears.

3. The Central Puzzle (book 2, section 12)

With this framework for understanding human motivation in place, Augustine begins the analysis of his special case: "Wretch that I was, what did I love in you, my theft, that nocturnal crime in the sixteenth year of my life? You were not beautiful, since you are theft" (2.12). Augustine focuses here precisely where we would expect him to focus, given the constraints he has just articulated. If his general account holds, then there must be some objectively recognizable delight motivating him to steal the pears. He suggests here at the beginning of section 12 that the theft itself is ineligible to fill this role. Theft, like the case of murder discussed in the previous section, insofar as it is recognized for what it is, neither is nor contains in itself anything delightful, anything naturally suited to attract us. The pears themselves would be appropriate objects of delight, but Augustine adamantly denies that they were what motivated him in this case: "The pears were beautiful, but my miserable soul did not desire them." The theft itself, however, is not an intelligible motivator; there is no beauty or dignity in it, as Augustine asserts for the second time in the space of a dozen lines of text: "And now, Lord my God, I ask what it was that delighted me in the theft. There is no beauty (*species*) in it." So if Augustine's account of human motivation holds generally, neither the theft itself nor the wickedness and shame it promises can have motivated him to steal the pears. His initial account of his motivation—confidently asserted in section 9 of the text (see A–E in section 2 above)—must be wrong. There must be some other delight that moves him to act in this case; the account of motivation he has sketched in sections 10 and 11 requires it.

This, I think, is the central puzzle Augustine sets for himself in the story of the theft of the pears. Are there genuine counterexamples to the general account of human motivation Augustine has just given us good reason to accept? Are there voluntary sinful human actions that are not merely heinous and perverse but also strictly unintelligible on the best account Augustine thinks we have?[19] The stakes here are extremely high for Augustine. His own hard-won and carefully wrought account of the nature of sin fits integrally with and relies essentially on the general account of human motivation sketched in sections 10 and 11. That account of sin provides Augustine the conceptual leverage he needs to overturn his Manichaean convictions: he comes to see that all of God's creatures are good and that sin, the first and fundamental evil in creation, arises from creaturely free choices that aim essentially (and inordinately) at genuine goods, things in which it is wholly appropriate to take some measure of delight. To allow that there are sins in which sinners aim at no good, sins in which sinners find no recognizable delight, would undermine the foundations of Augustine's theodicy and thereby the entire edifice of his Christian intellectual enterprise.[20] Reflection on the superficially banal story of the theft of the pears has led him to philosophical issues of profound importance. In my view, the most compelling reason Augustine has for including the story in book 2 of the *Confessions* is that it enables him, as the stories of his adolescent sexual exploits cannot, to raise this deep worry about human motivation.

The story of the theft of the pears allows Augustine to articulate the difficulty, but does reflection on it also enable him to resolve it? I want to suggest that Augustine seriously entertains two answers to the question "What did I take delight in in the theft?" The first appears in section 14. Since I think that commentators have for the most part failed to appreciate the importance of that part of Augustine's analysis, I devote most of my attention in what follows to it (see sections 5 and 6 below). The second, which Augustine develops in sections 16 and 17 of book 2, is the more explicit and, for that reason, better known of the two attempts. I begin briefly with it

4. The Allure of Camaraderie (book 2, sections 16–17)

In section 16 Augustine appears to emerge from the discussion of the theft of the pears and to begin pulling together the various threads of book 2: "What fruit did I ever get, wretch that I was, from these things that I now blush to recall, especially from that theft in which I loved the theft itself and nothing else?" The expression "these things that I now blush to recall" is intended to be general and to shift our attention from the single case he has been focused on since section 9 to the broader variety of sins he has identified and lamented in book 2. The theft of the pears remains in the foreground ("*especially* from that theft"), but Augustine here reminds us that it is one case among others. He is moving toward a general conclusion to his reflections on his adolescent sins.

This opening question in section 16 ("What fruit did I ever get . . . from these things . . . especially from that theft?") also reminds us of the puzzle that was raised but not resolved in section 12 ("What did I love in you, my theft?"). The two questions differ in perspective. The earlier question, in section 12, focuses attention on Augustine's motivation. It asks what he wanted (prospectively) to enjoy or what good he expected to obtain by means of the theft. By contrast the question here in section 16 seems to ask about the benefit or enjoyment he actually derived from the theft (and his other sins).[21] Augustine's answer to this later question is that he received no benefit at all. What he loved was the theft itself, and since the theft itself is nothing, he gained nothing by having got what he loved—in fact he was made more miserable still.[22] But this reference to what he loved in the theft, leads Augustine back to the question of motivation, which he goes on to address:

> Nevertheless, I would not have done it by myself—I remember that this was my state of mind at the time—I would in no way have done it by myself. Therefore I also loved there the camaraderie of those with whom I did it. . . . If at that time I loved the pears that I stole and wanted to enjoy them, I could have committed the wickedness by which I achieved my satisfaction even by myself, if the love was strong enough. I would not have needed to inflame the itch of my desire by the stimulation of my peers. But because my satisfaction did not lie in the pears, it lay in the crime itself committed in league with a gang of sinners.

The observation that he would not have stolen the pears by himself leads to a kind of break-through. On the basis of that observation Augustine immediately draws a conclusion that offers a direct answer to the question from section 12: "Therefore I also loved there the camaraderie of those with whom I did it." It had seemed to Augustine as if he had loved the theft itself and nothing else, but it is now clear to him that he also loved the camaraderie. Since apart from the gang he would not have done it, it follows, he suggests, that it was his love of camaraderie that provided the critical impetus: "[My satisfaction] lay in the crime itself committed in league with a gang of sinners." This is Augustine's final word on his motivation for stealing the pears.

Augustine accomplishes at least two important things with this last observation. First, he (finally) brings the story of the theft of the pears under the main theme of book 2. At the beginning of book 2 Augustine told us that at this time in his adolescence he was burning to be satiated with the lowest sort of goods. "And what was it that I was taking delight in," he goes on to ask (22), "except loving and being loved?" It is immediately clear how his sexual adventures and his bragging to his peers about them satisfy this general description. Here at the very end of the book Augustine shows us how the theft of the pears, too, can be understood as a misguided and disordered attempt at loving and being loved. Hence, his final verdict on the case: "O utterly hostile friendship, unfathomable seducer of the mind! . . . When someone says 'Come on, let's do it!' one is ashamed not to be shameless" (2.17).

Second, Augustine salvages the theoretical account of motivation that the story of the theft of the pears threatened to undermine. Contrary to initial appearances, the objectively undelightful theft was not what moved him to act as he did (at least it was not sufficient by itself). There was something else moving him: delight in the camaraderie of those with whom he did it.[23] Moreover, in contrast with the theft itself, camaraderie—loving and being loved—is a recognizable and intelligible good, the sort of thing human beings naturally take delight in. Hence, in the theft of the pears Augustine is, after all, moved by an objective delight. The good of friendship (in this case what is really false and hostile friendship) affects him inordinately and perversely, but the desire for friendship nonetheless satisfies the constraints imposed by Augustine's own account of motivation. He appears to have found a suitable answer to his question in section 12, "What did I love in you, my theft?"[24]

This resolution of what I have called the central puzzle occurs at the very end of both the account of the theft of the pears and book 2 (at sections 16–17). But Augustine seems to offer a different resolution earlier in the account, at section 14.

5. Imitation of God (book 2, sections 12–14)

After raising the central question in the opening line of section 12 ("What did I love in you, my theft?") Augustine devotes the remainder of section 12 to searching for a plausible answer. The search is structured by the systematic account of human delights suggested in sections 10 and 11.[25] Augustine first rules out the relevant corporeal goods (the beautiful appearance [*pulchra*] of the pears, their taste). He then denies that the theft delighted him because of any kind of spiritual or intelligible goodness it possessed: it did not have the sort of beauty (*species*) possessed by the virtues (equity or prudence) or the faculties of the human soul (mind, memory, the senses, or the vegetative life); nor did it have the sort of beauty or attractive ordering (*speciosa et decora*) found in the motions of the stars and the regular laws and cycles of nature. He finally appears to deny even that the theft possessed the sort of "defective and shadowy beauty found in the deceptive vices."[26]

The introduction of this notion of deceptive vices causes Augustine to leave off his search for the elusive delight in his theft in order to elaborate. He lists fifteen different deceptive vices, explaining in each case how the particular vice involves an attraction but one that is based on deception insofar as each seeks an object that is only a defective and shadowy imitation of something that is to be found genuinely only in God. He tells us that *pride* imitates exaltation (whereas only God is exalted above all things); *ambition* seeks honor and glory (whereas only God is worthy of honor before all things and eternally glorious); sloth seeks a kind of rest (whereas certain rest is found only in God); avarice seeks possessions (whereas only God possesses all things) and so forth.[27] The list is something of a mixed bag and the uniform analysis Augustine subjects it to seems strained in places.[28] But the general point Augustine wants to derive from the brief account does not depend on the details: "In this way the soul fornicates when it is turned from you and seeks apart from you things which it finds pure and clear only when it returns to you" (2.14).

Augustine has taken the time to introduce and explain the deceptive vices because they give him, in the notion of misguided or illusory imitation, an important new tool for understanding the structure of sin. The model Augustine had been working with up to this point in book 2 identifies sin as the *inordinate* desire for something that is genuinely good. What the fornicator or the glutton seeks is a good, but each person sins in preferring the genuine but lower good at which his fornication or gluttony aims to things of greater value: "Sin is committed for the sake of all these [lower goods] . . . when by virtue of a desire that is inordinate (since these are the lowest sort of good) better and higher things are abandoned. For these [lowest goods], too, have their own delights" (2.10). The goods identified here are genuine goods, despite their being of the lowest kind, and they have their own delights—that is why they can straightforwardly and directly motivate sinners to sin. But the deceptive vices give us a slightly different perspective on sin. The avaricious person, for example, seeks possessions and, presumably, does so inordinately—to that extent avarice has the structure of fornication and gluttony. But in the case of avarice there is an additional twist: the avaricious person's pursuit of possessions constitutes (in a defective and shadowy way) an attempt to possess all things, that is, to be like God in respect of possessions. The person who is subject to a deceptive vice, then, inordinately desires some object and *in so doing* seeks to have what can be had only by being or being in God. Deceptive vices call our attention, as it were, to two objects in the relevant sins: the sinner's direct object (possessions or power or honors and glory) and what we might think of as his indirect object (being like God in the relevant respect).

Having provided a new tool for thinking about the nature of these sins, Augustine brings it to bear on his own theft of the pears. Here is the relevant text:

> All who set themselves apart from you and extol themselves over against you imitate you perversely. But even when they imitate you in this way they indicate that you are the creator of all natures and that there is no way they can escape from you. What was it, then, that I took delight in (*dilexi*) in that theft, and in what way did I imitate my Lord viciously and perversely? Was it pleasing (*libuit*) to do something against the law at least deceptively (since I could not do it by sheer force), so that by doing with impunity what was not permitted I might imitate, in a dim likeness of omnipotence, the shackled freedom of a prisoner? Behold, this person is a slave who flees his master and hides in the shadows. What rottenness! What a monstrous life and abyss of death! Could what is not permitted have been pleasing for no other reason than that it was not permitted?
>
> (2.14)[29]

There is no mistaking the fact that Augustine intends here to identify his own theft of the pears as a case of perverse imitation of God, on the model provided by the deceptive vices. He begins with a general principle (at lines 1–2) that is clearly meant to encompass his own case. He has been describing himself since the opening lines of the *Confessions* as the prodigal who travels far from home, who sets himself apart from God.[30] Moreover, here in the story of the theft of the pears he has portrayed himself as the thief who brazenly flaunts the law God has indelibly inscribed on human hearts. So Augustine has set himself apart from God and extolled himself over against God. In the theft of the pears, then, it must be that he is imitating God perversely.[31]

But how exactly is his petty thievery a perverse imitation of God? Augustine raises the question (at line 5) and links it with the question he had left aside at the end of section 12 when he digressed to explain the deceptive vices. The suggestion is that the two questions must be treated together, that their answers will also be linked. Augustine goes on straightaway to offer an account (at lines 6–10) designed, apparently, to answer both questions. In breaking God's law with impunity he has grasped at freedom and power (his direct object) in a way attempts to be like God (his indirect object)—it is as if he were asserting "I can do whatever I want!" "Not even divine law can restrict what I do." But the freedom is sham—it is the shackled freedom of a prisoner who can move only as far as and only in the manner in which his shackles permit him to move. And the power he claims for himself is at best a dim likeness of omnipotence. The whole affair, Augustine suggests, is predicated on the illusion that in flouting God's law he is asserting or claiming for himself a kind of freedom and power that he does not and cannot possess. He acts as if he alone determines the limits of his actions. He thereby imitates omnipotent God perversely.

It is clear, then, how Augustine's account answers the question "In what way did I imitate my Lord viciously and perversely?" It also seems clear that it answers the question "What was it, then, that I took delight in in that theft?" According to the account Augustine entertains here in section 14, he took delight in the idea of possessing the radical freedom and power his act of impunity was intended to express. That sort of freedom and power—found only in the divine omnipotence—is a genuine good, a divine attribute, and recognizably delightful. Of course Augustine's idea that he himself could possess or manifest it is an illusion. But it seems reasonable to suppose—and Augustine's account seems to suggest—that that idea nevertheless delighted him and motivated his theft of the pears. In this way, both Augustine's subjective and objective requirements on explaining motivation are satisfied by the analysis of the events he sets out here. The puzzle of the motivation of the theft seems resolved.

I claim, then, that in section 14 Augustine uses the notion of the illusory imitation of God suggested to him by his account of the deceptive vices to unlock a resolution to the central puzzle of the theft of the pears. That conclusion is confirmed, I think, by a striking parallel from another of Augustine's texts. In *De libero arbitrio* Augustine argues that the first evil in creation occurs when one of God's rational creatures—the devil—freely turns away from God, loving certain created goods in preference to God himself who is the highest good. Near the end of the book Augustine raises and tries to resolve the difficulty that account unavoidably suggests: Why would the devil, who knows that God is the highest good and that his own happiness consists in loving God as the highest good, freely choose lesser, created goods in preference to God? What could possibly motivate the devil to act in this patently irrational and self-defeating way? Here is Augustine's reply:

> In its contemplation of the highest wisdom (which of course the [devil's] mind is not, since the highest wisdom is unchangeable), the [devil's] mind (which is changeable) also observes itself and, in a certain way, comes before its own mind. This would not happen unless there were a difference by virtue of which it is not what God is and nevertheless

> is something that can be pleasing (*placere*) next to God. Now, it is better when the mind forgets itself in the presence of the love of the immutable God or considers itself of little value in comparison with it. But if, insofar as it encounters itself, it pleases (*placet*) itself to the point of perversely imitating God so that it wills to enjoy (*frui*) its own power, then to the extent to which it desires to be greater, to that extent it becomes less. This is "pride, the beginning of all sin" (Ecclesiasticus 10:13).
>
> (*De libero arbitrio* 3.76)[32]

Augustine's account of the way in which his own theft of the pears constitutes a perverse imitation of God precisely tracks this account of the motivation for creation's very first sin. As Augustine explains it, the devil, who is first distracted from contemplation of God by his own genuine goodness, then takes inordinate delight in it, willing to enjoy his own power in such a way that he perversely imitates God.[33]

The parallels between these two accounts are significant for two reasons. First, they show clearly that Augustine intends us to take seriously his analysis of the theft of the pears as perverse imitation of God's power. The motivations Augustine details for the theft are not unique to this case nor are they idle conjectures he entertains briefly only to leave aside. Rather they conform to an important pattern, the prototype of which is found in the fall of the angels. Moreover, the pattern is intended, as the account of the devil's fall shows, to provide a genuine answer to the question of what motivates sinners to imitate God in this way. They are moved by the delight they take in the idea of the utter self-determination that betokens omnipotence. We should conclude, then, that understanding the theft of the pears as imitation of divine omnipotence constitutes Augustine's answer to the question "What was it, then, that I took delight in in that theft?"

Second, seeing that the account of the theft is modeled closely on the account of the devil's fall puts us in position to see an important reason Augustine has for including the story of the theft of the pears in book 2 of the *Confessions.* At the end of the account of the devil's fall (quoted above), Augustine identifies the devil's sin as pride, and quotes a biblical text identifying pride as the beginning of all sin. We can see the point in calling perverse imitation of God "pride." The devil's sort of self-assertion—his choosing, on his own accord, to prefer a created good to the highest good—constitutes the placing of one's own choices and their objects (in this case one's own power) above all other things. That, one might say, is the paradigm of pride. Moreover, Augustine supposes that the devil's first sin is appropriately called "the beginning of all sin" not only because the devil's prideful act is in fact the very first evil in all creation but also because pride is at the root or is the source of all other sins. The story of the theft of the pears is crucial to book 2 of the *Confessions*, therefore, because it allows Augustine to identify and explain an idea without which he thinks no account of sin can be complete: the idea that imitation of God in the form of prideful self-assertion is at the bottom of all sin.[34] The story of the theft of the pears is designed to push Augustine's explanation of the nature of sin to this its deepest level.

In what sense is pride the root or source of every sin? Augustine has argued that each sin consists in loving a lesser good in preference to God; that is what it is for a person to turn away from God and toward created things. At the first level of explanation, then, Augustine tells us that the sinner takes delight in some created thing (bodily pleasure, temporal honors, the sweetness of companionship) and loves it disproportionately. But we might reasonably go on to ask *why* or *for what reason* the sinner loves this thing too much? Augustine supposes that that question moves us to a deeper level of explanation. When sinners (irrationally) prefer lesser goods to higher ones, they are in essence determining for themselves how goods are to be ranked relative to one another, disregarding their objective values and rankings. But that is an act of self-assertion, claiming for oneself a power one does not and cannot possess, the power to determine by one's own will the relative values of things. All sinners, then, whatever the species of their sin, insofar as they love something inordinately, exemplify the sort of over-reaching self-assertion that Augustine calls pride.[35]

If I have understood Augustine's views about pride correctly, then it follows that his account of sin as the sort of perverse imitation of God in which pride consists and his account of sin as inordinate desire for created goods are in fact complementary. Each is correct and illuminating of sin's nature. They function, as it were, at different levels.

6. Augustine's Reticence

There is an obvious difficulty for the position I have just defended. Having identified a satisfactory motive for the theft, as I have argued he does in section 14, why does Augustine not proclaim that fact clearly and close the investigation. Why does he conclude section 14 by asking, "Could what is not permitted have been pleasing for no other reason than that it was not permitted?" If he had indeed just shown that there was something in the theft in which he took delight—the assertion of his own freedom and power—this question would be out of place. If I am right, we can see the significance of his insisting on having stolen the pears *because* it was forbidden. The fact that it was forbidden is crucial to the action's constituting the sort of prideful grasp at power that Augustine wants us to focus on. But he ought no longer to suppose that he did what he did *for no other reason* than that is was forbidden. He ought to suppose instead that he did it because it was not permitted and also because of the illusion of omnipotence it presented him. Similarly, when he returns to these issues in section 16 (see section 4 above), why does he seem to assume that he still lacks an answer to the question I have claimed he has resolved here in section 14?

I think Augustine has two reasons for insisting even after the analysis in section 14, that he stole the pears for no other reason that than it was not permitted. First, the action's being forbidden is crucially constitutive of and not merely instrumentally or accidentally tied to its expressing the sort of pride Augustine has identified. In a certain sort of way the allure of doing what is forbidden *just is* the allure of asserting one's own freedom and power. So when Augustine continues to maintain that there was no reason for his action other than that it was forbidden, he need not be taken to be denying thereby that he did it for the sake of asserting his own imagined omnipotence. Granted, the two *descriptions* of his motives are different and, on one way of looking at it, that is sufficient for ascribing two different motives to him.[36] But on another way of looking at it—the way I think Augustine chooses to adopt here—the two descriptions do not ascribe different motives since the one description merely specifies the feature of the action (its being forbidden) that is crucially constitutive of the action's satisfying the other description (its being an expression of radical freedom and power). So Augustine has some justification for continuing to maintain that he was motivated by nothing other than the fact that the theft was forbidden even while acknowledging that he was motivated by a desire for a kind of limitless power.

Second, there is another sense in which Augustine is right to say that there is nothing else motivating him. Insofar as he was motivated by delusions of his own omnipotence, there was nothing actually corresponding to his delusions. He was not in fact omnipotent nor was it possible that he become omnipotent. What moved him, then, was in reality nothing at all, a mere delusion, something utterly illusory. For that reason it is, in a way, correct to say that he was motivated by nothing other than the fact that the theft was forbidden. Of course illusions (as distinct from what the illusions are illusions of) can and do motivate us, and that is why it is also correct to say that the shadowy illusion of unlimited power moved him to commit his crime. He was moved by the prospect of an omnipotence that is impossible to attain.

Moreover, Augustine has good rhetorical reasons for availing himself of these less than entirely transparent philosophical maneuvers. In general he wants the story of the theft of the pears to emphasize the depravity of his soul at this stage of his life. He wants by the end of book 2 to be able to claim that the prodigal has reached his nadir. The insistence that he stole the pears only because the act was forbidden serves that purpose well.

He also has good reason to postpone the suggestion that the puzzle has been finally resolved. In fact he thinks that the explanation is not yet complete at the end of section 14. As we have seen, the allure of camaraderie plays a crucial, role in moving him to act, and that component of the account is still to come. Augustine's insistence that he stole the pears only because the act was forbidden allows him space to return to the question of motivation for the final time in section 16. As I have claimed, that insistence is only part of the truth

Augustine has revealed to us in section 14. But Augustine the skilled rhetorician is happy to emphasize just the parts of the truth that best advance his project.

7. Salvaging Intelligible Motivation

Commentators have sometimes suggested that Augustine believes that in its most radical cases sin is utterly unintelligible, that no intelligible motivation can be found that would explain—in the sort of way reasons-explanations explain—the actions of sinners in these cases.[37] The account of the theft of the pears can seem to support that view. It can seem that Augustine presents the theft of the pears precisely as a counterexample to the claim that all voluntary actions are motivated by an intelligible delight, and that his lengthy discussion of the case leaves the counterexample standing. It would follow that in radical cases of sin rational creatures choose what is evil for its own sake and for no other reason.

I have argued here that Augustine is interested in the theft of the pears for just the reason these commentators suppose—because it appears to present a counterexample to what Augustine himself holds to be the best account of the motivations of voluntary action—but that his search for intelligible motivations in this case is *not* fruitless. Augustine succeeds in uncovering two motivations for his thievery which, in his analysis, work crucially together. He stole the pears because doing so seemed to him a way of expressing or claiming for himself a kind of limitless freedom and power. But given that that motive was not sufficient by itself to move him to the deed, his action also required the motivation provided by his desire to be included in the fellowship of rogues—to love and be loved.[38] These are the two components of the composite motivational state Augustine's analysis of the theft of the pears reveals. Each of these motivating factors constitutes an intelligible motivation of the sort required by Augustine's own account of motivation. Each identifies something that an agent might reasonably take to be a good and therefore take delight in, even if doing so involves significant error or illusion.

Augustine's analysis of the theft of the pears therefore shows us how his action on that occasion is in fact intelligible. The analysis also makes clear that his motivations were neither simple nor immediately transparent. Augustine thereby succeeds in showing that the complexity and depth of the human psyche requires that any search for the motivations of voluntary action be patient, subtle, and resourceful.[39]

Notes

1. For example, Oliver Wendell Holmes: "Rum thing to see a man making a mountain out of robbing a pear tree in his teens" (as quoted in Starnes [1990], 37).

2. For useful general discussion, see Courcelle (1968), O'Connell (1989) ch. 4, James J. O'Donnell (1992) vol. II, Starnes (1990) 37–51 and Wills (1999) 10–15. See also the notes to *Confessions* book 2 in Gibb and Montgomery's edition (Augustine 1927) and those by Solignac (1998).
3. In references to the *Confessions* I omit the (redundant) chapter numbers in favor of the more precise section numbers. Hence "2.9–18" refers to book 2, sections 9–18.
4. See Luke 15:11–32 The parable of the prodigal son is prominent throughout the *Confessions* but especially here in book 2. See Ferrari (1971).
5. Boulding's translations (Augustine [1997]).
6. See Augustine's systematic analysis of the concept of sin in *De libero arbitrio.* In book 1 of that work Augustine begins his analysis by asking what constitutes the evil in adultery (1.6). His preliminary suggestion is that it is lust (*libido*) (1.8). He then goes on to generalize on that suggestion: the evil in sin in general is inordinate desire (1.18–20). See my discussion of Augustine's account of sin in MacDonald (1994).
7. Augustine follows biblical practice in referring to sin generally as fornication: the Old Testament often describes Israel's breaking of the covenant with God as fornication.
8. Translations are my own except where noted. I have used O'Donnell (1992) vol. I: "Introduction and Text."
9. It is significant that the object of assessment throughout the account is Augustine's heart and not the act of theft itself. Augustine holds that the morally significant element in sin—what makes it sin—is a feature of the agent's motivation (see *De libero arbitrio* 1). See also Mann (1994).
10. The feeding of the pears to the pigs in Augustine's story is perhaps meant to remind us of the Gospel's prodigal son who finds himself utterly destitute and far from home slopping another man's pigs.
11. See Starnes (1990) 45 and Wills (1999) 14–15. (Wills remarks that no one has seen this key point [p. 14], but Starnes's observations, for one, antedate Wills's by nearly a decade.)
12. The language reflects Isaiah 14:12ff. and Ezekiel 28:13ff. O'Connell (1989) emphasizes the similarities with Plotinian language and themes.
13. See Ferrari, (1970).
14. See my "Primal Sin" (1994).
15. *De sermone Domini in monte* dates from 393, most likely four or five years prior to the *Confessions.* Compare: *De libero arbitrio* 329; 3.74–75; *De trinitate* 12.17–18.
16. In the passage from *De sermone Domini in monte*, Augustine focuses on suggestion, delight and consent; presumably there is a phenomenon mirroring this one that consists in suggestion and something like aversion and rejection.
17. Augustine develops the idea more fully in *De musica* 6. I am grateful to Charles Brittain for this reference.
18. *Pace* Hume.
19. William E. Mann (1978) agrees that Augustine is worried about the intelligibility of the motivation alleged to obtain in the case of the theft of the pears, but his analysis of the locus of the worry is different from mine. Although Augustine does worry (elsewhere) about how an agent can come to prefer a lesser good to a greater good, I do not think that is the issue in the front of Augustine's mind in the theft of the pears.
20. The account of sin that appears to be challenged here by the possibility of voluntary action that aims at no good is first developed in detail in *De libero arbitrio* 1, perhaps as much as a decade prior to the writing of the *Confessions.* He continues to endorse that view here in the *Confessions* (the free-will theodicy articulated in book 7 relies on it, for example) and throughout his career (see, for example, *De civitate Dei* books 10–14, written more than a decade after the *Confessions*).
21. Augustine's use of the term 'fruit' (*fructus*) here achieves several rhetorical ends. It echoes Paul's reflection on the fruits of a life of sin at Romans 621: "But then what return did you get from the things of which you are now ashamed?" (*quem ergo fructum habuistis tunc in*

quibus nunc erubescitis; compare Augustine: *quem fructum habui*. . . *in his quae nunc recolens erubesco*). It reminds us of Adam and Eve's sin in the garden: "[Eve] took of [the tree's] fruit and ate; and she also gave some to her husband, and he ate" (Genesis 3:6). Moreover, in virtue of the etymological connection of 'fructus' with the verb 'fruor' (to enjoy), it plays on the relation between what one aims at (what one aims to enjoy) and what one actually gets (the fruit of one's actions).

22. Augustine here draws on his metaphysics of evil. On his view, evils are not realities, not substances or natures, but corruptions or privations in substances or natures. Insofar as his theft is evil, then, it is not a reality in its own right but a corruption or privation and, hence, metaphysically a nothing. See my account of Augustine's metaphysics of evil in "Primal Sin" (1994).
23. Is it intelligible? Augustine goes on in the next section to reflect on the curious phenomenon he has just uncovered: "Why, then, did I take delight in that which I would not have done by myself?" Since that material is not directly relevant to my purposes here, I leave it aside. For especially illuminating commentary, see Starnes, *Augustine's Conversion*, 43–5.
24. O'Connell, however, has doubts. See O'Connell (1989) 49, n. 2.
25. See section 2 above.
26. *Defectiva species et umbratica vitiis fallentibus* (last line of 2.12). There is reason to doubt whether the denial in this case is entirely genuine. I return to this question below, see n. 31.
27. The deceptive vices mentioned in section 13 are: pride, ambition, the brutality of those in power, the flatteries of lascivious people, curiosity, ignorance (simplicity), foolishness (innocence), sloth, luxury, extravagance, avarice, envy, anger, insecurity, and sorrow. See Starnes (1990) 41.
28. See O'Donnell (1992), "Commentary on Books 1–7," 136–7 for some principles of organization.
29. This is all of section 14 excepting only the section's first sentence (already quoted just above). The editions begin the new section with the preceding sentence ("In this way the soul fornicates when it is turned from you and seeks apart from you things which it finds pure and clear only when it returns to you"), but the sense of the text would be clearer if the new section began with the sentence that begins this quotation ("All who set themselves apart from you . . ."). The former sentence should be read as concluding section 13's digression into the deceptive vices; the latter sentence begins a new thought, adapting the results of that discussion to the special case at hand.
30. *Omnes qui longe se a te faciunt.* The language reflects the Gospel account of the story: *adulescentior filius peregre profectus est in regionem longinquam.* It also has affinities with Plotinian texts; see O'Connell (1989) 48–9.
31. Hence, it seems clear that Augustine does indeed suppose that the theft conforms to the model of the deceptive vices. What, then, to make of the last clause of section 12 where he seems to deny that his theft had even the defective attraction of the sort manifested in the deceptive vices? Perhaps that last clause should be taken as a question: "Does it lack even the defective and shadowy beauty found in the deceptive vices?" The question's answer ("no, it does not lack even that") would then be found here in section 14.
32. Book 3 of *De libero arbitrio* was composed sometime between 391 and 394, roughly five years prior to the writing of the *Confessions.* In the passage immediately preceding the text quoted here, Augustine puts the question as one about where the *suggestion* on which the devil ultimately acted comes from (3.74–5). He clearly has in mind the tri-partite analysis of sin (suggestion, delight, consent) articulated in the passage from *De sermone Domini in monte* quoted above (see section 2).
33. The notion of imitation of God is a feature of all three prominent Old Testament accounts of creaturely falls: Genesis 3, Isaiah 14:12ff., and Ezekiel 28:13ff.
34. See my "Primal Sin" (1994). See also Green (1949).

35. It is important that sinners who desire things inordinately do so in some sense voluntarily or by virtue of their wills. Otherwise their inordinate desire could not be construed as *self*-assertion of the appropriate sort, that is, the sort on which moral responsibility attends. See my discussion in "Primal Sin" (1994).
36. Given the intensionality of ascriptions of motive.
37. O'Connell seems to take this line, for example; see O'Connell (1989) 49, n. 2.
38. See Starnes (1990, 43–5) for an illuminating argument that these two motivating factors are *essentially* interdependent. The idea is that imitating God can be appealing only when an audience is present (when there is someone to acknowledge one's freedom and power). That would explain why the motivation identified in section 14 is not sufficient apart from the motivation identified in section 16.
39. I presented earlier versions of this chapter at the Catholic University of America and at the Cornell Summer Colloquium in Medieval Philosophy. I am grateful to the audiences on those occasions for helpful comments. I am also grateful to the participants in a graduate seminar on Augustine I taught at Cornell in fall 2001 for their useful discussion of this material. I have learned a great deal about the *Confessions* over a number of years from my colleague Charles Brittain. I thank him for many hours of stimulating conversation.

CHAPTER 2

Wanting Bad Things

GARETH MATTHEWS

In a famous passage in one of Plato's dialogues (*Meno* 77b), the character Meno is made to suggest that virtue is (i) wanting noble things (*ta kala*) and (ii) having the power to acquire them. Socrates gets Meno to agree that by 'noble things' he simply means good things. Then Socrates asks, in seeming bafflement, whether Meno thinks that, although some people want good things, others actually want bad things. His point is that, unless, conceivably, some people actually do want bad things, the first half of Meno's suggestion as to the nature of virtue, namely, wanting good (or noble) things, will be empty and so will not play any role in marking off virtue from nonvirtue.

Meno, for his part, thinks it obvious that some people do want bad things. But Socrates presses him hard by drawing a distinction: "Do you mean," Socrates asks Meno, "that some people want bad things believing them to be good, or is it that some people want bad things knowing them to be bad?" (77c). "Both," replies Meno, simply.

Socrates expends very little effort in the dialogue trying to show that nobody wants bad things, thinking that they are good. His idea seems to be that if one mistakenly supposes that an object of desire is good, when it is really bad, then the real object of one's desire is not the actually bad object one *seems* to want, but rather the good object one has pictured for oneself.

What, now, about the other kind of case that Socrates identifies? Can we ever want bad things, knowing that they are bad, or even believing that they are bad? Here Socrates assumes that my wanting bad things, if it were possible, would be my wanting things that it would be bad for me to get. Thus, he seems to reason, my wanting bad things *believing* them to be bad would be wanting them *believing* that they would be bad for me to get. (We might wish to question that inference.) Getting bad things, he adds, would be getting harmful things that would make one miserable. Socrates gets Meno to agree that no one wants to be harmed or made miserable.

Here all sorts of complications set in. Can I want another smoke, knowing that, *in the long run*, smoking is bad for me even if, in the short run, I would enjoy the pleasure of a smoke? Surely I can. Socrates does not discuss this kind of case in the *Meno*. But we can easily imagine what he would say: Doing such a thing would only be possible by putting out of one's mind the long-term badness and focusing on the short-term goodness, which would then be the true object of one's desire.

Perhaps I have said enough about the *Meno* passage to make clear that Socratic reasoning can easily lead us to conclude that wanting bad things requires either ignoring or else simply being ignorant in some crucial way about the badness of what one wants. That conclusion fits well with the Socratic idea that virtue is a kind of knowledge and that vice, wanting what are, in fact, bad things, is a kind of ignorance. That idea is made plausible by the somewhat more general thought that one could not want a thing except by thinking that it would be, in some way or other, a good thing to do or have. One wants whatever one wants, it is sometimes put, "under the form of the Good" – that is, conceived as something good. Let's call this thesis "(W1)" and formulate it in the following way:

> (W1) Wanting something is always wanting something one believes at the time to be good.

Augustine seems to have been the first important philosopher to question (W1). He does this by telling a rather ordinary story about a prank he participated in as an adolescent. Before he tells the story, however, he explains a bit about the context. In his *Confessions*, he writes, "During my sixteenth year there was an interruption in my studies. I was recalled from Madauros, the nearby town where I had first lived away from home to learn literature and oratory. During that time funds were gathered in preparation for a more distant absence at Carthage, for which my father had more enthusiasm than cash, since he was a citizen of Thagaste with very modest resources" (2.3.5).

Finding himself on a sort of extended holiday before being sent off for higher education in Carthage, Augustine did things he would later regret. Looking back on this year three decades later, when he wrote his *Confessions*, he could say:

> T1. At one time in adolescence I was burning to find satisfaction in hellish pleasures. I ran wild in the shadowy jungle of erotic adventures.
>
> (2.1.1)

Augustine describes this year as one of idleness in which he began to "show signs of virility and the stirrings of adolescence" (2.3.6). "Among my peer group," he writes, "I was ashamed not to be equally guilty of shameful behavior when I heard them boasting of their sexual exploits" (2.3.7). He continues:

> T2. Such were the companions with whom I made my way through the streets of Babylon. With them I rolled in its dung as if rolling in spices and precious ointments . . . The reins were relaxed to allow me to amuse myself. There was no strict discipline to keep me in check, which led to an unbridled dissoluteness in many different directions.
>
> (2.3.8)

With a buildup like T1 and T2 we might expect a story in which Augustine disgraces his family by making the underage daughter of a local landowner pregnant. But what follows is something very different. Here is the story that forms the centerpiece of *Confessions* 2:

> T3. There was a pear tree near our vineyard laden with fruit, though attractive in neither colour nor taste. To shake the fruit off the tree and carry off the pears a gang of naughty adolescents and I set off late at night after (in our usual pestilential way) we had continued our game in the streets. We carried off a huge load of pears. But they were not for our feasts but merely to throw to the pigs. Even if we ate a few, nevertheless our pleasure lay in doing what was not allowed.
>
> (2.4.9)

This incident seems somehow too ordinary to be the focus of a whole book of Augustine's *Confessions.* Yet Augustine invests it with great significance. In this theft, he writes:

> T4. I became evil for no reason. I had no motive for my wickedness except the wickedness itself. It was foul, and I loved it. I loved the self-destruction, I loved my fall, not the object for which I had fallen but my fall itself. My depraved soul leaped down from your firmament to ruin. I was seeking not to gain anything by shameful means, but shame for its own sake.
>
> (2.4.9)

It is difficult to take the rhetoric of this passage seriously. Yet Augustine seems to want us to do so. He seems to be deadly serious when he claims that

(a) he became evil for no reason;
(b) his motive was to achieve wickedness;

(c) what he did was foul and he loved it; and
(d) he was seeking to do something shameful for the sake of doing something shameful.

There could hardly be a more emphatic rejection of (W1) than this.

Augustine seems to realize that we readers will be baffled by his account of his motivation in stealing the pears. How can we be expected to believe that anybody would become evil for no reason, or that Augustine's motive was to achieve wickedness, or that he loved what was foul, or that he was seeking to do something shameful for the sake of doing something shameful? How could anyone believe such claims?

Somewhat surprisingly, Augustine begins his attempt to make his motivation comprehensible by talking about beauty. Thus T4 is followed immediately by this:

> T5. There is beauty in lovely physical objects as in gold and silver and all other such things. When the body touches such things, much significance attaches to the rapport of the object with the touch. Each of the other senses has its own appropriate mode of response to physical things. Temporal honour and the power of giving orders and of being in command have their own kind of dignity, though this is also the origin of self-assertion.
>
> (2.5.10)

What is going on here? First Augustine gives a baffling account of his motivation for stealing pears with his adolescent gang. Then he starts talking about beauty. How is beauty relevant to understanding the pear episode?

The relevance of beauty, I suggest, is this. Often we can explain why some person, A, chose to ø by making clear how A could think of øing itself, or what A might hope to get by øing, as beautiful, or, at the very least, as attractive. For example, most of us think gold and silver and things made of them are beautiful. We can understand that someone who sees an unguarded gold or silver cup might want to steal it. The implicit thesis here is something like this:

> (W2) If A chooses to ø, then, other things being equal, the fact (if it is a fact) that A thinks øing is an attractive thing to do, or else thinks øing is a good way to get some attractive object, explains why A chooses to ø.

If Augustine can make clear how he could think stealing is an attractive thing to do, or else that stealing is a good way to get some attractive object, then he has, other things being equal, an explanation for why he chose to steal.

Augustine goes on to say this:

> T6. The life which we live in this world has its attractiveness because of a certain measure in its beauty and its harmony with all these inferior objects that are beautiful.
>
> (2.5.10)

The mention of inferior objects that are, nevertheless, beautiful in their own way, invites us to consider whether a wrongful act might be understood as an agent's being attracted to something that has its own beauty, even though its beauty is outshone by that of an alternative, but superior, object. Augustine writes:

> T7. When a crime is under investigation to discover the motive for which it was done, the accusation is not usually believed except in cases where the appetite to obtain (or the fear of losing) one of those goods which we have called inferior appears a plausible possibility. They are beautiful and attractive even if, in comparison with the higher goods which give true happiness, they are mean and base.
>
> (2.5.11)

Even the actions of that most wicked Roman senator, Catiline, Augustine tells us, can be understood as motivated by an attraction to lesser goods, and objects of inferior beauty:

> T8. It was said of one brutal and cruel man [Catiline] that he was evil and savage without reason. Yet the preceding passage gave the motive: "Lest disuse might make his hand or mind slow to react." . . . His objective was to capture the city by violent crimes to obtain honors, government, and wealth. . . . No, not even Catiline himself loved his crimes; something else motivated him to commit them.
>
> (2.5.11)

So does the example of the evil and wicked Catiline help Augustine to understand his own sinful act? Apparently not. Addressing his act of theft as if it were another person he says:

> T9. There was nothing beautiful about you [my act of theft].
>
> (2.6.12)

Adding to his puzzlement Augustine draws on his understanding of evil as a deficiency, a mere "nothing," to ask, plaintively, "Do you exist at all for me to be addressing you?"

The pears he stole, Augustine concedes, were beautiful as being part of God's creation. But, he insists, it was not really the pears that he was attracted to. He had better ones at home. The ones he picked, he tells us, he picked solely with the motive of stealing. He threw the pears themselves away. "My feasting," he goes on, "was only on the wickedness which I took pleasure in enjoying" (2.6.12). But wickedness, it seems, cannot be understood as a lesser good with its own beauty. And Augustine makes no effort to get us to conceive it that way.

At the very end of this section Augustine tells us that vice is sometimes a "flawed reflection of beauty" (2.6.12). What he means by that comment is presumably brought out in the next section. "Pride imitates what is lofty," he tells us, "but you alone are God most high above all things" (2.6.13). Augustine then goes on to produce a list of what he seems to consider vices, including ambition, cruelty, soft endearments, and [mere] curiosity. The point of this list seems to be summed up in the next section, where Augustine tells us, "In their perverted way all humanity imitates you" (2.6.14). That observation leads Augustine into a line of explanation that he seems to accept. Addressing God, he says this:

> T10. In their perverted way all humanity imitates you. Yet they put themselves at a distance from you and exalt themselves against you. But even by thus imitating you they acknowledge that you are the creator of all nature and concede that there is no place where one can entirely escape from you. Therefore in that act of theft what was the object of my love, and in what way did I viciously and perversely imitate my Lord? Was my pleasure to break your law, but by deceit, since I had not the power to do that by force? Was I acting like a prisoner with restricted liberty who does with impunity what is not permitted, thereby making an assertion of possessing a dim resemblance to omnipotence? Was it possible to take pleasure in what was not allowed for no other reason than that it was not allowed?
>
> (2.6.14)

Here we have the picture of a prisoner who, frustrated and resentful at being under the rule of another, acts as if free from constraint in a futile effort to prove his freedom. The prisoner's action is, in a way, perfectly understandable. Perhaps we ourselves have on occasion acted in futile defiance of a parent or teacher or other authority figure. Although understandable, the action may be irrational in that it has no chance of changing the power relationship. The action may also be self-destructive, even deliberately self-destructive. Since it seeks no worthwhile goal, it is nihilistic. Let us call a person who acts out of this sort of motivation a "Rebel Without a Cause," after the movie of that name starring James Dean.

The Rebel Without a Cause wants to perform an action without believing either that the action, or what the action may achieve, is either good or beautiful. Thus the Rebel Without a Cause is a counterexample to (W1). Moreover the Rebel's action does not fall under the explanatory schema (W2). This Rebel acts, not even according to a Nietzschean transvaluation of values, but simply from resentment and frustration.

So here, at last, we have a somewhat plausible explanation of Augustine's theft. Perhaps he was rebelling, in a futile and foolish way, against God and God's morality. His theft was, perhaps the act of a perverted will.

In the final stage of his argument, Augustine turns to what at first glance may seem to be a much more satisfying explanation. He was, after all, taking part in a gang action. Maybe what Augustine sought was the camaraderie of the gang. Augustine writes:

> T11. What fruit had I, wretched boy, in these things which I now blush to recall, above all in that theft in which I loved nothing but the theft itself? The theft itself was a nothing, and for that reason, I was the more miserable. Yet had I been alone, I would not have done it – I remember my state of mind to be thus at the time – alone I would never have done it. Therefore my love in that act was to be associated with the gang in whose company I did it. Does it follow that I loved something other than the theft? No, nothing else in reality because association with the gang is also a nothing.
>
> (2.8.16)

This is a difficult passage to interpret. But Augustine seems here to commit himself to these claims:

(C1) In his act of theft, he loved nothing but the act of theft itself.
(C2) What he loved in that act of theft was to be associated with the gang.
(C3) He would not have performed the act of theft except in the company of others.
(C4) Yet he loved nothing other than the theft.

(C2) and (C4) seem to be in direct conflict. I shall try to show, a little later, how we might try to resolve that apparent conflict.

We might have expected that Augustine would supplant his suggestion about the Rebel Without a Cause with the explanation that he acted out of a desire to be approved by the gang. But what he does is something different from that. For one thing, he never withdraws his insistence that his pleasure lay in committing the act itself. Here is part of the next section, in which he elaborates on (C2) and (C3):

> T12. Had I been alone, it would have given me absolutely no pleasure, nor would I have committed [the act]. Friendship can be a dangerous enemy, a seduction of the mind lying beyond the reach of investigation. Out of a

> game and a jest came an avid desire to do injury and an appetite to inflict loss on someone else without any motive of personal gain on my part, and no pleasure in settling a score. As soon as the words are spoken, "Let's go and do it," one is ashamed not to be shameless.
>
> (2.9.17)

But T12 does more than elaborate on (C2) and (C3). It adds these claims:

(C5) He would not have taken pleasure in the act of theft, if he had been alone.
(C6) He had an avid desire to do injury and an appetite to inflict loss on someone else without any motive of personal gain on his part, and no pleasure in settling a score.

Can any sense be made of the conjunction of (C1) through (C6)? For starters we might think of mob actions, for example, lynchings, or gang rapes. It may very well be that many members of a given gang seek the approval or admiration of other gang members. But perhaps some participants in, say, a gang rape, find that the effect of acting in a gang is primarily, or even solely, to remove their inhibitions and free them to assault an innocent woman without other cause or motive except the sadistic desire to assault a woman. It may also be especially exhilarating to act in consort with others. What I have in mind is not that the gang member is seeking the approval of the others. It is rather that the group action, in which the individual is participating has a special thrill it would not have if the individual were acting alone.

If we want to see mob evil on a large screen, we might think of the horrendous horrors of the twentieth century – the Holocaust, the killing fields of Cambodia, the massacres of Rwanda. No doubt the motivation of individuals who participated in those horrors were often very complicated and very diverse. But these examples of mass evil seem to illustrate the point that mob action unleashes motivational forces that go well beyond wanting to be accepted or admired by the mob. And at least sometimes, it seems plausible to say that the atrocities are committed for the sake of committing atrocities, even though the participants would not have committed such atrocities on their own.

Of course a gang's theft of some pears is relatively insignificant in comparison with a gang rape, let alone a massacre. Yet the motivational structure of vast horrors may be mirrored in something as tame as stealing some pears from someone against whom one has no grudge, and then throwing those pears willfully to the swine.

So here is my suggestion as to how Augustine understands his act of theft. First, he leaves standing his "perversion account," the Rebel Without a Cause. He was throwing over the traces of God's morality, but without substituting for it any new morality of his own.

Augustine then supplements the Rebel story with an account of mob action. In concert with the gang he did something he would never have done on his own. But he does not see himself as acting so as to receive the approval or admiration of the gang. What he loved was the act itself, but performed in concert with the gang.

In the coda to *Confessions* 2, the very last section, which is only a short paragraph, Augustine does two more things. First he expresses exasperation at his own best attempt to understand his theft. He writes:

> T13. Who can untie this extremely twisted and tangled knot? It is a foul affair, I have no wish to give attention to it; I have no desire to contemplate it.
>
> (2.10.18)

Then, in the very last sentence of Book 2, he makes this summary judgment on his moral and. religious state at the time of this theft:

> T14. I became to myself a region of destitution.

I take T13 to express Augustine's lingering perplexity about his action and his dissatisfaction with his best efforts to understand it. Something like this is a feature of the horrors of the twentieth century. We are puzzled and perplexed at how people who, before their participation in, say, a great massacre, can seem to be, indeed, can be, such ordinary people. They are the person next door. Even more scarily, they are me! How did such ordinary, seemingly decent people, come to participate in such horrendous acts of evil? It boggles the mind. We want to say with Augustine, "Who can untie this extremely twisted and tangled knot?"

It is interesting to me that Joel Feinberg, in a recent discussion of evil, claims that such perplexity is partly constitutive of what he calls "pure evil." Feinberg writes:

> The purely evil wrongdoer may be taken by surprise by his own voluntary action. His conduct will seem mysterious to other people and likely will remain mysterious even after extensive study. If his conduct . . . remains a mystery, it may remain a mystery to *him* as well as to everybody else. His harmful action, having no motive intelligible to him or to anyone else, was done for no apparent reason and seems even to him to be incomprehensible. That must be what pure evil feels like from the inside. At its best, it is an astonishingly opaque phenomenon. At its worst it is, well, plain evil, nothing more, nothing less.[1]

I take T14 to express Augustine's anguish, both at his recognition that gang action can bring out such profound evil in him, and that he had at this time no real moral moorings. He was a Rebel Without a Cause. Without any effective moral moorings he was able to have "an avid desire to do injury and an appetite to inflict loss on someone else" without cause.

I suggest that the graphic portrayals of evil available to us today on our living-room TV sets should prepare us to find in Augustine's account of an adolescent escapade a small but clear window into the dark recesses of the human psyche. Through that window we can perhaps see that a not unusually evil person might sometimes do wrong just for the pleasure of doing wrong, especially when that wrongdoing is done in exhilarating concert with others.

There is a final paradox and perversity about the act Augustine has focused his attention on. Although that act is a counterexample to (W1) and stubbornly resists falling under the explanatory schema (W2), the very opacity of the act, to use Feinberg's expression, is a tribute to the attractiveness and plausibility of (W1) and (W2). We naturally seek to understand an action as something that the actor, at least at the time of action, believed to be a good thing to do. When we have to confront an action that resists being understood in that way, we naturally respond with Augustinian despair: "Who can untie this extremely twisted and tangled knot? It is a foul affair, I have no wish to give attention to it; I have no desire to contemplate it."

Note

1. Feinberg (2003) 150.

PART II
Anselm on Free Will

Editor's Introduction

Medieval, modern, and contemporary philosophers generally agree that free will is something valuable. On what it is, or why it's valuable, there is considerably less agreement. Some thinkers argue that free will liberates us from aiming at causally determined courses of action, affording us the capacity to choose indeterministically from among competing alternatives. Others argue that it frees us from having to opt for bad or morally neutral options, enabling us instead to choose courses of action that are right or good. Still others contend that our will is free if we exert the right sort of control over the desires that move us to action.

Anselm defines free will (or "free choice," *liberum arbitrium*) as the power to preserve rectitude of will for its own sake. At first glance this appears most like an account of the second sort. However, Katherin Rogers argues that after fuller exploration we must also understand it as an account of the third sort. More precisely, it anticipates by nine centuries key elements of Harry Frankfurt's influential view, according to which our will is free if we have the desires that move us to act because those are the desires we *want* to move us to act. Anselm holds that each human being has an "affection for justice" (*affectio iustitiae*), which Rogers takes to be a second-order desire (that is, a desire whose object is another desire) that the desires moving us to act accord with God's will. When that is the case, we have these desires precisely because we *want* to have them. Moreover, Rogers observes, Anselm's version of this account escapes difficulties that beset Frankfurt's. While Frankfurt cannot easily explain why we do not have to question the freedom of our second-order desires by moving to ever higher orders, Rogers observes that, because of the unique nature of the

Anselmian second-order desire, the threat of such an infinite regress simply vanishes.

Looking at the very same texts that lead Rogers to affirm a proto-Frankfurtian reading of Anselm, Williams argues for an interpretation that eschews any appeal to higher-order desires. In fact, he argues, the texts offer greater support for an account of freedom that is "flat" rather than hierarchical. What's more, the hierarchical account is best suited to address philosophical issues that Anselm isn't interested in. Why, then, read Anselm as a precocious Frankfurt? As Williams sees it, if we think of the history of philosophy as the story of visiting and revisiting a set of perennial problems, it becomes more plausible that philosophers at nine centuries' distance might come up with more or less the same solution. But on Williams' view, at any rate, this story is a fairy tale.

Note on References

Harmony = *On the Harmony of God's Foreknowledge, Predestination, and Grace with Free Choice* = *De concordia*
On Freedom of Choice = *De libertate arbitrii*
On the Fall of the Devil = *De casu diaboli*
On Truth = *De veritate*
S = the Schmitt critical edition of Anselm's works

Further Reading

- Harry Frankfurt (1971). "Freedom of the Will and the Concept of a Person."
- Stan R. Tyvoll (2006). "Anselm's Definition of Free Will: A Hierarchical Interpretation."

CHAPTER 3

The Purpose, Definition, and Structure of Free Choice

KATHERIN ROGERS

Augustine bequeathed to later Christians a number of difficult theological questions related to the issue of free will; was the original sin of Satan and Adam due to an inevitability of their nature such that the real responsibility lies with God? Does the human will play any active role in receiving saving grace? Can freedom be reconciled with divine foreknowledge? If all God's knowledge is causal, is not He the real agent behind all created choices? All of these questions are aspects of the broader and more fundamental question: in the universe of traditional, classical theism, is it possible that the rational creature can possess a free will such that it is the genuine source of its choices in a robust enough sense to ground moral responsibility?

Anselm of Canterbury does not find in the work of his predecessors an adequate analysis of how the absolute divine sovereignty of traditional, classical theism can be reconciled with true free agency, what I have termed 'primary' agency, on the part of the rational creature. In the time since Augustine the issue had surfaced in various guises and occasioned some bitter debate, but those engaged in the question failed, for whatever reason, to deal with it in the radical way required to achieve a workable solution—radical in the literal sense. They did not go to the roots of the problem. Whether it was due to lack of training or of interest or of innate ability, no one between the times of Augustine and Anselm took the necessary step back to address systematically the preliminary philosophical questions of the definition and workings of created free will. But without knowing what the created free will is and how it works, the task of showing how it can exist in the universe of traditional, classical theism cannot even be begun, much less completed.

Anselm's work is truly remarkable. Though he is operating within the framework of certain traditional, classical theist premises, when it comes to his project of systematically developing a philosophy of free will, he strides into uncharted territory armed only with his own analytic genius. He would perhaps eschew the label 'original', which was not a compliment in his day. But the fact is that he is the first to propose a metaphysics of freedom which can allow for the reconciliation of divine sovereignty and created agency and solve the problems that had troubled Christendom since Augustine's day. This is of tremendous historical significance, of course, but even more importantly Anselm's work is so careful and so sophisticated that it prefigures and engages with issues and arguments in the contemporary philosophy of free will. His analysis of freedom may still be the most adequate for the classically minded theist today.

The Purpose of Free Will

When contemporary philosophers ask about the value of free will, they often attempt to do so without admitting to any particular world view or background metaphysics. A standard position is that we must ascribe free will to human beings, for otherwise we could not hold one another morally responsible and praise and blame one another as we in fact do. But why is the status quo regarding assigning merit of any value? Does it signal some metaphysical superiority of the human animal over our non-responsible planet-mates? Is it just a useful convention, conducive to human comfort? Perhaps our penchant for praise and blame is based on a primitive illusion which we would be better off without. In the absence of any commitments regarding the nature of reality, the question of the value of freedom cannot be adequately answered.

Anselm does not attempt to set his world view aside. Rather his stated goal is to spell out a doctrine of free will within the framework of traditional, classical theism. And so, for him, the question of the value of freedom is to be put this way: why did God give us free will? Like many contemporary philosophers and like Augustine before him, Anselm holds that without free will we could not be morally responsible. And a morally responsible creature is inherently superior to one that cannot choose and act as we do. But there is more at issue than just our metaphysical superiority to other creatures. The point of being morally responsible is so that we might be just. (To avoid misunderstanding, note that Anselm offers a non-standard analysis of the term 'justice' not to be confused with the traditional, 'giving each one his due'. Anselm's understanding of 'justice' will be discussed later in this chapter.) And justice, in turn, is requisite for our achieving the goal for which God made us: eternal happiness in His presence. And why is justice necessary? Because only by choosing justice can the rational creature 'polish' the image of God in himself and become a genuine *imago dei* [image of God], meriting the happiness for which he was made.

From the beginning of his work on free will, found in his discussion of 'justice' in *De Veritate* 12, Anselm is clear that what he is interested in is the sort of freedom which can ground moral responsibility.[1] He notes that a horse can will, and even will rightly, but it cannot be just. The 'justice' in question, of which he is here seeking a definition, exists only in a rational will, and '. . . is that to which praise is due; just as blame is due to its opposite, that is injustice'.[2] The morally significant freedom which can ground praise and blame is his consistent concern throughout the next two dialogues, *De libertate arbitrii* and *De casu diaboli*, which Anselm asked to have bound together with *De Veritate* in the preface to that work. In the first chapter of *De libertate arbitrii* the student interlocutor expresses the worries that motivate the dialogue: is freedom of choice 'the ability to sin or not to sin', and do we always have it? If we always have it, why do we need grace? But if we do not always have it, how can we be blamed for our apparent 'sins'?[3] And *De casu diaboli* begins with an expression of the problem occasioned by Augustine's treatment of the first sins of Satan and Adam and Eve. If the bad angels could not hold fast to the good without receiving perseverance from God, and if God does not give it, how are they blameworthy?[4]

Anselm reiterates the point that his concern is only with the sort of free will which can ground moral responsibility in a later treatise, *De concordia*. Here he distinguishes various meanings for 'choice' (*arbitrium*) and 'freedom' (*libertas*). For example, one might be able to speak or keep silent and so have 'freedom of choice' in that regard, but in the absence of some moral import to the choice, this bare ability to choose one thing or another is not the sort of 'freedom of choice' which concerns him. He is interested only in that free choice '. . . which is the seat of justice' and which is relevant to salvation and damnation.[5] But exactly what is the connection between moral responsibility and the ultimate goal of the created agent?

Justice, about which a great deal more will be said later, is an inherently good thing. In the first chapter of his first philosophical work, the *Monologion*, Anselm argues for the existence of God through the basic platonic claim that our recognition of various good things proves that there is a *summum bonum*, and in support of this, as if it were a more obvious point, he says that all just things are just through justice, and argues later (*Monologion* 16) that God is Justice Itself, the source of all created justice.[6] In *Proslogion* 5 when he begins his project of analyzing the perfections of God, it is divine justice which comes first. So justice is a valuable prize for the creature to possess. Anselm argues in *De Veritate* 12 that justice can only be had by a creature that can recognize and choose it, and moreover, choose it for the right reasons and through its own power. It is our free will, Anselm argues in *De libertate arbitrii* 2, that enables us to choose justice. Thus, as Anselm points out in *De casu diaboli* 16, the free agent is intrinsically superior to lesser natures, which may be very good in their way, but cannot possess justice. Even the created agent who has lost justice and so is in a state of blameworthy debt bears the mark of the justice which he has lost and hence has a greater natural dignity than the creature which is not capable of justice. Though it must be added that while the nature is superior and more praiseworthy, the unjust *person* is that much more blameworthy.[7]

Not only is the rational agent intrinsically superior to other creatures, but its freedom fits it for a destiny superior to theirs. Anselm, like Augustine and, to my knowledge, most medieval, Christian philosophers, held that the ultimate goal for the rational creature is happiness—perfect, everlasting happiness with God. Some scholars, focusing on Anselm's claim that our morally significant choice decides between justice and benefit, see him as departing from standard medieval eudaemonism. I shall argue later in this chapter that this non-eudaemonistic interpretation rests on a misunderstanding of Anselm's proposed objects of choice. On the contrary, Anselm takes as one of his major premises in the *Cur deus homo* that '. . . man was made for happiness'.[8] But he insists, in this work, in the earlier dialogues on freedom, and in the later *De concordia*, that a rational nature should not, and in fact cannot, be happy unless it deserves to be, that is, unless it is just. '[One] neither is able nor ought to be happy unless he wills it and unless he wills it justly.'[9] 'God's intention, then, was to make rational nature just and happy so that it might enjoy Him. But it could not be either just or happy without the will for justice and for happiness.'[10] Exactly why this is so will become clear later in the discussion of Anselm's analysis of what it means to be just. Here suffice it to say that the just will conforms to the will of God, and failure to do so inevitably entails misery.

The rational, free agent is intrinsically a better sort of thing than other creatures and is able to enjoy an eternal beatitude not open to them. It is a closer image of God. None of this signals a departure from the standard medieval view developed by Augustine. But on the question of the importance of created freedom Anselm goes further. His view endows the created agent with a unique dignity which marks a radical departure from Augustine's position on the relationship of creature to Creator. As explained in Chapter 2 of Rogers (2008), Augustine says it is absurd to hold that the created agent, angelic or human, might make itself better on its own. Anselm disagrees. The very reason God gave rational agents free will was so that they might become more perfect images of God by helping in their own creation! In *Monologion* 68 he writes that the very point of our being rational is that we should be able to distinguish the just from the unjust so that we might love God.[11] And our greatest obligation to God is that we should work to see to it '. . . that that [divine] image which was impressed by natural power should be formed (*exprimere*) as a result of the will'.[12] In *De casu diaboli* 18 he explains that the reason God gave each angel freedom which entailed the ability to hold onto or to reject the justice given by God was so that, should he hold onto it when he could reject it '. . . he would be able, in a way, to give justice *to himself* [my italics]'.[13]

And then in *Cur deus homo* 2.10 he offers the clearest expression of the point that the rational agent, through its free will, shares in God's aseity. The issue under discussion is the freedom of Christ, who, according to Anselm, is free although he cannot sin.[14] The interlocutor is puzzled since Anselm, in previous works, had made it plain that the freedom of men and angels entails, at some point in their history, the power to reject or hold fast to justice. Didn't we say, asks the interlocutor, that if the good angels could not have rejected justice, then they would have no merit in clinging to it? How then can Christ be free? Anselm responds: 'Those angels are not to be praised on account of their justice due to the fact that they were able to sin, but rather due to the fact that, in a way, they have it *from themselves* [my italics] that they are [now] unable to sin; in this they are, to some extent, similar to God, who has whatever He has from Himself (*a se*),'[15] The crucial requisite for freedom and praiseworthiness, divine and human, is not open options, but rather *aseity*. This does not conflict with the claim, examined in detail in Chapter 4 of Rogers (2008), that for the *creature* to have freedom it must choose between genuinely open alternative possibilities. God has given the rational creature freedom of choice, which in the created nature entails the ability to cling to or reject justice, in order that it might, by holding on when it could let go, be just *from itself*, in an imitation of divine aseity necessarily unique to free creatures.

Thus Anselm, contrary to Augustine, embraces the view that the created agent imitates God in being a genuine cause, what I have called a primary agent. Though all that happens is permitted by God, there are some events in this universe not causally willed by God, but rather willed by, and originating from, the created agent. In the later *De concordia* when Anselm addresses the questions of divine foreknowledge, predestination, and grace, the questions to which Augustine's answers had occasioned such controversy, it is clear that he stands by this radical (at least for an Augustinian) claim. Unlike Augustine, Anselm is willing to allow that the choice of the created free agent can be the source of divine knowledge and that it is open to the human being, through its own choice, to cling to or abandon God's grace. All that has ontological status is made by God. Creatures do not produce things or even their own choices *ex nihilo*. And yet in created agency there is a trace of independence through which God has given the rational creature the ability to participate in His aseity by freely maintaining a justice it could abandon. How this is possible in the universe of traditional, classical theism is a complex story, the telling of which finds a logical beginning in unpacking Anselm's careful definition of free will.

The Definition of Free Will

I shall argue that in terms of the actual workings of free will, Anselm subscribes to a sort of libertarianism today labeled the 'self-causation' view: for a choice to be free it must originate with the agent himself and not be fully traceable back to further causes outside of the agent.[16] In spite of Anselm's adherence to the claim that all that has ontological status is immediately caused by God, there is a sense in which the agent can bear 'ultimate responsibility' for his choices. I adopt Robert Kane's phrase because it seems to me that Anselm's analysis prefigures Kane's in that the locus of 'self-causation' is found in the winning out of one desire over another, where the conflicting desires themselves are explicable in terms of preceding causes. All that is up to the agent is the ultimate preference of one option over the other. But this is enough to ground the claim that the agent chooses 'from himself' in a way sufficient to allow for moral responsibility.[17]

In order to defend this 'self-causation' interpretation, a thorough examination of Anselm's insistence on the importance of alternative possibilities and a discussion of his analysis of the causes of sin are required. But these issues must wait until we have looked at his definition of free will. This is because the alternatives, motives, and choices in question occur within a complex framework. Anselm offers a definition of free will which involves a hierarchy of choice, prefiguring that recently proposed by Harry Frankfurt.[18] According to Anselm, the point of freedom is to choose justice, and the choice for justice is what the contemporary literature, following Frankfurt, calls a 'second order' volition. It is a choice about what desires one wishes to have and to embrace. One becomes a real moral agent, in Frankfurt's terms, a 'person', only when one can step back from one's immediate desires, examine them, and then choose to identify with certain of them.

Anselm is not the first to propose some version of such a schema. Chapter 2 of Rogers (2008) noted Eleonore Stump's suggestion that Augustine adopts a hierarchical account of free will. I argued that Stump's conclusion that the early Augustine could be read as a qualified libertarian is mistaken, but the view that he accepts some sort of hierarchical approach is quite plausible. In *Confessiones* he discusses being torn between 'two wills'.[19] Not, he is quick to point out, that there were two warring powers within him, as the Manicheans had proposed, but rather that he longed to surrender to the new Christian lifestyle which he had come to believe held the path to happiness, yet at the same time he was loath to give up his old habits which kept him mired in his former way of life. The hierarchical element comes in when he meditates on the fact that there seems to be a self which in some sense transcends these conflicting desires and judges between them. And at this point in the *Confessiones* Augustine says that this self has come to identify with and embrace the desire for the new life. In Frankfurt's terms, Augustine has a second order desire for his longing to commit to Christianity. None the less he is addicted to his old lusts and does not act upon the desire with which he most fully identifies. Foreshadowing Frankfurt, who argues that freedom consists in being able to act upon the desires which one endorses, Augustine considers himself a slave while he follows the old desires he would like to banish. It is only when he is able to bring his behavior into line with the desires with which he identifies that he considers himself truly free. It should be noted that the comparison with Frankfurt here rests on a bit of equivocation on the terms 'slave' and 'free'. Frankfurt locates freedom in the harmony of first and second order volitions, while Augustine believes that he has free will, if not 'true freedom', whichever set of desires he follows. Still, this discussion in Augustine is an interesting, if not exact, prefiguring of Frankfurt's analysis of freedom and personhood.

Anselm certainly knew the *Confessiones* and may have been influenced by Augustine's meditations. However, Anselm's hierarchical working out of free will, though it depends on orders of desires, is very different from Augustine's. For one thing, Augustine's discussion concerns the post-lapsarian condition in which addictive bad habits can play a role. Anselm introduces his division between first order and second order desires in constructing his definition of free will, so the issue is not a fallen will drawn upwards or downwards. Moreover, Augustine, like Frankfurt, is a compatibilist. Anselm, on the other hand, proposes the hierarchical schema as a situation which permits libertarian free choice, while safeguarding the traditional, classical theist position that all of the existents involved in the choice are from God. So, while it is possible to find a sort of prefiguring of Frankfurt's views in Augustine, the use to which Anselm puts the hierarchical schema is really quite original. This is, of course, an interesting claim historically, but the more important point is that Anselm's proposal is plausible and philosophically fruitful if one is set on reconciling traditional, classical theism with libertarian freedom. Anselm constructed his definition of free choice very deliberately, and a careful unpacking will reveal the hierarchical framework he proposes for created freedom.

We have seen that for Anselm the point of free will is that it should be just and allow the agent a measure of aseity by which it can imitate God. Thus Anselm agrees to some extent with those contemporary philosophers who define freedom as an ability which is aimed at some good.[20] In *De libertate arbitrii* 1 the student interlocutor suggests, as a standard definition, that free will is the ability to sin or not to sin.[21] We have already noted that open options play an important role in Anselm's analysis of created free will. However, Anselm is adamant that it would be incorrect to *define* free will as the ability to choose between good and evil. Neither God, nor the good angels in their present state, can choose evil, and yet we call them free.[22] The student goes on to suggest that God and the good angels may possess a different sort of freedom from ours, subject to a different definition. But Anselm responds, in a clear demonstration of his view that language is used univocally of God and creation, that if the same word is used, there must be a single definition which can apply properly to all instances.[23] Not only does the ability to sin not figure in the definition of free will, but the will as more free when it is unable to sin![24] He will argue later that, unlike the situation with God, in order for a rational creature to have morally significant free will there must be some time in its history when the choice between good and evil was a genuinely open option for it, but that is a point *entailed* by the definition given the facts about the world, it is not a part of the definition itself. In *De libertate arbitrii* 3 Anselm derives the definition of free will from the purpose for which it was given to rational creatures. Free will is 'the power for preserving justice', and justice is 'rightness of will preserved for its own sake'. So free will is 'the power for preserving rightness of will for its own sake'.[25]

Before we can ask what 'rightness of will' is, there is the more fundamental question of 'rightness' *per se*. Some translators have rendered Anselm's term *rectitudo as* 'rectitude', 'uprightness', or 'righteousness'.[26] This is misleading in that in modern English these terms all bear moral connotations, whereas Anselm's *rectitudo* has a much broader meaning, better captured by 'rightness'. This point will bear significant philosophical fruit. Moreover, in order to grasp what Anselm means by 'rightness' one needs to begin not with his discussion of free will in *De libertate arbitrii*, but with *De Veritate*, the work that precedes it in the three-volume set Anselm asked to have bound together. It is important to read the works in the order Anselm requested because it is in the first work that Anselm develops the concept of rightness, which constitutes the initial step in building the definition of free will. In *De Veritate* Anselm holds that every existent thing, whether proposition, object, or action, has its own truth by participating in the Highest Truth, which is God. This truth is its 'rightness', its proper orientation to the divine standard, its being as it ought to be. Thus even inanimate things can have rightness. For example, fire acts rightly when it warms things and a falling stone acts rightly when it falls.[27]

It will be well, before addressing the question of rightness of will, *rectitudo voluntatis*, to say a word about Anselm's term *voluntas*. As Anselm uses the word it can bear at least three different meanings, which he enunciates in *De libertate arbitrii* 7, and again at more length in *De concordia* 3.11. *Voluntas* can mean the faculty by which we will something, *instrumentum volendi*.[28] It can also mean the fixed inclination, *affectio*, of that faculty which moves it to will something. I think it is correct to translate *voluntas* in this second sense as 'desire', but Anselm is very clear to say that the *affectio* need not be occurrent. It can be a sort of constant attitude of desire. He says, for example, that we have the *affectio* for health even when we are not thinking about it, and then as soon as it comes to mind we do want it.[29] The third meaning is the use of the faculty, *usus instrumenti*. This is the actually occurrent desire or choice: 'As when one says "I now have the will for reading" that means "I now will to read".'[30] (I do not distinguish 'desire' and 'choice' as two entirely different and separate phenomena because, for Anselm, as I explain in Chapter 2 of Rogers (2008), a choice is essentially the 'winning out' of one desire over another.) Thus *voluntas* can mean the faculty of will itself, the fixed inclination of the will, or the occurrent desire or choice, and the proper translation will depend upon the context.

And so to *rectitudo voluntatis:* will desiring what it ought to desire. Anselm explains in *De Veritate* that rightness of will can be possessed only by creatures capable of desire and choice, but it is important to note that it is not reserved exclusively to *rational* creatures. Many lower animals have desires and choose in accordance with them. When they desire and choose what is proper for them they have rightness of will. The horse which wants to go graze is willing what it ought.[31] And the dog which loves its puppies or the master who is good to it possesses rightness of will.[32] Clearly rightness of will here does not connote moral rectitude or uprightness. Anselm explains that lower animals are not capable of justice because they do not *recognize* and *choose* to have rightness of will, rather they simply have it by nature.[33] To put this in contemporary terms, borrowed from Frankfurt, according to Anselm the horse and the dog possess and act upon the proper first order desires, but they cannot step back to a higher level and evaluate and endorse those desires. They cannot form second order volitions *about* their own desires.

In order to have justice and hence be morally responsible in a way which allows for praise, one must keep rightness of will *for its own sake.* This is Anselm's definition from Chapter 12 of *De Veritate:* Justice is rightness of will kept for its own sake (*Iustitia igitur est rectitudo voluntatis propter se servata*).[34] It is important to note here that Anselm's term *iustitia* is used in a unique and very specific way which rules out many ordinary uses of the term 'justice'.[35] We often speak, for example, of a just court decision or a just treaty, meaning that each party has been given its due. But a court decision or a treaty does not have a will, and a decision or treaty which gives each one his due could be produced by people who are not motivated by any desire to do what they ought to do, and so do not have rightness of will. Such a decision or treaty would not be 'just', even indirectly, by Anselm's definition. In Anselm's terminology, the court decision and the treaty that give each his due, and so are as they ought to be, are 'right' rather than 'just'. In Chapter 12 of *De Veritate,* the student remarks that rightness and justice seem to be the same thing, but Anselm disagrees. He points out that the *iustitia* that he is trying to define here is that which '. . . ought to be praised; just as its contrary, namely injustice, ought to be blamed'. But only a person can be praised or blamed. That is, we do not credit the court decision *itself* or the treaty *itself* for its merits or defects. So he holds that the rightness which is *iustitia* can only be in a rational nature (*non est nisi in rationali natura*).[36]

Nor, continues Anselm in that same chapter, is it the person's knowledge or their actual deeds that are directly praiseworthy or blameworthy in the final analysis. It is the will. Anselm asks: 'Suppose there were someone who understands rightly (*recte*) and acts rightly, but does not will rightly. Would anybody praise him for justice?' The student answers, 'No', and that is the correct and obvious answer in Anselm's view.[37] Nor is it enough simply to *possess* rightness of will and hence will what one ought to will. As we have seen, the horse and the dog can do that. The just will must step back and will that very rightness of will. 'Whatever does not *will* rightness [my emphasis], even if it has it, does not deserve to be praised because it has rightness.'[38] The dog can will what it ought, but it cannot will to *will* what it ought. It can possess the appropriate first order desires which make it a good dog, naturally motivated to do what its Creator made it to do. It cannot possess the second order volition that it should have the desires which make it a good dog.

But even willing to have rightness of will is not enough for justice, since at the second level, one might have a non-praiseworthy motive for desiring and choosing the correct desires. For example, says Anselm, still in Chapter 12 of *De Veritate*, one who feeds the poor out of a desire for vain glory wills that he ought to will what he wills (. . . *vult se debere velle quod vult*).[39] But his choice is not praiseworthy. Justice requires that one possess the proper motive at the second level and hold on to rightness of will for its own sake. Again: *iustitia igitur est rectitudo voluntatis propter se servata.*

As we have seen, God gave the rational creature free will in order that it might be just. Having developed the definition of 'justice' in *De Veritate*, Anselm can go on in *De libertate arbitrii* 3 to define 'free will' as 'the power to preserve rightness of will for its own sake'. In this treatise he goes on to explain at length that this power is inalienable, that it must act from itself (*sponte*), and that it cannot be moved by any sort of necessity, even the necessity of natural inclination. I cover these issues in Chapter 4 of Rogers (2008), where I defend the claim that Anselm is a libertarian of a self-causation variety. Here I would like to continue the discussion of Anselm's analysis of free choice as a hierarchical ordering of levels of desires looking at *De casu diaboli* and *De concordia.* This is important in appreciating his doctrine of free will, and will also cast light on his views about what constitutes proper behavior for the rational creature.

The Two *Affectiones*

In *De casu diaboli* Anselm argues that in order for the rational creature to gain merit and in a sense make itself even better than it was made by God it must have the option to cling to or abandon justice. As I explain in Chapter 4 of Rogers (2008), this allows for a sort of self-causation without falling into Pelagianism. In Chapter 4 he proposes that in order to have this option the will must receive from God two sorts of desire: the desire for benefit (*commoditas*) and the desire for justice.[40] In this post-Kantian age one might anticipate that the analysis would then go something like this: the creature, confronted with conflicting desires for mere self-interested advantage versus disinterested virtue, can choose rightly, i.e. the latter, or not-rightly (wrongly or in some morally neutral way), i.e. the former. Thus one would interpret Anselm as a sort of proto-Kantian, saying that a choice motivated by the desire for advantage cannot also be a choice motivated by the desire for virtue. And vice versa, if a choice is motivated by a desire for virtue it is not motivated by desire for advantage.

What I call the Kantian interpretation of Anselm's two *affectiones* may go back at least as far as Duns Scotus, who cites Anselm by name and seems to see the two 'wills' as having very different objects. Scotus writes that through the *affectio* for justice the will '. . . is able to will some good not oriented to self. According to the affection for what is advantageous, however, nothing can be willed save with reference to self.'[41] But this Kantian interpretation represents a serious misunderstanding leading to mistaken conclusions regarding Anselm's views—not only about the structure of created freedom but also about the nature of good behavior and the just will.[42] For Anselm it is not that there are two mutually exclusive sets of objects of desire, the beneficial on the one hand and the just on the other. Rather there is the set of objects of first order desires, that is the benefits. Anselm holds that everything capable of desiring desires these. It is through possessing benefits that one achieves happiness. 'The happiness which all rational nature desires lies in benefits.'[43] And happiness, recall, is the goal of rational existence. In Chapter 12 of *De casu diaboli* he is clear that, 'no one desires (wills) *anything* [my italics] unless he judges it to be in some sense beneficial for him.'[44] Rightness of will consists in the desire for benefits in conformity with God's plan for the creature, as in the examples of the horse that wants to graze and the dog that loves her puppies. The desire for justice is a desire for 'rightness of will preserved for its own sake'. It is therefore a second order desire that one's first order desires for benefits should be properly ordered, should be as they ought to be. It would follow front the point that we only desire and will what we judge to be in some sense beneficial, that if we will justice we must recognize that it is in some sense beneficial. It seems correct to suppose that Anselm would hold that it is to our advantage to be just, since the ultimate end of justice is happiness. Ordinarily when Anselm speaks of benefits (*commoditates*) he seems to be referring to the naturally desired objects of first order desires, but it seems correct to allow that Anselm distinguishes these objects, what we might call 'first order benefits', from the 'second order benefit' of justice. But in any case, to will justice entails that one desire to will benefits in the right way, so one cannot possibly will justice without willing benefits.

This interpretation is reinforced in *De casu diaboli* 4 when Anselm explains that the injustice of the bad angel consists not in willing injustice *per se*, but in willing benefits which he should not have willed; '. . . by inordinately (*inordinate*) willing something more than he had received he extended his will beyond justice (*voluntatem suam extra iustitiam extendit*)'.[45] On the other hand, the justice of the good angels lies not in their willing rightness as somehow *opposed to* benefit, but rather in their containing their desires so that they will only those benefits already bestowed on them by God, benefits they were supposed to will.[46] But there is absolutely nothing intrinsically bad or tainted about the forbidden benefit. It is not some selfish advantage intrinsically opposed to justice. Rather it '. . . was something which [the good angels] were able to grow towards (*crescere*), which they did not receive when they were created, in order that they might achieve it on account of merit (*ut ad illud suo merito proficerent*)'.[47] The reward for the good angels' holding fast to justice is that they now possess everything which could possibly benefit them and so cannot desire anything which they ought not desire.[48] Again, Anselm's point is that it is always the desire for some benefit which motivates. The good angels now cannot be motivated to will anything but what they have received, since they have received the maximum benefits. Yet he calls them just. The only thing one might desire besides benefits is one's own justice, but justice itself consists in willing to will the appropriate benefits.

Prima facie this might seem like an excessively self-centered schema: we are motivated only by our desire for some benefit, and justice consists in willing to will the benefits which we ought to will. But I take it that Anselm's *commoditas* covets far more than mere selfish advantage. Anselm never wrote a treatise on ethics or values, nor does he devote any time to enumerating the sorts of benefits rational creatures might desire. In *De casu diaboli* the topic is the first sin of Satan, and Anselm wisely declines to theorize about the exact nature of the benefit which Satan desired to his downfall.[49] But it is probably safe to hold, in the absence of evidence to the contrary, that Anselm's thinking on human desires and motivations is close to Augustine's.[50] The effort to clarify or develop Augustine's thought is often the cited or implicit impetus for Anselm's work, and it may be that Anselm did not see any need to discuss human values because he may have felt that Augustine had said enough. In Augustine's view we are always drawn to will what we will by desire, but this is not self-centered. We are social animals with a natural love for other human beings. The very reason that God made the entire race from a first human being is so that we would have the natural love of kinship for all mankind.[51] But then an individual's will for his own benefit can include a desire for the good of his family, his neighbors, and indeed all of humanity. If we find this natural and universal love scarce in the world, that is a consequence of sin, not of human nature. In modern thought it is common to see the individual as discreet and atomic, essentially unconnected with those around him. For such a creature the desire for benefit would indeed be selfish. But this is not Augustine's view of humanity.

And there is at least some textual evidence to support the conclusion that Anselm is an Augustinian on this point, as on so much else. In *De conceptu virginali* 17 Anselm addresses the question of why God chose to redeem the children of Adam rather than simply starting over with a new race of human beings, or with miraculously conceived and hence sinless members of the race of Adam. He answers that God prefers to complete the work He began originally: '. . . lest, if none of Adam's natural progeny would be saved, God would appear to have created Adam's reproductive nature in vain and to have corrected, so to speak, what He had created imperfectly'.[52] The literal, biological kinship that Augustine saw as the source of a universal love is crucially important in Anselm's view. Or see Chapter 25 of the *Proslogion*, in which Anselm almost sings of the joys of heaven, in which all of the desires of body and soul are satisfied, and then multiplied for each individual by the number of citizens of the City of God, since all will rejoice in the joy of those they love as in their own happiness, and each one will love all the others as he loves himself. There is no reason to think that when Anselm says that no one wills something unless he judges it beneficial he is arguing that the only efficacious motive is a private and self-centered advantage.

In *De casu diaboli* 13 Anselm proposes a telling hypothesis: what if an angel had been given only the desire for benefits without the desire for justice? That is, on my interpretation, what if it had been given only the first order desire for benefits without the second order desire that its desires be ordered according to God's command? Anselm says that then it would will only happiness, and it would will the greatest happiness possible which is to be like God. Though this would be an inappropriate thing to will and certainly not just, we could not call it *unjust* either because the angel wills from necessity (this point is discussed at length in Chapter 4 of Rogers (2008)). And if, unable to have the higher goods, it should, like a lower animal, desire whatever lower pleasures occurred to it, still it would not be unjust since it does not have the capacity to select among its desires.

Anselm continues, in *De casu diaboli* 14, what if an angel had received only the will for rightness (*sola accepta sit voluntas rectitudinis*)?[53] That is, what if God had simply given it the desire to will what is appropriate for it? Note that, were the Kantian interpretation correct, the complement to the hypothesis in Chapter 13 in which the angel is given only the will for benefits, would be the hypothesis that God gives the angel only the will for *justice* and not any will for benefits. On my interpretation that would be an impossible hypothesis since the desire for justice is a desire regarding which desires for benefits one has, and Anselm does not propose it as a possibility in Chapter 14 or anywhere else. Moreover, the point of the chapter is that the one who can will only rightness has neither a just nor an unjust will, since he cannot will otherwise.[54] It is possible for God to give a creature only the will for rightness, but in doing so He has not, and in fact could not, give it a just will. The case is the same as that in which the angel receives only the unqualified desire for benefits. Like the dog who has rightness of will naturally, the angel who wills rightly as a matter of necessity is neither just nor unjust.

It should he noted that: earlier, in Chapter 5 of *De casu diaboli*, Anselm had considered the hypothetical situation in which the angels could not sin but rather 'preserve justice by necessity' (*necessitate servaverunt iustitiam*).[55] He says in that case they don't deserve any special merit. But does even raising the possibility that the angels could be just without the option to choose the wrong thing signal a conflict in Anselm's thought? I think not. He concludes by saying that these necessarily sinless angels, 'if you consider it properly, are not correctly called just' (*Sed nec iusti recte, si bene consideres, dicerentur*).[56] This important sentence is omitted in the Oxford translation, though it is there in the Schmitt edition from which the translation is taken.[57]

Having established the necessity of the two wills, Anselm continues in *De casu diaboli* 14 to explain their relationship. He writes that '. . . [the rational creature] is not able, nor ought, to be happy unless he wills it, and wills justly' (*nisi velit et nisi iuste velit*).[58] Note the adverb here. There is no suggestion of an inherent conflict between happiness and justice. The implication is that happiness is to be willed in the proper way, i.e. justly. 'Thus it is necessary that God make each will converge in him, so that he wills to be happy, and he wills justly (*beatus esse velit et iuste velit*). To the extent that added justice tempers the will for happiness it limits the excesses of that will, but it does not take away its ability for overreaching.'[59] The will for justice does not aim at some object opposed to benefit. It operates at a higher level, curtailing the excesses of the first order desires for benefits.

In a later work, *De concordia* (book 3, 11–13), Anselm again discusses the two wills for benefit and rightness, and again it is easy to see why one might attribute to him a Kantian view which opposes duty to benefit, especially if one came to *De concordia* without *De Veritate* in mind, or if one is working from the Oxford translation which translates *commoditas* as 'advantage' and *rectitudo* as 'uprightness' and 'righteousness'. Anselm explains that the will as instrument has two inclinations or *affectiones*. One is for willing benefit; the other for willing rightness. He writes: 'Certainly the will which is the instrument does not will anything unless it is either benefit or rightness' (*nisi aut commoditatem aut rectitudinem*).[60] The 'either/or' phrasing might suggest that the two inclinations move the will towards opposing objects, and that rightness involves disinterested duty, as the Oxford translation of *rectitudo* as 'righteousness' suggests, such that if one wills benefit one does not will rightness and if one wills rightness one does not will benefit. This would conflict with my interpretation that the will for rightness is not directed towards duty *as opposed to* every benefit, but is rather a second order desire for willing the appropriate benefits.

It should be noted first that if the Kantian reading of *De concordia* were correct it would conflict with the earlier dialogues. Anselm explicitly says that the dog and the horse have rightness of will, but surely they are not 'righteous' or 'dutiful'. If *rectitudo* in *De concordia* refers to an uprightness or righteousness which does not on some level take benefit as its object then the term seems to be used in a different way from the earlier dialogues. Further, the Kantian interpretation entails that if a choice is aimed at 'righteousness' it cannot be aimed at benefit. And yet, as I noted above, in *De casu diaboli* 12 Anselm argued that no one chooses anything unless he judges it to be a benefit. One might hold that Anselm's views had changed from the earlier writings, but in *De concordia* he refers the reader back to his analysis of 'justice' in *De Veritate*, so he seems to stand by the earlier work.[61]

More importantly, the discussion in *De concordia* supports my interpretation that Anselm sees the desires for benefit and justice as hierarchically ordered. To motivate the concept of the will as instrument having two inclinations, he gives an analogy with sight. Just as the will has two 'aptitudes' (*aptitudines*) which are its inclinations (*affectiones*), sight has many *aptitudines*, '. . . namely for seeing light, and through light for seeing figures, and through figures for seeing colors'.[62] The analogy is telling. It is not that vision's many aptitudes are directed towards contrary objects such that in seeing the color one would not be seeing the figure, or in seeing the figure one would not be seeing the light. Rather the objects of the different aptitudes of vision are 'nested' such that one sees the figures through the light and the colors through the figures. This suggests that the objects of the will's two inclinations are 'nested' rather than opposed, and so the analogy points to the hierarchical interpretation.

And in this same chapter he makes a point similar to one he had made in *De casu diaboli* 12 that we do not will anything unless we think it likely to prove a benefit. Here he writes, 'Indeed, through the inclination which is for willing benefit man *always* [my italics] wills happiness and to be happy' (*Per affectionem quidem quae est ad volendum commoditatem, semper vult homo beatitudinem et beatus esse*).[63] And this becomes important for the hierarchical interpretation when he sums up how the will as instrument became unjust. He never says, or even hints, that the will becomes unjust by choosing benefit *per se*, rather than the wrong benefit. On the contrary, the will for benefit itself was made good, and becomes unjust, 'because it is not subject to justice, without which it ought not to will anything' (*quia non est subdita iustitiae, sine qua nihil velle debet*).[64] In the last chapter in *De concordia*, Anselm explains that God created free will in man and joined justice to it so that whatever he wills, he should will it justly (*ut nihil nisi iuste vellet*).[65] But if we always will benefit, the implication is that we can will benefit *justly*. But then there can be no opposition between willing justice and willing benefit. This seems to be the same point he made in *De casu diaboli* 14 where he explains that it is the role of the will for justice to temper the excesses of the will for benefits.

Anselm is addressing a different issue in this late work, and so he does not offer the painstaking analysis of *iustitia* that we find in *De Veritate*, moving from rightness, to rightness of will, to rightness of will preserved for its own sake. But what he does say accords with the earlier works and supports the interpretation that the will for rightness is a second order desire that one's first order desires for benefits should be properly ordered and limited in accord with the divine will. Thus he is not espousing a sort of proto-Kantianism which pits duty against self-interest and natural inclination. The purpose of created freedom, then, is that the rational agent be able to step back and consciously choose to identify with the motivations which accord with God's will. In this way free creatures enhance the image of God in themselves, even to the extent of participating in the divine aseity by helping to cause their own justice. That Anselm is proposing a genuine, self-causing, libertarian sort of freedom will become clear in Chapters 4 and 5 of Rogers (2008) when we look at the role of alternative possibilities and at the source of sin.

Notes

1. Alfred Mele takes it as a serious criticism of Robert Kane's analysis of free will, an analysis prefigured in Anselm, that Kane, 'explicitly limits free choices to choices made in the face of internal conflict' (Mele [1995], 207). Mele points out that common sense allows that we freely make all sorts of mundane choices without feeling conflicted. Certainly that is true, but it is an unfair criticism. Kane and Anselm are not engaged in the project of canvassing the common uses of the term 'free'. Rather they are very deliberately concerned to see whether or not human agents have what Kane calls "ultimate responsibility' and whether or not we can engage in what he refers to as 'self-forming actions'.
2. S.I p. 132, ll. 27–8.
3. S.I p. 207, ll. 6–10.
4. S.I p. 234, ll. 22–7.
5. S.II p.256, ll. 2–12.
6. In this earlier work he may be using the term 'justice' in a broader and more standard way than in the later works on free will. I do not think this possible difference affects his arguments.
7. S.I pp. 259–60, ll. 28–7.
8. *Cur deus homo* 1.10, S.II p. 67, 1. 13.
9. *De casu diaboli* 14, S.I p. 258, ll. 20–1. The 'one' in question is a hypothetical angel.
10. *De concordia* 3.13, S.II p. 285, ll. 15–17.
11. S.I p. 78, ll. 21–5.
12. S.I p. 78, ll. 14–16.
13. S.I p. 263, ll. 13–14.
14. I discuss the question of divine freedom in Chapter 10 of Rogers (2008).
15. S.II p. 107, ll. 27–9.
16. Thomas Williams and Sandra Visser suggest that Anselm proposes two definitions of freedom: a normative one, where it is the power to hold on to what is fitting; and a descriptive one, where it is the power for self-initiated action (Visser and Williams, [2001], 221–44). Both of these elements are important, but I think it hews closer to the text to treat them as aspects of one understanding of freedom. As Williams and Visser remark, in Anselm's work the 'two definitions' are equivalent (240).
17. Robert Kane (1996). For ultimate responsibility see pp. 60–78. For the concept of 'self-forming willings' see pp. 124–8. For 'plural voluntary control', that is for the view that the free agent struggles to bring about one or another incompatible outcomes see pp. 133–44. Though Kane and Anselm share a concern to analyze a choice in terms of preceding desires, Anselm does not share Kane's commitment (pp. 115–17) to offering a libertarian analysis which does not invoke any categories or kinds of entities not also required for nonlibertarian accounts. The created, primary agency which Anselm ascribes to human beings is something new in the world.
18. 'Freedom of the Will and the Concept of a Person' (1971). Pages cited refer to reprint in Fischer (1986). I argue for the similarity in Rogers (2005). There is significant overlap between this article and the present chapter, though in the former I also try to make the case that Anselm's theory is immune from a number of criticisms one might bring against Frankfurt's. The similarity between Anselm and Frankfurt was first brought to my attention by Stan Tyvoll in "Anselm's Conception of Free Will: A Hierarchical Interpretation," presented

at the Twenty-fourth International Conference on Patristic, Mediaeval, and Renaissance Studies, Villanova University, 1999. My reading of that similarity is significantly different from Tyvoll's.

19. *Confessiones* 8.5–10.
20. Susan Wolf is a prime proponent of the position that the value of freedom has nothing to do with open options, but radier with our choosing in accordance with the true and the good; (Wolf [1990]).
21. This definition is expressed by Julian of Eclanum in Augustine's *Opus imperfectum contra Julianum* 1.80–1 and 6.10, where Augustine makes the same argument against it that Anselm does. We cannot know that Anselm had read this work, though an *Augustinus contra Julianum* is listed among the works in the library at Bec, the monastery in northern France where Anselm did much of his philosophical writing, in the twelfth century (*Patrologiae Cursus Completus, Series Latina* 150, p. 779). But Augustine had written two works on this theme with similar titles. Anselm does offer the same argument, but he does not suggest that the definition smacks of heresy. Scotus Eriugena gives a similar definition of free will in his *De divina praedestinatione* (5.9, ll. 207–8; *Corpus Christianorum Continuatio Mediaevalis* 50, p. 41), not listed at Bec. Some of Anselm's arguments resemble Eriugena's but we cannot know that Anselm had read this work.
22. S.I p. 207, ll. 4–13.
23. S.I p. 208, ll. 1–7.
24. S.I p. 208, ll. 18–26.
25. S.I p. 212, ll. 13–20.
26. In the Oxford World Classics edition (Anselm 1998), Anselm's term *rectitudo* is translated as 'rectitude' in the translations of *De Veritate, De libertate arbitrii,* and *De casu diaboli,* and as 'uprightness' and 'righteousness' in the translation of *De concordia.* Hopkins and Richardson begin in *De Veritate* by translating *rectitudo as* 'rightness', but change to 'uprightness' when the will is introduced (Hopkins and Richardson 1967).
27. *De Veritate* 5 (fire), S.I p. 182, ll. 3–6; 12 (stone), S.I p. 192, ll. 11–21.
28. S.II p, 280, ll. 1–10.
29. S.II p. 280, ll. 10–17.
30. S.II p. 280, ll. 18–19.
31. *De Veritate* 12, S.I p. 192, ll. 22–3.
32. *De libertate arbitrii* 13, S.I p. 225, ll. 20–2.
33. *De Veritate* 12, S.I p. 192, ll. 24–33.
34. S.I p. 194, l. 26.
35. In chs. 9–11 of the *Proslogion* Anselm ponders the question of how God can, in justice, punish some evildoers, but forgive and save others. It is understandable, he says, that God should return good for good and evil for evil, as 'the very order (*ratio*) of justice seems to require this' (*Proslogion* 9, S.I p. 107, ll. 18–19). One might suppose that here Anselm is using 'justice' in its standard sense of 'giving to each his due'. The 1998 Oxford edition would reinforce this since the translation for *ratio* in this sentence is 'definition' (p. 92). If Anselm *defines* 'justice' in the *Proslogion* as giving good to the good and bad to the bad, then his understanding of the definition undergoes a significant change before he writes *De Veritate.* But two things need to be noted. First, *ratio* does not necessarily mean 'definition'. It has a much broader application, for example it could be translated 'reason', or 'principle', or, as I have done, 'order'. In his later works where he is actually *defining* justice and freedom Anselm uses the term *definitio,* so I do not think we need conclude that in the *Proslogion* he actually defines 'justice' as returning good for good and bad for bad. More importantly, his point in these chapters is that God's mercifully saving some of the wicked is *not* unjust. Ultimately he concludes that God is just 'not because you repay us our due, but because you do what is fitting to your supreme goodness' (*Proslogion* 10, S.I p. 109, ll. 4–5). In the final analysis 'The just is only what you [to God] will, and the unjust is only what you do not will' (*Proslogion* 11, S.I p. 109, ll. 18–19). And this conclusion accords with the definition given in *De Veritate:* Justice is rightness of will kept for its own sake, where the standard for rightness is the will of God.

36. S.I p. 192–3, ll. 27–2.
37. S.I p. 193, ll. 9–11. In *De coceptu virginali et de originali peccato* 3 Anselm argues that sin is only in the rational will, and in 4 he makes the interesting argument that if sin were a property of the act rather than the will, then when the act is past the sin would be gone; S.1I p. 145, ll. 4–5.
38. S.I p. 192, ll. 31–2.
39. S.I p. 193, ll. 28–30.
40. S.I p. 241, l. 13.
41. *Ordinatio* III, suppl. dist. 26. I am following the Allan B. Wolter translation (Wolter 1986, 179). I am not competent to assess Scotus's complex and sophisticated discussion of the role of the two wills, and it may be that he ultimately offers something like Anselm's hierarchical analysis. This does not seem to be the view of Scotus scholars, however, See Cross (1999, 87), and Williams (2003, 345–7).
42. Jeffrey Brower defends the Kantian interpretation in arguing that Anselm, moves away from the eudaemonism characteristic of many medieval thinkers (Brower 2004). Stanley G. Kane also proposes the Kantian interpretation, and finds that on this interpretation Anselm's doctrine of morally significant freedom is inconsistent (Kane [1981], 86–7).
43. *De casu diaboli* 4, S.I p. 241, ll. 13–14.
44. S.I p. 255, ll. 11–12.
45. S.I p. 241, ll. 19–23.
46. *De casu diaboli* 14, S.I p. 258, ll. 21–3.
47. *De casu diaboli* 6, S.I p. 244, ll. 3–5.
48. *De casu diaboli* 6, S.1 p. 243, ll. 20–2. As Stanley Kane (1981) makes clear, on the Kantian interpretation, Anselm's view that the good angels are praiseworthy for possessing inalienable justice seems problematic when the fact is that they cannot sin only because they have all the benefits they could possibly desire (93–4).
49. *De casu diaboli* 4, S.I p. 241, ll. 19–20. The devil willed 'some good', which is not described. The rest of the chapter points out that in so doing he willed to be like God in a way.
50. Although I argue that Anselm's analysis of freedom is very different from Augustine's, on most of the basic metaphysical and epistemic issues Anselm follows Augustine. A glance at Schmitt's notes to the critical edition of Anselm's *Opera Omnia* makes the case clearly. See also Rogers (1997).
51. *De civitate Dei* 12.22.
52. S.II p. 158, ll. 17–19.
53. S.I p. 258, l. 6.
54. S.I p. 258, ll. 13–16.
55. S.I p. 243, l. 1.
56. S.I p. 243, ll. 3–4.
57. Anselm (1998), 203.
58. S.I p. 258, ll. 20–1.
59. S.I p, 258, ll. 18–24.
60. S.II p. 281, ll. 5–8.
61. *De concordia* 3. 12, S.II p. 284, l. 21.
62. *De concordia* 3.11, S.II p. 281, ll.3–5.
63. *De concordia* 3. 11, S.II p. 281, ll. 10–11. The Oxford translation insists upon the most Kantian interpretation beyond what the Latin requires. It reads (p. 469), 'Indeed when disposed to will their own advantage, people always will their gratification and a state of happiness.' 'Advantage' often connotes a benefit at someone else's expense, which *commoditas* does not. 'Their own gratification' has negative connotations which *beatitudo* does not. And the Latin does not require that 'always' be qualified by, 'when disposed to will their own advantage. . . .' The Oxford translation is not impossible, but the more obvious reading says just that we always will happiness.
64. *De concordia* 3.13, S.II p. 287, ll. 2–3.
65. *De concordia* 3.14, S.II p. 288, ll. 1–3.

CHAPTER 4

Anselm: Free Will and Moral Responsibility

THOMAS WILLIAMS

Sometimes an interpretive dispute is no more than that; nothing more is at stake than how one understands a philosopher's view of some particular topic. Sometimes, however, what looks like a dispute over some particular point of interpretation is actually something much bigger. The debate over Anselm's account of free choice is an example of the second sort of dispute. On the surface, it is no more than a debate about whether Anselm had a hierarchical understanding of will; but, when we probe more deeply, we find underlying disputes about the ways in which, and the purposes for which, the history of philosophy ought to be pursued, as well as about the proper role of philosophical assessment in philosophical historiography.

Many interpreters of medieval philosophy are taken with Harry Frankfurt's account of the hierarchical structure of the will (Frankfurt 1971), finding Frankfurtianism in authors as disparate as Augustine and Aquinas. Most recently, the Frankfurtians have erroneously claimed Anselm for their cause. But Anselm does not recognize a hierarchy of first- and second-order desires in the will, and (consequently) he does not analyze the will's freedom in terms of the relation between first- and second-order desires. I shall argue against the Frankfurtian reading on three grounds: textual, philosophical, and historiographical: The Frankfurtian reading relies on tendentious textual analysis and troubling eisegesis; it destroys whatever is philosophically attractive in Anselm's view and leaves him unable to answer the very questions that motivate his interest in free choice; and it represents an abuse of philosophical historiography.

The Textual Case

Before I turn to my main task, I must lay out a few important matters of definition. Let us understand a first-order desire as a desire whose object is not itself a desire or will, and a second-order desire as a desire whose object is a desire or will. This is a broader definition than either Frankfurt or his acolytes typically give—they generally define first-order desires as desires to perform an action—but the broader definition is considerably more useful. For example, my desire to escape censure for an intemperate outburst, my desire to be a successful teacher, and my desire for a widespread return to eastward-facing celebrations of the Eucharist may, under suitable circumstances, lead me to perform a particular action; but just as such they are not desires to perform any action. Yet they certainly seem to be first-order desires—they're desires, after all, and their objects are not other desires, so what else should we call them? (I'll come back to this.) When a desire is effective, we call it a volition. A first-order volition, then, is a first-order desire that produces an action; and a second-order volition is a second-order desire that produces a conforming first-order volition.[1] Persons have freedom of the will, Frankfurt argues, when they are able to have the wills they want to have: that is, when they are able to have first-order volitions that conform to their second-order volitions. And persons act freely when they act from first-order volitions that conform to their second-order volitions.

I can now turn to an analysis of the texts of Anselm on which the Frankfurtian reading ostensibly rests. This part of the paper is complicated by the fact that the two interpretations I'm considering impose the alien Frankfurtian scheme on Anselm's texts in very different ways. Stan R. Tyvoll (2006) identifies both of the fundamental inclinations of the will, the affection for justice and the affection for advantage, as second-order desires. Katherin A. Rogers (2008), by contrast, makes the affection for justice a second-order desire and resolves the affection for advantage into a plurality of first-order desires.[2]

I shall begin with one key passage on which both authors rely. The passage is from *Harmony* 3.11:

> 'Will', in fact, appears to be said equivocally. It has three senses: the instrument for willing, the affection of the instrument, and the uses of that instrument. The instrument for willing is the power of the soul that we employ for willing, just as reason is the instrument for reasoning that we employ when we reason and sight is the instrument for seeing that we employ when we see. The affection of this instrument is that by which the instrument itself is disposed in such a way to will something (even when one is not thinking of what it wills) that if that thing comes to mind, the instrument wills it, either immediately or at the appropriate time.... And the use of that instrument is what we have only when we think of the thing we will.

There is no dispute here that by the "instrument for willing" Anselm is talking about the will itself. Nor is there any unclarity about "the uses of that instrument," which Tyvoll, Rogers, and I agree are particular occurrent first-order desires. Our interpretations part company over the second sense of "will," "that by which the instrument itself is disposed," and over how to understand the contrast between the second sense and the third sense. I argue that the dispositions or affections of the will – there are at bottom just two, Anselm tells us later in this passage: one for willing advantage and one for willing rectitude – are general dispositional desires, whereas the uses of the will are particular occurrent desires. Tyvoll and Rogers say, however, that the contrast Anselm intends is between second-order and first-order desires. Though the two authors differ in their understanding of the disposition for willing advantage, they agree that the disposition for willing rectitude is a second-order desire. For Tyvoll, "the inclination for uprightness is . . . a second-order desire for morally upright first-order volitions" (Tyvoll 2006, 159). Rogers, who prefers to translate *voluntas* in its second sense as "desire," claims that the "desire for justice" is "a second order desire that one's first order desires for benefits should be properly ordered, should be as they ought to be" (Rogers 53).

I shall look first at the evidence Tyvoll offers in favor of the claim that the affection for justice is a second-order desire. So far as I can find, his entire case for reading the two affections as second-order desires is found in the following paragraph, which I quote in full:

> What sort of desires are the inclinations? Clearly, they are not desires for specific actions; they are neither first-order desires nor first-order volitions. For it is through the inclinations that first-order desires and volitions come about. Rather, the inclinations are desires of the second order; they are second-order volitions. So, for example, Anselm refers to the inclination for happiness as the "will" (*voluntas*) for "willing benefit" (*ad volendum commodum*), and to the inclination for uprightness as the "will" (*voluntas*) for "willing uprightness" (*ad volendum rectitudinem*). Hence, each inclination is a second-order desire for a will, and when effective, a second-order volition.
>
> (Tyvoll 2006, 159)

This is an exceptionally weak case. First, from the fact that the affections are not desires for specific actions, it does not follow that they are not first-order desires or first-order volitions. One can have a first-order desire for something general or abstract. One might desire a successful career without yet having decided which career to pursue or how exactly to pursue it. One might desire health without desiring to take any particular concrete steps toward achieving or attaining it. These are "not desires for specific actions," to use Tyvoll's words, but they are all first-order desires; their objects are possible goods or states of affairs, not other desires.

The fact that Tyvoll speaks here of "desires for specific actions" suggests that he may have succumbed to a false dichotomy. If (contrary to my earlier arguments) one insists on restricting the label "first-order desire" to desires to perform particular actions, the affections of the will will not be first-order desires. But we cannot immediately conclude that they are second-order desires, as if that were the only other option. For in addition to first-order desires to perform particular actions, and second-order desires to have a certain kind of will, there will be these other, general desires, which are not desires to perform particular actions but nonetheless have as their objects possible goods or states of affairs, not other desires.

Tyvoll offers a second reason for thinking that the affections of the will are second-order desires: "it is through the inclinations that first-order desires and volitions come about." But this reason is no better, since not every desire through which a first-order desire comes about is a second-order desire. Suppose I desire a successful career. Finding upon reflection that I have no talent for anything but philosophy, I come to have the desire to study philosophy. My first-order desire to study philosophy derives from my desire for a successful career; but the latter desire is, as I have already argued, itself a first-order desire. This is no contrived example, but exactly the kind that Anselm himself uses again and again to explain how will-as-use derives from will-as-affection. For example, in *On the Fall of the Devil* 12–13 Anselm explains that an angel who had only the affection for happiness would be moved thereby to will whatever particular goods he might think of as means to or constituents of happiness.

Rogers's case for the Frankfurtian reading emerges primarily from her elucidation of Anselm's definition of free choice as the power to preserve rectitude of will for its own sake, because, she says, "a careful unpacking will reveal the hierarchical framework he proposes for created freedom."[3] She writes:

> The horse which wants to go graze is willing what it ought. And the dog which loves its puppies or the master who is good to it possesses rightness of will. Clearly rightness of will here does not connote moral rectitude or uprightness. Anselm explains that lower animals are not capable of justice because they do not *recognize* and *choose* to have rightness of will, rather they simply have it by nature. To put this in contemporary terms, borrowed from Frankfurt, according to Anselm the horse and the dog possess and act upon the proper first order desires, but they cannot step back to a higher level and evaluate and endorse those desires. They cannot form second order volitions *about* their own desires.[4]

To begin with Rogers's last point: There is nothing about stepping back, evaluating, and endorsing desires in either of the examples from Anselm she invokes here (the horse from *On Truth* 12, the dog from *On Freedom of Choice* 13). Indeed, there is hardly anything about stepping back, evaluating, and endorsing desires anywhere in Anselm. This is a point that can hardly be overemphasized. It is an important part of Frankfurt's philosophical agenda that personhood involves a certain capacity for reflection on and criticism of one's own motives and desires. This is why Frankfurt will talk about persons as "identifying with" certain of their first-order desires and not with others. Rogers's book is full of such language. But this is simply not Anselm's agenda. Though no doubt human rationality as Anselm understands it does give us the capacity to reflect on our desires, Anselm never attributes human freedom to our capacity for taking up some cognitive or volitional stance toward them.

If what's distinctive about human beings isn't our ability to "step back, evaluate, and endorse" our desires, what is? The two passages to which Rogers alludes in the paragraph I've quoted give two complementary aspects of Anselm's answer. Anselm uses the example of the horse in *On Truth* 12 to draw a contrast between two different ways in which a creature might preserve rectitude. Rational creatures can deserve praise for preserving rectitude because they can "perceive," or "know," or "be aware of" rectitude and can therefore will it; non-rational creatures such as the horse cannot know rectitude and therefore cannot will it, so they are not praiseworthy if they preserve rectitude. To be aware of rectitude is simply to be aware that a given action is right. The horse is distinguished from human beings not because it lacks a hierarchically structured will but because it lacks the capacity for beliefs of the form "I ought to φ." So the horse example has no tendency to show that the power to preserve rectitude of will for its own sake depends on a hierarchically structured will.

Anselm offers the example of the dog in *On Freedom of Choice* 13, where he comments on the significance of each element in his definition of free choice. The dog enters the picture in Anselm's commentary on the phrase "for the sake of rectitude itself." The dog preserves rectitude of will, but not for the sake of rectitude itself, because it preserves rectitude *naturally*. This example would help Rogers's case only if she could show that Anselm thinks our capacity for evaluating or endorsing our desires is what allows us to act spontaneously, rather than naturally; and there isn't the slightest bit of textual support anywhere in Anselm for that notion.

It will be helpful here to distinguish between two different senses in which Anselm uses the expression "will rectitude." In one sense, to will rectitude is to will what is in fact right. In another sense, to will rectitude is to will something under the description 'right' (or under a description under which it is right). We might speak of the first as willing rectitude *materially* and of the second as willing rectitude *formally*. I will rectitude materially when I keep my appointment because I fear reprisal; I will rectitude formally when I keep my appointment because it's the right thing to do. The fact that "willing rectitude" can have these two senses explains why Anselm in one place affirms (*On Truth* 12), and in another places denies (*On Freedom of Choice* 13), that a non-human animal can will rectitude: it wills rectitude materially but not formally.

Up to this point Rogers has been arguing that the power to preserve rectitude of will for its own sake involves the power to form a second-order volition for rectitude of will; having such a second-order volition is a necessary condition for having a just will and thereby being a proper object of moral praise. She goes on to argue that a second-order volition for rectitude of will is not a *sufficient* condition for justice (see above, 52). Once again, the "second level" to which Rogers appeals here is her own invention. The vainglorious almsgiver in Anselm's example does not "have a non-praiseworthy motive for desiring . . . the correct desires"; he has a non-praiseworthy motive for *doing the right thing* – giving alms. Even on Rogers's own reading, the object of the vainglorious will is not a desire or a willing, but a moral fact: according to her, "he wills that he ought to will what he wills." A more apt translation of the passage, with a bit more context to flesh out Anselm's point, would go like this: "Someone who gives food to a starving pauper for the sake of an empty reputation wills that he be under the obligation to will what he in fact wills. For he is praised because he wills to do what he ought to" (*On Truth* 12). Anselm's point is that this person wills what he ought to will and even wills it *because* he ought to will it (because he wills praise for doing what he ought to do, and he can't get such praise unless he ought to do it), but he doesn't will it *for the sake of* rectitude. There's no hierarchy or "second level" here; there is simply the point that one can will rectitude materially without willing it formally, and this will would be a first-order volition.

The next element in Rogers's case for the Frankfurtian reading is her analysis of Anselm's arguments in *On the Fall of the Devil.* Anselm argues, she says, that "in order for the rational creature to gain merit . . . it must have the option to cling to or abandon justice" (see above, 52). That option in turn requires that God give rational creatures two desires: the desire for benefit and the desire for justice. We must not, however, think of benefit and justice as "two mutually exclusive sets of objects of desire" (see above, 53). For Anselm says that creatures do not will anything unless they judge it to be in some way beneficial for them (*Nam nullus vult nisi quod aliquo modo sibi putat commodum*). So Anselm must hold that all first-order desires are for benefits. The desire for justice is a second-order desire for first-order desires that conform to the dictates of justice (see above, 53).

It would take us too far afield to explain what Anselm means in this context when he says *nullus vult nisi quod aliquo modo sibi putat commodum*, but we can be quite sure that he does not mean that every choice is for the advantageous, because Anselm repeatedly denies that.[5] That denial is the cornerstone of his explanation of the fall of the devil: the good angels rejected something advantageous for the sake of justice, whereas the bad angels chose something advantageous at the expense of justice. The conditions of the primal angelic choice as Anselm explains it in *On the Fall of the Devil* require that the good angels' choice to preserve rectitude of will was *not* a will for some benefit, but precisely the spurning of a benefit. Furthermore, if the good angels *had* chosen to preserve rectitude of will because they judged it to be beneficial, they would (on Anselm's view) have been preserving rectitude of will for the sake of benefit rather than for the sake of rectitude itself – and they would therefore not have been just or praiseworthy and would not have merited the gift that, Anselm tells us, God gave them as a reward for their justice.

Furthermore, Anselm repeatedly makes clear that if one wills *x* for the sake of rectitude, it is most proper to say that one wills not *x* but rectitude; and that if one wills *y* for the sake of benefit, it is most proper to say that one wills not *y* but benefit.[6] So the contrast between willing rectitude for its own sake and willing rectitude for the sake of some external good is, in Anselm's mind, most properly described as a contrast between willing rectitude and *not really willing rectitude at all*—not as a contrast between a second-order volition for an upright will and the lack of such a second-order volition. Note too that Anselm's whole impetus is to flatten all our willings into one level, not to create hierarchies. To will *x* for the sake of *y* is, properly speaking, to will *y*—not to will a will that wills *y*.

Moreover, Rogers is simply wrong in denying that Anselm regards justice and benefit as two different kinds of good. Just a few lines up from the words Rogers cites, Anselm says that

> we commonly speak of two goods and of two evils that are contrary to them. One good is that which is called 'justice', whose contrary evil is injustice. The other good is what I think can be called 'the advantageous'; its opposite evil is the disadvantageous.[7]

And when Anselm discusses the two affections of the will in *Harmony* 3.11, he treats justice and advantage as alternative objects of first-order volitions and the affection for justice and the affection for advantage as parallel to each other.

The Philosophical Case

In the course of rebutting the textual case, we have seen enough of Anselm's theory of free choice that the philosophical case can be dispatched pretty quickly. Conceptually speaking, the key objection to the Frankfurtian reading is that Frankfurt and Anselm have two very different sets of goals in mind for their theories of the will and its freedom. Frankfurt's theory is designed to secure philosophical results in which Anselm displays no interest at all, and Anselm is keen on establishing conclusions that Frankfurt's theory notoriously fails to support.

The evidence that Frankfurt and Anselm are a horrible match philosophically speaking is not hard to find in both Tyvoll and Rogers. Tyvoll, for example, begins his paper by observing that:

> One advantage of the hierarchical analysis of desire and volition is that it serves to illuminate a familiar philosophical tradition in free will theory, according to which an agent is free if he is able to do or will as he wants to do or will.
>
> (Tyvoll 2006, 161)

But that tradition is a compatibilist tradition, and Anselm is unambiguously an incompatibilist. And as Tyvoll elaborates his point about the importance of being able to will as one wants to will, the misfit between Frankfurt's view and Anselm's becomes even clearer.

Tyvoll argues that on Anselm's view, "by willing what is morally right, agents have the will that they want to have and ought to have, and they have it because they want to have it; hence they enjoy freedom of will" (Tyvoll 2006, 164). Furthermore,

> someone whose first-order volitions cannot be contrary to her second-order desire for morally upright volitions (someone who is unable to sin) is freer than someone whose volitions can be contrary to that second-order desire (someone who is able to sin). The ability to sin decreases free will because it is an ability to have a will that we do not want to have.
>
> (Ibid)

But this is simply wrong. Even if Tyvoll's interpretation of the affection for happiness as a second-order desire were correct, it would turn out that those who sin have a will they want to have, just as much as those who preserve rectitude. For according to Anselm, every sin is committed for the sake of happiness. And anyone who wills to sin for the sake of happiness has a will she wants to have, since (if Tyvoll's own interpretation is correct) she has a first-order volition for happiness that accords with the (alleged) second-order volition for happiness. Furthermore, someone who chooses justice over happiness in a situation relevantly like that of the angels would, on Tyvoll's analysis, have a will he both does and doesn't want to have: a first-order volition for justice that accords with the second-order volition for justice but conflicts with the second-order desire for happiness. So no philosophical advantage is had in reading Anselm as part of a philosophical tradition that understands freedom as the ability to have the will one wants to have; on the contrary, such a reading makes a complete hash out of Anselm's arguments.

Tyvoll also argues that the Frankfurtian reading helps makes sense of Anselm's claim that someone who cannot sin is freer than someone who can, for such a person "is perfectly able to will and do as she wants to will and do" (Tyvoll 2006, 164). But Anselm nowhere says that such a person is freer because she has the ability to will and do as she wants to. He says such a person is freer because she *can't lose rectitude*, or more accurately, because she has the power to preserve rectitude of will for its own sake in such a way that she can't lose it. Freedom understood in that way does not require a hierarchy of second-order and first-order desires. Such a hierarchy doesn't even help—and as Tyvoll's analysis makes clear, the principal reason for introducing the hierarchy is to secure a conclusion that Anselm's isn't at all interested in.

So what *is* Anselm's chief concern? A careful look at *On Freedom of Choice*, *On the Fall of the Devil*, and *Harmony* shows very clearly that he means to develop a theory of freedom that secures the free agent's ultimate responsibility, both causal and moral, for sin.[8] Now as both Tyvoll and Rogers acknowledge, the strongest objection to Frankfurt's theory is precisely that it fails to secure the free agent's ultimate responsibility for his actions. Tyvoll, for example, addresses the objection that the hierarchical "mesh" between first- and second-order desires could be produced by mechanisms that clearly undermine the agent's responsibility for the resulting action. The account of freedom must therefore

> include the additional condition that the alignment is in some sense ultimately up to the agent himself. . . Hence, we must include the condition of ultimate responsibility as a supplement to the hierarchical account of Anselm's definition of free will.
>
> (Tyvoll 2008, 167–168)

But philosophically speaking this is completely askew. The ultimate responsibility condition isn't just a supplemental condition to be secured by extraneous fiddling. The whole purpose of Anselm's account of free choice is to preserve ultimate responsibility. And if one can secure ultimate responsibility without adopting a hierarchical view of the will, is there any good philosophical reason to attribute the hierarchical view to Anselm?[9]

I shall make one final philosophical point about how alien the Frankfurtian scheme is to Anselm's thinking. In arguing that Anselm's version of the hierarchical view escapes various problems that beset Frankfurt's views, Katherin Rogers accidentally supplies the conceptual wherewithal to eliminate the hierarchy altogether. Rogers notes that Frankfurt himself raises the difficulty that, theoretically speaking, there is no upper limit on the number of levels of desires. But for Anselm, she claims,

> there is no threat of an infinite regress of orders of desire. God's will is the absolute standard of value and once one, at the second level, has chosen to select one's first-order desires against that standard, there is no

> higher value to appeal to. Reflective self-evaluation is a means to the end of choosing justly, but there is no virtue in continuing beyond the second level. Moreover, it is not, on Anselm's analysis, really possible to do so. What would a third-order desire consist in? The desire to desire rightness of will for its own sake, i.e. the desire to desire justice. But, at least according to Anselm, all desires are aimed at something. What motivates this third-order desire? If it is the desire for justice, then this is really just the second-order desire reiterated.[10]

Notice that if she's right, her argument equally entails that the second-order desire collapses into the first-order desire. The second-order desire, according to Rogers, is supposed to be a desire to conform one's will to the requirements of justice. So we can ask what motivates this desire. If it is the desire for justice, then this is really just the first-order desire reiterated. Remember, Anselm always talks about preserving rectitude of will for its own sake—i.e., for the sake of rectitude itself. On Anselm's analysis of the *what* and the *why* of willing, willing rectitude of will for the sake of rectitude *just is* willing rectitude. We never get past the first level.

The Historiographical Case

There are, to oversimplify the matter grossly, two basic approaches to the history of philosophy. One approach views the work of the historian of philosophy as that of a "curator in the museum of ideas," to steal a phrase from D. S. Hutchinson. The aim of the historian on this view is to dust off the accretions of misunderstanding that have accumulated on a philosopher over the centuries and display him in his pristine condition, properly labeled and catalogued, and carefully presented in his historical context. This sort of historian has no official interest—no interest *qua* historian of philosophy—in the plausibility of the views thus presented, the success of the arguments deployed to support them, or the possibility of bringing the philosopher into some contemporary discussion. The other sort of historian, by contrast, reads older philosophy in the same spirit in which the non-historian reads the current journals: as a source of ideas and arguments to advance discussions in the contemporary sphere. Let us the call historians of the first sort "contextual historians" and historians of the second sort "argumentative historians."

These are two ideal types—two extremes—but a great deal of work in the history of medieval philosophy falls very close to one or the other of these two extremes. Both approaches have their uses, but both also have their characteristic abuses, failures, and besetting sins. The textual and philosophical mistakes into which the defenders of the Frankfurtian reading of Anselm have fallen represent errors to which argumentative historians are particularly prone. I do not say this by way of arguing for the superiority of contextual history, for I am an argumentative historian myself. It would appear that Tyvoll and Rogers have yielded to the temptation, so alluring to our sort of historian, to think of philosophical or theological disputes as generic "perennial questions." If a historian thinks of the questions we find in an author as nothing more than perennial questions, and of the available answers as nothing more than possibilities permanently residing in logical space, then why not go looking in Anselm for views that we find in contemporary metaphysics and philosophy of religion?

At the very least, it is tempting for argumentative historians to suppose that views we know from contemporary philosophy are somehow "out there" as solutions to *the* mind-body problem or *the* problem of free will or what have you. Thus, when we look at older texts that engage with *a* mind-body problem or *a* problem of free will, we both overlook the historical particularities that make it *a* problem rather than *the* (generic, perennial) problem and, consequently, expect what we find in the older texts to conform to the contours of contemporary debate. It is then no surprise to find Harry Frankfurt meeting us in the pages of Anselm.

But it *should* be a surprise. It would indeed be a thing most wonderful if a view first proposed in the context of early-1970s Anglo-American debates on the freedom of the will should be found ready-to-hand, lacking only the name of its author, in texts from the late-11th and early-12th centuries. The fact that the textual case for the Frankfurtian reading of Anselm is so weak—there simply is, as I have tried to show, nothing whatever to be said for it—suggests that this interpretive dispute is at bottom a dispute about philosophical historiography. If one finds in Harry Frankfurt a helpful tool for understanding *the* problem of free will, and one expects to find in Anselm a discussion of that very problem, for which the very same tools will be helpful in the very same way, it seems perfectly reasonable to expect to find Frankurt in Anselm. And, as both Tyvoll and Rogers demonstrate, the texts can be made to appear to cooperate with what one expects to find. Remove that expectation, however, and the eisegesis is exposed.

Notes

1. This is how the Frankfurtian interpreters of Anselm define second-order volitions, though Frankfurt himself defines them differently (Frankfurt 1971, 10).
2. See esp. chapter 3, "The Purpose, Definition, and Structure of Free Choice" (55–72), reprinted as chapter 3 in this volume. This discussion develops the interpretation offered in Rogers, 2005.
3. See above p. 49. I have severely abbreviated my treatment of Rogers's reading; for a much fuller account, see my review of *Anselm on Freedom* (Williams, 2009).
4. See above p. 51 (emphasis in original).
5. Rogers (see above, p. 57) also interprets *Harmony* 3.11 as saying that we always will for the sake of benefit, because Anselm says that through the affection for advantage we always will happiness. But since the very next sentence adds that through the affection for rectitude we will rectitude, the context militates very strongly against Rogers's interpretation.

6. Examples abound, but see in particular *On the Fall of the Devil* 13 (I:256) and *Harmony* 3.11 (II:281).
7. *On the Fall of the Devil* 12 (I:125).
8. Rogers, to her credit, realizes this fact, arguing that Anselm is chiefly concerned to develop an account of free choice that allows created agents "a measure of aseity" (see above, p. 49).
9. Rogers argues in a similar vein that Anselm secures ultimate responsibility in a way that Frankfurt fails to do. See Rogers, 2005, 264–266.
10. Rogers, 2005, 262–263.

PART III
Is Abelard's Ethics Conceptually Impoverished?

Editor's Introduction

Shakespeare's *Julius Caesar* depicts the role played by Brutus, a leading Roman citizen, in Caesar's assassination. The play invites us to look at this deed from different perspectives. Brutus believes himself to be motivated by honor and depicts the assassination as the deliverance of Rome from a rising tyrant. Whether his motives are really so noble is unclear. In convincing him to join the conspiracy, Cassius says he will turn the eyes of "many of the best respect in Rome" on Brutus to act as mirrors that reflect his "hidden worthiness." Is Cassius stirring a modest Brutus to act on the motive of honor? Or has he instead discovered Brutus's pride and envy of Caesar? The assassination itself is the same deed, and yet what we think of Brutus will vary depending on what his intention is in carrying it out. So Brutus himself discovers: When the crowd at Caesar's funeral thinks he was motivated by concern for the public good, they want to crown him emperor; but when Marc Antony convinces them that it was Caesar who was the public-minded figure, they conclude that Brutus's intentions were self-serving and they begin to riot. What Shakespeare shows is that our moral evaluation of an act depends crucially on the agent's intention.

Robert Sokolowski urges caution in the way we apply this insight about the moral relevance of intention. We should not think of an intention as an act that takes place in some shadowy "inner" space, while the deed takes place in the outer public space. He agrees with Thomas Aquinas that an intention is instead a sort of rational wanting that forms part of a whole human action that includes the deed. After reflection, our reason articulates an end as an end, in view of which we will determine the means to or constituents of that end. When we desire that end as a goal to be pursued by taking those means or achieving those constituents, we have elicited an intention. Although Sokolowski offers a mild criticism of Aquinas for his apparent requirement that an intention have a different object from the deed it informs, he reserves harsh criticism for Aquinas's predecessor Peter Abelard. Not only does Abelard distinguish the intention from the deed, but he argues that only the intention is morally relevant; all deeds are morally neutral. His ground for this view, according to Sokolowski, is the further contention that what matters morally is only our faithfulness to God's commands, which is a matter of our hidden interaction with God. If we are obedient, we act well, if we are disobedient, we act badly, and there is nothing further to articulate about moral goodness and badness beyond that. The result is that morality is seriously impoverished. The rich moral conceptual scheme we find in Aquinas—who characterizes acts as generous or miserly, charitable or slothful, magnanimous or pusillanimous—can find no place in Abelard.

In "Peter Abelard and St. Thomas Aquinas on Moral Intention," Ian Wilks first responds to Sokolowski by pointing to the appeal of internalist ethical views. Drawing on Abelard's own arguments, Wilks points out that we sometimes perform deeds in ignorance of the sort of act we are performing. Someone who has every reason to think her divorce is legal, when in fact it isn't, is not morally responsible for bigamy when she marries again. According to Abelard, this sort of case shows that accurate moral assessment depends on the agent's intention and not the deed. Furthermore, Wilks argues, Sokolowski should not infer that Abelard's internalism reduces ethics to a matter of thoughtless obedience or disobedience. It is instead an ethics of charity, a rich explanatory concept that underlies all the moral law's injunctions. Since an agent whose intentions are characterized by love of neighbor will under ordinary circumstances perform deeds that express this love, Abelard's ethics does not turn out to be a dark and mysterious transaction between the agent and God, but involves thoughtful and loving transactions with one's neighbors. Finally, Wilks argues that when understood correctly, Abelard's and Aquinas's views are not as different as Sokolowski has made them out to be: Abelard's ethics is not conceptually impoverished, and Aquinas turns out to have strong internalist leanings.

Note on References

For an explanation of how to read references to Aquinas, please see the Editor's Introduction to Part VII.

Further Reading

- David Gallagher (1995). "Will and deed in Abelard and Aquinas."
- Peter King (1995). "Abelard's Intentionalist Ethics."
- John Marenbon (1997). *The Philosophy of Peter Abelard.*

CHAPTER 5

Intentions and the Will: Aquinas and Abelard

ROBERT SOKOLOWSKI

I.

In his discussion of human action, St. Thomas uses a distinction that seems at first glance to be inappropriate. He contrasts the interior act of the will with the exterior human act. The distinction is conspicuous; it is found in many particular passages and an entire *Quaestio* in the *Summa Theologiae* is entitled "On the Goodness and Badness of the Interior Act of the Will" (1–2 19). Another is entitled "On the Goodness and Badness of Exterior Human Acts" (1–2 20). Aquinas says that the interior act is directed primarily toward the purpose or end, the *finis* that the agent has in mind, while the exterior act is defined or specified by what it is about, by being a certain kind of act: eating, walking, giving someone shelter, striking someone, stealing, lying (1–2 20.1 reply). The exterior act, moreover, is commanded by the interior act; the exterior act is called the *actus imperatus*, the commanded act, while the interior act is called the *imperium*, the command. The exterior, commanded act is related toward a purpose by the interior act that commands it and that is itself directed toward an end in view.

This double orientation of human behavior means that a human act can be evaluated in two ways: as regards the exterior act, we can ask whether the kind of thing being done is good or bad; as regards the interior act, we can ask whether the purpose the agent has in mind is good or bad. Both dimensions are morally relevant: a wicked exterior act is wrong even if done for a good purpose, a "good" exterior act can be part of a bad performance if it is done for a bad purpose. In fact, changes in the interior act can bring about numerically distinct acts even as we continue the same exterior behavior. Aquinas gives this example: suppose I set out to attend church so that I will be seen there and praised by others; then my walking to the church is part of an act of vanity. But if on the way I come to my senses and realize that I should attend church out of piety, and if I decide that I will indeed do so, then as I continue to walk I begin to act out of religious reverence and my vain conduct ceases (1–2 20.6 response to 1). The walking is one but the moral acts are two. This shows that although both the interior and exterior dimensions are morally significant, the interior act, the orientation toward a purpose, is the more important. It serves as the form for the performance and identifies each act that we do.

Aquinas goes into great detail in his analysis of other aspects of moral behavior. He says we first become aware of purposes, then discover means of achieving them, then deliberate about the means, then select the best means available, then begin the execution of the act by commanding the exterior performance. In these descriptions, however, the sharp distinction between the interior and the exterior acts remains troubling. It seems to break the human performance into two separate acts, one the act directed toward the purpose and the other the actual bodily conduct; one the interior act of the will, the other the visible behavior. We almost seem to be left with a Stoic division between the external performance and the internal attitude. But in fact, Aquinas does not leave us with this dichotomy. He has an article entitled "Whether the Command and the Commanded Act are One Act or Different Acts?" (1–2 17.4). In this article he develops some thoughts about different senses of unity and diversity, then he discusses the moral act and concludes, "The command and the commanded act are one human act the way a whole is one; but multiple as regards its parts." So despite the many passages that seem to imply that the interior and exterior acts are two, Aquinas says they are only two faces of one single act, with the interior aspect being the primary and formal one.

For Aquinas, an "act of the will," the interior act of the will, is not an internal thrust, shadow action, impulse, or decision. It is rather the kind of wanting, the kind of inclination—*inclinatio quaedam*—that follows when we are able to articulate a situation thoughtfully (1–2 6.4 reply). Our ability to think allows new kinds of desires to surface within us, inclinations that would not occur to a creature that merely perceived and imagined things. Aquinas calls this willing or wanting the "elicited act" of the will, the *actus elicitus*. It is our response to what is displayed in our thinking. The thoughtfulness that makes willing possible involves the appreciation that we can do some things through other things, that we can do more than merely react to whatever is around us. It is the appreciation of ends as ends and means as means, and it includes shaking out means and ends in our current situation. Such articulation permits a special kind of wanting, which is called the rational desire or the will. An act of willing is therefore the kind of desire that arises when a coherence takes shape in our practical thinking. However, this act of willing is also a command: it initiates a performance and does not merely long for something. It also therefore initiates the signing of a check, the putting of clothes on someone who is cold, the feeding of someone, the running away. And since the interior and exterior acts are only two aspects of one act, we can say that the feeding of someone or the running away is the act of generosity or cowardice.

We must introduce one more topic in Aquinas's description of moral behavior, the concept of intention. Aquinas defines an intention as an act of the will, the act by which the agent is related to an end ("The intention is the act of the will in respect to the end"; 1–2, 12.1 response to 4). The intention is our wanting or willing the end in view of which we conduct ourselves. However, the end in view, whether it be the thing desired or our use or enjoyment of the thing desired, has to be presented to the will by reason. That is, the end has to be articulated as end and understood as a good in view of which we will make choices. This purpose, presented as such, is sometimes called the *intentum,* the thing or action intended. For Aquinas, therefore, the intention is not a proposition or an intellectual presentation; it is an act of willing, but an act that requires a propositional or intellectual articulation. He says that not all intentions are directed toward the final end. Some intentions can be directed toward ends that are not final, but all intentions are "of an end" of some sort or other (1–2 12. 2 reply.)

Aquinas goes on to say that some acts are good or bad in their species (giving alms, feeding the hungry; stealing, murdering), but there are also some forms of behavior that are morally indifferent, such as lifting a straw from the ground or walking in the fields (1–2 18.8 reply). However, he says, although such acts may be indifferent in their species, no human act taken as an individual performance is morally indifferent, because every thoughtful act is done for some end, some *finis,* and this end in view will make the act to be either good or bad (1–2 18.9 reply). Aquinas admits that there are some performances that do not proceed "from deliberative reason, but from an imagination; for example if someone strokes his beard or moves his hand or foot" (ibid.). That kind of behavior is morally indifferent, but it is also not a thoughtful human act. Every thoughtful act is directed toward some end and therefore is good or bad.

It is at this point that a discrepancy arises between our description of moral action and the analysis given by St. Thomas. His analysis does not seem to provide enough space for simply voluntary actions that are thoughtful. All actions seem to have to be done for a purpose distinct from themselves; all actions seem to require an exterior act and an interior act of the will that is directed toward a purpose different from the exterior act. But there can be acts in which, so to speak, the intention collapses into the exterior act, in which the interior act of the will does not aim at anything more than the exterior act that is commanded. In such acts we do something simply because we want to do it or because it should be done in itself. Such cases do not seem to be adequately considered in Aquinas's analysis. Acts of friendship, acts of malice, exercises of skill, can be done in and for themselves, and they are not merely behavior based on imagination. And we cannot say that such acts are really composed of a choice plus an end in view; we cannot say that, for example, handing something over to someone is just an exterior act performed in view of an act of friendship as its end, for then the single voluntary act of friendship would be broken up into two parts, into a choice and an intention, and the simplicity of the voluntary performance would not be respected. The way the material performance, the handing over, both expresses and embodies the moral performance, the act of friendship, is not adequately formulated when we take one to be chosen in view of the other.

Aquinas emphasizes the intention so much that he seems to require a distinct intention, different from the exterior act being performed, in the case of every human action. Perhaps his theological concern with the final end makes him inclined to do this; when the issue of the final end is introduced, then any action that we perform, even an act that is being done entirely for its own sake, can always become subordinated to the overriding purpose, to the final end as a purpose distinct from this act. This theological concern certainly highlights the role of intentions, but it may have obscured the phenomenon of acts in which the purpose is in the action itself. In such simply voluntary acts the two faces of human action (the interior, commanding, elicited act, the intention; and the exterior, commanded act) collapse into one.

In other respects our description of moral behavior is in agreement with the essentials of Aquinas's psychology of moral conduct, except for a difference of emphasis. Aquinas stresses the interiority of human action; the term "interior act" indicates this. The practical reasoning that precedes action is said to be an activity carried on by the practical intellect, and its results are said to be proposed or presented to the will. Such expressions, obviously, must be appropriately interpreted; but they do convey the impression of mental activities going on quite completely in the mind as if in some inward place. Thomas's psychology of cognition confirms this: the phantasm, the impressed species of the possible intellect, the expressed "mental word" through which we know the object of our cognition, are all mental beings. They are all "similitudes" of objects (1 85.2). Through them, it is true, we are said to be referred to things, but they remain there as psychological and as intervening between us and things. The description of moral thinking that we have given places the categorialities of reasoning in things, as forms of presentation and identification and differing *of* things; and consequently it places thoughtful human behavior with and in things as well. Both the appraisals an agent makes of situations and the moral categorialities that inform the act (taking the good or bad of another as my good or bad) are said to be articulations of the presencing of things. Our difference with Aquinas on this point stems not just from a difference of opinion about the structure of the mind; it stems from a different appreciation of intentionality or of presencing (of presence and absence), and also from a different appreciation of the kind of reflection and the kind of discourse that occur in philosophy.

II.

Although Aquinas does not let the two faces of a moral act, the exterior and the interior, collapse into one, he does insist that the two are only two dimensions, not two separate acts. And he says that the moral character of the performance depends both on the kind of act being performed and on the intention of the agent; both faces together constitute the goodness and badness of the individual action. But in the moral theology of Abelard,[1] the two faces are separated and the intention alone is said to determine the good or bad character of a performance: "For God thinks not of what is done but in what mind it may be done, and the merit or glory of the doer lies in the intention, not in the deed" (p. 29; see pp. 43–45). Abelard states, quite emphatically, that "the addition of the performance of the deed adds nothing to increase the sin" (p. 15), and says that in good acts as well as bad everything is determined by our intention and consent: "It does not in fact matter to merit whether you give alms to the needy; charity may make you ready to give and the will may be there when the opportunity is missing and you no longer remain able to do so . . ." (p. 27).

Abelard can make such statements because he is discussing not the moral exchanges that occur among human agents but the relationship between the human agent and God. He discusses sin and salvation, not simply vice and virtue. His attention is concentrated on merit or reward, not on the internal goodness or badness of the act being performed. Moreover, he describes the relationship between God and man as a relationship between the lawgiver and one who obeys or disobeys the laws. Thus the essential exchange takes place between the divine intention and the human intention, between God's will and human obedience or contempt; it occurs internally and not in the acts that are publicly performed.

Abelard says that human beings have some desires that are directed toward things that have been forbidden in God's revealed commandments. If someone is aware of these commands and still consents to such desires, he expresses contempt of God; such contempt is sin (pp. 5–7, 17). The performance of the deed does not add anything to what we have morally "done" by our consent and contempt. This internal "doing" is the only thing that defines, redefines, or confirms our relationship to God. The external action is morally neutral: in fact, an action that is prohibited—eating something, taking something from someone, sexual intercourse—can in other circumstances be done without guilt (pp. 17–33), and God sometimes prohibits an action at one time and commands it at another (p. 19). God can command us to do deeds that seem bad, as he did when he ordered Abraham to kill his son; in such cases "the intention of the command alone, not the execution of the deed, excuses God, since he did will to command what is not a good thing to be done" (p. 31). Thus even in God's actions it is the intention that makes the act good.

In a passage that could have been written by a Stoic, Abelard says that if a deed added anything to our guilt, it would be "as if an exterior and corporeal act could contaminate the soul" (p. 23). He continues, "nothing pollutes the soul except what is of the soul, the consent which alone we have called sin, not the will [i.e., desire] which precedes it nor the doing of the deed which follows." Abelard says that all men are beset with desires for what is bad, but such desires are not morally bad; only consenting to them is wicked. In fact, "through this [men] have the material for a struggle so that triumphing over themselves through the virtue of temperance they may obtain a crown" (p. 5; see p. 13). Our inclinations to what is bad constitute "a certain weakness which is now necessary" (p. 7). Our "bad will" must remain as an occasion for conquest: "But in order that there be a fight, it is evident that there must be an enemy who resists, not one who actually gives up." We struggle against our desire, "but we do not really extinguish it, so that we always have it to fight against" (p. 13).

Finally, Abelard says that we as men judge the external acts that others perform, but we do not get to the substance of the performance, as God does; we are concerned with public order and public examples, not with moral guilt: "We, however, who are not capable of discussing and assessing [the intentions and consents of others], direct our judgment particularly to deeds, and we punish not so much faults as deeds, and we strive to avenge in someone less what harms his soul than what can harm others, in order to prevent public rather than individual injuries . . ." (p. 43). The domain of intentions and consents is visible only to the agent himself and to God; it cannot be perceived by others: God "particularly sees there where no man sees, because in punishing sin he considers not the deed but the mind, just as conversely we consider not the mind which we do not see but the deed which we know" (p. 41).

Abelard wrote over a century before Aquinas, before Scholasticism flourished in rigor and depth. His analysis of human action is unsophisticated, but it does capture the raw elements of problems that arise when moral action is placed within the context of revealed religion. His discussion may be unwieldy, but it is interesting precisely because it is so simple. In his analysis, as in that of the Stoics, the moral categories of self-control and weakness of self-control (*enkrateia* and *akrasia*) preponderate, but whereas the Stoics sadly concede that disturbing impressions will always be with us, Abelard rejoices in their presence because they offer an opportunity to win a reward. Neither Abelard nor the Stoics think that reason can suffuse passion and make its desires to be orderly. For both Abelard and the Stoics the passions and our external acts are "not our own," but while at least reason is "our own" for the Stoics, the divine commands according to which we regulate our desires are for Abelard not ours: we receive them from God and may not even understand why they are given; we as agents are identified with neither passion nor reason but serve as middlemen between the two, located between impenetrable obscurity and unending assault. It is in such an anthropology that intentions and acts of the will become the exclusive elements in moral conduct, the only thing left as really our own, the only thing for which we can be praised or blamed, rewarded or punished. Our task then is not, as for the Stoics, to strengthen our reason and make it conform to the cosmic *logos,* but to cultivate our obedience to God, who is displayed to us in his decisions rather than in his intellect. Because the reasons for his commands may be obscure to us we only can choose to obey; the obedience is not based on our understanding. Thus whereas the Stoic assent and dissent to appearances are acts of thinking, Abelard's consent to or struggle with passion is a decision.

If obedience and disobedience toward God's commands are the only two moral possibilities, then moral action is formalized to an excessive degree. It is not differentiated into the many various kinds of moral acts, good and bad: we no longer have acts of kindness, gratitude, and courage, or spite, cruelty, and murder.[2] There are only the neutral external performances on the one hand and the internal, awesomely secret exchange between the agent and God on the other. The agent does not become like his actions: he is made to be good or bad not by the weight of his performances but only by the intentions he has. And the internal action is so intensely moral that it, so to speak, drains all the morality from public action and from the public domain, which becomes merely utilitarian, concerned only with order and not with virtue.

One of the reasons why Abelard deprives public action of a moral form is that he deprives moral action generally of its thoughtful articulation. He does not acknowledge that an act is good, for example, because in it I truly identify your good, as such, as my good. As we have said, this moral categoriality, which informs a material performance, is what makes an act public, because thinking and the mind are public. Moral categoriality is an identification achieved by the agent, and as an identification it can also be achieved by others, provided they too are able to think morally. But Abelard leaves no room for this categorial dimension; the act we are commanded or forbidden to do is merely the material performance—the pushing or the taking or the killing—without the form of being recognized as your good or bad and done, as such, as my good or bad. For Abelard the only categoriality we can attach to the performance is the form of "being commanded" or "being forbidden," and there is nothing intrinsic to the performance that shows why it is commanded or forbidden; the performance is not taken as a substrate that, in these circumstances, demands that form; we are merely told it is to be identified as such. The being of a moral transaction is severely distorted by such an interpretation; the essentials are taken away. Abelard's analysis implies that the agent must forgo the moral thoughtfulness, the moral recognition, that constitutes an act as moral and makes it a publicly identifiable transaction. The place of moral categoriality is taken by an act of the will, by a hidden obedience or contempt.

Abelard's account of moral action represents a failed attempt to reconcile moral action and belief in revealed religion. In Christian belief, everything we experience is understood to have been created by God, who also reveals himself to man. There is an element of choice and command in creation and in revelation, but the kinds of choices and commands at issue must be clarified. They are not like the choices and commands we engage in as human beings, the choices and commands that must be contrasted to "nature." It is easy, but misleading, to turn the divine commands and choices into things that neutralize the necessity and integrity of natural things. Abelard does this; in his work the philosophical and theological articulations are not properly worked out. Aquinas has much more successfully developed the relationships between natural and philosophical necessities and theological truth.

Notes

1. See *Peter Abelard's Ethics* (1971). We will give page references to this edition of Abelard; references will be given directly in our text, and Luscombe's translation will be used.
2. Thus Abelard prefers to say that an agent acts well or badly (*bene* or *male facere*) rather than to say he does good or bad (*bonum* or *malum facere*), because it is not what is done but how it is done that matters. See Blomme (1958), 140–41.

CHAPTER 6

Peter Abelard and St. Thomas Aquinas on Moral Intention

IAN WILKS

Peter Abelard's philosophical tendencies were such as to incite controversy at every turn. In his treatment of logical theory this controversy confined itself to academic debate. In his treatment of theology and moral theory, by contrast, it occasioned a papal decree of excommunication. Most of the articles of heresy circulated against Abelard on the occasion of his final condemnation (Council of Sens, 1140) invoke theological positions. But in the transmitted lists of these heresies—numbering fourteen in one tally, nineteen in another—we do find three entries directed to points arising from his moral theory, implying for this part of his intellectual output an important role in the legacy of rejection he created for himself.[1]

What was found so contrary to orthodox belief in Abelard's moral theory? The most basic of the three views cited is that actions do not make someone better or worse; what does do so, Abelard argues, is the quality of intention from which those actions arise.[2] A second view simply accepts the implications of the first in the face of a highly controversial example: the crucifiers of Christ did not sin by their actions, because their intent was marked by ignorance of the true character of the deed they committed. A third view rules out certain internal properties of human experience as morally relevant; so, for example, the pleasure arising from a deed has no bearing on the moral quality of its performer. The central theme that underlies these three views, indeed the core claim of Abelardian moral theory, is that intention must be regarded as the sole and central object of moral assessment.

This theme is certainly striking. But it is not foreign to the period. Christian doctrine is rich in references to sin and merit, punishment and reward, and philosophical discussion of these leads moral theory in a direction quite apart from the treatment of virtues and vices inherited from antiquity. Augustinian moral psychology, with its attention to issues of freedom and choice, consolidates a tradition of viewing sin and merit as chiefly constituted by actions of the will. Physical actions arising from the will remain in the picture, but in a diminished role. Anselm, for example, holds that actions are considered unjust not in themselves but through the unjust will that underlies them; but at the same time he claims there are actions like perjury which could *only* be accompanied by an unjust will (*De conceptu virginali et de originali peccato*, 144).[3] In this way he affirms paramountcy of the will in moral assessment, but does so without going the whole way to ruling the physical act irrelevant. All medieval moral theorists share emphasis on moral intention. But most preserve some link to physical action. Abelard, and after him William Ockham, are noteworthy for trying to sever the link.[4]

Abelard's reputation as a moral theorist suffers by comparison with a figure like Aquinas, who puts quite a bit of work into distinguishing the internal from the external act, trying to ascribe some kind of role to each in the moral act as a whole. The Thomistic approach on this matter represents orthodoxy, and against that standard Abelard's divergence seems to some a great aberration. Ralph McInerny, an unswerving adherent of the Thomistic tradition, offers an assessment of Abelard's moral theory driven by that comparison. Abelard, he tells us, "maintained with almost perverse glee that morality consists in intention alone and that the things we do . . . are, apart from our intention in performing then, morally neutral. . . . Abelard's little book is a seed bed of confusion and sophistry" (McInerny 1982, 84). The question for this chapter is whether that theoretical reliance on intention really is so unredeemable an approach to moral theory – and whether, specifically, Abelard really does emerge as such an outlier in the medieval tradition, as compared with a canonical figure such as Aquinas.

For this project the commentary supplied by Robert Sokolowski is of great interest. Sokolowski actually finds both Abelard and Aquinas wanting in their analyses of human action, though Abelard much more so than Aquinas. The comparison is instructive, since it suggests a perspective on which these two figures may display a common tendency. I shall examine Abelard first, and then Aquinas, endeavoring along the way to take stock of Sokolowski's assessments.

Sokolowski's commentary on Abelard occurs as part of his work *Moral Action* (Sokolowski 1985). His subject matter there is action theory, especially as applied to moral action. A key theme is the inalienable role of the physical act as part of the moral act. Just as "there cannot be an ace in tennis without a ball being hit" (49), he argues, so in general there can be no "moral transaction" unless "it involves a material performance" (71). This is a fundamental divergence from Abelard, and from others; Sokolowski devotes a series of appendices comparing his viewpoint to that of the Stoics, Abelard, Aquinas and Kant. Chapter 5 of this volume reproduces the appendix that discusses both Aquinas and Abelard.

As noted, Abelard's view is that the moral act is entirely internal and has an existence independent of whatever physical behavior may ensue; as such it is nothing over and above the formation of an intention to act. Once that intention is formed, Abelard argues through a series of examples, the die is set; the moral act is complete, and the aftermath that unfolds in the physical realm is mere by-product. "Truly," says Abelard, "it is not a sin to kill a man nor to lie with another's wife; these sometimes can be committed without sin" (*Ethics*, 27).[5] Circumstances may arise where the physical act is committed without awareness of the kind of act it is, as when a judge orders the execution of someone mistakenly thought guilty, or a man has sex with a woman he mistakenly identifies as his wife. In such cases the physical act fails to be a register of what is intended by the moral agent and thus fails to be useful for the purpose of moral assessment. Cases like this may be rare, but their mere existence—in fact, their mere possibility—is enough to point to intention as the only consistent basis for accurate moral assessment.

Sokolowski's emphasis on the role of the physical act in moral life will not allow him to accept these results. Allowing for moral assessment that has no reference to physical acts is problematic enough, in his view; but Abelard then develops this theme in a radical way that seems to go even further in suppressing core intuitions of a well-rounded moral theory. These lines encapsulate Sokolowski's reply:

> If obedience and disobedience toward God's commands are the only two moral possibilities, then moral action is formalized to an excessive degree. It is not differentiated into the many various kinds of moral acts, good and bad: we no longer have acts of kindness, gratitude, and course, or spite, cruelty, and murder. There are only the neutral external performances on the one hand and the internal, awesomely secret exchange between the agent and God on the other.
>
> (see above, p. 83)

This pronounced focus on obedience and disobedience to God seems to exclude from the picture other aspects of moral life normally held important. If pressed to identify the goals of moral life, one would normally cite the happiness of other humans as an absolutely key one, to which the performance of actions suitably beneficent to others would present itself as means. But for Abelard this concern for altruistic outcomes seems to disappear; the point of moral life seems *only* to involve cultivating an appropriate state of loving God through the formation of law-abiding intentions. Sokolowski sees this account as endorsing a single-minded attitude of blind obedience to divine injunction to the exclusion of enlightened concern for the well-being of others. The whole conception of moral life thus proposed strikes him as lacking "moral thoughtfulness" (174).

To what degree may Abelard be defended from this line of attack?

Let us start with the notion that what is supposed to matter to the moral agent under this system is really just obedience, not beneficence. One may question whether, given Abelard's acceptance of a moral system deriving from Christian revelation, the two issues of obedience and beneficence really come apart in this way. His starting point as a moral theorist is a set of Christian moral teachings already presumed by all in his milieu to operate to the betterment of the human condition. In this setting it is natural to suppose that one need simply act in accordance with those teachings, and one's actions will be oriented toward beneficent outcomes. So it is not clear why Abelard would have any reason to question the parallel view expressed for intending: one need simply *intend* in accordance with those teachings, and one's intentions will likewise be oriented toward beneficent outcomes – in which case obedience and beneficence will indeed remain in a close relation. Abelard is giving us a theory about what counts as complying with Christian moral teachings (i.e., compliance as fully achieved at the level of intention); that sort of theoretical interest leaves the underlying character of those teachings intact, and in particular implies no change to what they prescribe as fit and proper attitudes to other human beings. The whole issue of how moral decisions orient themselves toward human well-being may occupy a lesser place in Abelard's discussions just because of the sheer obviousness of the matter for someone working within this tradition, where it would doubtless seem unclear how intending obedience to the word of God could fail to be a powerful impetus toward developing an attitude of beneficence.

And indeed Abelard is quite capable of advocacy for exactly this attitude. The lack of moral thoughtfulness Sokolowski finds in his work—its seeming indifference to the moral aim of altruism—is belied in a passage like the following, which seems to address that very theme:

> The blessed Augustine carefully considered this and reduced every commandment or prohibition to charity or cupidity rather than to deeds, saying: "The Law ordains nothing except charity and prohibits nothing except cupidity." Hence also the Apostle says: "All the Law is fulfilled in one word: Thou shalt love thy neighbor as thyself." And again: "Love is the fulfilling of the Law."
>
> (*Ethics*, 27)

The various Christian commandments manifest a common deeper understanding of the moral situation. Fulfilling the Law is presented here as being more than just a matter of obeying it. The required attitude is more than just acquiescence to authority. Morally acceptable intentions do not just relate to the well-being of others when they *happen* to issue in beneficent action. Such intentions require an in-built attitude of charity, an attitude from which beneficent action can for the most part (but not always, due to unforeseen circumstances) be expected to flow. This is not just so of *some* right intentions. The notion of charity – equivalently construed here as a notion of loving one's neighbor – distills the essence of *all* positive laws enjoining action, and so must likewise infuse *all* right intentions. Abelard's intention-based moral theory is one which thus appears to celebrate the formation of intentions along altruistic lines, and cannot fairly be regarded as lacking orientation to the well-being of others.[6]

So, consider the comparison between (i) the moral agent whose aim is to bring about an internal state of loving God, and (ii) the moral agent whose aim is to bring about actions with beneficial effects on others. Abelard does not appear to regard these outlooks as distinct. The intention bears moral value, not the action; but the content of the intention makes reference to the action. The content of the morally acceptable intention must refer to action in a manner consistent with divine command. And so for him it likewise seems that the objective of loving God will in practice involve the objective of intending actions beneficial to others. These results do not appear to offer an unorthodox account of how we ought to live.

That seems to me the key point against Sokolowski. Reading settled moral laws not as directives about how to act, but as directives about how to intend to act, does not make material difference to the laws themselves and the overall system they comprise. The difference between being directed not to commit adultery and being directed not to intend to commit adultery certainly affects how we assess conformity to that directive. But that difference implies no change to our understanding of what adultery is, and why it is presented as a sin. The same point holds for other moral laws. Textual evidence suggests that Abelard's focus is on how to judge conformity to law, not on proposing novel views about the content of law. Whatever is really unorthodox about his moral theory will be found not in his views about how we are to live, because what he is chiefly addressing is how we are to be *judged* for how we live.

To pay due attention to that latter issue I turn to the comparison with Aquinas. Abelard's unorthodoxy on these points, if any, should appear in relief against the settled orthodoxy of Aquinas's corresponding views. So it is these I now consider.

In question two of *On Evil*, Aquinas asks whether sin consists "chiefly of acts of the will" (q.2, a.3).[7] The answer is yes. But he also asks whether sin consists "solely of the will's act" (q.2, a.2), and the answer is no. The will's act is the key factor, but not the only relevant one, in constituting sin. The contrast with Abelard's viewpoint seems obvious. But in fact some of the content in the second article of this question suggests otherwise.

The first point to notice is the distinction between evil (*malum*), sin (*peccatum*) and moral wrong (*culpa*). As listed these notions are in order of decreasing generality, "evil" marking out most broadly "the privation of form or right order or due measure in anything" (q.2, a.2 reply). A sin is an *act* that is evil—an act lacking due order, form or measure. A moral wrong is then a *voluntary* act that is evil—in other words, a voluntary sin (i.e., a voluntary evil act). Having a crooked leg is an evil, says Aquinas, since it is a privation in the due order of the human form; limping is the corresponding sin—it is an action that is evil, an action lacking in due order. Obviously a sin so construed is not at all associated with what we think of as a moral wrong.[8] So when Aquinas talks about sin we must be careful to grasp what he says in light of the above definitions. In this case, when he queries the relationship between *sin* and acts of the will, it is not the same question as querying the relationship between *moral wrong* and acts of the will. This is an important point, because it is the latter question that Abelard pursues, not the former.

So, consider the former: does sin consist solely of the will's act? We might answer in the affirmative, says Aquinas, but that would make sense only if we were limiting our notion of sin to the sort of sin involving wrongdoing.[9] From this limited perspective there is indeed an element of truth in answering that question affirmatively, but for a better answer still we need to work with the notion of sin in its full scope of application. We need to be able to talk about sin not *just* in terms of wrongdoing, and if we do this we end up with a negative answer to that question: sin does not consist solely of the will's act. Such is the core argument Aquinas makes in this article.

But as it stands the argument is not a challenge to Abelard's position. Abelard is asking about what Aquinas calls wrongdoing. Does *it* consist only of the will's act? Of course Abelard says yes (although his answer is not expressed in terms of the will). Does Aquinas actually say no to that question here? Consider these lines, again from the reply in q.2, a.2:

> The act is deformed because it is at variance with the requisite rule of reason or of God's law. And there can be such a deformity in both internal and external acts, although it is because of the will that we impute external deformed acts to human beings as moral wrongs.[10]

Deformed acts are evil acts, ones marked by lacking due order, form or measure, as prescribed by reason or divine law. The point of the article is to argue that humans can commit such acts—in other words, they can sin—independently of what they may be willing. But the final clause of this remark reminds us that *wrongdoing* is not committed independently of what is willed. We think of an external act of sinning as a moral wrong only on the basis of the act of will which underlies it. In other words, moral wrongness wholly derives from the internal act of the will. On the question that Abelard is actually raising, this claim seems to have a lot in common with his answer.[11]

So is there any sort of role which the external act plays in determining one's moral standing? Aquinas addresses this question through the topic of reward and punishment. When we start with a laudable internal act, and then bring it to completion through the corresponding external act, do we merit additional reward because of that external act? Aquinas answers that we do indeed merit additional reward. But he also specifies that it will be a reward of a distinct kind, one which adds nothing to the kind of reward already merited through the internal act. The same point is made for internally and externally merited punishment. Here is a key text:

> A person who has the will to give alms and does not do so for lack of opportunity, merits in relation to the essential reward, that is, joy in God, just as much as if the person were to give alms, since this reward corresponds to charity, which belongs to the will. But in relation to the accidental reward, that is, joy in any created good, persons who both will to give and do give merit more, since such persons will rejoice both because they willed to give, and because they gave, and because of all the benefits that resulted from the giving.
>
> (*On Evil*, q.2, a.2, response to 8)

There is essential reward available here, and also accidental reward. Essential reward is deserved in all cases of appropriate willing—whether or not accompanied by appropriate doing—and takes the form of greater closeness to God, greater "joy in God." When there is *both* appropriate willing *and* appropriate doing this essential reward is still deserved, of course, but in addition an accidental reward is deserved as well: it is of this world, and takes the form of rejoicing here and now in the act and its consequences. Corresponding points can be made about sin. Inappropriate willing makes one deserve the essential punishment of greater separation from God, whether the willing is accompanied by action or not. But *if* accompanied by action then secondary (that is, accidental) punishment is deserved as well: "The person who sins by the will and by an external act incurs more demerit, since the person will suffer both for having willed evil and for having done evil and for all the evils that result from the person's evil deeds" (*On Evil*, q.2, a.2, response to 8).[12] Secondary punishment, like accidental reward, is of this world, and has no bearing on the all-important status of the agent's relation to God.

On the matter of sin and moral wrong, the above views sum to this: that part of sin which is voluntary and counts as moral wrong is punished in relation to God; and that part of sin which is not voluntary and does not count as moral wrong is punished in relation to the world.[13] Now let us see how this result matches up with Abelard's theory. If we think again in terms of his more rudimentary language of intention and action, Abelard seems to have something very much like essential reward/punishment in mind as what is deserved according to the quality of intentions. Speaking of joy in God as this reward seems pretty comparable to what I described earlier as an "internal state of loving God"—which for Abelard is the product of appropriate intentions. Speaking of separation from God as the corresponding punishment likewise maps well onto Abelard's notion of contempt of God as the product of inappropriate intentions. Both for Abelard and Aquinas these states are earned regardless of whether what is intended is brought to action or not. So on this point there is much comparability; the positions obviously differ in detail but not in general outline.

What about the kind of reward and punishment that Aquinas himself deems accidental and secondary? Here is Abelard's corresponding account:

> We do not, however, deny that in this life something is bestowed for those good or bad works, so that by a ready return in the form of profit or penalty we may be spurred on to good things or drawn away from evil, and so that some should follow the examples of others in doing what is fitting or in avoiding what is unfitting.
>
> (*Ethics*, 49, 51)

The point here is that there is something like accidental/secondary punishment and reward at work in Abelard's account as well, understood as being meted out in this world, not the next; he refers to these as "profit" (*premium*) or "penalty" (*pena*). They have nothing to do with the moral agent's relation to God, which is already determined by the intention. They are worldly attainments, in keeping with the worldly status of the physical action that motivates them. As so far described these profits and penalties seem to work in parallel with the rewards and punishments spoken of by Aquinas. At the same time there is clearly a difference. In Abelard's account these outcomes seem to be justified as chiefly motivational in character, since the agent's tendency to perform good acts will be consolidated by their being followed by profits, and contrariwise with evil acts and penalties. Profits and penalties do not seem, as with Aquinas, to represent something that the agent simply *deserves*, but rather something which *it would be appropriate for the agent to have* so as to consolidate pre-existing moral tendencies or weaken pre-existing immoral ones. In either case the physical action does appear to make a difference to the situation of the agent, a difference registered in the sort of reward (profit) or punishment (penalty) that is called for during the earthly phase of one's existence. The phrase "called for" does not express exactly the same relation in Aquinas and Abelard, but the difference is far from putting their respective theories in fundamental opposition.[14]

The above comparison suggests that between Abelard and Aquinas there is more similarity in approach to the problem of moral intention than may first meet the eye. So here again I am in disagreement with Sokolowski, whose comparative treatment of the two figures does not reveal the commonality that Abelard shares with Aquinas on these matters. A key element of Sokolowski's presentation is to sketch the Thomistic distinction between internal and external acts, intending to show how the distinction lets us condemn certain external acts *even if* they are done for good purposes (see above, pp. 77–8). But while the definitions supplied in *On Evil* let us condemn such acts as *sins* they do not let us condemn them as *moral wrongs*; this is the key distinction inherent in the Thomistic position I have outlined above. Abelard does not have the conceptual resources to capture this distinction, and his focus is squarely on what Aquinas is calling moral wrongs, not on what Aquinas is calling sins. But when it comes to moral wrongs, Abelard seems to be of one mind with Aquinas in claiming that they are to be judged *only* by what is done at the level of intention. Without due emphasis on this point the reader is left with the sense that Abelard is a radical outlier in medieval times on the matter of moral intention, and in this regard Sokolowski conveys a fairly standard impression. The truth seems to be that Abelard is not so radical an outlier, in that even a figure like Aquinas seems to share his tendency to make intention (or, in Thomistic language, acts of will) the basis for judgments about moral wrongs. The difference between the figures seems to be that Abelard relishes this doctrine, openly embraces it, even celebrates it, while Aquinas is much more guarded in his acceptance, and in his accounts of sin and evil is careful to provide the external act with other roles within his moral theory. In this Aquinas is like most medieval moral theorists, who proceed with caution on these matters—and unlike Abelard, and Ockham after him (and Immanuel Kant long after both), who do not.

In general, an understanding of human action that takes intentions as formed independently of physical actions, and as making up a distinctly separable domain, is going to push moral theory in the direction of emphasizing the primacy of intention over physical action in moral assessment. A great merit of Sokolowski's discussion is that he emphatically draws attention to the implications of separating the internal from the external acts, and indeed takes issue with Aquinas for tending to confer too much independence upon the internal aspects of action (although not as much, of course, as he takes issue with Abelard on this point).[15] In fact, so central is the notion of physical behavior in Sokolowski's analysis that he considers it possible for a genuinely voluntary external act to arise with no preceding internal phase: "there can be acts," he says, "in which, so to speak, the intention collapses into the exterior act" (see above, p. 79). Elsewhere in his work he has cautioned against seeing too stark a distinction between the internal and external aspects of action, and here he suggests that Aquinas "emphasizes the intention so much that he seems to require a distinct intention, different from the exterior act being performed, in the case of every human action" (see above, p. 79). If Aquinas errs by stressing "the interiority of human action" (see above,

p. 80), then it should not be surprising that in the end some of his views align with those views of Abelard that derive from the same tendency.

So is there enough difference between Aquinas and Abelard on the issue of moral intention to regard the one a model of Catholic orthodoxy and the other a complete outlier within the medieval tradition of moral theory? It seems not. My argument above is testament against so stark a view.[16]

Notes

1. In the longer list of nineteen heresies (*Capitulum haeresum xix*) the three entries pertaining to moral theory are #10, 13 and 19. See *Capitulum haeresum* (1969), and Mews (1985, 109–110).
2. Abelard speaks not only of intentions but also of consents. These terms have rough parity in his moral thought, but are nonetheless distinguishable at some level. William Mann, for example, suggests that consenting is the same as *forming* an intention (Mann 2004, 285). For other comments on this point see Blomme (1958, 133–136), King (1995, 214, n. 4), Adams (1995, xix-xx), and Cameron (2007, 335–336). Since nothing in this chapter rides on the distinction I shall simply use "intention."
3. The text is found in Anselm (1968), a translation in Anselm (1998).
4. Ockham's account along these lines is present in *Quodlibet septem* I.20.
5. References are to Luscombe's translation accompanying his Latin edition (Abelard 1971).
6. This aspect of Abelard's moral theory is discussed in Marenbon (1997, 282–297).
7. Translations of *On Evil* are from Aquinas (2001).
8. Aquinas does not give us an example of a corresponding moral wrong here, but this may serve: using the limp to create sympathy as part of a confidence scheme.
9. In q. 2, a. 2, reply, Aquinas is comparing the correct answer ("sin consists both of an internal act of the will and of an external act") to two others ("no act is a sin"; and "sin consists solely of an internal act of the will"); he says that although the correct one "is more true, still all are in some measure true." The third he holds to be true if one considers "only that whereby sin had the nature of moral wrong"—a claim that seems to correspond to Abelard's viewpoint.
10. The external act for Aquinas is not just physical behavior. It is external to the will and mobilizes powers of the soul and body in pursuit of an end. An internal act, by contrast, is exclusively an operation of the will in adopting an end. See also *Summa theologiae* I-II, q. 18, aa. 2–11. For helpful discussion of these doctrines see Gallagher (1990, 122) and Pilsner (2006, 76–91). Osborne (2007) gives wider-ranging background on the medieval history of this distinction. See also Hoffmann (2003).
11. Gallagher (1995, 684) and Hause (2007, 253–254) comment on this commonality between Abelard and Aquinas.
12. The shift from "accidental" to "secondary" reflects a shift in the original from *accidentalis* to *secondarius*; for the purposes of my argument, these terms are interchangeable.
13. One might object that sin is not always punished in relation to the world, and that likewise accidental reward is not always forthcoming. These claims are obviously true, but not really relevant; the point of introducing the notions of secondary punishment and accidental reward is to facilitate the distinction between sins and moral wrongs; we understand the distinction better by grasping how what we deserve for a sin differs from what we deserve for a moral wrong. Whether we always get what we deserve in the former case is beside the point.
14. Space does not permit discussion of another intriguing element of this passage: Aquinas's discussion of the person who "wants to kill saints in order to render obedience to God" (q. 2, a. 2, response to 8). This bears an obvious parallel to Abelard's discussion of the Jews who persecuted Stephen and crucified Christ (*Ethics* 59, 63) but is analyzed to opposite effect; in Aquinas's example the person cited is not excused, but in Abelard's the Jews *are* excused.

Is Aquinas actually disagreeing with Abelard here? I would argue not, because there is a key difference in their respective treatments of this example. In Abelard's case the Jews are characterized as sinning through ignorance—ignorance of the true nature of the person being persecuted. In Aquinas's case the problem seems to be not mistaken identity but a mistaken principle of action (that killing saints can be a way of rendering obedience to God); the mere fact of possessing a conscience makes one responsible for mistaken principles of action.

15. See especially Sokolowski (1985, 66–70) for his argument that intentions are formed over time and continuously shaped by actions occurring in that time, and therefore cannot be regarded as having an existence independently of action.
16. Thanks to Jeffrey Hause and Sarah Hogarth Rossiter for helpful comments on earlier versions of this chapter.

PART IV

Avicenna: Abstraction and Emanation

Editor's Introduction

In the most enigmatic chapter of his formidable *On the Soul* (3.5), Aristotle contends that our thinking involves both a passive (or "possible" or "material") intellect as well as a more active intellect, whose job is somehow to separate intelligible forms from sensory images so that these forms may be impressed on the possible intellect, allowing us intellectual understanding. Aristotle says little that is definitive about the nature of this mysterious active or "agent" intellect (are there many or just one? is it part of the soul or a separated substance?), leaving later thinkers the task of explaining what it is. Many of those who took up the challenge—including al-Farabi, Maimonides, Averroes, Pomponazzi, and Avicenna—conclude that the active intellect is not a human capacity, but a unique, super-human intelligence.

Avicenna maintains that this active intellect influences the workings of our own intellect, although its precise role has been the subject of dispute among scholars because Avicenna appears to contradict himself. On the one hand, he explains that humans abstract intelligibles from sense data; on the other, he asserts that intelligibles flow into human intellects by emanation from the active intellect. On the first reading, the principal source of intelligibles is something internal to us, and the active intellect plays a subsidiary role in helping us to perform the abstraction. On the second reading, the principal source of intelligibles is something external to us, and abstraction is either reducible to emanation or a process that prepares us to receive the intelligibles by emanation. In this pair of essays, Dag Hasse defends the first line of interpretation, while Deborah Black pursues the second.

Hasse proposes to resolve the apparent contradiction by exploring the way in which Avicenna develops the insights he inherits from his Aristotelian predecessors and, more tellingly, the way Avicenna's own thoughts develop from his early to his mature stage. In comparison with his predecessor al-Farabi, Avicenna offers a far more detailed account of abstraction as the vehicle for grasping intelligibles even in his early *Compendium on the Soul*, where he explains that the human intellect derives intelligibles from sensory forms and does so "when it wishes." In his mature works, Avicenna develops fuller accounts of abstraction from the elements he offers in the *Compendium*. It is in these later works that Avicenna offers the active intellect a more prominent but still subsidiary role in human cognition: The human intellect is still the agent of abstraction in the formation of intelligibles, but the active intellect must serve as a mediator that connects the human intellect with imagination, thus enabling the intellect to abstract the intelligible. The active intellect and abstraction are thus partners in human cognition, but abstraction is the principal partner.

Hasse argues persuasively that talk of abstraction cannot be just a way of talking about emanation. Black agrees, adding that abstraction plays a crucial causal role in cognition by preparing us to grasp intelligible objects. However, while she agrees with Hasse that intellectual cognition results from an unequal partnership between abstraction and emanation, in her view, it is abstraction that is the lesser partner. The principal cause of our acquiring intelligibles is by emanation from the active intellect. To say that abstraction is a necessary condition for acquiring intelligibles is just to say that we must prepare to receive them through the effort of different sorts of sensory attention. When Avicenna maintains that, as we proceed up the scale of human powers from the senses to the intellect, the higher powers "abstract" the form from the matter, he does not mean that these powers strip away an object's material aspects by succeeding stages until at last an intelligible is produced. Rather, he means that at each level of this scale, what is cognized is in some respect less material until, at the highest level, what the intellect cognizes is entirely immaterial. Because Black finds Avicenna to be a systematic philosopher whose thought on this topic does not change significantly over his career, she argues for her interpretation by explaining that it renders Avicenna's thought more consistent than alternatives. In particular, she argues, those who reject the emanationist account of concept formation will have considerable trouble making sense of Avicenna's account of intellectual memory, which depends on the emanationist thesis.

Note on References

References to Aristotle's text are by book and chapter number, followed by the more precise Bekker pagination and line numbers. This latter system of reference stems from the influential 1831 edition of Immanuel Bekker. For instance, when Black cites *Posterior Analytics 100a3-b4*, this constellation of letters and numbers refers to the selection from Bekker's edition starting on p. 100, column a, line 3 and ending on line 4, column b of the same page.

Avicenna's encyclopedic work *The Healing* (Al-Shifa') is divided into different units on different fields of philosophy, such as physics, metaphysics, and psychology. The unit on psychology is called the *Psychology* (or *De anima* or *Al-Nafs*) of *The Healing*.

Further Reading

- Cristina D'Ancona (2008). "Degrees of Abstraction in Avicenna: How to Combine Aristotle's *De Anima* and the *Enneads*."
- Jon McGinnis (2006). "Making Abstraction Less Abstract."

CHAPTER 7

Avicenna on Abstraction

DAG NIKOLAUS HASSE

I

The theory of abstraction is one of the most puzzling parts of Avicenna's philosophy. What Avicenna says in many passages about the human intellect's capacity to derive universal knowledge from sense-data seems to plainly contradict passages in the same works about the emanation of knowledge from the active intellect, a separately existing substance. When he maintains that "considering the particulars [stored in imagination] disposes the soul for something abstracted to flow upon it from the active intellect",[1] he appears to combine two incompatible concepts in one doctrine: either the intelligible forms emanate from above or they are abstracted from the data collected by the senses, but not both.

The standard reaction to this problem among modern interpreters is to believe Avicenna on emanation and to mistrust him on abstraction: abstraction is "only a *façon de parler*"[2] for emanation of intelligibles, it is "not to be taken literally":[3] "intelligible thoughts . . . flow directly from the active intellect and are not abstracted at all";[4] Avicenna "was unable to explain intellectual abstraction in knowledge"; the activity of the human intellect "can only dispose the mind to be receptive of new concepts".[5] This certainly is not only a well-established line of interpretation, but also a powerful one: it measures Avicenna's theory against a systematic concept of abstraction, as we know it from intellectual history, and finds that it falls short of the criteria and hence cannot be properly called a theory of abstraction.

Nevertheless, I think this interpretation cannot stand as it is. One of its unpleasant consequences is that Avicenna would not have achieved what he thought to have achieved, namely the development of a theory of abstraction.

With good philosophers such as Avicenna, who knows his Graeco-Arabic sources, this is a dangerous hermeneutical standpoint. In addition, one wonders whether Avicenna also falls short of speaking properly about emanation: the active intellect makes the forms flow upon the human intellect, but it does so by serving as a mediator in the process of intellectual perception, as a kind of immaterial light which helps the soul to see;[6] hence, concluded Anne-Marie Goichon some sixty years ago, "en rigueur de termes" the intelligibles are neither abstracted by the soul nor given to it by the active intellect.[7]

If one wants to avoid this negative double conclusion, it seems advisable, first, to focus again on Avicenna's own usage of terms from the semantic field "abstraction"—as some previous interpreters did before they decided that Avicenna should not be taken literally. Admittedly, this presupposes some intuition about what we are looking for—i.e., some notion of "abstraction"—but this notion may be taken broadly as referring to every transformation of sense-data into intelligibles. Secondly, it appears sensible to attempt a developmental explanation of Avicenna's theory; an explanation that does not consider his philosophy a system but follows the formation of the theory from the writings of his youth to that of his age. This approach is possible because, since Dimitri Gutas' study of Avicenna's oeuvre and its subsequent discussion by Michael Marmura and Jean Michot, there exists a basic scholarly consensus about the relative chronology of Avicenna's philosophical works (with the exception of *al-Ishārāt wa al-tanbīhāt, Ḥāl al-nafs* and the autobiography).[8] Ideally, a developmental interpretation would start with the sources which Avicenna had at his disposal, but that would transgress the boundaries both of this article and of my competence, given that the history of the concept of abstraction has not yet been written. The important article "Abstraktion" in the *Historisches Wörterbuch der Philosophie* of 1971 remains the best survey available, being particularly strong on the Western Middle Ages, but less so on Arabic philosophy.[9] Still, one of Avicenna's predecessors on the topic shall briefly be discussed because his theory is sometimes compared to that of Avicenna: Abū Naṣr al-Fārābī (d. 339 AH/950 AD).[10]

II

Al-Fārābī's standpoint may be illustrated by reference to two works of his, the "Principles of the Views of the Citizens of the Best State" (*Mabādi' ārā' ahl al-madīna al-fāḍila*), a major and influential treatise of comprehensive philosophical character written towards the end of his life, and his earlier, short tract "On the intellect" (*Fī al-'aql*). The *Mabādi'* do not contain much more than one sentence on the subject of abstraction, which on the one hand is not surprising since the book touches upon many philosophical areas without going into detail, but which on the other hand shows us that abstraction is not a topic important enough to be given a section of its own in this late work (as is the case with, for instance, the various members of the body). Al-Fārābī assumes, just as Avicenna after him, that the active intellect is a separately existing substance, the tenth and last of the incorporeal intelligences of the universe. Using the Peripatetic comparison of this intellect to the sun, he explains that, due to the influence of the active intellect, potentially intelligible things become actually intelligible. And he proceeds:

> When, then, that thing which corresponds to light in the case of sight arises in the rational faculty from the Active Intellect, intelligibles [arise] at the same time in the rational faculty from the sensibles which are preserved in the faculty of representation (*al-quwwa al-mutakhayyila*).[11]

One may note that al-Fārābī does not describe the rational faculty as an active participant in this process, and that the terminology used to describe the transformation of sense-data into intelligibles is restricted to intransitive verbs: intelligibles arise from (*ḥaṣala ʿan*) the sensibles, the intelligibles in potentiality become (*ṣāra*) intelligibles in actuality. Terms such as "discovering/deriving" (*istanbaṭa*), "abstracting" (*jarrada*), "divesting" (*afraza*), or "extracting" (*intazaʿa*), that Avicenna half a century later would use with respect to the intellect, do not appear in this context in *al-Mabādiʾ*. The phrase *al-instinbāṭ* is used when al-Fārābī comes to speak about rational actions, following upon the appearance of the intelligibles: then "a desire to find out things" arises.[12]

If one cannot say that there is anything close to a coherent theory of abstraction in this treatise, the case is different with the earlier *Fī al-ʿaql.* One must bear in mind, however, that this work does not necessarily present al-Fārābī's own philosophy but rather different usages of the term "intellect" among ordinary people, theologians and Aristotle. It is in the section on Aristotle's *De anima* that al-Fārābī mentions the abstracting activity of the human intellect: one of the definitions of the potential intellect, al-Fārābī says, is that its essence is disposed or able "to extract (*intazaʿa*) the quiddities of all objects and their forms from their matter".[13] He comes back to this when speaking about the second of Aristotle's intellects, as al-Fārābī understands them, the intellect in actuality:

> When we say that something is known for the first time, we mean that the forms which are in matter are extracted (*intazaʿa*) from their matter and that they receive an existence different from their previous existence. If there are things that are forms to which does not belong any matter, then this essence [i.e., the intellect] does not need to extract (*intazaʿa*) them from matter at all but finds them as something abstract (*muntazaʿ*).[14]

In this passage, Al-Fārābī takes up a doctrine stemming from Aristotle about the difference between those objects of thought that are in matter and those that are not.[15] Apart from this, we can see that al-Fārābī takes a view on the issue of the intellect's activity of "extracting": the form of something is separated from its matter and in virtue of this enters a new mode of existence. Alternative positions would be, for instance, that the forms in matter are imitated in the intellect (as Avicenna once mentions) rather than put into a new mode of existence, or that intelligibles arise from sense-data, as al-Fārābī says himself in the *Mabādi'*, or that the active intellect is involved in the process, as again in the *Mabādi'*. It is true that al-Fārābī has an elaborate passage on the separate active intellect in *Fi al-'aql*, but as to its role in the process of abstraction he maintains no more than that the active intellect makes potential intelligibles become actual intelligibles.[16] He never in this treatise explicitly connects the abstracting activity of the human intellect with the influence of the separate active intellect. Hence, one cannot say that according to *Fī al-'aql* the light of the active intellect "enables the human intellect to abstract".[17] Al-Fārābī also keeps silent about the transformation of sense-data, presumably because sense-perception falls outside the scope of this treatise on the intellect. In sum, al-Fārābī's remarks about abstraction remain sketchy and are in danger of being overinterpreted.

III

Compared with his Arabic predecessor, Avicenna appears a champion of abstraction theory. This is already apparent in a very early treatise, with which he began his career as a writer, the *Maqāla fī al-nafs 'alā sunnat al-ikhtiṣār* or *Compendium on the Soul* (dating probably 386/996–387/997).[18] The work certainly does not present Avicenna's mature thoughts on the topic of abstraction, but it contains *in nuce* several pieces of doctrine that are later developed into fully-fledged theories, such as the cooperation between the intellect and the internal senses (and the limits of this cooperation); the distinction between common and special, accidental and essential forms; the involvement of a separate universal intellect in the intellective process; the thesis that all perception, sensual as well as intellectual, is the abstraction of forms from matter; the comparison of the different modes of abstraction in the senses and in the intellect. And in general we encounter a notable interest in the transformation of sense-data into intelligibles:

> The faculty which grasps such concepts (*i.e. intelligibles that are not self-evident*) acquires intelligible forms from sense-perception by force of an inborn disposition, so that forms, which are in the form-bearing faculty (*scil. common sense*)[19] and the memorizing faculty, are made present to [the rational soul] with the assistance of the imaginative and estimative [faculties]. Then, looking at [the forms], it finds that they sometimes share forms and sometimes do not, and it finds that some of the forms among them are essential and some are accidental. An example of the sharing

of forms is that the forms[20] 'man'[21] and 'donkey'—in someone forming concepts[22]—share life, but differ with respect to reason and non-reason; an example for essential [forms] is 'life' in both of them, an example for accidental [forms] is 'blackness' and 'whiteness'.

When it[23] has found them being forms in this way, each of these essential, accidental, common, or special forms becomes a single, intellectual, universal form by itself. Hence it discovers by force of this natural disposition intellectual kinds, species, differences, properties and accidents. It then composes these single concepts by way of first particular and later syllogistic composition; from there it concludes derivations from conclusions. All this [the rational soul is able to do] with the service of the animal faculties and the assistance of the universal intellect, as we will explain below, and with the mediation of necessary, intellectual axioms[24] that naturally exist in it.

Even though this faculty receives help from the faculty of sense-perception in **deriving** (*istinbāṭ*) intellectual, single forms from sense-perceived forms, it does not need such assistance in forming these concepts in themselves and in composing syllogisms out of them, neither when granting assent to, nor when conceiving the two propositions, as we will explain below. Whenever the necessary corollaries have been **derived** (*istanbaṭa*) from sense-perception through the afore-mentioned natural disposition, it dispenses with the assistance of the faculties of sense-perception; instead it has enough power by itself for every action dealt with by it.

Just as the faculties of sense-perception perceive only through imitation of[25] the object of sense-perception, likewise the intellectual faculties perceive only through imitation of the object of intellection. This imitation[26] is the **abstraction** (*tajrīd*) of the form from matter and the union with [the form]. The sensible form, however, does not come about when the faculty of sensation wishes to move or act, but when the essence of the object of sensation reaches the faculty either by accident or through the mediation of the moving faculty; the **abstraction** (*tajarrud*) of the form [occurs] to the faculty because of the assistance of the media which make the forms reach the faculty. The case is different with the intellectual faculty, because its essence performs the **abstraction**[27] of forms from matter by itself whenever it wishes, and then it unites with [the form]. For this reason one says that the faculty of sense-perception has a somehow passive role in conceiving [forms], whereas the intellectual faculty is active,[28] or rather one says that the faculty of sense-perception cannot dispense with the organs and does not reach actualization through itself, while it would be wrong to apply this statement to the intellectual faculty.[29]

The first thing to note about this passage is that its terminology of abstraction can hardly be read as a *façon de parler* for emanation of intelligibles. Avicenna uses much transitive vocabulary: the rational faculty acquires (*istofāda*), finds (*wajada*), derives (*istanbaṭa*) and abstracts (*jarrada*) intelligible forms; they do not "arise" in it, as al-Fārābī put it in *al-Mabādi'*. In addition, Avicenna plainly states that in contrast to sense-perception, the rational faculty is an active faculty which can perform (*fa'ala*) the abstraction of a form at will. The power to form concepts is innate.

Nevertheless, Avicenna also mentions that the intellect needs the help of the senses, of the universal intellect and of naturally inborn axioms (the latter are needed for syllogistic forms of reasoning).[30] Later in the *Compendium on the Soul*, he elaborates upon the axioms and also adds a sentence on the separate intellect's role in intellection, when invoking the traditional analogy of light: Light is similar to this intellect in that it enables the faculty of sight to perceive without, however, providing it with the perceived forms:

> This substance (*i.e. the universal intellect*), in turn, supplies by the sole force of its essence the power of perception (*idrāk*) unto the rational soul, and makes the perceived form arise (*ḥaṣṣala*) in it[31] as well, as we have said above.[32]

The cross-references in this passage and in the previous quotation ("as we will explain below") make it plausible that these remarks about perceived forms refer to the same forms that were before said to be abstracted. Here, then, is the core of the problem which troubled so many interpreters of Avicenna, the collaboration of two very different powers in the process of abstraction, the human intellect and the separate universal intellect. But even if the rather casual sentence on the supplying activity of the separate intellect is taken very seriously—it reminds one of al-Fārābī and is certainly much less original than the long passage on the human intellect—it does not allow us to make the separate intellect the main protagonist in the process of intellection. For the relation between the human and the universal intellect is clearly described as an act of "assistance" (*a'āna*): "All this [the conceptualizing faculty is able to do] with the service of the animal faculties and the assistance of the universal intellect". Without doubt, in this early version of Avicenna's theory of abstraction, it is the powerful abstracting force of the human intellect which is the focus of the theory. The senses are indispensable, for they provide the necessary sense-data. The universal intellect is indispensable as well; its function is hardly described at all but seems to consist in somehow providing the necessary intellectual surrounding for the activity of the rational soul, in a manner similar to light with respect to the human ability to see. Hence both the senses and the universal intellect are necessary accompanying conditions rather than powers active in the process.

IV

In later writings of Avicenna—in the mature works of his middle period[33]—one can observe that one part of abstraction theory receives a formulation that Avicenna obviously considered perfect: it appears in four different works in almost identical wording: *Ḥāl al-nafs al-insāniyya* ("The State of the Human Soul", also called *al-Maʿād*, "The Destination"), the *De anima* part of *al-Shifāʾ* (dating probably 412/1022–414/1024),[34] *al-Najāt* ("The Salvation"), and the *Mashriqiyyūn* ("The Easterners").[35] This piece of Avicennian philosophy treats four different degrees of abstraction in sense-perception, imagination, estimation and intellect.

Two other doctrines familiar from the *Compendium on the Soul* are developed identically in these four treatises: the theory that the animal faculties assist the rational soul in various ways and especially in abstraction, and, connected with it, the theory that a soul with much acquired knowledge can dispense with the assistance of the senses.

Significantly, the case is different with the doctrine of the separate active intellect and its participation in the abstraction process: the treatises *Ḥāl al-nafs al-insāniyya* and *al-Najāt* do not go much beyond the *Compendium on the Soul* but similarly state that a power is issued from above and that imaginable forms become intelligible forms. Avicenna obviously felt the need to reformulate and develop the doctrine, for both in *De anima* and in the *Mashriqiyyūn* he gives a long and famous explanation of the active intellect's mediating role in intellection.

It is characteristic of Avicenna's working method that these three groups of doctrines (degrees of abstraction—assistance by the senses—function of the active intellect) that once were treated together in a single passage of the early *Compendium*, have now become fully-fledged theories of their own which are only loosely connected with each other. The increasing theorization of Avicenna's philosophy is accompanied by fragmentation. In *Ḥāl al-nafs*, for example, the three theories are treated in chapters three, six and twelve, in *De anima* they appear in chapters II,2, V,3 and V,5.

What then is the effect of this development on the content of Avicenna's theory of abstraction as present in the works of the middle period? The passage on the four degrees of abstraction, to start with the first group of doctrines, is too long to be given in full; the reader may be referred to the translation by Fazlur Rahman.[36] For the present purposes, suffice it to quote the beginning (on abstraction in general) and the end (on intellectual abstraction) only:

> It seems that all perception is but the grasping of the form of the perceived object in some manner. If, then, it is a perception of some material object, it consists in an apprehension of its form by **abstracting** (*tajrīd*) it from matter in some way. But the kinds of **abstraction** are different and their degrees various. This is because, owing to matter, the material form

> is subject to certain states and conditions which do not belong to [the form] by itself insofar as it is this form. So sometimes the **abstraction** (*naz'*) from matter is effected with all or some of these attachments, and sometimes it is complete in that the concept[37] is abstracted (*jarrada*) from matter and from the accidents it possesses on account of the matter.[38]
>
> [. . .]
>
> (*There follows the example of the abstraction of the concept "human being" and the description of the increasingly higher degree of abstraction among sense-perception, imagination and estimation.*)
>
> The faculty in which the fixed forms are either the forms of objects which are not at all material and do not occur in matter by accident,[39] [or the forms of objects which in themselves are not material but happen to be so by accident],[40] or the forms of material objects though purified in all respects from material attachments—such a faculty obviously perceives the forms by grasping them as **abstracted** (*mujarrad*) from matter in all respects. This is evident in the case of objects which are in themselves **free** (*mutajarrad*) from matter. As to those objects which are present in matter, either because their existence is material or because they are by accident material, this faculty completely[41] **abstracts** (*intaza'a*) them both from matter and from their material attachments and grasps them in the way of **abstraction**; hence in the case of 'man' which is predicated of many, this faculty takes[42] the unitary nature of the many, **divests** (*afraza*) it of all material quantity, quality, place, and position. If[43] [the faculty] did not **abstract** (*jarrada*) it from all these, it could not be truly predicated of all.[44]

It is obvious that important parts of the doctrine have changed since the *Compendium on the Soul*. First, in the early *Compendium*, the main difference between sense-perception and intellection is described in terms of passivity and activity: the senses are not able to grasp a form at will, as is the intellect. In the later formulation of the doctrine, the difference lies in the faculties' widely diverging powers to divest forms of their material attachments. Second, there is no explicit link to the theory of the separate active intellect in the passage from the middle period. Third, no mention is made of "imitation" or "assimilation" (*tashabbuh*), as was the case in the *Compendium*. Fourth, Avicenna now connects the fully abstracted status of a form with its predicability of many. Fifth, the terminology of "form" and "matter", though present in the *Compendium* ("This imitation is the abstraction of the form from matter"), had not yet served to develop a theory about the ontological status of concepts, which is a major concern of Avicenna's in his works of the middle period. What Avicenna means when he speaks of abstraction from matter, is once illustrated with an example: the rational soul divests the concept of man of "all material quantity, quality, place and position". Hence, the soul distinguishes between what is accidental to the form and what belongs to the form "insofar as it is this form"—which shows us that the discussion of concepts here is a development of the distinction between the essential and the accidental made in the *Compendium*.

Avicenna calls these accidents "material" because they occur to the form only in virtue of its presence in matter in an externally existent object. But what exactly is the nature of this form, which is the object of abstraction? It is with respect to this topic that Avicenna adds an important feature to his abstraction theory (in a sentence not yet quoted in the above doctrine of the four degrees of abstraction):

> To give an example: the form or essence (*māhiyya*) of man is a nature in which all the individuals of the species share equally, while in its definition it is a single unit: although it is merely by accident that it happens to exist (*wujida*) in this or that individual and is thus multiplied.[45]

Multiplicity is only accidental to the form. This theory clearly touches upon the metaphysical topic of the nature of intelligible forms and the distinction between essence and existence,[46] which Avicenna spins out in greater detail in the *Metaphysics* and the *Logic* part of *al-Shifāʾ*, written also in the middle period.[47] There is one passage in the *Metaphysics* which directly tackles the issue of abstraction in the context of the theory of forms; here he explains that both universality and particularity are accidents to the intelligible form. This passage is a good illustration of what Avicenna says in other works on abstraction, but it is an illustration only; Avicenna himself does not treat both theories—of abstraction and of forms—together, probably because he considered them to belong to different disciplines, psychology and metaphysics:

> The single form in the intellect is related to a multiplicity, in this respect being universal, while being a single concept in the intellect; there is no variation in its relation to whatever animal you perceive. That is, the form of every animal is made present in imagination with some disposition, then the intellect **extracts** (*intazaʿa*) an **abstraction** (*mujarrad*) of its concept from the accidents, [and] this form itself comes about in the intellect. This form is what derives from the **abstraction** (*tajrīd*) of animality from some individual [form in] imagination, which is grasped from an object outside (or something similar to an object outside), although it is not found itself outside but is created by imagination. This form, though universal with respect to the individuals, is particular with respect to the particular soul, being one of the forms in the intellect.[48]

Avicenna here says more clearly than in his psychological works that neither multiplicity nor particularity belong to the form as such. Embedded in this theory is a lucid description of the process of abstraction: the intellect works on data presented to it by the senses and stored in imagination; these data themselves are not imported from outside but are creations of the senses. The form that is in the intellect is a single concept only with respect to the intellect; it is universal with respect to the objects outside, and in itself it is neither universal nor particular, since—and here the distinction between essence and existence is involved again—it is independent of its existence outside and inside the intellect: as Avicenna says in his psychological works, it is the "unitary nature of the many" or "a nature in which all the individuals of the species share equally".

One may with some justification call this—the doctrine of the four degrees of abstraction plus the related discussion of intelligible forms in the *Metaphysics*—Avicenna's classical formulation of the process of abstraction: classical in the sense that he himself repeats it in several works and in that it was influential historically.[49] With respect to intellectual abstraction, the human rational faculty appears as fully capable of performing the act of abstraction by itself: a comparatively broad range of transitive vocabulary is employed to describe its abstracting and divesting activity (*intazaʿa, jarrada, afraza*).

One does not hear anything, however, about a collaboration with other entities involved in abstraction, neither with respect to the senses nor with respect to the separate active intellect. This collaboration is the topic of the two other groups of doctrines that Avicenna developed in the works of the middle period. The passage on the role of the senses appears identically in the four works mentioned above. Despite its brevity, one can easily spot that its roots lie in the early *Compendium*:

> The animal faculties assist the rational soul in various ways,[50] one of them being that sense-perception brings to it particulars, from which four things result in [the rational soul]: One of them is that the mind[51] **extracts** (*intazaʿa*) single universals from the particulars, by **abstracting** (*tajrīd*) their concepts from matter and the appendages of matter and its accidents, by considering what is common in it[52] and what different, and what in its existence is essential and what accidental. From this the principles of conceptualization (*taṣawwur*) come about [in] the soul: and this with the help of its employing imagination and estimation.[53]

The passage contains much that is already familiar: the use of the terminology of "form" and "matter" (but not the language of "essence" and "existence"); the explanation of the process of abstraction as the distinction between the common and the special, the essential and the accidental; the abstraction of forms as the starting-point for further intellectual activities such as the combination of concepts, and, most importantly, the usage of the term "assist" (*aʿāna*) for the role played by the senses. In this text as well as in the *Compendium*, it is the human intellect which is the active force in the process of abstraction, while the senses' main function is auxiliary: to present particulars, i.e. sense-data, to the intellect. The intellect is even said to "employ" or "govern" (*ista'mala*) the internal senses in this operation. One sees that Avicenna has not changed the basic features of his theory since the *Compendium* with regard to the intellect's relation to the senses. Instead, he has added new material. After the above quoted passage Avicenna adds two pieces of doctrine: the first maintains that the intellect returns to the senses only when forced to acquire an intelligible form not yet known to it—which is Avicenna's important distinction between the first acquisition of forms and their later reacquisition; for the latter, it suffices to reconnect to the active intellect[54]; the second is the example of the riding animal (*dābba*) which ceases to be useful when the place of destination is reached, just as there is no need for the senses when one has attained the intelligibles needed for further reasoning.[55]

If this group of doctrines does not undergo a revision in Avicenna's major writings, the opposite is true of the third topic, which concerns the role of the active intellect in the process of abstraction. One recalls that the *Compendium* contained very brief statements (reminiscent of al-Fārābī) about the universal intellect having an assisting function in the process: the active intellect supplies the power of perception and makes the forms arise in the human intellect. In two of Avicenna's later works, *Ḥāl al-nafs* and *al-Najāt*, the doctrine reappears without much alteration; it follows upon the standard Peripatetic analogy with light issuing from the sun:

> Likewise, there emanates from the active intellect a power and proceeds to the imaginable things that are potentially intelligible, in order to make them intelligible in actuality and to make the intellect in potentiality an intellect in actuality.[56]

What is missing, though, is the terminology of "assistance" which Avicenna had retained when explaining the function of the senses. This may simply be the effect of the increasing fragmentation of Avicenna's philosophy, that is, of the development of separate sets of doctrines (on abstraction and on the active intellect) loosely connected with each other, but when one turns to two other works of the middle period, the *De anima* of *al-Shifā'* and the *Mashriqiyyūn*, one finds that Avicenna, significantly, has substituted "mediation" for "assistance". These latter works, in fact, present a fully-fledged theory of the roles of the soul and the separate active intellect in abstraction, a theory of which there is not yet any sign in *Ḥal al-nafs* (and *al-Najāt*, which has the same text); this may indicate that *Ḥāl al-nafs* was composed earlier than *De anima*.[57] Avicenna obviously felt the need to revise what he had said earlier on the topic, and, even more, to give a proper theoretical foundation to a key doctrine of Peripatetic philosophy: the role of the active intellect in intellection. He tackles this problem at great length in chapters V,5 and V,6 of *De anima*, which present Avicenna's most important treatment of the issue in his entire work, given that he never returns to it with the same detailed attention and systematic approach (as will appear below).

On the basis of the evidence from earlier Avicennian writings laid out above, it can be demonstrated that the first part of chapter V,5 is not simply about the active intellect but about its involvement in abstraction (in contrast, the section on intuition in chapter V,6 does not employ abstraction terminology).[58] The passage in V,5 not only contains—in sequence—the analogy of light (pp. 234–5) and the theory about the transformation of sense-data into intelligibles (p. 235), hut also the doctrine that the human intellect separates the essential from the accidental (p. 236), and the theory that the concept "man" is a single concept with respect to the human intellect and a universal concept with respect to the objects outside (pp. 236–7). Without doubt, these are by now familiar ingredients of Avicenna's theory of abstraction. The last doctrine even contains an explicit reference to the *Metaphysics* passage translated above, which touches upon abstraction in the context of the theory of forms. A developmental interpretation of Avicenna's oeuvre, therefore, should make us very sceptical that this passage in *De anima* V,5 can be called in as principal witness for the "façon de parler" thesis: one can, of course, still claim that the vocabulary of abstraction in this passage should not be taken literally, but it seems impossible to claim that this is how Avicenna wanted to be understood, since the same vocabulary appears in the same doctrinal contexts in earlier or contemporary works of his which clearly deal with abstraction (and some of which do not mention the active intellect at all).

Let us turn to the crucial part of chapter V,5, the passage on the transformation of sense-data into intelligibles (p. 235); it contains the well-known sentence cited at the opening of the present article, in which Avicenna appears to combine incompatible notions of abstraction and emanation:

> (1) When the intellectual faculty considers the particulars which are [stored] in imagination and the light of the above-mentioned active intellect shines upon them in us, then the [particulars] are transformed (*istaḥāla*) into something **abstracted** (*mujarrada*) from matter and from the [material] attachments and get imprinted in the rational soul, (2) but not in the sense that the particulars themselves are transferred from imagination to our intellect, nor in the sense that the concept buried in [material] attachments—which in itself and with regard to its essence is **abstract** (*mujarrad*)—produces a copy of itself, but in the sense that looking at the particulars disposes the soul for something **abstracted** (*al-mujarrad*) to flow upon it from the active intellect. (3) For thoughts and considerations (*al-afkār wa al-taʿammulāt*) are movements which dispose the soul for the reception of the emanation, just as the middle terms in a more

> certain way dispose [it] for the reception of the conclusion (although the two happen in different ways, as you will understand later). (4) When some relation towards this form occurs to the rational soul through the mediation of illumination (*bi-tawassuṭi ishrāq*) by the active intellect, then from [the form] something comes about in the soul, [something] of [the form's] kind in some way and not of its kind in another way—just as when light falls upon coloured things, it produces in vision an effect which is not of its nature[59] in all aspects. The imaginable things, which are intelligible in potentiality, become intelligible in actuality, though not themselves, but that which is **collected** (*iltaqaṭa*) from them. Or rather:[60] just as the effect, which is transmitted through the medium of light from the sense-perceptible forms is not identical with these forms but something different, related to them, [something] which is generated through the mediation of light in the corresponding receiver, likewise when the rational soul looks at these imaginable forms and [when] the light of the active intellect makes contact with them in some way, [the rational soul] is disposed to have appear in it, due to the light of the active intellect, uncontaminated **abstractions** (*mujarradāt*) from these forms.[61]

Compared with the brief remarks in Avicenna's previous works, or with what we know from al-Fārābī, or with the passage in Aristotle's De *anima* III,4–5 which is at the origin of the problem, this is an impressively systematic theory of the active intellect's role in abstraction. The basic assumption of all three authors is that the active intellect renders potentially intelligible thoughts actually intelligible; in addition, they somehow connect this with the difference between intelligibles in matter and intelligibles freed of matter. Al-Fārābī added that it is the sensibles stored in an internal faculty from which arise the intelligibles through the influence of the active intellect. Avicenna does not leave it with this: section one in the above quotation gives a more precise description of the process by saying that the particulars stored in the faculty of imagination are "transformed" (*istaḥāla*) into something "abstracted" from matter and hence are imprinted in the intellect. Avicenna also mentions two conditions for this process: the human intellect needs to consider the particulars and the light of the active intellect needs to shine upon them. Note that he does not speak of "assistance": both intellects seem equally important for a successful transformation.

This is comparatively precise, but it is not yet Avicenna's main contribution to the discussion, which follows in section two. Here he distinguishes between three different possibilities for such a transformation: either the particular imaginable form travels from imagination to the intellect, or a copy is produced of its immaterial core, or an abstraction of it comes from the active intellect, for which the soul is disposed through its consideration of the particulars. Avicenna chooses the third and last possibility and justifies it in the long section four (after a brief explanation of what is meant with disposition). The abstracted form which arrives in the human intellect is partly of the kind of the imaginable form and partly not: it is not the imaginable form itself which becomes intelligible, but something taken or collected (*iltaqaṭa*) from it. Avicenna compares this process to vision: the effect produced in the receiver and transmitted through the medium of light is "different" from the sense-perceptible form of the object, but "related" to it. There cannot be much doubt that Avicenna here tries to pin down the exact meaning of intellectual abstraction—the Latin *abstractio* / "drawing from" is a very apt translation in this case—and to distinguish it from other possible forms of the transformation of sense-data: no simple transportation of them to the intellect, and no imitation (*mithl*) either—remember the term "imitation" (*tashabbuh*) in the *Compendium*—but a kind of derivation.

What are the respective roles of the human and the active intellect in this process? Note the terminology employed to describe the active intellect: its light "shines upon" the particulars in imagination; something abstracted "flows from" it (*fāḍa*) upon the soul; the forms occur to the soul "through the mediation of" its illumination; its light "makes contact with" the imaginable forms; abstractions of these forms appear in the soul "due to the light of the active intellect". The human intellect, in turn, "considers" the particulars stored in imagination; "looking at" (*ṭālaʿa*) the particulars disposes the soul for an abstraction; thoughts and considerations are "movements" which dispose the soul for the reception of the emanation; the form "occurs to" or "comes about in" (*ḥadatha*) the rational soul; it "looks at" the imaginable forms and hence is "disposed" (*istaʿadda*) to have "appear in it" abstractions from these forms.

A number of points need to be underlined: first, in contrast to the senses, which remain powers with an auxiliary function only, the active intellect is granted a more important role than in earlier writings of Avicenna: its traditional role was to give the power of intellectual perception to the rational soul and to make the intelligible forms arise in it—which is a Peripatetic version of Aristotle's idea that thinking needs to be triggered, needs to be turned from potentiality to actuality; its function now, much more specifically, is to make abstractions appear in the human intellect which are derived from the particulars stored in the soul's imagination. Second, the rational soul still is the main protagonist, even though there is a notable increase in passive vocabulary ("occurs to", "comes about in", "appears in" or "flows upon"). While the active intellect assumes the function of an indispensable intellectual surrounding and mediator, the human intellect is the power in action: it considers the particular forms stored in imagination and produces "thoughts and considerations", which eventually lead to the acquisition of a new intelligible form. Third, although Avicenna speaks of emanation and illumination, the vocabulary of light does not serve a theory of illumination in the strict sense: the light of the active intellect does not make contact with the human intellect only and not even primarily; rather, it shines upon the particulars stored in imagination and thus creates a connection between imagination and human intellect. Hence, the analogy of light is employed for the specific purpose to explain the role of the active intellect in the process of abstraction. When Avicenna maintains in section two that an abstraction emanates from the active intellect upon the soul, then this is an abbreviation—describing the entire process from one end of the process only, namely the human intellect—for the sentence in section four which maintains that abstractions from the imaginable forms appear in the soul due to the light of the active intellect.

In the traditional reading of the translated passage, the human intellect's attention towards the imaginable forms *only* disposes (*aʿadda*) the soul for receiving an emanation of intelligibles from above. This emphasizes the limitation of the soul's power of abstraction,[62] which, however, is not Avicenna's point. There is no "only" in the text.[63] As shown above, the core of the argument runs: no transportation of the imaginable form, no copying, but an abstraction mediated by the active intellect. The disposition of the soul is part of the theory, but it is not the gist of it, and there is no indication that Avicenna conceives of the soul's power of abstraction as something limited. One of the impossible consequences of the traditional line of interpretation is that—on account of the analogy used by Avicenna—the soul also would not *see* in the proper sense of the word, because turning towards the object only disposes the eye to have visible forms appear in it due to the light of the sun; which is clearly not what Avicenna means.

It is not correct to say that for Avicenna "human intelligible thought comes directly from the active intellect", or that "intelligible thoughts . . . flow directly from the active intellect and are not abstracted at all".[64] Apart from the fact that this interpretation rests on a misunderstanding of the term *fikr* ("reasoning") as referring to one of the internal senses only,[65] it is countered by Avicenna's explicit statement in section three: "thoughts" (*al-afkār*) are movements of the human intellect produced before the reception of abstract forms. When Avicenna speaks about abstraction and emanation, he means the acquisition of an intelligible "form" (*ṣuwar*) such as "man", not of thought in general. Moreover, as shown above, Avicenna unambiguously states that intelligible forms ultimately derive from the particulars in imagination and still resemble them: they are partly of their kind and partly not. It is true that one often finds in Avicenna's works the expression that the intelligibles flow from the active intellect, especially in the context of the reacquisition of a form which had been intellected before; but when the phrase is used with respect to the first acquisition of a form, it should not be misunderstood as excluding abstraction. On the contrary: to have given a clear definition of abstraction, to have described the function of the active intellect in it and to have distinguished abstraction from other modes of transforming sense-data, counts among Avicenna's major contributions to the history of epistemology.

V

For the present purposes, the late period of Avicenna's oeuvre shall be defined as comprehending works which postdate the psychological section of *De anima* and which present a theory of abstraction not identical with the version of the middle period. The *Najāt* and the *Mashriqiyyūn*, though clearly written after *De anima*, advance the same theory and thus belong to the middle period, considered from a doctrinal point of view. This is different with three later works which do not simply copy the doctrine: the *Dāneshnāme* (written in Iṣfahān between 414/1023 and 428/1037),[66] *al-Ishārāt wa al-tanbīhāt* ("Pointers and Reminders") and *al-Mubāḥathāt* ("Discussions").

These treatises are of very different character: the *Dāneshnāme* is a summary of philosophy written in Persian for the ruler 'Alā ad-Dawla; the *Ishārāt* is traditionally considered Avicenna's last *magnum opus*, peculiar for its style of giving hints and pointers rather than fully-fledged arguments; the *Mubāḥathāt* are a loosely organized series of answers to miscellaneous questions concerning Avicenna's philosophy. It is characteristic of these treatises that they treat abstraction less systematically and less comprehensively than the works of the middle period. The relevant passages are shorter and state a doctrine rather than argue for it. What makes them interesting for the present investigation is that they show us what Avicenna considered worth selecting or altering, be it for the readership of a ruler or of an intellectual élite.

We meet two familiar groups of doctrines in the *Dāneshnāme*, on the degrees of abstraction and on the participation of the active intellect in abstraction. The topic of the senses' assistance seems to be dropped; what is left, is the passage on the senses becoming a hindrance to the intellect, including the example of the riding animal.[67] With respect to the degrees of abstraction, Avicenna takes over the basic features of what was called above the classical formulation of the doctrine: the faculties' varying powers of abstraction, the omission of any reference to the active intellect, the language of "form" and "matter", the interest in the ontological status of concepts. He has reduced, however, the vocabulary of abstraction itself, shifting the focus towards different modes in which forms are perceived—rather than abstracted.[68] Another significant alteration concerns the metaphysical doctrine of forms, which Avicenna had woven into his theory of abstraction in various passages of the middle period. That multiplicity and particularity are extraneous to the form, is not a topic discussed in relation with abstraction theory in the *Dāneshnāme*.

If the section on the various degrees of abstraction (or, rather, perception) is a digest of the mature version of the doctrine—which is not surprising, given the addressee of the book—the same holds true of the passage on the active intellect. Here we meet with a number of features clearly taken from *De anima* (or *Mashriqiyyūn*): the light of the active intellect falls upon the imaginable forms; abstractions are taken from these forms; they are presented to the (human) intellect. Remember that in *Ḥāl al-nafs* and *al-Najāt* Avicenna had only spoken of imaginable forms being made intelligible in actuality. Avicenna has, however, skipped the entire discussion of the various possible ways of the transformation of sense-data; only the third possibility is left, which is abstractions from imaginable forms. No mention is made of the intellect being disposed to receive these forms.[69]

It is in the *Ishārāt* that one finds the most important development of the theory in Avicenna's late period. The *Mubāḥathāt*, in contrast, do not contain anything close to a *theory* of abstraction, to the best of my knowledge.[70] Of course, one finds various pieces of doctrine deriving from the thematic groups of the middle period, such as: imagination does not grasp concepts completely abstracted from matter (p. 177); the bodily senses can be compared to a riding animal (p. 232); consideration of what is stored in imagination is needed to receive an emanation from above; this consideration consists in thoughts and reasonings that prepare the soul for the emanation (p. 239). It is tempting but hermeneutically hazardous to combine these scattered sentences to a coherent picture of Avicenna's theory in *Mubāḥathāt*; the collection of response obviously is not meant to offer a systematic treatment of philosophical questions. The same *caveat* should be kept in mind when sentences from *Mubāḥathāt* are used to explain Avicenna's position in other works of his without proper consideration of context and the precise nature of the question asked.[71]

Turning to the relevant passages in the *Ishārāt*, one finds that the text has much in common with the *Dāneshnāme* (which corroborates the late dating of the *Ishārāt*):[72] it has about the same length; it does not say much on assistance by the senses but all the more on degrees of abstraction and on the active intellect; it does not use the terminology of "multiplicity" and "particularity" of forms; it draws on *De anima* for the theory of the active intellect in abstraction but omits the discussion of the exact nature of the transformation of imaginable forms. The first passage is the following:

> Sometimes a thing is perceived [via sense-perception] when it is observed; then it is imagined, when it is absent [in reality] through the representation of its form inside, just as Zaid, for example, whom you have seen, but now is absent from you, is imagined by you. And sometimes [the thing] is apprehended intellectually when the concept 'man', for example, which exists also for other people, is formed out of Zaid. When [the thing] is perceptible to the senses, it is found covered by things which are foreign to its essence and which, if they had been removed from it, would not affect its core essence (*māhiyya*). As, for instance, with place, position,

> quality, and quantity itself: if something else had been imagined in their place, it would not affect the reality of the essence of its humanity.
>
> Sense-perception grasps [the concept] insofar as it is buried in these accidents that cling to it because of the matter out of which it is made without **abstracting** (*jarrada*) it from [matter], and it grasps it only by means of a connection through position [that exists] between its perception and its matter. It is for this reason that the form of [the thing] is not represented in the external sense when [sensation] ceases. As to the internal [faculty of] imagination, it imagines [the concept] together with these accidents, without being able to entirely **abstract** it from them. Still, [imagination] **abstracts** it from the afore-mentioned connection [through position] on which sense-perception depends, so that [imagination] represents the form [of the thing] despite the absence of the form's [outside] carrier.
>
> As for the intellect, it is able to **abstract** (*tajrīd*) the essence which is enclosed[73] in extraneous accidents that individuate it,[74] securing it as if [the intellect] were acting upon the sense-perceptible [form] in a way that would make it intelligible.[75]

This is, indeed, a very dense fusion of various strands of abstraction theory as present in Avicenna's works of the middle period. It starts off, just as in the *Dāneshnāme*, with a distinction between different kinds of perceptions rather than abstractions. But shortly afterwards Avicenna touches upon the familiar doctrine of forms: imagine (and this is the more speculative tone of the *Ishārāt*) that one would give a different place, position, quality etc. to the essence of humanity, the essence itself would not be affected in any way. Avicenna here gives a new expression to the distinction between the forms' essences and their existence and even invokes the corresponding vocabulary, without however mentioning the forms' existential independence also of the intellect.[76]

There follow the three increasing degrees of abstraction; they are reduced from four to three by omitting estimation from the scala. Although this is a heavily abbreviated version of the doctrine, the vocabulary (*jarrada, tajrīd*) and line of argument show that the topic is the same as in the middle period: the difference between external senses, internal senses and intellect with regard to perception is explained in terms of varying powers of abstraction. A development of doctrine can be seen in the prominence given to the phrase "connection through position" (*'alāqa waḍ'iyya*) existing between perception and matter, that is, the fact that there is no sense-perception if the object is not present. In earlier versions, Avicenna had also mentioned a "relation" (*nisba*)[77] between object and perceiver as characteristic of sense-perception, but he had not yet spoken of this relation as something necessarily "grasped" by the senses and "abstracted" by imagination. We see him here elaborating a theoretical concept not yet fully developed in the middle period in order to create the highly condensed doctrine of the late *magnum opus*.

The passage in the *Ishārāt* ends with a sentence on intellectual abstraction which sounds just as a conclusion to the present article: the explicit use of abstraction terminology, the transformation of sense-perceptible forms into intelligible forms, the invoking of essentialist vocabulary with respect to the abstracted forms, and, above all, a reference—present in Avicenna's work since the early *Compendium*—to the very active part played by the human intellect: abstraction means that the intellect "acts upon" (*'amila bi*) the sense-perceptible form "in a way that would make it intelligible".

If the human intellect's activity is a constant feature of Avicenna's theory, this is not true of the role of the separate active intellect which changes from assistance to mediation, as we have seen. The *Ishārāt* give a final twist to the story:

> The multiplicity of the soul's occupations with sense-perceptible imaginable forms and connotational images,[78] which are in the form-bearing and the remembering [faculties respectively], with the help (*istikhdām*) of the estimative and cogitative faculty, makes the soul obtain a disposition for the reception of **abstractions** of them [i.e., of the imaginable forms and images] from the separate substance through some kind of relationship between the two. Observation and inspection of the issue verify this. These occupations [with imaginable forms and images] are those which give [the soul] a perfect disposition that is specific for [the reception of] each individual form, though an intellectual concept may [also] provide this specific [disposition] for [the reception of] another intellectual concept.[79]

One recognizes elements of doctrine central to Avicenna's abstraction theory since his earliest works: for instance, the role of "assistance" performed by the internal faculties; the soul's consideration of sense-data. But what is missing, is the analogy of light and, with it, the doctrine of the active intellect as a mediator—not to speak of an assisting factor—in the process of abstraction. In this *al-Ishārāt* differ from all other works treated, including the *Dāneshnāme*; it may be an indication of Avicenna's gradual emancipation from the Peripatetic tradition. The result, from a doctrinal point of view, is a theory that appears to reduce the consideration of imaginable forms to a mere preparation for an emanation of abstractions. Upon closer inspection, however, this interpretation does not hold: for Avicenna has taken over from *De anima* (or *Mashriqiyyūn* or *Dāneshnāme*) the phrase "their abstractions" (*mujarradātihā*), that is, abstractions from the afore-mentioned forms stored in imagination and memory. Even in the *Ishārāt*, no doubt is left about the origin of these intelligible forms: they ultimately derive from sense-data. The concept of the active intellect as mediator is still in force.

One also notes that there is only one active power in the process, the human intellect: it turns towards the imaginable forms and acts upon them—which is the sense of *taṣarrufāt fī*, "occupations with". These occupations give to the intellect a particular disposition to acquire a specific form; they particularize or "customize" (*mukhaṣṣiṣa*) the intellect for its reception. In other words, by looking through the many data furnished by the senses, the intellect assumes a focus that allows for the discernment of a specific intelligible form. Clearly, the protagonist in abstraction remains the human intellect.

VI

Is Avicenna's language of abstraction a *façon de parler* for emanation, and should we hence refrain from taking him literally in this context? Does he himself negate the reality of abstraction as a cognitive process? Or is he simply unable to explain intellectual abstraction in knowledge? *Pace diligentiae* of those who have given affirmative answers, mine can only be negative. It seems impossible to deny that Avicenna was convinced of the human power of abstraction, that he meant what he said and that he was fully capable of developing a theory of impressive quality, if measured against al-Fārābī's or those of his thirteenth-century Latin readers.[80]

Modern interpreters have perhaps been too impressed—and thus misguided—by some salient features of Avicenna's philosophy: the ample usage of emanation terminology, the fact that the active intellect is not part of the soul but nevertheless plays an essential role in human intellection, and the denial of intellectual memory, or rather the attribution of this function to the active intellect. It seemed impossible to integrate an actively abstracting human intellect into such a system—which however is exactly what Avicenna did. He achieved this not by turning one or the other of his discourses into a metaphorical, non-literal one, but rather by giving a new sense to transmitted vocabulary and a new explanation to traditional doctrines. Since abstraction is a complex phenomenon and since Avicenna developed his position gradually, one can find passages relevant to the topic in many different contexts of Avicenna's oeuvre. Combining these passages does not yet give us a clear picture of the theory: the increasing complexity of his philosophy makes it difficult to decide which pieces of doctrine are interrelated and which are not. This is why it seems advisable to attempt a developmental interpretation by describing the gradual transformation of groups of doctrines.

It is an entirely different question—and certainly not an interesting question for everybody—whether Avicenna's theory of abstraction deserves its name if compared to a systematic concept of abstraction derived from the longue durée of intellectual history. In view of the fact that Avicenna is a major factor in the historical shaping of the concept, one feels reluctant to believe that he falls short of speaking properly about it.

Notes

1. Avicenna (1959) ch. V.5. p. 235, line 7.
2. Rahman, (1958), p. 15. Cf. Gardet, (1951), p. 151: 'Il n'y a donc pas abstraction proprement dite'.
3. Davidson (1992) p. 94.
4. Davidson (1992) p. 93.
5. Weisheipl (1982) p. 150. Cf. Black (1997) p. 445: '. . . he denies the reality of abstraction as a cognitive process'. Cf. as probable sources for this line of interpretation. F. Brentano, (1867) p. 14 ('das Sinnliche hört auf die Quelle des geistigen Erkennens zu sein') and Thomas Aquinas, *Summa contra gentiles*. 2.74, and idem, *Summa theologiae*, 1.84.4 reply.
6. *De anima* V.5 (Avicenna [1959]) pp. 235–6.
7. Goichon (1937) p. 309: "Mais l'intelligible est-il abstrait par l'âme ou donné par l'intellect actif? En rigueur de termes, ni l'un ni l'autre".
8. See Gutas (1988) pp. 79–145, Marmura (1991), pp. 334–336, Michot (1997) pp. 153–163. Cf. also Michot's earlier book (1986) pp. 6–7, and Goodman (1992) pp. 1–48.
9. See Aubenque et al. (1971). On Thomas Aquinas's distinction between *abstractio* and *separatio* see "Metaphysics and *Separatio* in Thomas Aquinas" in Wippel (1984), pp. 69–82. Cf. also (on Alexander of Aphrodisias, Boethius, Abelard and Avicenna) De Libera (1999).
10. For comparisons of al-Fārābī and Avicenna on abstraction see F. Rahman (1963) vol. 1, p. 495, and Davidson (1992) p, 93. For the late Greek and early Arabic tradition see Arnzen's commentary on Ibn al-Bitrīq's paraphrase (extant in a revised version) of Aristotle's *De anima* in Arnzen (1997) pp. 335 and 451–2.
11. Al-Fārābī (1985) pp. 202–203.
12. Al-Fārābī (1985) pp. 204–205.
13. Al-Fārābī (1938) p. 12. Cf. the Latin translation, *De intellectu et intellecto*, edited by E. Gilson in Gilson (1929) p. 117: ". . . vel aliquid cuius essentia apta est abstrahere quidditates omnium quae sunt et formas eorum a suis materiis."
14. Al-Fārābī (1938) p. 20, line 6. Cf. Latin tr., *De intellectu et intellecto* (Gilson [1929]) p. 120, line 185.
15. Aristotle, *De anima* III.4. 430a 2–6.
16. Al-Fārābī (1938) p. 27, line 6. Cf. Latin tr., *De intellectu et intellecto* (Gilson [1929]) p. 122, line 265.
17. As maintained by Davidson (1992) p. 93.
18. The early dating is well established: see Landauer (1875) pp. 336–9, Michot (1986) p. 6, Gutas (1988) pp. 82–4, Marmura (1991) p. 341.
19. For textual comments the following abbreviations are used: La = Landauer's edition. Ah = al-Ahwānī's edition, A = manuscript A in Landauer, B = manuscript B in Landauer, tr. Al = Alpago's Latin translation, tr. La = Landauer's German translation in "Die Psychologie" (1875). The phrase 'form-bearing' translates *al-mutaṣawwira* (La, Ah, tr. Al: *informativa*); this does not refer to the rational soul and its power to form concepts, but is an alternative term for common sense in the *Compendium* (cf. ed. Landauer [1875] p. 352, line 13, p. 359, lines 4–5). In later writings, Avicenna uses the term *al-muṣawwira* for the faculty of imagination, the storing-place of sense-data (see the *Lexiques* in Avicenna (1968a) pp. 244–245).
20. 'forms': *ṣuwar* (Ah); 'form': *ṣūra* (La), *formae vel speciei* (tr. Al).
21. 'man': *insān* (B, Ah); *zayd* (A, La); *Platonis* (tr. Al).
22. 'in someone forming concepts': *fī mutaṣawwir* (La, Ah); 'wenn man an den Begriff . . . denkt' (tr. La); *in forma* (tr. Al).
23. 'it': *wajadat-hā* (conj. La), 'inuenit eas' (tr. Al); *wajadnā-humā* (A, La, Ah); *wajada-humā* (B).
24. 'axioms': *al-badā'ih* (B, La, tr. Al: *principiis*); *bidāya* (A, Ah).
25. 'the object of sense-perception . . . imitation of: om. Ah.
26. 'assimilation': *al-tashabbuh* (B, La, Ah); *al-tashbīh* ('comparison': A).

27. 'performs the abstraction': *taf'alu . . . tajarrud* (La, tr. Al: *operatur . . . denudando*); *ta'qilu . . . bi-tajrīd* ('knows the abstraction': Ah).
28. 'For this reason . . . active'; om. tr. Al.
29. Avicenna, *Compendium on the Soul*, edited by Landauer, in Landauer (1875) p. 362, line 16; edited by A. F. al-Ahwānī (Avicenna 1952b) p. 169, line 10; Latin translation by A. Alpago in Avicenna (1969) p. 23v; alternative English translation by E. A. van Dyck in Avicenna (1906) p. 72.
30. On Avicenna's theory of axioms and primary intelligibles see Hasse (1999) pp. 31–36.
31. 'in it [scil. the rational soul]': *fī-hi* (La with footnote: "suffixum masc.?"; Ah); cf. tr. Al: "in ea", scil. *virtus rationalis*, tr. La: "in ihr", scil. "denkende Seele".
32. Avicenna, *Compendium on the Soul*. ed. Landauer (1875) p. 371, line 9; ed. al-Ahwānī (Avicenna [1952b]) p. 177, line 3; Latin tr. (Avicenna [1969]) *Compendium de anima*, p. 34r, line 6.
33. For matters of chronology in general, see the references in n. 8 above.
34. Gutas (1988) pp. 41 and 103–106; the earliest possible dating for *De anima* is 1015, but since in 1021 only 20 folia of the section on natural philosophy had been finished (as reported by Jūzjānī, Avicenna's secretary; see the translation in Gutas (1988) p. 41), the later dating (1022–4) is more probable. Michot (1997) argues for a dating earlier than 1021; see p. 1.57, n. 58.
35. Avicenna, *Ḥāl al-nafs al-insāniyya*, ed. al-Ahwānī, *Aḥwāl* (1952b). pp. 69–73: Avicenna, *De anima* II,2 (1959) pp. 58–61 (= the Latin *Liber de anima seu Sextus de naturalibus* (1968a) pp. 114–20); Avicenna, *al-Najāt* (1938) pp. 168–71; Avicenna, *al-Mashriqiyyūn*, MS Istanbul, Ahmet III 2125, fols 665v–666v.
36. Rahman (1952) pp. 38–40.
37. 'concept': *al-ma'nā* (*De anima, Mashriqiyyūn*); om. (*Ḥāl, Najāt*).
38. Avicenna. *Ḥāl al-nafs al-insāniyya* (in Avicenna [1952b]) p. 69; = *al-Shifā': De anima* (1959) II,2, p. 58, line 4; = Latin tr., ed. Van Riet (1968a) p. 114, = *Mashriqiyyūn* MS Ah. fol. 665v, = *Najāt* (1938) p. 168, line 22, translation by Rahman, slightly modified, p. 38.
39. 'by accident': *lā ya'riḍu* (*Ḥāl, Najāt*); *lā 'araḍa* (*De anima, Mashriqiyyūn*).
40. [. . .]: *Ḥāl, Najāt, Mashriqiyyūn*; om. *De anima*.
41. 'completely': *min kulli wajhin* (*Ḥāl, Najāt, Mashriqiyyūn*); om. (*De anima*).
42. 'takes': *fa-ta'khudhu* (*Najāt*); *fa-ya'khudhu* (*Ḥāl*); *wa-ḥattā yakūna qad akhadha* (*De anima, Mashriqiyyūn*).
43. 'if': *wa-law* (*De anima, Mashriqiyyūn*); *thumma* (*Ḥāl, Najāt*).
44. Avicenna, *Ḥāl al-nafs al-insāniyya* (in Avicenna [1952b]) p. 72; = *al-Shifā': De anima* (Avicenna [1959]) II,2, p. 61, line 5; = Latin tr. (Avicenna [1968a]) p, 120, = *Mashriqiyyūn* MS Ah, fol. 666r-v, = *Najāt* (Avicenna [1938]) p. 170, line 20, translation by Rahman, slightly modified, p. 40.
45. Avicenna. *Ḥāl al-nafs al-insāniyya* (in Avicenna [1952b]) p. 69; = *al-Shifā': De anima* (Avicenna [1959]) II,2, p. 58, line 11; = Latin tr. (Avicenna [1968a]) p. 115, = *Mashriqiyyūn* MS Ah, fol. 665v, = *Najāt* (Avicenna [1938]) p. 169, line 4, translation by Rahman, p. 38 (slightly modified).
46. On these doctrines see Rahman, (1963), pp. 483–6.
47. For the *Logic* part see: Avicenna (1952a), ch. I,12, pp. 65–9 (on particularity and universality as accidents to the essential concept).
48. Avicenna (1960), V.1, p. 205 (= Latin tr. [1977–83] vol. II, p. 238).
49. At present state of research, the influence has only been documented for the Latin tradition; see the references to Dominicus Gundissalinus, anonymous *De anima et de potentiis eius*, Jean de la Rochelle. Alexander of Hales, Albertus Magnus, Vincent of Beauvais, Petrus Hispanus and Anonymous (MS Siena) in Hasse (2000) pp. 200–203 and Index Locorum II.2.b-g.
50. The *Mashriqiyyūn* write: 'The rational soul, however, sometimes employs the help of the animal faculties: they assist it in various ways'.
51. 'mind': *dhihn* (*De anima, Mashriqiyyūn*); *nafs* (*Ḥāl, Najāt*).

52. 'in it': *fī-hi* (*De anima, Mashriqiyyūn, Najāt*); *fī-hā* ('in them': *Ḥāl*).
53. Avicenna, *Ḥāl al-nafs al-insāniyya* (in Avicenna [1952]) p. 87 (= *al-Shifā': De anima* (Avicenna [1959]) V,3, p. 221, line 17, = Latin tr. (Avicenna [1968a]) p. 102, = *Mashriqiyyūn* MS Ah, fol. 685r–v, = *Najāt* (Avicenna [1938]) p. 182, tr. Rahman (1952) pp. 54–55).
54. Cf. Rahman's (1952) translation p. 56: "When not so diverted, [the soul] does not need the lower faculties for its special activity, except in certain matters wherein it specially needs to refer once more to the faculty of imagination for finding a new principle in addition to what had already been obtained, or for recalling an image" (for references to the Arabic text see next footnote). The theory of acquisition and reacquisition is discussed most fully by Avicenna in *De anima* V,6, esp. p. 247; it is put in context in Hasse (2000) pp. 174–49, esp. pp. 186–7.
55. Avicenna, *Ḥāl al-nafs al-insāniyya* (in Avicenna [1952]) p, 89, line 4 (= *at-Shifā': De anima* (Avicenna [1959]) V,3, p. 223, line 8, = Latin tr. (1968a) p. 105, = *Mashriqiyyūn* MS Ah, fol. 685v, line 18, = *Najāt* (Avicenna [1938]) p. 183. line 7, tr. Rahman (1952) p. 56). Some of these editions or manuscripts erroneously read *dhāt* instead of *dābba* (*Ḥāl, Najāt* and *Mashriqiyyūn*; corrected on the basis of better manuscripts by Rahman (1952) p. 125). The example of the riding animal is briefly discussed by Davidson (1992) p. 104.
56. Avicenna. *Ḥāl al-nafs al-insāniyya* (in Avicenna [1952]) p. 112; = *Najāt* (Avicenna [1938]) p. 193, = translation by Rahman (1952) p. 69.
57. Gutas argues for an early dating of *Ḥāl al-nafs*; see Gutas (1988) pp. 99–100. See Michot (1986) pp. 6–7, n. 29, for the contrary opinion.
58. Such terminology is also missing in the Avicennian treatise on prophetic knowledge called *Fī ithbāt al-nubuwwāt* (Avicenna [1968b]).
59. *jumla* here means 'gist', 'essence', not 'all', 'whole' (the Latin has *similis*).
60. 'or rather': *bal* (*De anima*); om. (*Mashriqiyyūn*).
61. Avicenna, *De anima* V,5 (Avicenna [1959]) p. 235, line 2; = Latin tr. (Avicenna [1968a]) p. 127; = *Mashriqiyyūn* MS Ah, fol. 688v.
62. Cf. Weisheipl (1982) p. 150: "According to Avicenna, human teachers and books can only dispose the mind to be receptive of new concepts from the dator formarum, the 'agent intellect'"; and Davidson (1992) p. 93; "Activity leading up to the ostensible act of abstraction thus does not come to fruition in a true act of abstraction. It rather prepares the way for the reception of abstract concepts from the emanation of the active intellect".
63. *Pace* Rahman (1958), who translates (p. 15): ". . . but *only* in the sense that its consideration prepares the soul so that the abstract form should emanate upon it from the Active Intelligence" (my emphasis).
64. Davidson (1992) pp. 102 and 93.
65. Davidson (1992) takes *fikr* ("reasoning", "cogitation") to refer only to the cogitative faculty (*al-mufakkira*); see pp. 95–102. In fact, Avicenna's use of the term is varied and it refers to reasoning processes both in the animal soul, where the cogitative faculty resides, and in the rational soul. At one point in the *De anima* (IV,2, p. 175, line 9) he even implies that intellectual reasoning (*al-fikr al-nuṭqī*) is hindered by the imaginative/cogitative faculty of the animal soul. Further, one of the key passages for Davidson's interpretation (1992 p. 96) is *Mubāḥathāt Discussions* (pp. 122–239 in Avicenna [1947]) p. 199, line 12, where it is said that *fikr* consists in seeking the perfect disposition to make contact with the active intellect. But this passage is adopted from *De anima* V,6, p. 247, line 3, where the term is not *fikr* but *ta'allum*: "acquiring knowledge", or "acquiring an intelligible form". See also Gutas (2001).
66. Gutas (1988) p. 114, suggests the year 1027; Michot (1986) p. 7, and (1997) p. 161, places it between 1030 and 1034.
67. Avicenna (1974), vol. 2. pp. 125–6; cf. the French translation (1986) p. 79.
68. Cf. the first sentences of the doctrine in its classical formulation (translated above, reference in n. 38) with the opening paragraph in *Dāneshnāme* (Avicenna [1974]) p. 102, tr. Achena/Massé (Avicenna [1986]) p. 66: "Toute connaissance que nous acquérons est la quiddité, l'idée et la forme de telle chose que nous appréhendons. L'on saisit de diverses manières la forme d'une chose. A cette fin, prenons comme exemple l'humanité."

69. Avicenna, *Dāneshnāme* (Avicenna [1974]) vol. 2, p. 124, tr. Achena/Massé (Avicenna [1986]) p. 78: "Mais tant que tout d'abord les sensations et les imaginations n'existent pas, notre intelligence ne vient pas à l'acte. Et quand les sensations et les imaginations viennent à l'existence, les formes se mêlent à des accidents qui leur sont étrangers, et elles sont alors voilées comme les choses qui se trouvent dans l'obscurité. Mais ensuite le rayonnement de l'intelligence active tombe sur les imaginations, de même que celui du soleil tombe sur les formes [des choses] qui se trouvent dans l'obscurité. Puis, partant de ces imaginations, les formes **abstraites** se présentent à l'intelligence, de même qu'à cause de la lumière les formes visibles se présentent dans le miroir ou dans l'oeil: comme ces formes sont **abstraites**, elles sont universelles; en effet, si tu retranches de [la perception] d'humanité les parties superflues, il en reste le concept général, tandis que les particularités individuelles disparaissent".
70. The references are to the edition of Badawī (1947). A similar case is Avicenna's *Marginal Notes on the De anima* (edited by Badawī in the same volume. pp. 75–116): it is doubtful whether a collection of passages employing abstraction terminology (e.g., *Marginal Notes*, pp. 96.4, 110.4, 111.7–8) or an analysis of key passages (such as p. 110, lines 10–12, on the light of the active intellect falling upon forms stored in imagination with the effect of their abstraction) will offer us more than heterogeneous pieces of a theory which Avicenna treats systematically elsewhere.
71. Cf. n. 65 above.
72. The anonymous Longer Bibliography, which is based on a list by Jūzjānī, calls it "the last and best work he wrote on philosophy, to which he held steadfastly", edited and translated in Gohlman (1974), pp. 96–97. Gohlman dates the book to 1024–37 (ibid., p. 154); Gutas (1988), p. 140, argues more specifically for the years 1030–34. Michot (1997) pp. 153–163—against his earlier view on the problem (cf. Michot [1986] p. 7)—prefers a date as early as 1016, but acknowledges that the *Ishārāt* postdate the *De anima* and the logic part of *al-Shifā'*, which was begun in 1015 at the very earliest and completed in 1027. However, in view of the enormous scale of *al-Shifā'* and of its intellectual complexity, which would demand a longer period of composition, and on the basis of the internal evidence laid out in the present article, the traditional dating seems much more probable.
73. 'enclosed': *maknūfa*; cf. the passage in *De anima* II.2, p. 61, line 4: *maknūfa bi-lawāḥiqi al-mādda* (Latin tr.: 'stipatam accidentibus materiae').
74. 'that individuate it': *mushakhkhaṣ* (misprint in Dunyā: *mushakhkhash*).
75. Avicenna, *al-Ishārāt wa al-tanbīhāt* (1960–68), vol. 2, p. 367. Cf. the French translation by A.-M. Goichon (Avicenna [1951]), p. 314.
76. On the object of perception see also the preceding paragraph in *al-Ishārāt* (Avicenna [1960–68]), vol. 2, pp. 359–66 (tr. in Avicenna [1951] pp. 311–12).
77. Avicenna, *De anima* II,2 (Avicenna [1959]) p. 59, lines 11–12.
78. 'connotational': *al-ma'nawiyya* (Dunyā; ='intentional', refers to the objects of estimation); *al-ma'qūla* (Goichon: 'intelligibles').
79. Avicenna, *al-Ishārāt wa al-tanbīhāt* (1960–68) vol. 2, p. 403; cf. Ṭūṣī's comment, ibid., footnote 1. Cf. tr. Goichon (1951) p. 333.
80. For general information on the history of abstraction theory, see notes 9 and 49 above. See also Rohmer (1928).

CHAPTER 8

How Do We Acquire Concepts? Avicenna on Abstraction and Emanation

DEBORAH BLACK

The Islamic philosopher Avicenna (Ibn Sīnā, 980–1037) had a profound impact on the metaphysical and psychological teachings of Western theologians, including not only Thomas Aquinas, but also many of his predecessors and successors. When Avicenna's psychological masterpiece, the *Psychology* (*Al-Nafs/De anima*) of *The Healing* (or *Cure*, *Al-Shifā'*), was first encountered by theologians in the early part of the 13th century, its account of how humans acquire concepts was viewed as complementary to the traditional Augustinian theory of divine illumination and thus generally favorably received.[1] Even Aquinas originally drew on Avicennian arguments to support his own account of how a subsistent intellective soul could be conjoined to a body (*see* Pegis 1934). But he eventually distanced himself from Avicenna's dualistic principles, in part because of their association with Avicenna's thesis that intelligibles must be obtained by emanation from the active or agent intellect, which Avicenna, like many other Islamic and Greek philosophers, held to be a separate mind or intelligence outside the individual human soul, rather than a faculty internal to it. Yet more recently, many Avicennian scholars, inspired by Dag Hasse's reading of Avicenna, have come to question the interpretation of Avicenna accepted by most of his medieval Latin readers, arguing instead that Avicenna too takes abstraction, and not emanation, to be the main process by which humans acquire intelligibles.[2] By contrast, I will argue that the traditional reading of Avicennian psychology is the correct one, since it is the only reading that allows us to give a systematic account of Avicenna's theory of concept acquisition that can make sense of his use of both emanative and abstractive language to describe the production of intelligibles.[3]

The Aristotelian Background

Medieval authors, including Avicenna, framed their cognitive theory around Book 3, chapters 4–8, of Aristotle's *De anima*. In particular, they accepted Aristotle's basic division of the soul into two parts or powers, a receptive one that came to be known as the potential or material intellect (discussed in *De anima* 3.4), and an active one, the agent intellect (discussed in 3.5).[4] As noted above, the standard view of the agent intellect in the Arabic tradition was that it is not a faculty in the individual soul, but a separate substance whose function is to aid in the production of intelligibles. It is important to note that Aristotle himself is not explicit about either (1) the relation between the agent intellect and the individual human knower, or (2) the process by which the agent intellect enables the production of all intelligibles. Aristotle instead resorts to analogies to describe this part of the intellect, likening it first to art, and secondly to light (*De anima* 3.5, 430a10–17). Nor is "abstraction" used in Aristotle's account of how we acquire the principles of knowledge "by induction" in *Posterior Analytics* 2.19 (100a3-b4). In short, "the notion of abstracting a universal or 'essence' from singulars . . . does not occur in Aristotle" (Owens 1978, 382). Rather, in Aristotle, talk of "abstraction" (*aphairesis*) is almost exclusively employed to describe how the mathematician considers the unique features of the objects of his science (Cleary 1985; Owens 1978, 383). So within the Aristotelian tradition, to downplay the role of abstraction in accounting for how we acquire knowledge of intelligible universals is not, in itself, problematic. But the assumption that a theory of abstraction is a desideratum seems in large part to motivate Hasse's interpretation of Avicenna's cognitive psychology, since Hasse claims that the traditional view "measures Avicenna's theory against a systematic concept of abstraction, as we know it from intellectual history, and finds that it falls short of the criteria and hence cannot be properly called a theory of abstraction" (Hasse above, 102).

This is not to say that the notion of abstracting intelligibles is simply foreign to Aristotle. It is an easy step to move from the identification of mathematicals as "abstract objects" to the claim that all universal intelligibles are "abstract," that is, immaterial. Aristotle provides warrant for viewing intelligibles as abstract objects when in the *De anima* he describes cognition as "the reception (*to dektikon*) of the form of the perceived object without its matter" (2.12, 424a17–19).[5] Putting all these texts together, it is not hard to see how the idea that we acquire knowledge by *abstracting* forms from matter came to be treated as the canonical Aristotelian doctrine. Yet even these Aristotelian texts seem to provide support for a notion of abstraction that pertains principally to the status of the *object known*. What we possess when we have universal knowledge is an abstraction, a representation or instance of the form of the object known stripped of some or all of its material features. Aristotle himself nowhere suggests that the process by which the knower comes to acquire such intelligibles can be described as an "abstracting" or "stripping" of the form from its material attachments, whether that process be accomplished by some faculty in the knower herself or by an agent intellect external to her.

Avicenna himself is well attuned to these nuances in Aristotle, and like Aristotle he employs abstraction-talk first and foremost to describe the cognized object. But since Aristotle does not say much about the process of acquiring intelligibles, Avicenna provides his own theory to supplement Aristotle. According to that theory, intelligibles must ultimately be received directly into the human intellect from the continual flow of intelligibles that emanate from the separate agent intellect. The agent intellect is the *principal*, though not the sole efficient cause of intelligibles in human minds. For while emanation is necessary for knowledge acquisition, it is normally not sufficient.[6] The capacity to receive emanation is in turn dependent upon the prior activities of the external and internal senses within the individual human soul. These prior activities are what determine which intelligibles the individual will obtain, and when she will receive them. These activities are, as the traditional view claims, preparatory and ancillary causes of knowledge, and they are what Avicenna means when he speaks of "abstraction."

The Metaphysical Foundations of Emanation: Mental Existence and Agent Causality

Before I turn to Avicenna's account of how we acquire knowledge, it will be helpful to highlight two principles of Avicenna's metaphysics which require that we recognize emanation as the principal way in which intelligibles are produced in individual human souls: (1) the distinction between the essence or quiddity and its two modes of existence; and (2) the distinction between physical and metaphysical agent causality.[7]

Essence and Existence

Avicenna's distinction between essence and existence is well known for its pervasive influence in Western medieval philosophy.[8] Avicenna holds that the concepts of "essence" and "existence" are irreducibly primary and distinct from each other in all beings but God. Avicenna argues for this distinction by observing that any essence or quiddity[9]—for example, "humanity" or "horseness"—is in itself neutral with respect to existence, and hence existence adds some positive content to the quiddity.[10] The neutrality or indifference of the quiddity is illustrated by the fact that essences can exist either as concrete singular things in the external world, or as objects of cognition in the souls or minds of knowers. But by simply examining the quiddity—that is, by looking at what is contained in the definition of "horseness" or "humanity"—we cannot tell whether what we are considering is really existent (like a horse), or merely a fictional being in the mind (like a phoenix). As Avicenna puts it:

> [Horseness] in itself is nothing at all except "horseness"; for, in itself, it is neither one nor many and exists neither in concrete things nor in the soul, existing in none of these things either in potency or in act, such that [these] are included in "horseness". Rather, in terms of itself, it is only "horseness".
>
> (*Metaphysics*, 5.1, §4, 204)

The essence–existence distinction is important for cognitive psychology because it claims that the objects we know have a special mode of existence in the mind. Just as concrete individuals have physical properties, such as position, size, and shape, so too mental beings have properties in virtue of their existence in minds. So when a quiddity exists in an intellect, it becomes an immaterial universal, i.e., an abstract entity. Universality and abstractness, then, are properties conferred on quiddities by their mental existence.

There is some sense, then, in which we could say that a universal *just is* the quiddity as a mental existent, in the same way that an individual *just is* the nature as a material existent. But it is more correct to say that mental existence is a necessary but not a sufficient condition for universality, because in addition to mental existence, universality requires the knower to recognize the relation of the conceived quiddity to multiple individual existents outside the soul:

> That [aspect] of "human being" that is intellectually apprehended in the soul is the universal. Its universality is not due to its being in the soul but due to its relating to many individuals, existent or imagined, concerning which the judgment in the soul is a single judgment (*ḥukm*).
>
> (*Metaphysics* 5.2, 159, slightly modified).[11]

This relational aspect of universality requires Avicenna to retain some role for abstraction in order to establish the link between the intelligible in the mind and the material singulars upon which its property of universality depends. Were it not for the preparatory activities of sensation and imagination, the universal in the mind could not be recognized as one nature shared by many individuals.

Agent Causality

A second pillar of Avicennian metaphysics, however, requires the introduction of emanation as the ultimate causal explanation for how humans acquire intelligibles—namely, Avicenna's theory of efficient or agent causality, which is closely connected to the distinction between essence and existence. For intelligibles in minds are themselves individual *instances* of the quiddities conceived through them: "This form, although a universal in relation to individuals, is an individual in relation to the particular soul in which it is imprinted, being one of the forms in the mind" (*Metaphysics* 5.2, §29, 157). For this reason the production of intelligibles requires the same creative act by an agent on which the production of any new *existent* depends. Such agent causality is reserved by Avicenna for separate substances, whom he calls "the cause[s] that endow the forms" (*Metaphysics* 6.2, §5,202). Thus, Avicenna argues, in ordinary examples of agent causality, such as a father begetting a son or a builder erecting a house, the father and the builder are not the sole nor even the principal agents of their effects, since physical causes are unable to confer either existence or continued subsistence on what they produce.[12] Still, physical agents are necessary for the generation of physical effects, though Avicenna describes their causality as "accidental" (*bi-al-ʿaraḍ*), "ancillary" (*muʿīnāt*), or "preparatory" (*muʿiddah*; *Metaphysics* 6.2, §5, 202; *Physics* 1.10, §3, 65).[13] Sons would not be born without fathers, and houses would not be built without builders. More importantly for our purposes, it is the activity of the preparatory causes that determines *which* quiddities will be instantiated: if the preparatory cause is a human, a human child will be born; if it is a canine, the offspring will be a puppy.

There are two points that emerge from this account of agent causality that are important for understanding the relations between abstraction and emanation in Avicenna's psychology. The first is that "ancillary," "preparatory," and "accidental" are technical terms for Avicenna. When they appear in his psychological texts, that provides strong prima facie grounds for assuming that Avicenna intends to evoke his official metaphysical account of the distinction between agent and preparatory causes. And this is exactly the sort of language that Avicenna uses when describing how abstraction paves the way for the emanation of intelligibles into human minds, as we'll see below.[14] The second is that when a process is described as preparatory or ancillary, this does not imply that it is *not* an authentic instance of natural agency. So the claim that Avicenna rejects abstraction as an account of how intelligibles come to exist in the mind does not entail that abstraction plays no causal function at all, any more than the claim that the builder or the father are not "causes for the subsistence of their effects" (*Metaphysics* 6.2, §1, 201) entails that their contribution to physical generation is merely illusory or metaphorical. Supporting causes are necessary conditions preparing their respective materials to receive the action of the separate causes. To say that Avicenna's cognitive psychology does not contain a theory of abstraction entails no more—and no less—than this.

With these principles in mind, we are now in a position to turn to the account in Avicenna's psychological writings of the process by which human knowers acquire intelligibles. My presentation of Avicenna's theory of knowledge acquisition will focus primarily on the *Psychology* of Avicenna's most comprehensive philosophical work, *The Healing*. I will not give much attention to developmental issues, which feature prominently in Hasse's account, since Avicenna's mature works do not seem to me to exhibit any major doctrinal differences on this point.[15] I will begin by offering an alternative reading of *Psychology* 2.2, where Avicenna outlines his scale of abstraction, and of *Psychology* 5.5, the key text in which Avicenna qualifies the claim that abstraction is what accounts for the *production* of intelligibles in the human intellect. I will then consider Avicenna's much-discussed denial of intellectual memory in the following chapter of the *Psychology* (5.6), which makes sense only in an emanational context.[16] Hasse treats this text only in passing, since on his reading it applies *only* to the reacquisition or reactivation of intelligibles previously learned—a view that unnecessarily fragments Avicenna's cognitive psychology by ignoring the argumentative continuity of Avicenna's text.[17]

The Grades of Abstraction

One of the passages that is often invoked to show that Avicenna upholds a theory of abstraction occurs in *Psychology* 2.2 and a number of parallel texts, where Avicenna discusses the various grades of abstraction within the human soul's cognitive powers.[18] The chapter begins with the claim that all perception or apprehension (*idrāk*) involves the grasping or taking (*akhdh*) of the form (*ṣūrah*) of the thing apprehended, a description that is clearly meant to evoke Aristotle's description of perception (*aisthēsis*) as the reception of the object's form without its matter (*De anima* 2.12, 424a17–19). Avicenna explains further that "If the apprehension is of something material, it consists of grasping its form abstracted from matter (*mujarradah 'an al-māddah*) in some way" (2.2, 58). In the explication that follows, Avicenna goes beyond Aristotle in explicitly holding that immateriality and abstractness admit of degrees, and he ascertains four distinct levels of abstractness in human cognition, each associated with a particular faculty: (1) the external senses; (2) the imagination; (3) the estimative faculty; and (4) the intellect. The metaphysical basis for Avicenna's scale is his distinction between the quiddity (which Avicenna here calls the "form"), for example, humanity or horseness, and its two modes of existence which I discussed in the previous section. The scale of abstraction can be viewed as a description of the various ways in which the quiddity enjoys mental existence.[19] Thus while Avicenna describes each subsequent level on the scale as one in which the faculty in question "abstracts" or "strips" the form of its material attachments, what the scale primarily describes are the levels of materiality that the *object known* manifests insofar as it's cognized in that particular faculty. This is especially evident from the fact that the notion of "abstraction" is equivocal across the four grades of abstraction, since what it means for each level to be more or less abstract than the one below it is different in each case. Moreover, according to Avicenna's accounts of the nature of the other faculties that make up the scale, it's clear that not all of them actually perform an operation on their objects: in some cases the quiddity becomes more abstract simply because of the way it exists in that particular faculty.

This is especially clear if one compares the level of abstraction of the external senses to that of the imagination. Sensation, Avicenna claims, is the least abstractive faculty for two reasons: (1) because it apprehends a particular in its particularity, qualified by all its material accidents of color, size, shape, and so on; (2) because it depends upon the material *presence* of the cognized object in order to perceive. I cannot see an object unless it's in my visual field, or touch it unless I come into physical contact with it: "The sense thus takes the form from matter together with these attachments, and with the occurrence of a relation with matter such that if this relation ceases, the perception stops" (*Psychology* 59). Imagination, on the other hand, is more abstract than sensation simply because it can retain the image of the sensible object when that object is absent from the perceiver's physical surroundings. But the image, like the sensible, nonetheless represents the object as a material particular with all its material qualities. So the only thing that distinguishes imaginative abstraction from sensible abstraction is the imagination's freedom from the object's physical presence: "Thus [the imagination's] apprehension of the form would constitute a complete severing of the connection between [the form] and matter, except that the imagination would not have abstracted it from material attachments" (*Psychology* 59). In this case, then, the objects of the two faculties are "abstract" in exactly the same way, but their respective relations to the extramental object differ. In neither case is there any abstraction in the sense of "stripping" forms from matter.

The third place on the scale is occupied by the estimative faculty (*al-wahm*), an Avicennian innovation posited to account for the capacities of both human and non-human animals to apprehend information about the external world that cannot be neatly categorized as either a proper sensible (an item exclusive to one of the five senses) or as a common sensible (an item perceived by two or more senses, such as shape, size, motion, rest). Avicenna calls these features of the world "intentions" or "meanings" (singular *ma'nā*), and his favorite example is the hostility that a sheep perceives in a wolf. According to Avicenna, intentions are "not essentially material," that is, they are not physical or corporeal properties of things, although they somehow attach or adhere to bodies:

> As for estimation, it would progress a little beyond this degree of abstraction because it attains the intentions that are not in themselves material, even though they happen to be in matter. This is because it is not possible for shape, color, position and the like to be unless in corporeal matters, whereas good, evil, agreeable, hostile, and the like are things that in themselves are immaterial, even though it may happen to them to be in matter.
>
> (*Psychology* 61)

Since the estimative faculty only apprehends things like hostility or friendliness as attached to the image of a particular wolf or lamb, however, its objects remain particularized and to that extent not fully abstract or immaterial, despite the nature of the perceived intentions themselves.

In all these cases, then, Avicenna describes the cognitive power as "abstracting" the form from matter. But when he discusses the operations of sensation, imagination, and even estimation, he does not present these faculties as performing any sort of stripping operation on the objects they cognize. The estimative faculty, for example, doesn't strip away what the other inner senses perceive; rather, both sensible forms and intentions are present in sensation and imagination, but these faculties do not have the capacity to *recognize* them. This is possible only for the estimative faculty, whose cognitive act is one of judgment or discernment, not one of abstraction. Estimation doesn't disregard the material attachments of sensory images, but rather, it recognizes that the intention is associated with them.

Thus, when Avicenna talks about the imagination, estimation, or intellect "abstracting" the form or quiddity from matter in this context, this cannot be taken as the description of a process or operation that is being performed on an object to render it more immaterial. That does not mean that abstraction is a metaphor for something else: it is rather a description of the relation that holds between the object of one faculty and that of the faculty immediately below it on the scale. The scale of abstraction, then, provides no evidence for the claim that Avicenna upholds a theory of abstraction as an account of how intelligibles are *produced*. It simply tells us that what the intellect ultimately understands is entirely free from matter.

Abstraction as Preparation for Emanation

In *Psychology* 5.5, Avicenna introduces emanation in order to clarify the function played by the agent intellect in human knowledge. His account begins in standard fashion, with a brief argument for the necessity of positing an intellect which, as Aristotle says, "makes all things" (*poiein panta*; *De anima* 3.5, 430a12) by bringing the human potential intellect into actuality:

> For when the intellectual faculty peruses the particulars in the imagination and the light of the agent intellect in us, which we have mentioned, shines upon them, they become abstracted from matter and its attachments and imprinted on the rational soul, *not in the sense that they themselves are transferred from the imagination to the intellect in us, nor in the sense that the intention immersed in the [material] attachment—being in itself and from the perspective of its own essence abstract—produces a likeness* (mathal) *of itself, but in the sense that perusing [the particulars] prepares the soul for having that which is abstract emanate on it from the agent*

> *intellect*. . . . For the images which are intelligibles in potency become intelligibles in actuality—*not themselves, but what is received from them*. Rather . . . when the rational soul peruses these forms in the imagination and the light of the agent intellect conjoins with it in some way, [the soul] becomes prepared for the forms abstracted from [material] contaminations to be produced in it (*ḥadatha min-hā fī-ha*) from the light of the agent intellect.
>
> (*Psychology* 5.5, 235, emphasis added)[20]

The first thing to note about this passage is that just as he did in the case of the scale of abstraction, here too Avicenna takes care to apply abstractive descriptions primarily to the state of the intelligible *object* that results from the activities of the agent intellect, and not to the process itself by which they become dematerialized. The second thing is that when Avicenna does use abstractive language of that process, he immediately qualifies the description in the phrases I have italicized, lest the reader interpret "abstraction" incorrectly. Avicenna recognizes and rejects two possible versions of a theory of abstraction. The first theory, which I will call the Transference Account, involves the transfer and imprinting of dematerialized images into the potential intellect.[21] The second theory, which I will call the Latency Account, takes abstraction to be a process of *stripping* or *peeling* away layers of material accidents so as to allow a latent immaterial intelligible already present in the image to emerge.[22] Both accounts are in some way incompatible with Avicenna's basic metaphysical principles outlined in section 2 above.

On the Transference Account, one and the same particular item—the image—is transformed into a different *kind* of item—an intelligible—whereupon it is then transferred from one faculty to another. The problem here is that particular things cannot be transformed into other things different in kind without undergoing a substantial change; and once a substantial change is involved, a *new* individual has been produced. This is clear from the terminology that Avicenna uses when he attempts to clarify the function of imagination in the abstraction, which is deliberately evocative of the theory of agent causality. The impression of an intelligible on the rational soul is described as a production or origination (*ḥudūth*),[23] and the soul's perusal of its store of images is described as a "preparation" enabling that production to occur. But, as we've seen, Avicenna's metaphysics stipulates that such productions, insofar as they result in something new coming into being, require the intervention of a separate cause, an agent intellect. The Transference Account is thus the cognitive analogue of the *Metaphysics*' example of the father producing a child. While the father plays an indispensable causal role in the process of conception, the conceived child is not simply something into which the father's semen is transformed, but a new individual sharing the same nature as the preparatory cause. Like the father and son, the image and intelligible are both instances of the same quiddity (an image and a concept respectively of a horse, for example); and like the father's semen and the son, the image and the intelligible are also two different kinds of entities. This, then, is what Avicenna means when he says that it is what is received from the image, not the image itself, that becomes the intelligible.

The Latency Account, by contrast, seems to run into problems when viewed against the backdrop of Avicenna's theory of universals, which distinguishes between the essence or quiddity as such, and the universal as a mental existent in the intellect of the knower. While the quiddity itself is existent in singular things, where it is qualified by material accidents, the universal, abstract intention as such is *not* actually present in singulars. So the kind of thing that one cognizes—a universal—is not latent in the image ready to be unveiled simply by peeling the material accidents away. And because the nature is not actually present as a universal in the image, a representationalist account, whereby a *likeness* of the nature is produced from the image, is also impossible. The only likeness a particular image could produce would be another particular image.

Still, as we've seen, for Avicenna the nature *is* present both in material singulars and in universals in the mind; it is also present in the images of singular things found in the internal senses. And it is precisely this fact that permits abstraction to play the preparatory role that Avicenna assigns it in the acquisition of intelligibles. This is especially clear in Avicenna's interpretation of Aristotle's famous account of how we acquire the principles of knowledge in *Posterior Analytics* 2.19:

> And this is also because that which senses the particulars would in some respect sense the universal, for what senses "Socrates" would also sense "human," and likewise whatever else it conveys. For it conveys to the soul "Socrates" and "human," except that it is a vague human mixed with accidents, not pure human. Then if the intellect peels and removes from it the accidents, there remains of it the abstract human from which Socrates and Plato are not distinct. And if it were the case that sensation did not perceive human being in some way, then estimation in us and in the animals would not [be able to] distinguish between the individuals of one species and [those of] another species, so long as there was no intellect.
>
> (*Demonstration* 4.10, 332)[24]

To sum up, then, if by a theory of "abstraction" we mean a theory that holds that the intellect's extraction of some intelligible core from sense images, or its transformation of those images into intelligibles, is what produces abstract concepts in the human mind, then Avicenna does not have a theory of abstraction. Such a process is unable, on its own, to offer a satisfactory causal explanation of how actual universals are impressed on the minds of individual knowers. It does not follow from this that abstraction is an illusion or a metaphor for Avicenna. Nonetheless, since the abstractive theories available to Avicenna would have involved one of the two incomplete or inaccurate causal accounts that Avicenna has rejected in *Psychology* 5.5, it seems misleading to ascribe to Avicenna, without qualification, a theory of abstraction.

Emanation and the Denial of Intellectual Memory

On the version of the traditional interpretation of Avicenna that I am defending, abstraction is a preparatory causal operation necessary but not sufficient for the acquisition of intelligibles. What it prepares for, as Avicenna clearly indicates in many places, is the emanation from the separate agent intellect of an abstract intelligible sharing the same quiddity as the images to which it corresponds. To ignore the implicit and explicit references to emanation in the texts where Avicenna discusses abstraction is to leave his theory of concept-acquisition incomplete. And it makes it almost impossible to make sense of Avicenna's revisionist account of intellectual "memory" in *Psychology* 5.6, an account which depends upon the thesis that actually contemplated intelligibles are not abstracted from images, but rather flow into the human intellect directly from the agent intellect.[25]

At the beginning of *Psychology* 5.6, Avicenna argues that when the human mind is actually considering intelligibles, it does not, as some had argued, become in some way identical with them. Avicenna heaps scorn upon this doctrine as a mystical and poetical rambling, claiming instead that "the forms of things take up residence in the soul, beautifying and adorning it" (*Psychology* 240).[26] Avicenna then proceeds to outline three ways in which actual conceptualization of this sort takes place. The first of these is straightforward, as when the intellect is actively entertaining some thought, such as "Every human is an animal." The second is when one has acquired knowledge of some intelligible, but at the present time one has turned one's attention away from that intelligible to consider something else. This is what we would normally think of as intellectual memory or the storage of previously learned intelligible concepts. The third way, which is not directly relevant to the present topic, is when one is on the verge of solving a problem but has not yet articulated the solution either to herself or an interlocutor (*Psychology* 242–44).

The problem posed by intellectual memory is simple. After we have first acquired a new intelligible—that is, once we have learned something—there is an obvious sense in which we can say that we *actually* know it in a way that we did not before. But as finite, temporal minds, we are unable to be actively thinking all the intelligibles we have learned all at once. What, then, is the status of those intelligibles that we have in our possession but are not actually using, for example, our knowledge of French when we are speaking English? Where are they stored when not in use? The most obvious answer would be that once any intelligibles have "taken up residence" in our souls, they remain there permanently ready for us to consider whenever we wish. Such a position would model intellectual learning and retention upon sense memory, i.e., our ability to recall particulars which we have encountered in the past. But Avicenna rejects this as incompatible with the nature of the intellect.

This is because Avicenna, like almost all philosophers within the medieval Aristotelian tradition, held that the intellect is an immaterial faculty that operates independently of any sensory organ. By contrast, the senses depend on bodily instruments in order to perform their operations. Memory, according to Avicenna, is an "internal" sense faculty, that is, one that is spatially localized in a part of the brain. But the intellect does not have a bodily organ in the brain in which it could store intelligibles which it is not actively thinking. And as Avicenna twice emphasizes in this chapter, thinking just is the *presence* of the intelligible in the mind; so if intelligibles remain active in our minds, then we will be thinking everything we know at all times:

> This is because it is impossible for us to say that this form [that is no longer being considered] is existent in the soul in perfect actuality and that [the soul] does not understand it in perfect actuality, since the meaning of "it understands it" is nothing other than that the form exists in it. And it is impossible for the body to be a storehouse for [the form]; it is also impossible for [the soul] itself to be its storehouse, since its being a storehouse for it is nothing other than that this form is understood and existent in it; but its understanding also occurs in this way. . . . For the existence of the intelligible form in the soul is its very perception of it.
>
> (*Psychology* 246)

How is this account of intellectual memory relevant to the emanational theory of cognition? Having ruled out the possibility of the intellect having its own storage facility for intelligibles that it is not actually considering, Avicenna is left with two other possibilities. One is that the intelligibles are separate Platonic Forms which are reflected in the individual intellect whenever it thinks them. Avicenna rules this out rather quickly, reminding the reader of his refutation of Platonism in his *Metaphysics*.[27] The remaining possibility is that the intelligible forms reside continually in a mind that *is* always actually thinking them, that is, the separate agent intellect, whom Aristotle had already described as "not sometimes thinking and sometimes not thinking" (*De anima* 3.5, 430a22).

On this view, learning occurs when an intelligible emanates from the agent intellect into the individual rational soul for the first time. It is a matter of establishing a relation to the form in the agent intellect that corresponds to the images which the intellect has "perused" in its preparatory abstractive activities. Remembering what one has learned is a matter of re-establishing the connection to the agent intellect whenever one wishes:

> Learning would then be seeking the complete preparation for conjoining [with the agent intellect] so that from it there would come about the simple understanding from which the differentiated forms emanate into the soul through the mediation of cogitation. Thus the preparation would be incomplete prior to instruction and complete after instruction. . . . Thus the first instruction is like the treatment of the eye. For when the eye becomes healthy, then whenever it wishes it looks upon the thing from which it takes some form, and whenever it turns away from it, that thing comes to be in proximate potency to actuality. And as long as the ordinary human soul remains in the body, it is impossible for it to receive the agent intellect all at once. Rather, its condition is as we have said.
>
> So when it is said, "So and so knows the intelligibles," its meaning is that he is such that whenever he wishes he can make its form present in his own mind. The meaning of this is that whenever he wishes he has it in him to conjoin with the agent intellect by a conjunction in which he will conceptualize that intelligible from it, not in [the sense] that that intelligible is present in his mind and conceived in his intellect in actuality always, nor [in the sense that his state] is like it was prior to being instructed.
>
> (*Psychology* 5.6, 246–47)

In this passage Avicenna makes it clear that conjoining with the agent intellect and having an intelligible emanate into the soul occurs in *both* the original act of learning and in acts of intellectual recall. Learning, however, requires abstraction and discursive thinking (i.e., cogitation) to precede the first reception of the intelligible. Once an intelligible has been acquired, no further preparatory activity is required on the part of the senses and the imagination, and the intellect is now able to access the emanation whenever it wishes.[28]

In explaining the role of emanation in the context of intellectual memory, Avicenna makes an important point about how emanation is to be understood that may not be clear from his discussion of abstraction in the preceding chapter. The flow of intelligibles into human minds is not an intermittent process that occurs at the whim of the agent intellect: like the sun, the agent intellect always pours forth forms simply in virtue of the fact that as a pure intellect, it's always thinking. It is the voluntary acts of individual humans turning towards and away from the agent intellect that determines when and if thinking occurs.

On Avicenna's view, then, dispositional or habitual knowledge is just that. It is not a matter of amassing a personal hoard of intelligibles through abstraction, but of developing a disposition to receive intelligibles at will by connecting with their continual outpouring from the agent intellect. It is important to emphasize that on this account the agent intellect cannot be said to function as a *supernatural* force, if by that we mean a providential entity who determines which individuals are permitted to receive an influx of intelligibles.

Rather, emanation is a natural mechanism which Avicenna posits to explain how immaterial universals can come to be present in an embodied intellect. Nonetheless, Avicenna's agent intellect is not simply a *natural* cause: it is, as we've seen, required by the properly *metaphysical* analysis of efficient causality which requires that any new instance of a quiddity—even if it be in a mind—be explained not only with reference to material causes, but also with reference to immaterial, agent causes of existence.

Conclusion

While one might, in the light of the foregoing consideration, agree with Hasse that Avicenna does have a theory of abstraction, Avicennian abstraction functions quite differently from the way it was understood to work by most of his fellow peripatetics. Avicennian abstraction cannot stand on its own as an explanation of how we acquire or recall intelligibles: a complete causal account of the production of intelligibles always requires a further appeal to an emanation from the agent intellect.

Since the Avicennian texts seem to be unequivocal on this point, one might wonder what motivation Avicenna's interpreters would have for attempting to bring him into the abstractionist fold. I believe part of the answer lies in the attacks to which the emanational aspects of Avicenna's theory have been subjected from at least the time of Aquinas.[29] One way to meet such attacks is to banish the offending views by claiming that they stem from a misreading of Avicenna. Yet this does not seem to me to be the best response. As I noted at the beginning of my discussion, it is not at all clear that abstraction is the bona fide Aristotelian account of knowledge acquisition that Aquinas claimed it is. Nor, as I have tried to argue, is emanation a form of "spooky" causality as its detractors seem to assume. Rather, it is a principled theory that represents an application of Avicenna's innovative metaphysical theses to the realm of cognition.

Nor does it seem to me that Avicenna's critics from Aquinas onwards have adequately refuted his account or responded to the problems that the emanational features of his theories were meant to address. With his usual penetrating insight, Avicenna lays out the serious problems that beset theories of abstraction when they try to account for how material images can be transformed into abstract intelligibles. The same is true of the conceptual difficulties posed by the idea of memory or storage as a way of accounting for dispositional knowledge in an immaterial intellect. It is possible, of course, that the problems Avicenna raises are endemic to the Aristotelian theory of intellect, or more broadly to any immaterialist account of the mind. But if that is the case, those same problems will be faced by those peripatetics who, like Fārābī, Aquinas, and Averroes, adopted a theory of abstraction. It is to Avicenna's credit that he recognized that a theory of abstraction is in many ways a poor fit within an immaterialist philosophy of mind.

Appendix: Avicenna, *The Healing: Psychology* 5.6[30]

On Memory and the Intellect

As for things that are imagined and what is connected with them, when the soul turns away from them they are stored in faculties that are [made] for storing, and they are not in fact perceived; otherwise [those faculties] would simultaneously be both perceiving and [functioning as] a storehouse. Rather, they constitute a storehouse to which, if the perceiving, judging faculty—be it the estimation, the soul, or the intellect—returns, it will find [the forms] realized [within]. If [these faculties] do not find them, then they must be retrieved through sensing or remembering. If this were not the explanation, then in the case of every soul which is unaware of a form, it would be necessary to doubt whether this form exists [actually] or whether it is only existent in potentiality. It would also be necessary to doubt how it is retrieved, and if it were not with the soul, [to ask], "In what thing will it be?" and "With what thing would the soul conjoin so as to make this form return?"

But the animal soul has divided its faculties and made a separate organ for each faculty. Thus it has made a storehouse for the [imagined] forms to which the estimation may be inattentive, and a storehouse as well for the intentions to which the estimation may be inattentive, since the estimation is not a place for the permanence of these things, but rather it is what judges them. So let us say that the estimation may either peruse the forms and intentions stored in the domain of these two faculties, or it may turn away from them. What, then, should we now say concerning the human soul and the intelligibles which it acquires and then forgets for others? Do these exist in it in perfect actuality? For then it would necessarily be understanding them in complete actuality. Or does it have a storehouse in which it preserves them, that storehouse being either itself, or its body, or something corporeal belonging to it?

We had said that its body and what is connected with its body is not suitable for this since it is not suitable to be a place for the intelligibles. Nor is it suitable for the intelligible forms to have position; yet their conjunction with the body would make them have position, and if they came to be in the body having position, then it would nullify their being intelligibles.

Alternatively, we might say that these intelligible forms are things which are subsistent in themselves, and each form among them is a self-subsisting species of some thing.[31] The intellect would consider them at one time and turn away from them at another. When it considers them, they are represented in it, and when it turns away from them they are not represented. The soul would then be like a mirror, and [the intelligible forms] would be like external things. For sometimes they appear in it and sometimes they do not appear, this being in proportion to the relations that obtain between the soul and them.

Then again, the agent principle [i.e., the agent intellect] might emanate one form after another on the soul in accordance with the soul's seeking, such that when [the soul] turns away from it, the emanation ceases. But if this is the case, then why doesn't it need to learn again from the beginning each time?

We say: The truth is the last option. This is because it is impossible for us to say that this form is existent in the soul in perfect actuality and that [the soul] does not understand it in perfect actuality, since the meaning of 'it understands it' is nothing other than that the form exists in it. And it is impossible for the body to be a storehouse for [the form]; it is also impossible for [the soul] itself to be its storehouse, since its being a storehouse for it is nothing other than that this form is understood and existent in it; but its understanding also occurs in this way. Memory and the formative faculty [i.e., the imagination] are not like this. For the perception of this form does not belong to them, but rather, its retention alone. For its perception only belongs to another faculty. Nor does the existence of the remembered and imagined forms in something constitute their perception, just as the existence of the sensed forms in something does not constitute sensation. This is why the [external] bodies containing the sensible forms are not perceptive. Rather, perception must belong to something whose function is to be impressed by these forms in some way insofar as it is a perceptual capacity. As for memory and imagination, the forms are only impressed in them insofar as they are organs and have a body that preserves these forms close to the bearer of the perceptual capacity, namely, estimation, so that it considers them whenever it wishes, in the same way as what preserves the sensible forms close to the sense so that the sense may consider them whenever it wishes.

Memory and the imaginative faculty can support this interpretation, whereas the soul cannot support it. For the existence of the intelligible form in the soul is its very perception of it. Moreover, we shall make clear later in first philosophy [i.e., metaphysics] that this form is not subsistent in isolation.[32] Hence, it remains that the correct option is the last option. Learning would then be seeking the complete preparation for conjoining [with the agent intellect] so that from it there would come about the simple understanding from which the differentiated forms emanate into the soul through the mediation of cogitation. Thus the preparation would be incomplete prior to instruction and complete after instruction. So when one has been instructed, it would be one's nature that if something conjoined with the intelligible being sought should come to mind and the soul turns in the direction of theoretical reflection—the direction of theoretical reflection being the return to the principle that bestows the intellect[33]—it will conjoin with [this principle], and thus the power of the separate intellect emanates on it, upon which follows the emanation of what is differentiated. When the soul turns away from it, it returns and this form becomes [a form] in potency, but a potency very proximate to actuality. The first instruction is therefore like the treatment of the eye. For when the eye becomes healthy, then whenever it wishes it looks upon the thing from which it takes some form, and if whenever it turns away from it, that thing comes to be in proximate potency to actuality.

And as long as the ordinary human soul remains in the body, it is impossible for it to receive the agent intellect all at once. Rather, its condition is as we have said. So when it is said, "So and so knows the intelligibles," its meaning is that he is such that whenever he wishes he can make its form present in his own mind. The meaning of this is that whenever he wishes he has it in him to conjoin with the agent intellect by a conjunction in which he will conceptualize that intelligible from it, not in [the sense] that that intelligible is present in his mind and conceived in his intellect in actuality always, nor [in the sense that his state] is like it was prior to being instructed. Attaining this type of intellect in actuality, namely, the power that is realized in the soul through which it understands whenever it wishes, [is such that] whenever it wishes, it conjoins with [the agent intellect] and the intelligible form emanates on it. That form is in reality the acquired intellect, whereas this power is the intellect in actuality in us insofar as it is up to us to understand.

Notes

1 For one medieval account of illumination, see Noone's contribution to this volume (chapter 12). This acceptance of Avicenna was dubbed "Avicennizing Augustinianism" in Gilson (1929–30), although some of the details of Gilson's interpretation are controversial.

2 Articles accepting some version of the account in Hasse (2001), reprinted above, are Gutas (2001), Adamson (2004), McGinnis (2006), and D'Ancona (2008). McGinnis and D'Ancona both offer modifications of the thesis that attempt to address the non-abstractive elements in Avicenna's accounts of knowledge-acquisition.

3 Hasse (see above, 103) disavows a systematic approach in favor of a developmental one. McGinnis (2006, 169–70), rightly notes that "Avicenna himself thought he had a philosophical system."

4 In Avicenna's case Neoplatonic sources, in particular the Arabic Plotinus, are also influential. See D'Ancona (2008) and Adamson (2002).

5 This description of cognition is offered by Aristotle as an account of perception (*aisthēsis*), so even here there is no essential link to the process of abstracting universals from particulars. Avicenna is interpreting this formula in *Psychology* 2.2, discussed in section 3.

6 The qualification of "normally" may be required to address Avicenna's theory of intellectual prophecy. See Marmura (1963, 1964); Rahman (1958, 30–91).

7 Hasse (see above, 110–111) and McGinnis (2006, 170–71) both discuss the essence-existence distinction as it relates to abstraction.

8 On the various aspects of the essence-existence distinction see Marmura (1979, 1984a, 1992). For the account in Avicenna see *Metaphysics* 1.5 and 5.1, as well as *Isagoge* 1.12, translated in Marmura (1979). This distinction has a long legacy in the Latin West, where it is embraced by Aquinas, Henry of Ghent, and Duns Scotus, to name just a few prominent examples. The most well-known adaptation of the distinction is found in Aquinas's *On Being and Essence*, especially chapters 1, 3–4.

9 Avicenna uses many different terms for the essence: in addition to "quiddity" or "whatness," he sometimes calls it a "nature," a "reality" or a "form."

10 *Metaphysics* 1.5, §31, 226: "It is evident that each thing has a reality proper to it, namely its

quiddity. It is known that the reality proper to each thing is something other than the existence corresponding to what is affirmed."

11 Cf. *Isagoge* 1.12, in Marmura 1979, 47–49.

12 Avicenna seems to take it for granted that only separate causes can confer and conserve existence. The underlying rationale seems to be that since existence *per se* is not a function of matter, only causes whose own subsistence is independent of matter are able to effect changes that involve more than changes within a material subject.

13 For Avicenna's theory of efficient causality, see Marmura (1984b), Richardson (2008 and forthcoming).

14 *Psychology* 5.3, 221–22, trans. in McGinnis-Reisman (2007), 192; 5.5, 235, trans. in McGinnis-Reisman (2007), §1, 200. See also Rahman (1952), 54–55. Hasse above cross-list 57 emphasizes that Avicenna does not say that abstraction "only" prepares the soul in these passages. This seems forced, however: preparation language by its very nature is delimiting—it implies that the preparer is a partial cause to which something else must be added to complete the causal story.

15 Hasse (see above, 112) speaks of the "fragmentation" in Avicenna's theory of abstraction from his earlier to later works. This can't be a good thing for any philosophical theory, and I don't think one need read Avicenna that way. The theory is complex and it depends upon a number of interrelated theses in psychology and metaphysics. The appearance of fragmentation is the result of Avicenna's desire to elaborate on the component parts of the theory in the texts that are most detailed (such as the *Healing*), which often dictates treating them in conjunction with psychological doctrines that are given only cursory treatment in more compressed works.

16 For a translation of this text see the Appendix to this chapter.

17 Hasse (see above, 112, and 124), distinguishes between "the first acquisition of forms and their later reacquisition," claiming that "for the latter, it suffices to reconnect to the active intellect." But on Hasse's reading, which seems to make abstraction *sufficient* for the first acquisition of intelligibles, it's not clear how intellectual memory would involve a *re*connection to the agent intellect, nor why the agent intellect would need to act as a storehouse of intelligibles if we had abstracted them through the agent intellect's illumination. Avicenna's denial of intellectual memory is a corollary of emanation, not a supplementary theory. The attempt in Hasse (2000, 186–88) to interpret *Psychology* 5.6 as harmonious with a theory of abstraction does not attempt to address these philosophical concerns.

18 See Hasse (see above, 108–109 and 118–119) and in D'Ancona (2008). An English translation of the parallel text in Avicenna's *Salvation* can be found in Rahman (1952, 38–40).

19 For mental existence in Avicenna see Black (1999 and 2010).

20 For a full translation of this chapter, see McGinnis-Reisman (2007, 199–202).

21 The language of "transfer" (*intiqāl*) used here is characteristic of Fārābī's brief description of abstraction in his *Letter on the Intellect (Risālah fī al-'aql)*, and it is later taken up by Averroes. See Taylor (2006).

22 Avicenna continues to employ "stripping" or "peeling" as a metaphor to describe the preparatory activities of abstraction, for example, in *Demonstration* 3.5, 222–23.

23 *Ḥudūth* ("origination", "creation") indicates the coming-into-being of something insofar as it involves a temporal process, and thus it refers primarily to the activity of preparatory causes (*Metaphysics* 6.1, 263).

24 For the "vague individual" see Black (2012). While the passage quoted mentions only abstraction, a bit earlier in the discussion Avicenna has already indicated that abstraction must be joined to emanation: "But when one of us acquires the simple [terms of propositions] from sensation and imagination in the aforementioned way and their composition appears to him, these [terms] in themselves are the cause of our assent to [the propositions] *when conjoined to the divine emanation from which the preparation is not detached*" (*Demonstration* 331, emphasis added).

25 For the full text of Avicenna's discussion of intellectual memory, see the Appendix to this chapter.

26 For Avicenna's denial of cognitive identification, see Black (1999, 58–60).

27 For Avicenna's arguments against Platonic Forms, see Marmura (2006).

28 On this point, which is a major departure from Aristotle's dictum that the soul never thinks without an image (*De anima* 3.7, 431a16–17; 431b2; 3.8, 432a3–10), see *Psychology* 5.3, 222–23, and 5.5, 236–37.

29 See, for example, *ST* 1.84.4, 1.79.6. Aquinas assimilates Avicenna's view to Platonism in 1.84.4; he criticizes the implications for intellectual memory in 1.79.4.

30 From *Avicenna's De anima, Being the Psychological Part of Kitāb al-Shifā'*, ed. Rahman, 244–48. The passage follows shortly after excerpt 8, paragraph 5, in McGinnis and Reisman 2007, 204. Paragraph 6, on "The 'Sacred' Intellect," begins immediately after the excerpt translated here.

31 The second alternative Avicenna is considering here (which he goes on to reject) is that the intelligibles are Platonic forms.

32 See *Metaphysics* 7.2–3, 243–56.

33 I.e., the agent intellect.

PART V
Cosmogony and Prophetology in Maimonides

Editor's Introduction

Like their ancient predecessors, medieval philosophers generally saw themselves as seekers after wisdom. They therefore concerned themselves with uncovering and expounding truths in various subdisciplines of philosophy and science. However, as adherents of the Abrahamic religions of Judaism, Christianity, and Islam, these philosophers generally recognized a double source of truth: philosophical study and divine revelation. The allegiance to this double source grew problematic when propositions from Scripture appeared to be in tension with the conclusions of philosophical reasoning. Should philosophy guide the thinker, whose task is to interpret propositions from Scripture as harmonizing with philosophy? Or should Scripture serve as guide, providing an anchor in truth that prevents the philosopher from drifting into error? Like other philosophers in the Abrahamic tradition, Maimonides addresses these questions in his *Guide of the Perplexed*. What distinguishes Maimonides from most others is that he intentionally obscures his answers to them.

It is hard for 21st-century readers to appreciate a thinker's motives for intentionally obfuscating hard-won discoveries. We might find that such intentional dissemination of "misinformation" shows a lack of respect for the audience. However, many ancient and medieval writers looked at the matter differently. Some held the truths they had uncovered in such high regard that they wanted to shield them from the unworthy, who might misunderstand or denigrate them. Hence, they cloaked these truths with difficulties that only those with virtue and insight could penetrate. Others found certain truths too dangerous to spread broadly, since they would serve to confuse or demoralize the general population. They must therefore be kept hidden from all but those morally and intellectually prepared to learn them.

In the Introduction to the *Guide*, Maimonides explicitly informs the reader that he too will conceal certain findings, worried about their potential harm to the naive reader. The truth of his esoteric doctrine can be uncovered only by those both intellectually and morally prepared—those who can be trusted with it. One field in which Maimonides says he deliberately conceals his view is cosmogony. He sets out three competing accounts about the origin of the world—the scriptural, the Platonic, and the Aristotelian—and then proceeds to defend the scriptural view against the Aristotelian. But if the promotion of the scriptural view and the refutation of the Aristotelian constitute his exoteric teaching, what is his esoteric teaching?

Maimonides himself offers one tantalizing hint: He notes that his discussion of cosmogony parallels his discussion of prophecy, in which he likewise sets out three alternatives: the view of the vulgar, that of the philosophers, and that of (sophisticated) Judaism. Piecing together the various considerations for and against each cosmogonal view, and unearthing the connections between them and the parallel views on prophecy, Warren Zev Harvey argues that Maimonides opts for the view that best explains the phenomena, namely, the Aristotelian view that the world is eternal. This account might seem to contradict the evident teaching of the Scriptures, which report that God brought the world into existence. However, Harvey explains, Maimonides can reconcile the Aristotelian and scriptural accounts. As Maimonides points out, when Genesis asserts that God created the world "in the beginning," the Hebrew expression may be taken to mean not that God brought the world into existence *after* its nonexistence, but rather *from* its nonexistence. In that case, the claim that God created the world in the beginning would amount to the assertion that the world depends on God for its existence. Since an eternal world would depend on God's continuous causal power no less than a world of limited duration, Maimonides' esoteric view can be reconciled to the Scriptures.

Tamar Rudavsky agrees with Harvey that Maimonides strives to develop an account of creation grounded in the best philosophy and science available, which is, in his view, Aristotelian thought. Since the Aristotelian theory of time is more easily reconciled with the view that the world is eternal rather than limited in duration, Maimonides rejects the scriptural account. However, as Rudavsky points out, Maimonides' reflections on God's creating the world "in the beginning" include not just philological observations, but an engagement with the rabbinic tradition that tried to understand this scriptural claim in the light of an Aristotelian theory of time. Maimonides' openness to certain elements of this rabbinic tradition suggests that he subscribes not to the Aristotelian, but rather to the Platonic view, a view that is consistent with the Aristotelian theory of time but not incompatible with the foundations of Judaism as understood in the rabbinical tradition.

Note on References

References to Maimonides' *Guide of the Perplexed* are to book and chapter numbers.

Further Reading

- Herbert Davidson (1979). "Maimonides' Secret Position on Creation."
- Lawrence Kaplan (1977). "Maimonides on the Miraculous Element in Prophecy."
- Howard Kreisel (2001). *Prophecy: The History of an Idea in Medieval Jewish Philosophy.*
- T.M. Rudavsky (2010). *Maimonides.*
- Roslyn Weiss (2007). "Natural Order or Divine Will: Maimonides on Cosmogony and Prophecy."

CHAPTER 9

A Third Approach to Maimonides' Cosmogony-Prophetology Puzzle

WARREN ZEV HARVEY

I

Maimonides' *Guide of the Perplexed*[1] is a book of puzzles. Worried lest his radically intellectualist teachings harm the unschooled reader incapable of replacing naive faith with reasoned conviction, Maimonides took extraordinary precautions to conceal them from him. He cut up his arguments as with a jig saw, placed the pieces in careful disarray, and tossed in a goodly number of extra pieces which seemingly fit but do not. His presupposition, of course, was that any reader keen enough to piece together his puzzles would be intellectually prepared to cope with his teachings. No one will gainsay that Maimonides did a superb job of concealment. After almost eight centuries, students of the *Guide* are still trying to figure out how to solve its puzzles.[2]

One puzzle in the *Guide* concerns the relationship between cosmogony and prophetology. In *Guide*, 2.13, Maimonides describes three opinions on the creation of the world; then in 2.32, he describes three opinions on the phenomenon of prophecy, and remarks: "The opinions of people concerning prophecy are like their opinions concerning the eternity or creation of the world. I mean by this that just as the people to whose mind the existence of the deity is firmly established have, as we have set forth [in 2.13], three opinions concerning the eternity or creation of the world, so are there also three opinions concerning prophecy."[3] Maimonides does not say anything more about the relationship between the two sets of opinions, but it seems reasonable to infer that there is a correspondence between the three opinions on creation and the three opinions of prophecy.[4] What this correspondence might be, however, is certainly not evident. The puzzle before us, therefore, is: just *how* do the three opinions on creation correspond to the three opinions on prophecy? Our puzzle is particularly confusing because Maimonides' teachings on both creation and prophecy are themselves puzzles, and scholars remain until this day in wide disagreement as to what Maimonides really believed about these two subjects. To solve the puzzle of the cosmogony-prophetology correspondence, therefore, involves solving—at least in part—the two puzzles of creation and prophecy.

The cosmogony-prophetology puzzle has recently received detailed attention in two independently written essays: Lawrence Kaplan's "Maimonides on the Miraculous Element in Prophecy"[5] and Herbert Davidson's "Maimonides' Secret Position on Creation."[6] According to the solution endorsed by Kaplan, the first opinion on creation corresponds to the third opinion on prophecy, the second opinion on creation to the first on prophecy, and the third opinion on creation to the second on prophecy; i.e., 1:3, 2:1, 3:2. According to Davidson, the correspondence is 1:1, 2:3, 3:2.[7] The current discussion of this puzzle would, I think, be lacking if some words were not said in favor of the most obvious correspondence, namely, 1:1, 2:2, 3:3, and this is what I intend to do in what follows. In fact, it seems to me that this most obvious of correspondences is indeed the one intended in Maimonides' esoteric teaching.[8]

II

Before I adduce my arguments in favor of 1:1, 2:2, 3:3, it will be helpful here to set down briefly Maimonides' comments on each of the two sets of three opinions. In his presentation of both sets, Maimonides describes not only the opinions themselves but also those who hold them. The three opinions on creation in 2.13, are briefly: (1) creation of heaven and earth after absolute nonexistence[9] by God's will, (2) creation in time of heaven and earth out of eternal matter, (3) eternity *a parte ante* of heaven and earth. These three opinions are said to be held respectively by: (1) "all who believe in the Law of Moses," (2) "all of the [modern?] philosophers of whom we have heard reports and whose discourses we have seen" and also Plato, (3) Aristotle and the Aristotelians. The three opinions on prophecy in 2.32, are briefly: (1) God turns whomsoever he wishes into a prophet, (2) prophecy is a natural human perfection, (3) prophecy is a natural human perfection but can be miraculously prevented by God. These three opinions are said to be held respectively by: (1) the vulgar both among the pagans and among those who profess our Law, (2) the philosophers, (3) us, i.e., this opinion is "the opinion of our Law and the foundation of our doctrine."

Let us now proceed to the arguments in favor of 1:1, 2:2, 3:3.

III

The argument for the correspondence of 1:1 is obvious, and has been stated succinctly by Davidson: "The parallelism is perfect: both the existence of the world and the appearance of a prophet are construed as sheer miracles, the coming into being of something from nothing."[10] To be sure, 1:1 almost certainly implies that Maimonides' attribution of the first opinion on creation to "all those who believe in the Law of Moses" is not to be taken at face value, but should be revised to read: "*the vulgar* among those who believe in the Law of Moses"; for if the first opinion on creation corresponds to the vulgar opinion on prophecy, then it seems that it too is a vulgar opinion. Such a revision of Maimonides' attribution of the first opinion on creation indicates, of course, that while in his exoteric teaching Maimonides advocated this opinion, in his esoteric teaching he rejected it. This, in fact, is Davidson's view,[11] and I believe that it is correct.[12]

Kaplan, as indicated above, prefers 1:3 to 1:1, and this is of course in accordance with Maimonides' explicit claims that the first opinion on creation is held by "all who believe in the Law of Moses" and that the third opinion on prophecy is "the opinion of our Law." According to 1:3, 2:1, 3:2, the correspondence favored by Kaplan, it would seem that all believers in the Law of Moses, including Maimonides himself, hold 1:3. Kaplan, however, does not commit himself to this proposition, since he leaves open the possibility that Maimonides esoterically held 3:2. Kaplan's analysis is based on the premise (which I consider correct) that prophecy according to Maimonides is a natural human perfection. Kaplan argues accordingly that *if* Maimonides did indeed hold the belief that the world was miraculously created after absolute nonexistence by the will of God, then it would follow that he should hold that God is able to perform miracles in nature, and that God is thus able to prevent miraculously the occurrence of the natural phenomenon of prophecy (i.e., Maimonides would hold 1:3). However, Kaplan concomitantly argues, *if* Maimonides held the Aristotelian theory of eternity, then he would not be able to speak of miracles, and would simply hold that prophecy is a natural phenomenon, period (i.e., Maimonides would hold 3:2). Kaplan is forced to leave open the possibility that Maimonides held 3:2 instead of 1:3, because he does not wish to deny the possibility that Maimonides held the Aristotelian theory of eternity.[13] To my mind, however, it is inconceivable that *if* Maimonides held 1:3, 2:1, 3:2, he would endorse 3:2, for this would suggest that he was dissociating himself from the unequivocal position of the Law of Moses (viz., 1:3), i.e., that he was *rejecting* the Law of Moses in favor of Aristotelian philosophy.[14] What seems correct to me (for reasons which will be given below) is that Maimonides did hold the Aristotelian theory of eternity, but that he did not consider it to be in conflict with the true doctrine of the Law (i.e., he held 3:3). As for the argument that if Maimonides held the Aristotelian opinion on cosmogony (3) he could not speak of miracles, and thus could not hold the opinion of "the Law" on prophecy (3), it is sufficient to remark that although the Aristotelian theory of eternity, as Maimonides understands it, does indeed seem to rule out supernatural phenomena, Maimonides' mention of miracle in his presentation of the opinion of "the Law" on prophecy need not be taken as referring to a *supernatural* miracle.[15]

IV

The argument for 2:2 is based on the clear correspondence of attributions: each of the corresponding opinions is attributed to "the philosophers." Now, with regard to the second opinion on cosmogony, it is evident that "the philosophers" must be understood as "the *non-Aristotelian* philosophers," since according to Maimonides the Aristotelian philosophers did not hold the second opinion, but rather the third. If, then, Maimonides as a good Aristotelian held the third opinion on cosmogony (which I think he did, as I shall explain below), he would in effect here be setting his own opinion (3) in contradistinction to that of "the philosophers" (2). Similarly with regard to prophetology, Maimonides sets his own opinion (3) in contradistinction to that of "the philosophers" (2).

With regard to the attributions, therefore, the relationship between 2 and 3 in cosmogony seems to be analogous to that between 2 and 3 in prophetology. Moreover, there is a similar analogy with regard to the subject matter. In both the cosmogony and the prophetology discussions, 3 is presented as being like 2, with one exception. In the cosmogony discussion, it is reported that those who hold 3, like those who hold 2, assert that "something endowed with matter can by no means be brought into existence out of that which has no matter," *but* that unlike those who hold 2, they assert that "the heaven is in no way subject to generation and passing away."[16] In the prophetology discussion, similarly, it is reported that 3 is identical with 2 "except in one thing," viz., that according to 3 "it may happen that one who is fit for prophecy . . . should not become a prophet."[17]

If we are justified in arguing that the relationship between 2 and 3 in the cosmogony discussion is analogous to that between 2 and 3 in the prophetology discussion, we would certainly be justified in going one step further, and in arguing that the relationships between 1, 2, and 3 in the two discussions are analogous. Thus, 1 in both discussions is the vulgar opinion; 2 in both discussions is the "philosophic" opinion; and 3 in both discussions is the "philosophic" opinion with one exception.

Davidson, as indicated above, argues for 2:3, and thus attributes to Maimonides the Platonic view on creation (although he allows that Maimonides might after all have held 1:3).[18] That Maimonides could have held the Platonic view on creation is emphatically rejected by Kaplan, who argues (I think decisively) that in Maimonides' judgment "a doctrine that affirms that the heavens are subject to generation and passing-away in effect denies the possibility that there exists a rational, natural order," and such a doctrine would have had to have been rejected by Maimonides, who, like Aristotle, believed in "a fixed natural order."[19] Kaplan's pairing 2:1 is based on his conclusion that for Maimonides the Platonic view on creation is unscientific, and thus it should correspond to the unscientific opinion of the vulgar concerning prophecy.[20] Kaplan's argument for 2:1 is compelling, except that it is not at all clear that the second opinion on cosmogony is more unscientific than the first.

V

In my judgment, Maimonides held 3:3. In other words, he held the Aristotelian position on cosmogony (3), in spite of his exoteric support of the position that the world was created after absolute nonexistence (1); and he held the position on prophecy which he said he does (3).

The question of whether Maimonides, despite his many disclaimers, did hold the Aristotelian theory of eternity was debated by medievals and continues to be debated by moderns. As we have seen, for example, Kaplan leaves the question open (maintaining that Maimonides held *either* 1:3 or 3:2) and Davidson answers negatively (maintaining that Maimonides held 2:3 or alternatively 1:3).[21] It seems to me, however, that there is ample evidence in the *Guide* to indicate that Maimonides did advocate the Aristotelian theory, and some of this evidence will be summarized presently. Before this summary, however, two comments are in order.

First, to avoid a common misunderstanding, it should be emphasized that to conclude that Maimonides held Aristotle's theory of eternity is *not* to say that he denied creation, and it is *not* to say that he denied religion; rather, it is to say that he denied what he considered to be the vulgar notion of creation and the vulgar notion of religion. Thus already in the thirteenth century, the philosophically astute kabbalist Abraham Abulafia argued in his esoteric commentary on the *Guide* that it is an error to consider the creation and eternity of the world as exclusive disjuncts, for the world may be *both* created (*ḥadaš*) and eternal *a parte ante* (*qadmon*).[22] According to Abulafia, the notion of continuous or eternal creation is found, for example, in the words of the morning prayer, "He creates [*mĕḥaddeš*] each day continuously [*tamid*] the work of creation."[23] The compatibility of creation and eternity was not infrequently affirmed in the medieval Maimonidean literature. In his well known commentary on the *Guide*, for example, the fourteenth-century Maimonidean philosopher, Moses of Narbonne, speaks of the crucial theological importance in Maimonides' system of the proposition of "the eternity of the world, which is to say, the eternal creation [*ha-bĕri'a haniṣḥit*]."[24]

Second, it should be remarked that to conclude that Maimonides held Aristotle's theory of eternity is *not* to say that he thought that the theory had been proved. His explicit statements to the effect that the theory has not been proved are, it seems clear to me, to be accepted as straightforward expressions of his true opinion.[25] However, if Maimonides thought that the theory had not been proved, he *also* thought that Aristotle himself did not think it proved.[26] Maimonides, as far as I understand him, embraced the theory of eternity for the same reason that he thought Aristotle had embraced it: namely, it conforms to the nature of what exists, i.e., it conforms to our empirical observation of the continuous motion of the heavens.[27]

We turn now to our summary of the evidence on behalf of Maimonides' advocacy of the Aristotelian theory of eternity.

To begin with, Maimonides states in *Guide*, 1.71, that in his proofs for the existence, unity, and incorporeality of God (in 2.1–2), and in his discussion of these subjects in his works on rabbinic law (e.g., *Mišne Tora*, Yĕsode ha-Tora, 1), he always presupposes the *eternity of the World* in order "not to cause the true opinion . . . to be supported by a foundation [viz., the doctrine of creation after nonexistence] that everyone can shake and wish to destroy, while other men think that it has never been constructed."[28] Maimonides, it is true, claims that his presupposition of the eternity of the world is merely methodological, and does not imply his commitment to it.[29] Nevertheless, an examination of Maimonides' proofs in Guide, 2.1–2, testifies that *our knowledge of God* is based on the Aristotelian premise of eternity.[30] More significantly, in my opinion, an examination of Maimonides' statements in his great Code, the *Mišne Tora*, reveals that the Aristotelian premise of eternity is indeed *required* for the fulfillment of the divine *commandments* to know God and to know that he is one,[31] and that Abraham our father had in fact come to know God on the basis of the Aristotelian premise of eternity.[32]

Again, an examination of Maimonides' comments in the *Guide* on the biblical narrative of creation shows that for him the Hebrew word *bara'* ("created") in the first verse of Genesis does not designate coming into being *after* nonexistence (Arabic: *ba'd al-'adam*), but rather coming into being *from* nonexistence (Arabic: *min al-'adam*), which seems to mean that it designates the continuous ontic dependence of creation on Creator, or if you will, the continuous information of matter by the Form of the world.[33] Similarly, according to Maimonides, the first word in Genesis, *bĕ-rešit* ("In the beginning"), does not refer to a *temporal* beginning, but rather to a "principle" (Arabic: *mabda'*) in the philosophic sense of the Greek *archē*.[34] Moreover, the Arabic word *al-bāri'* ("Creator") occurs in the *Guide* more than twenty times in contexts which are at least compatible with the Aristotelian theory of eternity, but *not even once* in a context suggesting the doctrine of creation after nonexistence.[35]

Again, Maimonides reports in *Guide*, 2.28, that "many adherents of our Law" attributed to King Solomon the belief in the eternity of the world. Although Maimonides makes a point of protesting that Solomon could not have harbored such a belief, his explication of the scriptural verses in question gives the distinct impression that Solomon did indeed hold the Aristotelian position.[36]

Again, Maimonides hints that three distinguished rabbis held the theory of eternity. On the basis of a dictum in the *Chapters of Rabbi Eliezer*, Maimonides suggests in *Guide*, 2.26, that the tanna Rabbi Eliezer ben Hyrcanus held that the "throne of glory" is the heavens (i.e., the celestial spheres or, perhaps more precisely, the diurnal sphere), and that it is eternal *a parte ante*.[37] On the basis of dicta of the amoraim Rabbi Abbahu and Rabbi Judah ben Simon, Maimonides suggest in *Guide*, 2.30, that they held the eternity *a parte ante* of time.[38]

Finally, what on the face of it appears to be fundamentally objectionable to Maimonides in the Aristotelian theory of eternity is that it denies God's will and affirms necessity.[39] Inspection of the relevant texts, however, shows that Maimonides does speak of God's "volition" (Arabic: *irāda)* in his presentation of Aristotle's theory of eternity.[40] Besides, Maimonides' teaching that God's will, wisdom, and essence are one and inscrutable effectively strips the concept of God's will of any cognitive meaning.[41] Similarly, Maimonides claims that as opposed to Aristotle who had held that all things exist by divine necessity, he holds that they exist by divine *purpose*.[42] However, he completely neutralizes this claim when he subsequently pronounces that the word "purpose" is used equivocally when applied to the purposes of men and of God.[43] Moreover, in several critical texts Maimonides openly advances the doctrine of divine necessity.[44] It is noteworthy in this connection that in explaining Aristotle's notion of the necessary derivation of the world from God, Maimonides writes in *Guide*, 2.20, that "this necessity is somewhat like the necessity of the derivation of an intellectum from an intellect,"[45] words which recall his own position put forth in 1.68, concerning the unity of intellect and intellectum in God.[46] In fine, if both Aristotle and Maimonides maintain the doctrine of divine necessity, and if both also speak about divine will, then on the allegedly crucial question of divine necessity and divine will there is no evident difference between Aristotle and Maimonides. What had been thought to be Maimonides' fundamental objection to Aristotle's theory of eternity now appears to be no objection at all.

Much more could be said in support of the proposition that Maimonides held the Aristotelian theory of the eternity of the world, but this is not the place to elaborate on the problem, and in any case the preceding summary of the evidence suffices for our purposes.[47] Having indicated the grounds for assigning to Maimonides the third opinion on creation, let us now examine the grounds for assigning to him the third opinion on prophecy.

At the outset, we may state that Maimonides' position on prophecy is not nearly as problematic as his position on creation. Surely he did not hold the opinion of "the vulgar" (1). It is imaginable, however, that despite his explicit affirmation of the opinion of "the Law" (3), he really held the opinion of "the philosophers" (2). The view that Maimonides esoterically held the opinion of "the philosophers" has been entertained by some medieval and modern commentators, and—as we have seen—it is left open as a possibility by Kaplan.[48] However, there does not seem to me to be any good reason to reject Maimonides' explicit affirmation of the opinion of "the Law." For as Kaplan's highly sensitive reading of Maimonides' statements on prophecy in *Guide*, 2.32, shows conclusively,[49] there is no essential distinction between the theory of prophecy of "the philosophers" (2) and that of "the Law" (3). Now if there is no essential distinction between 2 and 3, then there would seem to be no good reason to insist that Maimonides held 2 instead of 3. The proviso mentioned in Maimonides' presentation of 3 which is not found in his presentation of 2, viz., that God can miraculously prevent prophecy, has—as Kaplan explains—nothing whatsoever to do with the theory of prophecy proper. The point of the proviso is simply that according to the Law miracles *can* happen (even though they may be interpreted as purely natural phenomena), and thus just as God (to use Maimonides' own examples) miraculously prevented King Jeroboam from moving his hand (1 Kgs 13:4), and just as he miraculously prevented the soldiers of the King of Aram's army from seeing (2 Kgs 6:18), so too he can miraculously prevent a person naturally fit to prophesy from prophesying.[50] The question of just what Maimonides had in mind by his curious reference to the miracle of preventing prophecy need not detain us here.[51] What is important is only that according to Maimonides the Law has a notion of miracle and the philosophers do not, and that Maimonides—for reasons which have nothing to do with his epistemology of prophecy—accepts the notion of miracle (even if he interprets all miracles as natural phenomena).[52]

In affirming that there is no essential distinction between the theory of prophecy of "the philosophers" (2) and that of "the Law" (3), we are in effect pointing to a significant parallel between 2 and 3 in cosmogony and 2 and 3 in prophetology. For with regard to the opinions on cosmogony, Maimonides tells us explicitly that in essence there is "no difference" between the opinion of "the philosophers" (2) and that of Aristotle (3), since both entail the belief in eternity *a parte ante*,[53] or—to put it another way—both preclude the doctrine of temporal creation after nonexistence, and both cohere with that of eternal creation, i.e., with the doctrine that "creation" refers to the ontic or causal dependence of the world upon God.[54] We have already observed (see above, section IV) that in both the cosmogony and prophetology discussions, 3 is presented as being just like 2 but with one exception. It now appears that we may add that in both cases this one exception is not essential to the issue at hand. Just as with regard to cosmogony the essential choice is between the unscientific opinion of "creation after nonexistence" (1) and the scientific opinion of eternal creation (2, 3), so with regard to prophetology the essential choice is between the unscientific opinion of prophecy as a supernatural phenomenon (1) and the scientific opinion of prophecy as a natural phenomenon (2, 3). Moreover, it seems that both with regard to cosmogony and prophetology Maimonides chose 3 over 2 for reasons which have to do with his naturalistic theory of miracles,[55] or more generally with his belief (which is neither part of his doctrine of creation proper nor part of his doctrine of prophecy proper, but which of course influences both these doctrines) that *all* phenomena are to be understood in accordance with "the nature of what exists."[56]

VI

In what has preceded, I have tried to present the basic arguments for the correspondence 1:1, 2:2, 3:3, as the solution to the cosmogony-prophetology puzzle of *Guide*, 2.13 and 32. Admittedly, solutions to the puzzles of the *Guide* are never apodictic. It can always be argued that wrong pieces have been crassly forced into critical places in the puzzle, and that the pretty picture intended by Maimonides has been distorted out of recognition. However, I believe that a comparison of the three suggested solutions will show that 1:1, 2:2, 3:3 is not less likely than 1:3, 2:1, 3:2, or 1:1, 2:3, 3:2; and even if it is concluded that all three are equally likely, then I believe the nod should be given to 1:1, 2:2, 3:3, simply because it is, after all, the obvious correspondence, and unless there are reasons to think otherwise it may be supposed that this is the correspondence that Maimonides had in mind.

In any case, my purpose in writing down the foregoing comments on the cosmogony-prophetology puzzle was simply to contribute to the current discussion of the puzzle by presenting a third approach for the consideration of students of the *Guide*. I do not delude myself that I have solved the puzzle to everyone's satisfaction, and I know that even those readers who will agree with me about the solution may disagree with me about the reasons I have put forth in its defense, and perhaps they will find even better reasons.

Notes

1. Page references to the *Guide* will be to Shlomo Pines's English translation (Maimonides [1963]), although in quotations this translation may sometimes be modified.
2. In his Introduction to the *Guide* (pp. 5–20), Maimonides advises his philosophic reader (cf. p. 10, l. 21, and n. 24) on how to uncover the esoteric meaning of the book. E.g., he writes: "If you wish to grasp the totality of what this treatise contains . . . then you must connect its chapters one with another; and when reading a given chapter, your intention must be not only to understand the totality of the subject of that chapter, but also to grasp each word that occurs in it . . . even if that word does not belong to the intention of the chapter. For the diction of this treatise has not been chosen at haphazard . . . and nothing has been mentioned out of its place, save with a view of explaining some matter in its proper place" (p. 15). A valuable key to Maimonides' esoteric teaching in his discourse on the "seven causes" of contradictory and contrary statements (pp. 17–20), and perhaps in particular his comments on the *seventh* cause: "In speaking about very obscure matters, it is necessary to conceal. . . . Sometimes . . . this necessity requires that the discussion proceed [in one place] on the basis of a certain premise, whereas in another place [it] proceeds on the basis of another premise contradicting the first one. In such cases, the vulgar must in no way be aware of the contradiction; the author accordingly uses some device to conceal it by all means" (p. 18). On the esotericism of the *Guide*, see Leo Strauss (1952) 38–94; and his "How to Begin to Study *The Guide of the Perplexed*," in Pines's translation of the *Guide*, xi–lvi.
3. *Guide*, 360.

4. As Isaac Abrabanel observes in his Commentary on *Guide*, 2.32, if the only similarity between the two sets of opinions were the number 3, then Maimonides might as well have said that the opinions on prophecy are like the Patriarchs, or like any other trio. See *More Nĕbukim* (Maimonides [1872]) 66a. Abrabanel's observation is translated in Reines (1970) 4–5.
5. Kaplan (1977).
6. Davidson (1979).
7. The solution endorsed by Kaplan was, it seems, first explicitly suggested by the sixteenth-century rabbinic scholar Mordecai Jaffe, and has been held in the present century by S. Atlas and J. Kafih (see Kaplan, [1977] 249–50). The solution endorsed by Davidson is what Kaplan calls "the standard explanation of the correspondence"; it was explained in detail by Abrabanel and has been accepted by modern scholars like S. Munk, M. Friedländer, Z. Diesendruck, and Reines (see Kaplan [1977] 251–52 n. 42).
8. I have not seen this solution suggested in either the medieval or modern literature. However, it is perhaps implicit in the esoteric comments of some of the medievals.
9. This opinion, according to which the world was created "*after* absolute pure nonexistence (Arabic: *ba'd al-'adam al-maḥḍ al-muṭlaq*)" (p. 281, 11. 8–9), is *not* identical with the opinion that the world was created *ex nihilo* (Arabic: *min al-'adam*). It implies that *before* creation there had been nonexistence, whereas the opinion of creation *ex nihilo* may be interpreted to signify the continuous creation of existence out of nonexistence, or the eternal information of matter (=*nihil*). In other words, it is incompatible with the with the theory of the eternity of time, whereas the opinion of creation *ex nihilo* is compative with it. See Klein-Braslavy (1978) 81–90. The distinction between creation after nonexistence and creation *ex nihilo* is ignored by both Kaplan and Davidson, as well as by most scholars who have written on Maimonides' cosmogony. On concepts of creation in mediaeval Arabic literature, see Wolfson (1976) 355–72.
10. Davidson (1979) 23. "Nothing" must be understood here as "no matter" (see previous note).
11. Ibid., 24–26. On p. 36, however, Davidson expresses reservations about this view (and, indeed, about his entire analysis of Maimonides' position on creation), both on the grounds that the evidence he has assembled is "not unambiguous," and on the grounds that Maimonides may have been "less immune to error and carelessness than he and his readers through the centuries have imagined." While on the cosmogony Davidson thus expresses uncertainty as to whether Maimonides held 1 or 2, he voices no doubt that on prophetology Maimonides held 3. In his view, therefore, Maimonides' own position on the cosmogony-prophetology correspondence is if not 2:3, then 1:3. That 1:3 is (according to his own analysis) composed of *non*-corresponding opinions would presumably be taken by Davidson simply as evidence that Maimonides did not, as the "thoroughgoing esotericists" suppose, write the *Guide* with "exceeding precision" (see p. 25).
12. With regard to the possible objection that Maimonides had to have held the first opinion on creation since it is necessary for his conception of prophecy, see Maimonides' instructions to his reader in *Guide*, 1.71: "You should not ask how prophecy can be true if the world is eternal, before you have heard our discourse concerning prophecy" (p. 181). This comment, as Pines observes, "tends to produce the impression that prophecy can be true (or valid) even if the world is eternal" (Introduction to his translation of the *Guide*, cxxviii n. 115). However, whatever "impression" this comment produces, its plain meaning is that until the reader has studied Maimonides' discourse on prophecy, he has no right to conclude that the doctrine of creation after nonexistence is necessary for Maimonides' conception of prophecy. Now, Maimonides' discourse on prophecy begins at *Guide*, 2.32, and ends at 2.48. Since Maimonides' presentation of the three opinions on prophecy appears in 2.32, right at the beginning of that discourse, it is obvious that in examining that presentation the reader has no right to presume that only the first opinion on creation is compatible with Maimonides' conception of prophecy. See also Maimonides' affirmation of the compatibility of prophecy and eternity in *Guide*, 2.16, p. 294.
13. Kaplan (1977) 256.

14. That Maimonides considered Judaism and philosophy to be mutually exclusive has admittedly been maintained by Leo Strauss in several works; e.g., *Persecution* (1952) 42–43, and "How to Begin to Study the *Guide*" (Maimonides [1963]) xiv. Strauss thereby raises the question of whether Maimonides in his esoteric doctrine did indeed ultimately reject the Law of Moses for Aristotelian philosophy. Cf. also Pines's remark: "that Maimonides realized the true issue between philosophy and religion, or religious Law, does not necessarily mean that . . . he . . . chose religion" (Introduction to his translation of the *Guide* [1963] cxxviii). Nonetheless, I think that there is no justified doubt about Maimonides' uncompromising commitment to the Law of Moses, even if it is *also* true (as I think it is) that his commitment to philosophy was likewise uncompromising. On the integration of Judaism and philosophy in Maimonides, see Twersky (1967) and (1980); Hyman (1967) and (1976); Hartman (1976); and see my review of Hartman's book (Harvey [1979]) and Harvey (1980).
15. In *Guide*, 2.25, p. 328, Maimonides comments that Aristotle's theory of eternity would not contradict the Law if miracles are "interpreted"; and in 2.29, pp. 345–46, he suggests that miracles are "in nature." See also Maimonides' *Eight Chapters* (1912) 90–91 and in Maimonides (1975) 87–88.
16. *Guide*, 2.13, p. 284.
17. Ibid., 2.32, p. 361.
18. See above, n. 11.
19. "Maimonides on the Miraculous Element," 250, 253.
20. Ibid., 249–51.
21. Kaplan's view that on cosmogony Maimonides held 1 or 3 but surely not 2 is corroborated with extensive evidence by Klein-Braslavy (1978) (summary of findings, 256, 266). Davidson's view that on cosmogony Maimonides held 1 or 2 but surely not 3 has been held recently by some other scholars, e.g., Feldman (1971); however, the evidence for this view is not convincing, being based on unargued rhetorical statements of Maimonides, e.g., at *Guide*, 2.25, p. 330. Cf. below, n. 55.
22. *Sitre Tora*, MS. Paris, hébr. 768 (Hebrew University Microfilm, no. 12327) 137b–40b; MS. Paris, hébr. 774 (Hebrew University Microfilm, no 12332) 147b–49b.
23. Ibid., MS. 768, p. 140a; MS. 774, p. 149a. A similar use of this phrase (from the *yoṣer 'or* blessing preceding the morning reading of the *Šĕma*) is found, e.g., in Isaac Albalag (1973) 31, 1. 1; in *Or Adonay* book III A, 1, 5, (24viii, 1. 16 in Crescas [1555]); in Joseph Solomon Delmedigo (1631) 97b, 1. 20; and in modern times in Rosenzweig (1971) Introduction and 2.111. Another liturgical text cited by Abulafia (*loc. cit.*) as indicating the notion of eternal creation is "today is the birth of the world" (Additional Service, New Year, after sounding of ram's horn).
24. Moses Narboni (1852) Introduction, lb, 1. 18. Cf. "Epistle on *Shi'ur Qomā*" (Altmann [1967b]) 259, 1. 128 (trans., pp. 276–77), where Narboni—like Abulafia (see preceding note)—cites the prayer, "today is the birth of the world." On the compatibility of creation and eternity in the medieval Hebrew philosophic literature, cf. also, e.g., the references to Albalag, Crescas, and Delmedigo in the preceding note. A recent study of the theory of eternal creation in late Antiquity and in the Middle Ages is Feldman (1980). Feldman, however, does not consider the possibility that Maimonides held the theory (cf. above, n. 21).
25. E.g., *Guide*, 1.71, p. 180; 2. Introduction, 241; 2.15–16; 2.17, p. 298; 2.19, pp. 307–8; 2.22. p. 320; 2.23, p. 322; 2.25, pp. 328, 330. On Maimonides' general skepticism, see Pines (1979).
26. *Guide*, 2. Introduction, 240; 2.15, pp. 289–92; 2.19, pp. 307–8.
27. "For [Aristotle's] opinion [concerning eternity] is nearer to correctness than the opinions of those who disagree with him insofar as inferences are made from the nature of what exists [Arabic: *min tabī'at al-wujūd*]" (*Guide*, 2.15, p. 292; cf. 3.17, p. 468). "That which exists [al-wujūd] does not conform to the various opinions, but rather the correct opinions conform to that which exists" (ibid., 1.71, p. 179). Similarly, Maimonides remarks that his proofs for the existence, unity, and incorporeality of God—which presuppose the eternity of the world (see following note)—are "derived from the nature of existence [*min tabī'at al-wujūd*] that

can be perceived and that is not denied except with a view to safeguarding certain opinions" (ibid., 182). Cf. Maimonides' summation of the arguments for creation after nonexistence put forward by the Kalam: "they have abolished the nature of what exists [*tabī'at al-wujūd*] and have altered the original disposition of the heavens and the earth by thinking that by means of these premises it would be demonstrated that the world was created in time . . . [and thus they] have destroyed for us the demonstrations of the existence and oneness of the Deity and of the negation of His corporeality, for [these] demonstrations . . . can only be taken from the permanent nature of what exists [*min tabī'at al-wujūd*], a nature which can be seen and apprehended by the senses and the intellect" (ibid., 1.76, pp. 230–31; cf. 1.71, pp. 179–81). In sum, science has no choice but to base itself on "that which exists," even when dealing with questions which apparently cannot be absolutely decided on that basis.

28. *Guide*, 1.71, p. 182.
29. Ibid., Cf. also 1.76, p. 231; 2. Introduction, 235, 239.
30. I.e., on premise 26 ("time and motion are eternal, perpetual, and existing *in actu*"), *Guide*, 2. Introduction, 239–40. Not only does this premise figure critically in Maimonides' proofs, but apparently there can be no such proofs without them, "for [these] demonstrations . . . can only be taken from the permanent nature of what exists" (see above, n. 27).
31. See Maimonides (1962), Yĕsode ha-Tora 1:1–7, where God's existence (1:5) and unity and incorporeality (1:7) are inferred from the empirical observation that "the [diurnal] sphere spins continuously"; that this phrase is understood by Maimonides as denoting the Aristotelian theory of eternity is clear from Maimonides' remarks in *Guide*, 2.2, p. 252. Cf. Harvey (1981a). Cf. also Strauss (1967) and Twersky (1980) 448 n. 224.
32. *Book of Knowledge*, 'Akum 1:3, where Abraham (in the spirit of Yĕsode ha-Tora 1:7; cf. preceding note) is portrayed as having inferred the existence of God from the continuous spinning of the diurnal sphere.
33. *Guide*, 2.30, p. 358; 3.10, p. 438. Cf. above, n. 9. And see Klein-Braslavy (1978) 81–82, 86–87.
34. *Guide*, 2.30, pp. 348–49. Cf. Klein-Braslavy (1978) 114–31. And cf. Hasdai Crescas's interpretation in Wolfson (1929) 290–91, 664 nn. 34–35.
35. See Nuriel (1964); cf. I. Ravitsky's (1966) response. The word *ai-bārī'* occurs in *Guide*, 1.10, p. 36; 1.15, p. 41; 1.22, p. 52; 1.51, p. 113; 1.53 (twice), pp. 119, 122; 1.56, p. 130; 1.68, p. 165 (overlooked by Nuriel); 1.69 (four times), pp. 169–70; 2.11, p. 274; 2.12, p. 279; 2.14, p. 288 (in explicit reference to the Aristotelian theory of eternity); 2.19, p. 302 (in explicit reference to the Aristotelian theory of eternity); 2.20, p. 313 (in explicit reference to the Aristotelian theory of eternity); 3.12, p. 446 (cf. p. 443, 1. 3, where the underlying Arabic is *bāri'hu*); 3.13 (twice), pp. 448, 451. Maimonides, it may be remarked further, shows similar care with regard to the use of the Hebrew *bore'* ("Creator") in the *Book of Knowledge*. Strauss (1967) has called attention to Maimonides' avoidance of the Hebrew root *br'* in Yĕsode ha-Tora 1 (n. 31, 272). The first text in which a derivative of this root is predicated of God is Yĕsode ha-Tora 2:3, where the verb *bara'* is used in a context identical to that of *al-bāri' in Guide*, 2.11.
36. Thus, Maimonides states (p.334) that "people thought" that Solomon's words, "And the earth abideth forever [*lĕ'olam*]" (Eccl 1:4), indicate the eternity *a parte ante* of the world. However, he goes on to explain that "the word '*olam* does not signify [only] eternity *a parte post* unless it is conjoined with the word '*ad*"; but in the verse in question '*olam* is *not* conjoined with '*ad* (p. 335). It seems to be implied, therefore, that these words of Solomon's—as well as similar texts where '*olam* appears without '*ad* (e.g., Eccl 3:4, cited on pp. 335–36; but perhaps Gen 21:33, cf. references on p. 645)—do indeed indicate the eternity *a parte ante* of the world.

    Maimonides' exegeses in *Guide*, 2.28, are followed closely by Spinoza in *A Theologico-Political Treatise*, 6 (Spinoza [1951]) 96 (on Ps 148:6, Jer 31:35, and esp. on Eccl 1:1–9 and 3:14). On Eccl 1:9, cf. also Maimonides *Eight Chapters* 8 (1912), p. 90, and Weiss-Butterworth (1975), p. 87.
37. See also *Guide*, 1.9 and 70. Note the different interpretations of Lam 5:19 in 1.9 (p. 35; cf. 1.10, p. 37) and in 2.26 (p. 331); in this verse '*olam* appears without '*ad* (see preceding note),

and so its meaning is not restricted to eternity *a parte post*. In 3.2 (p. 422; on Ezek 1:26), the throne of glory has been understood by some medieval and modern commentators as symbolizing the convexity of the diurnal sphere. On the throne of glory in the *Guide*, see Klein-Braslavy (1978), 89, 132; Ravitzky (1977) 258–63, cf. 236 n. 1; Wolfson (1942) 78–79, (2. 115–16 in the 1977 reprint); Wolfson (1979) 113–20. Cf. G. Vajda (1962) 412, s.v. "Trône (de Gloire)"; M. Idel (1975) 150, 152–53.

38. Cf. Klein-Braslavy (1978) 228–45.
39. See *Guide*, 2.19–21.
40. Ibid., 2.13, p. 284, lines 30–31 ("all that exists has been brought into existence . . . by God through his volition").
41. Cf. ibid., 1.53, p. 122; 1.69, p. 170; 2.18, p. 302; 3.13, p. 456.
42. Ibid., 2.19, p. 303; 2.21, pp. 316–17.
43. Ibid., 3.20, p. 483; cf. 2.18, p. 301; 2.21, p. 315.
44. E.g., "the works of the Deity . . . are of necessity permanently established as they are, for there is no possibility of something calling for a change in them" (ibid., 2.28, p. 335; note the exegesis of Deut 32:4 on p. 336, and cf. 1.16, p. 42, and 3.25, p. 506). Cf. below, n. 46.
45. Pp. 313–314.
46. Cf. "His knowledge of things is not derived from them. . . . On the contrary, the things . . . follow upon His knowledge, which preceded and established them as they are. . . . He also knows the totality of what necessarily derives from all His acts" (3.21, p. 485.)
47. As Klein-Braslavy remarks, the very existence of ambiguities in Maimonides' position on creation is itself evidence that he held the theory of eternity: "If Maimonides had been of the opinion that the world was created [after nonexistence], he would have said it . . . explicitly and unequivocally, for the opinion of creation [after nonexistence] is the view acceptable to the vulgar man" (1978, 256). If Maimonides' ambiguities were intended to conceal something from the vulgar, it surely was not the doctrine of the creation of the world after absolute nonexistence!
48. See above, n. 13. Regarding the medievals, see Kaplan (1977), 240.
49. Ibid., 247–48.
50. "[W]ould anyone argue," asks Kaplan rhetorically, "that it is a fundamental principle of [the Law's] theory of vision that God can miraculously blind a person or that it is a fundamental principle of [the Law's] physiology that God can paralyze a person's arm?" (ibid., 248).
51. See ibid., 238–48, 252–53. However, *pace* Kaplan (237–38 n. 18), I suspect that Yĕsode ha-Tora 7:5 *does* underlie Maimonides' reference to the miraculous prevention of prophecy (cf. Yĕsode ha-Tora 7:5 with the problematic phrase in *Guide*, 2.32, discussed by Kaplan on 246–47 n. 38). See following note.
52. It may be argued that since according to Maimonides *all* miracles (including of course those recorded in 1 Kgs 13:4 and 2 Kgs 6:18) are natural phenomena (see above, n. 15), the provision about the miracle in the opinion of "the Law" (3) on prophecy is wholly meaningless, and that consequently there is *absolutely* (i.e., not only essentially) no distinction between the opinion of "the philosophers" (2) and that of "the Law" on prophecy. However, it seems to me that it is a mistake to equate the naturalistic interpretation of miracles with the denial of all meaning to the notion of miracle, just as it is a mistake to conclude that a thoroughgoing physical determinist can have no use for terms such as "will," "accident," or "luck." In point of fact, Maimonides himself seems to have been a thoroughgoing physical determinist (see Pines [1960] and Altmann [1974]), and there are analogies and connections between his treatment of will, accident, and luck, and his treatment of miracle (cf., e.g., *Guide*, 2.48). Altmann (1974) 41 has called attention to the "striking parallel" between Maimonides' comments in *Guide*, 2.32, concerning the miraculous prevention of prophecy, and his comments in *Eight Chapters*, 8 ([1912] 95–96, [1975] 90–91) concerning the miraculous prevention of human choice. While in *Guide*, 2.32, Maimonides likens the prevention of prophecy to the prevention of motion from Jeroboam's hand and the prevention of sight from the King of Aram's soldiers, in the *Eight Chapters* he had likened the prevention of prophecy to the

prevention of motion from Jeroboam's hand and the prevention of sight from the Sodomites (Gen 19:11). It is most likely that the case of both the miraculous prevention of human choice and the miraculous prevention of prophecy (which itself may be seen as an instance of the miraculous prevention of human choice), Maimonides had in mind a certain phenomenon (probably psychological, but possibly physical or political) which prevents human beings from acting in accordance with their natural abilities. Regarding the prevention of human choice, see also *Book of Knowledge*, Tĕsuba 6:3. On the relationship between Maimonides' theory of human choice and his statement that God may miraculously prevent prophecy, cf. Goldman 1970. According to Goldman's analysis of Maimonides, "the divine will which is spoken of in connection with prophecy is none other than the choice of the prophet" (210), and similarly the divine will which can prevent prophecy is none other than "human choice, whose source is the preeternai divine will" (208–9).

53. *Guide*, 2.13, p. 285.
54. Maimonides' statement (ibid., 283) that according to the opinion of "the philosophers" (2), "there exists a certain matter that is eternal . . . and that [God] does not exist without it, nor it . . . without Him [cf. 1.9, p. 35, on Lam 5:19; cf. above, n. 37] . . . [but that this matter does not have] the same rank in what exists as He . . . but He is the cause of its existence," holds good also according to the Aristotelian opinion (3).
55. Regarding cosmogony, the only "argument" mentioned by Maimonides in favor of 2 as opposed to 3 is that according to 2 "all the [biblical] miracles [taken literally] become possible" (*Guide*, 2.25, pp. 329–30); but given Maimonides' views on the "fixed natural order" (cf. Kaplan's remarks cited above, n. 19), it seems that this is really an argument *against* 2! Davidson (1979), to be sure, thinks otherwise (see 20–22); cf. above, n. 21. Similarly with regard to prophetology, it is the theory of miracles (however it is to be understood) which separates the otherwise identical 2 and 3.
56. See above, n. 27.

CHAPTER 10

Cosmogony and Prophetology in Maimonides' *Guide of the Perplexed*: A Reappraisal

T. M. RUDAVSKY

1. Introduction

Maimonides' major philosophical work *The Guide of the Perplexed*[1] was addressed to his student Joseph son of Judah, who had travelled from afar to study with him. When Joseph returned to Aleppo, Maimonides wrote the *Guide*, he tells us, as a "guide" for Joseph and other scholars like him. Maimonides' work is both literally and figuratively a guide, an intellectual road leading the philosophically perplexed individual back to the center, back to truth. But Maimonides complicates matters by distinguishing in the work itself two levels of interpretation, exoteric and esoteric, suggesting that it is sometimes incumbent upon a philosopher to conceal his own esoteric position behind the veil of exoteric doctrine. He enjoins his own student not to divulge his secret teachings to others. Maimonides thus introduces an ambiguity into the very reading and understanding of his texts, an ambiguity that has persisted to this day.

Nowhere is this ambiguity more apparent than in Maimonides' discussion of creation and prophecy, two topics that have received much critical attention in recent years. Maimonides characterizes the doctrine of creation as an extremely challenging as well as volatile topic, precisely the sort of issue deserving of an esoteric presentation. Prophecy, one of the "mysteries of the Torah" (*Guide* 1.35:80), is included among the obscure matters as well, suggesting to the astute reader that Maimonides will present many, often contradictory, positions on the nature of prophecy. Warren Zev Harvey's article (chapter 9, this volume) represents a recent attempt to reconcile the often cryptic comments pertaining to the relationship between cosmogony and prophetology. In what follows, we shall first lay out the basic features of Maimonides' twofold discussion, and then turn to a critique of Harvey's interpretation.

2. Creation and Prophecy Models in Maimonides

Guide 2.13 presents three opinions on creation, followed in *Guide* 2.32 by three opinions on prophecy; Maimonides notes that "the opinions of people concerning prophecy are *like* their opinions concerning the eternity of the world or its creation in time" (*Guide* 2.32:360, emphasis mine). Scholars throughout the centuries have jumped upon the apparent equation between these two listings and have wondered about the significance of the word "like." Is the word "like" supposed to posit a one-to-one correspondence between the two sets of opinions, or does it merely signify that both prophecy and creation can be reduced to three opinions? If the former, can Maimonides' own position be linked with any one set of correspondences, or is his allegiance split? In answer to these questions, interpreters have suggested every possible combination of opinions, and have offered every possible strategy for determining which is Maimonides' own view. Readers of the *Guide* who turn to chapters 2.13–30, which are devoted to creation, have thus been forewarned by the author to expect a modicum of ambiguity at best, or outright secrecy at worst.

The three standard views of creation can be summarized as follows:

> (C1) *The scriptural view*: that the universe was brought into existence by God after "having been purely and absolutely nonexistent"; through his will and his volition, God brought into "existence out of nothing all the beings as they are, time itself being one of the created things."
> (*Guide* 2.13:281)

> (C2) *The Platonic view*: that inasmuch as even God cannot create matter and form out of absolute nonexistence (since this constitutes an ontological impossibility and so does not impute impotence to God), there "exists a certain matter that is eternal as the deity is eternal. . . He is the cause of its existence . . . and . . . He creates in it whatever he wishes."
> (*Guide* 2.13:283)

> (C3) *The Aristotelian view*: that matter cannot be created from absolute nonexistence, concluding that the heavens are not subject to generation/corruption and that "time and motion are perpetual and everlasting and not subject to generation and passing-away."
> (*Guide* 2.13:284)

Each of these views carries with it both metaphysical and theological implications. The first (C1) clearly reflects the first words of Genesis and postulates creation after absolute nonexistence. Maimonides notes that this position is incompatible with the eternity of time, and entails not only that God brought the world into existence after absolute non-existence but that time itself is created. The last position (C3) can be seen as postulating an eternally beginningless universe; in other words it contradicts (C1) in that according to Aristotle the universe was not created. Finally, (C2) postulates both a creator as well as an eternal material substance out of which the universe is formed. That is, it represents a version of eternal creation, adopting features of both (C1) and (C3).

Let us compare this tripartite taxonomy with that of prophecy, presented by Maimonides in *Guide* 2.23. Again, Maimonides distinguishes three positions on prophetology:

> (P1) *The view of the "vulgar" masses*: "God chooses whom He wishes from among men, turns him into a prophet, and sends him with a mission."
>
> (*Guide* 2.32:360)

> (P2) *The view of Islamic and Aristotelian philosophers*: Prophecy is the result of moral, rational, and imaginative perfection. On this model, once the necessary qualifications have been satisfied, a person "will necessarily become a prophet, inasmuch as this is a perfection that belongs to us by nature."
>
> (*Guide* 2.32:361)

> (P3) *The Law*: Even one who has perfected his or her intellectual, moral, and imaginative faculties can fail to ascend to prophecy if God withholds it: "It may happen that one who is fit for prophecy and prepared for it should not become a prophet, namely, on account of the divine will."
>
> (Ibid)

Several implications stand out. On the first view (P1), prophecy is completely dependent upon the divine will. (P2) represents a completely naturalistic process; note that no mention of divine will is made in (P2). The third view (P3) opts for a middle ground between the total agency of God espoused in (P1), and the total naturalism of (P2) in that it combines the naturalism of the second view with the divine intervention of the first.

We noted above Maimonides' statement that "the opinions of people concerning prophecy are *like* their opinions concerning the eternity of the world or its creation in time" (*Guide* 2.32:360, emphasis mine). Is Maimonides trying to suggest that unpacking the proper correlation between the two sets of lists will yield his own (esoteric) view on the two topics? Or is he simply making the more straightforward exegetical point that in each case, we can iterate three options? Let us line up the two sets of views:

Three Views of Creation	Three Views of Prophecy
(C1) position of Torah – that God has created the world ex nihilo	(P1) position of the "vulgar" – that God can will anybody to receive prophecy
(C2) position of Plato – that the Demiurge creates the world out of eternal matter	(P2) position of the philosophers – that only one with the proper intellectual perfection can receive prophecy
(C3) position of Aristotle – that both matter and the world are eternal	(P3) position of "our Law" – that God can will to withhold prophecy from somebody who otherwise satisfies the requisite perfections

Reflecting Maimonides' own stated concern with esotericism, many scholars have assumed an implicit correlation between the two sets of views, and have come up with various parallels in order to uncover Maimonides' "real" views on both creation and prophecy. To cite several recent examples, while Lawrence Kaplan holds a C1:P3, C2:P1, and C3:P2 correspondence, arguing that Maimonides probably held the first option, Herbert Davidson has lined up a C1:P1, C2:P3, C3:P2 correspondence, emphasizing the similarity between (C2) and (P3), namely that (C2) and (P3) are both "mixed" views, incorporating elements of their respective extremes (Kaplan 1977; Davidson 1979). In response to Davidson, Warren Zev Harvey suggests a correlation between C1: P1, C2:P2 and C3:P3, arguing that "this most obvious of correspondences is indeed the one intended in Maimonides' esoteric teaching" (chapter 9, this volume, 151). Of the reasons adduced by Harvey for a C3:P3 reading of the *Guide*, the most important center around whether Maimonides held the Aristotelian theory of eternity and whether Maimonides allows for miraculous events in prophecy; both of these beliefs appear in the *Guide*, according to Harvey's reading. And so we must turn to eternity and miracles.

3. Eternity and Creation: An Alternative Reading

Maimonides specifies several important observations concerning the relations among these three characterizations. First, contrary to those who "imagine that our opinion and his [Plato's] opinion are identical," Maimonides is quick to disabuse those who are tempted to posit a connection between (C1) and (C2).The Platonic view, he states, cannot be substituted for Mosaic doctrine, even though there appear to be superficial similarities—most notably the postulation of a creator—between the two. But is the similarity in postulating a creator in both positions really that "superficial?" in fact it might be argued that this in itself is a crucial point and should not be so quickly discarded.

Secondly, Maimonides' attitude toward the relation between (C2) and (C3) is itself equivocal at best. Maimonides first contrasts the two positions on the grounds that the Platonists believed that the entire heaven is subject to generation and passing-away, whereas the Aristotelians believed that only the sublunar sphere is subject to such generation and passing-away. But he then dismisses (C2) as not worthy of serious consideration on the grounds that "[both] believe in eternity; and there is, in our opinion, no difference between those who believe that heaven must of necessity be generated from and pass away into a thing or the belief of Aristotle who believed that it is not subject to generation and corruption" (*Guide* 2.13:285). That is, after dismissing the original grounds for contrast between (C2) and (C3), he then argues that if Aristotle can be refuted, so too can Plato's theory be disqualified as a justifiable creation theory. In short, Maimonides appears to equate the positing of eternal pre-existent matter with the positing of an eternally beginningless universe. Having dismissed (C2) as a weaker version of (C3), Maimonides argues that the scriptural account is no more flawed than is the Aristotelian account. Then, pointing to the possibility of (C1), coupled with its Mosaic (and Abrahamic) sanction, Maimonides argues that the very plausibility of Scripture suggests that Aristotle's view is far from necessary.

Maimonides lays out in chapter 25 several ostensibly pragmatic reasons for supporting the Mosaic view of creation over that of Plato and Aristotle. The most important of these is that (C3) would destroy belief not only in the Law but in miracles and prophecy as well: Aristotle's view that

> the belief according to which the world exists in virtue of necessity, that no nature changes at all, and that the customary course of events cannot be modified with regard to anything—destroys the Law in its principle, necessarily gives the lie to every miracle, and reduces to inanity all the hopes and threats that the Law has held out.
>
> (*Guide* 2.25:328)

Maimonides is quick to point out, however, that the Platonic view is not nearly as devastating as that of Aristotle: the opinion of Plato would "not destroy the foundations of the Law and would be followed not by the lie being given to miracles, but by their becoming admissible" (*Guide* 2.25:328). Why, then, does Maimonides not appear to accept the authority of Plato? What he tells us is that the Platonic view has not been demonstrated: "In view of the fact that it has not been demonstrated, we shall not favor this [Plato's] opinion, nor shall we at all heed that other opinion [Aristotle's], but rather shall take the texts according to their external sense" (*Guide* 2.25:329). It might appear, then, that the scriptural account of creation of the universe out of absolute nonexistence (C1) is Maimonides' final view. But as we shall see, (C1) represents an exoteric reading.

Given Maimonides' explicit support of (C1), the view of Scripture, why not simply accept this as Maimonides' "real" view on creation? Let us return to Maimonides' original demarcation between exoteric and esoteric readings of controversial issues. Maimonides has given readers ample ammunition to interpret his support of (C1) as an exoteric conceit and has encouraged readers to search for the underlying, or concealed, theory of creation. I am suggesting that Maimonides has introduced many contradictions, false starts, and misleading comparisons between Plato and Aristotle. And as commentators working through these chapters have demonstrated, textual evidence abounds to support either Plato or Aristotle as an alternative expression of Maimonides' esoteric view of creation.

In fact I argue that Maimonides recognizes that the creation account in Scripture (C1) is ultimately untenable. In this context, it is important to point out that Maimonides has offered no demonstrative arguments in favor of (C1), the view of Scripture. Demonstration cuts both ways, and Maimonides has offered his reader no indubitable foundation upon which to accept either (C2) or (C3). Although epistemological skepticism would not be quite as heretical as espousing either (C2) or (C3), it nevertheless constitutes a provisional rejection of (C1), which is tantamount to a rejection of the Mosaic theory found in Scripture.

In further support of my reading, consider what Maimonides has to say about time and temporality. The most pointed discussion of time occurs in *Guide* 2.13, in the context of delineating the scriptural view of creation and temporality. Having stated that (C1) involves the creation of all existence, including time, "time itself being one of the created things" (*Guide* 2.13:281), Maimonides raises several puzzles having to do with the relation between God's actions and the domain of temporality. Surely, Maimonides claims, no temporal predicates can be used to describe God's activities or nature before the creation, since before creation there is no time: "Accordingly, one's saying: God "was" before he created the world—where the word "was" is indicative of time—and similarly all the thoughts that are carried along in the mind regarding the infinite duration of his existence before the creation of the world, are all of them due to a supposition regarding time or to an imagining of time and not due to the true reality of time" (*Guide* 2.13:281). Several points are worth noting in this passage. First, Maimonides is suggesting that, inasmuch as God transcends the temporal sphere and does not operate in a temporal context, God's duration must be characterized in atemporal terms. Although "duration" suggests temporal spread, in the case of God, duration eschews temporality altogether. Secondly, and more important for our purposes,

Maimonides' use of the terms "supposition" or "imagining" of time brings to mind his dismissal of the Mutakallimūn on the grounds that they were unable to distinguish between imagination and intellect. Maimonides is suggesting that (C1) involves one in a crude or vulgar understanding of time based on imagination, one which is contrasted with the "true reality of time."

Let us summarize our discussion to this point. With respect to creation, Maimonides maintains that "God's bringing the world into existence does not have a temporal beginning, for time is one of the created things" (*Guide* 2.13:282). Maimonides does not want to suggest that time itself is eternal, but neither will he claim that the creation of the world is a temporally specifiable action, for on the Aristotelian definition of time, the world must be beginningless in the sense that it has no temporal beginning. While supporting on an exoteric level the scriptural reading of creation, on an esoteric level Maimonides is suggesting that an Aristotelian theory of time (which he accepts) is more consistent with an eternity model of the universe. But does this mean that Maimonides is supportive of (C3)? If so, then the radical esotericists are right that Maimonides is a closet Aristotelian with respect to creation. Before acceding to this reading, let us first examine Maimonides' analysis of the first word/s of Genesis, "In the beginning" (*be-reishit*).

The first words of Genesis designate the fact that there was a beginning. But positing a beginning instant carries with it assumptions about what preceded this instant, and how this instant is reflected in Scripture. The theological implications of these issues become apparent when we turn to the following midrashic text from *Genesis Rabbah*:

> ["And there was evening and there was morning," (Genesis 1:3)] Said R. Judah b. R. Simon, "Let there be evening" is not what is written here, but rather 'and there was evening.' On the basis of that formulation we learn that the sequence of time had already been laid out." Said R. Abbahu, "on the basis of that same formulation we learn that the Holy One, Blessed be he, had been engaged in creating worlds and destroying them prior to the moment at which he created this one." Then he said, "This is the one that pleases me, but those did not please me."
>
> (Neusner 1985, 33)

This rabbinic statement became the focus of profound philosophical speculation among Jewish philosophers wishing to ground Scripture in scientific legitimacy. More specifically, commentaries on this passage crystallized the attempt of Jewish philosophers to reconcile rabbinic dicta and sentiments with an Aristotelian theory of time. Why, Maimonides asks, does Scripture start with the phrase "In the beginning God created . . ."? Maimonides explains the term "beginning" as referring not to a temporal priority, but rather to the ontological separation between nonexistence and existence (chapter 9, this volume, 155). Having postulated the nontemporal mode of creation, Maimonides turns to those rabbis who understood the Creation account in Genesis to postulate a domain of temporality before the creation event. Maimonides subsumes their comments as corollaries of Rabbi Eliezer's view, whose commentary on creation postulated creation by means of pre-existent matter. Maimonides depicts this commentary as admitting "the eternity of the world, if only as it is conceived according to Plato's opinion" (*Guide* 2.26:331). Interestingly enough, Maimonides does not reject Eliezer's statement; his only response to it is to claim that it may "confuse very much indeed the belief of a learned man who adheres to the Law. No persuasive figurative interpretation with regard to it has become clear to me." Uttered by an individual who is generally not at a loss for interpretative prowess, for whom the "gates of interpretation" are rarely if ever closed, Maimonides' stance suggests that perhaps he is not as uncomfortable with Eliezer's statements as one might expect.

Maimonides concludes his analysis of the rabbinic comments by dismissing their authority: "To sum up: you should not, in considering these points, take into account the statements made by this or that one" (*Guide* 2.30:349). Here Maimonides seems to be suggesting that in considering the issues of time and creation, one ought not be misled by the opinions of sundry rabbis. If this is so, what sense, then, should we make of Maimonides' overt espousal of the scriptural reading of creation on the basis of Mosaic authority? At least Plato and Aristotle both have other considerations in their favor. Despite his dismissal of the "sundry rabbis," Maimonides has pointed to a way of reconciling their views with that of Plato, in that the rabbinic statements adduced above provide an alternative way of reading Scripture. In fact, these final chapters point to the credibility of Plato's view on creation as a compromise between that of Scripture and Aristotle. Unlike the view of Aristotle, Plato's view, as Maimonides has reminded us, does not undercut the foundations of Judaism, but is still consistent with an Aristotelian theory of time. (C1) has no demonstrative underpinnings, and in *Guide* 2.30 Maimonides has undercut rabbinic authority. And so given that we will never be able to demonstrate creation with absolute certainly, Maimonides is *inclined* to follow the position most consistent scientifically with Aristotelianian thought, but least capable of undermining Jewish belief. This position he identifies with Plato. Maimonides is a skeptic in the sense that he realizes there can be no definitive proof either way, but on this score the scientific views of Aristotle fare no worse than the views found in Scripture.

5. The Relation of Creation to Prophecy

Having considered arguments in support of a (C2) reading of creation, let us turn now to the identification, if any, that might hold between creation, prophecy and miracles. Maimonides turns in *Guide* 2.36 to a technical and philosophical account of prophecy that, couched in Aristotelian epistemology and psychology, focuses on the prophetic activity itself rather than the one who attains to prophecy. Maimonides defines prophecy as follows:

> the true reality and quiddity of prophecy consists in its being an overflow from God . . . through the intermediation of the Active Intellect, toward the rational faculty in the first place and thereafter toward the imaginative faculty. This is the highest degree of man and the ultimate term of perfection that can exist for his species; and this state is the ultimate term of perfection for the imaginative species.
>
> (*Guide* 2.36:369)

Maimonides' point is that, under ideal conditions, any imaginative experience without the contaminating effect of the senses has the potential to provide a prophetic vision. In his quest for moral and intellectual perfection, the prophet epitomizes an ascetic lifestyle; eschewing all corporeal pleasures, he lives in solitude and avoids human interaction. When such an individual is overcome by emotions, or when his imagination is weak, he is unable to receive prophetic revelation.

So far Maimonides' exposition of prophecy has been almost entirely naturalistic, and his view has tended toward the philosophical position (P2). But where does Maimonides stand with respect to the effects of divine will in the acquisition of prophecy? Let us recall that Harvey wants to read Maimonides as a supporter of (P3), namely the view that while prophecy is primarily a naturalistic event, God can withhold prophecy from one who in all other respects has satisfied the requirements. And in fact Maimonides does suggest that divine will occasionally prohibits a person from exercising prophecy; this is the position expressed in (P3). Maimonides tells us that "it may happen that one who is fit for prophecy and prepared for it should not become a prophet, namely, on account of the divine will" (*Guide* 2.32:361). He then compares this intervention to a miracle: "this is like all the miracles and takes the same course as they" (ibid).

What are we to make of this passage? On a strictly philosophical account of prophecy (P2), anybody with a perfected rational and imaginative faculty can be a prophet; these two criteria are both necessary and sufficient for prophecy. But in *Guide* 2.32, Maimonides claims that God can stand in the way of the natural order, in that God can prohibit this final step from being actualized. In this sense, God's standing in the way of prophetic actualization can be seen as a "negative miracle." It would appear that the only way God could withhold prophecy would be to interrupt the activity of the Active Intellect. But Maimonides has already told us in *Guide* 2.18 that the actions of the Active Intellect are perpetual: any obstacle to its action results from a material disposition and not from the Intellect itself (*Guide* 2.18:300). And so, if we take *Guide* 2.18 at face value, then God cannot withhold prophecy, and Maimonides' apparent support of (P3) collapses into (P2).

Most of the medieval Jewish commentators (including Kaspi, Narboni, Shem Tov, Efodi and Abravanel) read Maimonides as adopting a purely naturalistic view of prophecy (P2), one in which an individual can achieve prophecy by actualizing inner perfections, without any intervention on the part of God's will. They argued that Maimonides himself did not believe in God's miraculous withholding of prophecy: on the medieval interpretation of Maimonides, God has for all time established the natural order in a way that incorporates what the vulgar are inclined to call "miraculous" events. The supernatural aspect of prophecy thus depends upon whether we think that Maimonides believed in supernatural miracles. Take Maimonides' example of the biblical figure Baruch who took all the human steps necessary to become a prophet, but was prohibited by God from doing so; was God's intervention "miraculous"? There are several ways to read this example. The first, which returns us to the views of the "vulgar," is that God has intervened in the process of prophecy. Another approach emphasizes the view that God has established the laws of nature, and that the "miracle" adduced here is introduced for the untutored masses. Finally, it might be that the miracle represents an occurrence already embedded within the laws of nature.

While a full examination of this topic is beyond the confines of this short study, let us consider several details supportive of a naturalistic reading of miracles. While Maimonides' early halakhic writings present a straightforwardly naturalistic view of miracles, his later works, including the *Guide* and *Essay on Resurrection*, appear to reflect a shift from a totally deterministic, naturalistic system to one that at least appears to make room for miracles. In fact, however, there is textual evidence to support the claim that Maimonides allows for God's theoretical withholding of prophecy only in the case of one who is not truly deserving. On this reading, when Maimonides says "to my mind this is like all the miracles and takes the same course as they," his point is theoretical: it is within the logical realm of possibility that God withhold prophecy, but there is no scriptural evidence supporting God's ever having done so. Maimonides makes this point explicitly in *Guide* 3.32:

> Though all miracles change the nature of some individual being, God does not change at all the nature of human individuals by means of miracles. . . We do not say this because we believe that the changing of the nature of any human individual is difficult for Him . . . Rather it is possible and fully within his capacity. But according to the Foundations of the Law, of the Torah, He has never willed to do it, nor shall He ever will it.
>
> (*Guide* 3.32: 529)

On this reading, when Maimonides' says in *Guide* 3.17 that "it is possible that he should not become a prophet" (Hebrew: *efshar she-lo yitnabeh*), what he seems to be suggesting is that *de jure* the possibility exists that an otherwise qualified individual may not become a prophet, but *de facto* any person with the requisite perfections will become a prophet. *Guide* 3.32 tells us explicitly that God would not withhold from an individual what he has otherwise deserved, if only because God will not change a person's nature by means of a miracle.

In short, I am arguing that the status of (P3) is dependent upon supernatural miracles, and thus cannot be accommodated to "natural law." If one believes that Maimonides does not support supernatural events, then when Maimonides says "to my mind this is like all the miracles and takes the same course as they," he in effect correlates (P3) with the class of "vulgar" views (P1).

Might it be argued that several passages in the *Guide* do evince evidence for the recognition of the *possibility* of miracles? As I have noted elsewhere, Maimonides is clearly perplexed by the existence of natural irregularities observable in the cosmos (Rudavsky 2010). How does Maimonides reconcile the notion of miracles (the existence of which are intimated in *Guide* 2.19 and 2.25) with the Aristotelian naturalism espoused in *Guide* 2.11, 2.13, and 2.28? One way is by claiming that although miracles are voluntary acts of God, nevertheless they are predetermined at the time of creation, and do not indicate a *change* in God's will or wisdom. A miracle represents a unique occurrence of an event that can still be understood within the causal nexus. On this reading, the *Guide* reinforces the idea that miracles do not represent the abrogation of the laws of nature. Thus what we might be tempted to call "miraculous events" are already contained in embryo in nature, and will be revealed to the prophet shortly before they occur.

Maimonides both naturalizes and subjectivizes many so-called miracles described in Scripture, claiming that the events in question occurred in the agent's mind and not in reality. Take for example, Jacob's wrestling with God, or Balaam's ass speaking. In both these cases, Maimonides reminds us that the event in question happened in a vision of prophecy and not in reality, thus undermining the objective status of the event (*Guide* 2.42). Other miraculous accounts are reduced to natural events as well, as in the case of Daniel's surviving in the lion's den (*Guide* 2.6). In the case of the revelation at Sinai, Maimonides offers the reader several ways to understand the miracle: either as a prophetic vision rooted in intellectual apprehension, or as a prophetic vision that incorporated sight as well, or one that incorporated hearing as well. "Choose whatever opinion you wish," says Maimonides (*Guide* 1.21), signaling that even this event is not necessarily rooted in objective fact. Again, in the case of explaining the extraordinary life-span of certain individuals, Maimonides gives us the option to explain such an anomaly either naturally or supernaturally:

> Only that individual who is mentioned lived so long a life, whereas the other men lived lives that had the natural and usual duration. The anomaly in the individual in question may be due either to numerous causes attaching to his nutrition and his regimen or is due to a miracle and follows the laws thereof.
>
> (*Guide* 2.47:408).

In all these cases, Maimonides is providing his readers with different ways of understanding miracles, depending on their intellectual sophistication: the "vulgar" will cling to the supernatural interpretation that reinforces miraculous events, whereas those initiated in philosophy and science will recognize that none of these events contravenes the natural order.

6. Conclusion

I have tried to argue in this chapter that theological speculation about creation of the universe has been shaped and influenced by philosophical considerations of time and cosmology. Much of Maimonides' effort has been aimed at showing not only that the scriptural view of creation is inconsistent with an Aristotelian theory, but that the "accepted" views on prophecy are inconsistent with a naturalized conception of the universe. Aristotelian cosmology represents the acme of modern science for Maimonides, and presents a coherent alternative to creation *ex nihilo* as presented in Scripture. And yet, Maimonides is unwilling to support Aristotle altogether, as reflected in his comments on Rabbi Judah. Maimonides realizes that the Aristotelian eternity thesis has not been definitely demonstrated. Thus while both Platonic and Aristotelian theories of time and matter are important in shaping Maimonides' modes of discourse pertaining to creation, they are interwoven along with rabbinic material to create an inter-textual garment which takes on a life of its own. Maimonides does not want to give up a creator deity altogether, but Maimonides' God is not the God of Genesis. Maimonides is drawn to an Aristotelian theory of creation, but one tempered by Platonic underpinnings (C2). Because Maimonides recognizes that neither can be demonstrated definitively, he leaves open the door to further inquiry. Given the centrality of demonstrative argument to Maimonides' analysis, it is clear that the doctrine of Scripture does not pass the test of scientific certainty.

Similarly, I have proffered arguments in this chapter for a naturalistic understanding of prophecy. While many modern scholars, Harvey included, have agreed that Maimonides' real view of prophecy is (P3), they disagree about whether the miraculous element in (P3) can be naturalized or not. I have argued in favor of a (P2) reading according to which prophecy has been naturalized in a way that minimizes God's direct intervention. This position does not deny the incorporation of anomalies into the natural order, but it does underscore a rationalist and naturalized understanding of both cosmogony and prophetology.

Note

1. References to the *Guide* will be to Shlomo Pines's English translation (1963) and will include part, chapter, and page.

PART VI

Bonaventure's *Itinerarium*: Philosophy and Divine Illumination

Editor's Introduction

Medieval thinkers often devoted themselves to both philosophy on the one hand, and divinity or (as it came to be called) theology on the other. What distinguished the one field from the other was sometimes unclear, and that unclarity opened the door to debates about the boundaries of these two disciplines—debates that are ongoing even in the 21st century. However, no one doubted that Bonaventure's *Itinerarium mentis in Deum*, his *Mind's Journey to God*, was a work of Christian theology, outlining a journey to God which a spiritual pilgrim makes by drawing not just on her natural capacities, but also on her capacities reformed by grace. Nevertheless, some of the finest philosophy in the Middle Ages is found in works of theology, and both Gregory LaNave and Timothy Noone point to Bonaventure's important philosophical contributions in this theological work. As LaNave explains, the work explores two trajectories: knowing God *through* things, and knowing God *in* things. In exploring the first trajectory, Bonaventure makes ample use of philosophical arguments, arguments that do not depend on any sort of divine revelation. Noone echoes LaNave's observation and develops it in a way congenial to the thrust of LaNave's contentions: Even Bonaventure's theological arguments are infused with philosophy. In fact, as Noone points out, Bonaventure uses the philosopher Avicenna's argument linking delight, proportionality, and beauty as the cornerstone on which he constructs his theological argument that our minds rise to the consideration of God in the process of sense perception.

One prominent doctrine in the *Itinerarium* that might strike contemporary readers as theological is that of divine illumination, the view that humans need the "divine light" to form concepts or judgments. However, as LaNave explains, Bonaventure depicts this illumination as a natural process.[1] When our minds form concepts and pass judgments, they also appeal to the ideas in God's mind, and this appeal makes it possible for us to know with certitude. Noone develops LaNave's observations by detailing two related arguments for this natural process of illumination found in the *Itinerarium*. Before we can know anything, we must first have a grasp of being; after all, whatever exists or can be an object of thought is a being of some sort. However, Bonaventure does not stop at the conclusion that being is what is first known. More precisely, he contends, all our knowledge requires a grasp of pure being. Since only God is pure being, all our knowledge requires a grasp of God, whether we are aware of it or not. Bonaventure therefore leaves us with a doubly astonishing conclusion: This knowledge of God underlies all our thinking, and it does so even if we are blind to the fact that it is God that is first known.

Note on References

For a brief explanation of medieval commentaries on the *Sentences* and a key to decoding references to these commentaries, see the Note on References to Part VII.

Note

1. Cf. Deborah Black's observations in chapter 8 (138–139) about the way in which the emanation from the agent intellect in Avicenna is likewise a natural process.

Further Reading

- Jay Hammond (2001). "Order in the *Itinerarium mentis in Deum*."
- T. Noone (2010). "Divine Illumination."

CHAPTER 11

Knowing God Through and in All Things: A Proposal for Reading Bonaventure's *Itinerarium Mentis in Deum*

GREGORY F. LANAVE

Scholars of Bonaventure's thought labor under the difficulty that the Seraphic Doctor is more widely admired than read. Yet there is one advantage they may claim: the immense popularity down through the centuries of his *magnum opus:* the *Itinerarium mentis in Deum*, "The Journey of the Mind to God." The text is poetic, concise, and dense. It summarizes many points in Bonaventure's philosophy, theology, and spirituality—indeed, it has sometimes been called a *summa* of his spiritual theology.

In the present chapter, I offer a proposal for reading the *Itinerarium.* I do so with two types of readers in mind. One is the Bonaventure scholar, for whom I make certain arguments concerning the logic of the text and its relationship to other works of Bonaventure. The other is the non-specialist who wishes to teach the *Itinerarium* as a significant part of the Christian theological patrimony. To the latter, I offer a schematic to understand the different elements of the text in their relationship to each other. This guided reading will, I hope, help the teacher to present the scientific (in the Aristotelian sense) power of Bonaventure's theology.[1]

I. Preliminary Note

My preliminary claim is that the *Itinerarium* is best understood as divided into two trajectories: one involves the three stages of seeing God *through* the visible world, the soul, and what is above the soul; the other involves the three stages of seeing God *in* the visible world, the soul, and what is above the soul. This claim might be criticized by readers of the text. Bonaventure gives several possibilities for understanding the structure of the text in the first part of chapter 1, and does not state that one should be privileged above the others.[2] However, as he goes on to explain each stage, the division that keeps reappearing is that of seeing God *through* and *in* the visible world, the soul, and what is above the soul.[3] I therefore regard that division as the most significant.[4] In what follows, I first examine certain antecedents to the *Itinerarium*'s structural argument in earlier works of Bonaventure. I then outline the first trajectory, highlighting its similarities and differences with those earlier works, and then the second trajectory, highlighting its uniqueness and proposing a key by which it may be understood. I close with a brief statement of the significance of my reading in light of some recent scholarship.

For reference, one may use the following chart, delineating the trajectories.

	Knowing God *through*	**Knowing God *in***
what is below the soul	chap. 1: the consideration of God through his vestiges in the universe	chap. 2: the consideration of God in his vestiges in this visible world
the soul	chap. 3: the consideration of God through his image imprinted on our natural powers	chap. 4: the consideration of God in his image reformed through the gifts of grace
what is above the soul	chap. 5: the consideration of the divine unity through its primary name which is Being	chap. 6: the consideration of the most blessed Trinity in its name which is the Good

II. Antecedents to this Kind of Consideration of God

A. Knowing God Through and In

The distinction between seeing God *through* and *in* is not unique to the *Itinerarium.* It occurs earlier, in the *Commentary on the Sentences,* in two places. Though the contexts and the language are slightly different, the content of the distinction is the same.[5] To know God *through* creatures is "to be raised from the knowledge of the creature to the knowledge of God as by way of a intermediate ladder." To know God *in* creatures is rather to know "his presence and influence in the creature." Bonaventure says further that knowing God *through* creatures is characteristic of wayfarers, and is a knowledge that is always available to them, even after the fall, though the fall darkened the mirror of creatures. To know God *in* creatures is characteristic of the blessed, though it can be experienced partly in this life. Both kinds of knowledge are therefore suitable to the created intellect, and possible to us in this world. On the other hand, the sense in which the creature serves as a mediator is apparently different in the two cases, though Bonaventure does not elaborate on this point. Moreover, knowing God *in* is more of its nature dependent upon the action of grace.[6]

B. Knowing God by Reason and by Faith

A different kind of antecedent to the *Itinerarium* may be found in the first of the disputed questions *De mysterio Trinitatis.* No distinction is made here between knowing God *through* and *in*, but Bonaventure does identify two distinct ways of approaching the knowledge of God. The question is divided into two articles. The first asks whether the existence of God is an indubitable truth. The second asks whether the doctrine of the Trinity is a congruous and necessary belief. Each article presents three types of arguments in support of its contention. Structurally, therefore, this question shows at least a *prima facie* similarity to the two threefold trajectories of the *Itinerarium.* Moreover, the focus of each set of arguments is echoed in the *Itinerarium.* The terminus of each argument in the first article of *De mysterio Trinitatis* is the divine Being, which is likewise the terminus of each stage of the *Itinerarium*'s first trajectory. The terminus of each argument in the second article is the Trinity—and this is certainly the case in the second trajectory of the *Itinerarium* as well.

In his recent book on Bonaventure, Christopher Cullen addresses the oft-discussed question of Bonaventure's philosophy by asserting that:

> Bonaventure's thought presents us with genuine philosophy, whose content and spirit can be studied without entering formally into theology, in part, because he carefully distinguishes between arguments from reason and those from authority.[7]

The disputed question we are looking at here seems to present just such a distinction.

In the first article, Bonaventure offers twenty-nine arguments for the existence of God, divided into three ways:

> The first way says: Every truth that is impressed in all minds is an indubitable truth. The second way says: Every truth proclaimed by all creatures is an indubitable truth. And the third way says: Every truth which, in itself, is most certain and most evident is an indubitable truth.[8]

The three ways might be called the way of illumination, the way of causality, and the way of ontological affirmation. Each of these ways consists of a thoroughly philosophical approach to the question. All creatures proclaim the existence of God their cause; all rational minds are illumined by the impression of the divine Mind; and the most certain and evident truths, considered in themselves, show the indubitability of God's existence.[9]

The second article presents a somewhat greater range of argument. The credibility of faith in the Trinity is testified to through three "books": the book of creation, the book of Scripture, and the book of life. In the book of creation we see that creatures are either vestiges of God, which in one way or another point to a threefold distinction in God—that is, the Trinitarian appropriations—or images of God, in which the relationship of the powers of memory, intellect, and will function as an image of the Trinity. In the book of Scripture, there is an implicit witness to the Trinity in the Old Testament, and an explicit witness in the New Testament. The book of life refers to the illumination of the human mind. Bonaventure distinguishes here between the innate light of the mind and an infused light. Both come from God; the innate light belongs to us by creation, the infused light by grace. These two cooperate in our thinking about God, so that we can reason, in a way reminiscent of Richard of St. Victor, to the credibility of the Trinity.[10] In brief, one is bound to think of God in the highest and most reverent manner possible. If one were to deny that God is capable—that he has the power—of producing an eternal beloved and co-beloved, one would not be thinking of him in the highest manner; if one were to admit that he is capable of this but deny that he wills to do so, one would not be thinking of him in the most reverent manner. The innate light of reason and the infused light of grace cooperate in this argument.[11]

Cullen's distinction between philosophy and theology seems to be verified here, in that the proofs of God's existence in the first article are all philosophical, and the arguments for the credibility of the Trinity in the second article are theological—if not based on arguments of authority, they at least require the illumination of faith in order to reach their conclusion.

The content of this question can be summarized in the following outline:

De myst. Trin., q. 1, a. 1: Whether the existence of God is an indubitable truth of reason

- The way of illumination: "Every truth that is impressed in all minds is an indubitable truth."
- The way of causality: "Every truth proclaimed by all creatures is an indubitable truth."
- The way of ontological affirmation: "Every truth which, in itself, is most certain and most evident is an indubitable truth."

De myst. Trin., q. 1, a. 2: Whether the doctrine of the Trinity is credible (i.e., congruous for belief and worthy to be believed)

- The book of creatures: creatures are either vestiges or images of God
  - Vestiges point to the Trinitarian appropriations
  - The intellectual soul, as image, points to the Trinitarian relations
- The book of Scripture: the testimony of faith
  - In the Old Testament, the Trinity is presented figuratively
  - In the New Testament, the Trinity is presented clearly
- The book of life: the light that shines on our minds
  - In the innate light of nature, thinking of God most highly, we see that he is able to produce an eternal beloved and co-beloved.
  - In the infused light of grace, thinking of God most reverently, we see that he does will to produce this eternal beloved and co-beloved.

C. The Relation of Creatures to God: Vestige, Image, Likeness

A final, typical way Bonaventure has of schematizing his doctrine of our rising to the consideration of God is based on a triple distinction he makes between creatures. This is what Etienne Gilson has called Bonaventure's doctrine of "universal analogy."[12] Every created thing can be described as a vestige, an image, or a likeness of God. In brief, non-rational natures are vestiges of God, the intellectual soul is an image of God, and the soul that has received grace is a likeness of God. Thus one may come to the knowledge of God through any creature; but the kind of knowledge that results depends on whether the creature is considered as a vestige, an image, or a likeness.

This kind of argument occurs in several texts.[13] Other texts simply refer to a distinction between the vestige and the image.[14] It is typical of all these texts that they are not primarily concerned with constructing demonstrative arguments for the existence of God. Some of them have broader epistemological concerns, showing how true knowledge is possible for man because he is made in the image of God. Others have more to do with unfolding the different kinds of representations of God. Yet in the *Breviloquium* Bonaventure states forthrightly an integral point of his doctrine of creation: in the state of innocence, God could have been known on the basis of this universal analogy.[15]

III. First Trajectory: Knowing God Through

The bulk of my argument concerning the reading of the *Itinerarium* concerns the second trajectory. The first trajectory is rather more straightforward, and certainly is related to some of the other texts mentioned above. In this section, therefore, I will limit myself to drawing out those connections and commenting on a few distinctive marks of the first trajectory.

Before turning to the individual chapters of the *Itinerarium*, one may make a more general comment. Looking at the antecedents of the *Itinerarium* in the

Sentences commentary and *De mysterio Trinitatis*, one may expect that Bonaventure will equate knowing God *through* and knowing him in the way of philosophy. In fact, the *Itinerarium*'s retrieval of the earlier material is more complicated. Below is an outline of the first trajectory of the *Itinerarium*, showing its correspondence to *De mysterio Trinitatis.*

Itin. 1: Through the vestiges of God in the visible world one sees
- the existence of the first principle (= *De myst. Trin.*, q. 1, a. 1 [the way of causality])
- the Trinitarian appropriations (= *De myst. Trin.*, q. 1, a. 2 [the book of creatures]).

Itin. 3: Through the image of God (i.e., the rational soul) one sees
- God as the object of its powers (= *De myst. Trin.*, q. 1, a. 1 [the way of illumination])
- the Trinity by the relationship of its powers (= *De myst. Trin.*, q. 1, a. 2 [the book of creatures]).

Itin. 5: Ontological argument for the existence of the highest Being (= *De myst. Trin.*, q. 1, a. 1 [the way of ontological affirmation])

In addition to the philosophical arguments, the first trajectory of the *Itinerarium* draws upon the disputed question's theological arguments regarding the book of creatures.

A. Chapter 1

The vestiges of God are, most basically, a "distinction of essential properties" that point to the Trinitarian appropriations, not to the personal properties or the persons themselves. This is the teaching laid down in the *Sentences* commentary, and followed strictly in *De mysterio Trinitatis* and *Itinerarium* 1.[16] Every sensible reality allows one to rise to the consideration of its efficient, formal, and final cause, namely, the power, wisdom, and goodness of God. "The supreme power, wisdom, and benevolence of the Creator shines forth in created things as the bodily senses make this known to the interior senses" (*Itin.* 1.10).[17]

A striking point of the *Itinerarium*'s treatment of this topic is the broad range of things that are included under the "vestiges of God." In common with his fellow Schoolmen,[18] and St. Augustine before them, Bonaventure finds support for the idea that every created thing is a vestige of God in the Vulgate translation of Wisdom 11:21: "You have disposed of all things in measure and number and weight." This triad, and others like it,[19] which may be found in all creatures, points to the Trinitarian appropriations. The presence of such an argument here is only to be expected. More striking is the fact that

Bonaventure includes as well the consideration of things that can be known only in faith. The believer comes to the power, providence, and justice of God in considering the origin, development, and end of the world (*Itin.* 1.12). Furthermore, he comes to the immensity of divine wisdom in considering the order of divine laws, precepts, and judgments in Scripture, and the immensity of his goodness in considering the order of the divine sacraments, graces, and rewards (*Itin.* 1.14). If this trajectory of the *Itinerarium* were concerned only with philosophical ways to God, such considerations would be entirely out of place, resting as they do on faith. Nevertheless, the terminus of such arguments is the same as the others in chapter 1: they come to the Trinitarian appropriations, not the Trinitarian relations.[20]

B. Chapter 3

In chapter 3, Bonaventure turns to the "image of God." The key consideration is that Bonaventure means two things when he speaks of this image. Generally speaking, "image" refers to similarity in configuration, the distinction and relationship of parts—as opposed to "likeness," which refers to a similarity in quality.[21] In this way, the rational soul is the image of God. Furthermore, as the image of God, the human soul has God as its object; it is invariably oriented toward him.[22] The soul without grace has lost the likeness to God, but it bears God's image (*imago creationis*) because (1) it is one substance with three powers, and (2) these native powers, however deformed by sin, are ineluctably turned toward God.

These distinctions, familiar from earlier texts, are recapitulated in *Itinerarium* 3.[23] Thus the consideration of God to which one is raised through the soul is twofold. In line with the sense of image as orientation to God, we rise from the soul to consider the reality of the divine Being, known in accord with Bonaventure's philosophical doctrine of illumination.[24] In line with the sense of image as configuration, we rise from the soul to consider the Trinitarian relations, seen by faith through considering the analogy of the Trinity in the relation of the powers of the soul. There is no question here of a philosophical proof of the doctrine of the Trinity. It is thanks to the purification of the mind through faith that one sees the proper force of the *analogia Trinitatis*.[25] As in chapter 1, Bonaventure does not restrict himself to a purely philosophical argument.

C. Chapter 5

Turning above the soul, in chapter 5, we come to a more direct consideration of the divine Being. This is the ontological consideration, the raising of the mind to that which is implied in its fundamental understanding of being, and therefore cannot be thought not to be. Anselm's ontological argument lurks in the background, obviously. And not for the first time. In fact, there are clear antecedents for this chapter in *De mysterio Trinitatis*, with the philosophical proof from that which is most certain, and in the *Sentences* commentary.[26] Although we are not at this level looking at particular created beings, we may still speak of a knowledge of God *through*—that is, through the way that he is present to us. The object is the "light that is impressed upon our minds" (*Itin.* 5.1; my translation), also called the "similitude of the divine light" (*Itin.* 7.1).[27]

Distinctive about the *Itinerarium*'s treatment is that it does not stop at the affirmation of the existence of the divine Being, but goes on to say something about the essential attributes of that Being. The "most pure Being" is first, eternal, most simple, most actual, most perfect, and supremely one.[28] Bonaventure is not interested in a mere enumeration of these attributes. The point of this chapter is the way in which simple attentiveness to that which is implied in everything we know brings us to the thought of God. The terminus of the argument here is, as it was clearly in chapter 1, and more implicitly in chapter 3, the power, wisdom, and goodness of God (*Itin.* 5.7). It is not sufficient for Bonaventure to point to pure being and say, "and this is God." Only when we recognize the divine qualities, and what is implied in them, do we really gain an insight into the Trinitarian appropriations. The way this works in chapter 5 is as follows. First we come to recognize the divine qualities mentioned above. Then we come to realize that these imply other qualities. The pure being is first, and also last—and last precisely because it is first:

> For since it is first, it does all things for its own sake. Thus the first being is of necessity the final end, the beginning and the consummation, the *Alpha* and the *Omega*.
>
> (*Itin.* 5.7)

Again, the pure being is eternal, and also most present, and present because it is eternal:

> Because it is eternal, it does not come from another, and of itself it does not cease to exist, nor does it move from one state to another. Therefore it has neither past nor future, but its being is only in the present.
>
> (*Itin.* 5.7)

The same can be said of all the other qualities.[29] All of these considerations flesh out the teaching that God is First Cause, Final End, and Exemplary Cause of creation—or in other words, that he is all-powerful, all-good, and all-wise.

We will see later that the consideration of the Trinity (in chap. 6) is even more important to Bonaventure's conception of God. To anticipate, recognizing God as good involves seeing in the relations of the divine persons the principle of self-diffusive goodness; but this only comes insofar as one enters into the life of God. Here, the argumentative reduction is not to the inner life of God, but to his creative essence. And that essence is seen most clearly in recognizing the fullness of God's relation to the world.

Cullen's claim regarding the distinction of philosophy and theology in Bonaventure is verified in this trajectory of the *Itinerarium*, for one can clearly distinguish those things that are known by way of reason and those things that are known by way of faith. But as part of the same trajectory they fall under a more encompassing category. In brief, I suggest that the knowing of God *through* in this trajectory of the *Itinerarium* is based in the consideration of what things are. If knowing what something is—for example, the course of history, or the image of the Trinity in the soul—requires faith, so be it. If the knowledge of what something is does not require faith, then it can be thought of on the level of philosophy simply, and opens the possibility for a philosophical demonstration of the terminus of the argument, that is, the existence of the divine Being. In either case, one is called to consider in the most precise—even analytical—manner possible, the nature of things, and to come to three distinct kinds of knowledge of God as a result.

IV. Second Trajectory: Knowing God *In*

If the first trajectory has to do with what things are, what is left for the second trajectory? Something new is going on in these chapters of the *Itinerarium*. In the *Sentences* commentary we read that to know God *in* a creature is to know his presence and influence in the creature, and it is a knowledge that appears to depend on grace; but little more is said there. The theological way of approaching the knowledge of the Trinity in *De mysterio Trinitatis* is mostly not on display here. A different key must be found for this trajectory.

I suggest that key is Bonaventure's doctrine of sensation. In chapter 2, he lays out this doctrine. Sensation involves three processes: *apprehension, pleasure,*[30] and *judgment*. The sensible object generates a similitude, or likeness, of itself, which is apprehended by the perceiver. The received similitude causes pleasure in the senses, in accord with its proportionality to its source, its medium, or the object on which it acts; thus Bonaventure distinguishes three kinds of pleasure: beauty, sweetness, and wholesomeness. Finally, the received similitude is purified and abstracted from its sensible particularity by judgment so that it may enter the intellective faculty.

All of these activities, Bonaventure says, "are vestiges in which we can see our God." This explains why he deals with them in this chapter, which is on the consideration of God in his vestiges. The ramifications of the doctrine of sensation extend further, however, through the other stages of this trajectory. The considerations of God in his image reformed by grace (chap. 4) and in the name of the blessed Trinity, which is Good (chap. 6), are likewise marked by the qualities of sensation. They include a direct *apprehension* of God in the soul and in what is above the soul, a capacity to receive *pleasure* in that apprehension, and a formation of the soul in conformity to what it perceives (corresponding to *judgment*). The following outline gives a summary of the function of the moments of sensation at each level of this trajectory.

Itin. 2: Knowing God in his vestiges in the visible world

- Apprehension—The apprehension of an object through its similitude "manifestly suggests" the eternal generation of the Son from the Father.
- Pleasure—The experience of beauty "suggests" the perfect beauty which is the perfect correspondence between the Son and the Father. This perfect beauty is also seen to be most sweet and most wholesome.
- Judgment—Judgment is possible because our minds are by nature oriented toward the eternal Truth in God.

The fact of judgment points "in a way that is more excellent and more immediate" to that Truth, which we know in faith as the Word of God, the Second Person of the Trinity.

Itin. 4: Knowing God in the soul reformed by grace

- Apprehension—Through grace, the soul has a direct apprehension of the Son, whether as mediator between God and man; as the uncreated, incarnate, and inspired Word; or as the Bridegroom.
- Pleasure—The soul is able to apprehend the Son in these various ways insofar as it is informed by the theological virtues, the spiritual senses, or the spiritual transports.
- Judgment—The soul thus informed becomes "a house of God," conformed to the angelic hierarchy, a dwelling-place for the Word.

Itin. 6: Knowing the Trinity in its name which is Good (cf. *De myst. Trin.*, q. 1, a. 2)

- Apprehension—Through its conformity to the Word, the soul perceives that he is the generated similitude of the Father because the law of the Trinity is the law of goodness. To see the goodness of God truly is to see that God must be a Trinity.
- Pleasure—Such perceptions fill the soul with amazement. The goodness of God displayed in the incarnation and crucifixion calls forth even more wonder. And the soul's delight is made perfect when it sees that through the incarnation and crucifixion it is made capable of union with God.
- Judgment—Union with God is accomplished through conformity to the Crucified. The pattern for contemplation is St. Francis, who was inflamed with love for Christ and so able to be conformed to him.

A. Chapter 2

If chapter 2 is the key to what is new in this trajectory, it is also the most difficult to understand. Bonaventure begins the chapter by talking about contemplating God in sensible creatures, "in as far as God is present in them by essence, power, and presence" (*Itin.* 2.1). This triad was well known to the Schoolmen, inherited from a comment in the *Glossa ordinaria* on Song of Songs 5:17. It was taken by them to refer to God's omnipresence, and Bonaventure indeed adverts to it in that context in his commentary on the *Sentences.*[31] When he speaks of knowing God *in* creatures earlier in the same commentary, however, he uses a different expression: to know God *in* creatures is to know "his presence and influence in the creature."[32] He also adds that this knowledge is perfect in the blessed and is partially accessible to man *in via.* As I have noted above, this suggests that such knowledge is in some way dependent on grace—and therefore is distinct from a purely philosophical knowledge of God's omnipresence. Bearing this in mind, we must suspect that whatever Bonaventure means by seeing God in creatures in his essence, power, and presence, he does not mean simply that God's causal power can and should be seen in the creature. This is a philosophical vision that has already been dealt with in chapter 1.

The key to the chapter is Bonaventure's appeal to the doctrine of sensation. What does it mean—what *could* it mean—to say that one rises to the consideration of God in the process of sensation?

One possible interpretation, which is indeed followed by some commentators, is as follows. It is simple enough to say that what we find in apprehension, with the object generating a similitude of itself, is like the perfect generation of the Son from the Father. Since I, as a Christian, know the fact of the eternal generation of the Son, I can be raised to the thought of it when I reflect on what happens in sensory apprehension. The natural generation of a similitude is thus a suitable analogy for the Trinitarian procession.[33] So much may be easily admitted. There is no difficulty in supposing that the human knower, especially as influenced by grace, can move so swiftly from the perception of a creaturely reality to the idea of God that he seems to find the very idea of God in the thing.[34]

My own reading is that our knowledge in faith of the Trinity is directly implicated in natural sensation. Our knowledge of the perfect generation in the Trinity conditions our experience of sensate apprehension, our knowledge of supreme delight in the Son conditions our experience of sensate delight, and our knowledge of the Son as the Eternal Art in whom lies the truth of all things is directly implicated in the judgments we make upon our sensations.[35]

It is most revealing to begin with judgment, which Bonaventure says points to God "in a way that is more excellent and more immediate" than do apprehension and delight. Judgment naturally occurs through our direct relationship to God. "Through [Eternal Art] our mind comes to judge about all those things which enter into it through the senses." Bonaventure is expressing here his version of Augustinian illumination theory. Briefly, the truth of any sensible thing lies in three places: in the thing itself, in our minds, and in the mind of God (the "Eternal Art"). Only in God does that truth exist immutably, and so only by reference to God's idea of the thing is the truth of the thing known with certitude. Sensory cognition therefore involves two aspects: the intellectual abstraction of the form from the thing, and comparison of this abstracted form to its eternal exemplar. This is a thoroughly natural process. The mind, created in the image of God, is ineluctably directed toward God, and therefore toward his eternal knowledge of things. From the fact of judgment we therefore rise, "in a way that is more excellent and more immediate," to the consideration of the eternal exemplarity of things in God.[36]

Judgment absolutely requires recurring to the Eternal Art. Delight and apprehension do not absolutely require advertence to the eternal procession of the Son or his perfect proportionality to the Father—indeed, to claim that they do would suggest the kind of natural proof of the Trinity that Bonaventure steadfastly eschews. Instead, delight and apprehension are conditioned by the eternal procession and proportionality.

Regarding delight, Bonaventure says the Son, the eternal Likeness of God, is perfectly proportioned to the Father, and therefore is most beautiful, most sweet, and most wholesome. Moreover, "it is in God alone that the fontal and true delight is to be found. So it is that from all other delights we are led to seek him" (*Itin.* 2.8; translation modified).[37] There is clearly an analogy between my natural experience of *beauty*—the proportion of a similitude to the object that generates it—and the perfect proportionality between the Son of God and the Father. But there are also the delights of sweetness and wholesomeness. That is experienced as most *sweet* which is best proportioned to the perception of the recipient, and most *wholesome* which best fulfills the needs of the recipient. Bonaventure says here that these qualities may be attributed to the Son, but he does not spell out how. The recipient in question is certainly the human being. If I, the perceiver, am to regard the Son as most sweet and most wholesome, it must be because I sense his proportion to my perceptive power and my needs.

To make sense of this, I would introduce another key Bonaventurean theme, one we find elsewhere in the *Itinerarium* and throughout his works: to speak of the Son of God is to speak at once of the uncreated Word, the inspired Word, and the incarnate and crucified Word. Each of these corresponds to an element of Bonaventure's description of delight. The uncreated Word is most beautiful since he is the perfect expression of his source, the Father; the inspired Word is most sweet because the revelation of God[38] is perfectly proportioned to the perceptive power of fallen man; and the incarnate and crucified Word is most wholesome because it is in these forms that the Word satisfies our deepest need—namely, the need for redemption. Therefore, when Bonaventure says that the experience of delight "suggests" the idea of the perfect delight in the primal similitude, I understand him to be saying that our experience of the Word in these various forms conditions our experience of sensible delight.[39]

Regarding apprehension, Bonaventure says that the process whereby an object generates a similitude which is united with the receptive organ of the perceiver "manifestly suggests that the Eternal Light begets of himself a Likeness or co-equal, consubstantial, and co-eternal Splendor . . . which is united by the grace of union to the individual of rational nature" in the incarnation.

> If, therefore, it is in the nature of all knowable things to generate a likeness of themselves, they clearly proclaim that in them as in mirrors can we see the eternal generation of the Word, the Image, and the Son eternally emanating from God the Father.
>
> (*Itin.* 2.7)[40]

What is most notable about Bonaventure's account of apprehension is his introduction of the idea of the similitude. We apprehend sensible objects not directly, but only through the mediation of a similitude. This is an original solution of a dispute between an Augustinian and an Aristotelian account of sensation.[41] But it raises a philosophical problem: how can the perceiver be sure that the similitude truly represents the object? One can perhaps give a philosophical solution, but Bonaventure does not do so here, at least explicitly. Instead, he offers a theological solution. The Christian knows the Trinity, and thus knows the perfect, eternal generation of the Son from the Father. This knowledge governs our sense of the natural generation of similitudes by objects. The fact of this natural generation need not turn us into Kantians or skeptics, for we have seen the perfect, utterly resplendent instance of generation. At the same time, all instances of this creaturely generation fall short of the divine generation, and therefore we know the former's deficiencies.

In summary, knowing the truth of the Trinity modifies one's sense for what happens in natural sensation. Natural apprehension involves the reception of a similitude generated by an object, and therefore is always a mediated access to the object. But there is no need for skepticism about the object, because in our knowledge of the Trinity we see the possibility of the generation of a perfect similitude. Natural delight satisfies our sense of proportionality—whether to the object, to our sensitive capacity, or to our felt need. But when we know in faith that all of these things are perfectly and supremely satisfied by the Son of God—most beautiful in his perfect proportion to the Father, most sweet in his revelation, most satisfying (or wholesome) in fulfilling our needs in the redemption (incarnation and crucifixion)—the Son becomes the standard by which we judge instances of natural beauty. Thus Bonaventure can say that apprehension and delight "suggest" their eternal referents, while judgment leads us "in a way that is more excellent and more immediate . . . to see the eternal truth with greater certainty" (*Itin.* 2.9).

It would be more dramatic, and would verify my proposal for reading this chapter, if Bonaventure claimed that there is some kind of presence of the Trinity in the things we perceive in the world outside of us that is directly accessible by our senses. He does not say this here, and his choice of words militates against such an interpretation. Natural apprehension "manifestly *suggests* [*insinuat*]" the eternal generation of the Son from the Father; natural pleasure "*suggests*" the beauty of the Primal Similitude. We do not sense God; instead, what we experience in sensation allows us to rise to the consideration of God.[42] But in chapters 4 and 6 of the *Itinerarium*, which form the rest of this second trajectory, he does speak of a transformation of the power of sensation, which allows for a direct apprehension of God in the soul and in what is above the soul, a capacity to receive pleasure in that apprehension, and a formation of the soul in conformity to what it perceives. I will therefore briefly outline how I see this logic of sensation playing out in these chapters. My claim is that Bonaventure is turning our attention to a capacity within the person that is sensitive to the divine presence and able to be formed by it.

B. Chapter 4

Chapter 4 concerns the "consideration of God in his image reformed through the gifts of grace." As in chapter 3, we have moved from the sensible world outside and below the soul to a consideration of the soul itself. Chapter 3 deals with the soul as the natural image of God, chapter 4 with the soul as the image of God reformed by grace. In chapter 3, "image" refers to the soul's natural orientation to God and its Trinitarian configuration. In chapter 4, the transformation wrought by grace makes the soul the similitude of God, which affects both its orientation and its configuration. The orientation is no longer to God simply, in the form of the Trinitarian appropriations; it is rather specifically to the Second Person of the Trinity. The configuration is no longer simply the *imago Trinitatis;* it is the hierarchized soul, "flooded with . . . intellectual lights" (*Itin.* 4.8).

Grace first enters the picture in chapter 4, and with it the transformation of the pilgrim. In earlier works Bonaventure lays out an elaborate doctrine of sanctifying grace, with the virtues, the gifts of the Holy Spirit, the beatitudes, the fruits, the spiritual senses, and the sacraments.[43] Though aspects of much of this material are incorporated into the *Itinerarium*, Bonaventure's purpose in chapter 4 is to show how in the reform of the soul's powers through grace the soul rises to a distinctive consideration of God. He does not delineate the habits of sanctifying grace, but evokes the place of Christ as medium of grace and object of the transformed soul. Through the theological virtues, the soul grasps Jesus Christ, the Mediator between God and man. By means of the spiritual senses, the soul is related to Christ as the uncreated, inspired, and incarnate Word. And in spiritual transports, the soul is devoted to, admires, and exults in Christ the Bridegroom (*Itin.* 4.3). In each of these ways, we see the interplay of that apprehension and delight that belong to the logic of sensation. The infusion of grace puts us in a certain relationship to Christ, who thus becomes the object of our *apprehension*. What follows upon this is a sense of *delight*, which varies according to the various degrees of grace infused. The soul is given a sense for God, concretized in its apprehension of the reality of Christ; epistemologically, this is the primary result of the transformation wrought by grace.

The presence of *judgment* on this level is not so obvious, but it can be seen by comparison with the role of judgment in corporeal sensation. Judgment is the means by which the transient experience of corporeal sensation is purified of its sensible particularity. By judgment, perceptions become the stable possession of the receiver. In corporeal sensation this requires going beyond the sensible thing to its truer existence in the Eternal Art. When we turn to the spiritual sensation of Christ, however, there is not the same need for "going beyond." The soul that senses the Word is caught up in that sensation, which is not deficient in the way that the sensation of corporeal objects is deficient. At the same time, there must be a transformation in the soul, so that the spiritual sensation of the Word becomes the stable possession of the perceiver. This we find in chapter 4 in Bonaventure's description of the soul as hierarchic. By grace, the soul is made to conform to the ecclesiastical and celestial hierarchy, thus becoming the "house of God" (*Itin.* 4.8).[44]

The divine presence sensed at this level is that of the Word, who comes to us as the self-expression of God, raises the capacities of our soul to be able to delight in him, and seals us with the representation of the heavenly hierarchy.

C. *Chapter 6*

In the penultimate stage of the *Itinerarium*, we rise to the consideration of God in what is above the soul. This involves the "contuition of the most Blessed Trinity," in which we see the meaning of the divine goodness, which is "the most basic foundation for our contemplation of the emanations" (*Itin.* 6.1). The chapter begins with a reasoning to the reality of the Trinity on the basis of the principle "the good is self-diffusive" (*bonum est diffusivum sui*).

Though the principle belongs to the realm of philosophy, Bonaventure is not here, any more than he is anywhere else, offering a purely philosophical proof of the Trinity. In a manner reminiscent of Richard of St. Victor and Anselm, Bonaventure sees that full knowledge of goodness, and therefore the force of the maxim, requires the influence of grace—that there is a difference between the philosophy of the non-believer and the philosophy of the believer.

It seems clear enough that once the believer knows the truth of the Trinity, he can see how it is related to the selfgivingness of the divine goodness. But Bonaventure goes further here. The conclusion of chapter 4 was that the human soul is transformed by grace into a likeness of God, and thereby rejoices in the presence of the divine self-expression in Christ. In chapter 6, this trajectory reaches further. By virtue of our graced conformity to God, we see, not that Christ is the self-expression of God, but that within God himself there is an order of procession, that God in himself is a mystery of self-diffusive goodness.

Bonaventure makes much the same argument in the disputed questions *De mysterio Trinitatis*, when he speaks of the credibility of the doctrine of the Trinity as testified in "the book of life": that is, by the innate light of reason we think of God "most highly" and thus must hold that God can communicate himself, and by the infused light of faith we think of God "most reverently" and thus must hold that he does communicate himself. In both texts, the argument is more or less that if God is good, and if goodness is self-diffusive, then God must be a Trinity.

Given the similarity, it is worthwhile to highlight two other points about the texts: one similarity and one difference. The difference lies in the purpose of the texts. In *De mysterio Trinitatis*, Bonaventure is speaking of the credibility of the doctrine of the Trinity—that it is a doctrine "fitting, necessary, and worthy of belief."[45] He is not concerned (at least directly) to show that it is not contrary to reason. Rather, he is looking for those things that testify to its truth—summarized in the book of creation, the book of Scripture, and the book of life. This is really an argument addressed to all Christians, or perhaps all nascent theologians. The fact of the doctrine of the Trinity must be firmly implanted in all Christian minds, and anyone who would strive to understand the doctrine must reflect on the various reasons why we hold the doctrine to be true. The whole discussion is really a preliminary to the study of the Trinity.

This is quite different from the purpose of the *Itinerarium*. Here we are speaking not of the beginning of Christian theology, but of the end of Christian insight. What is the highest thing that one can see of God, having been raised and transformed by the power of grace? It is the inner life of the Trinity—something that every Christian knows to be true, but of which few come to have a sense in a compelling, self-evident way. There is a difference between the apprehension of the truth of the Trinity on the part of the beginner and on the part of the perfect.[46]

The hidden similarity between the two texts is that even in the disputed question Bonaventure reveals the possibility of an *itinerarium*. After identifying the testimonies of the book of creatures, the book of Scripture, and the book of life, he asks what is the primary reason that motivates our belief in the Trinity. Perhaps surprisingly, it is not the book of Scripture, but the book of life.

> Therefore if it is asked what it is that moves us to believe this—is it Scripture, or miracles, or grace, i.e., the eternal truth itself—the answer should be that that which moves us principally is the illumination which begins in the natural light and finds its consummation in the infused light, for

> this leads us to think of God not only in a lofty manner but also in a reverent manner, because this illumination proceeds from the eternal light itself which takes our intellect into obedient captivity; in capturing the mind, it subjects it to God in worship and veneration and renders it ready to believe what pertains to the divine honor and veneration, even though such things be beyond our reason. This becomes clear from experience if one turns to the secret things of one's own mind.[47]

Graced illumination is not a one-time offering, which makes the recipient ready to believe what is revealed. It is a continual and progressive working of God in the soul that draws it on the itinerary of understanding. The deeper one goes, the better one understands. Ultimately, our experience of God will guide our perception of the truth he reveals.

There is no doubt that the *Itinerarium* is a more detailed account of this journey than is the disputed question. But this is consistent with Bonaventure's thought more generally. The nature of Bonaventure's theology does not differ greatly from the beginning to the end of his career. The principles are there in the beginning; but the insight into the principles, and a more thorough sense of their reality and implications, grows over the course of his writing.[48]

Turning back to the text of *Itinerarium* 6, we may now begin to identify how the moments of sensation are operative here. The moment of *apprehension* occurs when the Word is seen, not as the Christ in whom God is revealed, but as the Son who is the self-expression of the Father within the divine life itself. Following from this is the apprehension of the interrelated mysteries of the Trinity: distinction of properties with unity of essence, supreme communication and true origin, etc.

If this is what is apprehended, what follows? *Delight*, says the logic of sensation. The mysteries apprehended are only partly grasped—or rather, following Bonaventure's use of St. Paul, these mysteries take us captive. The delight that follows is a delight in what superexceeds our comprehension; the words Bonaventure uses to describe this, repeatedly, are amazement and admiration. In chapter 7 he adds the descriptions "praise" and "rejoicing." In other words, we are not only seized with wonder, but we gladly enter into praise of that which we see, for it is proportioned enough to us for us to see its praiseworthiness. Thus one might verify the presence of the elements of beauty (proportion to the source, in this case calling forth our stunned admiration) and sweetness (proportion to our capacity, seen in this case in our response of praise). Yet more ultimate than these is the element of wholesomeness, the proportion to our need. How can the inner mysteries of the Trinity be experienced as fulfilling our need? Perhaps they cannot. But those mysteries are enfleshed in Christ, the incarnate and crucified Word. One does not cease to be amazed at them; if anything, it is more remarkable that the mysteries be enfleshed than that they exist in the heavenly Trinity. But in the crucifixion, the Word has made the supreme call on our affection.

The result of this is the possibility of being united to Christ. It is the means by which one may pass over into God. In short, the ultimate delight comes in being united with the divine Word, in whom the full mystery of the Godhead has been opened to us—a union made possible in the cross.

Finally, there is the moment of *judgment*, the stabilization of the perception, participation in and conformity to what has been perceived. At this level, this can only mean conformity to the expressivity of the divine self-gift. This is the ultimate Franciscan moment in Bonaventure's itinerary, for the conformity comes about through union with the crucified Word, the expression of divine love—a union which Bonaventure suggests here, and makes clear later in the *Life of Francis*, is exemplified in Francis's reception of the stigmata. The expressivity that lies at the heart of the Godhead has become most visible to the world in the Crucified, and in those like Paul and Francis (see *Itin.* prol.3) who showed, each in his own way, the marks of the Crucified. It is through such conformity that the soul reaches the height of its sensing of God, confirming its apprehension of and delight in the divine Beloved.

V. Presenting the *Itinerarium*

Commenting on the structure of the *Itinerarium* is a kind of cottage industry among Bonaventure scholars. To set my proposal against all other opposing claimants would require an argument vastly extended beyond the bounds of the present argument. Nevertheless, I would highlight two aspects of my proposal: the structural connections between the *Itinerarium* and other of Bonaventure's works, which indicates the distinctiveness of his second trajectory, and the interpretation of that second trajectory consistently in terms of sensation. The value of the latter may be seen more clearly in contrast with a tendency of some other recent proposals.

Scholars such as Ewert Cousins, Zachary Hayes, Jay Hammond, and Ilia Delio have described the *Itinerarium* in terms of a symbolic approach to theology, which has two key aspects.[49] First, this is a theology that seeks the intelligibility of the things of faith by means of symbols. Hammond puts it this way: Bonaventure "does not employ symbols to prove anything, rather, he resorts to the effusive nature of symbols to demonstrate ineffable mysteries that elude easy description." These symbols are not "merely" symbolic; they are in fact ways to penetrate the real metaphysical structure of the realities in question.[50] Second, the mystery revealed in any such symbol points to the whole of the mystery, never to any one part in isolation. For example, one may speak about creation and its relationship to the single creative activity of the Creator; but one must at the same time know that Creator to be the Trinity, and see the analogous presence of the Trinity in the creature.[51] Analytical thinking might try to separate these elements; symbolic thinking always strives to see them implied in each other.

My own claim, by contrast, is first that Bonaventure is turning our attention not to symbols that evoke God, but to a capacity within the person that is sensitive to the divine presence and able to be formed by it; and second, that this is best understood according to the canons of a scientific theology (in the Aristotelian sense).[52]

My reading of the first trajectory of the *Itinerarium*, in light of earlier treatments of the same subject, indicates that Bonaventure draws on both philosophical and theological arguments in construing how we know God *through* things. This very fact suggests that something new is going on in the second trajectory. My proposal for reading it is based on the possibilities of the objectivity of sensation. Apprehension points to the importance of what is really there. Pleasure points to our capacity to receive what is really there. And judgment points to the possibility of our transformation in the reception of what is really there.

I do not maintain that the *Itinerarium* is a kind of manual of scientific theology. It is not. However, I do maintain that it is animated by a theological intelligence that is conscious of the scientific character of theology. Thus, for example, one should not expect from the *Itinerarium* a rigorous deduction of the existence of God, convincing to all clear-minded readers. But with respect to the first trajectory one should expect to see a rigorous explanation of what it means to see God *through* things, consistently applied. With respect to the second trajectory, one should expect to find a precise explanation of our capacity to see God in things, and what one may know of God in this way. And such is the case: Bonaventure exhibits great care in describing the means by which God may be known in the various levels of the *Itinerarium*, and the kind of knowledge that results.

The symbolic reading of Bonaventure has undoubted merits, not least of which is its attempt to do justice to his deft use of an array of symbols in his theology.[53] My own reading pushes in a different direction. If one dares to speak of a "perennial theology," Bonaventure may enter the lists as a worthy contestant, or at least a worthy dialogue partner for those claimants, such as Aquinas, that have a more obvious scientific sense of theology. Like Aquinas, Bonaventure insists that the terminus of the knowledge of God *through* creatures is the Trinitarian appropriations; like Aquinas, he believes that it is possible to prove the existence of God, though his grounds for such arguments differ from those of Aquinas. Like Aquinas, he recognizes that revelation provides a yet higher knowledge of God, which requires some working of grace in the human knower in order for it to be received; but unlike Aquinas, he develops an elaborate theory of the sensing of God. Bonaventure's distinctive contention is that God is present in the things to which the soul attends, in such a way that that presence, if the knower is attuned to it, has a definite transformative power. This aspect of his theology will be seen much better if it is understood scientifically, not symbolically.

Notes

1. Translations of the *Itinerarium* will be taken from Bonaventure (2002), except where otherwise noted. For a distinction between a symbolic and a scientific reading of Bonaventure, see below, section 5. With respect to the *Itinerarium*, the question for a scientific approach is, what exactly is the way in which, at each level, the mind is raised to God? And what are the metaphysical and epistemological claims that are necessary for this itinerary? Implicit is a further question: how do these claims compare to those of other Christian thinkers who speak about our natural and graced knowledge of God?
2. Fundamental to all the possibilities is the idea (*Itin.* 1.2) that the world is divided between more distant and nearer representations of God, and so there is a threefold progression: from the world (vestige, corporeal, temporal, outside of us), to our mind (image, spiritual, everlasting, within us), to the First Principle (eternal, absolutely spiritual, and above us). Bonaventure compares this triple progression (*Itin.* 1.3) to three days' journey in the wilderness, the threefold enlightenment of a single day (evening, morning, noon), the threefold existence of things (in matter, in the understanding, in the eternal art), and the threefold substance of Christ (corporeal, spiritual, divine). Then come three principal *aspectus* of the mind (*Itin.* 1.4): animality, spirit, and mind. Each of these three can be divided into two (*Itin.* 1.5): by considering God as Alpha and Omega; by considering him as through and as in a mirror; or by considering each way in itself or in conjunction with another. Having thus established six stages, Bonaventure speaks of six corresponding powers of the soul (*Itin.* 1.6): senses, imagination, reason, understanding, intelligence, and synderesis.
3. In chapter 7 he summarizes what he has done as follows: "our mind has beheld God outside itself through and in vestiges, in itself through and in the image, and above itself through the similitude of the divine light shining on us and in that light" (*Itin.* 7.1; my translation).

   The language here is a little deceptive, insofar as it suggests the following order of the text: stages one and two, vestiges; stages three and four, image; stages five and six, similitude. To be sure, the distinction of vestige, image, and similitude is a key Bonaventurean theme, but the way he commonly understands it does not correspond to such a division in the *Itinerarium*. The image of God is treated in stage three, insofar as the soul is both oriented to God as its object and is configured like God; the similitude of God is treated in stage four, insofar as the soul through grace has become like God. Stephen Brown has noted this in his commentary on the *Itinerarium* (Bonaventure [1993], 47). What "similitude" means with reference to stage five is not clear.
4. For an attempt to correlate all of these possible divisions of the text, see Hammond (2001).
5. In I *Sent.*, d. 3, p. 1, a. un., q. 3, in *Omnia Opera*, I, 74–75. The question is whether God can be known through creatures in every state of man—innocence, fallen, redeemed, glorified. In III *Sent.*, d. 31, a. 2, q. 1, response to 5, in *Omnia Opera*, the question is whether faith is empty in the state of glory. The specific objection in the latter instance refers to St. Paul in the First Letter to the Corinthians, with a distinction between seeing now as in a mirror, but then face to face. The first text distinguishes knowing God through and in *creatures*; the second text distinguishes knowing God through and in a *mirror*.
6. The fact that in the *Sentences* commentary both kinds of knowledge have to do with creatures signals a difference with the *Itinerarium*: in the latter, the end of each trajectory is the consideration of God not through and in a creature but through and in what is above the soul.
7. Cullen, (2006), 35.
8. *De myst. Trin.*, q. 1, a. 1 (Bonaventure [1979], 107).
9. For a detailed analysis of these types of proofs, see Noone and Houser (2005).
10. Cf. Richard of St. Victor, *De Trinitate*, book 3, (Richard of St. Victor [1958]).
11. In a reply to an objection, Bonaventure says that fallen reason thinks that God cannot be both one and three, that innocent reason dictates something consonant with this, and that reason elevated by grace dictates the very truth itself. The argument is based not on reason in the light of nature, but on "elevated reason."
12. Gilson (1940), ch. 7.

13. *De scientia Christi*, q. 4; *Breviloquium* 2.12; "Christus unus omnium magister," 16 17.
14. I *Sent.*, d. 3, p. 1, a. un., q. 2, response to 4; II *Sent.*, d. 16, a. 1, q. 1; *De myst. Trin.*, q. 1, a. 2.
15. *Breviloquium* 2.12.4. Nevertheless, this knowledge is made possible through grace: "when the image was not yet spoiled but rendered God-like through grace, the book of creation sufficed to enable human beings to perceive the light of divine Wisdom" (Bonaventure [2005], 97).
16. I *Sent.*, d. 3, p. 1, a. un., q. 4, response to 3.
17. See also I *Sent.*, d. 3, p. 1, a. un., q. 2, response to 4.
18. See, e.g., Thomas Aquinas, *Summa theologiae* I, q. 45, a. 7.
19. For a comprehensive listing of the possible triads, see I *Sent.*, d. 3, p. 1, dub. 3. (1) Considered in itself according to the substance of its principles the creature consists of matter, form, and composition. (2) Considered in itself according to its situation it is disposed by number, weight, and measure. (3) Considered with respect to other creatures in terms of its natural action it acts by substance, power, and operation. (4) Considered with respect to other creatures in terms of its spiritual action it consists of that by which it is, that by which it is fitting, and that by which it is distinct. (5) Considered with respect to God in terms of its simple reference to him it exists by mode, species, and order. (6) Considered with respect to God in terms of both its reference and assimilation to him it exists by unity, truth, and goodness.
20. Hammond (2001) 228, in his symbolic reading (I will say more about this in section 5), does not wish to make too great a distinction between God as First Principle and God as Trinity. He puts it this way: "while God always relates to creation as one principle (*primum*), this one principle always remains a Trinity of persons (*primitas*)." What then is the terminus of the mind's ascent to God through his vestiges? God as First Principle, indeed, but the Trinity as well, inasmuch as, according to Hammond, one should never think of the one entirely without the other. To end at a pure First Cause that could just as well be unitarian as Trinitarian would undercut the symbolic value of this line of thought. Therefore, this view sees the power, wisdom, and goodness of God not so much as Trinitarian appropriations, but as pointing to—though not proving—the Trinitarian persons. Yet it is striking that, as Hammond acknowledges, there is only one explicit mention of the Trinity in this section (*Itin.* 1.14); see Hammond (2001) 232 n. 139.
21. Bonaventure, II *Sent.*, d. 16, a. 1, q. 1; d. 16, a. 2, q. 3.
22. See also Bonaventure, *De scientia Christi*, q. 4.
23. See also *Breviloquium* 5.4.4.
24. For a good account of this, see Speer (1993). Bonaventure's epistemology draws from both Plato and Aristotle. From Aristotle he takes the notion of abstraction, and from Plato he takes the notion of illumination. Briefly, the soul is able to know things with certitude because it abstracts the form from the object known and judges it in light of the soul's orientation to God's knowledge of the form.

    Similarly, in discussing the powers of the soul in chapter 3 of the *Itinerarium*, Bonaventure speaks of their orientation to God. For example: the memory contains within itself simple forms that must be infused from above (*Itin.* 3.2); the intellect can know with certitude only by means of an unchanging, uncreated light (*Itin.* 3.3); and the will can judge one thing as better than another only with an implicit appeal to the notion of the highest good, which is impressed on the soul (*Itin.* 3.4). This is again suggestive of the Trinitarian appropriations, with the will pointing to the highest goodness, the intellect to the highest wisdom, and the memory to the highest being (rather than power).
25. On this point, the *Itinerarium* is perfectly consistent with the earlier view of the *Sentences* commentary: I *Sent.*, d. 3, p. 2, a. 2, q. 3.
26. Bonaventure, *De myst. Trin.*, q. 1, a. 1; I *Sent.*, d. 8, p. 1, a. 1, q. 2. See Noone and Houser (2005) section 5, "God."
27. This is to be distinguished from the rational creature as similitude of God, which is the subject of *Itinerarium* 4. See note 3, above.
28. *De mysterio Trinitatis* likewise treats of the qualities of the divine Being (*De myst. Trin.*, qq. 2–7), though the order is a little different: God is supremely one, most simple, infinite,

eternal, immutable, and necessary. The significance of these orders requires further study. See Perdrix (2007).

29. Cousins (1978), famously called this the "coincidence of opposites," a term that has been picked up by such scholars as Jay Hammond and Ilia Delio. Insofar as the phrase suggests that the chief point of enumerating these mutually implied qualities is that Bonaventure would have us contemplate them as a symbol that brings us to the consideration of the divine, I find it uncongenial to my own reading of Bonaventure.
30. Following Hayes's translation, I use "pleasure" (*oblectatio*) and "delight" (*delectatio*) interchangeably in what follows.
31. I *Sent.*, d. 37, p. 1, a. 3, q. 2. For an exposition of Bonaventure's thought on this point, see Fuerst (1951) 146–70.
32. See note 5, above.
33. Hammond (2001) 233–34 gives a very strong presentation of this line of argument. He reads the three moments of sensation in terms of a symbolic evocation of the Trinity. The content and ordering of the symbols is important. Hammond wants to find a one-to-one correlation between the moments of apprehension, pleasure, and judgment and God's essence, power, and presence. According to this view, Bonaventure is pointing to the mystery in an ordered and evocative way. This is neither simply a philosophical understanding of the creature, nor a theological eisegesis into the book of creation. It is a cooperation between the light of nature and the light of faith, each pointing to the other.
34. Aquinas, *De Veritate*, q. 18, a. 2 speaks of a cognition like this belonging to Adam before the Fall: "there were thus in man two kinds of knowledge of God, one, by which he knew God as the angels do, through an internal inspiration; the other, by which he knew God as we do, through sensible creatures. However, this second knowledge of his differed from our knowledge as the investigation of one who has the habit of a science and proceeds from things he knows to a consideration of things which he had once known differs from the investigation of one who is learning and strives to proceed from what he knows to things which he does not know."
35. Contrary to a more symbolic reading, I would highlight the possibilities inherent in the strict objectivity of sensation. In apprehension I am really confronted with an object. My sense of pleasure comes from my capacity to be properly attuned to that object, and in judgment my perceptions are made firm and secure. In general, my argument is that this whole second trajectory of the *Itinerarium* ought to be seen in terms of a logic of sensation: Bonaventure is pointing us, in various ways, to a real object, a real capacity for that object, and a real transformation in us in relation to that object.
36. See Speer (1993). Hammond (2001) 234, in his attempt to understand judgment symbolically, says that the natural experience of judgment is an analogy revealing that a thing's existence is eternally present in the Eternal Art. I do not see the analogy. Perhaps, if I judged a sensible object simply on the basis of the idea of the object pre-existing in my mind, then there would be an analogy between this and the pre-existence of all ideas in the divine Mind. But in fact Bonaventure's epistemology requires us to turn immediately to the ideas in the divine Mind. This is what allows us to judge.
37. Hammond (2001) 233, explains this by saying that "the divine emanation is the primordial source of all earthly delight." Furthermore, he says, delight reveals the Trinitarian influence upon a thing's power or operation. That is, visible things are beautiful because the delight they evoke in us points in a symbolic way to the primal beauty which is the Son, the perfect Image of the Father. So far as it goes, this reading is plausible. But Hammond's treatment of delight here is incomplete, precisely because in focusing on the correspondence between Father and Son, he attends only to the sense of beauty, and not those of sweetness and wholesomeness.
38. This revelation occurs in a variety of ways, most notably in Scripture and in the imitation of Christ that pertains to the life of the evangelical counsels.
39. See Gregory LaNave (2005), 104: "when the believer, who knows the supreme wholesome-

ness of redemption, experiences wholesomeness in the perception of sensible objects, he is made to think of the supreme wholesomeness, for it is that which conditions his whole experience of the wholesome. To the unbeliever, the experience of pleasure in natural sensation will seem to be something quite other than what he perceives in the incarnation or the crucifixion, even if he is willing to concede that these doctrines say something about the goodness, or the humility, of God. The crucifixion in particular he might well judge to be ugly or distressing. But when one knows and loves what is present in the crucifixion, one has a different judgment about what is truly pleasureable."

40. Hammond's reading of this (2001) 233 is that in apprehension we perceive the essence of things, and find in there a symbol—namely, the object's generation of a similitude—that analogously represents the divine Trinitarian essence.
41. See Lang (1986).
42. I have argued elsewhere that Bonaventure later (viz., in the *Collationes in Hexaëmeron*, 2.23) comes to precisely this point: to see visible things properly is to apprehend God's self-expression in them; see LaNave (2005) 179–80. But this is not yet his teaching in the *Itinerarium*.
43. III *Sent.*, d. 34, p. 1, a. 1, q. 1; *Breviloquium* 5.1–6.
44. See LaNave (2005) 112: "The reformation of the soul by grace not only transforms the soul's capacity to apprehend and delight in the presence of God (in the form of the Word), it also produces a permanent form in the soul, whereby it receives and corresponds to the ecclesiastical and celestial hierarchy. The soul is thereby the recipient of the influence of the grace communicated from Christ (the supreme Hierarch) through the nine orders of angels, sealing (*insignitur*) the soul with the nine grades of orders."
45. *De myst. Trin.*, q. 1, a. 2.
46. For a comment on the way theology satisfies both these classes, see Bonaventure, I *Sent.*, pro., q. 2.
47. Bonaventure, *De myst. Trin.*, q. 1, a. 2 (Bonaventure [1979] 132).
48. See LaNave (2005) 186–92.
49. See e.g., Cousins (1978), Hayes (1994), Hammond (2001), Hammond (2002), Delio (2001).
50. Hammond (2001) 198. See also Cousins (1978) 168.
51. See Hammond (2001) 228–29.
52. Certain points are uncontested between these two views. There is no doubt that Bonaventure makes extensive use of symbols in his theology in a way that a more obviously scientific theologian such as Aquinas does not. On the other hand, each of the scholars mentioned would acknowledge that Bonaventure is well aware of the possibility of describing theology as an Aristotelian *scientia*. Not only does he on occasion explicitly speak of theology this way, he is more favorable to that approach to theology than were his Franciscan teachers (the *Summa halensis* [lib. 1, tract. intro., q. 1, c. 1] and Odo Rigaud [*Quaestio de theologia* I, q. 1] explicitly deny that theology is a *scientia*). Finally, it is generally agreed that it would be a mistake to limit Bonaventure's theology properly speaking to his early university works, which are more obviously Scholastic, and to relegate later works to the realm of "spirituality." The *Itinerarium* is one of these later works. It certainly describes the various states of the journey of the mind to God, and in that sense might properly be called a work of "spirituality," but in doing so it makes definite, substantive claims about creation, redemption, the human soul, grace, the angels, Christ, and God, and in that sense is inescapably theological.
53. This must be said not only of the *Itinerarium*, but also, as Joshua Benson has recently argued, of such an example of strict Scholastic theology as the disputed questions *De scientia Christi*. Benson aptly notes that many scholars who write on these questions focus almost exclusively on question 4, on epistemology. See Benson (2004).

CHAPTER 12

St. Bonaventure: *Itinerarium Mentis in Deum*

TIMOTHY B. NOONE

> . . . all creatures of this sensible world lead the mind of someone contemplative and wise to the eternal God . . . inasmuch as they are traces, images, and displays put forth and signs divinely given, causing us to catch a glimpse of God . . .
>
> (Bonaventure, *Itinerarium mentis in Deum* chap. 2 n. 11; ed. Boehner, 60–61)

Anyone reading the text of Bonaventure's *Itinerarium mentis in Deum* for the first time must find the experience overwhelming to some degree. Even scholars whose area of specialization is the Middle Ages—whether that be medieval history, theology, or philosophy—are likely to find themselves mired in the details, trying to decide what different literary sources, biblical or patristic images, and theoretical points Bonaventure is combining in various measures throughout his text. Despite its small size—a mere 18 pages in the Quarracchi critical edition—the work has produced a considerable literature of its own: translations into multiple modern languages, sizable commentaries in English, French, and German, as well as numerous scholarly articles. As we shall see, there are sharp disagreements about how to read the work and what to make of it: is it a work of mystical theology, a work partially philosophical and partially theological, or a wholly theological work, laying the basis for a rigorous approach to speculative theology?

If we pay attention to the themes and the structure of the text, encompassing as it does a prologue and seven chapters, there can be little doubt, formally speaking, the work is one that is primarily theological. The work fits, moreover, into a genre of literature well known throughout the Middle Ages, namely, a spiritual guide, leading the mind of the reader to contemplate God and the highest things. Works of this sort within the Christian tradition date back to the patristic period with the *Mystical Theology* of Pseudo-Dionysius and certain writings of St. Augustine, but were heavily associated with the monastic tradition in the Latin West, including St. Bernard of Clairvaux's *The Steps of Humility and Pride* and the *Benjamin Major* of Richard of St. Victor. Such spiritual guides, furthermore, are found even outside Christianity in the schools of pagan philosophy (Hadot, 2002).

Yet Bonaventure's *Itinerarium* is quite distinct, even within this genre of writings. Its most salient characteristic in this regard is its point of departure: the life and religious experience of St. Francis of Assisi with its constant focus on the center of reality in Christ. Bonaventure himself tells us that the work was originally composed when he visited Mount Alverno in October, 1259, some two years after he became Minister General of the Franciscan Order, and that the immediate inspiration was his reflection on the vision of the crucified six-winged Seraph that Francis had at the time of his reception of the stigmata in September of 1224. The six-winged Seraph provides the framework for the first six chapters of the *Itinerarium*, and the figure of Francis and his journey back to God the model for how to make the journey.

Yet if the work is so thoroughly theological, one might question whether it is suitable for inclusion in a book of the present sort, devoted to the study of philosophy in the Middle Ages. The answer to such a question is actually twofold: first, Bonaventure's own approach to theology is, generally speaking, quite philosophical, especially so, if the point of comparison is more recent theology; second, Bonaventure quite consciously distinguishes between philosophy and theology in his own thought and in particular introduces philosophical arguments into the *Itinerarium* as part of the work's aim to raise the mind to God. As so often in medieval philosophy, we are in the position of having to isolate philosophical arguments and themes from a broader theological work, but in the present case the methodological warrant for our doing so is, at least in part, the recognition on the part of the author himself of a properly philosophical realm of discourse with its own canons of legitimacy.

The present chapter will be divided into two parts. In the first, we shall review the structure of the *Itinerarium* as a whole, indicating alternative ways of reading that whole and adjudicating to some extent a recent scholarly controversy in that regard. In the second, we shall focus our attention upon one philosophical theme present in the text's various chapters, divine illumination, and note how its treatment within the *Itinerarium* parallels and differs from its treatment elsewhere by Bonaventure.

I. The *Itinerarium* as a Whole

The work comprises a prologue and seven chapters. Both the prologue and the final chapter are, however, outside, so to speak, the main sequence followed throughout the work inasmuch as the prologue gives an overview of the work and the seventh chapter is not itself a step along the journey but rather represents the terminus of the journey. The main sequence or the journey proper is organized around two principles: the first principle of organization, originating from the writings of St. Augustine, locates the parts of the journey in three levels (or stages) of reality: things outside the soul, things in the soul, and things above the soul; the second principle of organization, found elsewhere in Bonaventure's writings, subdivides each of the levels or stages into two distinct aspects: seeing God through creatures and seeing God in creatures. The combination of these two principles yields the total of six steps, corresponding to the six chapters.

It is in this connection that we find a major disagreement between two recent interpreters of the *Itinerarium*, Gregory LaNave and Jay Hammond. Writing chronologically first, Hammond argues that the subdivision into knowing God through and in things amounts to knowing God as *primum*, that is as the source of created being as first efficient, exemplar, and final cause inasmuch as we know God through creatures, and knowing God as *primitas* in terms of his inner life as Trinity, inasmuch as we know God in creatures (Hammond, 2001, 217–218; 225–229). LaNave criticizes Hammond's approach as creating too much of a dichotomy between the philosophical and theological aspects (see LaNave, above, 187 and 191; 277–278; 284–285). LaNave advances a way of reading the *Itinerarium* that finds its chief organizing principle in the 'in' versus 'through' (LaNave, above, 181–182), but then seeks two different sources as background to these distinct 'trajectories' of the work: the 'through' sequence (chaps. 1, 3, and 5) finds its background in parallels in Bonaventure's earlier work, *Disputed Questions on the Mystery of the Trinity*; the 'in' sequence (chaps. 2, 4, and 6) takes its lead from within the *Itinerarium* itself in the doctrine of sensation found in chapter 2 and its three qualities of apprehension, pleasure, and judgment (LaNave, above, 189–290).

Although this disagreement is about the work as a whole and not precisely about the meaning of a particular philosophical doctrine, the disagreement does touch upon the presence of philosophy within the work and what significance to assign to the philosophical sections. In what follows, the reader will have to judge for herself which of the intepretations does justice to the work by re-reading the *Itinerarium*, consulting the relevant literature, and (re-)assessing the overview given here.

If we turn our attention to the prologue and first section of the first chapter (up to n. 8), the intention and the scope of the work are adequately disclosed to us. The word 'peace' occurs no less than five times within the space of the first three paragraphs; Bonaventure interprets Francis's earthly striving as ordered to the peace of the heavenly Jerusalem and the anticipations of it that can be experienced in the present life. His own stay at Mount Alverno was for the sake of finding the 'peace of the spirit' and the meditation he proposes to us gives us, in the six stages of the journey modeled on the six wings of the crucified Seraph, the six steps or stages of reaching the peace that can be experienced within this life. Since the end of the work is the attainment of peace by the reader, it may be said to be a work of practical and even mystical theology, not a work whose sole aim is investigation and contemplation. This is not to say, of course, that there are not speculative arguments to be found within it, but their order and purpose is to raise the mind to higher and higher levels of contemplation so that, at the end of the process, the reader may pass beyond contemplation to an experience of divine peace.

This practical purpose also explains why Bonaventure places so much emphasis upon desire and prayer at the outset of the work. In the prologue in particular, he lets us know that adequate preparation on the part of the reader and a certain attitude towards the text are required to achieve the end at which the work aims (Bonaventure, *Itin.* prol. n. 4; ed. Boehner, 32–33). What this means is that we need to adopt a certain discipline in order to appreciate the work in the manner that Bonaventure intends. In part, this discipline involves preparation for reading, a point that Bonaventure reinforces in the penultimate paragraph of the prologue, where he notes that the 'speculations' he submits to ourselves as lovers of divine wisdom are of no consequence unless the mirrors of our minds are wiped clean and polished by moral effort. But the discipline also requires reading the text in a certain slow, we might say meditative, way:

> I ask, accordingly, that the aim of the writer be weighed more than the work itself, more the sense of what is said than the uncouth speech by which that sense is expressed, more the truth of the statements than the beauty of their sound, more the exercise of the will of the reader than the instruction of his intellect. For this to come to pass, the progress of these speculations should not be run through hurriedly, but quite slowly meditated upon.
>
> (Bonaventure, *Itin.* prol. n. 5; ed. Boehner, 34–35)

Turning to the first part of the first chapter, where in effect, we get a description of the main sequence to be followed through to the end of the sixth chapter, we find Bonaventure describing the three major steps that are to be taken in raising the mind to God. Before he does so, however, he reminds us of the importance of two things: the need for divine assistance through grace and the corresponding need for prayer on the part of the one taking the journey. Nothing could indicate more clearly the theological and religious character of the work than Bonaventure's insistence upon both of these points.

The three major levels or stages are depicted as steps upon a ladder whose rungs are the levels of reality found within the universe: some creatures are traces, while others are images; some are bodily, others spiritual; some are temporal, others are everlasting. These distinctions suggest that we begin with the former members (traces, bodily, and temporal things), rising to the latter members of the dichotomy (images, spiritual, and everlasting things), but only in order to surpass them, rising still further to things above (*res extra nos, intra nos, supra nos*). What these divisions mean needs to be carefully understood. Strictly speaking, for Bonaventure, all creatures are traces inasmuch as they are related to God as the First Efficient, Exemplary, and Final Cause, the Source of their being, unity, truth, and goodness. In other words, strictly speaking, even the things that are images, such as humans and angels, are also traces. But the reason that Bonaventure begins with things that are only traces and not images is to start with those creatures that are the furthest from the First Principle in order to show the way that even they point to and reflect their the Divine Source.

The main trichotomy of below us, within us, and above us answers to three different ways in which the rational mind apprehends things: through sense powers common to humans and animals (*animalitas seu sensualitas*), rational spirit (*spiritus*), and mind (*mens*). But each of the ways in which the three levels of reality are so apprehended is, in turn, bifurcated in accordance with another principle, namely, whether the First Principle or God is arrived at through creatures or seen as reflected in creatures. Bonaventure uses the biblical example of Jacob's ladder to indicate this distinction; seeing God through creatures is compared to climbing up Jacob's ladder and seeing God in creatures is compared to coming down the ladder. We should note that what this means is that, in conformity to Augustine's doctrine of signs, signs are things which, though themselves known, bring to mind or convey our mind to other things; this is knowing God through creatures. The other member of the bifurcation is found in the reverse process. Having glimpsed God in whatever fashion we can through creatures at the pertinent level of reality, we see reflected in the very same creatures their Divine Source.

What this bifurcation of the three levels gives us in the end is a sixfold division: knowing the things below us in such a way as to reach God through them (chap. 1, after n. 8); knowing God in the things below us (chap. 2); knowing God through rational creatures that contain His image (chap. 3); knowing God in rational creatures as reformed by grace (chap. 4); knowing God through the things above us understood through the notion of being as a likeness of the divine reality (chap. 5); and knowing God in the things above us through the notion of goodness as a likeness of the divine reality (chap. 6). Once again, at the transition to the first substantive section of chap. 1, at n. 8, Bonaventure reminds of the importance of grace and prayer but also points forward to the final and seventh chapter which will be contemplation of the divine Source through grace and mercy.

Reviewing the first level or step towards God in both the aspect of knowing God through lower things and knowing God in lower things will help us in coming to grips with LaNave's suggestion that sensation holds the key to reading chapters 2, 4, and 6 correctly.

After n. 8 of chapter 1, Bonaventure begins his examination of things below us inasmuch as we may understand God through them. His argument is remarkably quick in its inferences. Sensible things viewed as a sensible world disclose features that point to God. For example, the weight, measure, and number of things (Wisdom 11:21) indicate God's infinite power, wisdom, and goodness, while mutable things point to something unchangeable. In what is practically a paraphrase of Augustine's approach to God, Bonaventure claims in the final section of this first chapter that anyone who fails to notice these creaturely features as leading to God is foolish (*Itin.* chap. 2 n. 15; *Opera omnia* V, 299).

A different tack in regard to sensible things is taken in chapter 2. Here the focus is not so much the features of sensible things, but their communication to humans as sentient creatures. As Lang has noted in her excellent article, Bonaventure is quite concerned to emphasize that sensible things enter into the sense faculties through their immaterial likenesses and this places his doctrine of sense cognition within more an Aristototelian, than an Augustinian, framework (Lang 1986, 77–80). But actually both Lang and, following her, LaNave have missed something quite important to Bonaventure's doctrine that delight follows immediately upon sensation and leads from the act of sensation to judgment: the key text comes from Avicenna's *Metaphysics*, not Aristotle nor Augustine. It is Avicenna who links the experience of delight to the proportionality between the object sensed and the sense power, while also delineating the relationship between delight, proportionality, and beauty since his treatment of delight is embedded in a treatise in which he is attempting to show, among other things, that the First or Necessary Being is most Beautiful (Avicenna, II: 431–432). What Bonaventure seems to be doing in chapter 2, accordingly, is exploiting the Avicennian connection between delight and sensation, understood as conditioned upon proportionality between object and sense power, to see another sign pointing to God in the very process of sense cognition.

What does this all of this mean for the controversy between Hammond and LaNave? In his reply to LaNave's article, Hammond is correct to suggest that the theological and philosophical aspects of the work are interwoven, and this is a point that LaNave, too, acknowledges (Hammond, 2009, 317; LaNave, above, 199). Furthermore, although the two authors differ on precisely what reading of the work they prefer, both acknowledge that the work may, and perhaps should, be read in various ways and at different levels of sophistication. (For a completely different way of reading the work, see Blohm, 2011, 25–28.) My own finding is that, so long as we are aware that the work is primarily aimed to bring the reader to the goal of experiencing, to the extent possible in the present life, some foretaste of divine peace and that it is in this sense a work of practical theology, many different interpretations are legitimate. As to LaNave's claim that the second chapter is presenting us with a description of a certain, particularly Christian, capacity for perception, I would say that, if this is so, it is based upon an Avicennian model of how sense awareness is structured and that it uses that model as an analogue for describing the capacity. Even so, the language towards the end of the second chapter suggests quite strongly that Bonaventure is reading the whole process of sense cognition as another level of signs reflecting the Divine Source.

II. A Philosophical Theme

One philosophical theme that is quite prominent within the *Itinerarium* is divine illumination. Although the doctrine of divine illumination has been subjected to drastically different interpretations in recent scholarship (Petersen-Boring, 2010, 40–45; Schumacher, 2011, 2–24), the interpretation assumed here will be the one that is more in line with earlier scholarship: divine illumination is a philosophical theory that identifies one of the necessary conditions of natural intellectual knowledge in the presence of the divine light to the human intellect in its activity of knowing (Noone, 2010, I: 369–371). This description of 'divine illumination' leaves open entirely the mode of the presence of the divine light to the human mind; whether as a light cast upon the object of knowledge or the knowing subject or both, and whether the illumination is operative in concept (re-)formation or judgment or both are entirely open-ended matters. Historically, the theory of divine illumination, as opposed to the view, rather commonplace in late antique and later Arabic authors belonging the Peripatetic tradition, that some less than divine mind enlightened the human mind, is traceable back to certain writings of Augustine as interpreted by Anselm among other Latin writers. Bonaventure endorses the theory of divine illumination, defending the need for such a divine light cooperating with human intellectual powers despite the ability of the latter to abstract intelligible forms from sensible things. The basic reasoning he gives in his *Disputed Questions on the Knowledge of Christ* is that eternal truths are the term of natural intellectual awareness and that the kind of certitude and necessity that are the earmarks of knowing such truths exceed what any creature could provide inasmuch as no creature is eternal.

In the *Itinerarium* Bonaventure first alludes to the doctrine of divine illumination immediately after the text in chapter 2 on sense cognition that is so central to LaNave's interpretation of the *Itinerarium*. He argues that judgment, in order to be certain and necessary, must transpire through a feature (*ratio*) that abstracts from time, place, and the potential for change. But this must mean that we judge through some principle that is entirely unchangeable, immutable, and unlimited, that is to say, something eternal. Yet the only thing that is eternal is God. Hence the ground for our judging even sensible things is the divine light, here portrayed, as it so often is by St. Augustine, as the law according to which we judge, not the thing being judged (Bonaventure, *Itin.*, chap. 2 n.9; ed. Boehner, 57–58).

Much more extensive is the presentation of divine illumination in chapter 3. Since the theme of the chapter is seeing God through the image of Him imprinted on the natural powers of the human soul, Bonaventure's discussion is centered around the three parts of the image: memory, understanding, and will. In each of these parts of the soul, Bonaventure finds that their proper activities involve the divine light. Memory, understood in the way that Augustine did as the root of our self-awareness and the source of our fundamental notions as well as our knowledge of the past, points to the presence of the divine light to our minds, since, among other things, our holding fast to primary propositions whose truth is unchangeable is disproportional to our minds being, as changeable, the source of such truth. Understanding does the same in our knowing unchangeable truth in general; even necessary inferences that hold whether the logical subjects exist or not point to the conclusion that a divine art is behind the inferences since they would hold independently of ourselves or our acts of knowing. Even the power of will, as part of the divine image, points to the presence of the eternal light to the human mind, inasmuch as all value judgments presuppose acquaintance with not only the good but the Best as the precondition to assigning relative values and the judgments are made in terms of moral laws that are unchanging (Bonaventure, *Itin.*, chap. 3 n. 2–4; ed. Boehner, 62–68).

What is distinctive about Bonaventure's version of the divine illumination theory here as opposed to the version in the *Disputed Questions on the Knowledge of Christ* is the way he uses a distinct thesis that was well known in his time but to which he did not clearly adhere in earlier writings: the thesis that God is first known. Bonaventure first indicates his adherence to the thesis in chapter 3. The reasoning involved in this first occurrence of the doctrine begins with the claim that the first things grasped by the mind are terms. Yet the definitions of terms involve the categories and the categories, in turn, are various ways in which things are (or, if you wish, they are modes of being). Even if we would argue that the other categories besides substance are traceable back to substance on the grounds that they depend on substance for their being and, at least by extension, their meaning, we still have to cope with substance understood as 'being *per se*' (*ens per se*). But understanding being *per se* involves conceiving well the notion of 'being': this means not simply being aware of the transcendental properties of being, but also the features that will, in subsequent philosophical history, be called 'disjunctive', such as being as act/potency, perfect/imperfect, absolute/dependent, simple/composite, and so forth. To fully resolve the notion of being requires some primitive acquaintance with the more perfect member of each of these couplets: being as most actual, most perfect, most absolute, and most simple. But such a being is God. Hence, although being is first known, what is actually first known through being is God.

A second presentation of the thesis of God as first known occurs in chapter 5. In this text, the parallel argument does not refer to being through the concrete term (*ens*), but through the abstract term (*esse*, or 'to be'). We must recall that chapters 5 and 6 concern the stage of the journey in which the wayfarer is seeing God in the things above herself and that here the concept of 'to be' involves seeing God through the things above ourselves, just as 'goodness' (*bonum*) involves seeing God in the things above ourselves. The argument here seems to trade on a distinction between the concrete and the abstract, though how this difference is ultimately to be understood is not so clear (For discussion, see Goris, 2011, 86–89; Metselaar, 2009, 52–59). The reasoning moves from considering the notion of being as most certain—since the non-existence of being is unthinkable—to the conclusion that to be, as the pure act of being, is the first thing known; then, from that conclusion to the further conclusion that divine being (*esse divinum*) is what is first known. The first step requires that we understand being as most certain, but it can only be such if it is grasped as being in its purity. But being in its purity means being with no aspect of non-being involved in its notion. That in turn means being understood as purely actual since being as potency always involves some mixture of non-being in being. But being as purely actual is pure act. The second step then is the working out of the implications in this claim: such a being cannot be a particular being since that is necessarily limited being and thus partakes of potency, but it cannot be analogical being, that is to say, being understood as common to substance and accident or God and creature since that has even less a degree of actuality. Hence, the purely actual being that is understood by us is the divine being (*esse divinum*).

Here we may be puzzled what this line of reasoning has to do with divine illumination. But Bonaventure clarifies this point in *Itinerarium* chapter 5 n. 4 (ed. Boehner, 82). Although he does not refer to his earlier discussion at chapter 3, he obviously proceeds on the assumption that being is what underlies all of our categorical and transcategorical concepts. If that is so and if 'to be' as divine being is what underlies the concept of being as concrete, then the mind, he tells us, must be remarkably blind, for this notion of being as pure and divine actually is the starting point for all of our intellectual knowledge, yet the human mind seems to be entirely oblivious to this fact. This hidden but maximally operative notion is, then, the illumination of our mind, though we perceive it as a mist (*summa caligo*). Bonaventure compares it to the human eye which does not notice the purest light, even when it sees it; rather if it perceives just light the eye seems to see nothing (*Itin.* chap. 5, n. 4; ed. Boehner, 82).

Both the arguments of chapters 3 and 5 are philosophically interesting inasmuch as they arrive at the conclusion that, if we maintain that being is the starting point of our intellectual knowledge and the reference point of all of our concepts, the notion of being involves our knowing pure being, which, in turn, involves our knowing God, though unwittingly. The actual process of the argument here seems to trade on the understanding of being as a nature along the lines that Avicenna conceives of it; that is, what belongs to a notion setting aside all else that is connected or concomitant with it. If we apply this approach to the notion of being, Bonaventure maintains, we must conclude that God, as the pure expression of being, is what underlies our thinking. Historically speaking, Bonaventure's argument regarding divine illumination, combining as it does this epistemological theory with the thesis that God is first known, was to have a substantial impact on later philosophy. For it presses readers to offer an alternative account for the connection between the concept of being, what is first known, and God, if they are unwilling to accept Bonaventure's own way of organizing them, endorsing both divine illumination and God, and not simply being, as the first thing known by the human mind. Readers from Henry of Ghent in the late thirteenth century to Husserlian phenomenologists in the twentieth have felt the attraction as well as the challenge of Bonaventure's views (Cator, 1934, 183–187).

PART VII
Aquinas on Analogy

Editor's Introduction

The topic of analogy drew the interest of both logicians and theologians in the Middle Ages. Reflecting on Aristotle's distinction between words used univocally (with the same sense) and words used equivocally (with different senses), medieval logicians distinguished various sorts of equivocity. Some words were used in completely unrelated senses, as when we say that "Carissa's bat cracked when she struck the ball" and "Carissa's bat eats citrus fruit." On the other hand, some words are used in related senses, as when we say: "Beulah the cow is healthy," "Beulah's urine is healthy," and "Beulah's medicine is healthy." According to the first proposition, Beulah is the subject of health; according to the second, her urine indicates that she has health; and according to the third, her medicine will cause her health. These three uses of "healthy" are neither univocal nor purely equivocal. They are analogical.

Theologians appealed to analogy to address problems in language about God. Medieval Jews, Christians, and Muslims take God to be unlike any creature in that he is absolutely simple and transcendent. To say that Socrates is just or wise is to say that Socrates has the property or "accident" of goodness or wisdom, and has it to a limited degree. However, when we say that God is just and wise, this claim cannot have the same sense. God cannot have any accidents, since he would then be a compound of substance and accident. Rather, he is good and wise by his very essence and without limitation. What if we do not ascribe any accident to God but merely describe his relationship to creatures? Even in that case we face difficulties. We can say without difficulty that Socrates is Plato's guide, since Socrates and Plato are relevantly alike. But if we say that God is Socrates' guide, that claim must have a very different sense since God is transcendent and cannot be captured by the Aristotelian categories. One possibility, then, is that language about God is purely equivocal. In that case, however, we would have no idea what words such as "wise", "just", or "powerful" meant in the case of God, and religious discourse would be largely pointless. To resolve this problem, many medieval theologians, including Aquinas, maintained that language about God falls midway between univocity and pure equivocity. It is analogical.

Ralph McInerny's goal is to offer a full, clear description of Aquinas's account of analogy; once we have that, we can then use it to understand the doctrine of religious language that is embedded in it. McInerny explains that Aquinas's account of analogy is a logical rather than a metaphysical doctrine. Although this doctrine is closely tied to Aquinas's metaphysical views about reality, it is because of the way we think and speak about those real things that we call them analogous (or equivocal or univocal). He then sets out Aquinas's explanation of how a name can be used in multiple senses that are partly the same, but partly different. Each name has a *ratio*, that is, the intellect's conception of what that name signifies. That *ratio* is a function of both what the name signifies (the *res significata*) and the name's mode of signifying (its *modus significandi*). When a word is used analogously, its uses have senses that are partly the same and partly different. Aquinas explains this phenomenon, McInerny argues, by noting that in each case what the name signifies is the same, but the mode of signification is different. That is why each analogous use of a name has a *ratio* that is partly the same as, yet partly different from, the others.

On the face of it, McInerny's plan is eminently sensible: Explain Aquinas on language about God by appeal to the broader account of analogy in which this theological language is grounded. However, E. J. Ashworth argues that this plan is flawed because Aquinas has no broader account that is complete and stable enough to play this role. What Aquinas says about analogy undergoes significant changes over time, and what he says about analogy is restricted to his limited needs in any particular context. More importantly, she argues that McInerny misunderstands some of Aquinas's central claims about analogy. While he recognizes that Aquinas forms his own views in a historical context and expresses his views in a technical language, he pays too little attention to that context and language and as a result produces an account of analogy that Aquinas never held.

Note on References

Aquinas wrote three major syntheses of his thought. The earliest is his commentary on the four-book *Sentences* of Peter Lombard, a broad work that raises a vast number of issues in theology. At the time Aquinas attended university, all students seeking a doctorate in theology were required to lecture on, and write a detailed commentary on, Lombard's *Sentences* as the culmination of their graduate studies. In Latin, Aquinas's commentary is called the *Scriptum super Libros Sententiarum* and references to it take a form such as this: "*In 3 Sent.* 22.1.3," which refers to the commentary on Book 3, distinction 22, question 1, article 3 of the *Sentences.* The second of Aquinas's syntheses is the work we know as the four-book *Summa contra gentiles* (abbreviated as CG or SCG). Standard references to this work refer to the book, chapter, and chapter subdivision. The third synthesis is the *Summa theologiae* (sometimes called the *Summa theologica*). This work is divided into three parts, abbreviated as I, II, and III (or 1, 2, 3; you may also sometimes see Ia, IIa, and IIIa, for the Latin *Prima Pars, Secunda Pars,*and *Tertia Pars*). The Second Part is so large that it is itself divided into two parts, descriptively called I-II (the First Part of the Second Part, sometimes abbreviated as IaIIae) and II-II (the Second Part of the Second Part, sometimes abbreviated as IIaIIae). Hence, "ST I 13.4" refers to the First Part, question 13, article 4.

References to Aquinas's various commentaries on earlier works (such as philosophical texts by Aristotle or Boethius, as well as books of the Bible) often follow the same pattern as references to his commentary on the *Sentences.* For instance, "*In 11 Met.*" refers to Aquinas's commentary on book 11 of Aristotle's *Metaphysics.*

For references to Aristotle, see the Note on References in Part IV.

PL = Patrologia Latina. References in Ashworth and McInerny to Boethius are to PL vol. 64.

L = Leonine edition of Aquinas's work (in Latin). The Leonine edition, which is not yet complete, is a great improvement over prior complete editions of Aquinas's work.

Further Reading

- William P. Alston (1993). "Aquinas on Theological Predication: A Look Backward and a Look Forward."
- E. J. Ashworth (1991). "Signification and Modes of Signifying in Thirteenth-Century Logic: A Preface to Aquinas on Analogy."

CHAPTER 13

Analogous Names

RALPH MCINERNY

Whenever Thomas lays out what he means by a word's being analogous, he refers us to univocal and equivocal terms and notes that the analogous term can be located between these two as extremes.[1] Aristotle's discussion of equivocal and univocal terms at the outset of his *Categories* provided the point of reference for the discussion of analogous terms.

Equivocals

"Things are said to be named equivocally when, though they have a common name, the definition corresponding with the name differs for each."[2] It is, of course, the Latin translation of this sentence that influenced Thomas Aquinas. *Aequivoca dicuntur quorum solum nomen commune est, secundum nomen vero substantiae ratio diversa.*[3] To be named equivocally is not a property things possess independently of our knowing and talking about them. Names attach to things insofar as they are known.[4] Doubtless this is why, in the Aristotelian definition, things are *said* to be equivocal: *dicuntur, et non sunt.*[5] If man with his distinctive mode of knowing did not exist, there would be no equivocal things—that is, things named equivocally. No one would be talking.

Things named equivocally are said to have only a name in common; as soon as we look beyond the shared name, we see diversity. The common term does not signify the same definition in each use. The English translation relies on a loose use of "definition", something avoided by the Greek λόγος [*logos*] and Latin *ratio.*[6] A definition in the strict sense, one composed of a proximate genus and specific difference, is not necessarily intended by *ratio* in the definition of equivocals. If it were, the apparent purpose of speaking first of equivocals and then of univocals would be defeated. Aristotle is preparing to speak of the ten supreme genera of which "being" is said, not univocally, but equivocally. Since the supreme genera cannot have a definition in the strict sense, they could not be said to be named equivocally if *ratio* had the strict sense.

Aristotle's definition begins from things, and these things are said to be equivocal. They are not equivocal in themselves, as things, but insofar as they are talked of in a certain way.[7] Nevertheless, Aristotle is not talking about equivocation but about equivocals, about things named equivocally. The *Categories* divides things, not as they exist, but as they are known and named by us. That is why it is a logical work. What is categorized is the real; categorization is logical.[8] The division is in terms of the different mode of existence (and hence of signification) that things have in our mind. Things are said to be equivocal or univocal because of what happens to them due to our mode of knowing them and talking about them.[9] This is the reason for the distinction mentioned by Cajetan[10] and John of St. Thomas,[11] though not original with them, between *aequivocum aequivocans* (the name) and *aequivoca aequivocata* (the things). Because things are equivocal as named and thus as known by us, this is a logical designation.

A difficulty can arise in understanding Aristotle's claim that equivocals have the same name. What constitutes a name as a name is the fact that it signifies something, and that something is either the *ratio* or a thing via the *ratio*. A name is the name it is, is individuated, so to say, by its meaning. How then can we speak of the same name where there are different meanings? It would seem that we should speak of the same *vox* rather than the same name in discussing equivocals and the Latin would read "quorum solum vox communis."

St. Albert goes into this problem at some length and suggests a distinction between a first and a second form of the name. The physical sound, the *vox*, is what is material, and the first form specifying it is accent, pronunciation, and, as written, letters and syllables, its orthography. The first form adds to the mere vocal sound, modulating and articulating it so that one sound differs from another. It is thanks to this formation that the sound is a word or name, an element of language. In this sense, Albert suggests, things named equivocally can have the same name.[12] It is the same articulate sound and, as written, has the same spelling. Unless the *vox* has received this first form, it is not apt to take on the further form of signification and, since it can retain this first form even when its significations vary, we can say that the same name is retained. It is, of course, essential to the understanding of the definition of equivocals that the second form of the *vox*, its signification, be understood as well. In things named equivocally, the *vox* has not only received the first determination of accent, letters and syllables, it is also taken as signifying. The point is that it signifies different things. Thus the same name in one sense becomes different names in another sense of the term. Support for this explanation of Albert can be found in Thomas.[13]

With regard to the phrase in the definition "secundum nomen substantiae ratio diversa" ["the account of the thing that is associated with the name is different"], St. Albert seems to be the only one who has referred this to the dictum "omne nomen substantiam significat cum qualitate" ["Every name signifies substance with quality".[14] The *ratio substantiae* is that which the name is imposed to signify; the quality of the name is that *a quo nomen imponitur* [that from which the name is imposed]. The substance of the name is that to which it is attributed, or that for which it supposits (what it means thanks to the meaning or *ratio* of the name).[15]

In his definition, Aristotle insists that it is according to the name that equivocals have in common that they are said to be named equivocally. Given another name, it could happen that things named equivocally would be named univocally.

Examples abound of shared names that do not get the same account.

Ducks have bills, and one should pay his bills.
Cinderella, dancing on the balls of her feet at the ball, was having a ball until she slipped on a ball.
Before he would bowl, he had to have a bowl of beer.
Can girls who can can-can?
Darn she cried and darn she did, and here are the socks to prove it.
Hail to the chief they cried, just as hail began to fall.

Language is an inexhaustible source of equivocation, and to know a language is to know that. Formal logic was once unctuously recommended as a way of overcoming the fatal ambiguity of ordinary language. But ambiguity is an ordinary, not a fatal, aspect of language, a constant source of fun and puns. And, of course, the humorless logician must first sort out all the meanings before he can assign them different symbols. In doing that he will find he already has the skill to recognize equivocation. Aristotle does not discuss equivocation as an unfortunate and removable aspect of the way we talk of things. To ignore it is productive of all kinds of strange theories. This was his complaint against Plato. There is, of course, the fallacy of equivocation, but the cure for fallacies is not the invention of an artificial language.

Univocals

"On the other hand, things are said to be named univocally which have both the name and the definition answering to the name in common."[16] Once again, Aristotle begins from the things named, and once again there is community of the name. But here, in contrast to equivocals, the community extends beyond the name to the *ratio* or definition signified by it. When a man and an ox are called animals, they have the name "animal" in common, and what is signified by the name is shared by each and, from this point of view, shared equally. Both a man and an ox are "animate sensitive substance." The term "animal" is imposed to signify what man and ox have in common with a generic community.

The elements of the definitions

*Aristotle

ὄνομα χοινόν
λόγος τῆς οὐσίας
λέγεται
αὐτός, ἕτερος

Equivocally named = only the shared name the same, the account given of the substance different

Univocally named = shared name the same, the account given of the substance the same

*Boethius:

nomen commune
ratio substantiae
dicuntur
diversa, eadem

*Edghill

common name
definition
are named
differs, is the same

*Ackrill

name in common
definition of being
different, same

What these definitions enable us to do is to distinguish lists like:

1. Desdemona is a wife.
2. Xanthippe is a wife.
3. Lady Macbeth is a wife.

from lists like:

1. The monkey climbed the pole.
2. The cardinals elected a Pole.

and

1. There is no ace in this deck.
2. The boy stood on the burning deck.

But is the example of the *Categories,* a man and his picture, like these last two lists? There seems to be no connection whatsoever between the things called pole or deck, whereas a man and his painting had better be alike. In fact, it would be difficult to explain what we mean by the likeness of a man without referring to the man it is like. That is why "to cow one's opponents" and "to milk a cow" may not seem as distant as pole and deck, no more than do "the miller mills" and "the crowd mills about." While these latter terms would get different accounts, they seem related nonetheless.

Boethius, therefore, introduces a distinction (166A–B) between *aequivoca a casu* [equivocals by chance] and *aequivoca a consilio* [deliberate equivocals]. His example of the first is a proper name that happens to be shared by different individuals. The second, he says, is exemplified by the example Aristotle gives in the text. This distinction has as its consequence that the opposition at the outset of the *Categories* is not between purely equivocal terms and univocal terms but between deliberately equivocal terms and univocal terms. The significance of the distinction is this: taken as such, the discussion at the outset of the *Categories* does not give us the extremes that analogous names are midway between.

How things named equivocally and those named univocally differ is now clear. The latter have a common name, and the same *ratio* is signified by the name as it is used of each. In equivocals, on the other hand, although they have a common name, the name signifies different *rationes* as applied to them. A point of extreme importance, which warrants repetition, is that things are said to be (*dicuntur*) equivocals or univocals. In themselves, *in rerum natura,* they are neither, for in order to be univocals or equivocals they must be known and named by us. We are talking about things signified insofar as they are signified. That is why the doctrine of equivocals and univocals is called a logical one.

In the interest of exhausting the possibilities if not the patience of the reader, let us take note of the fourfold division proposed by Boethius.[17] He observes that things may be *univoca, diversivoca, multivoca,* or *aequivoca.* That is, they have one name that signifies the same *ratio;* or they have different names that signify different *rationes*; or one thing receives many names that signify the same *ratio* (what we mean by synonyms; Aristotle's *synonyma* is translated as *univoca*); or many things have one name that signifies diverse *rationes.* It is with the last, the equivocals, that analogy is located.

Analogates

We have seen that, for St. Thomas, analogy is a kind of equivocation, but, when we spoke of equivocals, we said nothing of analogy. How can room be made for analogy among things spoken of equivocally? In addressing that question, I want to look at what Boethius and Albert, and Cajetan too, have to say before turning to St. Thomas himself. They commented on the *Categories* whereas

Thomas did not; but, by referring the analogy of names to the discussion of equivocals, he explicitly calls into play what Aristotle had to say about them. That is why we have been approaching Thomas via the *Categories*.

The clearest case of equivocals is had when things share a name that gets a totally different account as said of each of them. 'Pen' said of a writing instrument and of an enclosure for pigs is used equivocally. But when a cow and a picture of a cow are both called 'animal', the notions signified by the name, while diverse, are not wholly so. Let us say that the example of 'pen' gives us a case of pure equivocation, while that of 'animal' does not. In the case of 'pen', as in the sentences given above, it seems that the same orthographic symbol just happens to be used in that way, as having several wholly unrelated meanings. Having the same name is adventitious. Asking why 'bill' is used to mean the beak of a duck and a demand for payment would not be a good research project. Demanding that we nail down the reason why 'nail' has the meanings it does may not be rewarding. There may be lost connections, of course, and they can delight us when they are ferreted out. This rediscovered link (as between a chain and a golf course) may suggest that there really are no accidents and thus no examples of pure equivocation, and that would be a great leap indeed. Consider the examples of 'ball' and 'can' above, and imagine the sentences that we might form with 'stick' and 'gum' and 'page' and on and on. While some uses may wrongly be taken to exemplify pure equivocation, it is inescapable that different meanings have been assigned to the same term without rhyme or reason, but the example Aristotle gives of equivocals does not seem one of pure equivocation. 'Animal' is not fortuitously used to speak of a cow and her portrait. True, it would not mean exactly the same thing in each use—it isn't univocal—but its meanings are not unrelated. That is why Boethius picks up from Aristotle elsewhere the distinction between chance equivocals and equivocals by design.[18]

Commentators are unanimous in seeing Aristotle's example of equivocals as other than pure equivocation. It is only fitting that it not be when we consider the purpose of the discussion as prologue to discussing the supreme genera of being. Nonetheless, Aristotle's definition can be taken to cover two types, pure equivocation and equivocation by design, depending on whether the diversity of the notions is complete or partial.[19]

Where there is only partial diversity in things named equivocally, there must also be partial sameness. The sameness is had, St. Albert notes, in this, that the name principally signifies one of the equivocals and signifies the others insofar as they refer in some way to what is principally signified. He illustrates this point with the familiar Aristotelian examples of 'being', 'medicine', and 'medical'. Furthermore, Albert uses the term 'analogy' to set off intended equivocation from chance equivocation. "Et hic quidem modus vocatur multiplex dictum secundum analogiam, sive proportionem ad unum quod principaliter in nomine significatur."[20]

Not without interest is the fact that Cajetan, in his commentary on the *Categories,* says quite explicitly that analogy is a kind of equivocation. Having pointed out that *diversa* in the definition of things named equivocally should be understood as comprising both complete and partial diversity on the part of the *rationes* signified by the common name, he goes on to say that the example given by Aristotle is one of "aequivocatio a consilio seu analogia."[21] It is precisely here that he promises a separate treatise on this kind of equivocation.[22] That separate treatise was to be the *De nominum analogia,* and in it analogy, which is a kind of equivocation, unaccountably becomes something metaphysical. In turning now to the texts of St. Thomas, we will find the resources to decide whether Cajetan was explaining equivocation or employing it.

Let it be recalled that St. Thomas devoted no special treatise to the question of analogous names. We have been proceeding as we have in this chapter because of Thomas's placement of analogous names between purely equivocal and univocal names. Let us then fashion a definition of analogous names, or of things named analogously, on the model of the definitions of the *Categories.*

> Things are said to be named analogously when, though they have a name in common, the definitions corresponding with the name are partly the same and partly different, with one of those definitions being prior to the others.

Here is precisely how Thomas puts it:

> Et iste modus communitatis medius est inter puram aequivocationem et simplicem univocationem. Neque enim in his quae analogice dicuntur, est una ratio, sicut est in univocis; nec totaliter diversa, sicut in aequivocis; sed nomen quod sic multipliciter dicitur, significat diversas proportiones ad aliquid unum; sicut *sanum,* de urina dictum, significat signum sanitatis animalis, de medicina vero dictum, significat causam eiusdem sanitatis.
> (*ST,* I, q.13, a.5)

> This type of community is midway between pure equivocation and simple univocation. In things named analogously there is neither one account, as with univocals, nor totally diverse accounts, as with equivocals. Rather a name said in many ways in this manner signifies diverse proportions to some one thing. For example, 'healthy' as said of urine signifies a sign of the health of the animal, but said of medicine it signifies the cause of the same health.

We notice that it is the *proportion* or *analogy* of secondary meanings to the primary meaning that explains Thomas's use of the term analogy to speak of common names of this type.

> . . . in omnibus nominibus quae de pluribus analogice dicuntur, necesse est quod omnia dicantur per respectum ad unum: et ideo illud unum oportet quod ponatur in definitione omnium. Et quia ratio quam significat nomen est definitio, ut dicitur in IV *Metaphys.*, necesse est quod illud nomen per prius dicatur de eo quod ponitur in definitione aliorum, et per posterius de aliis, secundum ordinem quo appropinquant ad illud primum vel magis vel minus: sicut *sanum* quod dicitur de animali, cadit in definitione *sani* quod dicitur de medicina, quae dicitur sana inquantum causat sanitatem in animali; et in definitione *sani* quod dicitur de urina, quae dicitur sana inquantum est signum sanitatis animalis.
>
> (*ST*, I, q. 13, a. 6, reply)

> In all names said analogously of many, it is necessary that all are said with respect to one and that that one be placed in the definition of all. Because the account the name signifies is a definition, as is said in *Metaphysics* IV, it is necessary that the name be said first of that which is put into the definition of the others, and secondarily of the others, in the order in which they are more or less proximate to that first thing: for example, 'healthy' as said of animal enters into the definition of 'healthy' said of medicine, which is called healthy insofar as it causes health in the animal; and in the definition of 'healthy' said of urine insofar as it is the sign of the health of the animal.

Aristotle sometimes says that 'being' is predicated equivocally of substance and the other categories; just so, Thomas notes, he will say that 'animal' is predicated equivocally of an animal and its portrait. But these are both instances of analogous name. Thomas seldom speaks of analogous names without contrasting them with equivocal and univocal names. He exemplifies pure equivocation by 'dog' said of an animal and a star.[23] He also adopts the contrast between chance equivocation and equivocation by design.[24] Unlike Boethius, he takes two men having the same proper name as an obvious case of chance equivocation.[25]

> Quandoque vero secundum rationes quae partim sunt diversae et partim non diversae: diversae quidem secundum quod diversas habitudines important, unae autem secundum quod ad unum aliquid et idem istae diversae habitudines referuntur; et illud dicitur analogice praedicari, idest proportionaliter, prout unumquodque secundum suam habitudinem ad illud unum refertur.
>
> (*In IV Metaphysic.*, lect. 1, n. 535)

> Sometimes, however, according to accounts that are partly diverse and partly not diverse: diverse insofar as they involve diverse relations, but

one insofar as these diverse relations are referred to one and the same thing; that is said to be predicated analogically, that is, proportionally, insofar as each in its own way is referred to that one thing.

Terminology

We see a technical, that is, logical, terminology emerging. We can say that the analogous name signifies a plurality of *rationes* which are related *per prius et posterius;* that is, one *ratio* is primary and presupposed by the others, this being revealed by the fact that the first *ratio* enters into the others. These secondary *rationes* signify diverse *proportions* or *analogies to* the first; they are said *per respectum ad unum* [with respect to one].

Question: In the favored example of 'healthy', there seems to be vacillation between saying, on the one hand, that the one thing to which all the *rationes* refer and which they all contain is 'health', and, on the other hand, that there is one meaning of 'healthy' (viz. the health of the animal) that is the per prius with respect to which, on an analogy with which, other meanings of 'healthy' are formed. Which is it?

This question is sharpened when we consider the universal rule about analogous names stated in *ST,* I, q. 16, a. 6: "Sed quando aliquid dicitur analogice de multis, illud invenitur *secundum propriam rationem* in uno eorum tantum, a quo alia denominantur" ["However, when something is said analogically of many things, it is found in just one of them according to its proper account; from this one the others are denominated"]. What is the *ratio propria, sanitas* (health) or *sanitas animalis* (healthy)? *Response:* [a] Both the abstract ('health') and the concrete ('healthy') term involve complexity, because the form or *res significata* is not subsistent, (cf. *ST,* I, q. 13, a. 1 response to 2). The account or ratio of 'health' is 'that whereby a thing is called healthy'; the account or ratio of 'healthy' is 'that which has health'. As Thomas pointed out in the *De ente,* the form or essence is predicated of the individual only as concretely signified, never as abstractly signified.[26] The analogous term is one predicable of many things; the analogous term is a concrete term.

[b] The concrete term is a way of signifying (*modus significandi*) a form or perfection (*res significata*). The analogous name has a plurality of rationes, each of which signifies the same form or perfection (*res significata*), but in different ways. This form is the *id a quo nomen imponitur ad significandum,* that which is picked out by the word to designate the thing.

More Logical Terminology

Analogous names thus have the same *res significata* and diverse *modi significandi.* Each *ratio* involves both the *res significata* and a way of signifying it. The *ratio propria* is not the *res significata,* but the primary and controlling way of signifying the *res significata.*[27]

Thus, all of the *rationes* of the analogous name are sometimes said to refer to, to be proportioned to, the same *res significata,* but this is an elliptical way of saying that the secondary meanings are ways of signifying the *res significata,* which relates or proportions them to the primary way of signifying the form.

The *ratio propria,* therefore, is not *sanitas* but *sanum* taken as meaning *sanitas animalis.*

We see now the precise meaning of saying that the many rationes of the analogous name are partly the same and partly different. They are the same as to the *res significata;* they differ as to the *modi significandi.* . . .

Notes

1. "Et iste modus communitatis medius est inter puram aequivocationem et simplicem univocationem" (*ST,* I, q. 13, a. 5, reply).
2. *Categories,* 1a1–2. [Editor's note: A stricter translation of the sentence would be: "Things are called 'equivocals' when just their name is common, while the account of the thing that is associated with the name is different."]
3. The Latin translation by Boethius continues: ". . . ut animal homo et quod pingitur. Horum enim solum nomen commune est, secundum nomen vero substantiae ratio diversa. Si quis enim assignet quid sit utrumque eorum, quo sint animalia propriam assignabit utriusque rationem." Cf. Boethius, *In Categorias Aristotelis,* PL 64, 163C.
4. *On Interpretation,* 16a3–4. We have discussed this in the previous chapter.
5. [Editor's note: The Latin means "For they *are* not equivocal things, but they *are called* equivocal."] Cf. Boethius, *In Categorias Aristotelis,* PL 64, 164B: "Aequivoca, inquit, dicuntur res scilicet, quae per se ipsas aequivocae non sunt, nisi uno nomine praedicentur: quare quoniam ut aequivoca sint, ex communi vocabulo trahunt, recte ait, aequivoca dicuntur. Non enim sunt aequivoca, sed dicuntur."
6. There is a marked similarity between the various meanings of *ratio* given by St. Thomas in his commentary on the *De divinis nominibus,* lect. 5, n. 735, and those given by Boethius. "Ratio quoque multimode dicitur. Est enim ratio animae, et est ratio computandi, est ratio naturae, ipsa nimirum similitude nascentium, est ratio quae in diffinitionibus vel descriptionibus redditur. Et quoniam generalissima genera genere carent, individua vero nulla substantiali differentia discrepant, diffinitio vero ex genere et differentia trahitur, neque generalissimorum generum, neque individuorum ulla potest diffinitio reperiri. Subalternorum vero generum, quoniam et differentias habent et genera, difinitiones esse possunt. At vero quorum diffinitiones reddi nequeunt, illa tantum descriptionibus terminantur. Descriptio autem est, quae quamlibet rem propria quadam proprietate designat. Sive ergo diffinitio sit, sive descriptio, utraque rationem substantiae designat" (*In Categorias Aristotelis,* PL, vol. 64, col. 166A).
7. Joseph Owens, in his magisterial *The Doctrine of Being in the Aristotelian Metaphysics* (Owens 1978), has an extended discussion on this passage (pp. 107–135). His insistence that Aristotle's focus is on things rather than words or concepts may suggest that equivocity is a property of things *tout court.* Wherever the emphasis may lie in a given passage, equivocation requires several things, one word and diverse meanings.
8. De Rijk (1952), vacillates between calling the work logical and calling it ontological.
9. "Et dicuntur univoca per oppositum modum ad aequivoca, res scilicet univocatae in nomine uno, ut res ipsa ad dici et ad sermonem referatur, quia aliter non esset logicum quod dicitur: quia res in se considerata, non secundum quod stat sub dictione, non ad logicum, sed ad

Philosophum pertinet. Et ideo additur, *dicuntur,* et non dicitur univoca *sunt*" (St. Albert, *In praedicamentis Aristotelis* [Albert the Great (1890)] tract. I, cap. 3). See also Cajetan (1939), p. 9: "Signanter quoque dixit 'dicuntur' et non 'sunt', quia rebus non convenit aequivocari ut sunt in rerum natura, sed ut sint in vocibus nostris. Aequivocari enim praesupponit vocari, quod rebus ex nobis accidit."

10. Cajetan (1939), p. 8.
11. John of St. Thomas (1933) p. 478: "Sed quia non dicuntur aequivocata nisi ratione intentionis alicujus, quae dicitur aequivocatio, et haec, ut statim dicemus, non convenit rebus significatis nisi ut subsunt nomini, non vero conceptui ultimato, ideo traditur definitio per nomen, in ordine ad quod sumitur intentio aequivocationis."
12. Albert the Great (1890), cap. 2.
13. John of St. Thomas (1933, p. 579) directs our attention to *Quodlibet IV,* q. 9, a. 2: "Manifestum est autem quod unitas vocis significativae vel diversitas non dependet ex unitate vel diversitate rei significatae; *alioquin non esset aliquod nomen aequivocum:* secundum hoc enim si sint diversae res, essent diversa nomina, et non idem nomen."
14. Albert the Great (1890), cap. 2: ". . . et id quidem cui imponitur nomen est significata substantia ipsius; proprietas autem ejusdem rei sive substantiae quae afficit imponentem dum nomen imponit, est qualitas significata per nomen."
15. [Editor's note : We "impose" the names of things (that is, we turn sounds into significant speech) from certain "qualities" or forms on the basis of which we cognize those things. However, those qualities are not always what we impose the name to signify.] Cf. Boethius, PL, vol. 64, col. 165C: "Idem etiam in his nominibus quae de duabus rebus communiter praedicantur, si secundum nomen substantiae ratio non reddatur, potest aliquoties fieri, ut ex univocis aequivoca sint, et ex aequivocis univoca; namque homo atque equus cum secundum nomen animalis univoca sint, possunt esse aequivoca, si secundum nomen minime diffinita sint. Homo namque et equus communi nomine animalia nuncupantur, si quis ergo hominis reddat diffinitionem dicens, animal rationale mortale, et equi, animal irrationale hinnibile, diversas reddidit diffinitiones, et erunt res univocae in aequivocas permutatae. Hoc autem idcirco evenit, quod diffinitiones non secundum animalis nomen redditae sunt, quod eorum commune vocabulum est, sed secundum hominis atque equi."
16. "Univoca dicuntur quorum nomen commune est, et secundum nomen eadem ratio substantiae" (*Categories,* 1a6–7).
17. Boethius, PL, vol. 64, cols. 164–5.
18. Boethius, PL, vol. 64, col. 166: "Aequivocorum alia sunt casu, alia consilio. Casio ut Alexander Primari filius et Alexander Magnus. Casus enim id egit, ut idem utrique nomen poneretur. Consilio vero, ea quaecumque hominum voluntate sunt posita." The use of proper names to make the point may surprise. But then we have Alexander senior and Alexander junior. On the other hand, a random selection of men named John would be unlikely to turn up an eponymous instance of the name among them. Of course, if they are all Christians and were christened John after the same saint who is put before them as a model of the Christian life, we might judge differently. But there are, of course, many Johns in the calendar of saints.
19. Albert the Great (1890) spells this out "Quando ergo idem est nomen quantum ad ea quae sunt nominis in littera et accentu: et id quod significatur in nomine, non est idem vel aeque participatum ab ills quibus nomen imponitur, nec etiam proprietas a qua impositum est omnino eadem est, quamvis forte referatur ad unum: tunc nomen est aequivocum, quia ratio substantiae cui nomen imponitur (quae est ratio substantialis a qua nomen imponitur) sic duobus modis est secundum aliquid vel simpliciter diversa: substantia enim aliqua (ut diximus) est secundum aliquid per modum quo rationi substat, cui nomen ipsum imponitur: et illius ratio diversa est quando non penitus est eadem: et adhuc a quo nomen imponitur quod est nomimis qualitas, et substantialis ratio quae datur de nomine secundum illud quod nomen est. Quando ergo illa etiam non penitus est eadem, iterum ratio substantiae, hoc est, substantialis ratio nominis est diversa: ita quod nihil rei cui imponitur nomen, aequaliter

participant significata per nomen" (cap. 2).

20. Albert the Great (1890). Boethius too speaks of equivocals by design as representing an *aequivocatio secundum proportionem.* Cf. PL vol. 64, col. 166: ". . . secundum proportionem, ut principium, namque principium est in numero unitas, in lineis punctum . . . Alia vero sunt quae ab uno desccndunt. Alia quae ad unum referuntur . . ." It is interesting to see Boethius move easily from what might be called the proportionality of 'principle' to proportions *ad unum* and *ab uno.* It is noteworthy that Boethius distinguishes equivocation *secundum proportionem* from that *secundum similitudinem.* It is the last kind of equivocation that he feels is involved in the example given by Aristotle in the *Categories.*
21. Cajetan (1952), p. 10.
22. "Quot autem modis contingat variari analogiam et quomodo, nunc quum summarie loquimur, silentio pertransibimus, specialem de hoc tractatum, si Deo placuerit, cito confecturi" (Cajetan [1952], p. 11).
23. *In IV Metaphysic.*, lect. 1, n. 535; *In* X *I Metaphysic.*, lect. 3, n. 2197; *I Sent.*, d. 31, q. 2, a. 1 response to 2.
24. *In I Ethic.*, lect. 7, n. 95; *I* S *ent.*, d. 31, q. 2, a. 1 response to 2.
25. *In I Ethic.*, lect. 7, n. 95.
26. Et quia, ut dictum est, natura speciei est indeterminata respectu indiuidui sicut natura generis respectu speciei: inde est quod, sicut id quod est genus prout praedicabatur de specie implicabat in sua significatione, quamuis indistincte, totum quod determinate est in specie, ita etiam et id quod est species secundum quod praedicatur de individuo oportet quod significet totum id quod est essentialiter in indiuiduo, licet indistincte. Et hoc modo essentia speciei significatur nomine hominis, unde homo de Sorte praedicatur. Si autem significetur natura sperici cum praecisione materiae designate quo est principium induiduationis, sic se habebit per modum partis; et hoc modo significatur nomine humanitatis, humanitas enim significat id unde homo est homo [. . .] inde est quod humanitas nec de homine nec de Sorte praedicatur" (*De Ente et Essentia*, cap. 2. L vol. 43, p. 373, ll. 243–67; see *In VII Metaphysic.*, lect. 5, nn. 1378–9).
27. For a dissenting view on the importance of the distinction between *modus significandi* and *res significata* for the analogy of names, see E. J. Ashworth pp. 60–61.

CHAPTER 14

Aquinas on Analogy

E. J. ASHWORTH

In this short chapter, I hope to demonstrate the importance of paying very close attention to the historical context of the theory of analogy, and to the way in which technical terms were actually used when explicating Aquinas's theory of analogy. In addition, I intend to argue that McInerny gets Aquinas's theory wrong partly because he places too little emphasis on the fact that Aquinas was principally concerned with the names we use of God.

Introduction

Analogy is a notion with various uses. In epistemology one can speak of coming to know something new on the basis of an analogy or likeness between two things, and such analogies can form the basis for analogical arguments, including the argument from design for the existence of God. In ontology, the so-called analogy of being refers to the doctrine that reality is divided horizontally into the very different realities of substances and accidents,[1] and vertically into the very different realities of God and creatures, and that these different realities are related by some kind of likeness. However, for the purposes of this discussion, we are primarily concerned with analogy as a doctrine belonging to the philosophy of language, and most especially as a solution to the problem of religious language.

Aquinas has been hailed through the centuries as making a particularly important contribution, and recent philosophers of religion have taken his doctrines seriously (e.g. Swinburne 1977, Alston 1993). But there are various problems, many stemming from the fact that nowhere does Aquinas give a sustained account of analogy, but rather he employs the notion on an ad hoc basis to settle the issues under discussion in a particular place. One problem, which I shall touch on briefly below, is whether his account of analogy changed over the years. Two other problems have been discussed fairly extensively by McInerny. One is the question of whether it is a theory of language at all, or whether Aquinas was more concerned with the analogy of being; another concerns the truth of the long-held belief that Cardinal Cajetan's book on analogy, published in 1506, though written in 1498, gave an accurate account of Aquinas. McInerny has successfully argued that Aquinas was indeed concerned with analogical terms, even though his account had certain metaphysical views as its basis, and that Cajetan is not a good interpreter of Aquinas.[2] In what follows, I shall focus on another aspect of Aquinas: how his theory is embedded in specifically medieval semantics. It is here that the fourth chapter of McInerny's book (chapter 13, this volume) offers a useful object lesson in the importance of getting such matters straight. Aquinas wrote in a specific context, and he used terminology with an established meaning that his readers would have known. It is a mistake to read a thirteenth-century author (or any other, for that matter) as if he wrote in a vacuum, and as if his views were only related to thinkers such as Boethius, Cajetan, and John of St. Thomas, who were all far removed from him in time. The only author contemporary with Aquinas cited by McInerny is Albert the Great, and the references are not always helpful.

The Problem of Religious Language

Before we look at McInerny's chapter in more detail, we need to consider what the problem of religious language is, how it arises, and why analogy is supposed to offer a solution. In the Jewish, Christian, and Islamic traditions, God is taken to be a transcendent, all-good, all-powerful, all-knowing spiritual being. God cannot therefore be regarded as just like a human being, albeit more powerful, so the words we use of him cannot have exactly the same sense as those used of humans. If we say that God is wise, we cannot suppose that he acquired wisdom slowly through time and effort, and that his mental attitudes depend in some way on a physical brain. On the other hand, if we suppose that the words we use of God have a completely different sense, as does "pen" used of a writing implement and an enclosure for animals, then whatever we say about God will be pointless, since we do not know what the theological sense of the words is. It seems that if we are to utter truths about God, we will have to find some middle road, whereby terms are used of God and creatures in senses which are neither completely the same nor completely different, but which are related in some way or other. This is the path that Aquinas follows.

For medieval theologians, including Aquinas, these problems were complicated by the doctrine of God's simplicity, and also by the metaphysical background. To understand the latter, we have to start with Aristotle. He had transmitted a metaphysics of real natures, both genera (such as animal) and species (such as horse) which existed in some way or other independently of the thinker. In addition, he transmitted the doctrine of ten categories (whether of words or things), including substance, quantity, quality, and relation, which would allow us to speak of reality in the appropriate way. Aristotle's ontology was enriched by the later neo-Platonists in a way that is important for our purposes. First of all, they emphasized the hierarchical nature of reality. Beings were ranked in accordance with the degrees of perfection, including existence, that they exhibited. For a Christian neo-Platonist, or those, such as Aquinas, influenced by neo-Platonism, that meant that God was the one who existed most fully, who was the most unified, and hence the most simple, and who was the highest good. All these perfections were essential to God's nature, whereas inferior beings enjoyed their lower degrees of existence, unity, goodness, and so on only through some appropriate degree of participation. Especially in his *Commentary on the Sentences*, Aquinas relates participation to imitation, but the relationship between God and creature was richer than that of a simple reflection in a mirror. Causality was also extremely important, and a principle that Aquinas enunciates frequently throughout his works is "All agents produce effects that resemble them" (*omne agens agit sibi simile*). The distinction between having an essential perfection and having a participated perfection is crucial to his doctrine of analogy, as is the doctrine of divine unity and simplicity.

In the *Summa theologiae*, Aquinas's discussion of religious language in ST I 13 comes after two important developments. First, he sketches five proofs for the existence of God (ST I 2), and then he builds on his proofs to establish certain claims about God's nature (ST I 3–11), while noting that we can know God, at least in this life, only through our experience of creatures (ST I 12). He argues that no distinction can be made between the nature that God has and what receives or exhibits that nature. God is identical with his essence or nature, and furthermore, that essence is identical with God's *esse* or existence. God can have no accidental properties, and all of his essential properties are in a sense the same. Whether we are talking about God's justice or God's goodness, and whether we say "God is just" or "God is justice," we are speaking of one and the same absolutely simple reality. A further consequence of these claims is that God could not be placed within an Aristotelian genus, and a fortiori could not be regarded as belonging to or characterized by a species, accident, differentia, or property.[3] Hence anything we say about God must transcend the Aristotelian categories that were supposed to provide the framework for all our descriptive language. Yet Aquinas believed that for words to be called univocal they had to fall within the Aristotelian framework, by functioning as genus-terms, species-terms, accident-terms, differentia-terms, or property-terms (CG I 32.4).

Medieval Semantics

This last remark brings us to the topic of medieval semantics. The focus was on individual words, for we must form words before we can form phrases or propositions, and in what follows I shall concentrate on ordinary nouns and adjectives, leaving aside verbs and syncategorematic terms, that is, terms such as "all" and "none" that perform special functions in a proposition. I shall also leave aside terms such as "nothing," "blindness," and "chimera" that raise special problems of interpretation. The basic semantic notion was signification, which is a psychologico-causal property not to be confused with meaning.[4] For a word to signify was for it to function as a sign, to represent or point to something beyond itself, and this does not fit well with the notion of meaning. To give the meaning of a term is not to name some item to which the word is related in some way, but we can sensibly say that a spoken word signifies or makes known an item, whether mental or physical, conceptual or real, universal or particular. In accordance with standard accounts based on Boethius's Latin translation of Aristotle, *On Interpretation* 16a3–8, spoken words were said to be signs of concepts, and concepts were in turn said to be similitudes of things (cf. ST I 13.1). How the references to concepts and things were interpreted varied, but Aquinas wrote that the *ratio* signified by a name was the intellect's conception of the thing signified (*res significata*),[5] and this in turn was a common nature, whether substantial or accidental, that existed by virtue of characterizing unspecified individuals. Thus "human being" signifies the intellect's conception of humanity as it belongs to humans, but Socrates and Plato themselves are not signified as such.[6] On the other hand, in a propositional context, the term "human being" may well refer to or supposit for Socrates or Plato (the term's *supposita*), and this kind of reference was called personal supposition. Aquinas also frequently remarked that the *ratio* that a name signified was a definition (ST I 13.6), namely whatever it was that captured the real essence of the thing spoken of, or at least, approximated to that. Here we must remember that Aquinas allowed human thinkers to progress from a confused and indistinct apprehension of a thing to a clearer and more distinct conception of the very same thing, but that he was in general quite sceptical about our ability to come up with fully-fledged Aristotelian real definitions.

Some semantic complications were introduced by terms that did not seem to fit into the framework of Aristotle's division of the ten categories into substance and nine types of accident. One problem concerned accidental or adjectival terms, such as "white." The abstract accidental term "whiteness" clearly belongs to the category of quality, but the term "white" does not seem to belong to any of the categories, although, especially when it is the subject of a sentence, its presence clearly indicates that there is something which is a composite of substance and quality. For instance, the Latin sentence "*Album currit*" (literally "White runs"), when said of a polar bear, signifies that a substance characterized by the quality whiteness is running (for similar examples, see the *Commentary on the Posterior Analytics* I 33.281). There were various views about how to construe adjectival terms, whether they occurred in subject or predicate position, but Aquinas belonged to the school that held them to signify form alone.[7] In his *Commentary on the Sentences*, he wrote that "substantive terms signify not only a form, but also the bearer (*suppositum*) of the form . . . but adjectives only signify the form,"[8] and in the *Summa theologiae*, he wrote that "the difference between substantive terms and adjectives is that substantive terms carry their *suppositum* with them, <and> adjectives do not, but they apply the thing signified (*res significata*) to a substantive thing."[9] These remarks have an obvious bearing on the favourite medieval example of an analogical term, the adjective "healthy" (*sanum*). For Aquinas this term signifies the form of health (*sanitas*) while at the same time indicating that a thing of some sort is related to health in some way.

Other terms that did not fit neatly into the framework of Aristotle's ten categories were the so-called transcendental terms such as "being" (*ens*)[10] and "good" (*bonum*). These were called "transcendental" because they transcended or went beyond Aristotle's categories in that they could be said of any substance or accident: both a polar bear and whiteness can be called a being, and both a human being and a quality can be called good. Like "healthy," both "being" and "good" were standard examples of analogical terms.

Equivocal and Analogical Terms

After these general remarks about signification, we can turn to the particular problem of what it was that distinguished analogical terms from other terms. This brings us directly to McInerny's chapter for, as he points out, the framework for Aquinas's discussion, and for that of everyone else, was provided by Aristotle's *Categories*, which opens with a brief characterization of things named equivocally, as when "animal" is said of real and pictured human beings, and things named univocally, as when "animal" is said of human beings and oxen. In the first case, the name is the same,[11] but there are two distinct significates or intellectual conceptions, but in the second case, both the spoken term and the significate (*substantiae ratio*) are the same. There are two things to be noted here. First, though no medieval author seems to have been aware of this, and McInerny does not mention it, the Greek word "*zoon*" is genuinely equivocal, for it means both a living being and a pictured object. Second, the phrase "*substantiae ratio*," literally "*ratio* of the substance" requires some explication. Logicians pointed out that "substance" here needed to be taken quite generally, as some words signify accidents, not substances. Moreover, as Boethius wrote in the untranslated passage quoted in McInerny's footnote 6 on p. 229, *ratio* should also be taken fairly generally to include not just definitions but descriptions or identifying features.[12] Thus the phrase roughly means "account of the thing spoken of."

McInerny's discussion of the phrase "*substantiae ratio*" does not help us to understand Aquinas. He refers (without identifying the source) to Albert the Great's use of the Roman grammarian Priscian's definition of the name or noun: "The property of a name is to signify a substance and a quality,"[13] and then mentions Albert's idiosyncratic attempt to relate this definition to "*substantiae ratio*" see pp. 221–2. Aquinas himself had explained Priscian's definition by saying that it meant that a noun signified a *suppositum* with the nature or determinate form in which it subsisted (ST I 13.1 response to 3). Earlier (*In 1 Sent.* 22.1.1 response to 3) he had pointed out that the definition was a grammatical one, intended to differentiate nouns from verbs, and that where the term "whiteness" was concerned, the word only signifies something *as if* it were subsistent. Moreover, we have already seen that this claim had to be construed rather differently in the case of concrete accidental terms, since their signification of a *suppositum* is indirect at best. Nor, of course, can we bring together, as McInerny does in the last sentence of his explication see p. 222, what a term signifies together with what it supposits for and with what it means. "Human being" can supposit for or refer to Socrates in such propositions as "The human being who taught Plato," but it neither signifies nor means Socrates.[14]

On p. 224, McInerny introduces Boethius's distinction, taken from Greek sources, between chance equivocals (*aequivoca a casu*) and deliberate equivocals (*aequivoca a consilio*). Where chance or pure equivocals are concerned, there is no relationship between different uses. In the case of deliberate equivocals, however, some intention on the part of the speakers was involved, and the occurrences of the equivocal term could be related in various ways. In order to understand Aquinas on analogy, we need to consider Boethius's four subdivisions, again taken from Greek sources.[15] The second subdivision involved analogy in the original Greek sense of a comparison between two relations, though the word "*proportio*" replaced the Greek word "*analogia*." Later authors, including Aquinas, often preferred the word "*proportionalitas*" to replace the Greek word, and used "*proportio*" in the very general sense of "proportion or relation." Boethius's example was the word "*principium*" (principle or origin) which was said to apply to unity with respect to number and to point with respect to a line. No common nature is involved here, and what allows the disparate things to be grouped together is a similarity of relations, for unity is to a number as a point is to a line (or so it was claimed). This type of analogy was later dubbed "the analogy of proper proportionality" by Cajetan, and he regarded it as the only true type of analogy, though he did not appeal to the example "principium" since it accorded ill with his view that the analogy of proper proportionality involved some kind of property that was intrinsic to all its referents.

The other subdivisions of deliberate equivocation given by Boethius were similitude, as exemplified by "animal" said of real and pictured human beings, of one origin, used of the word "medical," and in relation to one, used of the word "healthy."[16] Subsequently, there were two important developments. The first was the use of the Latin term "*analogia*" to refer to these last three subdivisions of equivocation, in a way that linked the term most closely with Aristotle's *pros hen* equivocation, or focal meaning rather than with Aristotle's own use of the Greek word.[17] The word in its new, non-Greek, sense was closely linked, or even identified, with the notion of being said in a prior and a posterior way (*secundum prius et posterius*). This phrase seems to have been derived from Arabic philosophy, and was used to express the main characteristic of those ambiguous terms that were intermediate between equivocal and univocal terms (see Wolfson 1938). One particularly important text is found in the *Logica* of Al-Ghazālī, translated in the twelfth century, which said:

> Terms associated by an agreement are intermediate between univocals and equivocals: for instance, being (*ens*) said of substance and accident [. . .] Being (*esse*) belongs first to substance, and then to accident. As a result, it belongs to them according to the prior and the posterior. This <type of term> is called "ambiguous".
>
> (*Logica*, 246)

Another important text is from Averroes's long commentary on Aristotle's *Metaphysics*, translated between 1220 and 1235, for it introduced the notion of attribution used in the phrase "analogy of attribution" as applying to the non-Greek sense of analogy. He wrote:

> The term "being" (*ens*) is said in various senses . . . that is to say, it is neither equivocal [. . .] nor univocal [. . .] but it belongs to those words which are said of things that are attributed to one and the same thing, and which are intermediate between univocals and equivocals.
>
> (*In Met.*, f. 65 rb)

In the same place, Averroes spoke of attribution to one end, or to one agent, or to one subject.

These texts, among others, lie behind the second important development, namely a new classification of deliberate equivocals, now equated with analogy, as including just three cases: from one origin or agent, as applying to "medical," in relation to one end, as applying to "healthy," and in relation to one subject, as applying to "being" (*ens*). The first two cases come from Boethius, with the addition of a reference to an agent, but the third was introduced to cover the case of being. Similitude was dropped, as was proportionality. We find this three-fold division in chapter 6 of Aquinas's very early work, the *Principles of Nature*, and also in his late commentary on the *Metaphysics* (*In 4 Met.* 1 537–8). However, it would be a mistake to overemphasize these passages, since Aquinas tended to change his presentation of divisions and examples of analogy depending on the context. It is more important to consider whether he changed his mind about how analogy should be used in relation to the problem of religious language, for neither of the two texts I have just cited dealt with that issue. Nor does McInerny deal with it except in an early brief reference (1996, 24–25) and in a very brief section on the divine names at the very end of his book (1996, 158–161), but what Aquinas says about religious language is crucial to the understanding of his account of analogy in his other texts.

Stages in Aquinas's Account of Analogy

I follow Montagnes (1963) in thinking that there are three stages in Aquinas's discussion of analogy as a solution to the problem of religious language. In his *Commentary on the* Sentences, Aquinas suggests that there are two kinds of analogy, one when the analogates share something in accordance with priority and posteriority (analogy of attribution), and one when one of the analogates imitates the other as far as it is able. It is the second that applies to God and creatures, and in saying that, Aquinas emphasizes the formal causality through which creatures participate in the perfections that God possesses through his essence (*In I Sent.* 35.1.4). The second stage is found in *On Truth* 2.11, where Aquinas argues that the analogy of attribution is insufficient because it involves a determinate relation between God and creatures, which is impossible. As a result, and leaving aside any recourse to the analogy of imitation, Aquinas appeals to proportionality, and claims that we should compare the relation between God and his perfections to the relation between creatures and their qualities. This solution is gravely flawed, because the problem of religious language largely arises from the radical difference that exists between God's relation to his perfections and the relation of creatures to their qualities. As a result, in the *Summa contra gentiles* and the *Summa theologiae*, Aquinas returned to the analogy of attribution. He reconciled this kind of analogy with the analogy of imitation by turning from formal causality to efficient causality, and placing his emphasis on the act by which God transmits his perfections to creatures. Recall the principle "All agents produce effects that resemble them." It is by his act of creation that God gives his creatures the perfections of existence, unity, goodness and so on, and it is also by virtue of that act that creatures resemble God whilst also being radically different from him.

McInerny's account of analogy is clearly a version of the analogy of attribution, and we now have to consider whether or not he gives an adequate explanation of how Aquinas used that kind of analogy to solve the problem of the language we use about God. I shall argue that he does not.

Problems with McInerny's Account

McInerny sums up his view as follows. In chapter four he writes pp. 228–9: "*Analogous names* thus have the same *res significata* and diverse *modi significandi.* [. . . .] The *ratio propria*, therefore, is not *sanitas* but *sanum* taken as meaning *sanitas animalis.*" In his final chapter, in the section entitled "Divine Names," he begins by saying:

> Just as, when many things are named healthy analogously, we have a plurality of meanings so that the same *res* (health) is involved in them all but there are different modes of signifying it (subject of—; cause of—; sign of—) with some modes invoking the primary mode or *ratio propria*, so too is it with names common to God and creature.
>
> (McInerny 1996, 159)

My main quarrel with McInerny, which relates closely to the reason why he has so little to say about divine language, has to do with his misconstrual of the notions of *modi significandi* and *res significata*, as well as the notion of *ratio propria*. We need to look at these notions in turn, starting with *ratio propria.*

We should first remind ourselves that, according to Aquinas, an adjective, such as "healthy" (*sanum*), signifies a quality alone, though it indicates in some way that the quality belongs to something or other. Accordingly, in its central sense, "healthy" does signify "health" (*sanitas*), and although there is indirect reference to the health of an animal, since only animals can have health, the word does not signify "health of an animal" (*sanitas animalis*). Words like "healthy" may also have extended uses, and here Aquinas sometimes speaks of just one *ratio* that includes different senses, and sometimes of several *rationes.*[18] In either case, what a word in its central use signifies can be called the proper *ratio*, though Aquinas more frequently speaks of a perfect *ratio*, as contrasted with the imperfect *rationes* signified by the terms used analogically.[19] In one place, he wrote that the proper *ratio* had to appear in the definition of an analogical term used in its extended sense (ST I 16.6), and so to call medicine healthy is to say that it causes health, the proper *ratio*. In other places, he put the same point differently, without reference to a proper *ratio.*[20] How definitional inclusion works in the case of divine language is somewhat problematic, but Aquinas seems to have in mind that although words such as "good" are given their signification on the basis of our experience of creatures, when we come to know God as the first cause and fully perfect being, we recognize that creaturely perfections are merely a reflection of God's perfections, and hence that God's goodness is prior to ours (ST I 13.6). The central sense of "good" would then be something like "absolute and essential goodness." I shall return to this point below.

Next, let us consider the *modi significandi*. It is important to notice that Aquinas speaks of various kinds of modes or ways. For instance, there are the *modi praedicandi*, the different ways in which terms in different categories are predicated in propositions (*In 1 Sent.* 22.1.3 response to 2, *In 3 Phys.* 5.15), and there are also different *modi relationis*, such as the different ways of relating urine, medicine, and diet to healthy animals (*In 11 Met.* 3.2196–7). *Modi significandi* are not to be confused with these other *modi*, for the notion of a way of signifying is primarily grammatical, and that is how Aquinas uses it in his discussions of divine language and only in his discussion of divine language. He explains that the problem of divine language involves *modi significandi*, the ways of signifying that are inextricably bound up with our *modi intelligendi*, or ways of understanding (CG I 30.3, ST I 13.1 response to 2, ST I 13.3). Our understanding begins with sense experience, and what we sense are concrete objects—objects in which substance and form are compounded or brought together.[21] Accordingly, the nouns and adjectives we use to name things signify concretely. We can also use abstract terms, such as "humanity" and "whiteness," but these do not name things as such, for these forms cannot subsist, that is, exist by themselves. As a result, our nouns and adjectives cannot be used to speak appropriately about God, for God is neither a concrete thing—he is not something that has qualities—nor an abstract form. If we say "God is good," we mistakenly use a concrete term, and if we say "God is goodness," we mistakenly use an abstract term, yet both our claims must be true. At no point does Aquinas appeal to *modi significandi* in his explanation of how such standard analogical terms as "healthy" work, nor did the logicians contemporary with him. Accordingly, McInerny's analysis of ways of saying "healthy" illustrates the modes of relation that Aquinas has talked about in other places, but has little to do with the *modi significandi* used by Aquinas in his account of religious language.

An even more important confusion characterizes McInerny's account of the *res significata*, which McInerny holds to be the same whether it is divine or creaturely. As I read Aquinas, he presents us with a two-stage process. First, we reflect on and articulate the inappropriateness of the *modi significandi* that attend all human language, and we cancel them out. This brings us to the second stage, for when the *modi significandi* have been cancelled out, we are left with the *res significata*. It is here that analogy enters the picture, for God's perfections are not like ours. As I remarked above, "good" said of God signifies absolute and essential goodness, and all God's perfections are absolute and essential. They constitute his very nature, but we have our perfections by participation, and they are lesser imitations of God's perfections. Aquinas insists over and over again on the difference: goodness and other perfections are in God in a higher way (*secundum modum altiorem*) (ST I 13.3), excellently (*excellenter*) (ST I 13. 5), and more eminently (*eminentius*) (ST I 13.6), and this is why, even when the *modi significandi* have been cancelled out, we can only speak of God analogically. The somewhat different examples of "healthy" and "being" (*ens*) are used to give us, not a precise blueprint of exactly how analogical language about God does work, but a suggestion about how it might work. Had McInerny paid more attention to the problem of divine language as presented by Aquinas he might have realized this.

Notes

1. Editor's note: Aquinas explains that, in contrast to a substance, an accident's mode of being is to exist in something else. For instance, a horse is a substance, but its size, color, and scent are accidents because their nature is to exist in something else.
2. While McInerny successfully dismisses Cajetan as an interpreter, he does not recognize that much of Cajetan's discussion is directed towards some fifteenth-century authors rather than Aquinas himself.
3. These are the five predicables discussed by Porphyry in his *Isagoge* or introduction to Aristotle's *Categories.* A differentia is what is added to a genus to produce a species, e.g. "rational" in "rational animal" (the human species). A property is something that all and only members of a species have, but which is not essential to them.
4. Unfortunately many, if not all, translations use the word "meaning" and its cognates when signification (*significatio*) is at issue.
5. ST I 13.4: "Ratio enim quam significat nomen est conceptio intellectus de re significata." Note that the meaning of "*ratio*" varies depending on the context, so that the word is almost untranslatable.
6. Nominalists insisted that terms signify individuals, and later Thomists tended to say that individuals were secondary significates.
7. For discussion of different medieval views about the use of adjectival terms, see Ebbesen 1988.
8. *In 3 Sent.* 5.3, expositio textus: "substantiva enim significant non tantum formam, sed etiam suppositum formae [. . .] adjectiva autem tantum significant formam [. . .]." See also *In 1 Sent.* 18.1.2 response to 3.
9. ST I 39.5 response to 5: "haec est differentia inter nomina substantiva et adiectiva, quia nomina substantiva ferunt suum suppositum: adiectiva vero non, sed rem significatam ponunt circa substantivum."
10. "Being" (ens) was normally regarded as a substantive term, though there was some recognition of its participial use, as in "Being an athlete, John trained hard."
11. McInerny reviews Albert the Great's discussion of what might be meant by "name" here (see above, p. 229) but in fact there were a number of views on the matter: see Ashworth 1992, 132–135.
12. See also Aquinas, *In 1 Sent.* 2.1.3.
13. Priscian, *Instit. gram.* II.IV,18: "Proprium est nominis substantiam et qualitatem significare."
14. The long untranslated passage from Boethius that McInerny gives in note 15 seems irrelevant to the discussion in the paragraph it is appended to, as in it Boethius clearly uses "*substantiae ratio*" as equivalent to "definition."
15. Boethius, *In Cat.* 166 B–C.
16. These examples are found in Aristotle, Metaphysics 4.2, 1003a33–1003b3. Boethius and others often use related terms such as "medicinal" and "healthful."
17. McInerny makes this point in his second chapter, but without any historical explanation of the new use.
18. For instance, *In 1 Sent.* 22.1.3 response to 4 he speaks of "wisdom" and "goodness" being said of God and creatures according to one *ratio* analogically, and in *In 11 Met.* 3.2197 he speaks of a *ratio* that is partly the same and partly different, whereas in the passage cited by McInerny p. 227, he speaks of several *rationes.*
19. See, e.g., *On Truth* 1.2 and ST I-II 88.1 response to 1. The notion of a proper *ratio* is most frequently used to distinguish the common *ratio* of a genus from the proper *ratio* of a species (e.g., *In Peri herm.* 1.8 n.6.)
20. ST I 13.6, ST I 13.10.
21. The Latin word "*concretus*" includes these senses.

PART VIII
Aquinas's Philosophical Theology

Editor's Introduction

Thomas Aquinas penned three extensive systematic works: his early *Commentary on the Sentences*, his mature *Summa theologiae*, and between these, a work that has come to be called the *Summa contra gentiles*. Contemporary scholars have a good understanding of Aquinas's purposes in writing these first two works. The *Contra gentiles*, by contrast, remains something of a mystery. It has a unique structure among Aquinas's works. Of its four books, the first three, which treat God's existence and nature, creation and rational creatures, human happiness, and divine providence, contain only arguments built from premises accessible to natural reason alone. In contrast, the arguments in the fourth book appeal to premises taken from Christian revelation. Why does Aquinas proceed this way? Is he providing a critique of natural reason, celebrating its powers while demonstrating its limitations? Is he providing his contemporary missionaries with a battery of philosophical arguments for Christianity that would be convincing to non-Christians before turning to arguments convincing only to his fellow Christians? Another mystery lies in the astounding number of arguments Aquinas offers for each thesis he aims to establish. Aquinas's other syntheses likewise consist of arguments, but they generally supply just one or two arguments for each thesis; the *Summa theologiae*'s famous "five ways" to prove God's existence are the exception. In contrast, the *Contra gentiles* assembles argument after argument not just for the most important contentions, such as God's existence or the nature of the intellect, but for its minor theses as well. There are, for instance, no fewer than four arguments for the conclusion that the consumption of food is not in itself sinful.

Mark Jordan attempts to solve these mysteries in "The Protreptic of *Against the Gentiles*." He ably demolishes the oft-repeated contention that Aquinas meant this work as a manual for missionaries. Instead, he maintains, the work is an anthology of arguments that show orthodox Christian believers ways they may effectively persuade their "adversaries"—whether pagans, Jews, Muslims, or heterodox Christians—to accept the truths of orthodox Christianity. This explains why Aquinas offers so many arguments: If one should fail to persuade, there are still others at the ready. It also explains the mysterious division of the work. The truths of Christianity are of two sorts: those our natural powers enable us to arrive at, and those we learn only through revelation because they surpass our natural powers to arrive at. Effective persuasion must respect this important difference, and so Aquinas divides book IV from the rest of the work on this rhetorical ground. We must nevertheless not think that the *Contra gentiles* offers nothing for the reader beyond a tutoring in the persuasion of adversaries. In fact, the work also aims to persuade the orthodox: it persuades them to the practice of Christian wisdom. This further goal governs other features of both the content and the structure of the *Contra gentiles*. In particular, Jordan points out that the flow of ideas in each of the work's four books builds to a discussion of the human good, which consists in the contemplation of God. This large-scale structural feature, repeated many times over in smaller-scale structures within the four books, suggests that the work serves its readers as a "protreptic to the contemplation of God," an exhortation to the practice of Christian wisdom.

Despite concerns about the speculative character of Jordan's interpretation, Cyrille Michon admits that it may well capture Aquinas's intentions and serve us as a fruitful reading of the text. Nevertheless, in his view, it fails to explain some important features of the *Contra gentiles*. He therefore proposes a different interpretation that better explains the structure and content of the work, yet does not discard Jordan's worthwhile speculations. Michon's chief interest is in explaining why Aquinas divides the work into its two main "parts": one concerning truths accessible by reason alone, and a second concerning truths available only through divine revelation. Michon points out that in each part Aquinas accomplishes his stated goal of making the truth known, but to different interlocutors. In the first part, Aquinas draws on the best philosophical tradition he knows to show that reason can establish many truths of religion, including some distinctive of orthodox Christianity. In this part, Aquinas addresses his arguments to any interlocutor, including those who reject some or all of his religious convictions. By contrast, in the second part (book IV), Aquinas uses both argument and appeal to authority to make the truth known to those who share his Christianity.

Note on References

For a general overview of references to Aquinas, see the Note on References in Part VII. For references to Aristotle, see the Note on References in Part IV.

References to the CG are to book and chapter number. Jordan uses section numbers from Aquinas (1961–67), while Michon uses section numbers devised by Gauthier and published in the French 1999 translation.
PL = Migne *Patrologia Latina* (1844–1855; 1862–65).

Further Reading

- Thomas Hibbs (1995). *Dialectic and Narrative in Aquinas: A Reinterpretation of the* Summa contra Gentiles.
- Norman Kretzmann (1997). *The Metaphysics of Theism, Aquinas's Natural Theology in* Summa contra Gentiles I.

CHAPTER 15

The Protreptic of *Against the Gentiles*

MARK JORDAN

Thomas pays respect to his authorities by transforming them without pretending to reproduce them. He does not swear allegiance to their reified doctrines. He constellates them with other authorities around sequences of topics that strain to trace out new pedagogical patterns. Across the span of his writing, Thomas experimented with at least five major patterns: Peter Lombard's *Sentences*, the writings of Boethius, those of Pseudo-Dionysius, the so-called *Summa against the Gentiles*, and the *Summa of Theology*.[1] The first and the last of these are more or less radical variations on the verbal professions called creeds. The others are patterns for interrogating not so much doctrine as the languages in which it can be taught. All of Thomas's experimental structures have been liable to misreading, but perhaps no structure has been misread so aggressively as the one mislabeled *Against the Gentiles*.

How is a serious reader meant to be moved by the structure of this experiment in persuasion? Who is addressed by the work? In view of which ends? Taking up these questions, I begin to show what it means for Thomas to transfigure authorities into pedagogies.

Circumstances

Circumstantial evidence about *Against the Gentiles* invites a fallacy of authorial intention.[2] Those who commit it classify the work as a missionary manual and include it in histories of missionary activity. In fact, the surviving evidence in no way decides the intention or even the title of the work known both as *Against the Gentiles* and *On the Truth of the Catholic Faith*.

In a narration of the deeds of James I of Aragon, as part of a reminiscence of Raymond of Peñafort, the Dominican chronicler Peter Marsilius recounts a story about the composition of *Against the Gentiles.*[3] Peter's text was finished on April 2, 1313; the frame for the story of Raymond is a narrative about Christmas, 1274; and the story itself lies even further back – more than 40 years before the date of writing. At that time, Peter says, Raymond asked Thomas to compose a work "against the errors of unbelievers (*contra infidelium errores*)" as an aid in conversion. "That master did what the humble rogation of such a father required; and he composed a *summa* called 'against the Gentiles,' which is believed not to have any equal for such material (*pro illa materia*)."[4] There have been some textual questions about this passage, but none is unanswerable.[5] Let the text stand as received, but then read it carefully. The story is introduced to illustrate Raymond's zeal for conversions and to show his influence within the order. Since the story is not repeated in the contemporary lives of Raymond or in any of the canonization proceedings for Thomas, it is presumed that Peter was relying on a local legend from the Dominican house in Barcelona, where he had worked with Raymond years before. We are presented with the only extant attestation for a bit of local hagiography. It has been argued that Peter would not have invented this story because there were many among his readers who would have had first-hand knowledge of the events mentioned.[6] This argument is weakened by remembering that flattering inventions are less likely to be contested than scurrilous ones and by comparing this tale with the sorts of things being told, less than six years later, in the canonization proceedings for Thomas.

If we were to assume that the story is a luckily preserved fact rather than a pious invention, difficulties would multiply. The first difficulty is simply to know what Peter means and, particularly, what he intends by the phrase "such material (*illa materia*)." What is the "matter" or material of *Against the Gentiles*? To speak more practically, where exactly does it fit into the well organized Dominican missionary effort? Peter's story might be saying at least three different things: *Against the Gentiles* is a book to be given to potential converts, or it is a manual for field-training missionaries, or it represents a reference work that refutes all errors of unbelievers compendiously. Of these three readings of *materia*, only the third has any plausibility—and then not much. Still let me take them in order.

Against the Gentiles cannot have been directed to potential converts. From the first line and then on every page thereafter, Thomas speaks as one Christian to another. His rhetorical address is evident in the use of scriptural and magisterial quotations, in a presumption of acquaintance with Christian letters, and even in the voice of the first person plural. Thomas argues in the prologue that the mysteries of Christian faith ought not to be presented argumentatively before non-believers for fear of making them think that faith depends only on probable arguments.[7] Precisely these arguments appear in the plan of the fourth book (as Thomas himself promises, 1.9 [no. 56]). How could Thomas have intended, then, that his book be placed into the hands of non-believers, without giving them offense and exposing Christian faith to scandal?

It is no more likely that *Against the Gentiles* was intended to train Dominican missionaries in the field. There are external and internal reasons. Externally, *Against the Gentiles* is an unsatisfactory missionary manual by Dominican standards of the thirteenth century. The life of Raymond himself offers counter-examples. Raymond not only founded schools for Oriental studies within the Dominican order, as Peter narrates, but also figured prominently in public debates with non-Christians. In 1263, for example, Raymond helped to set the rules for a debate between the Dominican Paul "the Christian" and Rabbi Moses ben Nachman of Gerona.[8] This Paul had converted from Judaism and his strategy was to argue from a detailed knowledge of rabbinical writings that the messiah had already come, that he was prophesied to be both divine and human, and that his advent had destroyed Jewish laws and ceremonies.[9] The strategy of refutation from within had been adopted by Dominicans in campaigns of Jewish conversion through the 1250s and 1260s in Spain and France.[10] They dealt similarly with Cathars and allied heretics.[11]

Equally expert devices and emphases figure in Dominican preaching to Islam. Here a central figure was another Raymond, Raymond Martí (Martinus, Martini).[12] As early as 1250, Martí appears in Tunis as founder of an Arabic school. In 1267, he published the *Muzzle of the Jews* (*Capistrum Judaeorum*), a detailed attack on Judaism much like the internal criticism practiced by Paul "the Christian." In 1278, Martí presented the *Dagger of the Faith* (*Pugio Fidei*), an attack on Islam and Judaism. The work has figured prominently in the history of *Against the Gentiles* because it borrows directly from Thomas.[13] Far from confirming Thomas's missionary intention, however, the borrowings show how little Thomas could be used in direct missionary activity. Martí turns to Thomas almost exclusively in *Dagger of the Faith* 1. That first book, only 10 percent of the whole, is intended to combat the errors "of the naturalists and the philosophers."[14] Martí uses Thomas against errors arising from the reading of Aristotle and the Peripatetics. Thomas supplies most of Martí's argument on the eternity of the world, God's knowledge of singulars, and the resurrection of the dead.[15] When it comes to a detailed consideration of the claims and counter-claims of competing canons, or to the intricacies of Islamic and Jewish theology, borrowings from Thomas almost disappear. According to the judgment of one expert missionary, Thomas's *Against the Gentiles* helps in philosophical preliminaries, but not in missionary work properly speaking.

External comparisons are confirmed internally by scattered remarks in *Against the Gentiles* about Islamic religion. In the "prologue" to the work (1.1–9), there are two pertinent passages. The first pleads Thomas's excuses for not being able to contest particular errors. He is not familiar with them, he says, nor can he proceed against all adversaries on the basis of common scriptural authorities

(1.2, nos. 10–11a). Thomas mentions the "Mohammedans and pagans" as not sharing any scriptural authority with Christians. The second passage contrasts the sober motives for accepting Christian revelation with improper persuasions to various errors. Thomas describes the inducements offered by Mohammed, namely "carnal pleasures" and easy living, which he promised in colorful fables, without the supporting evidence of miracles or previous prophecy, to a credulous and isolated people (1.6, no. 41). The description is backed by no particular knowledge of Islam. Indeed Thomas's source is not contemporary Dominican research, but the century-old *Summula* of Peter the Venerable.[16] Some readers have seen here a "singular discretion" on Thomas's part as he reduces Koranic religion to the preaching of violence, perhaps in order to justify the Christians' crusades.[17] It is simpler to suppose, as Thomas has admitted, that he knew little about Islamic belief, or, indeed, about the course of Islamic civilization.[18] How could he write a paradigmatic missioner's manual for an order that prided itself on expert acquaintance with the languages and beliefs of its adversaries? It was not only the ideal of the order. We have from Thomas himself a letter *On the Reasons of Faith against the Saracens, Greeks, and Armenians.*[19] Written just after completion of *Against the Gentiles,* it repeats charges against the infidels only as claims made by a correspondent. Thomas reminds him that no one ought to attempt a demonstration of the truths of the faith.[20]

Against the Gentiles is not a manual for training missionaries—and so we are left with the third possibility, that it was intended to provide a reference book of philosophical arguments against the conceptual errors instanced in unbelievers, to be read by Christians living in intellectual contact with them. Here again the story of Raymond's request must be reinterpreted, always assuming its credibility. Perhaps Thomas received such a request and wrote what he could, within the limits of his knowledge: a foundational work that would undergird any detailed missionary attack. Perhaps he already had a work of comprehensive pedagogy in hand that he adapted for Raymond's sake, adding topical references in the prologue and elsewhere.[21] Of course, a fundamental work structured according to the needs of Christian pedagogy is not easily classed as missionary, except in that sense in which every Christian reader is constantly being called to conversion. Any number of works, including the *Summa of Theology,* have been used as foundations for missionary activity. Such uses have not drawn them into the class of missionary manuals.

Circumstantial arguments about the work's intention have run aground. We must turn from them to the work itself in order to appreciate its experiment in persuasion.

The Prologue

On opening *Against the Gentiles,* the careful exegete would want first to consider the meaning of its title. Unfortunately, here too there is uncertainty, as is not unusual with medieval academic works. The title *Book* or *Summa against the Gentiles* appears in early lists from the Parisian booksellers ("stationers"), in the writings of Thomas's early exponents, and in catalogues of Thomas's works.[22] In the early copies of the work, however, there stands the title *Book of the Truth of the Catholic Faith against the Errors of Unbelievers* or variants of it.[23] Either title is easily derived from the text of the second chapter, where Thomas says "we propose as our intention to show, in whatever little way we can, the truth offered by the catholic faith (*veritatem quam fides catholica profitetur*), eliminating contrary errors" (1.2, no. 9). He then goes on to speak of the "errors of the Gentiles (*errores gentilium*)" (1.2, no. 10). Whether the book is a *summa* is not decided by the text (as it sometimes is elsewhere). The title "*summa*," even if authentic, would prove too equivocal for fixing rhetorical purpose. In the thirteenth century, "*summa*" covers a number of very different works, beginning with the simplest of collections. The decision among the various titles must be set aside, then, except insofar as the catalogue title raises a question about the meaning of "Gentiles."

M. M. Gorce argued more than 70 years ago that the Gentiles of Thomas's title referred immediately to the Parisian exponents of a radical Aristotle.[24] His evidence for the claim came from a Parisian document of 1277, which speaks of the "Gentiles" of the Arts faculty, and from the correspondences between heterodox views condemned in 1270 or 1277 and positions mentioned by Thomas. Gorce's arguments are unconvincing. He could not establish any direct connection between the coinage in the document and Thomas's use of the term, nor could he show that the correspondence of views is anything but the effect of a common philosophical problematic. Gorce does raise the issue, however, about what Thomas might mean by speaking of Gentiles in the prologue itself.

Elsewhere in *Against the Gentiles,* positions ascribed to the Gentiles are those of ancient Greek philosophy. Gentiles were misled by the "first natural philosophers" into holding a view that the heavens are animated by divinities (1.20, nos. 189–193). They relied on this error to defend their idolatry (1.27, no. 258). Gentiles also claimed some kind of eternity for the cosmos and, thus, a circular time (2.38, no. 1,150; 4.82, no. 4,171). When Thomas says in the prologue that Christendom's "ancient teachers (*antiqui doctores*)" could attack errors in detail because they had been Gentiles or were in conversation with them, he is thinking of such writers as Augustine, Ambrose, and Jerome—men who lived in or among the philosophic schools of late antiquity.

The same usage is found in others of Thomas's works and in "reports" or (edited) transcripts of his teaching. Thomas speaks of the Gentiles as exponents of pre-Christian learning. He writes that "the Greeks" is used metonymically for all Gentiles, since all received worldly wisdom from the Greeks.[25] He singles out the Platonists among the Gentiles because they posited a providence, though he holds that Gentiles typically recognized the existence of God.[26] Most interestingly, Thomas is reported as speaking about "Gentiles" in the present tense. He distinguishes them both from the (Byzantine) schismatics and from the (Islamic) infidels: "in the North (*in Aquilonari*) there are still many Gentiles (*gentiles*), and in the East many schismatics and infidels (*schismatici et infideles*)."[27] The reference must be to unevangelized tribes or groups, though here too Thomas may be speaking more from dated hearsay than from current fact. To summarize: "Gentiles" means for Thomas, historically, pre- or extra-Christian humankind and, metaphorically, the human mind under the tutelage of nature. The highest moment of tutelage is Greek philosophy. How do we understand an argument made by Thomas "against the Gentiles"? It is an argument that corrects the natural errors of mind especially as articulated by philosophers. Is this suggestion borne out in the work's prologue?

The prologue begins with an Aristotelian explication of a scriptural verse in praise of wisdom (1.1). The explication connects this verse and other passages in Scripture with Aristotle's hortatory depiction of wisdom at the beginning of the *Metaphysics.* Thomas argues for wisdom's usefulness and announces his intention to set it forth, despite difficulties (1.2). This is a standard topic in philosophical prologues. So is the claim that wisdom demands expression.[28] But how should wisdom be set forth? The next chapters answer this question in general (1.3–8), while the final introductory chapter draws out an implied table of contents (1.9). The whole prologue constitutes an extended teacher's preface or *accessus,* in which 1.2 gives the statement of intention while the remaining chapters describe the manner of proceeding in relation to the subject-matter. Understanding the matter requires a distinction between two types of truth in regard to God, a distinction that has provoked as much feuding as did the possibility of a missionary motivation.

The most recent round of the debate can be said to have begun as far back as 1924, when Guy de Broglie argued from the "general economy" of *Against the Gentiles,* as proposed in the prologue, to a formal distinction between philosophical and theological truths in it.[29] De Broglie's motive was not to comment on *Against the Gentiles* so much as to extract a polemical conclusion from it about the natural desire for God. Still De Broglie took Thomas as promising that the first three books of the work would deal only with "religious truths accessible to reason alone," thus constituting "a Christian philosophy that will have its own consistency."[30] De Broglie was answered instantly by Blanche, who argued that *Against the Gentiles* was an apologetic, theological work, which treated of everything under the formality of the revealed.[31] Blanche's brief comment was only the first of many.[32]

In the next year, Mulard, while rebutting De Broglie's main thesis at length, agreed with Blanche on the apologetic character of *Against the Gentiles* and added confirming evidence from its manner of citing Scripture.[33] Bouyges followed with a summary of the debate (after a heated two years) and the proposal that *Against the Gentiles* be regarded as a missionary apologetic structured by reference to the sensitivities of a non-Christian readership.[34] All specifically Christian matter is transposed into the fourth book, Bouyges wrote, while all matter common to Christians and non-Christians is arranged progressively in the first three books. For him, the distinction is not a formal division between two types of propositions characterized with regard to their demonstrability; it is an apologetic distinction between the "discussable and non-discussable" or between what is and is not "susceptible . . . of being established and defended, in different degrees, before non-Christian partisans of supposedly revealed religions."[35] Bouyges's hypothesis was substantially accepted in a general review of the debate published in 1930 by Balthasar and Simonet.[36] Since then, the tendency has been to argue for a wider audience and a larger intention.[37]

None of the positions taken on the two truths is entirely fair to *Against the Gentiles,* though Bouyges comes closest—not when he invokes the missionary character, but when he points to the rhetorical motivation of the division. Read in context, the famous division separates two possibilities for effective persuasion. The division is introduced, in 1.3, with an allusion to Aristotle's doctrine about the various ways disciplines produce conviction (no. 13). Since those who are wise teach truth so that it be learned and held, they must study the degree of conviction possible in any subject matter. The division is recalled again when Thomas says that there is a twofold mode of truth "in what we confess (*confitemur*) of God" (1.3, no. 14). The first truths "exceed every power of human reason"; the second truths "natural reason can also reach." These latter truths were "demonstratively proved" by the philosophers, "led by the light of natural reason" (1.3, no. 14). Note here that reason is said not to exhaust, but to touch these accessible truths. We must understand the demonstrative proofs of the philosophers not as Cartesian reductions, but as exemplary forms of rational instruction. To say that the philosophers proved the conclusions demonstratively is to say that they constructed fully rational pedagogies leading to them. Thomas stresses that some truths obviously exceed the power of human pedagogy because human beings do not now know God's essence and stand low in the hierarchy of created intelligences (1.3, nos. 16–17). They make daily mistakes even about sensible things (1.3, no. 18).

Thomas amplifies the warning in 1.4 when he concludes that truths of the second class are fittingly proposed for belief because of the weakness of human speculation. If even naturally accessible truths were left solely for philosophic demonstration, only a few would come to know God, and that after a long time and with much error mixed in (1.4, nos. 23–25). Thomas adapts these arguments from several sources, but especially from a longer list in Maimonides's *Guide of the Perplexed.*[38] Here he uses them to argue that the divine clemency acted therapeutically (*salubriter*) when it revealed naturally accessible truths to human pupils (1.4, no. 26). The converse argument is made in 1.5, where Thomas defends God for having revealed truths that exceed human reason altogether. He argues, first, that nothing will be desired or sought unless it is known. His examples are the promises of the Christian religion and the moral persuasion of ancient philosophy. The philosophers had to persuade their hearers to leave sensual pleasures for better ones by showing them that there were goods more powerful than the sensory; higher pleasures come with the exercise of active or contemplative virtues. Thomas gives no specific illustration, and there is none to be found in Maimonides's discussion of preparatory disciplines.[39] Thomas summarizes the project of "Gentile" persuasion to philosophic life, the pursuit of participation in the divine. As if to emphasize the Greek origin, Thomas takes three authorities from Aristotle—and then confirms them with two from Scripture.

The concern for justified persuasion leads to a distinction between sober and frivolous conviction (1.6, nos. 36–41), to analogies between divine and human teaching (1.7, no. 43), and to remarks on how useful and delightful it is to pursue what exceeds present capacity (1.8, no. 49). Persuasion stands forth most clearly in the final chapter of the prologue, where Thomas draws a conclusion for his own composition from the two modes of truth. Truths that the labor of reason can reach should be set forth by demonstrative reasons, "through which the adversary can be convinced" (1.9, no. 52). Higher truths cannot be reached by demonstrative reasons. The teacher ought not to try to "convince the adversary" by their means, but only to address or resolve difficulties (1.9, no. 52). Indeed, the only way of "convincing the adversary" in such cases is by the authority of Scripture, divinely confirmed through miracles (1.9, no. 53). For higher truths, the writer should provide verisimilitudes in order to exercise and comfort the faithful, not "to convince adversaries" (1.9, no. 54).[40] Thomas will write first about the truths that faith proffers and reason also investigates, using authorities from both philosophers and saints, "so that these truths might be confirmed and the adversary convinced" (1.9 no. 55). He writes only then about higher truths, in order to "resolve the reasonings of the adversaries" and to declare the truth of the faith by probable arguments and Scriptural authority (1.9, no. 56).

I have here reproduced Thomas's language, even at the risk of illustrating faulty repetition, in order to show that the phrase "to convince an adversary (or adversaries)" recurs five times in three short paragraphs. Thomas proposes the structure of *Against the Gentiles* in terms of a rhetorical or pedagogical efficacy.[41] Who is to be persuaded and about what? The audience is not the "adversary," not the prospective convert. Thomas wants to show rather how an adversary could be convinced. To whom will he show this? He will show it to believers who are concerned with the persuasion of unbelievers—that is, to all thinking believers whatever. The means by which he shows it to believers—this is a second order of persuasion, a higher rhetoric, by which he teaches those who would persuade. Thomas means to write an anthology of exemplary arguments divided by a distinction in persuasion. This is the conclusion of the prologue and, I think, of the debate over the two truths.

In order to teach believers about what can and cannot be demonstrated, Thomas undertakes a persuasive clarification of the truth of faith. While it teaches believers how to persuade, *Against the Gentiles* also persuades believers to become habituated in the whole of Christian wisdom. Where do we place a work with this kind of rhetorical purpose?

Genre

Genre analysis inevitably risks essentialism. The essences may be deep patterns of representation offered to readers or tidy models for composition offered to writers, but they are essences all the same. The more like an essence genre becomes, the less useful it is as a category for readers and writers. Elaborately defined genres, for example, are invariably subject to innovation, admixture, variation, and rejection of the definition.[42] For that reason, among others, ancient rhetoricians often condemn attempts to systematize genre—as Plato's Socrates silences the rhetorical manualists with irony (*Phaedrus* 271c) and Cicero's Crassus shrugs off their advice as unhelpful for real composition (*De oratore* 1.32.145–146). Their points should be made more sharply for prose didactic works, which were never properly analyzed even by the manuals.

In didactic writing, a "genre" is a fluid cluster of vocabularies, tropes, argumentative logics, discursive structures, and rhetorical purposes. It becomes a useful category for analyzing philosophical or theological rhetoric only when it is conceived as something below a text's surface disposition. Too often "genre" is made to refer to a bewildering range of textual features and responses to them. It is more helpful to pick out in that confusion the features and responses that have to do with persuasive relations, the relations of teaching in view of which a work is properly considered didactic. In looking for other texts that might illuminate the structure of *Against the Gentiles,* I am not hoping to squeeze Thomas's writing into an antecedent kind. For me, asking about a work's genre is not a request to affix a taxonomic label. I want instead an increasingly specific appreciation of a particular text's pedagogical choices.

Thomas's prologue already suggests three generic antecedents in its use of sources. The first is the explicit authority of Aristotle's *Metaphysics.* The second is an implicit reliance on Maimonides's *Guide.* The third is the invocation of Hilary's *On the Trinity.*

At least since Jaeger, modern readers have recognized the connection between the opening of the *Metaphysics* and Aristotle's (lost) *Protreptikos* or exhortation to the study of philosophy.[43] They have thus known, though they have not always appreciated, that the opening of the *Metaphysics* is related to a long line of similarly motivated writings. Exhortations to philosophy were written for a millennium after Isocrates.[44] Extant or partially extant examples are whole Platonic dialogues or sections in them (such as the conversation between Socrates and Clinias in the *Euthydemus*), the (lost) *Protreptic* of Posidonius, Cicero's (lost) *Hortensius*, the 90th of Seneca's *Moral Letters*, Iamblichus's *Protreptic*, and the 24th oration of Themistius. For many of these texts, which share at best a family resemblance, exhortation to the study of philosophy presupposes that undertaking inquiry or moral reform requires persuasion, that this persuasion must be undertaken against competing claims, and that the character of the persuasion foreshadows the character of the inquiries and virtues practiced after it.

Of ancient works that might be called protreptics, Thomas knew only a small fraction. He inherited a number of books by Cicero, but not, of course, the *Hortensius*.[45] He might have gathered some sense of Cicero's protreptic from the remarks on wisdom in *On Duties*[46] or from those on philosophy in the *Tusculan Disputations*.[47] Seneca enjoyed a wide reputation for moral teaching among Latin readers in the twelfth century, but he figures in Thomas chiefly as an authority on how the wise may conquer passion.[48] It might seem more likely that Thomas would have learned of ancient philosophic protreptic through its description and imitation by early Christian writers. Unfortunately, Thomas speaks no judgment about Augustine's praise for Cicero's exhortation, and he does not notice the protreptic structure of early Augustinian works including *Against the Academicians*. He does not advert to the persuasive drama of Boethius's *Consolation*. Perhaps he passes over these allusions to protreptic because of his generally harsh judgment on teaching rhetoric.[49] Augustine mocks his professors of rhetoric, then outdoes them in performing the art. Thomas, who had never been a Gentile, begins already within the Christian practice of persuasion.

Thomas does understand the importance of beginning persuasion rightly. For example, he applies the Ciceronian model of the *exordium* to the opening of Aristotle's *On the Soul* and its remarks on delight in learning.[50] He makes no such explicitly rhetorical approach to the *Metaphysics*, but he does attend to its persuasive purposes. In his exposition of the *Metaphysics*, finished some ten years after *Against the Gentiles*, Thomas paraphrases at length Aristotle's remarks on the desirability of wisdom.[51] More summarily, Thomas says that the purpose of Aristotle's prologue is to show the dignity and end of metaphysics.[52] In works prior to *Against the Gentiles*, Thomas frequently appeals to these same chapters to secure lofty characterizations of wisdom.[53] Thomas sees that Aristotle begins the *Metaphysics* not just with a designation of the study, but with its praise.

Of course, Thomas cannot simply copy any ancient exhortation to philosophy. Philosophic protreptics often presume citizenship in a pagan polity and move from it to the call of philosophy, variously conceived. Thomas's protreptic presumes Christian baptism, membership in the Church, and calls not to initial conversion, but to progress in the practice of Christian wisdom. The protreptic of Christian wisdom is internal to faith, but it is needed for the duration of our pilgrim state. Thomas could find Christian transformations of persuasion to wisdom in many places. There are sapiential exhortations in a number of Latin academic works familiar to the Parisian schools. Consider Hugh of St Victor's *Didascalicon*, Gundissalinus's *On the Division of Philosophy*, and William of Auvergne's *On the Universe*.[54] Among works of mendicant authors prior to 1260, such prologues can be found in Robert Kilwardby's *On the Origin of Sciences* and in Bartholomaeus Anglicus, *On the Properties of Things*.[55] Thomas himself uses such a prologue based on the fourfold division of wisdom for his *Scriptum* on the *Sentences* of Peter Lombard; a similar topic is treated in his inaugural lecture as regent master of theology.[56] Still, these Latin antecedents are no more helpful than allusions to Aristotle's *Metaphysics* when it comes to specifying the structure of persuasion in *Against the Gentiles*. While Thomas may share with his theological predecessors' faith in a revealed wisdom, he construes differently the consequences for teaching that faith. How is his specific notion of persuasion to revealed wisdom connected to his specific compositional structure?

The second genre model behind Thomas's prologue is Maimonides's *Guide*, with which Thomas shares both acceptance of revelation and familiarity with the Aristotelian tradition of wisdom. Are there structural parallels here? The suggestion gains plausibility because Maimonides particularly influenced Latin academic circles through Albert and Albert's students, including Thomas.[57] How then did Thomas regard Maimonides's persuasive project in the *Guide*? Absent explicit comment, only a structural comparison can show whether Thomas is imitating Maimonides.

The *Guide* begins, in Thomas's Latin version, with a blessing on a nameless student and a dedicatory epistle addressed to him. The student is beloved because he so earnestly desires wisdom, though his prior training had not prepared him for its study.[58] Maimonides is writing the *Guide* to complete a hierarchy of learning that has again been interrupted. There follows an invocation compounded from Psalm 143:8 and two verses from Proverbs (8:4, 22:17). Maimonides begins his proemium proper with a plain statement of intention: the *Guide* will explain difficult locutions in the prophets. After stressing that he does not write for all, Maimonides says more fully: "the intention of this whole book is that the law be understood along the way of truth (*per viam veritatis*). For the intention of this book is to purge (*experge-facere*) the mind of the just man . . ." (fol. 2r.). Scripture shows forth its secrets briefly and through the veil of symbols. Any teacher wishing to expound its truth should explain scriptural symbolism only with deliberate brevity and obscurity. Maimonides ends with specific instructions to the reader, including remarks on seven reasons for the semblance of self-contradiction in a book.

The prologue of *Against the Gentiles* may be said to agree with the opening of the *Guide* when it emphasizes wisdom, expresses desire to complete a hierarchy of knowledge, and subordinates philosophical study to Scripture. *Against the Gentiles* disagrees with the *Guide* crucially on private and public in spiritual teaching. There is no device of dedication to a single student in Thomas, though this was a common topic in earlier Latin prefaces; nor is there any long analysis of esoteric writing. On the contrary, Thomas begins with a scriptural quotation that emphasizes the public and disputatious character of wisdom. (Thomas's opening citation is also taken from Proverbs 8, though not from Maimonides's verse.) Moreover, Thomas's notion about a double mode of manifesting truth replaces Maimonides's more elaborate and pessimistic hierarchy of minds in relation to divine radiance.[59] Maimonides writes obscurely for the just; Thomas writes publicly for a community of believers.

If Thomas's prelude at once echoes and reverses the project of the *Guide*, a comparison of structures will show even more ambivalence. It is possible to take the first 70 chapters of the *Guide*, to delete most of the short sections that gloss particular scriptural locutions or passages, and then to match the remaining chapters with some plausibility against the topics of *Against the Gentiles* 1. Thomas's use of remotion to establish negative truths about God's simplicity corresponds to the reiterated emphasis in the *Guide* on God's incomparable incorporeality.[60] More particularly, Thomas's chapters on remotion (14), the metaphysics of divine simplicity (21–22), and divine bodilessness (20, 27) match chapters in *Guide* 1 exactly (respectively, 34 and 57, 56, 54 and 75). Again, Thomas's treatment of the divine names (30–36) corrects a similarly explicit treatment in *Guide* 1 (26, 51–52, 59, and 60–63 for the scriptural particulars). The main tenets of divine knowledge, divine causality, and divine life are also established in the *Guide's* first book (respectively 67, 68, and 45).

These correspondences, which can be explained in many other ways than as direct imitation, conceal great differences. The scriptural hermeneutic of the *Guide* is lacking in Thomas as a compositional motive. Thomas is not concerned in *Against the Gentiles* to gloss the obscurities of Scripture, except incidentally (e.g., 1.42, no. 353b). *Against the Gentiles* does not follow the *Guide's* order, either in sequence or division of topics. To take the obvious example: Thomas begins *Contra gentiles* 1 by reviewing demonstrations for the existence of God; Maimonides treats the demonstrations only at the beginning of the second book and then in the contexts of divine creation. Again, Maimonides tends to approach attributes of life before those of intellect and causality or will. Thomas's order is just the reverse. Thomas may be interested in Maimonides on the divine names, anthropomorphism, or specific details of the Islamic Aristotle, but he does not follow either Maimonides's structure or his general conclusions.

There is one peculiarity in the structure of the *Guide*, however, that points towards the central feature in the structure of *Against the Gentiles.* Maimonides ends with the following sequence of topics: providence, prophecy, the rationality of the Torah, and the implications of God's law for human life. So, too, *Against the Gentiles*, in all of its divisions, ends with depictions of the human good. The structure of *Against the Gentiles*, as of the *Guide*, is not so much a descending deduction as an ascending exhortation. The end of wisdom is an act, an exercise of life. Such wisdom is taught best not in a deduction to the last particular, but by tracing a route leading to the highest end. Thomas's chief rhetorical mode is not apodictic, but epideictic; not demonstrative, but hortatory. His work is a protreptic to the contemplation of God. It ascends to God through world and law in order to practice wisdom as vision. The protreptic of *Against the Gentiles* shares with ancient protreptics the use of persuasive devices as an introduction to the practice of contemplative virtues. It shares with Maimonides the structural suggestion that such virtues are completed beyond the simply natural by means of divine exhortation.

The third genre model for *Against the Gentiles* is *On the Trinity* by Hilary of Poitiers. Thomas invokes Hilary twice. In the first passage, Thomas quotes Hilary dedicating himself chiefly to knowledge and expression of God (1.2, no. 9). Towards the end of the introductory chapters, Hilary is invoked again to confirm the argument that it is both useful and pleasant for believers to reason about truths beyond reach of demonstration (1.8, no. 50). Joseph Wawrykow argues from these passages and others that Hilary's own *On the Trinity* guides the conception and construction of *Against the Gentiles.*[61] Thomas is more likely to be inspired in writing out the duty of wisdom by a patristic author than by Greek protreptic or by Maimonides. Thomas shares with Hilary not only creedal profession, but a tradition of elaborating Christian wisdom in the face of philosophical and heretical error.

Wawrykow's suggestion is a good one, but it raises again questions about Thomas's access to full texts of predecessor works. In both passages, Thomas turns to Hilary by a kind of word association. In the first, the word *officium* (office, duty) supplies an explicit link; in the second, it is the notion of presuming to comprehend the divine. Hilary appears, in other words, as the "author" of *sententiae* or excerpts already in circulation and already connected to certain topics, either literally (in an anthology) or virtually (by habit of memory). In thirteenth-century anthologies of patristic passages, the attempt to improve upon the sources by topical or indexical arrangement is balanced by the insistence on the importance of full citations and comparison with the original context.[62] As we have seen, and precisely on exegetical principle, Thomas prefers to know something of context whenever he deals with an authority. Still he is a medieval master, and he depends on quick access to an enormous range of usable text fragments. The suspicion that Hilary may be one of these is reinforced when the reader notices that *On the Trinity* is cited only one other time in the whole of *Against the Gentiles,* and then to support the notion that being is not an accident in God (1.22, no. 212). Is Hilary the inspiration for Thomas's structure or the remote source of a few loci useful for confirming discrete notions?

If Thomas had studied *On the Trinity* whole, he might have found it both interesting and unhelpful for his experiment in protreptic construction. Hilary declares his intentions and explains his structure in a prologue that adheres closely to Roman rhetorical models.[63] Hilary offers a symbolic autobiography that narrates his conversion from folly towards knowledge of God (1.1–14). God is disclosed progressively in creation and its philosophy, in the Old Law, and then decisively in the New. The stages of the narrative are fixed, formulaic, but the voice speaks as if in intimate autobiography.[64] Hilary tells of his own pedagogy through reflection on society and the discovery of a sequence of texts: Exodus 3:14, Wisdom 13:15, the opening of the Gospel according to John, and Paul in Colossians 2. There is no such autobiography in *Against the Gentiles,* because there was no such progressive discovery of Christianity in Thomas's life. The main conceit of Hilary's prologue is one that Thomas cannot use. Thomas notes that he lacks the familiarity with paganism possessed by some of the patristic writers. He means in part that he did not have their experience of conversion to Christianity.

After the prologue, Hilary turns from his curriculum of wisdom to the upsurge of heresies that deny the Trinity (1.15–19). He certainly agrees with Thomas on the importance of refuting dangerous errors. He agrees as well in wanting to lay out a work on the Trinity that persuades the reader to undertake a fluent ascent (1.20). Of course, Hilary's book is only about the Trinity. Its exposition begins with divine generation—that is, at the point Thomas reaches only in *Against the Gentiles* 4.2. If Hilary (among others) could offer Thomas some confirming sayings, an admonition to refute error, and an ideal of compositional unity, he could not help at all with an experiment in a comprehensive curriculum for Christian wisdom.

Thomas experimented with a new kind of structure. The structure's intention—not to say, its success—can be read off many features in the finished work beyond the prologue.

Protreptic Structure

If *Against the Gentiles* is a protreptic, it ought to be possible to find in it the structures and devices of persuasion to an end.[65] The most obvious persuasive structure is the ascent to the human good in 3.1–63. The argument rises from a general assertion of teleological order (1–16), through the thesis that God is the end of all creatures and of intellectual substances particularly (17–26), to a comparison of contemplation with all other possible claimants to human happiness (27–47). Thomas ends the sequence by representing the contemplation of God in beatitude, which is both heaven and the fulfillment of philosophic longing for unfettered contemplation (48–63; compare 41–44).

The ascent combines features from classical and Christian protreptic. One feature is the *synkrisis* or comparison of wisdom with alternate goods (27–36). Thomas has already remarked that philosophers must lure their hearers away from other pleasures (1.5, no. 29c). So Thomas rules out claims that happiness consists in the exercise of political virtues or liberal arts—just as Greek philosophers had to keep their hearers from succumbing to the rival pedagogies of sophists or poets. Thomas offers, in second place, a criticism of alternative descriptions of wisdom (41–44). This, too, is a kind of *synkrisis*, and it takes the place in Greek philosophy of the review of rival schools. Then Thomas adds, in third place, an evocation of the good to be attained in beatitude. He writes three lyrical chapters to show that the vision of God makes human beings eternal participants in divine life (61–62), even as it fulfills their every desire for knowledge, virtue, honor, fame, wealth, pleasure, immortality, and community (3.63, nos. 2,378–2,383). Thomas ends the peroration by juxtaposing Aristotelian and scriptural praises of wisdom, so that the reader might see the one perfected in the other (3.63, no. 2,383).

Against the Gentiles 3 does not stop with that evocation—and it is important that it does not do so. Thomas turns with the briefest of connecting passages to a long consideration of providence. Teaching about providence is required to assure the reader that the distant end of contemplation, which so little resembles human life here, is within the power of the cosmic ruler. God the end is also God the "governor" or "ruler" of the means.[66] God's governance is not coercive. The second thesis of the treatment of providence is that human agents are free from the coercion of celestial bodies (84–87) and separate substances (88–89); they may follow God without fearing fortune or fate (91–92). At much greater length, Thomas analyzes divine rule over intellectual creatures (111–113) in order to show the necessity for God's teaching (114–129) and the usefulness of God's counsels (130–139). The teaching on providence culminates in the argument that humans need divine grace to attain the end that has been proposed (147–163). *Against the Gentiles* 3 ends with a chapter on election and reprobation that emphasizes human freedom under or within God's glory. The last line of the books is a doxology from *Romans* 11:35–36. It seals the teaching that the human goal cannot be reached without God's help.

The evidently hortatory structure of Book 3 finds echoes both earlier and later in *Against the Gentiles.* At the end of the prologue to the whole work, Thomas writes that the first thing to be demonstrated is God's existence, "without which every consideration of divine things is removed" (1.9, no. 58). The last demonstrative arguments conclude that there is some being "by whose providence the world is governed" (1.13, no. 115). The existence of God is not a fact only, but a force over human life. When he turns to God's perfection, Thomas must treat again of the divine names, in order to secure resemblance between God and creatures (28–36). More specifically, he must show that his protreptic speaking about God is not "in vain" (1.36, no. 301). It is appropriate to a protreptic that it should center on God's understanding, willing, and living. God's understanding makes God the final end for intellectual creatures; God's willing grounds providence; God's life is the activity to which human beings are called. The last section of Book 1 concerns the divine life (97–102); the last chapter argues that God's beatitude exceeds every other beatitude (1.102).

It rejects false happiness and adds a doxology: "To the one who is singularly blessed be honor and glory unto ages of ages" (1.102, no. 850).

Against the Gentiles 2 aids the protreptic by establishing God's causality over creation and humankind's indispensable place in the hierarchy of intelligences. The preface promises as much. Thomas supplies four arguments to justify considering creatures within Christian wisdom: creatures imitate divine wisdom and so produce wonder and reflection (2.2, no. 859). Studying them leads to fear of God and reverence (2.2, no. 860). It kindles divine love (2.2, no. 861). Indeed, meditating on creatures produces a likeness of divine wisdom (2.2, no. 862). Knowing creatures also helps destroy errors that prevent contemplative ascent to God – by deifying matter, by exaggerating creatures, by exalting necessity, by debasing human teleology (2.3, nos. 865–868). Each of these four reasons is directly connected to the protreptic. Each supposes that *Against the Gentiles* means to bring right order to active pursuit of the divine. The considerations proposed hasten pursuit; the errors rejected would prevent it. The protreptic purpose is confirmed in the part's last section, which offers another doxology to the divine mind (2.101, no. 1,860). In the parts leading up to the third, then, Thomas frequently describes persuasion towards the highest good as a gracious gift from its possessor.

The order of *Against the Gentiles* 4 is often set out rather prosaically: the Trinity (2–26), the Incarnation (27–55), the sacraments (56–78), and the final resurrection together with the last judgment (79–97). Notice these structural peculiarities. The Trinity is introduced under the rubric of "generation" in God. Thomas shows how far God's life can be compared to that of other living things (4.2, no. 3,354c; compare 4.26, no. 3,629, "in living things"). The passage ends by reiterating the likeness of human thought to the Trinitarian processions (4.26, nos. 3,631–3,632). The treatment of the Incarnation ends with the question of its appropriateness or *convenientia* (4.53–55).[67] The positive arguments assert that God's incarnation is the most effective help towards beatitude (beginning in 4.54, no. 3,923). The sacraments appear as applications and manifestations of Christ's role in human healing (4.56, no. 3,962). The final sacrament to be treated is matrimony, which extends through time the human search for the good (4.78, nos. 4,119, 3,124). The resurrection and the last judgment are concerned quite literally with the end of human life—indeed, of human history. Although such topics frequently appear at the end of comprehensive theological works, Thomas here not only designates human life after resurrection, he describes it (82–88). Some of his hypotheses may seem extraordinary, but they aim to convince the reader that human desire will be satisfied in the city of glory (see especially 4.86). The last chapter of the entire work begins with these words, "Thus when the last judgment has taken place, human nature will be constituted completely in its end" (4.97, no. 4,285). *Against the Gentiles* ends with the divine proclamation of eternal joy and exultation (4.97, no. 4,292).

It would be possible—indeed, necessary for a satisfying argument—to consider Thomas's rhetorical structure in greater detail and to show how far other reasons, such as traditional arrangement, might account for some of these features. Let me enunciate that large task and then suggest how a reader could begin to discover the protreptic character of *Against the Gentiles* at closer range, in its details—for example, in locutions that introduce authorities, in arrangements of multiple arguments for a single point, and in choices about which topics will be treated at length.

Thomas's phrases or locutions for introducing scriptural authorities were mentioned by Mulard in the debate over De Broglie. Mulard's point was that they separated philosophical argument from theological authority.[68] The locutions are actually more complicated, at least before the fourth part, where they begin to sound more like rubrics for proof texts in doctrinal controversy. In the first three Books, the locutions clearly do not introduce scriptural texts as syllogistic premises for philosophic demonstration. Their steady repetition of "also" shows that the citations they introduce are supplements to the arguments.[69] More interesting are the verbs: the authority of Scripture or of the faith is said to "confirm," "give testimony," "agree" or "harmonize," "profess," "confess," "commemorate," "attest," "show," "proffer," and "protest."[70] The verbs suggest that citations add both evidence and emphasis. They add more evidence, because the Scripture already counts as true for the Christian reader. They supply emphasis, because the Scripture is supremely authoritative and beautifully moving. The most interesting locutions imply a causal connection: Scripture says something or faith holds something *because* of the reasons enunciated in the chapter.[71] Here the reader can see the protreptic connection between rational and authoritative persuasion. She has been led through a series of arguments; she has also been reminded that the same doctrine is found in the authorities of her faith. The complete persuasion to wisdom is accomplished when the reader grasps that the intelligibility of argument leads into the intelligibility of Scripture. The reasons of rational pedagogy pass over into the motives of Scripture.

A reader can see protreptic detail as well in the sequence of arguments. *Against the Gentiles* is remarkable for not conforming to the patterns of an academic dispute or commentary. In some sections, especially technical ones, Thomas falls back on the devices of the *quaestio*.[72] Much more rarely does he carry out a proper *lectio* (as in 2.61, 2.78). The typical chapter in *Against the Gentiles* has a short introduction or enunciation followed by a series of arguments that ends with confirming authorities or historical specifications or both. The multiple arguments are not interdependent. They can be grouped around certain basic premises, but they are better grasped as steps towards a cumulative persuasive effect. To show that the same conclusion can be derived from diverse premises makes it more plausible. Again, readers who are not convinced by one argument may be convinced by another. Thomas sometimes varies his starting points in the hope of casting a wider argumentative net. Finally, the last arguments in a chapter are sometimes more comprehensive or penetrating than the first.

A single passage can illustrate these persuasive structures. In 2.16, Thomas offers 12 arguments for creation *ex nihilo*, from no pre-existing matter. The first argument depends on a rule against regression in natural causes (no. 933); the second through the fifth invoke some principle of universality in effect and cause (nos. 934–937); the sixth through the ninth stress disanalogies or disproportions between matter and divine creation (nos. 938–941); the tenth and eleventh argue from God as first being (nos. 942–943). One might also say that the principles are: no regression (no. 933), universality of causation (nos. 934–935), peculiarities in the causation of being (nos. 936–937), peculiarities in the reception of effects by matter (nos. 938–940), and asymmetrical relationships (nos. 941–943). On either account, there is a movement in the chapter from physical causality through its expansions and distensions to basic ontological relations. Note too that the arguments are designed to address readers of the *Physics*, the *Metaphysics* of both Aristotle and Avicenna, and the *Book of Causes*.

The third and last detail in which a reader can recognize protreptic structure is the selection of topics for fuller treatment. Principles of selection appear on the surface of Thomas's other works. In the *Scriptum* on the *Sentences*, selection is determined remotely by the Lombard's text and directly by the tradition of commentary on it. In the large *Summa*, by contrast, Thomas announces that the principle of selection is pedagogical concern for beginners. What is the equivalent principle of economy in *Against the Gentiles*? The missionary hypothesis would explain its selection of topics by pointing to the confrontation with Islam. Gorce would explain it as a reaction to the "Latin Averroists." In fact, the selection is motivated by the aim of persuasion to the practice of Christian wisdom. The topics that are treated extensively and technically bear directly on persuasion to the highest good.

Thomas evidently chooses to concentrate in *Against the Gentiles* 2 on refuting false views about the human intellect (for example, 2.59–62, 73–78). Thomas treats these views extensively not out of a technician's delight in detail, or from love of contention, but because human participation in the highest good depends on the individuality of intellects. A fashionable denial of individuality requires extensive correction if readers are not to be prevented in advance from accepting protreptic persuasion. The conclusion of the arguments against separation or unity of intellects serves as a premise in the first, syllogistic proof for human immortality (2.70, no. 1,598). A similar reading can be given to the technical analysis of the beatific vision (3.51–60). Coming at the end of the ascent to the highest good, these chapters carry great weight. They must show that God can be contemplated directly, but only by divine gift—otherwise the rest of Book 3 will be beside the point. If there is no direct contemplation, Thomas's protreptic has no end. If there is no need for grace, the protreptic is in no way Christian. Similar reasoning directs Thomas's technical emphasis on divine cognition of singulars (1.63–71), on human freedom from creaturely determination (3.84–88), and so on.

In three kinds of detail, then, *Against the Gentiles* shows protreptic motivation. It uses authorities, arranges arguments, and chooses technical disputes in order to persuade readers towards full Christian wisdom. This wisdom requires the exercise of Christian virtues, both acquired and infused. Persuasion to the practice of a virtue will be sterile unless it can offer some opportunity for enacting it. For Aristotle, famously, virtues, including intellectual ones, are acquired by practice. The best Aristotelian protreptic would not only exhort, but engage; it would speak about the virtues to be acquired while it provided exemplary occasions on which to imitate them. Here, too, Thomas succeeds in constructing *Against the Gentiles.* The work presents the virtues of Christian wisdom above all by requiring that its readers practice them—in following its structures, learning its locutions, discovering the order of its arguments, and understanding its technical digressions. Perhaps most helpfully, *Against the Gentiles* applies in hundreds of particular arguments drawn from dozens of predecessor texts the intelligible principles that are the seeds of speculative virtue. Its protreptic structure is not only an exordium to wisdom, but a school for its practice—not least in the proper handling of authorities.

Notes

1. In this and similar passages, I omit the *Compendium of Theology,* in part because of its brevity (at least as we receive it), in part because it returns to much older structures, especially Augustine's *Enchiridion.* The notion that Thomas's various works should be read as part of a more or less unified project became fixed for me in the course of studying Corbin (1974). If I cannot agree with Corbin's Hegelian narrative of development, I remain completely persuaded by the project of his title.
2. The arguments that follow assume the generally accepted chronology for Thomas's writings, as in Weisheipl (1974), and Torrell (1993). I reject the elaborate reasonings by Pierre Marc that would advance the time of composition to the second Parisian regency. For a specific but abbreviated rejoinder to Marc, see the review by Clemens Vansteenkiste (1968), and fuller criticism in his unsigned review (1970). The proposal to redate the *Contra gentiles* to the second Parisian regency was not new; it had already been considered and rejected in Castagnoli (1928), especially pp. 491–492. Marc's redating did not win general assent; consider the summary chart for works published ten years after Marc in Review of Calogero Allegro (1981), 49. One favorable vote can be had in Thomas Murphy (1969).
3. The text is discussed and quoted extensively in Marc (1961–67) 1:72–77 and 612–613.
4. Barcelona, Bibl. centr. MS 1018, fol. 179r, as quoted in Marc (196–67) 1:73.
5. The issues are summarized in Marc (1961–67) 1:74–76.
6. See Burns (1971) at p. 1,410; Huerga (1974), especially pp. 551–552 and 556.
7. References to the *Contra gentiles* will be made parenthetically to Aquinas (1961–67). The citations will list book, chapter, and unique section numbers. This edition reproduces the text of Leonine *Opera omnia* vols. 13–15.
8. Chazan (1977), especially p. 826.

9. Chazan (1977) p. 826.
10. See Chazan (1974).
11. See Sanjek (1974); compare Kaeppeli (1947). In the prologues edited by Kaeppeli, it is interesting to note the remarks on recourse to *rationes naturales* in controversy with heretics (pp. 301–302); compare *Contra gent.* 1.2 (no. 11b).
12. See generally Berthier (1936), especially pp. 295–312 on Raymond's "method."
13. These resemblances led Miguel Asín y Palacio to argue that Thomas had plagiarized portions of the *Pugio*; see Asín y Palacio (1904), especially pp. 320–323. The charge was refuted almost at once by Luis G. Getino on the basis of chronology; see Getino (1905), pp. 8–19 generally, with replies to objections on pp. 19–27. The question of borrowings between Aquinas and Martí reappeared with Marc's redating of the *Contra gentiles.* Marc asserts a dependence of *Contra gent.* 1.6 on Martí's *Capistrum Judaeorum*; see Marc (in Aquinas [1961–67]) 1:65–72, and Burns (1971), p. 1,409, who adopts the thesis of redating apparently on the basis of Murphy's summary article. There is also the thesis of prior exchange between Aquinas and Martí in Casciaro (1969), p. 44, Saranyana (1973). These hypotheses become necessary only if one rejects the simpler explanation that Martí borrowed from Thomas in his *Capistrum* just as he would do later and at length in the *Pugio.*
14. Raymundus Martinus (1967), pp. 192–253.
15. Marc (Aquinas [1961–67]) provides an exhaustive summary of the textual relations in 1:62–65.
16. The *Summula* is edited in Migne *PL* 189:651–658; for the parallels to Thomas, see especially cols. 653D–655C, and compare Peter's Letter 4.17 to Bernard (*PL* 189:321–345). For the composition of Peter's anthology of Islamic writings, see d'Alverny (1947–1948), especially pp. 69–71, 74–79.
17. Van Riet (1974), especially p. 158.
18. See the conclusions of Louis Gardet (1976), esp. p. 140.
19. See Weisheipl (1974) p. 389, no. 63, and p. 394, no. 72.
20. *De rat. fidei* 1 (Leonine *Opera omnia* 40:B57, esp. ll. 25, 27, 41, 49) and 2 (40:B58, ll. 1–22).
21. The autograph of the text lacks the folios that would show Thomas's rewriting of the first nine chapters. Such traces of the first redaction as are preserved in the "pA" manuscript tradition provide only a few variants for chapters 1–4, none of which are substantive. See the critical apparatus in the Leonine *Opera omnia* 13:3–23, and the summary remarks, p. xvi.
22. For catalogues from around 1292 to 1375 with the title "*Contra gentiles*" or some variant, see Michelitsch (1913), pp. 101 (no. 46), 102 (82/251), 104 (127/295), 105 (131/299), 107 (175/1372), 109 (245/192), 110 (254/200), 111 (285/232), 112 (311/1559), 115 (75), 127 (14), 134 (4), 137, 140 (30), 143 (6), 145 (4), 149 (4), 156 (3). The title "*Liber de veritate catholice fidei*" appears in some of the later catalogues: see Michelitsch (1913) pp. 104 (117/286), 106 (165/1,083), 110 (268/214). Henry of Hereford, whose catalogue is dated 1292–1294, gives the conflated title *Summa contra gentiles de veritate catholice fidei*; see Michelitsch (1913) p. 125 (76). For a Parisian stationers' list of 1286, see Denifle and Chatelain (1889–97) vol. 1, no. 530, pp. 644–649, especially p. 646 ("Summa fratris Thome contra Gentiles").
23. See the summary in Leonine *Opera omnia,* 13:xii.
24. Gorce (1930a), particularly pp. 228–233; see also his retrospective remarks on the work in Gorce (1930b). Gorce's argument was attacked on its characterization of a persistent "Latin Averroism" by David Salman (1937).
25. *Expos. Pauli, I ad Cor.* 6.3; *ad Rom.* 1.5 and 1.6.
26. *Sent. De cael.* 1.4.5, *Sent. Ethic.* 9.10.3, *Post. Psalmos* 21.23.
27. *Post. Psalmos* 48.1. On the reliability and context of this text, see Weisheipl (1974) pp. 368–369, no. 26, and Torrell (1993) pp. 376–378.
28. See Curtius (1953), pp. 83–85 and 87–88.
29. Guy de Broglie (1924–25). The most pertinent remarks fall in the first two installments.
30. De Broglie (1924–25) p. 207; compare pp. 206–209, 482.
31. Blanche (1924) (appended to a report of a lecture by de Broglie).

32. Indeed, there were really two debates, one concerning the natural possibility for beatitude (together with such related notions as "obediential potency"), the other concerning the distinction of two truths in the *Contra gentiles.* I will here notice only the second debate. For a bibliography of the first, see Matthys (1936), at p. 201, n. 2. Matthys himself provides a rigorous but falsely schematic reconstruction of the argument for the two truths (pp. 203–213).
33. Mulard (1925), though Mulard there adds nothing further with regard to the structure of the *Contra gentiles.*
34. Bouyges (1925)
35. Bouyges (1925) p. 191 (of the separate pagination).
36. Balthasar and Simonet (1930), especially pp. 185 (n. 1), 186–188, 203. Balthasar and Simonet consider as well the views of De Broglie, Blanche, and Mulard, adding those of Berten (1928). Compare the reviews by H.-M. Féret (1930-33).
37. From the 1950 edition of his *Introduction* on, Chenu holds that the *Contra gentiles* is a theological apologetic, but also a deeply historical work, engaged in the concrete reality of the confrontation between Christianity and Islam (see Chenu [1974] pp. 247–251). Gauthier argues, to the contrary, that the intention of the work is the supra-historical "intention of wisdom"; see Gauthier (1961) pp. 87–99. In a persuasive essay, somewhat at odds with his introduction to the English translation of *Contra gent.,* Anton Pegis sees Thomas as transforming the Aristotelian project by ordering it to the Incarnation, see Pegis (1964), especially pp. 172, 181–182. Quintín Turiel argues that the work is intended to show educated believers the truth of what they hold by faith; see Turiel (1974). Among more recent works on *Contra gent.,* I can single out one for agreement and one for disagreement. I agree when Thomas Hibbs deftly traces the dialectical correction of philosophy by theology in Hibbs (1995). I must disagree when Norman Kretzmann argues a strictly philosophical reading in Kretzmann (1997) and (1999). According to Kretzmann, *Contra gent.* 1–3 is "the fullest and most promising natural theology ever produced" (as in the latter volume, p. vii; compare p. 1., n. 1, "the paradigm of a fully developed natural theology"). Natural theology is understood in turn as the branch of *philosophy* that investigates "by means of analysis and argument, at least the existence and nature of God and, in this fuller development, the relation of everything else—but especially of human nature and behavior—to God considered as reality's first principle" (p. 5).
38. For a schematic analysis of the six texts in which Thomas treats this question, see Synave (1930), particularly pp. 328–352. Synave concludes that the *Contra gentiles* marks Thomas's mature reformulation of Maimonides's five reasons (pp. 350–351).
39. Maimonides (1964), 1.33, fols. 13r–v. On the peculiarities of this Latin version, which reproduces that used by Thomas, see Kluxen (1954), especially pp. 32–35; and Kluxen (1966), especially pp. 156–157.
40. "Verisimilitudes" reminds the reader that another topic runs underneath this section of the *Contra gentiles:* the use of *rationes convenientiae,* of reasonings from appropriateness or aesthetic fittingness. On these, see now Narcisse (1997), especially pp. 127–132.
41. R.-A. Gauthier has cautioned that "*convincere*" in these paragraphs means, not persuasion, but the refutation of error. See his remarks in the Leonine edition of *Sent. De anima* (Leonine 45:289*–293*). Gauthier seems to understand persuasion as a sub-rational activity opposed to critique or counter-demonstration. He also pictures it happening in mid-air, outside of particular human minds. By contrast, I take teaching truths to particular human beings as the paradigmatic activity of (fully rational) persuasion. But the debate continues: for two recently on the side of a logical construal of Thomas's project of persuasion, see te Velde (1994), and (in much less detail) Schönberger (2001), notably at pp. 20–21; for one on the side of rational persuasion as concrete pedagogy, Levering (2000), at pp. 604–613.
42. Rosalie Colie has shown for Renaissance letters just how luxuriant the growth of types can be even in writers enamored of archaizing definitions. See Colie (1973).
43. Jaeger (1948), pp. 68–71.

44. For a recent survey of protreptic in ancient philosophy, see Schenkeveld (1997), at pp. 204–213.
45. Vansteenkiste (1959), especially pp. 378–379.
46. For example, *De officiis,* 1.4.13, 1.6.18–19, 1.44. 1.155–156.
47. For example, *Tusculanarum Quaestionum,* 1.4.7–8, 2.1.1–2.5.13, 3.1.1–3.3.7, 4.1.1–4.3.7, 5.1.1–5.5.11.
48. See, for example, *Scriptum Sent.* 1.46.4 *arg.* 1, 2.33.2.2 *sed contra* 2, 3.15.2.2 *quaestiuncula* 1 *arg.* 2, and 3.35.2.1 *solutio* 2. There are other references on moral matters (such as the naturalness of death) and on miscellaneous bits of ancient culture. Seneca is cited only once in *De veritate* and then for a definition of "idea" (2.1 *sed contra* 1). He is never cited explicitly in the *Contra gentiles.* I leave aside the question, how far this decrease might signify a different judgment on Seneca and how far it is the result of Thomas's tendency to simplify his handling of *auctoritates* after the *Sentences*-commentary.
49. There is an interesting exception in the *Contra impugn.* 3.5, where Thomas defends the utility of rhetoric in the setting forth of divine teaching.
50. *Sent. De anima* 1.1.
51. *Sent. Metaph.* 1.1, 1.2, 1.3.
52. *Sent. Metaph.* 1.4.
53. See, for example, *Super De Trin.* 2.2 *ad* l, 5.1 *ad* 2, 5.4 *sed contra* 3, 6.4 *arg.* 3.
54. Hugh of St Victor (1939) 1.1, p. 4; Dominicus Gundissalinus (1903), pp. 1–19; William of Auvergne, *De universo* 1. *prol.* and *cap.* 1, as in William (1963), 1:593–594.
55. Kilwardby (1976) *De ortu scientiarum* 1, pp. 9–10; Bartholomaeus Anglicus, *De proprietatibus rerum praef.,* as in Bartholomaeus Anglicus (1979). Examples of such prefaces after *Contra gent.* would include such diverse works as Gilbert of Tournai's De *modo addiscendi* 2, where it has a specifically pedagogical purpose, and Anonymous (1936), pp. 121–122.
56. *Scriptum Sent.* 1. *prol., Princ.* Grabmann approaches the prologue to the *Summa theol.* by comparison with other prologues in the genre, especially that of Robert of Melun; see Grabmann (1957), 2:340–358, for the text from Robert and Grabmann's comments on it.
57. See Kluxen (1955), especially pp. 157–165.
58. Maimonides (1964), fol. 2r.
59. See Maimonides (1964), *Dux prol.* fols. 2v–3r. Maimonides offers something like the doctrine of two modes of truth in *Dux,* 1.30, f. 11r. I return to the question of esoteric writing in Thomas in chapter 9 of Jordan (2006).
60. Of course, Maimonides is not the only source of the insistence against anthropomorphism. Thomas knows of it from many patristic sources, such as Augustine *De Trinitate* 1.1.1–3 and John Damascene *De fide orthodoxa* 1.
61. Wawrykow (1994).
62. Rouse and Rouse (1982), 170–176.
63. Hilary of Poitiers (1979), ed. P. Smulders. Smulders's edition of the first book is reprinted with a French translation and excellent notes by G. Pelland in Hilary of Poitiers (1999), 202–273.
64. Contemporary readers are likely to recognize this narrative pattern from its later reworking in Augustine's *Confessions,* but Hilary could have learned it already in Lactantius.
65. This claim has already been made by Allard (1974). Allard compares the structure in Thomas with the Ciceronian paradigms for deliberative discourse. I differ from Allard both in regard to the importance of any particular rhetorical paradigm and in his emphasis on the political. But it may be that I rightly belong alongside Allard in any typology of views on the *Contra gent.*; see, for example, Hoping (1997), pp. 45–48.
66. Thomas says exactly this in his prologue to the exposition of Job, which is contemporary with *Contra gent.* 2–3; see Weisheipl (1974), p. 368, no. 25, and Torrell (1993), p. 494. Thomas writes that the denial of providence is the destruction of all virtue and the fostering of vice; see *Expos. Iob prol.* (Leonine *Opera omnia* 26, ll. 41–48).

67. See the opposite order in *Summa theol.* 3, where the treatment of *convenientia* (q. 1) precedes the treatment of the manner of the Incarnation (qq. 2–19).
68. Mulard (1925), p. 8.
69. See 1.14 (no. 119), 39 (323), 44 (380), 50 (428), 67 (566).
70. In Book 1, for confirmation, see 14 (no. 199), 39 (323), 47 (402), 60 (505), 65 (539), 68 (574), 75 (646), 78 (666), 91 (764), 97 (815); for testimony, 15 (126), 43 (370), 55 (464), 57 (484), 66 (554); for agreement, 20 (188); for harmony, 58 (493), 70 (610); for profession, 22 (212); for confession, 44 (380), 72 (626); for teaching, 50 (428); for commemoration, 29 (271), 91 (765); for attestation, 49 (417); for showing, 67 (566); for proffering, 82 (698); and for protesting, 100 (835).
71. "Et inde est quod . . ." (1.29, no. 271); "hinc est quod . . ." (1.37, no. 308; 40, no. 328; 41, no. 334; 56, no. 472; 61, no. 514; 99, no. 827); "propter quod dicitur . . ." (1.38, no. 315).
72. See especially 1.10–11, 2.61/69, 2.74–75, 2.80–81, 2.88–89, 3.5–6, 3.8–9, 3.54, 3.68, 3.108–109, 3.131/134, 3.132/135, 3.136–137, 4.4.9, 4.10, 4.16/23, 4.25, 4.40/49, 4.51–52, 4.53–55, 4.62–68, 4.80–81. Note the preponderance of such sections in the fourth Book. This is due to the procedural limitation of answering objections against the mysteries of faith, as in 1.9, no. 56.

CHAPTER **16**

"To Make the Truth Known": The Aim and Structure of the *Contra Gentiles*

CYRILLE MICHON

The *Summa contra gentiles* (CG), the smaller but older sister of the *Summa theologiae* (ST), has always been recognized as serving a purpose different from that of the *Summa theologiae*: It is not just a synthesis of Christian doctrine, organized in a pedagogical order. True, both works cover more or less the same topics—the whole of Christian doctrine—and both can be seen as efforts to replace Peter Lombard's *Sentences*, the textbook used to teach theology since the end of the 12th century. However, the *Contra gentiles*'s most important and distinguishing characteristic lies in its structure. Superimposed on the work's division into four books is yet another important division into two parts: the first (books I–III) bears on truths that are naturally accessible to human reason, while the second (book IV) bears on the mysteries of faith knowable only through divine revelation. This remarkable organization, more original than that of other *summas*, including Aquinas's own *Summa theologiae*, has long been a subject of multiple interpretations and controversies: what was Aquinas's aim in giving this structure to the first synthesis of Christian teaching whose organization he was free to create himself? Appeals to the old distinction between a *summa philosophica* and a *summa theologica*, though influential, are not relevant since the *Contra gentiles* is, according to its author, a work of theology and is certainly not philosophical in its shorter, second part. After reviewing the main points of Mark Jordan's "rhetorical" interpretation, I will propose my own, which in contrast focuses on the main division of the work and on its declared aim of making the truth known (*manifestare veritatem*).

Jordan's Rhetorical Interpretation

In his impressive and erudite essay (chapter 15, this volume), Mark Jordan has added an important chapter to the long history of interpretations of the *Contra gentiles.* One can summarize it in two main points, a negative and a positive one. I concur with the first, which is Jordan's judgment about the legend, originating in a chronicle written by Peter of Marsilius in 1313, of the supposed command made to St. Thomas by his master St. Raymond of Peñafort to develop a missionary treatise to convert the "infidels". Following Gauthier (1993), Jordan shows why the legend is untenable.[1] Through a careful reading of the prologue to book I (chs. 1–9), which is a general introduction to the whole *Contra gentiles,* he characterizes the project of the work as aiming at wisdom and the meditation of truth (ch. 1), according to the main division between the two kinds of truths (ch. 3). Aquinas introduces this distinction by remarking that discussions must be based on shared premises, such as those found in the New Testament, which Catholics share with heretics, those found in the Old Testament, which they share with the Jews, and those that have only the authority of reason, which they share with those who do not recognize any of part of their scripture, such as the ancient pagans and Aquinas's contemporary Muslims (ch. 2). This remark might appear to sustain the "missionary" reading, but Jordan explains convincingly that Aquinas means to amass a reservoir of arguments so that Christian thinkers will have them ready to hand against all kinds of intellectual objections. The *gentiles* or "pagans" he is concerned with are thinkers and philosophers rather than than the general population.[2] And the "victory" he is aiming at (*convincere*) against his "adversaries" (see I, 9.2) is less personal than intellectual: arguments win over, and refute, errors.

Jordan's second and positive thesis about the *Contra gentiles* is certainly more controversial. He interprets the project of the book as a "rhetorical" one, that of giving a protreptic to Christian wisdom. By the term "protreptic" he means that the book has a "persuasive structure" aiming at leading the reader to the "contemplation of God" and even to "the practice of contemplative virtues . . . by means of divine exhortation" (see p. 260). Jordan compares the *Contra gentiles* with other protreptic forms, mainly in order to differentiate it from ancient protreptics (Aristotle, Cicero, Seneca), from Maimonides's *Guide for the Perplexed* (though similarities are noted, see below), and from patristic exemplars, such as Hilary of Poitiers' *On the Trinity,* quoted in the opening chapter. After remarking on the order of arguments within chapters, of chapters within each book, and on the locutions introducing the texts of the Scripture, he concludes: "The work presents the virtues of Christian wisdom above all by requiring that its readers practice them—in following its structure, learning its locutions, discovering the order of its arguments, and understanding its technical digressions" and moreover that this "protreptic structure is not only an exordium to wisdom, but a school for its practice . . ." (p. 266). These assertions strike me as highly speculative and less well grounded than his negative and historical thesis. Of course, this does not mean they are ungrounded, much less false.

In particular, Jordan does a very fine job of identifying different forms of "ascensions" organized according to chapter groupings. The most impressive are found in the long discussion on human happiness in book III (2-63): eliminating false candidates, gathering necessary conditions, and culminating in the vision of God, the whole book ascending to the necessity of grace and the doctrine of predestination which bears on the life to come. One can likewise see in book I another form of ascension: from the more general divine attributes, such as perfection and simplicity, to the more imitable ones, such as intellect, will, and finally the divine life we are called to share eternally. Book II is less representative, but it is largely devoted to the examination of human intellect, that is, again, the part of us that is immortal. Books I–III themselves contain an ascent from the proofs of God's existence, starting from empirical data, to the divine providence over our final destiny. In a similar way, book IV organizes the mysteries of faith so that we ascend from God's nature as Trinity, to his work in the Incarnation, redemption and the sacraments, and finally to the life of our resurrected bodies.[3] The "hortatory structure" of the *Contra gentiles* discovered by Jordan is then the structure of each book, of each of the two major parts, and finally of the whole *Contra gentiles.* But this is the structure considered from the point of view of the contents, and it does not explain the function given to the main division based on the two kinds of truths. However fertile Jordan's ideas about the different ascensions in the *Contra gentiles* turn out to be, they cannot be the whole story. And apart from the interpreter's own conception of theology, I can find no basis for his reading of the *Contra gentiles* as an invitation to the practice of the virtues (though I would not deny that it could have been Aquinas's objective).

In what follows, I will not so much discuss Jordan's interpretation as his dismissal of the traditional reading, recently revived by Norman Kretzmann, of books I–III as offering a philosophical treatise on natural theology.[4] And I will also offer another interpretation of the whole *Contra gentiles*, that might complement Jordan's, but should have as an effect, if it is correct, of leaving his "rhetorical reading" in place as a supplementary interpretation. I will be concerned with the interpretation of the *Contra gentiles*'s main structure: Why did Aquinas proceed the way he did?

Wisdom, Theology and Philosophy in the *Contra Gentiles*

As already noted, the general intention of the work is expressed in the first chapter: the meditation of truth, and the attainment of wisdom. Even though he begins with a quotation from the book of Proverbs, Aquinas illustrates and articulates this intention by implicit and explicit references to the works of Aristotle and describes wisdom in a way that is compatible with the Philosopher's account of first philosophy.[5] This meditation is said to culminate in the highest truth, that is, God, so that wisdom is contemplation of the divine, or "theology", since *theologia* is the Greek word used by Aristotle to refer to that supreme part of first philosophy. The reader understands that the project will depart from philosophy only when Aquinas adds that God, whose nature is far above human capacities of knowledge (a fact that is not denied by Aristotle), is known not just indirectly through the knowledge of sensible things by an *ascension* of the mind to the supreme reality. God is also the active source of knowledge that *descends* from the highest to the human mind, either indirectly through the channel of the prophets, and this is the work of *revelation*, or immediately as an object of perception in the beatific vision. The prologue does not insist on this triple form of knowledge of God. But it was common doctrine, which Aquinas had already treated in earlier works (*Commentary on the Sentences* I,1.1, *Commentary on the Trinity* 2.2) and would address later in this one (IV, 1). In the prologue to book I, Aquinas considers only the first two kinds of knowledge or truths, those that are accessible to us in this life, and, as we have seen, in chapter 2 he introduces the distinction between putative interlocutors who do and those who do not accept the whole catholic faith, along with the need to argue on a shared basis.

Though he implicitly differentiates between a natural knowledge of God and what we will call a supernatural one, Aquinas does not make an explicit distinction between the two institutional disciplines of philosophy and theology, nor between the theology of the philosophers (natural theology) and revealed theology, or sacred doctrine.[6] Since he aims at wisdom, that is, at the meditation of truth, and so of the highest truth, which is God, he is in fact aiming at meditating the whole of the catholic faith, which is co-extensive with the whole of the truth about God that is reachable in this life. In the first chapter he emphasizes the need to *manifest* the truth, and consequently to *refute* the errors opposed to it.[7] With the distinction between the two kinds of truths, this work can be done by building on propositions that are knowable by human capacities alone, or on those that require divine revelation and the act of faith. Using the labels devised by Norman Kretzmann, the distinction between a theology (discourse on God, science of the divine) *from the top down* (revelation) and a theology *from the bottom up* (philosophy) is grounded.

Even if reason is qualified by Aquinas as "weak" (*deficiens*) in divine matters (I, 2.3), it will nonetheless be the shared basis on which to argue with those who do not accept any scripture. In the *Contra gentiles* Aquinas relies as much as possible on human reason alone in the statement and defense of the catholic faith, as one can conclude from two obvious features of the work. First, the distinction between the two kinds of truths gives the main division of the whole. Second, the first part, the exposition of truths that can be known by reason alone, occupies the first three books, which amounts to more than three quarters of the whole. And one can confidently assume that this apportioning is not due to the numerical advantage, nor to the intellectual resistance, of pagans and "infidels", but rather to the large part of the catholic faith that can be defended on a natural basis. Book IV is concerned only with the "mysteries" of the Trinity, Incarnation and Redemption, the doctrine of the sacraments, and some speculations on resurrected bodies. That leaves much of the catholic faith to the first part, the truths accessible by human reason: not only the existence and the nature of God (book I), the creation and the nature of the human soul (book II), but most of what concerns God's governance (providence) of rational creatures, which includes the doctrine of grace and glory for both humans and angels (book III).[8] This seems fully to justify Kretzmann's thesis that the first three books of the *Contra gentiles* constitute an enterprise in natural theology, even though Aquinas does not say so.

The reason the *Contra gentiles*—not even the first three books—cannot be considered a work of philosophy by its author is that, on Aquinas's view, if the premises of an argument are naturally knowable by human reason, that is a necessary but not a sufficient condition for the argument to have a philosophical nature. One also has to take into consideration the perspective or the point of view from which the argument is made. In the prologue to book II (ch. 4), Aquinas opposes two perspectives on creatures: that of the philosopher and that of the believer or *fidelis*. Apparently, the philosopher considers creatures in themselves and aims at knowing them, and so develops all the parts of philosophy, which include what we nowadays call science: biology, meteorology, physics. The believer considers them only in relation to God, as revealing something of God, in his production of them. Special attention must be given to rational creatures, not only because they resemble God better than other creatures, but also because *we* have a special interest. But once again, this interest is not general; for instance, the believer does not have any special interest in the human body (as medicine does), nor in political government (as practical philosophy does). His special interest is in the immortal human soul, called to the beatific vision. And he is also concerned with individual ethics, since human actions, virtues, and vices lead to eternal happiness or damnation.

This sort of difference in perspective also leads to a difference in *agenda* (to adopt once again one of Norman Kretzmann's felicitous expressions), indicating the relevant topics and their order. The philosopher's *agenda* comprises a chapter on God (natural theology). But it is usually the last chapter, the summit which is reached after a long journey exploring the main features of reality, as happens with book XII (long considered the last one) of Aristotle's *Metaphysics*. The believer, or the theologian, does not wait so long: he begins with God, maybe with a proof of his existence that starts from the consideration of worldly phenomena (movement, causation, finality), but in order to make a quick ascent to the top and then to develop a study of the highest reality. If the believer takes up the nature and function of creatures, even that will be with reference to God, since he will treat creatures as proceeding from the divinity (creation), or as coming back to him (through the practice of the virtues, and piety). This very neo-platonic triple consideration—the principle in itself, the emanation from the principle (*exitus*), the return to the principle (*reditus*)—seems to fit well both with the distribution of the first three books (God in himself, as origin of things—Creation, as end—Providence), and with the interior plan of the fourth one (Trinity, Incarnation and Redemption, Resurrection and everlasting life of creatures). It is, so to speak, a "theological" order, rather than a philosophical one.[9]

Finally, there is a third reason to consider the *Contra gentiles* a theological work. One could call it a *mereological* reason. It can be split into two principles. First, if one part of a whole is theological in that it proceeds from revealed propositions, then the whole is theological.[10] Second, if a whole is theological, then each part of it is theological. One part of the *Contra gentiles*, the second one or book IV, proceeds from revealed propositions and is theological, so the whole *Contra gentiles* is a work of theology. So the first part (books I–III) and each subpart of it (each book, each chapter), is also theology. This is so, even if the arguments are intrinsically philosophical. And we can reproduce this two-step argumentation at the level of the chapters, since Aquinas ends nearly all of them with a "confirmation" that what has been argued for belongs to the catholic faith (which confirms the truth as well as the relevance of the conclusion). He does this with an argument from authority, usually quoting the Scriptures. We can apply the two aforementioned principles to each chapter: some essential part of it is theological, so the whole chapter is, and so the other parts (the philosophical arguments) are too. This *mereological* reason is not explicit in the *Contra gentiles*, but it can be based on what Aquinas says about *sacra doctrina* in the first question of the *Summa theologiae*, which is not new. The basic idea is that philosophy is considered an auxiliary, a servant, of theology. The major discipline can use the services of the secondary one without losing its nature (see ST I, 1.5 response to 2). Philosophy is absorbed into theology.

Now, all of this being said, one can nonetheless underline that books I–III seek to establish on the basis of reason alone a long series of propositions about God, creation and providence, and that the invocation of scriptural authority comes only as a confirmation, at the end of each chapter. There is no doubt that the arguments are *intrinsically* philosophical, even if they are only philosophical elements in a theological whole, and can be said to be theological by absorption. The *perspective*, the *agenda* and the *mereology* are extrinsic to the arguments themselves. Were they not included in a theological work, they would not be considered theology; by themselves, they are philosophical. And they certainly belong to *natural theology* when considered individually: to be accepted, their premises require only the natural light of reason, while revealed theology requires the light of grace, and the vision of the saints and the angels requires the light of glory. As such, those arguments constitute a reservoir of natural theology. This is why I think Kretzmann was correct in speaking of the *natural theology* of *Contra gentiles* I–III, and in referring to the *metaphysics* of theism (book I), of creation (book II), and of providence (book III). In order to keep in mind the importance of the point of view and of the agenda, he proposed to distinguish the natural theology developed in the *Contra gentiles* as a *philosophy from the top down*, in opposition to traditional *philosophy from the bottom up*.[11]

Aquinas's careful re-reading of Aristotle's texts, manifest in various chapters or chapter groups, offers external confirmation for the view that books I–III constitute a philosophical enterprise. The most evident case, as noted by Jordan, is the long disputation over the human intellect in book II, which includes the detailed discussion of Averroes' reading of Aristotle (56–90). But in that same book one could also point to the precise argumentation on the question of the eternity of the world, on its possible eternal creation (31–38), as well as the long series on human happiness in book III (25–63), concluding with the affirmation that only the vision of God could fulfill the human longing for happiness. Those three topics (human intellect, eternity of the world, human happiness) were the ones that attracted criticism and condemnation of Aristotle's philosophy during the 13th century, since the Philosopher seemed to defend views opposed to the catholic faith (no personal immortality, an eternal world, mere earthly beatitude).[12] They were also the topics that, from the 1260s onward, came to characterize what would be called "Latin Averroism".[13] When the masters at the Arts College in Paris expounded Aristotle's philosophy, they did so with the help of commentaries, above all, those of Averroes. In fact, their work defended or at least spelled out an Averroistic understanding of Aristotelian philosophy. It has appeared to many scholars that the writing of the *Contra Gentiles* provided Aquinas with the occasion of a careful re-reading of Aristotle's works—but not the last, since it precedes all his commentaries devoted to Aristotle (written between 1269 and 1273). It may have prompted the writing of those commentaries, which made Aquinas famous and respected among the arts masters. Some of them (like the *Commentary on the Soul*) pave the way for developments in the *Summa theologiae*.[14] And Aquinas certainly thought that Aristotle's philosophy was the most important speculative tool for the doing of theology. But this in another way of saying that he turned philosophy into a servant, and sometimes into a part, of theology. The *Contra gentiles* is a perfect illustration of that.

A Dialogue and a Controversy with the Philosophers

We have seen along with Jordan that the strictly "missionary" interpretation, which makes the *Contra gentiles* a conversion handbook, is quite implausible.

So why did Aquinas choose the distinction between natural (philosophical) knowledge and revealed (gracious) knowledge of God and his works to organize his summa? The prologue to book I largely explains the distinction, its grounds, and the reason why God has revealed both kinds of truth (chs. 4–5). But it does not say much about the reason why the book (*liber*, treatise, summa) should proceed that way. I think we can take advantage of what has been said before in order to offer an answer that is quite different from Jordan's "rhetorical" explanation.

We have seen not only that Aquinas split his exposition according to the distinction of the two kinds of truth, but that the first part, the "philosophical" one, is much more developed than the strictly theological one. We have also seen that it represents a very careful reading of Aristotle, often in competition with Averroes. Both results suggest the following hypothesis. Aquinas is showing through *Contra gentiles* I–III that a good reading of Aristotle, which amounts more or less to the same thing as a good employment of reason alone, or good philosophy, goes very far in showing the truth of Christian faith. Not the whole truth, since what is knowable only through revelation does not belong to the first part, but a good deal nonetheless. More importantly, it can establish truths that are accepted only by Christians, so that reason alone can establish (part of) the truth of the Christian faith, and not just truths the Christian faith shares with paganism, Islam, or even Judaism. And so it would be a mistake to think that reason alone must be misled as individual pagan philosophers, the *gentiles*, were.[15] And not only pagan philosophers but also individual philosophers who belong to other religious cultures: Muslim and Jewish philosophers.

Let us first consider the case of Islam. Aquinas does not fight against Islam, but against the best philosopher he knows from the Muslim tradition: Averroes. His philosophical debate with Averroes consists of purely philosophical arguments; but over and above that, since both admit Aristotle as their guide, as a sort of incarnation of reason, Aquinas is eager to prove that his own reading of Aristotle is superior to the one given by Averroes. A very large part of book II is devoted to Averroes's interpretation of Aristotle on the intellect, according to which there is just one intellect for all human beings. There, Aquinas is eager to show not only that this view is philosophically unsound, but also that such a reading of Aristotle is inaccurate. He attacks Averroes's reading, according to which the possible intellect is separated and common to all human beings (II, 61) and argues instead that, for Aristotle, the intellect is the form of the body (II, 70). And he also argues against Avicenna's reading of Aristotle, according to which, even if the possible intellect is proper to each human being and serves as the form of the body, the agent intellect is separated and unique (II, 78). The philological arguments serve the philosophical ones (see chs. 59, 60, 68, 69, 73 and 75 against Averroes's conception and 76 against Avicenna's). One might suspect Aquinas's scholarship of being influenced by his philosophical views, and his philosophical views of being influenced by his theological commitments, since it turns out that what he is defending against Averroes is the personal immortality of the human soul (II, 79–81). Whatever it may be, I just want to emphasize the importance of the discussion of Averroes, both as a philosopher, and as an exegete of Aristotle. Aquinas argues that Averroes is philosophically wrong and that a correct reading of Aristotle, and so correct philosophy, is favorable to Christian beliefs.[16]

What about Judaism? Maimonides, *Rabbi Moyses*, the only Jewish philosopher mentioned in the *Contra gentiles*, is quoted only twice.[17] This might give a false impression: in fact, Maimonides is so present in *Contra gentiles* I–III that, after Aristotle, one might say that he is the most influential philosopher on Aquinas, a view I will shortly argue for. But first I have to make clear that Aquinas does not argue against Maimonides the way he does against Averroes. One reason is certainly that Judaism is closer to Christianity than Islam and Paganism, and Aquinas regards it not as a false religion, but as an incomplete one. Another reason is that Maimonides' influence on Aquinas is very often constructive; after all, Aquinas borrows many of his own arguments from the *Guide of the Perplexed*. In the prologue to book I, Aquinas's explanation of God's revelation of truths that are accessible to human reason is an adaptation of Maimonides' five reasons to delay the study of metaphysics.[18] But it goes the opposite way: the reasons why metaphysics should not be learned first and by all become reasons for revealing, early and to all, natural truths we do not have easy access to. Aquinas's proof of the existence of God, mainly the first one based on motion, is taken from Aristotle, but very close to Maimonides's exposition of it (*Guide* II, introduction and ch.1). And then, in chapter 14, Aquinas embraces Maimonides' view that the only way to avoid any falsity in our language about God is to use negative predication. Even so, Aquinas countenances, with caution, certain positive predications about God as well, and the small treatise on analogy (I, 32–34),[19] the most explicit in Aquinas's works, can be taken as a criticism of Maimonides's view that all positive divine attributes are equivocal when said of both God and of creatures. In book II the discussion on the eternity of the world defends Maimonides's exoteric doctrine. Aquinas already followed the Jewish thinker in his *Commentary* on the *Sentences* (I, d. 44), but the treatise of the *Contra gentiles* is absolutely clear about a) the impossibility of proving that the world is eternal; b) the impossibility of proving that it is not eternal; and c) the fact of the beginning of the world, which is known only through revelation. In book III, it is obvious that Aquinas tacitly follows Maimonides when he echoes Maimonides' contentions about the compatibility of providence and human freedom (III, 111–113) and the doctrine on marriage (III, 122–126), taking from the *Guide* (III, 49) his own arguments against incest and marriage between members of the same family. The end of the book, by contrast, supports views that exceed the bounds of Judaism in general and Maimonides' thought in particular, including considerations on the double commandment of charity (116–117), on the obligation of the "true faith" (118), on the evangelical counsels of obedience, chastity and poverty (130–135), on vows (138), and on the necessity of grace for following the commandments (147–163). Even before treating those major doctrines that Judaism finds untenable (about Trinity, Christ and the Sacraments), Aquinas implies that reason alone has shown the truth of some doctrines that belong to Christianity alone.[20]

If my hypothesis is correct that Aquinas is in dialogue with Averroes and Maimonides through large parts of *Contra gentiles* I–III, while he engages in further debates with pagan philosophers (about God's immateriality at I, 20, about the intellect in book II, and implicitly about conceptions of happiness in book III), then the objective of *Contra gentiles* I–III is quite clear: reason alone, correct philosophy, including and based on correct reading and interpretation of Aristotle, leads to a large part of the catholic faith and sometimes establishes truths that are proper to it. Such a result is valuable in itself and can be used in different contexts of discussion, maybe not with a general population of "infidels" or potential converts, but with the intellectual elite. Books I–III are not polemical all the time, and most of book I on divine attributes progresses peacefully, proving each attribute one after the other. But that fits with the aim of giving natural (philosophical) arguments for the truth of the catholic doctrine: it may be against some particular philosophical position, but it does not have to be. Proof and refutation are the two means, and the two tasks to be fulfilled for the same end, as defined in the prologue.

The Aim of the *Contra Gentiles*: To Make the Truth Known

This does not give us a justification for the whole project, including book IV. The last book of the *Contra gentiles* argues in favor of those catholic truths that are not accessible to reason alone, those for which we must rely on the authority of the Scriptures. There, Aquinas is arguing for theological conclusions and also defending truth against errors, mainly heresies (and not Judaism). Some of these heresies date from antiquity (see the heresies on the Trinity of Photinus, Sabellius, and Arius in IV, 2–9, as well as Photinus, the Manicheans, Valentinus, Apollinaris, Arius, Theodorus of Mopsuestia, Eutyches, Macarius and Nestorius on the Incarnation in IV, 28–44) and others from more modern times (e.g. the controversy with the Greeks about the procession of the Holy Spirit in IV, 24–25, or about the Eucharist in IV, 69, all in addition to Aquinas's book I discussions of the pantheism of David of Dinant in I, 17, and Amalric of Bena in I, 26). It is quite clear that Aquinas is often arguing against positions he knows second hand, many of them through Augustine. His arguments sometimes rely on the authority of the Councils (21, 22, 24), but most often he uses rational deductions from revealed premises. Aquinas is not only expounding the catholic faith, but arguing for its truth. Consequently, the whole of the *Contra gentiles* appears as a massive argument or a body of arguments for the truth of the catholic faith. Most of them (I–III) take as premises naturally knowable truths (both empirical and rational ones), but those of book IV rely on revelation and defend its correct interpretation and articulate conclusions that can be drawn from it.[21]

The project of the whole *Contra gentiles* is then simply to manifest, to prove, to argue for, the truth of the catholic faith from the most widely acceptable premises. If we want to identify the particular character of the work, the emphasis has to be put not so much on its content, since the topics are more or less the same as in other syntheses, but on the chosen order and the declared aim: showing the truth, refuting errors. In so doing, Aquinas is economical in his resources, as far as possible; but everything is useful, and in book IV he does not refuse recourse to arguments from authority. All of this is in perfect conformity with the declaration of the prologue. There Aquinas says:

> We shall first seek *to make known that truth* which faith professes and reason investigates. This we shall do by bringing forward both demonstrative and probable arguments, some of which were drawn from the books of the philosophers and of the saints, through which truth is strengthened and its adversary overcome [books I-III].
>
> Then, in order to follow a development from the more manifest to the less manifest, we shall proceed *to make known that truth* which surpasses reason, answering the objections of its adversaries and setting forth the truth of faith by probable arguments and by authorities, to the best of our ability [book IV].
>
> (I, 9.3, emphasis mine)

Now we can see that his aim was exactly that: make the truth known.

It might be helpful to contrast the *Contra gentiles* with the *Summa theologiae* on this point. In the *Contra gentiles*, as we have seen, philosophy is allotted a large space, the space of truths accessible to reason alone. But we have also acknowledged that the work's overall goal and its agenda are theological, and so we have reason to say that philosophy is absorbed into theology. Of course, if we consider the nature of the arguments and their premises, there is no alteration in the discipline. Philosophy is present, but only as a part, and as a tool. In the *Summa theologiae*, Aquinas is writing for theology students, who already, in principle, admit the truth(s) of the catholic faith. The goal therefore is not so much to settle disputes over the truth as to reach understanding. In fact, in nearly every article, Aquinas separates the argument from authority into the *sed contra*, which is enough to settle the conclusion (since the interlocutors accept those authorities), from the demonstrative argument, or argument from reason, in the reply, which begins with naturally or supernaturally known premises, and leads to the conclusion via a valid deduction or at least a plausible justification. Of course, one could insist, as Aquinas himself does, that when the premises are not naturally knowable, this is no longer philosophy. He admits, nevertheless, that it can be *science*: in the first question of the *Summa theologiae*, devoted to the *doctrina sacra*, he shows that science must argue for true conclusions, via valid arguments, from true and self-evident premises. In the case of theology, since the premises are known (believed) by faith, they are not self-evident to us, but they are to other minds, namely, those of the angels, the blessed, and God himself. So, theology can be considered a science subordinated to another one, in the same way that music is subordinated to arithmetic and builds on premises that are not self-evident to the musician, but are self-evident or known by demonstration to the mathematician.

This is not the place to discuss this very demanding conception of science, nor the conception of the subordination of one science to another that cannot be had by minds like ours (ST I, 1.2). What is crucial for our purposes is to note the way the conclusions are reached: through argumentation, most often deductive arguments. Even if this is not strictly philosophy (because of the status of the premises), it is a philosophical move that allows one to go from premises to conclusions.[22] When theology consists of arguments, it adopts the procedures of philosophy. When it relies on authorities to manifest the truth, philosophy is absent. But when authority is invoked only to certify the premises, and one proceeds to conclusions afterwards by way of rational argumentation, it can be said that theology is absorbed into philosophy. And this method serves a different objective from that of making the truth *known*: it aims at making the truths of faith *understood*. What is reached is not so much truth, the truth of faith *per se*, but the *intellectus fidei*.

In a famous *Quodlibet* (IV, 9.3), relating a dispute that occurred after the writing of the *Contra gentiles*, and during that of the *Summa theologiae*, Aquinas distinguishes two kinds of disputation.[23] The first kind aims at answering the question "Is it true?" or "Is it so?" (*an ita sit*). In the resolution, one can proceed by any helpful means towards the conclusions that things are so (*quia est*), in particular one can use various authorities, as was said in the prologue of the *Contra gentiles* (I, 9). The other kind of disputation is, according to Aquinas, proper to the schools of theology (*magistralis in scholis*). Since the fact of the matter is already accepted and believed, the response aims to provide the understanding of what is believed (*intellectus veritatis quam credunt*). Authorities in that case are of no use, for they can establish the truth, but no more. Aquinas says that anyone who would believe on the sole basis of authorities would know the truth, but he would have an empty head (*vacuus abscedet*). To *understand*, whether fully or minimally, requires the work of reason. Certainly, in that case reason proceeds from revelation, is enlightened by faith, grace, supernatural light, but it is the same reason, following the same procedures as in natural philosophy.

Is it fair to say that the *Contra gentiles* illustrates the first kind of disputation, and the *Summa theologiae* the second one? Well, since the *Contra gentiles* is preoccupied in books I–III with truths that can be known by reason alone, and strives to proceed with that more limited scope, it settles its conclusions via philosophical arguments. In a way it is more strictly philosophical than the *Summa theologiae*. Nevertheless, its aim is different, and even if book IV offers lengthy refutations of others' arguments or uses arguments from congruency, Aquinas is in principle happy with arguments from authority. In contrast, in the *Summa theologiae*, the distinction between natural and supernatural premises is not emphasized, but arguments from authority are always distinguished from, and always followed by rational ones, which constitute the real points Aquinas wants to make. This should be sufficient to draw a contrast between the two *summas*, even though their content largely overlaps. They both synthesize the Christian doctrine, but one aims at making its truth known, the other aims at making it understood. The first one relies as much as possible on natural knowledge and philosophy and is philosophy made theology, the second proceeds only through rational arguments and is theology made philosophy or, better, philosophy of faith.

Notes

1. As I did myself in the General Introduction to my French translation of the CG: (Aquinas 1999, pp. 9–65), following R.-A. Gauthier's magisterial *Introduction* to Saint Thomas d'Aquin, *Somme contre les Gentils* (Gauthier 1993).
2. Jordan (pp. 252–3) reminds us also, in keeping with Gauthier and others, that Aquinas used "infidels" to mean those whom he took to reject Catholic teaching (such as the Muslims) rather than the unevangelized. See also Gauthier's "Introduction" (1993, chapter 3, pp. 109–130).
3. For a similar comparison of the structure of book IV with that of I–III, see D. Moreau "Introduction" in Aquinas (1999, IV La Révélation, p. 21). I am less sure of Aquinas's originality there, and even less of the book's orientation towards human beatitude. I see conceptual rather than rhetorical or hortatory reasons for studying divine life after the other attributes; book II ends with the separated substances, the angels, and the "ascension" follows the scales of being rather than human achievement.
4. Kretzmann (1997). See on p. 2 the declaration alluded to by Jordan: "Aquinas's ambitious project in *Summa contra gentiles* Books I–III is the most fully accomplished and most promising natural theology I know of." Kretzmann develops his interpretation of Aquinas's project in chapter 1 "Theology from the bottom up". My hope is that this chapter will help serve to rehabilitate Kretzmann's splendid commentary on the first three books against its rapid dismissal by Jordan, n. 37.
5. The first chapter refers three times to the *Metaphysics* and once to the *Topics* in order to illustrate and articulate the office of the wise man. By contrast, chapter 2 defines the author's intention with quotations only from Hilary and the Scriptures (but see Gauthier's "Introduction" [1993, p. 145], on the implicit presence of Aristotle in chapter 2).
6. See the first question of ST I on the *doctrina sacra* and the explicit distinction mentioned here in a2.
7. On this double task (*arguere, manifestare* and *convicere, revincere, refutare*), grounded both in Aristotle (*Soph. El.*165a24-27) and Paul (*Titus 1:9*), see Gauthier, "Introduction" (1993, pp. 147–156).
8. This short summary is given by Aquinas himself at the beginning of the third book (III, 1.11).

9. This plan is even better illustrated by the CG than by the ST, which is more often used as an example. It is not in any obvious way a rival to Jordan's "hortatory" and ascending structure, but it may be sufficient to explain the structure of the books.
10. Note two precisions: the whole must be structured, in that many parts contribute to the nature of the whole, and those parts must be considered as necessary or essential parts (by opposition to mere accidental ones such as added remarks, excursus, etc.).
11. Both are forms of natural theology, or theology from the bottom up (from naturally knowable premises), and differ only in their agenda. See Kretzmann, (1997), chapter 1.
12. The teaching of Aristotle's natural philosophy books had been forbidden as early as 1210.
13. This does not mean that the CG itself was directed at this "movement" (since it manifests itself later); on this, see Jordan (p. 252). Aquinas may even have had some responsibility in the creation of Averroist doctrines such as that of the double truth, which he invented in denouncing it. See de Libera (1994).
14. See Torrell (2005) for the dates.
15. See Jordan (p. 252, and footnotes 25, 26), and the idea that the *gentiles* might well be the philosophers, or the intellectual elite, of the pagan world.
16. In book III, the discussion of happiness goes against Averroes's thesis that beatitude consists, in this life, in the contemplation of intelligible substances (II, 43–45). Aquinas "proves" that this is not sufficient, and that happiness must consist in the eternal, otherworldly vision of God Himself.
17. Once for his error on the counting of angels in II, 92.12 and once for his providing information about certain Muslim thinkers' occasionalist doctrine on causality in III, 97.15.
18. *Guide* I, 34 (explicitly quoted in the *Super Boetium de Trinitate*, 2.2), see Jordan p. 254.
19. Jordan (p. 258) indicates closer parallels between chapters of CG I and *Guide* I.
20. See Jordan's remark (p. 259) that as a *proptreptic* the CG is closer to the *Guide* than it is to ancient proptreptics, or to his contemporary Latin ones, but differences are also to be observed (p. 259). For a more precise survey of parallels and differences, and the thesis that Aquinas has the *Guide* in front of him when writing the CG, see Wohlman (1988 and 1995).
21. In I, 9.2 Aquinas also says that concerning the second kind of truths, "there are certain likely arguments that should be brought forth in order to make divine truth known", but only for the consolation of the faithful, and not with the idea of refuting adversaries, "for the very inadequacy of the argument would rather strengthen them in error, since they would imagine that our acceptance of the truth of faith was based on such weak arguments."
22. In his Commentary on Boethius's *On the Trinity*. 2.2.6, Aquinas says that *science* makes the conclusion appear from the principles (by inference), but is not involved with the appearing of the principles (it is the work of *intellectus* to make the principles appear: that is to understand their immediate evidence), so that in the *appearance of science* (*apparentia scientiae*) which proceeds from the apparent (unjustified and maybe untrue) principles, the work of reason is the same as in science itself.
23. According to the editors, this question was disputed at Easter 1271 (during the redaction of ST II). Its response is very close to the first chapters of the CG. See Gauthier (1993, pp. 157–158).

PART IX
The Character of Aquinas's Ethics

Editor's Introduction

No one doubts the extraordinary influence of Aristotle's *Nicomachean Ethics* on Aquinas's ethical theory. That theory's eudaemonistic structure, its focus on moral virtue, its assertion of the virtues' reciprocal relationship, and the doctrine of the mean of virtue all establish Aristotle's stamp on Aquinas's system. In fact the individual elements of Aquinas's ethics, such as the accounts of voluntary action, virtue, vice, continence, and incontinence, have sometimes struck readers as little more than re-worked Aristotle or "Aristotle baptized." Aquinas's repeated citations of the *Nicomachean Ethics* do little to dispel the impression that he is Christianizing Aristotle's work for a scholastic audience. In fact, his occasional appeal to Aristotle's ethics as a guide to interpreting the Bible suggests an openness to understanding the Christian ethical life at least partly in Aristotelian terms. And yet even a cursory reading of Aquinas's ethical writings will reveal important divergences from Aristotle. The most obvious include Aquinas's arguments that our perfect happiness can be found only in the next life, that we attain this happiness through the exercise of the God-given virtues of faith, hope, and charity, and that we must appeal to the divine and natural law as ethical guides.

Subtler, more attentive readings of Aquinas have begun to emerge, offering more sophisticated, careful, and well argued defenses of the ways Aquinas is—and isn't—an important exponent of the Aristotelian tradition in ethics. Among these are the selections in this part by Terence Irwin and Bonnie Kent. Recognizing Aquinas's departures from Aristotle, Irwin also details many ways in which Aquinas embraces Aristotelian moral thought. Nevertheless, this embrace amounts to something more than, and more interesting than, a mere Christianizing of Aristotle's pagan virtue ethics. Instead, Irwin points out how Aquinas develops Aristotle's thought in ways that advance his own project while remaining faithful to Aristotle. Sometimes he makes connections among disparate elements in Aristotle's ethics, as when he unites observations about virtue that Aristotle makes in different contexts in order to develop his own account of the cardinal virtues, which serve as organizing principles of his virtue ethics. In other cases, he draws out the implications of Aristotle's arguments, and in still others he makes explicit or even adds features that (in his view) Aristotle needs for his system to be defensible, such as a concept of the will. In so doing, Aquinas shows himself to be a charitable expounder of Aristotle's thought as a major foundation of his own.

Bonnie Kent, by contrast, calls attention to the ways in which Aquinas departs from Aristotelian models, not just in minor details, but in central elements of his moral theory. For example, although Aquinas offers a eudaemonistic virtue ethics, his account of virtue departs radically from Aristotle's. Aristotle argues that we acquire moral virtues by a long process of learning and practice. Aquinas agrees that we acquire *some* virtues this way, but only imperfect virtues that can at best lead us to an imperfect happiness. We can acquire and grow in perfect virtue—the sort that leads to the perfect happiness of the next life—only by God's bestowing it on us. Moreover, Aquinas embraces un-Aristotelian elements in his psychology of virtue, most notably, in his claim that it is in a virtuous person's power not to exercise a virtue even when it is called for. These aspects of Aquinas's moral thought prove him to be more Augustinian than Aristotelian. But since the *Augustine* brand name does not sell as much product in our contemporary philosophical marketplace as the brand name *Aristotle*, there is no wonder why philosophers working on Aquinas's ethics are more eager to package it under the latter heading than the former. The irony, as Kent points out, is that much of what contemporary thinkers will find most plausible in Aquinas's ethics stems from his un-Aristotelian, more Augustinian side.

Note on References

For references to Aquinas's *Summa theologiae*, see the Note on References to Part VII.
DQ Card. Virt = *Disputed Question on the Cardinal Virtues*
DQ Virt. Gen. = *Disputed Question on the Virtues in General*
L = the Leonine Edition of Aquinas
M = the Marietti Edition of Aquinas
P = the Parma Edition of Aquinas
Met.= Aristotle's *Metaphysics*
For references to Aristotle, see the Note on References in Part IV. Aristotle's *Nicomachean Ethics* is sometimes abbreviated as NE, and sometimes as EN

(after its Latin title, *Ethica Nicomachea*). References to Aquinas's commentary on the *Nicomachean Ethics* in Kent's chapter direct the reader to the relevant book and *lectura* or commentary; Irwin directs readers to book, *lectura*, and section number in the Marietti (1964) edition.

Further Reading

- Tobias Hoffmann, Jörn Müller, and Matthias Perkams, eds. (2013). *Aquinas and the Nicomachean Ethics.*
- Terence H. Irwin (1999). "Splendid Vices? Augustine For and Against Pagan Virtues."
- Thomas Osborne, Jr. (2003). "The Augustinianism of Thomas Aquinas's Moral Theory."
- Andrew Pinsent (2012). *The Second-Person Perspective in Aquinas's Ethics: Virtues and Gifts.*

CHAPTER 17

Excerpts from *The Development of Ethics*

TERENCE H. IRWIN

1. Progress, Optimism, and Pessimism

(1) According to one extreme non-historical conception of ethics, there is no particular reason, besides convention or convenience or purely doxographical interest, for a historical treatment. If moral theories are defensible by arguments available to anyone who thinks carefully about the subject, and no more appropriate at one time than another, then the history of ethics simply gives us a list of the positions that have been held. While it may be historically interesting to see how one position develops out of, or in reaction to, another, this sort of fact does not tell us anything about the philosophical merits of the position itself.

(2) According to another extreme conception, a moral theory cannot be assessed timelessly, and there are no timelessly appropriate questions that different moral theories try to answer. There are different questions and problems raised by different historical and cultural circumstances, and moral theories cannot intelligibly be assessed except by their success or failure in dealing with these historically-conditioned problems. The moral virtues and principles that may seem to be constant throughout the history of ethics are really products of different backgrounds, circumstances, and traditions; and it is an illusion to think there is one set of problems to be studied or described in a history of ethics.

(3) On a third view, it might seem plausible to speak of the "evolution" of ethics, suggesting that we can see in the history of ethics a gradual approach to the principles that we have now discovered. On this view, we should be able to distinguish the "progressive" and "reactionary" elements in the moral

thinking of previous historical periods, and show how they evolved towards the present assured results. The history of science is sometimes written from this point of view.

(4) A fourth view might look for unity rather than evolution in the history of ethics. On this view, deeper examination of the apparently various and conflicting tendencies in ethical theory will reveal some considerable degree of agreement on the main principles; and this degree of agreement will constitute some argument for the principles. This view differs from the first in so far as it does not assume that philosophers are all addressing the same questions, so that we can evaluate their views in the way we would evaluate a debate among our contemporaries. The historian's task is to discover the relatively permanent principles expressed in different intellectual and cultural embodiments.

This sketch of some extreme positions may suggest some appropriate questions. Elements of these positions are present in some influential accounts of the history of ethics. The most successful and satisfactory history of ethics in English is Sidgwick's *Outlines* (1892), which is written from the third point of view, displaying the evolution of moral theory towards utilitarianism. The best-known recent history in English, Alasdair MacIntyre's *Short History* (1966), tends towards the second view; and he takes a similar view in his major works on moral theory, *After Virtue* and *Whose Justice? Which Rationality?* (1988).[1] A less extreme version of this view underlies Jerome Schneewind's more recent major work on the history of modern moral philosophy; he often warns us against assuming that the history of ethics consists of a series of efforts to answer the same questions (Schneewind 1997).[2] The fourth view may be found in T. H. Green's discussion of Greek ethics in *Prolegomena* (1883).

I am most inclined to agree with the fourth view. I believe we can usefully trace the discussions I have mentioned through the history of ethics, and that we learn something about the philosophical merits and resources of different positions by considering successive efforts to attack and to defend them, and to combine one position with another.

Reflexion on this history does not necessarily lead to a "Whig interpretation" (inspired by Macaulay's view on the development of the British constitution). I do not believe that moral philosophy has made continuous progress, or that all discarded theories belong in the dustbin. Historians of philosophy have the opportunity, and perhaps even the obligation, to point out occasions when a particular assumption or line of argument was abandoned for insufficient reasons, even when, or perhaps especially when, those insufficient reasons still influence us. The history of ethics displays more than one example of premature abandonment. Moralists of the 17th and 18th centuries were not always right about which parts of the mediaeval and Aristotelian outlook they should reject. Similarly, 20th century moralists have not always been right about which aspects of Hegelian idealism should be abandoned.

While I do not take an optimistic view about steady progress and improvement, I write from an optimistic point of view in one respect: I assume that if a particular philosophical position is widely criticized or widely dismissed by successors who were aware of it, this is not the result of foolish or uninteresting errors by the successors, but the result of some significant weaknesses in the position itself. For this reason I try to consider sympathetically the explicit and implicit objections that have been raised against different positions, on the assumption that they deserve consideration. This is why I devote some space to criticisms of the Aristotelian position of Aquinas, and, later, to criticisms of Kant and of utilitarianism. I proceed on the assumption that, whether or not the criticisms are strictly accurate, they point to some important issues that can legitimately be raised about these different positions.

In saying that I approach the history of ethics with some degree of optimism, I mean that I assume we can criticize an earlier theory constructively from the point of view of a later theory, and that in many cases a defender of an earlier theory can reasonably be expected to learn something from the criticisms of later theorists. This assumption is to some extent self-vindicating, since it requires us to focus on the aspects of theories that allow communication and mutual criticism, in contrast to those that do not. I have not, for instance, emphasized the deep and obvious differences between the general intellectual outlook of Aristotle and Aquinas, or of Aquinas and Hobbes, or of Hobbes and Rawls; I do not mean that these difference are unimportant, but I assume that they are not all-important. For I assume that the different theories are mutually comprehensible far enough to allow fruitful criticism and replies.

But this optimistic assumption is not wholly self-vindicating. For when we examine details, we may find that our expectation of constructive mutual criticism is unfulfilled. To fulfil our expectation, we must show that different theories actually allow mutual criticism. Fruitful mutual criticism is what we expect or hope for in dispute and disagreement among contemporary philosophers. An optimistic approach to communication among past philosophers suggests that the same expectation is fulfilled when we turn to them.

To treat past philosophers as though they were contemporaries engaged in a debate would be hopelessly un-historical if we pretended that the task of understanding them is the same as the task of understanding one of our contemporaries or that they should be judged by the standards we apply to our contemporaries. If we are to understand what they are saying, or how it bears on what other people are saying, we have to reflect on what they are trying to say, within the assumptions and options available to them. We ought not to focus on the ways in which they have failed to profit from reflexion on the later theories that were unknown to them. Our task is to look for the best statement we can find of their essential points, and of their bearing on points raised by later philosophers. In speaking of "best statement" and "essential points" we have to rely on philosophical judgment. That is why historians of philosophy cannot do without philosophy, if they try to discuss constructive mutual criticism. Nor can they do without specifically historical study, if they try to grasp what philosophers have to say to one another across historical divisions.

This degree of optimism does not imply that the critic is always right, or that a later theory is, all things considered, an improvement over an earlier theory. The history of ethics shows regress as well as progress. But to argue that the history of ethics takes some wrong turnings is not to take the reactionary view that we ought to ignore, as far as we can, the later views and try to stick firmly with the earlier position, as it was originally formulated. Here also I proceed on an optimistic assumption, that criticism usually identifies genuine weakness, or incompleteness in a moral theory, and that the theory needs to be modified and restated so as to take account of later developments. I argue, for instance, that the Aristotelian position and the Kantian position are not mutually antagonistic, and that a proper modification of the Aristotelian position ought to incorporate some of the major Kantian claims.

Some readers may regard this suggestion as a sign of unintelligent syncretism, betraying failure to grasp the basic differences between these different theories. It may seem more sensible to conclude either that it is mere nostalgia to defend Aristotle and Aquinas, or that the Aristotelian and Kantian positions offer us a clear choice that is not to be disguised by eirenic attempts to blur the conflict between them. Philosophers who try eirenic combinations sometimes appear to be well-meaning muddlers.[3] We will want to decide whether this verdict is justified . . .

2. Virtue and Freewill

According to Aquinas's account of the will, rational agents necessarily pursue happiness as their ultimate end. If a correct account of the will vindicates the role that eudaemonist ethical theory attributes to happiness, it should explain why happiness requires the cultivation of the virtues. Virtuous and vicious agents differ in so far as they make different choices about how to pursue the ultimate end.

The virtues are important because we have freewill. Aquinas claims that the pursuit of an ultimate end is essential for human freedom; he is right only if this ultimate end has the right characteristics. If our awareness of it included an exhaustive grasp of its contents and of the means to it, and if this grasp were independent of rational reflexion and deliberation, our actions would not express freedom of choice and we would not be in control of our actions (*ST* 1a q82 a2). We are in control of our actions by pursuing means to an ultimate end, because both our grasp of the content of the end and the choice of instrumental means to it are open to practical reason, and (in human beings) to deliberation.[4] We necessarily pursue happiness in so far as we necessarily pursue some end that we think is complete and achieves our own completion, leaving no good outside it. But we do not thereby have a clear conception of what constitutes this end or of how to achieve it. To form the correct conception of happiness, and to execute this conception, we need the moral virtues; for "the proper ends of the virtues are directed towards happiness as towards the ultimate end" (1–2 q13 a3 response to 1).

The will necessarily pursues happiness because happiness (the complete and comprehensive end) necessarily seems good to any rational agent, from whatever point of view it is considered. This is not true of the components of happiness, however. We pursue virtue, or wealth, or honour, only because we look at them in a certain way that is not necessary; our view of these constituents is alterable by rational reflexion and deliberation.

Both virtuous and vicious agents act on freewill. Aquinas agrees with Augustine that an act of virtue is the "good use of freewill" (q55 a1 response to 2); he infers that virtue is the state that is directed towards this good use of freewill. Both our rational pursuit of the ultimate end and our natural non-rational inclinations are beyond our control, but we still have free choice in being virtuous or vicious. Our non-rational inclinations do not incline us irresistibly, but are subject to the will, since we can still elect one of a number of options (1a q83 a1 response to 5; 1–2 q13 a6). Hence our character is up to our free choice.

The distinctive features of virtuous or vicious people must, therefore, be accessible to free choice, and so to deliberation. A state of the non-rational parts that is independent of the will cannot determine the end for deliberation. If it did, correct aiming at the end would not be a matter for deliberation, and so could not express freewill. Aquinas's account of the will, freedom, and happiness, as we have traced it so far, makes room for virtues as expressions of freewill. Rational agents share a schematic conception of the end. Deliberation must consider the different ends that constitute the ultimate end. These are questions to which virtuous and vicious people give different answers that explain their different choices.

These features of the will and of freedom explain why the virtues involve practical reason and deliberation. Aquinas also appeals to his conception of the will to explain why the virtues involve more than rational desire. Once we understand the nature of the passions and the will, we can see how the passions may agree or disagree with the will, and how the will may guide or neglect the passions. The right form of agreement and guidance depends on the moral virtues.

3. Will and the Formation of Character

If Aquinas's conception of the moral virtues fits his claims about the will and freedom, the will, rather than some non-rational condition independent of us, must make us virtuous or vicious. We have rational capacities for contraries, as

Aristotle describes them, because we can choose between contrary courses of action that are equally within our power.[5] Aristotle says that desire or election "controls" (*kurion*) the particular way in which a rational capacity is exercised (*Met.* 1048a9–11). This controlling election is the function of the will, as Aquinas conceives it. The will itself is not a capacity for contraries, but our having a will gives us this capacity. It would not be open to us to do a given action or its contrary unless we could deliberate on the merits of these contraries and could choose the one that appears better.[6]

To form states of character that exercise rational capacities in one particular direction, we need habituation (*ethismos*; *assuetudo*, 1–2 q63 a2; *In EN* ii 1, §247). Sometimes one might suppose that Aristotle identifies habituation with the sort of habit-forming training that a child might undergo, so that it precedes the sort of instruction that presupposes will, deliberation, and election. It is easy to suppose this, if one notices that Aristotle takes habituation to begin with the training of children (*EN* 1104b11–13; *In EN* ii 3, §268). But Aristotle does not intend purely non-rational training. For he believes that a virtue of character acquired by habituation includes the correct election, which requires prudence. If correct habituation did not ensure correct election, the virtue acquired by habituation would not include correct election. Hence habituation must be partly a rational process that, at some stages, presupposes will and election.[7]

Aquinas grasps the rational aspects of Aristotelian habituation; that is why he maintains that a state is formed by will rather than passion. Though it begins with non-rational training, the formative activities that he discusses are rational. They mould our non-rational tendencies, and form the sensory parts of the soul into a state, in so far as they "operate at the command of reason," and so "can be directed towards different <ends>" (1–2 q50 a3). The will can form a state, because a state is a capacity of reason and so can be directed in different ways towards action (q50 a5). It must be directed to some determinate goal, since our natural tendency towards the ultimate end is not directed to a sufficiently determinate end for us to achieve our ultimate end (q50 a5 response to 1).

The actions that form states of character are rational actions proceeding from the will: ". . . the states of the moral virtues are caused in the desiring capacities, in so far as they are moved by reason" (q51 a2). A state is formed in so far as reason succeeds in "overcoming" (*supervincere*) the desiring capacity. But it cannot do this in just one action, since a particular action is concerned with determinate circumstances and features of a situation (q51 a3). To "overcome" desire by forming the right state, we need to generalize correctly, "so that desire moves towards the same thing in most cases, in the way that nature does" (q51 a3).

"Overcoming" desire takes time because one's desires already have specific tendencies derived from passions; we modify, but we do not abolish, these tendencies, and this process takes time. We learn to recognize brave or generous actions in different conditions, so that we gradually learn which tendencies should be encouraged or restrained. In general, "the states of the desiring part are caused by the fact that reason naturally moves the desiring part" (q53 a1). In the case of the virtues, the relevant state "can be caused from human actions, in so far as such actions proceed from reason" (q63 a2).

Since habituation results from reason operating on desire, non-rational animals cannot form states. They can be trained, and to this extent they can be said to have states. But they lack the sort of state that is relevant to the virtues, because they do not control their actions, either in forming or in actualizing a state.[8] Control over one's actions is the mark of a rational agent, since such an agent can deliberate about what to do in the light of a conception of the ultimate end.

Since the appropriate state of character requires the proper exercise of the will in action, it requires the right aiming (*intentio*) and deliberation, leading to the right election. Hence Aristotle defines a moral virtue as a "state that elects" (*hexis prohairetikê*). This definition may appear too narrow for the range of actions that he recognizes as characteristic of virtue. Though actions on the right election are an important subset of the virtuous actions characteristic of the virtuous person, they are not the only ones. Aristotle assumes that many voluntary actions are produced by the non-rational parts of the soul apart from election, and that the virtuous person performs these actions, and not only actions on election, in a characteristic and distinctive way. The feelings and immediate reactions that the virtuous person has without election are, as Aristotle insists, important signs of the virtuous character.

According to Aquinas, election belongs to all fully voluntary actions. We act virtuously in so far as we act, on election, through the proper direction of the will by reason in the use of one's natural capacities. But he seems to allow voluntary actions that do not meet his strictest conditions, if they result from consent without election.[9] His claims about directly and indirectly voluntary actions allow the actions characteristic of virtues to include actions that are not the direct result of deliberation. His views about the sources of voluntary action influence his analysis of virtue and vice and of conditions related to them.

4. Reason, Passion, and Virtue

These features of Aquinas's position prepare us for an account of the virtues as expressions of the will that also include an important role for the passions as the source of indirectly voluntary actions that depend on the consent of the will. By introducing the virtues after the discussion of passions and states (1–2 q55), he follows Aristotle, who describes the virtues of character as states that regulate the passions in the ways that achieve the appropriate mean conditions. This emphasis on the passions distinguishes Aristotle's account from the Socratic and Stoic conception of the virtues as purely cognitive states. If Aquinas's account of the relations between the passions and the will is correct, it should explain how the passions are relevant to virtues that are elective states.

Aristotle's emphasis on the passions might seem to lead towards a strongly anti-Socratic view that makes non-rational desire the dominant element in virtue. According to this view, virtue is primarily a good condition of the passions; these form the right desires, and these desires are the basis for correct practical reasoning. Practical reason can be used well or badly, but it cannot regulate itself or turn itself in the right direction. It is turned in the right direction in so far as it agrees with well-trained desires.[10]

Aquinas is sympathetic to one aspect of this view. He believes that freedom is a property of the will, which is rational "by participation."[11] Since the virtues exercise our freedom, they belong to will, and not simply to intellect. But though he rejects an extreme intellectualist view, he does not make passions prior to the will in moral virtue.[12] If the direction of the will depended on the direction of the passions, and the direction of the passions did not depend on the will, we would not be free to direct either our passions or our will correctly, and so we would not be free to be virtuous or vicious.

Aquinas places freewill in the ability of the will to pursue one or another end through rational comparison resulting from deliberation. The virtues, then, include will, rational comparison, and deliberation, which belong to freewill. An extreme anti-rationalist picture of virtue, subordinating will and deliberation to passions, would destroy his cumulative argument about ethics. An extreme intellectualist picture, implying that virtue is simply a matter of knowledge and that vice is simply the product of non-culpable ignorance, would be equally damaging. He needs an account of virtue that fits his broader theoretical claims about freedom, reason, and the will.

5. The Passions as Subjects of Virtues

Since the passions both influence the will and are influenced by it, correct deliberation and choice requires the co-operation of the passions. Aquinas claims that some moral virtues are virtues of the non-rational parts, and not simply virtues that involve them; this is what he means by saying that the non-rational parts are the "subjects" of these virtues (1–2 q56 a4 *sed contra*).[13] He does not simply mean that a virtue requires passions to be trained or modified in some way. Bravery and temperance, for instance, involve bodily training, but they are not bodily virtues in the way that health and strength are, nor is the body the subject of these virtues. If the passions are subjects of moral virtues, they cannot merely provide suitable material or support.[14]

The passions are important because the actions characteristic of the virtues include the whole range of "human acts." These include not only actions that are the direct product of election, but also the actions that we control (*domini*).[15] These include actions resulting from passions, since passion does not prevent consent and election.[16] But since passions impede the use of reason in particular actions, purely intellectual virtues do not ensure right action.[17] A passion may make something appear so attractive that it is difficult to refuse one's consent to it; in such cases reason is "clouded," though not made ineffective.

This feature of the passions helps to explain why they are subjects, and not simply necessary conditions, of moral virtues. Parts of the body have no distinct principle of action that is capable of opposing reason, and so moral virtue does not belong to them; but since the passions have their own principles, they need their distinct perfections to prevent these principles from opposing reason.[18] Even if my arm or my leg does not move when I want it to, it does not impede me by presenting the attractions of not moving it. But if I am lazy, it appears pleasant to stay where I am, or irksome to move. These are principles that can oppose reason, and so I need to secure the co-operation of my passions. This is part of Aquinas's reason for treating the passions as subjects of virtue.

He recognizes, however, that his claim about the passions is open to question. One might argue that since sin does not consist in the having of a passion, virtue cannot consist in this either (*DQ Virt. Gen* a4 obj1). Aquinas grants the claim about sin, but maintains that the non-rational parts are subjects of virtues.[19] Both sin and virtue essentially consist in reason's "moving or consenting"[20] in right or wrong action, but the passions are relevant in so far as they influence the will towards right or wrong action. Virtue belongs to them only in so far as they obey reason (1–2 q55 a4 response to 3).[21] They do not have "the character of good or bad" in themselves, but belong to virtue only in so far as they conform to reason, and hence to election.[22] This is why Aristotle defines a virtue as a state concerned with election.[23]

6. Means, Ends, and the Virtues

To support his claim that the passions are subjects of moral virtues, Aquinas points out, following Aristotle, that moral virtue makes the end correct and prudence makes the means correct. He considers the argument that since the principal expression of moral virtue is election, which does not belong to the non-rational parts, moral virtue does not belong to them either (1–2 q56 a4 obj4). He rejects this argument, on the ground that correct election requires both correct aiming at the end and correct grasp of the means to it. Since correct aiming in relation to the passions belongs to the good arrangement of the non-rational parts, correct election partly proceeds from them too; hence moral virtue belongs to them, while prudence, concerned with the means to ends, belongs to reason.[24]

As Aquinas understands Aristotle, the practical intellect operates through the intellectual virtue of prudence. Since prudence is concerned with means to ends, it does not prescribe the ends for moral virtue.[25] It presupposes the moral virtues, which turn us towards the right ends (q58 a5); hence there can be no prudence without the moral virtues. If a purely intellectual virtue could provide a first principle for moral virtue, apparently the practical intellect itself would be a source of motivation, contrary to Aquinas's assertion that the will is irreducible to practical intellect. Just as the correct use of intellect requires the will directed to the right end, so also prudence requires the moral virtues directed to the right end, if the deliberation of the prudent person is to guide virtuous actions.

In the light of this assumption that practical reason depends on will, Aquinas defends Aristotle's claim that moral virtue is concerned with ends, and prudence with means to ends (*EN* 1144a6–9, 20–2; 1145a5–6; 1178a16–19).[26] Since Aquinas resists the assimilation of will to reason, he might appear to make the passions dominant in directing the will. If he were to accept this view, it would be reasonable for him to take the moral virtues to belong primarily to the non-rational parts.

He cannot, however, consistently accept this argument for treating the passions as the subject of moral virtues; it conflicts with his rationalist position about will and reason, and takes him too far in the direction of sentimentalism, making desire prior to reason.[27] Though he rejects the extreme intellectualist view that reason moves us without will, Aquinas does not agree that the will gets the right aim from passions that are independent of will; for if the passions were the source of the right aim, we would not be free to choose one or another end. Since we are free to choose ends, deliberation cannot have the narrow scope that we would assume if we thought that passions direct the will. Aquinas's claims about happiness and subordinate ends imply that we can deliberate about how to specify a schematic conception of an end; deliberation is not confined to cases in which we already have a definite conception of the end given to us through desires independent of will.

It is puzzling, then, that Aquinas argues from the role of moral virtue in setting ends to the claim that the passions are the subject of the moral virtues. If his claims about passion and virtue are consistent with his general view of the will and deliberation, he cannot claim that the passions are the subjects of moral virtue because they give us the correct ends.[28]

7. The Positive Contribution of the Passions

Since the passions tend to move us on the basis of considerations that also appeal to the will, Aquinas infers that they must have a distinct positive role in the virtues. He rejects the Stoic view that the passions are always bad, and that moral virtue requires their elimination (1–2 q24 a2–3; q59 a2–3). Passions are constituents of a virtue in so far as they are subject to reason and moved by reason (q56 a4).[29]

These relations to reason do not simply require the passions to be regulated by reason. Aquinas also believes that virtuous human beings are better off with well-trained passions than they would be if they were guided simply by practical reason and had no passions to interfere with it. Augustine is right, therefore, to argue that in a person with a good will it is better to have the right passions than to have no passions (*City of God* xiv 6a).

Aquinas discusses two contributions of the passions (1–2 q24 a3). First, reason is capable of regulating passions, and it produces a better good the more things it regulates. If the passions guide reason, they "cloud" it, and to that extent make actions worse by obscuring the appropriate grounds for action.[30] Secondly, passions improve actions when they are guided by reason.[31] They give greater intensity to our motives to act virtuously (cf. q30 a1 response to 1), and we may reasonably elect to have a certain kind of passion in order to act more eagerly, with the co-operation of the sensory appetite.[32]

The passions contribute most directly to virtue through this second function. A passion absorbs some of one's attention, and turns it away from other things that may appear to be as good as or better than the object of the passion; and it encourages a more favourable view of the object of the passion than one would otherwise take. This absorption of attention may sometimes distract us inappropriately, but it may also sometimes improve us. We need to form a state that predisposes us to react in a specific way to specific circumstances, instead of relying on our deliberative capacities to work out the right answer on each occasion by "radical" deliberation, setting out from the ultimate end.[33]

We can avoid any need for radical deliberation on each occasion if we have formed passions that are constituents or results of virtuous states, in so far as they are subject to the will.[34] This is why mercy (*misericordia*) may be a virtue; the passion of mercy is not a virtue, but if mercy proceeds from an elective state it acquires the character of a virtue (2–2 q30 a3 response to 4). Similarly, we may regard repentance (*poenitentia*) either as an elective state that produces the right regret on the right occasions, or as the regret that results from such a state; in the first case it is a virtue, and in the second it is the actualization of a virtue (3a q85 a1; cf. q84 a9). But if we regard shame (*verecundia*) simply as a passion, and not as the result of an elective state, we do not count it as a virtue (2–2 q144 a1 response to 1).

This connexion between will and passion explains why we can act virtuously even when we act "suddenly," without deliberation. Aquinas mentions two sorts of sudden action: (1) One sort results from the immediate response of a passion without the intervention of the will; this is a "sudden motion" that falls short of consent. (2) A second sort of sudden action results from the antecedent tendency of our state (*ex inclinatione habitus*). Aquinas illustrates this from Aristotle's example of people acting bravely in sudden emergencies, because such action proceeds from their state of character. The state has been formed by previous deliberation, so that new deliberation is not needed in an emergency when one needs to act at once.[35] A state has been completely formed only when it includes this capacity for immediate action.[36]

In the second case of sudden action, Aquinas agrees that, as in the first case, no deliberation immediately precedes the action, but he still regards the action as being elected, because previous deliberation has determined the end to be pursued in such situations. Hence, when something apparently suitable to the end appears in such situations, we choose it without farther deliberation; but our choice is still an election, because it is the result of our having formed an end by previous deliberation.

Radical deliberation on each occasion is foolish, not only because it takes too long and is so complicated that we may easily make mistakes, but also because fear, inclination, self-interest, and so on sometimes distort our view. When we form a state of character, we cultivate passions that tend to counteract the distorting effects of other passions and lead us to attend to the right features of different situations. We need correct attention to generalize correctly. According to the parable of the Good Samaritan, the requirement to love one's neighbour applies to cases where another person is alien to us in obvious ways; we need to attend to the fact that this is another person needing help, not to his being alien.

Well-trained passions not only help us to avoid distortion, but also turn us in the right direction. When we reflect at leisure, outside a situation where we need to make an immediate decision, we may notice that in some situations this or that feature deserves our attention. But if we leave it to our rational judgment to work this out by a scrutiny of the situation whenever we need to make an immediate decision, we may be, at the least, inefficient, since we may take an unreasonably long time to survey all the conceivably relevant aspects of the situation. Even if we take all the time we need, we may still act badly, since it is not always easy to see, when we are in a situation, the features that become clearer to us from a more detached point of view. We are better off with a passion trained to focus on the right features.

The passions do not merely remind us of what we have previously recognized as relevant. They may also bring to our attention an aspect of the situation that we had not thought was relevant, or had even dismissed as irrelevant. We might, for instance, have decided that we ought to punish a child for some misdeed, and that her distress at being punished is irrelevant. But once we actually see how distressed she is, we may wonder whether the punishment that we thought was fair is unnecessarily severe. A soldier might have no doubt that the war he is fighting is just even if it harms innocent civilians, but when he sees the extent of the suffering it causes, he may wonder whether it is really worth it. In some such cases, our passions may cause us to reconsider the ends we aim at, and in this respect may form our conception of the end.

We should not always have second thoughts whenever our passions revolt against the action that we have elected. If I decide I was wrong in a dispute with you, and ought to apologize to you, perhaps I still ought to do it even if I still dislike you and your reaction to the apology is ungracious. To explain the difference between this case and the cases where passions ought to change our mind, we need to estimate how reliable passions are in various situations. Our tendency to sympathize with other people's suffering is—in some people—a desirable tendency that has been formed in the right ways. Our tendency to find our enemies and opponents disagreeable may not be as desirable. The passions that we justifiably rely on in forming second thoughts about our elections are passions that have been formed by our states of character, and hence by our elections.

We sometimes benefit, then, from passions that cause us to attend to some aspects of a situation and to ignore others. Though these passions are not infallible, we may be better off if we sometimes follow them than if we always ignore them. The virtues turn the passions in a beneficial direction. The right passions prepare us to avoid evils and to pursue goods (q59 a3), and so prepare us for virtuous actions (2–2 q123 a9–10). If we have the appropriate passion, the situation appears good or bad in a particular way, in advance of rational reflexion about it, since the passions make us aware of different particular goods. It is often unwise to wait for rational reflexion to examine all the relevant features of a situation. If a well-trained passion helps us to focus on the right features without reflexion, we are better off.

If passions are directed towards certain particular goods, and are normally subject to the will, it is sometimes reasonable to develop a tendency to focus on certain particular goods. An account of the virtues, therefore, should identify both the rational desires we should develop, and the tendencies to selective attention that we should form in the light of our rational desires. In Aquinas's view, the non-rational tendency to focus on some features of situations is often the best way for practical reason to apply itself to particular situations (cf. 2–2 q123 a9–10).

The positive role of well-trained passions helps to explain why our having the right aim towards the end results from (*contingit ex*) the good state of the non-rational parts (q56 a4 response to 4).[37] We saw earlier that this claim might be taken to express a strongly anti-rationalist account of our choice of ends, implying that the passions, as opposed to will and deliberation, form our conception of ends. Such an account would raise grave difficulties for Aquinas, given his other views about the role of will and deliberation.

His remarks about the benefits of well-trained passions, however, do not conflict with his rationalist views on reason and will. Deliberation and practical reason discover the right conception of the end by finding the constituents of happiness. This role of deliberation allows an important role to the passions in maintaining and expressing our grasp of the right end. Since the passions absorb our attention, and so turn it in a good or bad direction, they make it easier or harder to attend to the right ends. If we are to attend to the right ends, we need well-trained passions to help us and to remove potential hindrances. None the less, practical reason discovers the right ends. The passions do not discover ends, but they help us to retain our grasp of the ends we have discovered. To make sure that passions do this on the right occasions, we should form them in the light of our rational conception of the good. Hence they must be subject to reason.

If we look back at the passage where Aquinas says that the passions determine the right ends (q56 a4 response to 4),[38] we might say that Aquinas overstates the role of the passions, and that we can see the overstatement if we compare this passage with his other remarks about prudence and the role of the passions. Alternatively, we might try to interpret this passage so that it fits his other remarks. We ought not to treat the passage, straightforwardly interpreted, as an accurate statement of his general position about the role of passions in fixing the right ends.

[. . .]

8. From the Ultimate End to the Cardinal Virtues

To show that prudence is unified, Aquinas needs to show that universal prudence, deliberating from the universal end, discovers the specific ends of each of the virtues, and that these ends are connected in such a way that understanding of one requires understanding of the others in their relation to the ultimate good.

Has Aquinas given deliberation too large a task, and too indefinite a starting point? We might agree that agents such as us need passions and wills guided by reason and virtue if they are to pursue their good correctly, but we might still have no clear view about what the virtues are—whether, for instance, they include the control of appetites or the formation of rational plans for the maximum satisfaction of appetites. As Aquinas remarks, we might agree that the human good requires us to act in accordance with reason, but still not agree that acting in accordance with reason requires temperance and bravery, as he understands them. It seems still more obvious that we might agree about acting in accordance with reason, but deny that such action includes action for the good of others that does not provide some antecedently-desired good for ourselves.

If our deliberation is to reach a definite result, do we perhaps need some principles, accepted apart from deliberation, that constrain the process of deliberation and introduce some definite moral content? Scotus and Ockham derive these further principles from the revealed will of God.[39] Others might derive them from some definite social facts, or collective preferences, or contingent psychological traits, that apply to some group of actual human beings but cannot be derived from Aquinas's general claims about rational agency. Any of these attempts to constrain deliberation rejects Aquinas's attempt to explain the virtues by reference to rational agency.

Aquinas believes that deliberation about one's ultimate end yields not only an account of virtue, but also a sufficiently detailed account of the virtues. Deliberation shows that the moral precepts of the Decalogue are required by the virtues, and that we have reason to care about the interests of other people for their own sakes. The considerations he has appealed to so far seem to him to support a detailed account of the virtues.

This detailed account is mostly presented in the Secunda Secundae. This Part discusses a bewildering variety of virtues and vices. Moreover, it clearly belongs to moral theology more than to moral philosophy, since it presupposes the supernatural additions (infused virtues, and so on) to the acquired moral virtues. Still, its main structure and aims are fairly clear; it tries to answer some of the questions about the virtues that we might ask when we reflect on the ultimate end, prudence, and deliberation.

The main argument rests on Aquinas's claim that the matter of morality is derived from the four distinct cardinal virtues.[40] In his view, the various traits that we recognize as virtues are either aspects or applications of the cardinal virtues. They have a definite structure that shows how they meet some general requirements of rational agency.[41]

9. The Nature of a Cardinal Virtue

The cardinal virtues express the "perfect character of virtue, which requires correctness of desire" (1–2 q61 a1). They are not necessary for every virtuous action, since not all virtuous action requires correct desire, and a mere capacity to perform some virtuous action does not imply the possession of a cardinal virtue. Aquinas's distinction between virtuous action and acting virtuously supports his claim that prudence is necessary for being a virtuous person (cf. q56 a3; q57 a5), and hence supports his defence of the reciprocity of the virtues.

To act virtuously, according to Aquinas, we must act on the cardinal virtues, no matter what special virtue we display in a particular action. Some virtues are cardinal (*cardinales*, from *cardo*, "hinge") because they are those "in which the moral life turns and is founded in a certain way." The moral life is founded on them because that is the life proper to a human being, in contrast to a non-rational animal or an angel; this is the life of practical reason, the "active life, which consists in the exercise of moral virtues." Aquinas infers the generic features of such a life from Aristotle's account of acting virtuously (*EN ii* 4; *DQ Card. Virt.* a1).[42] Aristotle's demand for knowledge introduces prudence;[43] his demand for correct election for the right end introduces justice; and his demand for firm and unshakeable election introduces temperance and bravery (2–2 q123 a11). Prudence is relevant because it provides the appropriate prescriptive (*praeceptiva*) knowledge, justice because it directs a person's actions to the right end, temperance and bravery because they produce the appropriate control (*moderatio*) and firmness.

These claims do not fit the passage in Aristotle that Aquinas cites, but they fit Aristotle's intentions in his account of virtue as a whole. The reference to prudence fits Aristotle's remark that the mean must be determined by the reason by which the prudent person would determine it. The demand for the right end fits Aristotle's claim that we need the right election. Firmness and control fit his demand for a firm and unchanging state. Firmness and constancy depend on the condition of our non-rational desires and passions; if they are misdirected, they will make us waver even if we make the correct (in some ways) election on occasions where strong passions are not involved.

We discover the virtues by examining the "formal principle," which is the good of reason. This consists, first of all, in consideration by reason itself, and, secondly, in the direction of other things by reason. These other things are actions and passions; the passions are those that can turn us away in bad directions or prevent us from going in good directions. We need prudence (for consideration by reason), justice (for right action), and temperance and bravery (for the proper regulation of potentially distracting and inhibiting passions). The same conclusion results if we consider the subject of the different aspects of the right formal principle. One subject has to be the rational part, of which prudence is the virtue. Another has to be the part that is rational by participation, and this is divided into the will, the spirited part, and the appetitive part (1–2 q61 a2).[44]

The cardinal virtues, therefore, are generic and pervasive; we do not need to look for particular occasions on which we are exercising prudence or temperance, say, as opposed to some other virtue. This feature seems to distinguish them from a virtue such as generosity or wit; if we are not in the right situation, we cannot display wit, but if we are in any situation that calls for any of the virtues, the appropriate action displays the formal principles of the different cardinal virtues (cf. 2–2 q123 a11; q141 a7).

Aquinas's view that the cardinal virtues mark pervasive features of all virtuous action is defensible by appeal to Aristotle; but it is more characteristic of Stoicism.[45] The Stoics claim that in every virtuous action we act in accordance with each of the cardinal virtues, even though we exercise some specific virtue in a way in which we do not exercise all the others. Aquinas argues that the four virtues are different specific virtues, so that we exercise temperance (e.g.) on particular occasions on which we do not (in the same way) exercise other virtues as well. This emphasis on the different occasions for the exercise of the four virtues is more clearly Aristotelian than Stoic, though the Stoics also admit that not all of the virtues are always exercised in the same way.

10. "Principal" Displays of the Cardinal Virtues

Aquinas claims that the cardinal status of these four virtues supports and justifies the Aristotelian view that they are different specific virtues displayed in distinct ranges of action. The goodness of the pervasive virtues is displayed "principally" or "especially" in different ranges of action.[46] Whenever we act virtuously, we must display the appropriate firmness, but we especially display it in facing the danger of death; hence it is appropriately displayed in bravery, which is the virtue concerned with facing this danger. A similar argument applies to temperance. The claim that these are special or "principal" displays of the relevant pervasive virtues supports the claim that these are distinct virtues with their own range of actions. . . .

11. Subordinate Virtues

Aquinas believes that other recognized virtues can be classified as either integral or subjective or potential parts of the cardinal virtues.[47] The integral parts "must concur to produce a perfect act of that virtue" (2–2 q48 a1), and so are aspects of the virtue, inseparable from it in the way that beams and foundations are inseparable from a house. The subjective parts are species of the virtue—for instance, the types of prudence that are displayed in different areas (2–2 q48 a1). The potential parts are "annexed virtues that are directed towards some secondary acts or materials, as not having the whole power of the principal virtue" (q48 a1). They apply the virtue to areas that are less difficult than the areas of the primary exercises of the virtues.

Aquinas's description of these potential parts assumes that the cardinal virtues are pervasive features of acting virtuously. Though the potential parts of each cardinal virtue are less difficult to exercise than the principal cardinal virtue itself, they are inseparable from the principal virtue; we cannot have magnanimity, for instance, without bravery. The circumstances in which magnanimity maintains firmness are less difficult than those in which bravery maintains firmness, but since they require the same sort of firmness for the same reasons, magnanimity is a part of bravery.[48]

By organizing the virtues around the cardinal virtues, Aquinas argues that the virtues do not conflict, and especially that recognized "pagan" virtues do not conflict with "Christian" virtues. His treatment of magnanimity and humility illustrates his strategy. Once we see the relation of these subordinate virtues to their cardinal virtues, we see that they do not conflict, Magnanimity strengthens us in the pursuit of appropriately great actions, while humility restrains us from the distractions that would result from illusions about our own importance; hence we need both magnanimity and humility to pursue the right ends without distraction.[49]

If we object to magnanimity because it includes contempt for others, Aquinas answers that this contempt is contempt for the evil aims of others. Such contempt prevents the magnanimous person from accepting or acquiescing in the evil projects of others, and so he needs it if he is to be independent enough to stick to the right course of action. This contempt for others is not opposed to humility; for we can honour other people in so far as they display the gifts of God, and we can recognize our own failure to use the gifts we have received from God.[50] Determination to use our gifts for great results, and rejection of the evil aims of others that would impede the proper use of our gifts and theirs, are two aspects of magnanimity.[51] In recognizing our own failure to use all our gifts, and in appreciating the gifts shown by others, we display aspects of humility.[52] Neither magnanimity nor humility can do its proper work without the other.

Humility also prevents a false sense of self-importance. This is why it does not always reject the sorts of actions that would sometimes show a lack of self-respect. Sometimes "abject" services are required by charity, and in these cases a person without false self-importance will not refuse to do them.[53] Hence it is not abject to belong to a mendicant religious order, even though it would be abject to beg from others simply from disinclination to support oneself (CG iii 135).[54] Humble people do not refuse the abject course of action in the right circumstances, though they do not accept it indiscriminately.

The connexion between magnanimity and humility answers some objections to RV [i.e., the thesis that the virtues are reciprocally connected]. We might well cite these two virtues to show why virtues sometimes conflict, and why traits required by one impede traits required by another. Aquinas answers that this appearance of conflict may mislead us about the relation between the two virtues. We can see that they do not conflict once we understand the circumstances in which contempt for others or belief in our own unworthiness is appropriate; for the two virtues have the same aim, and do not conflict, but complement each other. Recognition of the connexion between the virtues involves universal prudence, since it refers to the universal end promoted by the specific ends of the different virtues.

This example suggests how the cardinal virtues, as Aquinas understands them, make the other virtues intelligible. The subordinate virtues promote or facilitate or protect the goods pursued by the cardinal virtues. This arrangement of the subordinate virtues allows Aquinas's theory to be flexible. Different circumstances might produce different threats to the goods pursued by the cardinal virtues, so that the same subordinate virtues might have different contents, or different traits might actually become subordinate virtues. Aquinas's account shows why in different circumstances a particular subordinate virtue needs to be cultivated.

Prudence and temperance, for instance, do not always require saving money for tomorrow. If the rate of inflation is high, someone who merely saves impoverishes himself, and would be better advised to take a less conservative attitude to short-term financial risk. In these circumstances the attitude conventionally recognized as "prudent" may be ill-advised; but the virtue of prudence is not ill-advised. On the contrary, prudence advises a less conservative attitude to risk in these circumstances. The virtue of prudence, as Aquinas understands it, helps us to see why one subordinate virtue ought to be replaced by another.

His theory explains not only why certain traits are virtuous at a particular time, but also why it would be reasonable for subordinate virtues to change over time, within the constraints of the same cardinal virtues. He includes some details about the specific traits and actions required of virtuous people, and about the social roles and institutions that support these requirements. If we reject these details, we do not necessarily reject Aquinas's theory of the virtues. If he relies on some subordinate social or psychological assumption that either was always false or is no longer true, an objection to the details may not undermine the theory.[55] Once we understand the theoretical aspects of his account of the virtues, we can distinguish the acceptable from the unacceptable conclusions. If Aquinas's theory of the virtues works, it ought to allow us to argue effectively about the content and application of the virtues; if we can use his theory to give good reasons for rejecting his conclusions, we have vindicated the most important parts of his theory.

This point is relevant not only for the philosophical assessment of Aquinas's theory but also for understanding its historical fortunes. It was criticized, not surprisingly, for the particular description of rules and requirements that reflect its historical circumstances.[56] But the rejection of Aquinas's specific virtues does not justify the rejection of his theory of the cardinal virtues and subordinate virtues, and the way he tries to derive these from his conception of rational agency. We need to consider more closely whether the historically influential criticisms of Aquinas go beyond criticism of relatively superficial details that do not affect the main theoretical issues.

Notes

1. See MacIntyre (1981) 11: "We all too often still treat the moral philosophers of the past as contributors to a single debate with a relatively unvarying subject-matter, treating Plato and Hume and Mill as contemporaries both of ourselves and of each other. This leads to an abstraction of these writers from the cultural and social milieus in which they lived and thought and so the history of their thought acquires a false independence from the rest of the culture. Kant ceases to be part of the history of Prussia, Hume is no longer a Scotsman. For from the standpoint of moral philosophy as *we* conceive it these characteristics have become irrelevances. Empirical history is one thing, philosophy quite another."
2. In this book I display some sympathy with what Schneewind calls "the Socrates story": "Although we have not reached agreement about the basis of morality, we know the tasks that we moral philosophers should undertake. We are trying to answer the question Socrates raised: how to live. People have always had opinions on the matter, but it is very hard to get an indubitable answer based on an undeniable foundation" (1997, 535–6). I am also somewhat sympathetic to what he calls the "single-aim view" of the history of moral philosophy

(548). Schneewind introduces the Socrates story and the single-aim view in order to criticize them. I am more inclined to think that each of them alludes to true views about the history of ethics. I do not accept either of them, however, as Schneewind states them, since he includes in them a number of claims that I would reject (e.g., the search for an indubitable answer or an undeniable foundation).

3. It would not be too unfair to summarize Sidgwick's (1902) view of Green in these terms.
4. The claim about freedom does not mean that the content of the final good must be uncertain to every sort of free agent. See Irwin (2007) §§251 and 267 on God and the angels. Their certainty about the content of the final good does not threaten their freedom, because their grasp is not independent of their awareness of the rational merits of what they grasp. According to Scotus, Aquinas's attribution of necessity to willing the ultimate end is a threat to freedom. See Irwin (2007) §362 and Cajetan's discussion in §361.
5. "The rational capacities, which are proper to a human being, are not fixed (determinatae) on one <actualization>, but are related in no fixed way to many <actualizations>; but they are fixed on particular actualizations through states (habitus)" (q55 a1; cf. q49 a4). If we render "*habitus*" by "habit", we suggest misleadingly that a habitus is a mere tendency or custom (I may be in the habit of taking a particular route home, but this is not my habitus). See Kenny in BF xxii, pp. xxi–xxii (who favours "disposition").
6. For Scotus' interpretation of the claim about our capacity for contraries, see Irwin (2007) §369.
7. See Irwin (2007) §101.
8. "They lack the characteristic of a state as far as concerns the exercise of the will, because they do not have control over exercising or not exercising, which seems to belong to what is characteristic of a state" (q50 a3 response to 2).
9. See Irwin (2007) §252.
10. This anti-rationalist account of Aristotle is discussed in Irwin (2007) §89.
11. See Irwin (2007) §257.
12. On intellectualism, voluntarism, rationalism, and sentimentalism see Irwin (2007) §259.
13. "Temperance, however, in so far as it is a human virtue, is about appetites for sensory pleasures, which belong to the appetitive power. . . . And for that reason temperance, in so far as it is a human virtue, is in the appetitive part . . . But temperance is spoken of in <the angels> in so far as they display their will under control (*moderate*) in accordance with the standard (*regula*) of the divine will" (1a q59 a4 response to 3).
14. Aquinas's doctrine is examined by Graff (1934) esp. ii 64–73.
15. See *DQ Virt. Gen* a4 = M 717b: "Whatever action, therefore, is in a human being's control is a proper action of virtue; not, however, those actions that are not in a human being's control. . . . Therefore, in whatever is the source (*principium*) of action of the sort that is in a human being's control, there we can place human virtue."
16. To explain how these actions are in our control, he often quotes Aristotle's remark that reason exercises a political rather than a despotic rule over the non-rational parts of the soul (1a q81 a3 response to 2). Cf. *DQ Virt. Gen* a4 = M 717b: "just as kings and rulers of states are in control of free people who have the right and ability of rebellion in relation to some precepts of the king or ruler." On the political metaphor see Irwin (2007) §254.
17. ". . . the desiring capacity obeys reason, not altogether at its nod, but with some contradiction. That is why the Philosopher says that 'reason commands the desiring capacity by a political power', the sort by which someone is set over free subjects who have a certain right (*ius*) of contradiction. . . . And so for a human being to act well it is necessary not only for reason to be well disposed through a state of intellectual virtue, but also for the desiring capacity to be well disposed through a state of moral virtue" (1–2 q58 a2). I omit the cases in which a passion entirely takes away the use of reason. See Irwin (2007) §253.
18. *DQ Virt. Gen* a4: ". . . but in the lower desire, which is capable of rebelling against reason, something is necessary by which it follows without rebellion the action that reason commands."

19. At 2–2 q155 a4 Aquinas argues that the passions, rather than the will, are the subject of temperance, because they have been improved so as to be subject to reason (*ipse appetitius sensitivus est subiectus rationi*). If we treated the will as the subject of temperance, we would be assimilating temperance to continence.
20. *DQ Virt. Gen* a4 response to 1: *ratione movente vel consentiente.*
21. For Scotus' criticism of Aquinas see Irwin (2007) §372.
22. "... the movement of virtue has its principle in reason and its terminus in desire, in so far as it is moved by reason" (1–2 q59 a1).
23. When Augustine appears to identify some passions, such as pity, with virtues, Aquinas argues that he must be taken to mean that the tendency to pity in accordance with reason is virtuous (q59 a1 response to 3), Cf. below section 7.
24. "In election there are two things, namely, aiming at the end, which belongs to moral virtue, and the preferential choice (*praeacceptio*) of what is towards the end, which belongs to prudence. Now the fact that people have the right aim towards the end with reference to the passions of the soul results from the good disposition of the spirited and appetitive parts. And for that reason the moral virtues that are about the passions are in the spirited and appetitive parts, but prudence is in reason" (q56 a4 response to 4).
25. See 1a q22 a1 response to 3; q23 a4; q113 a1 response to 2; 1–2 q57 a5; 2–2 q47 a6; q56 a1.
26. Aquinas quotes *EN* 1144a6–9 at 2–2 q47 a6 sc. In Aquinas's terms, virtue has the correct *intentio* towards the end. See *in EN* vi 10 §1273 (cf. §1269). On *intentio* as aiming at the end rather than the means see 1–2 q12 a4.
27. See Irwin (2007) §259.
28. Cf. Bradley (1997) 239.
29. See esp. *Ver.*q26 a7; *Mal.*q3 a11; q12 a1.
30. ". . . for it is more praiseworthy if one does an act of charity from a judgment of reason than if one does it solely from the passion of pity" (q24 a3 response to 1). Aquinas's use of "*ex* sola *passione*" makes his point clear. His position is similar to Kant's in *Groundwork* 398–400.
31. "... by way of election, namely when someone by a judgment of reason elects to be affected by a passion in order to act more promptly, having sensory desire co-operating. And in this way a passion of the soul adds to the goodness of an action" (1–2 q24 a3 response to 1).
32. For this function cf. 1–2 q77 a6 response to 2; 2–2 q2 a10; *Ver.* q24 a12; *DQ Virt. Gen* a1 sc2.
33. The formation of such a state is relevant to Herman's discussion of a "deliberative field", in (1993) 193–5 (e.g.), and to Wiggins' remarks on "salience", (1975–76) 230–4.
34. ". . . virtue cannot be present except in those acts that proceed out of the command of will, even though they are also acts of the sensory parts" (*2Sent* d24 q3 a2 response to 3 = P vi 604b).
35. "For the activity is more from the state to the extent that it is less from premeditation. For things evident in advance, i.e., known in advance, someone will elect in advance from reason and thought without <the appropriate> state, but sudden actions are in accordance with one's state. But this is not to be understood as saying that the activity in accordance with a state of virtue can be altogether without deliberation, since virtue is an elective state, but that the one who has the state has the end in his election determined; so that whenever something arises as suitable to that end, it is at once elected, unless it is hindered by some attention and further deliberation" (Ver. q24 a12 = M 461a). Aquinas alludes to Aristotle on emergencies, *EN* 1117a17–22; see Irwin (2007) §86.
36. "For unless a rational capacity tends through a state in some way to one <actualization>, it will always be required, whenever it is necessary to act, for some inquiry about the action to precede; this is clear about someone who wants to consider, not yet having the state of scientific knowledge, and about someone who wants to act in accordance with virtue, lacking the state of virtue. Hence the Philosopher says . . . that sudden actions are from one's state" (*DQ Virt. Gen* a1 = M 709a). In the last sentence Aquinas cites *EN* v 3, which (in his capitulation)

begins at 1129b11. I do not know what he has in mind, unless he is taking some of the actions listed in this chapter to be "sudden".

37. ". . . In order to be in a correct state about particular principles of things that can be done, which are ends, it is necessary for a human being to be perfected through certain states in accordance with which it comes to be in a certain way connatural to a human being to judge correctly about an end. And this comes about through moral virtue; for the virtuous person judges correctly about the end of virtue, because 'such as a person is, so the end appears to him', as it is said in *Ethics* iii. And thereby, in order to have correct reason about things that can be done, which is prudence, it is necessary for a human being to have moral virtue" (1–2 q58 a5). Cajetan comments (L vi 377b, quoted by M 257b): "Prudence is not in reason without qualification, but as directed towards desire, and it depends essentially on desire, from which depends the precept, its actualization, and from which varies the appearance of the end, its principle."
38. Quoted in n21.
39. Ockham agrees with Aquinas in recognizing non-positive and positive elements of morality. But he takes the positive elements to include higher principles that Aquinas regards as non-positive. See Irwin (2007) §395.
40. See *3Sent.* d33 q2 a1 sol.4 = P vii 359ab.
41. Jordan (1999) 91–5, discusses the organization of *ST* 2–2, and emphasizes Aquinas's innovation in making the cardinal virtues the principle of organization.
42. He cites *Proverbs* 26:14 ("As a door turns on its hinge, so does an idler in his bed") as his Scriptural authority for the term "cardinal", and he cites Ambrose as his patristic authority for the use of "cardinal" for the canon of four virtues. See *DQ Card. Virt.* a1; *ST* 1–2 q61 a1 sc; *3Sent.* d33 q2 a1 sol.2 = P vii 358b.
43. Aquinas's interpretation does not fit; Aristotle seems to be demanding simply the sort of knowledge that is necessary for voluntariness. Aquinas recognizes this point about the passage in 2–2 q58 a1. At *in EN* ii 4 §283 he does not introduce his own interpretation of the demand for knowledge.
44. For objections to this classification see Irwin (2007) §290.
45. Ambrose relies on the Stoic division in *De Officiis.* He argues that the saints of the Old Testament display the cardinal virtues: "What duty (*officium*) belonging to the principal virtues was lacking in these men?" (i 115). In his view, the types of duties originate (*nascuntar*) in the four virtues (116). He uses Stoic arguments to show that each of the cardinal virtues deals with questions that can be answered only by appeal to the other cardinal virtues (i 126–9). See Ambrose (2001), ad i 115. On the treatment of the cardinal virtues in early Christian writers and in mediaeval writers before Aquinas see Lottin (1942–60) iii, ch. 12 (see esp. 154). The four virtues are mentioned in Wisdom 8:7 (referring to wisdom): "And if anyone loves justice, her labours are virtues; for she teaches temperance and prudence, justice and bravery, and nothing is more useful in life for human beings than these." On *4* Macc. see Irwin (2007) §203.
46. See 1–2 q61 a3; 2–2 q123 a11; 141 a7; *DQ Card. Virt.* a1.
47. 2–2 q48 a1; cf. q79; q80; q128; q143.
48. ". . . magnanimity agrees with bravery in so far as it confirms the mind about something difficult. But it falls short of bravery in this point, that it confirms the mind in something about which it is easier to preserve this firmness" (2–2 q129 a5).
49. "That is why a double virtue is necessary in relation to desire for a difficult good. One is needed to control (*temperare*) and to restrain the mind from an uncontrolled (*immoderate*) pursuit of high objects; and this belongs to the virtue of humility. The other is needed to strengthen the mind against despair, and urge it on after great things in accordance with correct reason; and this is magnanimity" (2–2 q161 a1).
50. Humility does not require false modesty. Aquinas (if he is the author of the prayer) prays that he will be "*humilem sine fictione*", P xxiv 242a.
51. Cf. 2–2 q21 a1 sc.

52. "In a human being one finds something great, which he possesses through the gift of God, and something defective, which belongs to him from the weakness of nature. Magnanimity, therefore, makes a human being think himself worthy of great things from consideration of the gifts he possesses from God. For instance, if he has great virtue of mind, magnanimity makes him pursue perfect works of virtue . . . Humility, however, makes a human being think little of himself from consideration of his own deficiency. Similarly, magnanimity despises others in so far as they fall short of God's gifts; for it does not think so much of others as to do anything inappropriate for their sake. But humility honours others and thinks them superior, inasmuch as it looks upon something of God's gifts in them. . . . And in this way it is evident that magnanimity and humility are not contraries, though they seem to aim towards contraries, because they proceed in accordance with different considerations" (2–2 q129 a3 response to 4). The attitude that Aquinas describes here is endorsed by Paul at Rm. 12:3; ". . . not to think of yourself more highly than you ought to think, but to think with sober judgment (*sōphronein*)."
53. "It is not, therefore, characteristic of humility, but of stupidity, if one accepts whatever is abject, but <it is characteristic of humility> if one does not refuse because of its abjectness what is necessary to do because of virtue. For instance, if charity demands that one carry out some abject task for one's neighbours, because of his humility one does not refuse to do this" (*CG* iii 135 §3097).
54. MacIntyre (1999) xi, mentions this aspect of humility (in "a prayer composed by Aquinas in which he asks God to grant that he may happily share with those in need what he has, while humbly asking for what he needs from those who have") in order to contrast Aquinas's outlook with Aristotle's views on magnanimity ("a prayer that in effect, though not by Aquinas's own intention, asks that we may not share some of the attitudes of Aristotle's *megalopsychos*"). He develops this contrast later (127). He may be referring to the prayer (of dubious authorship) in *P* xxiv 241b (*da bonum quod non habeo ab habentibus humiliter quaerere*).
55. Aquinas's discussion of usury in 2–2 q78 offers an example of such assumptions. He qualifies the general prohibition with the conditions set out in a2–3. The development of discussions of usury in moral theology is described by Jonsen and Toulmin (1988), ch. 9. It is summarized by Davis (1946) ii 373–7, who mentions "extrinsic titles" that justify the taking of interest on a loan (e.g., loss sustained by the lender, or real and unusual risk incurred by the lender).
56. For Machiavelli's objections to the Christian character of the virtues that Aquinas describes see Irwin (2007) §407. Hume expresses rather similar objections in speaking of the "monkish" virtues (*Enquiry Concerning the Principles of Morals* ix 3).

CHAPTER 18

Aquinas's Ethics and Aristotelian Naturalism

BONNIE KENT

No other medieval thinker gets nearly as much attention from philosophers as Thomas Aquinas. He dominates the literature on medieval philosophy to a degree that no single figure does the literature on ancient or early modern. Thanks to the renaissance in virtue-centered theorizing, Aquinas's ethics has attracted particular interest in recent years. The growing literature in this area can be a boon for readers unfamiliar with his works. Regrettably, it can also be a source of much confusion. Even though Aquinas's admirers greatly outnumber his critics, they themselves divide sharply on how his ethical theory should be understood. Some present it as Aristotelian, others insist that it is not, and scholarly controversy on the topic never seems to end. The scope of the disagreement makes it especially puzzling. While we often see disputes among experts about specific points of interpretation, rarely do we see heated, long-running debates about the overall character of someone's ethical theory.

In the first part of this chapter I argue that disputes about the Aristotelianism of Aquinas's ethics arise largely from conflicts over how, or even whether, to work at winning it recognition in mainstream contemporary philosophy. Philosophers concerned that his ethics might be dismissed as so much theology work to legitimize it by the secular standards of philosophy prevalent in their discipline today. In order to do so they commonly link it to Aristotelianism, even to Aristotelian "naturalism." The second part of the essay sets out some objections, philosophical as well as historical and religious, to Aristotelianizing interpretations of Aquinas's ethics. Here I argue that virtue-centered theorizing has expanded to encompass such a wide range of issues and approaches that Aquinas need not look Aristotelian to gain a hearing in philosophical circles today. Aquinas's disagreements with Aristotle hold at least as much philosophical interest as their areas of accord. The last part of the essay presents as an example Aristotle's dubious conclusion that prudence (or practical wisdom) requires all the moral virtues, and vice versa. Here I argue that Aquinas's account of the cardinal virtues and their "parts" enables him to avoid some standard philosophical objections that Aristotle's ethics cannot.

Divisive Questions

The most basic question about Aquinas's work is simply how, or even whether, it qualifies as *philosophy*—a question all the more contentious because we have yet to reach any clear consensus about what constitutes philosophy, as opposed to theology, history, empirical psychology, political theory, or something else. Some philosophers take an expansive view of the discipline, including work on the borders with other disciplines. Others define philosophy more narrowly and demand that its borders be policed. The disputed border between philosophy and theology proves especially troublesome for interpreters of Aquinas. Unlike some medieval thinkers, he never produced a treatise dedicated to logic, semantic theory, or any other topic indisputably "philosophical" by today's standards. His *Summa theologiae* is a theology textbook, and his commentaries on Aristotle focus mainly on explaining Aristotle's views, not his own. Of course, one can still discuss Aquinas's philosophy, even the philosophy in his *Summa*, but only by highlighting select passages and issues and downplaying or ignoring the rest.

A second contentious question concerns the relation between Aquinas's thought and Aristotle's: Is Aquinas's thought *Aristotelian*? While many well-known interpreters present it in this way, others resist, describing it as Augustinian or at least non-Aristotelian. Conflicts here arise partly from divisions on the previous question. Scholars who focus on some aspect of Aquinas's philosophy, as distinct from his theology, are the ones most likely to cast it as Aristotelian. Yet conflicts also arise because some give the term "Aristotelian" a much wider meaning than others do. Consider, for example, the article on Aquinas in the *Stanford Encyclopedia of Philosophy*. Having pronounced Aquinas "emphatically Aristotelian" as a *philosopher*, the authors elaborate on what they mean:

> He adopted Aristotle's analysis of physical objects, his view of place, time and motion, his proof of the prime mover, his cosmology. He made his own Aristotle's account of sense perception and intellectual knowledge. His moral philosophy is closely based on what he learned from Aristotle. . . . But to acknowledge the primary role of Aristotle in Thomas's philosophy is not to deny other philosophical influences. Augustine is a massively important presence. Boethius, Pseudo-Dionysius and Proclus

> were conduits through which he learned Neo-platonism. There is nothing more obviously Aristotelian about Thomas than his assumption that there is something to be learned from any author, if only mistakes to be avoided.
>
> (McInerny and O'Callaghan 2010)

The assumption that there is something to be learned from any author might well be called "open-minded," or possibly "generous," but "Aristotelian" is not a word that would normally come to mind. In literature on medieval philosophy, though, "Aristotelian" often figures as an expression of unqualified praise. Hence those who use it to describe Aquinas's thought are sometimes commending it more than actually describing it.

The "Aristotelian" label becomes especially controversial when applied to Aquinas's ethics, where his divergences from Aristotle are impossible to overlook. Unlike Aristotle, he argues that the ultimate end of human life lies in union with God in the afterlife. We can attain this end only through supernaturally 'infused virtues received as free gifts of grace (ST 1–2 62.1 reply). Aquinas accordingly bases his definition of virtue on Augustine's work, not Aristotle's (ST 1–2 55.4 reply). For him, as for Augustine, the paradigm virtues are gifts of God, infused by grace. Aquinas even denies that naturally acquired virtues differ from infused virtues only in their degree of perfection or completeness. He argues that they differ in kind from infused virtues, are intrinsically incomplete, and qualify as "virtues" only in an extended sense of the word (ST 1–2 65.2 reply). Indeed, people who receive God-given virtues might have no naturally acquired virtues at all (DQ Card. Virt. 2 resp. 3) Equally important, Aquinas follows the Christian tradition in arguing that all infused virtues are rooted in God-given charity or love, not naturally acquired prudence or practical wisdom. Where Aristotle awards his highest praise to virtues of the intellect acquired only by a select few, Aquinas awards it to charity, a virtue of the will given to many (ST 2–2 23.6, 2–2 24.1 replies).

Considering the massive differences, is it simply wrong to call Aquinas's ethics Aristotelian? Remember that scholars usually apply this label to what they consider his moral *philosophy*, as distinct from his moral theology. Thus they concentrate on his account of acquired virtues (or perhaps natural law), giving short shrift to infused virtues and other topics he discusses at much greater length than "philosophical" ones. In contrast, scholars who oppose the Aristotelian label usually have in mind Aquinas's ethics as a whole. Why, then, do the two factions get embroiled in such heated debates? Why not simply grant that they are arguing at cross-purposes? Partly because each tends to take a dim view of the other's purpose. One seeks to secularize Aquinas in order to win him attention in mainstream contemporary philosophy. It aims to prove, as Philippa Foot claimed, that his ethical works "are as useful to the atheist as to the Catholic or other Christian believer" (Foot 1978, 2). The other faction usually regards this campaign as a gross distortion of the historical Aquinas, a betrayal of the Christian values he held dear, or both.

Terence Irwin's account of Aquinas's ethics as the best statement ever given of "the Aristotelian approach to moral philosophy," including "Aristotelian naturalism," seems to me a classic example of the secularizing strategy.[1] Exactly what does "Aristotelian naturalism" involve? As Irwin uses it, "Aristotelian naturalism" does not commit itself to the claims about the definability of moral properties associated with G. E. Moore. Thus it does not refer to the kind of ethical naturalism commonly at stake in contemporary debates about metaethics. Neither does "Aristotelian naturalism" suggest that morality should be understood without reference to any God or gods. Obviously, Aquinas could not be considered a naturalist in this sense, Aristotelian or otherwise. What, then, does "Aristotelian naturalism" mean? Irwin explains:

> [Aristotle] defends an account of the human good as happiness (*eudaimonia*), consisting in the fulfillment of human nature, expressed in the various human virtues. His position is teleological, in so far as it seeks the basic guide for action in an ultimate end, eudaemonist, in so far as it identifies the ultimate end with happiness, and naturalist, in so far as it identifies virtue and happiness in a life that fulfills the nature and capacities of rational human nature. This is the position that I describe as "Aristotelian naturalism" or "traditional naturalism."
>
> (Irwin 2007, 4)

"Traditional naturalism" would be the better term, for Plato, the Stoics, and the Epicureans all hold the requisite positions. Even Augustine probably qualifies as a naturalist in Irwin's sense. Why, then, introduce "Aristotelian naturalism"? One reason is that it serves to commend Aquinas's work to contemporary philosophers. A fair number of them consider Aristotelianism in ethics a good thing, and most regard naturalism as a good thing. Indeed, so many philosophers want to be considered proponents of "naturalism" that they have stretched it wider and wider, to the point where the term no longer has any clear meaning at all (Papineau 2009). Even more important, "Aristotelian naturalism" aims to establish Aquinas's ethics as genuine moral *philosophy* and thereby legitimize the study of it in secular philosophy departments.

The problem here is not unique to Aquinas but shared by medieval thinkers in general. As Norman Kretzmann once observed, medieval philosophy has long been studied in a "philosophical ghetto," with most contemporary work in the field carried out in ignorance of achievements by medieval thinkers on the same topics (Kretzmann 1982, 3). His *Cambridge History of Later Medieval Philosophy* tried to remedy the problem by paying scant attention to theological issues and concentrating instead on the parts of medieval philosophy he judged most readily recognizable as philosophical by contemporary standards. This led to an overemphasis on logic and philosophy of language, a general neglect of ethics, and a virtual exclusion of theology, including natural theology. Had the volume taken a wider view of contemporary philosophical interests, it might have enjoyed a warmer reception.

The older legitimizing strategy, adopted by Irwin, portrays a medieval author's work as an extension of Aristotle's. Medievals rarely get stopped by the disciplinary border patrol when they arrive hand in hand with the most popular premodern philosopher of the West. The company they keep helps them prove their lineage, so that they pass as philosophers by present-day standards. If a medieval thinker can be cast as a proponent of Aristotelian naturalism, so much the better.

Granted, scholars of medieval philosophy might choose to ignore the legitimacy problem. Yet those who do run the risk of having their works fall dead-born from the press. Most of the best-known literature on medieval philosophy addresses the legitimacy problem by exaggerating Aristotle's influence. So why quarrel with a strategy that works?

Objections to Aristotelianizing Interpretations

However efficacious Aristotelianizing interpretations of Aquinas's ethics may be, they leave ample room for protest on religious grounds, historical grounds, and even philosophical grounds. The religious objection says that Aquinas's ethics differs not slightly but radically from Aristotle's. Although he awards a place to what Aristotle considered virtues, that place turns out to be quite modest, as it would have to be, given that Aristotle theorized in ignorance of the ultimate end of human life, the incarnation of Christ, and the need for God's grace. Alas, some scholars respond to the Aristotelianizing line of interpretation with an exaggeration of their own, claiming that Aquinas did not even regard Aristotelian virtues as real virtues. Alasdair MacIntyre made this claim in *Three Rival Versions of Moral Enquiry* but wisely dropped it in later works (MacIntyre 1990, 25). Eleonore Stump has recently revived it (Stump 2011, 31).

In fact, Aquinas devotes an entire article of his *Summa theologiae* to this very question and formulates a more nuanced position. Having argued that no virtue can be a true virtue *simpliciter* in the absence of (God-given) charity, he grants someone without charity can have a true virtue if it is directed to a genuine particular good, such as the preservation of the community. Such a virtue would be intrinsically imperfect or incomplete, because it is not directed to the ultimate end of happiness in the afterlife; but it would still be a real virtue, not just a false likeness of virtue (ST 2–2 23.7 reply).

In taking this position Aquinas moves a step away from Augustine, whose later works deny that pagan virtues are real virtues. On the whole, though, his theory of virtue still comes much closer to Augustine's than to Aristotle's.

Aquinas lays the ground for it by the conception of dispositions (*habitus*) he develops in the Prima Secundae (ST 1–2 49–54). Since he wants to classify all virtues as dispositions (ST 1–2 55.4 reply), he recognizes that a disposition cannot be by its very nature something produced by habituation. While it might be produced by habituation, it might also be produced supernaturally, through God's grace (ST 1–2 51.1, 1–2 51.4 replies). What, then, makes a disposition a special kind of quality? Aquinas mentions not only a disposition's resistance to change, the feature emphasized by Aristotle, but also its relation to the will. Appealing to Augustine's *On the Good of Marriage* and Averroes's *Long Commentary on De Anima*, Aquinas explains that a disposition is the sort of quality an individual uses *when he wills* (ST 1–2 49.3 sed contra, 1–2 50.5 reply). This understanding of a disposition enables him to argue that virtuous people can fail to exercise their virtuous dispositions when circumstances call for them. They can even choose acts they recognize at the time to be wrong (ST 1–2 53.1–3 replies). Unlike Aristotle, Aquinas endorses what today's philosophers call a probabilistic conception of virtue.

The historical objection to Aristotelianizing interpretations of Aquinas's ethics can take various forms. It might argue that he could have written "philosophical" works, as Albert the Great and other contemporaries did, but chose not to do so. Interpreters should respect his decision (Jordan 2006, 155). The objection might highlight Aquinas's large debt to sources other than Aristotle, whether ancient or Christian. Finally, it might argue that Aristotelianizing interpretations give short shrift to the most distinctive feature of his ethics: what John Inglis calls Aquinas's "replication of moral virtues" (Inglis 1999).

The last point merits needs some explanation. While Aquinas acknowledged the naturally acquired virtues discussed by Aristotle, he regarded them as intrinsically incomplete and "virtues" only in an extended sense of the word. He proceeded to posit a whole class of supernaturally infused moral virtues, many with the same names as naturally acquired moral virtues, but of a different species and given by God together with charity, as free gifts of grace. As he saw it, naturally acquired virtues dispose us to act according to reason, in order to attain the imperfect happiness possible in earthly life. The infused theological virtues of faith, hope, and charity direct us to God and eternal happiness, but they themselves do little to guide our behavior regarding created things. We accordingly need another kind of infused virtues—infused prudence and moral virtues—which dispose us to act according to divine law in earthly life (ST 1–2 63.3–4 replies).

Other thinkers of the period charged that Aquinas posited more virtues than a moral theorist needs to posit. Some added that he equivocated on the word "moral" in applying it to naturally acquired virtues as well as virtues given by grace, even to baptized babies. Only his most loyal disciples joined in positing both naturally acquired and infused moral virtues, instead of just one kind or the other (Kent 2010, 499–502). Whatever one might think of this aspect of Aquinas's ethics, it shows what a modest role he assigned to virtues that people develop through learning and practice. On his view, the only unqualified moral virtues are ones we can neither acquire nor even increase through our own efforts (ST 2–2 23.7).

We come at last to a philosophical objection to Aristotelianizing interpretations of Aquinas's ethics—namely that they overestimate the enthusiasm for Aristotle in contemporary philosophy. While no one doubts that Aristotle has a genuine moral philosophy, many doubt whether it is one worth supporting in the twenty-first century. Neo-Aristotelians face sharp criticism from Kantians, consequentialists, advocates of situationist psychology, and others convinced that Aristotle's ethics should be left in the past. Why bother studying Aquinas's ethics if one assumes that it has the same weaknesses?

No doubt there are places where Aquinas does follow Aristotle's teachings, at least about naturally acquired virtues; but if we try to resist the Aristotelian vision of his ethics and take a fresh look, we might notice solutions to some problems that contemporary philosophers see in Aristotle's ethics. In the next section we turn to one such problem—or rather a set of related problems—arising from Aristotle's famous argument for the reciprocity of the virtues: nobody can acquire any moral virtue without prudence, nor can someone acquire prudence without all the moral virtues. To be sure, a person might have some kind of "natural virtue" without prudence, on par with the kind of courage we might praise in a child or even an animal. A moral virtue, however, cannot exist in someone lacking the intellectual virtue of prudence. Prudence, in turn, cannot exist without justice, courage, temperance, and all the other moral virtues (*NE* 6.13).

Some philosophers concede that no real person can attain Aristotle's ideal but defend it nonetheless, insisting that it encourages and guides moral development. Others take a more negative view. Gary Watson thinks that Aristotle's argument for the reciprocity thesis draws too strong a conclusion. To possess one virtue completely one need not have all the other virtues completely as well (Watson 1984, 60). Susan Wolf argues that someone who has a moral virtue must have the knowledge required for other moral virtues but not the other virtues themselves (Wolf 2007, 156–61). Linda Zagzebski moves another large step away from Aristotle in claiming that someone can have a genuine virtue, as a Nazi might have the virtue of courage, even though the virtue does not make him a better person overall. Indeed, the virtue might make him a worse person overall (Zagzebski 1996, 92–3). At the very end of the anti-reciprocity spectrum stands John Doris, who argues that no real human being could ever acquire the kind of virtuous character Aristotle describes, because there is no such thing as moral character. Morally speaking, we are all mixed bags. We can indeed acquire situation-specific dispositions deserving of praise, but not the kind of "global" and "robust" character traits that Aristotle and his followers imagine (Doris 2002, 62–91).

Another line of criticism says that Aristotle allows for pitifully little diversity in virtuous character. Even supposing that he requires only ordinary generosity, not the large-scale virtue of magnificence, his account rules out people who are extremely poor. (By the time Aquinas was writing, this would have included those who chose to live by a vow of strict religious poverty and hence had literally nothing of their own to give.) Aristotle's understanding of courage likewise excludes many people we normally think of as having this virtue. Aristotelian courage is a virtue enabling one to face without fear the prospect of death in battle. Since Aristotle does not consider other kinds of deaths "noble," he denies that those who confront them fearlessly can properly be credited with the virtue of courage (*NE* 3.6).

What does Aquinas think of the reciprocity thesis? He endorses Aristotle's view that no moral virtue can exist without prudence, nor can prudence exist without moral virtue; but he stops short of concluding that prudence cannot exist without all the moral virtues. Aquinas's own account of virtuous character centers on the cardinal virtues,[2] and even in discussing these four he diverges from Aristotle's teachings.

Cardinal Virtues as a Threshold Concept

The idea of four cardinal virtues can be found in works by the Stoics, Macrobius, Cicero, and the Church Fathers. The four are always prudence (or practical wisdom), justice, temperance, and courage. The same virtues figure prominently in Aquinas's works. Indeed, he organizes his long treatment of virtue in the Secunda Secundae around the theological virtues and the four cardinal virtues. Aquinas recognizes, though, that even the idea of cardinal virtues cannot be found in Aristotle's works. He says so explicitly in his commentary on the *Nicomachean Ethics.* While Aristotle does describe the virtuous person as "foursquare beyond reproach," Aquinas denies that this expression refers to the four cardinal virtues (*NE Com.*1.16). Yet he himself considers the cardinal virtues so central to ethics that he introduces them into his commentary on the *Ethics.* In commenting on book II, chapter 7, where Aristotle ticks off a list of about a dozen moral virtues, Aquinas identifies four virtues as cardinals and the rest as merely secondary virtues. In order to do so he has to insert prudence, an intellectual virtue that Aristotle does not discuss in this part of the text (*NE Com.* 2.8).

The notion of cardinal virtues helps to preserve the common intuition that some virtues are simply more important to a person's character than others. Suppose, for example, we are accustomed to considering Smith a splendid colleague and all-round virtuous human being. He does his share of administrative work, never loses his temper, never drinks too much at social functions, and judges others fairly, both in his personal and his professional life. But over time, we notice that Smith routinely assents to unjust decisions by his bullying spouse; he never visits friend who are ill, from fear of "catching something"; and he thinks nothing of shirking his duties whenever he himself feels under the weather. We come to realize that Smith lacks courage, and his deficiency in this respect has more than trifling repercussions. Having discovered this flaw in his character, many of us would abandon our original opinion of him as a virtuous person. Some might even decide that the virtues they originally attributed to Smith are not genuine virtues. (How could anyone with the virtue of justice repeatedly assent to unjust decisions? How could he fail his friends when they sorely need his support?)

While cases like this make Aristotle's reciprocity thesis sound appealing, we need only change the example to show how the reciprocity thesis conflicts with common moral intuitions. Suppose what we find lacking in Smith is instead a different Aristotelian virtue, such as wittiness. (For all his splendid qualities, he turns out to be a boring companion.) Discovering this defect, hardly any of us would abandon our originally positive judgment of his overall character. We certainly would not start thinking that virtues he seems to possess cannot be genuine virtues. Why would we respond differently in this second case? Because courage is important to a person's moral character in a way that wittiness and various other virtues are not. Aquinas shares this view.

For Aquinas courage, justice, temperance, and prudence constitute the foundation of moral character. None of these virtues can exist without the others. To this extent he embraces the reciprocity thesis. On the other hand, he resists the conclusion that nobody can acquire prudence without acquiring all the moral virtues. Aquinas argues that all the other virtues are parts of the cardinals but distinguishes between three different kinds of parts (ST 2–2 48.1 reply). Virtues he calls integral parts are constitutive of a cardinal virtue, as a roof and walls are constitutive aspects of a house. What he calls subjective parts are instead different species of a cardinal virtue, as sheep and goats are different species of animal. (Hence people who choose not to have any sexual relations and people who have sex only with their partners can both be temperate.) Finally, there are the potential parts Aquinas classifies as secondary virtues that can be "annexed" to the cardinals. Most of the moral virtues listed by Aristotle have this status, and many discussed by other philosophers and patristic authors do, too.

Why does Aquinas think the cardinals matter more than those virtues he classifies as secondary? Aquinas says that "human life turns on them in a more important way, and the other virtues are founded on them" (DQ Card. Virt. 1. resp. 12). At the very least this represents a normative claim: the cardinals have more worth (*dignitas*) than secondary virtues (ST 1–2.66.4 reply). But why do they have more worth? Because they give a person the psychological order that she needs to meet the most difficult challenges of human life. Prudence helps one to reach correct moral judgments; justice inclines one to act on them; and the other cardinals moderate especially troublesome appetites and fears.

Aquinas follows Aristotle in arguing that we need courage especially to deal with our fear of death; but he diverges in thinking that this fear can affect our lives in many ways, so that bravery in combat represents only one possible manifestation of courage. People also need courage to help their communities during a hurricane, and perhaps even to visit a friend with an infectious disease.[3]

Together these four virtues give a person's actions and emotional reactions the kind of stability (*firmitas*) we rightly attribute to virtuous people (DQ Virt. Gen. a. 12, resp. 23). Stability matters all the more to Aquinas precisely because he rejects Aristotle's idealized notion of the virtuous person as someone who never does wrong through the influence of passion, let alone from deliberate choice. His probabilistic conception of virtue allows that people can sometimes succumb to temptation or otherwise behave badly without immediately losing their claim to be considered virtuous people.[4] So we would not need to change our favorable judgment of Smith's character if he turns out to be deficient only in some virtue with little significance for his life on the whole. Nor would we need to change it if he went along with an unjust decision or failed in other significant ways only now and then. On the other hand, if Smith repeatedly exhibited a lack of courage, we would indeed have to change our judgment of his character. Aquinas thinks we would even have to scrap the idea that Smith truly has the virtues of prudence, justice, and temperance.

While Aquinas does not expect virtuous people to be moral paragons, neither will he count as virtuous someone who lacks a cardinal virtue. The cardinal virtues together serve as the foundation for all the secondary virtues. A secondary virtue cannot stand as a virtue on its own, without the related cardinal, any more than the shutters or doors of a house could stand if the house lacked walls (an integral part) or the foundation supporting them. Thus all secondary virtues are "traced back" to related cardinals (*NE Comm.* 2.8). In contrast, a cardinal virtue—at least one we acquire naturally, through our own learning and practice—might well exist without at least some of the secondary virtues related to it. Aquinas makes this clear in declaring that justice can exist without magnificence; indeed, it can even exist without ordinary generosity (ST 1–2 66.4 resp. 1).

This is not to suggest that secondary virtues do nothing to improve a person's character. On the contrary, Aquinas routinely emphasizes their value. Even so, he distinguishes between what is morally owed, and hence necessary for moral integrity (or rectitude: *honestas*) and what is not. On his view, justice is so necessary that without it integrity of character cannot be preserved. The same does not hold for related secondary virtues such as generosity and friendliness. While they make us better than we would otherwise be, Aquinas thinks that integrity of character can be preserved without them (ST 2–2 80.1 reply). We might equally say that a house would be better if it had shutters and doors, although it would retain its structural integrity without them.[5]

Now we come to a problem in interpreting Aquinas: If the distinction between cardinal and secondary virtues matters so much, why does he sometimes seem to endorse Aristotle's claim that nobody can have prudence without all the moral virtues? One reason is just that he usually tries to avoid highlighting his disagreements with "authorities," striving rather to find some truth in what they say. Hence his *Summa* argues that prudence requires moral virtue and vice versa (ST 1–2 4–5), but only later explains that prudence does not require magnificence, magnanimity, or generosity. By the same token, his disputed question *On the Virtues in General* includes no question about the connection of the virtues. He prefers to discuss their connection when focusing on the cardinal virtues (DQ Card. Virt. 2).

Confusions also arise from the fact that Aquinas's remarks sometimes apply to naturally acquired moral virtues, sometimes to infused moral virtues, and sometimes to both. On his view, a virtuous person might acquire the cardinal virtues and some secondary virtues without acquiring other secondary virtues. She need not have all the secondary virtues in order to qualify as virtuous. In contrast, Aquinas thinks that God gives baptized Christians infused prudence and all infused moral virtues together, as dispositions (DQ Card. Virt. resp. 5). But even though they receive all these virtues through grace, they do not all possess them, much less exercise them, to the same degree (ST 1–2 65.2, 1–2 66.1 replies). Indeed, baptized babies cannot exercise their virtues at all.[6]

Notwithstanding the difficulties it presents, Aquinas's account of the cardinal virtues and their parts helps to address at least some objections that contemporary philosophers level against Aristotle's theory of virtue. So perhaps we need not exaggerate the Aristotelianism of his account in order to win it attention. Perhaps we could prescind from the question of intellectual lineage and just focus on philosophical issues.

Notes

1. Irwin (2007, 4). I do not mean to suggest that Irwin is the first philosopher to credit Aquinas with "Aristotelian naturalism." I flag the account in vol. 1 of Irwin's *The Development of Ethics* only because it is the most recent and will probably have more readers than earlier ones.
2. Aquinas uses the terms "cardinal virtue" and "principal virtue" interchangeably. For the sake of simplicity I stick with the first.
3. Although Aquinas argues for this view in 2–2 123.5, presumably with reference to the infused virtue of courage, I think his expansion of this virtue's scope applies equally to naturally acquired courage. Yet even as he demilitarizes courage, he stops well short of making it the kind of general virtue, concerned with fears of all kinds, that the Stoics do.
4. This clearly holds for acquired moral virtue, but even infused moral virtue allows for bad behavior. When Aquinas claims that a single mortal sin destroys all infused moral virtues (ST 1–2.65.3 reply), we must not overlook the qualifier "mortal." Someone with infused moral virtues might still commit many venial sins.
5. The main drawback to the house analogy, which Aquinas uses in flagging certain virtues as integral parts of the cardinals, is that it makes other ones he treats merely as potential

parts—secondary virtues that might be "annexed" to the cardinals—sound too peripheral. He himself compensates by shifting the analogy from architecture to psychology (ST 2–2.48.1 reply). Comparing these secondary virtues with the nutritive and sensitive powers considered potential parts of the soul, he emphasizes instead the idea of organic development.

6. Readers might also be a bit confused because some infused secondary virtues have naturally acquired counterparts, whereas others, such as the virtue of patience, do not.

PART X
Scotus on Cognition

Editor's Introduction

As he is about to murder King Duncan, Shakespeare's Macbeth has two very different sorts of perceptual experience. He perceives that he has a real dagger, the one that he draws to kill the king. But he also imagines a dagger floating before him, a figment, he supposes at one point, of his "heat-oppressed brain." In Duns Scotus's language, Macbeth has an "abstractive cognition" of the dagger he imagines, but an "intuitive cognition" of the real dagger he will use to murder the king. We have abstractive cognitions of sensible objects when the character of our cognition does not depend on whether the object really exists or is present to us. Intuitive cognition, by contrast, requires that the object really exist and be present. In what would be a highly controversial move, Scotus argues that not just our sensory powers, but likewise our intellect has intuitive as well as abstractive cognition. Without intellectual intuition, Scotus argues, we would be unable to explain how we know such contingent propositions as "The car is making a clanging noise." Nor would we know that our acts are *our* acts. Intuitive intellectual cognition, therefore, plays an important role in Scotus's epistemology.

However, Scotus's treatment of intuitive cognition has left a 700-year history of wide disagreement about how to understand the theory's details and significance. Scotus's commentators disagree about how to spell out the basic account of intuitive cognition, the range of objects it extends to, and the "mechanism" by which it works. It is this last issue that Douglas Langston focuses on in "Scotus's Doctrine of Intuitive Cognition." Scotus maintains that in abstractive intellectual cognition, the intellect understands through intelligible species which are a sort of representation needed for thought in the absence of the object itself. However, most commentators deny any role to species in intuitive intellectual cognition. According to Langston, that denial is motivated by their concern to ensure that the really existing object, and not its representation, be the object of knowledge. However, this concern is misplaced, since these representations are not themselves the objects of intuitive cognition, but the means through which we know the objects they represent. In fact, Langston argues, these intelligible species are *needed* for intuitive cognition. The basic account of intuitive cognition, therefore, cannot rely on the premise that intuitive cognition takes place in the absence of intelligible species.

In "Scotus on Intuitive and Abstractive Cognition," Giorgio Pini focuses on the more basic question of just how we should understand intuitive cognition. According to Pini, we have intuitive cognitions only when objects cause our knowledge without any causal intermediary; if an intelligible species caused our knowledge, it would be an abstractive cognition. Pini further argues that it is not abstractive cognition, such as the act of understanding, that is the pinnacle of intellectual achievement, but rather the contemplation that comes from intuitive cognition. If Pini is correct, Langston's view, which narrows the difference between intuitive and abstractive cognition, makes it hard to see how intuition is a more perfect sort of cognition.

Both Langston and Pini agree that William Ockham, Scotus's early admirer and frequent critic, should have been more cautious in his appraisal of Scotus's account of intuitive cognition. Langston contends that Ockham, who rejects any role for intelligible species, cannot explain how our intuitive cognition is about really existing objects precisely because he does not furnish a role for content in mental acts—the very role that the rejected species play in Scotus's theory. Pini, who denies that there are species in intuitive cognition, shows how Ockham's supposed criticism of Scotus can in fact be turned against Ockham himself. Evidently, Ockham himself later came to appreciate the force of Scotus's understanding, since Ockham alters his own view in ways that nudge it closer to the views of Scotus.

Note on References

Scotus worked his Oxford lectures on Peter Lombard's *Sentences* into his early *Lectura*. His *Ordinatio* (Ord.) is a more polished commentary on the *Sentences*, begun at Oxford and continued in Paris. His *Reportatio* consists of student notes (some later revised by Scotus himself) from Scotus's lectures on the *Sentences* at Paris. The critical "Vatican" edition (="Vat.") of Scotus's Latin texts is still incomplete, requiring scholars to use older editions, such as the Vivès edition, for many of Scotus's works. A good critical edition of Scotus's philosophical writings (*Opera Philosophica*, or OPh) was produced by the Franciscan Institute.

Ockham likewise published an *Ordinatio* (=Ord.), published as four volumes of his theological writings or *Opera Theologica* (=OTh) by the Franciscan Institute. His *Questions on the Second Book of the Sentences* is abbreviated as "rep." because it is a *reportatio.*

Further Reading

- Marilyn McCord Adams (1970). "Intuitive Cognition, Certainty, and Skepticism in William Ockham."
- Susan Brower-Toland (2007). "Intuition, Externalism, and Direct Reference in Ockham."
- J. B. South (2002). "Scotus and the Knowledge of the Singular Revisited."
- Allan B. Wolter (1990). "Duns Scotus on Intuition, Memory, and Our Knowledge of Individuals."

CHAPTER 19

Scotus's Doctrine of Intuitive Cognition

DOUGLAS C. LANGSTON

In his *De Anima,* Aristotle analyzed the views of his predecessors, the Presocratics, about how human beings come to have knowledge. He claimed that they shared a basic principle—only like is known by like—that was formulated in line with their basic metaphysical assumptions. The material monists held that human beings could know things because their souls were made of the one substance of the universe. Material pluralists held that human beings could know the various objects in the universe because their souls contain the same elements that make up the objects themselves.[1] Aristotle rejected such materialistic notions of the soul. Yet, he did not reject the basic principle that only like is known by like. In fact, he made it an important part of his view about how human beings have knowledge. For, according to Aristotle, the soul becomes like everything it knows. It accomplishes this by having reside in it the forms of what it knows. And thus it is often called "the place of the forms." This Aristotelian position is captured in the saying, the "soul is, in a sense, all things," and this expression became a basic assumption in the explanations of human knowledge offered by such medieval thinkers as Thomas Aquinas and John Duns Scotus.[2] The details of how Aquinas explains human knowledge of both universals and singulars are widely known and generally agreed on. He claims that the immaterial intellect knows directly general notions and knows material particulars only indirectly through an attention to phantasms. Likewise, it is generally known that Scotus seems to follow a basic Thomistic account of abstractive knowledge but also holds that the intellect has an intuitive cognition of particulars. The details of the mechanics of intuitive cognition, however, are not widely agreed on. Some authors maintain that intelligible species and phantasms can play no role in intuitive cognition. Others maintain that sensible material particulars are the objects of intuitive cognition. Still others maintain that only our own mental states can be intuitively conceived.[3] This range of views about Scotus's doctrine is disturbing. It is surely desirable that such an important doctrine in Scotus's works be clearly understood. By a careful examination of key texts, I hope to show in the first section what his doctrine is and is not. In the second section I will explore some of the implications of the doctrine.

1.

The *Quodlibetal Questions* are among Scotus's latest works. Despite their theological nature, they reveal certain aspects of Scotus's views about intuitive cognition. In particular, Question Six contains an important statement of the difference between abstractive and intuitive cognition:

> To understand better what is involved, it is helpful to distinguish two acts of the intellect at the level of simple apprehension or intellection of a simple object. One is indifferent as to whether the object is existing or not, and also whether it is present in reality or not. We often experience this act in ourselves, for universals and the essences of things we grasp equally well whether they exist extramentally in some subject or not. We also have [an empirical or] *a posteriori* proof of this, for scientific knowledge of a conclusion or understanding of a principle can be equally present to the intellect whether what they are about is existing or not, or is present or absent. In either case, then, one can have an equal understanding of that term on which an understanding of the principle or conclusion depends. This act of understanding which can be called "scientific," because it is a pre-requisite condition for knowing the conclusion and understanding the principle, can very appropriately be called "abstractive" because it "abstracts" the object from existence or non-existence, from presence or absence.
>
> But there is another act of understanding, though we do not experience it in ourselves as certainly, but it is possible. It is knowledge precisely of a present object as present and of an existing object as existing. Proof of this: Every perfection which is a perfection of cognition absolutely and which can be present in a faculty of sense knowledge can pertain eminently to an intellective cognitional faculty. But it is a matter of perfection in the act of knowing qua knowledge that what is first known be attained in itself and not just in some diminished or derivative likeness of itself. On the other hand, a sense power has such perfection in its knowledge, because it can attain an object in itself as existing and present in its real existence, and not just diminutively in a kind of imperfect likeness of itself. Therefore

> this perfection also pertains to an intellective power in the act of knowing. It could not pertain to it, however, unless it could know an existing thing and know it as present either in its own existence or in some intelligible object that contains the thing in question in an eminent way, which we are not concerned with at present.[4]

Scotus accomplishes several things in this quotation. In the first part, he presents a definition of "abstractive cognition." In general, it is a cognition indifferent to an object's present existence before a perceiver. Scotus also presents an argument from direct experience that we have such abstractive cognition, and he gives a proof for its existence from the nature of science. The definition, arguments, and proofs of this section are found elsewhere in Scotus's writings.[5]

The second section presents the basic definition of "intuitive cognition" found throughout Scotus's texts. It is knowledge of a present and existing object as present and existing. In this section, Scotus also offers an often repeated argument that a being possessing an intellect and sense knowledge also has intuitive cognition. The point of the argument is that, since the intellect is a power superior to the senses, it should possess any cognitive ability the senses possess. Because the senses can know an existing and present object, it follows that the intellect should likewise have the ability. While Scotus claims in this passage only that it is possible that human beings have intuitive cognition in their present state, it is clear that in other texts he states that human beings have intuitive cognition of particulars *in statu isto*.[6]

This long passage indicates that intuitive and abstractive cognition are to be distinguished in terms of the status of the object of cognition. In intuitive cognition, the known object exists presently before the perceiver. In abstractive cognition, the known object is not known as present and existing before the perceiver; rather, some representation of the known object, indifferent to the known object's present existence, is known as present and existing before the perceiver.[7] In commenting on the distinction between intuitive and abstractive cognition, Sebastian Day (1947) claims that neither phantasms nor intelligible species can be involved in an intuitive cognition. He argues that both of these entities can represent objects in their absence before a perceiver and so cannot be a part of this type of cognition. They are, of course, found in abstractive cognition, for the objects of this type of cognition are objects that are not present and existing before a perceiver.[8] Day is not alone in thinking that neither intelligible species nor phantasms can be involved in intuitive cognition. Etienne Gilson maintains that intelligible species do not enter into our knowledge of our own sensations, and Allan B. Wolter claims that neither intelligible species nor phantasms can be a part of our knowledge of our own mental states.[9] Clearly at the root of Day's view is the belief that if intelligible species or phantasms were a part of intuitive cognition, they would be what is known in the act of intuitive cognition, and so the mind would not be in a direct relationship to the particular object in the world. Yet this belief is mistaken, for Scotus understands intelligible species in intuitive cognition to be that *through which* the mind gets to particular objects. Intelligible species in intuitive cognition are not what is known in the act of cognition. Moreover, phantasms have a similar role in our knowledge of external, material particulars: they serve as means *through which* the mind gets to particular objects, and are not themselves what is known in the act of cognition. To see that Scotus is careful to distinguish between what we know and the means *through which* we know, we need to turn to other texts.

Question 14 of the *Quodlibetal Questions* is entitled "Can the Soul Left to Its Natural Perfection Know the Trinity of Persons in God?", and it involves a discussion of the cognitive powers of the soul in itself as well as in its different states (human, angelic, blessed). While the topic is a theological one, certain important philosophical points concerning the media of knowledge and of types of species are made. In the last part of the question, Scotus states:

> In answer to these I point out that a "medium of knowledge" or "means of knowing" can have two meanings: (1) the medium itself is known so that by knowing it something else is known, as is the case when a conclusion is known by means of a principle, (2) the medium itself is not known but it merely functions as a means of knowing, *in the way, for instance, that the sensible species in the sense faculty is a means of knowing.*[10] (My emphasis)

My emphasis is intended to stress Scotus's claim that some sensible species are media for knowing an object without being themselves known. For Scotus, the sensible species in the sense faculty (*in organo*), which include the species in the senses as well as the species of the phantasm in the imagination, are species *through which* objects are known. They are not themselves what is known. Their presence in intuitive cognition would thus not disrupt the direct relationship between the perceiver and the material object perceived, as Day would have us believe.

Day commits a similar mistake in regard to intelligible species. In *Ordinatio* II, d. 3, p. 2, q. 2, Scotus discusses an image (*imago*) that is a means of knowing something and is not itself known: "It is to be granted that the image that is only a means of knowing, not what is known, represents the object immediately, without reasoning (as is the case with visible species in the eye and intelligible species in the intellect)."[11] In his discussion he says explicitly that the intelligible species in the intellect are such images. It is thus clear that Scotus would regard intelligible species as that *through which* something is known in intuitive cognition, and not what is known. They do not interfere with the direct relationship between the perceiver and the object in intuitive cognition.

Other texts emphasize that intelligible species are not the objects of cognition. In Book I, question 2 of Scotus's first and second commentaries on Aristotle's *De Interpretatione*, he discusses whether words directly signify things in the world—the view he himself endorses on the basis of reason—or whether words directly signify concepts and indirectly signify things—which is the view he attributes to Aristotle.[12]

In the course of discussing the first view (the one he endorses from reason), Scotus tells us: "[T]he thing is understood principally, and not the species, unless through [some act of] reflection."[13] Similar passages appear in his second commentary on *De Interpretatione.*[14] The point of these passages seems to be this. We know things primarily and ordinarily. These are the objects of our thoughts and cognitions. We do not, on the other hand, know the species through which we know things. We can get to these species only by some sort of internal reflection on our mental state of cognition.

Thus if we accept the claims of Scotus's commentaries on *De Interpretatione*, it is very difficult to interpret him as claiming that species in the intellect are what is known in intuitive cognition. The species become what is known only in a reflective operation. Their normal role in intuitive cognition is to be that *through which* the objects of cognition are known.

The contention of Day and others that intelligible species cannot be involved in intuitive cognition becomes even more problematic when we turn to *Ordinatio* II, d. 3, q. 8, n. 9. For, here, Scotus explicitly denies the claim that "a sensible thing can immediately without any intelligible species cause intellection."[15] Scotus thus seems to affirm explicitly that intelligible species are required for the knowledge of sensible particulars in both intuitive and abstractive cognition. Day attempts to dismiss this passage by arguing on the basis of another text—*Ordinatio* I, d. 3, p. 3, q. 1—that Scotus thinks intelligible species are found only in abstractive cognition, so that the passage from *Ordinatio* II, d. 3 must be read as talking about abstractive cognition only. A careful reading of the text from *Ordinatio* I, d. 3, however, undermines Day's interpretation.[16]

This text is often examined as a source for Scotus's views about knowledge. In it Scotus treats the question whether the memorative part of the intellect properly taken has an intelligible species present to it prior to its act of understanding. As his main response to this question, Scotus focuses on our knowledge of universals and claims that intelligible species representing a universal must be present prior to the act of understanding in cases of abstractive cognition of universals.[17] Since we know universals through abstractive cognition, it is obvious that the text of *Ordinatio* I, d. 3, p. 3, q. 1 is principally about abstractive cognition. Yet, in his discussion in this text, Scotus says several important things about intuitive cognition. To see this we need only turn to the beginning of the text and examine his response to the second argument of the contra section.

This argument states that a species cannot be present to an intellect before its object is present to the intellect, since the existence of the species depends on the presence of the object.[18] It follows from this that the question asked in this section—whether the memorative part of the intellect properly taken has an intelligible species present to it prior to its act of understanding—must be answered in the negative. (It is important to note that the situation described in the argument is one of an intuitive cognition of a white object, and this fact gives plausibility to the general claim that an object must be present before the appropriate species is found in the intellect. For an object must be present to an intellect before there can be an intuitive cognition of the object.)

In response to this argument, Scotus states:

> To the second, concerning presence, I respond that the object in respect to the faculty first has a real presence, that is such an approximation that it can cause species in the intellect, which is the formal condition of intellection. Secondly, the object is present under the aspect of intelligibility or as representing, through this generated species, which is an image of what generates [it]. The first presence precedes naturally the second, because it precedes the impression of the species through which the second is formally present. . . .[19]

In these lines Scotus distinguishes the real presence of the object to the intellect (*praesentiam realem*), the presence of the object in the manner of the intellect (*ratio formalis intellectionis*), and the presence of the object as knowable (*praesens sub ratione cognoscibilis*). He also states that the presence of the real object must precede the presence of the object in the manner of the intellect. Scotus then goes on to state:

> When, therefore, it is granted that "the species in the intellect is not the cause of the presence of the object," I say that it is false of the presence under the aspect of intelligibility, at least in the case of abstractive cognition, concerning which we now speak. And when it is shown that "the object is present before the species," this is true of the real presence, by which the agent is present to the passive [faculty].[20]

Here Scotus states in the first sentence the rule that an object must be present prior to the existence of the relevant species is not true for the relationship between the presence of the object as knowable and the real object in *abstractive cognition*. In the second sentence, he affirms that in cases in which an object is really present, viz. intuitive cognition, the presence of the object must precede the presence of species (presumably of either the object in the manner of the intellect or of the object as knowable).

Scotus then ends his response by stating:

> And I understand [the matter] in this way: In the first instant (*signo*) of nature the object in itself or in a phantasm is present to the agent intellect. In the second instant of nature—in which they are present to the possible intellect as a passive agent—there appear species in the possible intellect, and then through the species the object is present under the aspect of intelligibility.[21]

In this passage, Scotus describes a two-step operation of intellection. The object in itself or in a phantasm is first present to the intellect.[22] Second, the intellect creates species in the possible intellect, and through these species objects are present as knowable objects to the intellect. It is clear, given its context, that the passage is, in fact, about intuitive cognition. For, immediately prior to this passage, he has stated how the case of abstractive cognition is unusual (viz., the knowable object precedes the presence of the real object), and he now explains in this passage how cognition occurs in the typical non-abstractive, i.e. intuitive, case. First, the object in itself or in a phantasm is present. Then a species is formed in the possible intellect, and it is through this species that the object as knowable is present to the intellect. It is quite clear, then, that Scotus thinks that intelligible species are essential in intuitive cognition, for it is through the intelligible species formed in the intellect by the real presence of the object that the real object is knowable. In fact, Scotus explicitly confirms this interpretation of the passage in *Ordinatio* II, d. 3, p. 3, q. 1.[23] In this text, Scotus discusses the knowledge an angel has of itself through its own essence. In his discussion Scotus handles the following accusation of inconsistency: his view about angels seems to suggest that a sensible object can itself directly cause an intellection without the presence of an intelligible species—a position he rejected in *Ordinatio* I, d. 3. In response, he agrees that an object existing in itself or in some species external to the possible intellect is not intelligible in itself. It must be made intelligible by some intermediary. Thus Scotus confirms that in *Ordinatio* I, d. 3, the text I have just considered, he argues that an intelligible species is required for the cognition of any object. Moreover, this text of *Ordinatio* I, d. 3 also makes it very clear that Scotus thinks we know material singulars in our present state.

Surprisingly, Allan B. Wolter has recently denied that Scotus thinks that in our present state we intuitively conceive material particulars. According to Wolter, Scotus claims that we intuitively conceive only our own mental states. In advancing this claim, Wolter argues that Scotus acknowledges two types of intuitive cognition in our present state: perfect and imperfect intuitive cognition. Perfect intuitive cognition is the knowledge of a singular as present and existing. Imperfect is either an opinion about the future or a memory of the past, which remains after perfect intuitive cognition.[24] Wolter emphasizes that the only examples Scotus provides of either type are the intuitive cognition of our own mental acts or states. He specifically does not provide any examples of the intuitive cognition of material singulars. Even in acts of memory in which we remember material objects, the remembered object is only a remote object; the act of the person who is remembering, which is of course a mental act, is the immediate or proximate object of knowledge. So even Scotus's texts on memory give no cases of the intuitive cognition of material objects.

As it turns out, Wolter claims, material singulars in the world are not known by intuitive cognition. A careful analysis of texts indicates that material singulars are known indirectly through abstractive cognition. This process involves both phantasms and intelligible species abstracted by and placed in the intellect.

On the other hand, according to Wolter, intuitive cognition, which is of our mental acts alone, involves neither phantasms nor intelligible species. Phantasms cannot be present, for our mental acts do not have the extension or spatiality required for phantasms. Intelligible species are not required because there is no need to make a non-material correlate of our mental acts available to the possible intellect, since our mental acts are already immaterial.[25]

Wolter's views about Scotus's doctrine of intuitive cognition are puzzling. As we saw in our discussion of *Ordinatio* I, d. 3, p. 3, q. 1, Scotus claims that intelligible species are required in both intuitive and abstractive cognition. Without a species in the intellect, the object known will not be present to the intellect and the act of the intellect will not be of the object. Of course, a phantasm will not be involved in our knowledge of our own mental states because we do not know our mental states through our senses. However, phantasms must be involved in our cognition of material particulars, because our knowledge of them comes through our senses. But Scotus did acknowledge this difference by claiming that in the first instant of nature of our cognition the object in itself or in a phantasm is present to the agent intellect.[26]

It is also puzzling why Wolter thinks that there are no texts in which Scotus acknowledges our intuitive cognition of material singulars. William Ockham, for example, refers us to a text in Scotus's writings that he believes shows that Scotus states we have such cognition of sensible objects.[27] This passage comes immediately after a passage Wolter (1982) analyzes in great detail. The text is:

> Assuming as certain there could be in us an act whereby the past qua object is known, I add that this act, which we call "remembering," is not immediately about any past event, but only about some act of the remembering subject, and to exclude vegetative acts, chance actions or imperceptible acts generally, we limit ourselves to human acts. For I only remember that you sat here because I recall I saw or knew you sat here. On the other hand, though I know I was born, or that the world was created, I don't remember either, for I recall no act of mine that had this or that

> as its object. "Remembering is cognition of some past act of the person remembering where the act is recognized as being past." Given this definition of the term, certain things follow from the fact it is known as past and others from the sort of past object involved. From the fact that this knowledge is of the past four conclusions follow: First, we must understand that the potency or capacity to remember has an act after a lapse of time, otherwise it would not be the past qua past that is remembered. . . . Second, memory perceives the flow of time between that instant or time in which the object remembered existed and the present instant of perception. Third, the remembered object confronting the person remembering is not present in itself, otherwise it would not be remembered as past. Fourth, since the object must in some sense be present to the act and it cannot be present in itself, it must be present in a likeness or species and then the memory will be conserving the species. . . . Because of the special character of the object remembered, however, namely that it is a past act of the individual who remembers, three more certain conclusions follow: First, remembering will involve a double object: one ultimate or remote (viz. the something about which the person remembering had at one time a conscious or human act), the other, the proximate (viz. the past human act whereby he reached out to that other object). Second, since the potency for remembering requires a species, speaking of what is required for remembering *in toto*, this could not be impressed by the object when the latter no longer exists or is actually present. But this proximate object is a human act of the past. Therefore, while it did exist, the necessary species was impressed. And since the species of a past human act could not be impressed in any potency other than that which had this act as object, it follows then that the past act of knowing has to be the object of the potency for remembering. Third, only what concerns one's own act—where this is human—is subject to remembrance, for it is only through knowing one's own act as proximate object that we know its object qua remote object. Hence a person cannot remember the same sort of act in another as he can in himself.[28]

This passage is extremely fruitful for understanding Scotus's doctrine of intuitive cognition. In the first place, the distinction between the remote and proximate objects of an imperfect cognition can be used to show that Scotus does hold that we have intuitive cognition of material particulars. The case presented in the passage is the imperfect cognition that I recall I saw you sit here. According to Scotus, the immediate or proximate object of this imperfect intuitive cognition is the mental act of seeing you sitting as represented through a species in the memory. Your sitting as represented in a species in the memory is the remote or mediate object of the imperfect intuitive cognition.

Scotus explicitly claims that an imperfect intuitive cognition of a past act requires that a perfect intuitive cognition has occurred.[29] So the imperfect intuition of recalling that I saw you sit there must rest on the past, perfect intuitive cognition of seeing you sitting there. But we must be careful about determining the object of this cognition, for whatever is the object of this perfect intuitive cognition is preserved as a species in the memory and is the remote object of the imperfect intuitive cognition. There are two apparent possibilities for the object of the perfect intuitive cognition: my act of seeing you sitting or your action of sitting. If my act of seeing you sitting is the object, this act of seeing you sitting preserved as a species in the memory is the remote object of the imperfect intuitive cognition. But Scotus claims that my act of seeing you sitting preserved as a species in the memory is the proximate object of the imperfect intuitive cognition. Since the remote object and the proximate object of an imperfect intuitive cognition cannot be the same, my act of seeing you sitting cannot be the object of the perfect intuitive cognition. Thus, your act of sitting must be the object of the perfect intuitive cognition. It is also clear that your sitting is an example of a material object in the world, and we can therefore conclude that Scotus does hold that we have intuitive cognition of material objects. Needless to say, the passage also clearly indicates that we have intuitive cognition of our own mental acts, but we cannot conclude from the passage that our intuitive cognitions are only about our own mental acts.

In the second place, in looking over the whole text we must be struck by Scotus's claim that the proximate and remote objects of the imperfect intuitive cognition are represented as species in the memory. These species in the memory are peculiar, for they seem to be both what we are aware of in our act of memory and what we must go through to get to what Scotus clearly labels as the proximate and remote objects of the imperfect intuitive cognition: my past act of seeing you sit there and the past fact of your sitting there. These, then, seem to be a type of intelligible species that impose themselves as the direct object of cognition between the perceiver and what the perceiver perceives. Of course, this is the kind of intelligible species that so bothered Day and led him to claim that intelligible species are not involved in intuitive cognition. But it is important to realize that in the case of imperfect intuitive cognition there is no present and existing object before the perceiver, for the imperfect intuitive cognition is about a past act and fact. So the intelligible species in the memory do not come between the perceiver and the perceived object but rather allow the perceiver to get to the past act and fact.

As we saw above, a similar situation arises in cases of the abstractive cognition of universals. According to Scotus, there must be intelligible species in the memory that represent the universal prior to the act of intellection. These intelligible species seem to be both the object of our cognition and the means by which we have the cognition of universals. Of course, these intelligible species are not problematic for they occur in an abstractive cognition, and in an abstractive cognition there are no presently existing known objects before the perceiver that the intelligible species can block from the direct awareness of the perceiver. There is thus little reason to argue that intelligible species and phantasms play no role in Scotus's doctrine of intuitive cognition. On the contrary, there are clear indications that Scotus thinks they play crucial roles in intuitive cognition. For it is through intelligible species that perceivers intuitively conceive their own mental acts, and it is through intelligible species and phantasms that perceivers intuitively conceive presently existing material singulars.

2.

One of the more surprising implications of Scotus's doctrine of intuitive cognition is that in intuitive cognition a perceiver grasps a certain property: the property of actual existence. Like Aquinas, Scotus is a moderate realist and holds that universals are real but not independent of the particulars in which they are found. Unlike Aquinas, Scotus did not regard matter as the principle of individuation. According to Scotus, non-material formalities such as species differences and individual differences (haecceities) contract the common being found in finite objects to give individuality.[30] While the human intellect in its present state cannot directly intuit these formalities and can know them only abstractively, it can know presently existing material singulars directly through intuitive cognition, as we have seen. Given Scotus's doctrine of the univocity of being, it is clear that it is the same concept of being that applies to all beings—whether they are actual or possible.[31] Yet, it is clear that actual beings are different from possible beings. In what does this difference lie?

In the first place, what beings are possible is independent of God's activity. God's intellect, as a natural agent whose sole function is to know all that is knowable, knows the infinite possibilities that exist; it is not the case for Scotus that some possibility obtains because God's intellect knows it.[32] From all the possibilities present to the divine intellect, God chooses some consistent set of possibilities to become actual. So actual beings are actual for Scotus by virtue of God's activity, and they become actual as elements of a larger set of actual objects.

There are, of course, a variety of actual objects. For Scotus, these actual objects include not only tables, cabbages, and kings, but also minds, souls, angels, the blessed, and, of course, God. In our present state we cannot understand the actual being of souls, angels, the blessed, or God. We can, however, through intuitive cognition grasp the actual being of presently existing material singulars and the actual being of our own presently existing mental states. We can also grasp the being of possible material objects and possible mental states. But we do not grasp them through intuitive cognition: we grasp them abstractively based on prior intuitive conceptions of presently existing objects. What we grasp in intuitive cognition, then, is the property of actual existence that an object has. For this property is all that distinguishes a real object from the merely possible. In the next life, according to Scotus, where our intellects are not joined to our material bodies, we shall be able to understand intuitively the actual being of separated substances such as the angels and the blessed. We shall also enjoy intuitive cognition of the divine essence. But it is the same property of actual existence we shall understand then as we grasp now.

It is, of course, difficult to specify the content of the concept of actual existence. For whatever the content is, it must be appropriate not only to material bodies but also to mental acts, separated substances, and God. But Scotus's doctrine of intuitive cognition provides a criterion for actual existence: an entity has actual existence if it can be intuitively conceived by an intellect that has at least as much power as a human intellect. The qualification about an intellect having "at least as much power as a human intellect" is necessary because, in mankind's present state, human beings can only intuitively conceive their own mental acts and presently existing material objects. But, as we saw above, the set of actual beings, according to Scotus, includes much more than human mental acts and material objects. These other actual beings—formalities, souls, separated substances, and so on—can be intuitively conceived by beings whose intellects far exceed the power of human intellects.

Yet, there seem to be difficulties with Scotus's claim that human beings can intuitively conceive the actual existence of external, material objects. Scotus thinks, as we have seen, that there are intelligible species that are both what is known and that by which we know. But if there are such intelligible species, is it not possible that what we take to be a case of intuitive cognition is only the cognition of a mind-dependent intelligible species? And does this not undermine a seemingly important function of the doctrine of intuitive cognition: to guarantee our certainty about the existence of the external world?

It is important to realize, however, that Scotus never intended his doctrine to be used to demonstrate the independent and present existence of the external world. On the contrary, he assumed that there is an independent and present reality that perceivers know. His doctrine was intended to explain how it is that perceivers have the perceptions they do, and, in particular, how perceivers can know particulars as our own mental acts and material singulars.

It is clear that his doctrine could not, for example, answer the skeptical question posed by Descartes' evil genius hypothesis. Such an entity could cause a human being to think that a certain situation was a case of the intuitive cognition of an external object when it was not. Yet, this is an unfair challenge to pose to Scotus since he was not interested in guaranteeing our knowledge of the existence of the external world.

Within his assumption that there is an external reality that we know, he provides a clear way of separating cases of intuitive cognition of external objects from other types of cognition. Scotus claims that there is a clear and strong phenomenological difference between the different acts. In intuitive cognition, memory plays no role in the knowing of objects. Rather such cognition provides material, i.e. species, that will be stored in memory. In other types of cognition, there is an awareness of the memory acting to provide material that will represent objects in their absence. There is, then, no danger of confusing knowledge of present and existing objects—intuitive cognitions—with other types of cognition—abstractive cognitions. So it is not the case that the important role Scotus assigns to intelligible species in intuitive cognition will undermine the knowledge we claim to have about the presence of external objects.

Scotus's emphasis on the role of intelligible species for human cognition and, in particular, for intuitive cognition serves to distinguish him from both Aquinas and Ockham. As I have argued above, Scotus thinks that the presence of intelligible species is required for every act of cognition. The reason for this is that the intelligible species are images of the object known, and with their presence the mind is directed to objects.[33] Scotus's claims are perhaps best understood as saying that the intelligible species give a content to the act of the mind cognizing, and this content directs the mind to the object cognized. The notion of directedness, of course, brings to mind the notion of intentionality.

It has been long recognized that modern conceptions of intentionality derive from the scholastics. Brentano, in fact, explicitly acknowledged his indebtedness to the scholastics in formulating his doctrine of intentionality. Interestingly, those concerned with the medieval notion of intentionality often focus on Aquinas's views about human knowledge.[34] This is an odd focus, however, as we can see from this passage from *Summa Theologiae* I, 86, 1:

> Our intellect cannot directly and primarily know particular material things. The reason is that the principle of individuation in material things is individual matter, but as was said above, our intellect understands by abstracting intelligible ideas from such matter. What is abstracted from individual matter is universal, and so our intellect is directly capable of knowing only universals. But indirectly and by a kind of reflection it can know individuals, because as was said above even after it has abstracted intelligible ideas, it cannot exercise them in acts of understanding without turning to phantasms. . . . Thus, by means of its ideas it directly understands the universal, and indirectly the particulars of which the phantasms are phantasms.

Aquinas thus holds that human beings never directly know particulars. They directly know phantasms and indirectly know the particulars in the world. Aquinas's emphasis on matter as the principle of individuation and his claim that intelligible species are directed only to universals and not particulars lead him to argue that our intellects are cut off from direct contacts with particulars. This claim seems counter-intuitive, and is at odds with the large number of modern proponents of intentionality, who take for granted that the mind is directly aware of singulars. Given Scotus's emphasis on our knowledge of singulars, he seems a more important source for the modern doctrine of intentionality than Aquinas. It is also Scotus's emphasis on the role of intelligible species that saves him from the difficulties implicit in Ockham's account of intuitive cognition.

Ockham defines intuitive cognition in the Prologue to his *Commentary on the Sentences* in this way:

> Intuitive cognition of a thing is that knowledge by virtue of which it can be known whether the thing exists or not, such that if the thing exists, immediately the intellect judges it to be and evidently knows that it is, unless by chance the intellect is impeded in judging by the imperfection of this knowledge.[35]

He goes on to extend this notion of intuitive cognition to knowledge of whether a contingent proposition about the present is true. Thus, in general, an intuitive cognition is that by virtue of which we can have evident knowledge of the truth of present contingent propositions.

In reaction to Scotus, Ockham insists that intuitive and abstractive cognition are not to be distinguished in relation to the objects they are about. Quite simply, for every object we can have an intuitive cognition of, we can also have an abstractive cognition of. Without going into too much detail, it is worth mentioning that part of the reason Ockham says this is that God can cause us to have intuitive cognitions of non-existent objects as well as of objects that exist but are not present. Moreover, God himself intuitively conceives merely possible objects. Ockham also insists that neither abstractive cognition nor intuitive cognition involves phantasms or intelligible species. In the case of intuitive cognition, all that is required are the perceiver's intellect, the existing object, and God's activity. For the object itself acts on the intellect directly to cause it to be apt to assent to the truth of a contingent proposition truly describing the object, e.g., it exists, it is white, and so on.

In coming to terms with the existence of universals as well as non-existent particulars, Ockham came up with two different positions.[36] The first position, called the objective existence theory, held that universals are concepts but that concepts are to be analyzed as mental acts that are directed to some objectively existing entity. Objective existence here is not to be confused with real existence, which Ockham labels "subjective existence." Rather, objective existence is something like intentional or mental existence. So we think of universals by virtue of thinking about objectively existing universals as redness, roundness, and so on. Similarly, our thought of a unicorn is directed to an objectively existing unicorn. In explaining how the act of the intellect is directed to the objectively existent object it is about, Ockham relies on notions of similarity and causality: the act is directed towards the objectively existent object it is most similar to and that is causally connected to the mental act.[37] So, my thought of the universal roundness is causally connected to the objectively existing roundness and is more similar to it than any other objectively existing object in the universe.

Ockham extended this analysis of concepts to talk about existing real particulars. He claimed that my act of intellect of, say, a red apple, is of the red apple because it is directed towards the red apple in objective existence—meaning by this that my act of intellect is causally related to the objectively existent apple and is more similar to it than any other objectively existing object in the world. This, of course, is quite peculiar. Ockham distinguishes objective existence from real existence. Yet, in trying to account for our knowledge of real objects, he has our acts of intellect being directed to objectively existing entities. So, oddly enough, on the objective existence view, our acts of intellect never get to the real objects in the world. It thus cannot be part of a theory of the intuition of real entities.

The distinct advantage of the objective existence theory is that the directedness of acts of the intellect is easily explained: the act is directed towards the objectively existing object it is of. The disadvantage is that, as a consequence, the act never gets to real objects. It would be tempting to eliminate this disadvantage by reducing the objectively existent object to the content of a mental act. Thus a mental act would be directed by the objectively existing object—its content—towards something in the real world. Ockham did not, however, make this reduction. On the contrary, he completely rejected the whole notion of objective existence and proposed a mental-act theory of concepts.

According to the mental act theory, an act of intellect is about some object if it is more similar to that object than any other object in the universe and, in the case of existing particulars, it is causally related to the object. It is difficult to understand the notion of similarity Ockham has in mind here. What is it to say that one mental act is more similar to roundness than to a unicorn? Resemblance cannot be a factor, for mental acts will resemble each other more than they resemble other entities. Moreover, unless it is already assumed that there is some content to the mental act, there is no reason to think that some mental act is more "of" some object than another. To be sure, if it is already assumed that the mental act is identified as being of some object, it will be of the object; but unless we know how it is identified as being a mental act of the object in the first place in a non-circular way, there really is only the semblance of an explanation. Can causality explain how a mental act can be of some particular? In a way, this is a very unusual question to ask relative to a discussion of intuitive cognition. For we are trying to explain how an intuitive cognition can be of the relevant particular that is causally related to a perceiver. To try to answer by appealing to causal relationships seems to be no answer at all. But there are other difficulties. How can Ockham explain intuitive cognition of non-existents since the non-existents cannot causally interact with the perceiver's mind? Or, for that matter, how can God's intuitive knowledge of particulars be explained in this causal way, since it is knowledge that is prior to all existence of real particulars?[38] Finally, how can simple causality explain why our intuitive cognition is of one particular rather than another? When we intuitively know Socrates' whiteness or existence before us, we are in contact with him not in isolation from other particulars but in the presence of many particulars, e.g., a chair, some books, and so on. Why, then, is a particular mental act of Socrates' whiteness and not of the book? Surely the book is as causally related to my mind as Socrates is. So causal explanations cannot be enough. To be sure, if I know already that I have a mental act of Socrates' whiteness, his causal relationship to the act is sufficient to explain why it is of Socrates in this circumstance. But, on pain of circularity, the identification of the act must be independent of the causal relationship itself. All of these considerations, of course, lead us inevitably to the conclusion that Ockham's mental act theory also fails to explain how our mental acts are of particulars.

What is missing in Ockham's account, of course, is an acknowledgment that mental acts have content and that it is through their content that they are directed to particulars. It is this failure that results in difficulties for Ockham's theory. Scotus, on the other hand, saw the need for a content in mental acts to direct the mental acts to the objects they are about. Intelligible species provide this content. It is therefore of little surprise that intelligible species play such a critical role in intuitive cognition, which, for Scotus, provides the chief link between our minds and the external world. Given the role Scotus assigns intelligible species in human cognition, his historical importance for issues surrounding intentionality is considerable.[39]

Notes

1. *De Anima*, Bk. 1, Chap. 2.
2. See *Ordinatio* I, d. 3, p. 3, q. 1 (Scotus, 1950, Vol. 3, p. 226) for Scotus's reference to Aristotle's views.
3. Sebastian Day (1947, Chap. 2) claims that neither phantasms nor intelligible species can be involved in an intuitive cognition. Etienne Gilson (1952, pp. 549–52) claims that intuitive cognition involves an intuition (without phantasms or intelligible species) of the content of our sensations and an abstractive cognition (involving intelligible species and phantasms) of the nature of what we intuitively conceive. (It is noteworthy that Gilson fails to show adequate textual support for his view.) Camille Berubé (1964, pp. 179, 190) claims that Scotus embraces the theory of Vital du Four concerning our knowledge of presently existing singulars and names it "intuitive cognition". Among the objects we can intuitively conceive are material singulars. Allan B. Wolter (1982) claims Scotus admits only that there is intuitive cognition of our own mental states and acts in our present state. Wolter is explicitly critical of Berubé and others who say that Scotus's doctrine is a development of the theories of Vital du Four.
4. This is Wolter and Alluntis's translation (1975, pp. 135–36). The Latin text is found in Scotus (1891, Vol. 25, pp. 243–44).
5. See F. M. Garcia (1974, pp. 148ff.) for other related texts in which the definitions occur.
6. Day (1947, pp. 58ff.).
7. The qualification "known as present and existing" is critical, for it may happen that an object is known abstractively when it exists presently before the perceiver. A case in point is

thinking about a long-lost friend when he, by happenstance, is in a crowd at an address you are giving. Given this complication, one can perhaps think of intuitive cognition in this way. The known object's presence before a perceiver is a *sine qua non* cause of intuitive cognition. The presence of the object is also not inconsistent with an abstractive cognition of it by the perceiver. But the present existence of the object known as present and existing before the perceiver is a necessary and sufficient condition of intuitive cognition and is inconsistent with an abstractive cognition of the known object.

8. Day (1947, pp. 53, 105ff.).
9. See note 3.
10. Wolter and Alluntis's translation (1975, pp. 340–41). The text is found in Scotus (1891, Vol. 26, p. 108).
11. Scotus (1950, Vol. 7, p. 551):

    Licet imago quae est tantum ratio cognoscendi, non "ut cognita" (sicut est de specie visibili in oculo et de specie intelligibili in intellectu), repraesentet obiectum immediate, absque discursu. . . .

    Day systematically fails to distinguish between species that are the object of knowledge and species through which one knows objects. Once this distinction is made, it becomes clear that the texts he cites to show that Scotus claims that intelligible species cannot be involved in intuitive cognition do not support his view. See, for example, the texts cited on pp. 105ff. Each one can be read as claiming that species that represent an object in its absence cannot be part of intuitive cognition. But species representing an object in its absence should not be equated with the intelligible species through which objects are known.
12. Scotus (1891, Vol. 1, p. 544):

    Prima via videtur probabilior, secundum auctoritates. Secunda secundum rationes.

    In *Ordinatio* I, d. 27, Scotus makes it quite clear that he embraces the theory that words signify things directly.

    I do not mean to equate signification with understanding. Scotus clearly separates the two notions. It turns out, however, that in this text describing the signification of terms and concepts Scotus talks about what it is that we understand in acts of understanding.
13. Scotus (1891, Vol. 1, p. 543):

    [Q]uod res intelligitur primo, et non species, nisi per reflexione[m].
14. Ibid. (p. 583).
15. Ibid. (Vol. 12, p. 186b):

    [R]es sensibilis posset immediate absque specie intelligibili causare intellectionem.

    Day (1947) discusses this text on p. 110. See note 7 above for distinctions about types of causation.
16. The question is found in Scotus (1950, Vol. 3, pp. 201ff.).
17. Ibid. (p. 225):

    Ad quaestionem ergo dico quod necesse est ponere in intellectu ut habet rationem memoriae, speciem intelligibilem repraesentantem universale ut universale, priorem naturaliter actu intelligendi. . . .
18. Ibid. (p. 202).
19. Ibid. (p. 232):

    Ad secundum, de praesentia, respondeo quod obiectum respectu potentiae primo habet praesentiam realem, videlicet approximationem talem ut possit gignere talem speciem in intellectu, quae est ratio formalis intellectionis; secundo, per illam speciem genitam, quae est imago gignentis, est obiectum praesens sub ratione cognoscibilis

> seu repraesentati. Prima praesentia praecedit naturaliter secundam, quia praecedit impressionem speciei per quam est formaliter secunda praesentia. . . .

20. Ibid. (p. 233):

> Quando ergo accipitur quod "species in intellectu non est causa praesentiae obiecti," dico quod falsum est de praesentia sub ratione cognoscibilis, saltem intellectione abstractiva, de quo modo loquimur; et cum probatur quod "prius est obiectum praesens quam species," illud verum est de praesentia reali, qua agens est praesens passo.

21. Ibid.:

> Et intelligo sic, quod in primo signo naturae est obiectum in se vel in phantasmate praesens intellectui agenti, in secundo naturae—in quo ista sunt praesentia intellectui possibili, ut agentia passo—gignitur species in intellectu possibili, et tunc per speciem est obiectum praesens sub ratione cognoscibilis.

22. Scotus says this to account for the difference between our knowledge of our own mental states and our knowledge of material singulars. While intelligible species are necessary for both cognitions, phantasms are involved only in our knowledge of material singulars since we know them through our senses. Our knowledge of our own mental states does not involve phantasms since we do not know them through our senses. Rather, the mental states in themselves are present to our mind.
23. Scotus (1950, Vol. 3, p. 527).
24. Wolter (1982, p. 82).
25. I take some interpretive license here. Wolter does not explicitly claim that immateriality makes the difference. But I can see no other reason why mental acts present and existing before the perceiver can be known by intuitive cognition and material singulars present and existing before the perceiver cannot. Thus my interpretation of Wolter.
26. See note 21.
27. In presenting his theory of intuitive cognition, Ockham refers to Scotus's doctrine as an antecedent of his own (Ockham, 1967, Vol. 1, p. 44).
28. Wolter (1982, pp. 93). The text is from *Ordinatio* IV, d. 45, q. 3 (Scotus, 1891, Vol. 20, pp. 326–27).
29. Wolter (1982, p. 82).
30. See Langston (1979) and Marilyn Adams (1987, Chap. 2) for discussions of Scotus's metaphysics.
31. See Wolter (1946) for a discussion of the univocal concept of being.
32. See Langston (1986, Chap. 1) for a discussion of God's creative activity. See Simo Knuuttila's discussion (Knuuttila and Alanen, 1988, pp. 33ff.) of the independence of possibility from God's knowledge.
33. See notes 19 and 21.
34. A good example of this focus is Ausonio Marras (1976).
35. Ockham (1967, Vol. I, p. 31).
36. My discussion of Ockham's views relies heavily on Marilyn Adams's discussion (1987, Chaps. 3, 4, 13) of these issues. Many of the arguments I offer here are advanced by her in this work.
37. Cp. Adams (1987, p. 80).
38. Ibid. (p. 140).
39. There are many people and institutions to acknowledge as helping me to complete this paper. Funds for researching this article were provided by a grant from the Division of Sponsored Research, University of South Florida. Princeton University gave me access to its libraries, through the help of John Gager. While at Princeton, I benefited from conversations with Calvin Normore, Victor Preller, Marilyn Adams, and Jeff Stout. While at the University of Helsinki, I benefited from conversations with Simo Knuuttila, Gyula Klima, Lilli Alanen, and the members of my seminar on intentionality of the later Middle Ages.

CHAPTER 20

Scotus on Intuitive and Abstractive Cognition

GIORGIO PINI

Scotus held that any non-complex occurrent cognitive state belongs to one of two kinds. The first kind includes perceptual states and is typically exemplified by the state of seeing a color. Scotus called those states "intuitive acts," where an act is an occurrent state as opposed to an ability or disposition (e.g. my seeing a color right now as opposed to my ability to see a color) and "intuitive" comes from the Latin verb *intueri*, "to see." The second kind is best illustrated by the state of imagining a color, but imagining a sound or a taste would be equally good examples. Scotus called those states "abstractive acts," because he thought that their defining characteristic was that, unlike intuitive acts, they "abstract" from the existence of their objects, i.e. maintain their identity whether their objects exist or not. While I cannot see a color if that color does not exist, I can imagine a color whether that color exists or not. Perceiving and imagining had been distinguished at least since Aristotle's times. Scotus's original contribution was to argue that that distinction exemplified a basic contrast cutting across *all* cognitive states, whether sensory or intellectual. He also tried to give a precise definition of each class of acts and explored some situations where it is important to distinguish between them.

There is no doubt that Scotus was successful in putting the distinction between intuitive and non-intuitive states on the map, as witnessed by both critics and followers of his views and as confirmed by a number of studies devoted to this topic. Some of those studies reconstruct the historical context of Scotus's distinction. Others address specific questions—e.g., did Scotus think that intuitive acts are about singulars? Did he think that we have intellectual intuitions in this life? And, if so, of what? What are the mechanisms of intuitive cognition? Specifically, do intellectual intuitions require an intelligible species? Less attention has been devoted to the most fundamental questions of precisely what intuitive and abstractive acts are and why their distinction matters. I will focus on these more fundamental questions.

This chapter has four sections. First, I consider Scotus's definition (or rather, definitions) of intuitive and abstractive cognition. Second, I turn to what is probably Scotus's most innovative but also most controversial contribution to this issue, namely his contention that the intellect and not just the sensory power is capable of intuitions. Third, I present Ockham's criticism of Scotus's account. Fourth, I sum up the main points I made in the previous sections.[1]

1. The definition of intuitive and abstractive cognition

In ordinary circumstances, it is not difficult to distinguish seeing a color from imagining a color. But finding a rigorous criterion to distinguish those two cognitive episodes turns out to be more difficult than expected. This is what Scotus tried to do. In this section, I first consider intuitive cognition. Then I turn to abstractive cognition.

1.1. Intuitive cognition

Scotus gave several descriptions of intuitive cognition. All those descriptions single out the existence and/or the presence of the object as the characteristic feature of an intuitive act. Thus, he held that an intuition is a cognition (a) of an object present as present and existent as existent;[2] (b) of an object as it is existent and present in some real existence;[3] (c) of something present according to its actual existence;[4] (d) of something present in its proper nature;[5] (e) by itself of something existing and such that it touches the object in its proper actual existence.[6] He also claimed that (f) an intuitive act occurs when a thing is actually present.[7]

From these descriptions, it can be gathered that a cognitive act is intuitive only if its object exists. I see a color only if that color exists. If that color does not exist, I may believe that I see a color, but as a matter of fact I do not see it. Rather, my act would be an act of imagining, daydreaming or hallucinating—which are all non-intuitive acts.

This feature, however, is not sufficient to identify a cognitive act as intuitive. I may well imagine a color that actually exists. That act, however, would not count as intuitive. Some other condition is required to single out intuitive from non-intuitive acts. It is this further condition that Scotus was trying to pin down in the somewhat convoluted phrases I have mentioned above. At least at first, it is not easy to see what Scotus had in mind.

Scotus himself warned us against taking a wrong track. Intuitive acts cannot be distinguished from non-intuitive acts simply because they pick out some special aspects of their objects. Specifically, and notwithstanding what several of the phrases I have mentioned above might suggest, Scotus explicitly denied that intuitive acts are identified as intuitive because they focus on the existence of their object or on their object as existent.[8] Scotus's point seems to be well taken. My cognitive act of something existent may be precisely targeted at its existence or at that thing as existent. Still, that act may not count as intuitive. I may well imagine a color as existent, when that color does exist. Similarly, if we turn from sensory to intellectual acts, I can conceive of something existent as existent by a non-intuitive act. Take for instance my thinking of that than which nothing greater can be thought. I can think of that than which nothing greater can be thought as existing. Still, that thought would not be intuitive (as is shown by the fact that when I think of that than which nothing greater can be thought as existing I am not enjoying the beatific vision).

What is still missing from the characterization of intuitive cognition is a clause introducing some sort of direct acquaintance between the cognizer and the thing cognized. The object is *present* in both abstractive and intuitive acts—i.e. both abstractive and intuitive acts are related to something as to their object. But those two kinds of acts differ because of the different way the objects are present in each of them.[9] How can we account for the different way the object is related to intuitive and abstractive acts, given the object's existence is not sufficient to single out intuitive acts?

Scotus held that we can account for the difference in the way the object is present in intuitive and abstractive acts, and consequently the difference between those two kinds of acts, only by referring to the *cause* of those acts. In intuitive acts, Scotus claimed, "the thing present in itself" is what moves the act and "the thing in its own existence is by itself what moves objectively."[10] What does that mean?

By using those formulas, Scotus was trying to identify the specific way an intuitive act is caused by its object. His point can be grasped more easily by contrasting the causal relation Scotus intended to pick out with the other way a cognitive act can be caused by its object. By stating that the cause of an intuitive act is the thing present in itself or in its own existence, Scotus was ruling out that an intuitive act is caused by its object by way of a causal intermediary that can continue to exercise its causal power even when the object has ceased to exist and through which the object can still cause the act "by proxy," so to speak. Let me illustrate this point with an example. The causal relation between the object of an intuitive act and that act is like the relation between the power coming from an electric outlet and the working of an alarm clock with no battery backup. If there is a blackout, the clock ceases to work. Similarly, if the object ceases to exist, the intuitive act ceases to exist. By contrast, think of the relation holding between the power coming from an electric outlet and the working of an alarm clock with battery backup. Even though electric power is necessary to start and charge the clock, once the clock's battery is charged, no more power coming from the outlet is needed to keep the clock working. Similarly, as we will see, in abstractive cognition the existence of the object is not necessary to keep the abstractive act about that object in existence. But in intuitive cognition, the object and the cognitive power are the sufficient causes of the cognitive act and no further causal intermediary device (such as an image or a species) is required or, indeed, admitted.[11]

Scotus held that, as a consequence of the way the object is causally related to an intuitive act, the intuitive act is linked to its object by a special relation, which he called "relation of contact" (*relatio attingentiae*). That relation is both actual and real (i.e. it is occurrent and obtains independently of whether it is being thought about or not).[12] Even though the relation of contact is different from the causal relation linking the object to the cognitive act and cannot be reduced to it, it nevertheless depends on the causal relation. As Scotus stated, the object is not perfectly attained—and thus, the relation of contact does not hold or does not hold as an actual and real relation—when the object is not touched in itself but in a diminished likeness caused by the object itself.[13] Something is present "in a diminished likeness" if it is present to the cognitive power—i.e., it is the object of a cognitive act—by way of a causal proxy for that object. By contrast, the relation of contact obtains as an actual and real relation between a cognitive act and its object when something is the object of a cognitive act by way of no causal proxy. As a consequence, the relation of contact obtains because of the specific way the cognitive act is caused.

Incidentally, a consequence of the way an intuitive act is causally related to its object is that the existence of the object is necessary not just for bringing the intuitive act into existence but also for keeping that act in existence. What Scotus had in mind is that the object of an intuitive act is what other thinkers will call a "cause with respect to existence" (*causa secundum esse*) and not just a "cause with respect to its coming to be" (*causa in fieri*) of the intuitive act itself.[14]

So all of Scotus's descriptions of intuitive cognition, if correctly understood, involve a mention of the way the object an intuitive act is about causes that act. In fact, it is because of the way an intuitive act is caused by its object that that act is about an *existent* object. A cognitive act is intuitive if and only if it is caused by its object through no causal proxy. That an intuitive act is about an existent object is not a separate necessary requirement that act must meet. Rather, it is a consequence of the special causal story that links the object and the act. Because nothing can replace the object in its causal role and the object must be "present according to its existence," as Scotus says, the existence of the object is necessary to keep the act in existence. So if the object does not exist, the act about it does not exist either.[15]

1.2. Abstractive cognition

Because Scotus held that the distinction between intuitive and abstractive acts is exhaustive, any cognitive act that is not intuitive is abstractive. Specifically, an abstractive act is described as failing to satisfy either the first condition (that its object exist) or the second condition (that its object be present in its existence and not by causal proxy). I will consider these two descriptions in turn.

(a) Scotus usually described an abstractive act as a cognitive act that is indifferent with respect to whether its object exists. So the object of a cognitive act may or may not exist. In other words, an abstractive act is related to its object in such a way that its existence and identity are independent of the existence of the object it is about. This is what Scotus meant by saying that such an act "abstracts" from the existence of its object.[16] That object may have ceased to exist—such as dodos and dinosaurs did. The act by which I imagine a dodo, or I think about what a dodo is, is the same kind of act by which I imagine a cat or think about what a cat is. Admittedly, the way I acquired my thought of what a cat is is probably different from the way I acquired my thought about what a dodo is. But this difference is not relevant to the identity of my thoughts. Thoughts about what cats and what dodos are are thoughts of the same kind. They are both abstractive.

While an intuitive act is linked to its object by the special relation of contact, at times Scotus suggested that such a relation is absent in the case of abstractive cognition. In abstractive cognition, the only relation holding between act and object is one that Scotus called "of measurability," which can roughly be equated to aboutness.[17] In another passage, however, Scotus seems to have held that there *is* a relation of contact even between an abstractive act and its object, because it is impossible to think of an act of abstractive cognition without thinking at the same time of its object as something occurrently present to that act. But such a relation is conceptual and not real, because its term (namely, the object of the act) may not exist (as when I imagine or think of dodos) and Scotus held that nothing can be really related to something that does not exist. Moreover, it seems that such a relation of contact between an abstractive act and its object holds just because the act can be *thought* and identified only if some reference is made to its object. So the existence of that relation of contact between an abstractive act and its object depends on an intellect thinking about the abstractive act.[18]

(b) Scotus also offered a causal account of abstractive cognition. He claimed that intuitive and abstractive cognition are different *kinds* of cognition because in abstractive cognition "what moves" is not the thing in its existence (like in intuitive cognition) but "something in which the thing has cognizable being"—usually, an image (in the case of an act of imagining) or the so-called intelligible species (in the case of an act of thinking).[19] Scotus had the following account in mind. An abstractive act is caused by its object via a causal intermediary, i.e. the image or the intelligible species. The object's causal power to produce a cognitive act in a suitable subject is transferred, so to speak, to that intermediary device, which can accordingly function as a causal proxy for the object. Think of the backup battery present in an alarm clock, which can keep that clock working even during a blackout. The power to keep the clock working is transferred from the power coming from the electric outlet to the battery. Similarly, the power to keep a cognitive act in existence is transferred from the object to the causal intermediary device, i.e. the image or the intelligible species.

Scotus took the causal account of abstractive cognition as explanatorily more fundamental than his definition in terms of indifference to the existence or non-existence of the object. For the causal story by which an abstractive act is produced accounts for that act's keeping its existence and identity no matter whether its object exists or not. When the causal proxy of the object is received in a cognitive power that can retain it even when the object has ceased to exist, then that power cognizes the object even when that object has ceased to exist.[20] Both the imaginative power and the intellect are such that they can retain causal proxies of their objects even when their objects have ceased to exist. Those proxies are images and intelligible species, respectively. Imagination and intellect are cognitive powers with a backup battery. Accordingly, those two cognitive powers can have occurrent cognitive acts about a certain object independently of that object's existence or non-existence—both imagining and thinking are forms of abstractive cognition. To use a terminology that will become common after Scotus, the object is not the cause with respect to the existence (*causa secundum esse*) of the image or of the intelligible species. Neither the image nor the intelligible species depends on the object for its continuing to exist. Rather, the object is the cause of the image's and species' coming to be (*causa in fieri*).[21]

The capacity of some of our cognitive powers for keeping a causal proxy of their objects even when those objects have ceased to exist plays a key role to account not just for daydreaming but also for some of our most important cognitive achievements. Specifically, this capacity accounts for our ability to achieve scientific knowledge (*scientia*), which is indifferent to whether its objects currently exist, as is the case with cats, or not, as is the case with dinosaurs.[22] Some other powers, i.e. our external senses (sight, hearing, smell, touch, and taste), do not have the capacity for retaining a causal proxy of their objects when those objects have ceased to exist. For that reason, those powers are actualized only when their objects exist and only as long as their objects exist. For example, I cannot see a color or hear a voice that does not exist anymore. But I can still dream or think about them.

It is important to notice that the intermediary device present in abstractive cognition—be it an image or an intelligible species—acts as a proxy for the object only from a *causal* point of view. That intermediary device can cause a cognitive act about a certain object even when that object has ceased to exist. But images and intelligible species do *not* replace the object as that at which the cognitive acts they cause are directed. In abstractive just as in intuitive cognition, what is cognized is a thing, not its representation. So even though there is an intermediary device in the causal process resulting in an abstractive act, there is no corresponding representational device intermediary between the cognitive act and its object. In other words, Scotus was not a representationalist. Neither the image nor the intelligible species is a representation, if by "representation" we mean something that is a direct object of cognition. Admittedly, it does not help that Scotus repeatedly called those intermediary devices "representations" or that he said that in abstractive cognition the object is present in something that represents it and that it is attained not in itself but in a diminished or derived likeness.[23] No matter how strongly those expressions seem to suggest that Scotus was indeed committed to a form of representationalism, in some of the very passages where he used those expressions he explicitly claimed that both abstractive *and* intuitive acts give *immediate* cognition of an object and not of something else by which that object is cognized.[24] This makes it clear that he thought that images and species are only causal vehicles through which the object is made present to the intellect but are not themselves what is immediately cognized.[25]

2. Intellectual intuitions

So far, I have considered intuitive and abstractive cognition as typically exemplified, respectively, by seeing and imagining. These are sensory acts. Scotus, however, claimed that the distinction between intuitive and abstractive cognition cuts across sense and intellect. Specifically, he contended that intuitions can be intellectual as well as sensory. Scotus's contention was at odds with the common view that the intellect was an exclusively abstractive power, which operated through concepts whose identity was independent of the existence or non-existence of their objects. The insight behind the common view was that the intellect's foremost and indeed defining achievement is *understanding*, and more specifically the sort of understanding that is reached in scientific knowledge (*scientia*). Scientific knowledge was usually described as that state in which one is able to understand the essences of things, i.e. what things are and why they behave as they do. Now it is a key feature of scientific knowledge that it extends beyond what exists here and now—its claims are universal and always true. For example, what I know about the essences of dodos and cats is true no matter whether there is any dodo or cat. So if the intellect is naturally geared for scientific knowledge, it is only fitting that it operates without taking into account whether its objects exist or not. In this framework, the abstractive nature of the intellect is actually one of its major assets, because it allows us to get free from the strictures of the here and now and to get a genuine understanding of the natures of things.

Before Scotus, a few thinkers had already suspected that this could not be the whole story about the intellect. The test case those thinkers took into account was the beatific vision, i.e. the face-to-face contemplation of God's essence that the blessed are believed to enjoy in Heaven. The beatific vision was commonly acknowledged to be or at least to involve an intellectual experience, but that intellectual experience could clearly not be described as an act of understanding God's essence in abstraction from God's existence. In fact, it seems to be a constitutive part of the beatific experience that God's essence be contemplated as present and existent. This feature of the beatific vision was stressed at least in part in order to distinguish the experience of the blessed in Heaven from the understanding of theologians on earth. Even the most learned theologian could not achieve, while on earth, the state of the blessed in Heaven. The difference between seeing God, on the one hand, and understanding what God is, on the other hand, is not a difference between understanding better and more and understanding worse and less. Rather, it is a difference between two *kinds* of cognitive state, only one of which can be described as an instance of understanding.[26]

Scotus himself took the beatific vision as the paradigmatic case of intuitive cognition. But unlike his immediate predecessors, he explored the deeper philosophical significance of the claim that the intellect is capable of intuitions. If the intellect is capable of intuitions, abstraction is not the only way the intellect can operate, but just one of two possible ways. Furthermore, it also appears that understanding should not be assumed as the intellect's paradigmatic state. Rather, contemplating something existent and present should be considered the better candidate, as Scotus explicitly claimed. Intuitive cognition is more perfect than abstractive cognition.[27]

Scotus was aware that extending the notion of intuitive cognition to the intellect was controversial. Several of his predecessors and contemporaries held that the intellect can pass from a potential to an actual state (i.e., that an intellectual cognitive state can occur) if and only if an intelligible species is present in the intellect. Scotus also noticed that Aristotle, whose main interest lay in the understanding of essences central to scientific knowledge, never mentioned intellectual intuition.[28] And Scotus granted that while the existence of abstractive acts can be established by an appeal to experience, there is more uncertainty concerning intellectual intuitions.[29] Undeterred by any of this, he gave some *arguments* to demonstrate that the human intellect is capable of intuitive cognition.

One of Scotus's arguments is theological. As I have mentioned, the very notion of intellectual intuition historically originated in order to account for the beatific vision as a "face-to-face" experience and differentiate it from the theologians' understanding of God's essence. So it is not surprising that one of the arguments to demonstrate the possibility of intellectual intuitive cognition is grounded on the notion of beatific vision. Seeing God's essence is an act of intellectual intuitive cognition; the blessed see God's essence; therefore, the human intellect must be capable of intuitive cognition.[30]

But Scotus also had some arguments of a purely philosophical character.

(a) By far Scotus's most common argument to demonstrate that the human intellect is capable of intuitions is based on the uncontroversial claim that we carry out sensory intuitions—we perform acts such as seeing and hearing. The argument runs as follows. (i) The senses perform intuitive acts. (ii) By an intuitive act, a cognitive power is related to its object as that object is really present in itself rather than by way of a likeness. (iii) To be related to an object as it is really present in itself rather than by way of a likeness is something that pertains to the perfection of a cognitive power. (iv) If something pertains to the perfection of a cognitive power and a lower cognitive power can do it, then a higher cognitive power is capable of doing it as well. (v) The intellect is higher than the senses. (vi) Therefore, the intellect is capable of performing intuitive acts.[31]

To put it mildly, interpreters have been unimpressed by this argument.[32] The hierarchy between cognitive powers, which is assumed without further evidence in premises (iv) and (v) sounds at best dubious. The same can be said about the notion of the perfection of a cognitive power, which is central to premises (iii) and (iv). Consequently, there seems to be no evidence for the claim that, if the senses can do something, the intellect must be able to do it as well.

An unprejudiced consideration of this argument, however, reveals some interesting aspects of Scotus's position.

So let us take a second look at what Scotus said. Premise (i) is uncontroversial and premise (ii) is just a consequence of Scotus's understanding of intuitive cognition, as was shown above. Scotus's contention in premise (iii) was that a cognitive power's optimal mode of operating occurs when that power is related to its object without the mediation of anything acting as causal proxy for its object. This claim is probably grounded on Aristotle's view that cognition is the identity between cognizer and thing cognized (*De anima* 3.4, 430a4). It seems to be preferable to achieve that identity with no causal intermediary intervening. So a cognitive power is better off if it can perform its act when its object is present in itself as opposed to by way of a causal proxy. Now abstractive cognition involves the presence of an intermediary that acts as causal proxy for the object—in the case of intellectual cognition, that intermediary is an intelligible species. By contrast, intuitive cognition obtains in the absence of any causal proxy. Therefore, there seems to be some evidence in support of the claim that intuitive cognition is more perfect than abstractive cognition and a cognitive power capable of intuitions is better off, *qua* cognitive power, than a power that is not capable of intuitions. As I have mentioned, contemplation rather than understanding is the paradigmatic cognitive state, according to Scotus. Intuition is cognition as it should be, abstraction is only the second best.

What about premises (iv) and (v)? The notion of a hierarchy of cognitive powers may sound antiquated, but by referring to it Scotus conveyed another key insight. His point was that the intellect is at least as well equipped as the senses to grant us access to the world in all its complexity. Scotus's claims in premises (iv) and (v) should be read as part of his larger project of vindicating the intellect in its autonomy from the senses as the best tool to reconstruct the structure of reality. Even though in this life the intellect may need to rely on the senses to grasp some key features such as existence, singularity, etc., in principle the intellect misses nothing—its scope encompasses anything whatsoever.[33]

(b) Another argument appears much less frequently in Scotus's writings but it will become Ockham's starting point in formulating a new theory of intuitive cognition. Unlike the previous argument, this argument is meant to establish not just that the human intellect is capable of intuitive acts, but also that it actually performs them. Scotus's idea was that we can account for our knowledge of contingent propositions (e.g. "Johnny is wearing a white shirt") only if we posit that our intellect performs intuitive acts. Scotus's argument runs as follows. (i) Our intellect knows that some propositions are contingently true (e.g., "Johnny is wearing a white shirt") and uses those propositions as premises in syllogisms. (ii) Forming a proposition, knowing that it is true, and engaging in deductive reasoning are all operations pertaining to the intellect. (iii) A contingent proposition can be known to be true only if the objects signified by its terms are cognized intuitively. (iv) Therefore, our intellect cognizes some objects intuitively.[34]

The idea behind premise (iii) is the standard view that necessary propositions are defined as propositions that are true by virtue of the signification of their terms—more specifically, in a necessary proposition the signification of the predicate-term is included in the signification of the subject-term (the common example was "A human being is an animal"). So in order to know that a necessary proposition is true, it is sufficient to know the signification of its terms. By contrast, contingent propositions are defined as non-necessary propositions—in contingent propositions, the signification of the predicate-term is *not* included in the signification of the subject-term. So, in order to know whether a contingent proposition is true, it is not sufficient to know the signification of its terms. It is also necessary to know that what is signified by the predicate term is actually joined to what is signified by the subject-term—in my example, that a white shirt is actually being worn by Johnny. But this additional knowledge can be gained only through an intuitive act—no amount of understanding what Johnny is and what a white shirt is will ever take me to the knowledge that Johnny is wearing a white shirt.[35]

Premise (ii) is particularly revealing. The view that forming a proposition, knowing that it is true, and engaging in deductive reasoning are all operations carried out by the intellect was not controversial. But Scotus was committed to a strong version of that view. His idea was not just that the intellect performs those operations, but that the intellect does so by itself and in complete autonomy from the senses. It may be true that right now the intellect has to rely on the senses to acquire information about the world. But if forming and assenting to propositions are activities pertaining to the intellect as its proper characteristics (Scotus uses the term *proprium*), the intellect must be capable of carrying them out without the help of any other cognitive power, at least in principle. So this premise takes us back to Scotus's vindication of the intellect's autonomy.

(c) Another argument for intuitive cognition is that, if our intellect were not capable of intuitions, we would not know that our acts are actually our own; but we do know that our acts are our own; therefore, our intellect is capable of intuitions.[36] The acts Scotus was referring to are "intrinsic acts," i.e. acts of our cognitive or volitional powers, such as seeing, thinking, loving, etc. Scotus established the second premise by an appeal to experience—I just know with certainty that the act of seeing a tree right now or of loving my siblings is *my own* act. Scotus even stated that, if somebody claims that she can doubt whether her acts are her own, she would not be a human being, because having an "interior vision" of one's own acts is experienced by all human beings and, so it seems, is a necessary feature of being human.[37]

(d) Connected with the previous argument is another argument for intellectual intuition that is mentioned very briefly in Scotus's works but is all the same worth relating. The argument runs as follows. (i) We have intellectual memory. (ii) Intellectual memory presupposes intellectual intuitive cognition. (iii) Therefore, we have intellectual intuitive cognition.[38]

By "intellectual memory," Scotus meant our intellect's capacity to remember some of its past acts. For example, I remember that I understood the Pythagorean theorem when I was eight. The idea behind premise (ii) is that an individual occurrence of an intellectual act, such as my understanding the Pythagorean theorem when I was eight, can be cognized only by an intellectual intuitive act. This seems plausible. Only the intellect is able to cognize its own acts. And the sort of cognition required in remembering is not an act of understanding what something is but the sort of direct acquaintance that only an intuition can give. I remember that I understood the Pythagorean theorem if I have an intellectual vision of my past act of understanding, not if I understand what understanding the Pythagorean theorem amounts to. Even though Scotus did not develop this point, his insight here is particularly interesting. The contention is that, whether or not we have intuitions of external objects, we certainly have intuitive access to our own acts.

* * *

As mentioned, Scotus's first and most common argument only establishes the human intellect's capacity for intuitions. By contrast, the other arguments establish that the human intellect actually carries out intuitions in this life. In this respect, Scotus probably changed his mind. At first, he explicitly ruled out that we have any intellectual intuition in this life. Later on, he came to the conclusion that even in this life the human intellect does perform some intuitive acts.[39] But a distinction should be drawn between intuitions of intellectual acts and intuitions of extramental objects. Scotus seemed to be pretty positive that our intellect intuits its own acts. As clear from the second argument reported above, Scotus also came to the view that intellectual intuition is necessary in order to account for our knowledge of contingent truths, which may concern extramental objects. But he seems to have thought that the intellect, while actually performing intuitions of extramental objects in this life, currently operates in conjunction with the senses, so that now intellectual intuitions are caused by prior sensory intuitions, and consequently every intellectual intuition of an extramental object is currently preceded or accompanied by a sensory intuition of the same object.[40] As to the question whether the object of an intuition is a singular or a common nature, Scotus held that it can be either.[41] Again, it seems that a distinction should be made between intellectual acts and extramental objects. With regard to intellectual acts, Scotus granted that the intellect intuits itself and its own acts as singulars. By contrast, with regard to extramental objects, Scotus's view seems to be that our intellect currently intuits common natures of extramental objects, so that it is possible to have numerically the same intuition of two distinct but indistinguishable singular objects.[42]

3. Ockham's criticism

Scotus's distinction between intuitive and abstractive cognition left a mark. Ockham was among those who took it over. Actually, it may be contended that intuitive cognition played a more important role for Ockham than it did for Scotus.[43] There are a number of differences between Ockham's and Scotus's accounts of intuitive and abstract cognition. For one, Ockham had none of Scotus's hesitations about our having intellectual intuitions in this life—he clearly stated that our intellect regularly performs intuitive acts, even though he added that our intellect can currently cognize material things only via the external senses.[44] He also held that intuitions are singular acts, i.e. their objects are individual things as opposed to universal concepts.[45] Moreover, Ockham rejected the view that abstractive cognition obtains by way of intelligible species. He held that not a species but a habit is the natural cause of abstractive cognition.[46] But more important is probably the different focus of Ockham's treatment of intuitive cognition. He took Scotus's brief mention that intellectual intuition is necessary in order to account for our knowledge of contingent truths as the centerpiece of his theory. For Ockham, the basic function of intuitive cognition is to provide the ground for evident knowledge of contingent propositions, where the knowledge of a true proposition is said to be "evident" if the knowledge of the simple terms that constitute that proposition is sufficient to cause the assent that the intellect gives to that proposition. The abstractive cognition of the terms of true necessary propositions is sufficient to cause our intellect's assent to their truth. For example, it is sufficient to know what "human being" and "animal" signify in order to assent to the truth of the proposition "A human being is an animal." By contrast, the terms of a true contingent proposition must be known by act of intuitive cognition if our intellect is to be able to assent to the truth of that proposition. For example, it is necessary to have an intuitive cognition of Johnny and of his white shirt in order to assent to the proposition "Johnny is wearing a white shirt."[47]

So, as Ockham himself was ready to admit, the raw materials of his theory of intuitive and abstractive cognition come from Scotus but they are put to a different use. In order to illustrate this point, I will consider Ockham's criticism of Scotus's definition of intuitive cognition.

As I have shown in the first section of this chapter, Scotus's account of intuitive cognition includes a mention of its cause. A cognitive act is intuitive if (a) its object exists and (b) the object causes the act by way of no causal proxy (so that, as a consequence, the existence of the object is necessary to keep the intuitive act about it in existence). Ockham lists no fewer than five different descriptions of intuitive cognition that Scotus gave in his works and criticized them all. His fundamental criticism, however, is directed at Scotus's causal account of intuitive cognition.

According to Ockham, Scotus failed to consider the possibility that God might directly cause an act of intuitive cognition. Acts of intuitive cognition are mental qualities. Because of his absolute power, God can sidestep secondary causes and cause directly any non-relative item (such as a quality). So, even though Ockham granted that, in ordinary circumstances, an intuitive act is caused by its object, he denied that this is necessarily so. Scotus's failure to take into account God's omnipotence was all the more surprising as he did not hesitate to rely on the view that God can cause directly any non-relative item in many other circumstances.[48]

As a consequence, Ockham gave an alternative definition of intuitive cognition, which was supposed to fix Scotus's blunder. Intuitive cognition must be defined not in terms of what causes it, but in terms of what it causes. Intuitive acts may or may not be caused by their objects. What is relevant to identify them as intuitive acts is that they cause the intellect's assent to contingent truths. As Ockham stated, an intuitive act is one by which the intellect is able to judge with evidence that a thing exists, if it exists, *or that it doesn't exist, if it doesn't exist*. The second clause of Ockham's definition points to a curious consequence of his shift of focus from the cause to the effect of intuitive acts. Since the actual existence of the thing cognized intuitively is contingent and irrelevant to the identity of an intuitive act about it, it is possible that God may cause an intuitive act about something that does not exist.[49] Even in that case, however, the intuitive act would still cause the intellect's assent to a contingent truth. Specifically, the intellect would assent to the contingent truth that the object of its intuitive act does not exist. So if God caused in me the act of seeing a patch of red when there is no patch of red to be seen, that act would still count as an intuition if and only if it made me assent to the proposition "The patch of red I am seeing does not exist."[50] Because even in that exceptional (indeed, miraculous) case an intuitive act would still issue in evident knowledge (i.e. the evident knowledge that what I am seeing does not exist), so Ockham's position does not have skeptical consequences.[51] From an historical point of view, however, it is probably accurate to say that it was Ockham who put the possibility of an intuition of non-existents on the philosophical map.[52]

Ockham's criticism of Scotus's views on intuitive cognition can be challenged on two accounts.

First, Scotus would grant that God can cause directly any non-relative item, but he would disagree that an intuitive act is *just* a non-relative item. Scotus's definition of an intuitive act in terms of its cause should not be read, as Ockham did, as a wrong definition of a quality but as the correct definition of an item composed of a quality *and* a relation, specifically, a relation to a cause. Similarly, if instead of considering the causal relation between an intuitive act and its object we focus on the intentional relation between that act and that object (which depends on the causal relation, as I have mentioned), an intuitive act can be considered as composed of a quality and a relation to an existing object. If the object does not exist, the relation does not obtain, and consequently, there is no intuitive act.[53] Since it is logically impossible for a relation to exist when its relata do not, Scotus would deny that God can cause an intuitive act when its object does not exist. Since an intuitive act is by its very nature caused by its object, if God caused an act directly in the human intellect, that act would not be intuitive, unless it were an intuitive act having God himself as its object (this is exactly what occurs in the beatific vision).

Second, Ockham was not always consistent in rejecting the way Scotus characterized intuitive cognition. Elsewhere, he contended that, even though God can cause an intuitive act directly in the human intellect, an intuitive act would still be "naturally suited" to be caused by a certain object—i.e. the object it is about.[54] This is an aspect on which the defenders of an externalist reading of Ockham's theory of cognition have insisted (according to such a reading, the content of acts of intuitive cognition is determined—at least in part—by the causal connection between those acts and their objects).[55] But then, Ockham helped himself with a way to define and distinguish intuitive acts that is very similar to what he criticized in Scotus. The only difference is that Scotus referred to the object's actual causation of the act whereas Ockham referred to the act's potential or dispositional power to be caused by a certain object. It may be contended that this is not a small difference. But the real question is, why didn't Ockham introduce a local fix to Scotus's account by reformulating it in terms of "natural suitability" to be caused by a certain object? Why did he prefer to replace Scotus's account with a different description in terms of what intuitive acts cause (i.e. assent to contingent truths)? Ockham's strategy against Scotus does not seem to be justified, as afterwards he seemed to realize that his own description should be supplemented with a reference to the natural cause of intuitive acts, i.e. their objects.[56]

So it is doubtful whether Ockham's criticism of Scotus was successful. But that criticism is extremely revealing of where Ockham's interests lie. Ockham focused on an intuitive act's ability to cause assent to a certain class of propositions. While for Scotus the primary instance of cognition was an act of contemplation of an existing object, Ockham's focus was on knowledge of propositions and mental language.

4. Conclusion

Scotus considered the distinction between intuitive and abstractive cognition to be a fundamental distinction cutting across both sensory and intellectual acts. He was also possibly the first to attempt a systematic account of the distinction between intuitive and abstractive acts. His different descriptions of intuitive cognition contain or imply a causal element—an intuitive act is caused by its object through no causal proxy, so that the existence of the object is necessary to keep that act in existence. By contrast, abstractive cognition occurs by way of a causal proxy for the object (an image or an intelligible species), which can cause the cognitive act even when the object has ceased to exist. Scotus's most original and controversial contribution was his claim that the human intellect is capable of intuitions. So intuitions can be intellectual as well as sensory. Several thinkers had already hinted at that possibility, but what they said had focused chiefly on the beatific vision. By contrast, Scotus built a theory that took intuitive acts as the paradigmatic instance of cognition. Abstractive cognition, typically exemplified by the act of understanding, turns out to be second best. A controversial but interesting aspect of Scotus's views on intellectual intuition was his vindication of the power of the pure intellect to grasp reality in all its aspects without the aid of the senses. Ockham's criticism of Scotus's account shifted the focus from the cause to the effect of an intuitive act, i.e. the assent to a contingent truth. It is doubtful, however, whether that criticism was successful. When not directly criticizing Scotus, Ockham himself resorted to a causal account of intuitive cognition not too different from the one Scotus gave.

Notes

1. I will base my analysis of Scotus's position on the following texts: *Lectura* II, distinction 3, part 2, question 2 (= *Lect.* II, d. 3, p. 2, q. 2), nos. 285–90 (Vat. XVIII, 321–23); *Ordinatio* II, distinction 3, part 2, question 2 (= *Ord.* II, d. 3, p. 2, q. 2), nos. 318–23 (Vat. VII, 552–54);

Lect. III, d. 14, q. 3, nos. 133–54 (Vat. XX, 349–54); *Ord.* III, d. 14, q. 3, nos. 107–13 (Vat. IX, 465–73); *Ord.* IV, d. 45, q. 3, nos. 17–21, ed. Wolter in Wolter and Adams (1993), 205–09; *Ord.* IV, d. 49, q. 12, no. 6 (Vivès XXI, 442); *Reportatio* IA, question 1, article 2 (= *Rep.* IA, q. 1, a. 2), nos. 153 and 164 (ed. Rodler, 88 and 143); *Quodlibet* (= *Quodl.*), q. 6, nos. 7–8 (Vivès XXV, 243–44); *Quodl.*, q. 13, nos. 8–10 (Vivès XXV, 521–22); *Quodl.*, q. 14, no. 10 (Vivès XXVI, 39); *Questions on the Metaphysics* (= *QMet.*) II, q. 2–3, nos. 80–81 and 109 (OPh III, 224–25 and 266); *QMet.* VII, q. 15, nos. 18, 27, 28, and 36 (OPh IV, 314–15, 317–18, 321). For the most comprehensive list of Scotus's and Ockham's passages on intuitive and abstractive cognition and a still valuable study (even though in need of several local revisions), see Day (1947). For more specific and updated works, see Richard E. Dumont (1968); Stephen D. Dumont (1989); Wolter (1990); Langston (1993); Pasnau (2003); and King (2007). In *Quodl.*, q. 13, no. 8 (Vivès XXV, 521), Scotus claimed that the distinction between intuitive and abstractive cognition can be applied not just to cognitive but also to appetitive acts (such as willing, loving, etc.). Unfortunately, he did not provide any example. In this chapter, I will consider exclusively cognitive acts.

2. *Quodl.*, q. 6, no. 8 (Vivès XXV, 244).
3. Ibid.
4. *Ord.* II, d. 3, p. 2, q. 2, no. 318 (Vat. VII, 552). See also *Lect.* II, d. 3, p. 2, q. 2, no. 285 (Vat. XVIII, 321).
5. *QMet.* II, q. 2–3, n. 109 (OPh III, 230–31).
6. *Quodl.*, q. 13, n. 8 (Vivès XXV, 521).
7. *Rep.* I-A, q. 1, a. 2, no. 153 (ed. Rodler, 88).
8. *Quodl.*, q. 13, no. 10 (Vivès XXV, 522).
9. *Ord.* IV, d. 10, q. 3, no. 404 (Vat. XII, 170).
10. Ibid. and *Ord.* IV, d. 49, q. 12, no. 6 (Vivès XXI, 442).
11. *Ord.* IV, d. 45, q. 2, no. 12 (Vivès XX, 305).
12. *Quodl.*, q. 13, no. 11 (Vivès XXV, 525).
13. *Quodl.*, q. 6, no. 8 (Vivès XXV, 244); *Ord.* II, d. 9, q. 1–2, no. 65 (Vat. VIII, 164–65). On Scotus's view that there is a relation between a cognitive act and its object that cannot be reduced to the causal relation ordinarily holding between them (even though in the case of the relation of contact, the former relation holds because the latter relation holds), see Pini (2011).
14. On the distinction between *secundum esse* and *in fieri* causes, see Garber (2001), 192 and Machamer and McGuire (2009), 45–6. The standard example of the latter kind of causation is the causal relation holding between a father and a child. The father is the cause of the child's coming into existence, but he is not necessary for the child's continuing to exist. The child can continue to exist even though her father dies. The role of the expression "objectively" in Scotus's description seems to be just to make it clear that the relevant thing to be considered in this causal account is the object of the intuitive act, i.e., what that act is about. For example, what should be considered in order to distinguish my act of seeing a color from my act of imagining a color is the way that color is causally related to both acts. Other things may play a causal role in the production of my acts (specifically, my sensory faculties). But those other causes are not relevant in this context.
15. In the light of my analysis, Scotus's account of intuitive cognition should be described as externalist, because the content of intuitive acts is determined by their causal connection to the objects in the cognizer's environment. It should be noticed that the object of an intuitive act is what is called a cause "with respect of the existence" (*causa secundum esse)* as opposed to just a cause "with respect to the coming to be" (*causa secundum fieri*) of the cognitive act. On that distinction, see Garber (2001), 192 and Machamer and McGuire (2009), 45–6.
16. *Quodl.*, q. 6, no. 7 (Vivès XXV, 243); q. 13, no. 8 (Vivès XXV, 521); *Ord.* II, d. 3, p. 2, q. 2, no. 318 (Vat. VII, 552); *QMet.* VII, q. 15, no. 18 (OPh IV, 299).
17. *Quodl.*, q. 13, nos. 13–14 (Vivès XXV, 539–41).
18. *Quodl.*, q. 13, no. 33 (Vivès XXV, 582–83).

19. *Quodl.*, q. 13, no. 10 (Vivès XXV, 522); *Ord.* IV, d. 49, q. 12, n. 6 (Vivès XXI, 442). See also Rep. IA, q. 1, a. 2, no. 153 (ed. Rodler, 88, n. 153), where Scotus stated that abstractive cognition occurs "by the species of an absent thing."
20. *QMet.* II, q. 2–3, no. 81 (OPh III, 225).
21. Notice, however, that God could create both an intelligible species and an abstractive act directly in an intellect. See Pini (2011).
22. *QMet.* II, q. 2–3, no. 113 (OPh III, 232). This is an objection, but Scotus agreed with its premise that there can be abstractive cognition when a cognitive power is able to retain the species in the absence of its object. For a similar point concerning sensory images, see *Ord.* IV, d. 45, q. 2, n. 12 (Vivès XX, 305).
23. *Quodl.*, q. 6, no. 8 (Vivès XXV, 244). See also *Ord.* IV, d. 10, p. 3, q. 2, no. 392 (Vat. XII, 168).
24. *Quodl.*, q. 14, no. 10 (Vivès XXVI, 29).
25. The point that Scotus is not a representationalist even in his account of abstractive cognition is rightly emphasized in Langston (chapter 19, this volume). But Langston wrongly held that scholars were induced to deny that an intelligible species is present in intuitive cognition because of their unjustified fear of making intuitive cognition an indirect form of cognition. Rather, the reason why scholars have held that there is no species in intuitive cognition is that Scotus explicitly said so. See for example *Ord.* II, d. 9, q. 1–2, no. 65 (Vat. VIII, 165) and *QMet.* II, q. 2–3, no. 109 (OPh III, 230–31). Scotus's claim fits well with the causal account that Scotus gave of intuitive and abstractive cognition as I have described it. The difference between intuitive and abstractive cognition is precisely that, because of the way our cognitive powers receive the causal action exercised by their objects, the existence of those objects is sometimes essential to the identity and permanence of those acts (if the acts are intuitive) and sometimes it is not, because of the presence of a causal intermediary (if the acts are abstractive).
26. See on these discussions Dumont (1989). Dumont also stressed that the claim that the blessed in Heaven have an intuitive cognition of God was repeatedly endorsed by Henry of Ghent, who was most likely Scotus's immediate source. See ibid., 583–4. The view that there is no intelligible species in the beatific vision had already been made by Giles of Rome, who was developing Thomas Aquinas's position. See for example Giles of Rome, *Quodl.* II, q. 21; *Quodl.* III, q. 14; *Quodl.* V, q. 9 (ed. de Coninck, 103–05, 171–5, 289–94). On Aquinas, see Torrell (1997).
27. *Ord.* II, d. 9, q. 1–2, no. 65 (Vat. VIII, 164–65); *De primo principio*, 4.89 (ed. Wolter, 149).
28. *QMet.* VII, 1. 15, no. 36 (OPh IV, 307) and *Ord.* IV, d. 45, q. 3, no. 17 (ed. Wolter and Adams, 205).
29. *Quodl.*, q. 6, nos. 7–8 (Vivès XXV, 243–44).
30. *Quodl.*, q. 13, no. 8 (Vivès XXV, 521); *Lect.* II, d. 3, p. 3, q. 2, no. 289 (Vat. XVIII, 322); *Ord.* II, d. 3, p. 2, q. 2, no. 322 (Vat. VII, 553). On the view that the blessed see God's essence, see Dondaine (1952).
31. *Quodl.*, q. 6, no. 8 (Vivès XXV, 243–44); q. 13, no. 8 (Vivès XXV, 521); *Lect.* II, d. 3, p. 2, q. 2, no. 287 (Vat. XVIII, 322); *Ord.* II, d. 3, p. 2, q. 2, no. 320 (Vat. VII, 552–54); *Ord.* IV, d. 49, q. 8, no. 5 (Vivès XXI, 306); *Ord.* IV, d. 49, d. 12, no. 3 (Vivès XXI, 440); *Rep.* I-A, Prol., q. 3, a. 2, no. 198 (ed. Rodler, 63); *QMet.* II, q. 2–3, no. 112 (OPh III, 231).
32. Pasnau (2003), 297.
33. See Pini (forthcoming).
34. *Ord.* III, d. 14, nos. 112–13 (Vat. IX, 467–69); *Ord.* IV, d. 45, q. 3, no. 17 (ed. Wolter and Adams [1997], 205). See also *Ord.* IV, d. 45, q. 2, no. 12 (Vivès XX, 305); *Lect.* III, d. 14, q. 3, nos. 149–51 (Vat. XX, 352–53).
35. *QMet.*, V, q. 5–6, nos. 60–65 (OPh III, 461–62). See Pini (2004).
36. *Ord.* IV, d. 43, q. 2, no. 11 (Vivès XX, 40); *Ord.* IV, d. 45, q. 2, no. 12 (Vivès XX, 305); *Ord.* IV, d. 49, q. 8, no. 5 (Vivès XXI, 306). See also *Quodl.*, q. 6, no. 8 (Vivès XXV, 244), where Scotus denied that a certain angel, say Michael, knows himself and his own acts in the same way he

knows another angel, say Gabriel, and the other angel's acts. While the first sort of knowledge is intuitive, the second sort of knowledge is abstractive and would remain the same even if Gabriel were annihilated.

37. *Ord.* IV, d. 43, q. 2, no. 11 (Vivès XX, 40).
38. *QMet.* VII, 15, no. 28 (OPh IV, 303).
39. Wolter 1990.
40. *Ord.* III, d. 14, q. 3, no. 117 (Vat. IX, 470). For the converse claim, namely that every sensory intuition is accompanied by an intellectual intuition, see *QMet.* II, q. 2–3, no. 114 (OPh III, 232); *Ord.* IV, d. 45, q. 3, no. 20 (ed. Wolter and Adams [1993], 208).
41. *Ord.* III, d. 14, q. 3, no. 111 (Vat. IX, 467).
42. *QMet.* VII, q. 13, no. 158 (OPh IV, 271). In that passage, Scotus claimed that the soul cannot mistake itself for another soul and that the same holds, perhaps, with regard to the soul's own acts. Notwithstanding the doubts Scotus cast on the knowledge of a soul's own acts as expressed by the adverb "perhaps," elsewhere he was quite confident in that respect, as I have mentioned above. See on this topic Pini (2008).
43. On Ockham's account of intuitive and abstractive cognition see Adams (1987), 501–15; Karger (1999); Panaccio (2004), 5–20; and Piché (2005) (which also collects Ockham's main texts on intuition and abstraction in both Latin and French translation).
44. Ockham, *Ord.*, Prol., q. 1 (OTh I, 27 and 67–68).
45. Ockham, *Quodl.* I, q. 13 (OTh IX, 73).
46. Ockham, *Ord.*, Prol., q. 1 (OTh I, 61).
47. Ockham, *Ord.*, Prol., q. 1 (OTh I, 6–7, 22–23, 31–32, 50 and 70).
48. Ockham, *Ord.*, Prol., q. 1 (OTh I, 33–38).
49. Ockham, *Ord.*, Prol., q. 1 (OTh I, 35, 38–39).
50. Ockham, *Ord.*, Prol., q. 1 (OTh I, 70–71). See Panaccio and Piché (2010). It would seem that a consequence of Ockham's view that God can cause an intuitive act even though its object does not exist would be that Ockham's account of intuitive cognition is internalist. See Brower-Toland (2007), contrary to King (2007); Normore (1990, 2003); and Panaccio (forthcoming). But for an answer to Brower-Toland, see Panaccio (2010).
51. Boehner (1943), Adams (1970).
52. Wood (1987).
53. Scotus held that a relation to an object pertains necessarily to both abstractive and intuitive acts, and in the case of intuitive acts the relation is both real and actual. See Scotus, *Quodl.*, q. 13, no. 11 (Vivès XXV, 525). As I have argued above, the special relation of contact holding between an intuitive act and its object is dependent on a causal relation between the act and its object, because it holds only if the object causes the act in a special way, i.e. as a cause *secundum esse.*
54. Ockham, *Quod.* I, q. 13 (OTh IX, 76); *Rep.* II, q. 12–13 (OTh V, 289).
55. See Panaccio (forthcoming).
56. Another perplexing aspect of Ockham's account of intuitive cognition is that the notion of intuitive cognition cannot be extended in a non-problematic way to non-human animals, as non-human animals are generally assumed to be unable to carry out judgments and to assent to propositions. But they clearly perform intuitive sensory acts, such as seeing, hearing, etc.

PART XI

Scotus and Ockham: A Debate over Universals and Individuation

Editor's Introduction

Suppose you are walking through a garden of red roses, all the same color. Suddenly you're struck by a puzzle: What exactly does it mean to say that they are all the *same* color? Your first thought is that if they're all red, there must be one property they all share in: redness. What could be plainer? But it then occurs to you that this answer is itself ambiguous. Is it numerically one property they all share? That would explain why you thought all the roses were the *same* color. But it would also be a metaphysically odd view, since it would require numerically the same color to be in many different items at the same time. Perhaps then what you are looking at in the roses are actually hundreds of different rednesses, all exactly alike. There would be no metaphysical oddity to that, since each instance of redness would be present in just one flower. But then you find yourself facing a new puzzle: What makes them all alike? If it's not a numerically single property of redness, then what do we mean when we say they are all exactly alike?

It is by reflecting on these sorts of questions that philosophers from classical Greece to our own time have raised those puzzles that make up the family of problems we call "the problem of universals." In the middle ages, treatments of the problem of universals reached new heights of sophistication. There is a consensus among contemporary scholars that two of the most important discussions are those by Scotus and Ockham. Yet if J.T. Paasch is correct, it is hard to assess that claim because it has not yet become clear just what Scotus's and Ockham's views actually are.

Paasch's investigation of Scotus and Ockham serves multiple functions for this volume. First, he outlines the various interpretive possibilities for understanding their views on universals, sketching the pros and cons of each alternative, thereby laying the foundation for debate over the correct interpretation. Second, in so doing, Paasch makes clear that many previous commentators have jumped to conclusions about what Scotus and Ockham think because they failed to see the different interpretive possibilities, together with their pros and cons. Third, Paasch offers some brief observations about how the medieval discussion is relevant to the contemporary debate over universals. Certain aspects of Scotus and Ockham's treatment map more or less squarely onto the contemporary discussion, and Paasch helps us to see how. However, the medieval debate took place in a very different intellectual milieu from ours, and so to understand Scotus and Ockham we cannot just look for ways in which their writings help us advance us in our projects. We must also become interested in *their* projects. Therefore, fourth, Paasch draws contemporary readers into the *medieval* debate by detailing William Ockham's criticisms of Scotus's and explaining how Scotus might reasonably reply to those criticisms.

Note on References

For works by Scotus and Ockham and their abbreviations, see the Note on References to Part 10. In his notes, Paasch cites both the Latin critical edition and (where relevant) the English translation in Spade (1994).

Further Reading

- Marilyn McCord Adams (1982). "Universals in the Early Fourteenth Century."
- Timothy B. Noone (1993). "Universals and Individuation."

CHAPTER 21

Scotus and Ockham on Universals and Individuation

JT PAASCH

It is sometimes said that the problem of universals is one of the key debates in medieval philosophy. It is also sometimes said that John Duns Scotus and William Ockham made some of the most important contributions to that debate.

Scotus's and Ockham's texts have been studied extensively, but it seems to me that a clear picture of their views has not emerged. The literature on the subject is vast, but sometimes it is confusing and hard to understand. Some of it is even riddled with technical ambiguities.

In situations like this, it can be useful to take a step back and identify the points of confusion as precisely as possible, for ambiguities and confusions are always easier to manage once we know what they are. In this chapter, I will not try to resolve any of the ambiguities and confusions. Rather, I simply want to identify them as clearly as I can.

In the first part, I will provide context by discussing the problem of universals in general, and by asking how Scotus and Ockham fit into that broader discussion. In the second and third parts, I will look at the specific views of Scotus and Ockham in turn.

1. The Problem of Universals, and where Scotus and Ockham Fit

When delving into the literature, one of the questions that comes to mind is this: what exactly *is* the problem of universals, and how do Scotus and Ockham offer solutions to it? The answers to these questions are not straightforward.

1.1 The Problem of Universals

Part of the confusion stems from the fact that the problem of universals is itself ambiguous. There are a number of different ways to interpret it, even in modern analytic philosophy. But allow me to restrict the scope and terminology by casting the problem as follows: how should we analyze sameness, or at least exact similarity?

We observe in the world around us that things are the same, or at least exactly similar, in a variety of ways. Electrons have the same charge, two apples might be the same shade of red, other objects might have the same size or shape, and so on. We can even speak like this about "natures"—i.e., the set of characteristics that define a species: all members of a species have the same nature, or at least exactly similar natures.

These kinds of observations can be expressed in a generic form. Whenever two things have a feature in common, one can say:

(1) For any *x* and *y*
that have some feature *F* in common,
the feature *F* of *x* and the feature *F* of *y*
are the same.

Or perhaps one would prefer to say:

(2) For any *x* and *y*,
x and *y* have a feature *F* in common if and only if
a feature F_1 of *x* and a feature F_2 of *y*
are exactly similar.

The basic question is, how should we analyze the notions of sameness or exact similarity that we find in these types of expressions? What does it mean to say that the *F* of *x* and *y* are the "same" or "exactly similar"?

1.2 Different Theories of Universals

One strategy is to ask: what are we referring to when we say two things have something in common? When we use expressions like (1) or (2), what does *F* refer to?

Does it refer to some *one* thing or entity in the world, outside the mind, which somehow stretches into both *x* and *y*? Or are there *two* exactly similar *F*s, one in *x*, and another in *y* (an F_1 and an F_2)? Or is *F* just a concept or linguistic category by which we sort *x* and *y* into the same group?

Those who say yes to the first question are called "realists" because they believe *F* refers to a real thing in the world that is present in many, and the term "universal" is the label given to such hypothesized entities.

There are, however, two different kinds of realists. Some think the universal exists outside individuals, as a kind of abstract entity that somehow gets reflected or cast onto each individual. These are called "extreme realists" or "Platonic realists" (since the view is allegedly inspired by Plato). Others maintain that the universal exists *in* the individuals, as a constituent or part of them. These are called "immanent realists" because they believe universals are immanent to (or present within) individuals.

Second, those who say there are two exactly similar *F*s (an F_1 and an F_2) are called "trope theorists." Since trope theorists do not believe in universals, they need a different label for each particular F_1, F_2, . . . F_n, and that is a "trope." (There are other labels for tropes, but "trope" is fairly standard, and I will use it here.)

Finally, those who say yes to the third question are often called "nominalists." This label can be ambiguous (more on that in a moment), but as I will use the term here, nominalists are united in their belief that there is no item in the world that corresponds to *F*. Rather *F* is just a general concept (concept nominalism), or perhaps even just a general linguistic predicate (predicate nominalism).

1.3 Strengths and Weaknesses

Each of these views has strengths and weaknesses. The realist has a straightforward way of parsing expressions of the form "the *F* in *x* and the *F* in *y* are the same." For those expressions will be true when *x* and *y* do indeed have a real connection with one and the same *F*.

On the other hand, universals are mysterious entities that are hard to believe in. If they are abstract, how do they get "reflected" in concrete space and time? (Abstract entities are precisely the kinds of things that do *not* exist in space and time.) Alternatively, if universals are immanent, how can they exist in many places at once—i.e., over here in *x*, but also over there in *y*? Surely a single item cannot exist in many places at once.

Trope theory can seem intuitive because we encounter, say, one patch of red over here (in one apple), and another similar patch of red over there (in another apple). So it seems natural to say we have encountered two (similar) patches of red.

Despite that, trope theory has difficulty explaining similarity. For the original question was "why are two things the same, or at least exactly similar?" To turn around and say, "because they are exactly similar" does not answer the question. It simply restates it.

Nominalism can be attractive because it does sometimes seem that much of the way we categorize the world is based on language, conceptual schemas, or even human convention. Nevertheless, are we really to believe that our categorizations correspond to nothing in reality? However much our linguistic, conceptual, and cultural conventions enter the picture, surely electrons have the same charge.

1.4 Confusing Labels

It is important to note that the labels "realist," "trope theorist," and "nominalist" as I am using them here are modern labels. But historians of philosophy sometimes use other labels that can lead to confusion.

One ambiguous label is "moderate realism." Some use it to refer to immanent realism, while others use it to refer to trope theory. Another ambiguous label is "nominalism." Some historians use it as I have here, but others use it to refer to trope theory.

So where do Scotus and Ockham fit into this taxonomy? As will become clear in what follows, the question is vexed. But even when we get past the labels, it is important to keep in mind that many still place Scotus and Ockham in different camps.

Sometimes the literature speaks of Scotus as if he were a realist[1]—and by that I mean an immanent realist, not a Platonic realist (so far as I know, nobody of note thinks Scotus is a Platonic realist).[2] On the other hand, the literature sometimes speaks of Scotus as if he were a trope theorist.[3] This is confusing, because immanent realism and trope theory are incompatible. Similarly, the literature sometimes speaks of Ockham as if he were a nominalist, but it also sometimes speaks as if he were a trope theorist.[4]

When it comes down to it, we are left with the question: which is it? Is Scotus an immanent realist or a trope theorist? And is Ockham a trope theorist or a nominalist?

2. John Duns Scotus

Scotus focuses on what I will call "individuals," that is, the everyday objects that Aristotle calls "substances," such as plants, animals, humans, or even sticks and stones.[5]

According to Scotus, every individual has two metaphysical parts: (i) a nature that it has in common with all members of its species, and (ii) a unique ingredient that no others have, which is typically called a "haecceity" or "individual difference."

This leads to three questions. First, in what sense do members of a species have a nature in "common"? Second, what role does the haecceity play in the individual? And third, how are the nature and haecceity connected in each individual?

2.1 Scotus on Common Natures

Scotus doesn't focus his questions around common natures. Instead, he focuses on individuals, asking: what makes them singular?[6] His views about common natures must be gleaned from that.

One of the options he considers is that individuals are intrinsically singular—they are singular in their very nature—and so they do not need to be *made* singular in any way.[7] Scotus rejects this view though, for as he sees it, members of a species must have a nature in common. If they didn't, absurd consequences would follow.

For instance, we would not be able to group things into species if every individual were so radically unique. Our concepts of various species would just be fictions of the mind, which Scotus thinks is absurd. Surely humans really are more like each other than they are like members of other species.[8]

Furthermore, we regularly make empirical observations which require some kind of commonality between things. We measure by standards that apply to more than one thing, and we judge that things are the same, similar, or equal in a variety of ways. None of that would be possible if every individual were totally unique, for nothing would really be the same.[9]

There is an ambiguity here. What exactly is the view Scotus is rejecting? There are two ways to interpret it. On the one hand, to say every individual is singular in its nature could mean that every individual has a *particular* nature rather than a *universal* nature. In other words, every nature is a trope:[10]

(3) For any physical individuals x and y
that are members of the same species S,

(i) the nature N_1 in x is a non-universal particular, and
(ii) the nature N_2 in y is a non-universal particular.

This does not necessarily imply that N_1 and N_2 will be unlike each other. They could be exactly similar, for tropes are commonly understood to be repeatable (natural forces can produce many individual copies of a trope, analogous to how a factory can produce many identical cars). The point is not that they are dissimilar; the point is that they are particulars.

Alternatively, to say every individual is singular in its nature could mean that each nature is utterly unique, and cannot be copied. In that case, N_1 and N_2 would indeed be dissimilar and unlike each other:

(4) For any physical individuals x and y,
the nature N_1 in x is not like the nature N_2 in y.

What Scotus thinks about common natures depends on which of these views he is rejecting. If he is denying that natures are particular (as (3) says), then he could be proposing they are universal:

(5) For any physical individuals x and y
that are members of the same species S,
the nature N in x and y is universal.

But if he is denying that each nature is unique (as (4) says), then he would simply be proposing that members of the same species have natures that are alike (whether they are universal or particulars):

(6) For any physical individuals *x* and *y*
that are members of the same species *S*,
the nature N_1 in *x* and the nature N_2 in *y*
are the same or exactly similar.

Unfortunately, the literature does not consistently distinguish between these two alternatives, and that can lead to confusion.

Scotus may offer some help, for he tells us how he defines universals. The mark of a universal, for him, is that we can identify it with each of its instances. As he puts it, we can say "this is this," where the first "this" refers to the instance, and the second "this" refers to the universal.[11]

This is a literal identification: when we identify each instance with the universal, we are saying each instance *just is* the universal. So, there is really just one of it, though it is wholly present in each individual that exemplifies it:

(7) For any nature *N*,
N is universal if and only if
for any *x* and *y* that have *N*,
N in *x* and *N* in *y* are numerically identical.

Given that definition of universals, Scotus goes on to claim that natures are *not* universal. As he sees it, only a generic concept can genuinely apply to each instance in this way, so only concepts can be "universal." In the physical world (outside the mind), nothing can be universal.[12]

The reason Scotus thinks universals are impossible seems to be that if they really did exist in many different things and places at once, then they would exist in many different states at once, which seems impossible. One rose might be flowering while another is dying, and how could a nature exist in both states?[13]

On the face of it, this suggests Scotus would reject (5) and opt for (6) instead, but we need to be careful here. It seems correct that Scotus's rejection of (7) means he rejects (5), but that doesn't mean he countenances (6), for he makes other claims that complicate the matter. Specifically, he says natures "of themselves" are neither universal nor particular, nor are they one or many. Of course, they always exist in some such state: they are always represented in the mind by universal concepts, and/or they are particulars in the world. But in and of themselves, natures are neither one nor the other.[14]

This can be read in two ways. On the one hand, Scotus could be making a negative claim: he could be proposing that natures *lack* any intrinsic restrictions on whether they can be represented with universal concepts, and on whether they can be copied in the world any number of times.

(8) For any nature *N*,
N has no intrinsic properties
that are incompatible with

(i) being represented by a generic concept, or
(ii) being instantiated as a particular *n* number of times.

On the other hand, Scotus could be making a positive claim: he could be proposing that natures have a special kind of intrinsic status where they are neither universal nor particular.

(9) For any nature *N*,
N exists such that intrinsically

(i) *N* is not universal, and
(ii) *N* is not one or more particulars.

Scotus further claims that, entirely apart from whether anyone ever thinks about them, natures really are common to a species, and they have a real intrinsic unity (it is, as he puts it, "less than numerical unity," but there is still some real unity there nevertheless).[15] This can certainly seem to buttress the idea that he thinks natures have a special kind of intrinsic status.[16]

If (9) were correct, Scotus would be neither an immanent realist, nor a trope theorist, for common natures would be neither universal nor particular. They may "become" universal (when we form generic concepts of them), and they may "become" particularized when they get instantiated, but prior to that, they intrinsically have a status that is neither.

Unfortunately, it is very hard to imagine what this special state could be like. If natures are neither universal nor particular, then what exactly are they? If they are not concepts or particular things in the world, then where exactly are they supposed to exist? Over here? Over there? (9) makes natures very mysterious sorts of beings.

Still, (9) would allow Scotus to differentiate between natures in this special state and natures in their particularized instantiations. Indeed, some have argued that Scotus thinks natures "of themselves" are potential with respect to their actual instances, and there is no contradiction in saying that qua potential, a nature is (or is not) universal, while qua actual, an instance is particular.

But this merely seems to relocate the problem. It is like stepping on a bump in the rug, only to find that it pops up somewhere else. For now we are left with natures that exist in a "potential" state, but that seems just as mysterious. What exactly are natures in this "potential" state supposed to be like? Are they ghostly or shadowy sorts of entities? And where are they supposed to exist?

On the other hand, if (8) were correct, Scotus would not be making any claims at all about whether natures are universal or particular. Rather, he would simply be claiming that there is nothing in a nature that prevents it from getting repeated or copied any number of times, and there is nothing in it that prevents it from getting represented by a generic concept.

It could also be that Scotus is trying to define repeatability. That is to say, he could be proposing that something is repeatable if there is nothing in it that is incompatible with it getting repeated or copied. (It would be *impossible* for it to be repeated or copied if it did have some intrinsic feature that were *incompatible* with repetition.) So, one could interpret (8) like this:

(10) For any nature *N*,
N is repeatable if and only if
N has no intrinsic feature *F*
that is incompatible with *N* getting repeated.

Given all these alternatives, what exactly does Scotus mean when he says a nature is "common" to every member of a species? Surely he does not think natures are immanent universals, since he explicitly rejects the possibility that numerically one and the same item can exist in multiple individuals at once.

But he could have something like trope theory in mind. In that case, a nature would be "common" to every member of a species in the sense that each has an exactly similar copy of it. Alternatively, he could be proposing that intrinsically, natures have a kind of hybrid status, where they are neither universal nor particular. So which is it?

2.2 Scotus on Haecceities

The other component in individuals is the haecceity, a component that is totally unique and not common to anything else. Throughout his career, Scotus discusses at least six different theories which each try to explain why physical substances are individuals, and he rejects all but the last (his own theory).

The most interesting of the rejected theories claims substances are individual through their bodies. As Scotus puts it, they are individual through their "quantity," or how much of them there is that takes up space.[17] This seems plausible enough, for bodies do seem to be unrepeatable. (Even if scientists could clone me, for example, they would still have to replicate my genes in separate cells.)[18]

But Scotus rejects this because bodies often change size. If an individual were tied so tightly to the physical size of its body, then a new individual would come into being every time its body grows or shrinks, which seems absurd.[19]

One way to remedy this might be to propose that individuality is due not to the specific size of the individual's body, but rather to the matter it is made from.[20] That way, even if a body gains or loses pieces of matter, it would still be the same (growing and shrinking) body so long as it is composed of the same (growing and shrinking) lump of matter.

Scotus rejects this too though, since the same pieces of matter can end up in different individuals. As natural forces operate on the basic matter in the universe, it is constantly getting formed into new things. What happens if two objects get formed (one after the other) from the same pieces of matter? Surely individuals cannot be tied so tightly to the matter they are composed of.[21]

Since individuality cannot be explained by the "bodies" theory (or any of the other first five theories he discusses), Scotus feels he must go with a sixth option: he must postulate a special entity to explain individuality, and that is a haecceity. Each haecceity is totally unique: there are no others like it.[22]

(11) For any haecceities H_1 and H_2,
H_1 and H_2 are not exactly alike.

Individuals that have a haecceity will also be unique. No matter how many other components two individuals might have in common, if each has a unique haecceity, they will be different at least in that respect.[23]

(12) For any physical individual x
that has a haecceity H_1 as an essential part,
and for any physical individual y
that has a haecceity H_2 as an essential part,
x and y are not exactly alike.

So for Scotus, a physical substance is an individual precisely because it has this special component that is totally unique to it, and it will remain that individual so long as it has that unique haecceity.

Still, there is an ambiguity here too, for haecceities function differently depending on whether natures are immanent universals, tropes, or neither. For example, if Scotus thinks natures are immanent universals (which is unlikely, as already noted, but bear with me for the sake of the argument), he would need haecceities to explain why members of the same species are numerically distinct. For they would need something besides their shared universals to individuate them:

(13) For any physical individuals x and y that share
the (numerically) same constituent F as an essential part,
x and y are (numerically) distinct if and only if

(i) x has a constituent G as an essential part,
(ii) y has a constituent H as an essential part, and
(iii) G and H are (numerically) distinct.

On the other hand, if Scotus thinks natures are repeatable tropes, he would not need haecceities to explain why each individual is distinct, for tropes are distinct particulars (by definition). Even if two individuals were composed of (exactly similar) bundles of tropes, they would still be distinct.

Nevertheless, one might believe individuals cannot be repeated in any strict sense. For instance, one might say that, even if scientists could clone me, the clone would not be another "me," strictly speaking. It would be another human being (who happens to look and act a lot like me).

But if that is right, then what is it about *me* that is so unrepeatable?[24] Scotus could say it is a haecceity, and that would explain why I cannot be copied, even if all of my other characteristics (tropes) can:

(14) For any physical individual *x*
that has one or more repeatable tropes *F*,
x cannot be copied if and only if
x has at least one unrepeatable trope *G*.

A third possibility: if Scotus thinks natures are shadowy entities that are neither universal nor particular, then the haecceity would presumably be needed to explain how natures get instantiated. For since natures would be neither universal nor particular in their purest state, they would somehow need to be drawn out of that into actual instantiations. And the haecceity would perform that role by "contracting" the nature into an actualized instance.[25] Something like this:

(15) For any physical individuals *x* and *y*
that share a nature *N*,
x and *y* are discrete individuals if and only if

(i) *x* has a unique haecceity H_1

that contracts an instance of *N* as N_1,

(ii) *y* has a unique haecceity H_2

that contracts an instance of *N* as N_2,

(iii) H_1 and H_2 are not (numerically) identical, and
(iv) N_1 and N_2 are not (numerically) identical.

In all of this, what is clear is that Scotus believes haecceities are unique, unrepeatable entities that are an essential component of each and every physical individual. What is less clear is how exactly they "individuate" those individuals.

2.3 Scotus on How Natures and Haecceities Combine

Scotus famously claims that a nature and haecceity combine to form an individual, and the result is that the two are "really the same," yet they are "formally distinct."[26] What does this mean? There are two parts to it. First, what does Scotus mean by "really the same," and second, what does he mean by "formally distinct"?

As for the first, he explains elsewhere that two items are really distinct if they can be separated—that is to say, if one can exist without the other:[27]

(16) For any *A* and *B*,
A and *B* are really distinct if

(i) *A* can exist without *B*, or
(ii) *B* can exist without *A*.

From this we can infer that two items are really the same if they cannot be separated:

(17) For any *A* and *B*,
A and *B* are really the same if

(i) *A* cannot exist without *B*, and
(ii) *B* cannot exist without *A*.

Separability can only be a sufficient condition, not a necessary one, for Scotus believes there are cases where the items in question are really distinct, even though they cannot be separated. For instance, he maintains that the persons of the Trinity are really distinct from each other, but they cannot be separated off so that one exists in isolation from the others.

In the physical world though, separability is sufficient, and that is what Scotus presumably has in mind for natures and haecceities: in an individual they are "really the same" in the sense that they cannot be pulled apart.

(18) For any physical individual *x*
that has a nature *N* and a haecceity *H*,
N and *H* are really the same if
N and *H* cannot be separated.

The second question is what does Scotus mean when he says the nature and haecceity are "formally distinct"? He explains elsewhere that two things are formally the same if (a) they are really the same (that is, they cannot be pulled apart), and (b) they have the same definition (or would have if they were definable).[28]

(19) For any *A* and *B*,
A and *B* are formally the same if

(i) *A* and *B* are inseparable, and
(ii) *A* and *B* have the same definition

(or would have if they were definable).

From this we can infer that two things will be formally distinct if (a) they are really the same, but (b) they have different definitions (or would have if they were definable):[29]

(20) For any *A* and *B*,
A and *B* are formally distinct if

(i) *A* and *B* are inseparable, and
(ii) *A* and *B* have different definitions

(or would have if they were definable).

So, when Scotus says the nature and haecceity in an individual are formally distinct, he means that although they cannot be pulled apart, they still have different defining characteristics.

Nevertheless, there are ambiguities here too. Sometimes specialists speak about the formal distinction as if it were a kind of identity. This can be confusing, for according to many modern accounts, identity satisfies Leibniz's Law: if *A* and *B* are identical, they have the same properties.

(21) For any *A* and *B*,
if *A* is identical to *B*,
then if *A* is *F*, *B* is *F*.

Formally distinct items, however, do not satisfy Leibniz's Law, for they will differ at least in the fact that each has a different definition. Hence:

(22) For any *A* and *B*,
if *A* and *B* are formally distinct,
then if *A* is *F*,
it is not necessarily the case that *B* is *F*.

Furthermore, identity is typically understood to be transitive:

(23) For any *A*, *B*, and *C*,
if *A* is identical to *B* and *B* is identical to *C*,
then *A* is identical to *C*.

But again, the formal distinction is not like this. If one thing is formally distinct from another, and that other is also formally distinct from a third, that does not mean the first is formally distinct from the third as well.

A case in point is the Trinity (again). Scotus maintains that each divine person (Father, Son, and Spirit) are really the same as, though formally distinct from, the divine essence. But that does not mean the persons are formally distinct from each other. Rather, they are really distinct from each other. So the formal distinction cannot be transitive:

(24) For any *A*, *B*, and *C*,
if *A* is formally distinct from *B* and
B is formally distinct from *C*,
it is not necessarily the case that
A is formally distinct from *C*.

Given that, it is hard to see how the formal distinction could count as a kind of identity. If it does not conform to Leibniz's Law and it is not transitive, then it seems to be something else altogether.

An alternative interpretation is to say the formal distinction is a kind of unification or unity relationship rather than a kind of identity. That is to say, it is not about two things being the *same*; rather, it is about two things being unified or bound together (very, very tightly).

Unification is a possible fit because it does not conform to Leibniz's Law, and it is not transitive. Indeed, if any two things are unified, they will still have their own properties, as (22) says. And if one thing is (directly) united to another, and that other is (directly) united to a third, the first need not be (directly) united to the third as well, as (24) says.

On this front too though, it is far from clear exactly what Scotus's view is. As we shall see, Ockham attacks Scotus's formal distinction, arguing that it is either incoherent in itself, or that it leads to incoherence. But it seems to me that we cannot decide whether this is so until at least some of the ambiguities discussed here are clarified.

3. Ockham on Universals

As many a student of philosophy knows, Ockham is history's token nominalist, even though the "nominalist" label is ambiguous. The reason typically given for Ockham's nominalism is that he rejects universals, insisting instead that every extant entity is individual or particular. As we shall see though, even this is ambiguous, for the precise sense of "individual" or "particular" is not clear.

3.1 Ockham Against Immanent Realism

In the *Ordinatio* and elsewhere, Ockham criticizes a number of different theories about universals, but the most relevant for this context are his critique of immanent realism, and his critique of Scotus's theory.

Ockham rejects immanent universals on the grounds that, as he sees it, no one thing can exist in other things (each of which are also one thing).[30] One might formulate the point like this:

(25) For any *x*, *y*, and *z*,
x cannot exist in *y* and *z* simultaneously if

(i) *x* is one thing,
(ii) *y* is one thing, and
(iii) *z* is one thing.

This, however, depends on what it means to be "one thing." The frame of a car extends into the front and back halves of the vehicle, even though the frame seems to be one thing, and the front and back halves each seem to be one thing too. The scope of (25) needs to be restricted.

Suppose we assume "one thing" refers to items that can occupy only one region of space at a time:

(26) For any *x* in the physical world
x is "one thing" if and only if
for any time *t* during *x* 's lifespan,

(i) *x* occupies one region of space R_1, and
(ii) *x* occupies no other non-overlapping region of space R_2.

Then (25) should be reformulated along these lines:

(27) For any *x*, *y*, and *z*,
each of which are "one thing",
x cannot exist in *y* and *z* simultaneously if

(i) *x* occupies one region of space R_1,
(ii) *y* occupies another region of space R_2,
(iii) *z* occupies another region of space R_3, and
(iv) none of R_1, R_2, or R_3 overlap.

That proposition seems evidently true, for if an item can occupy only one region of space at any given time, then of course it could not be "in" other individuals that occupy different regions of space simultaneously.

But the immanent realist would say:

> You're begging the question. Universals are not "one thing" in the sense specified by (26). The whole premise of immanent realism is that univer-

> sals *are* capable of wholly existing in many places at once. So, of course items that are restricted to *one* place cannot exist in *other* places too, but immanent universals are not like that.

Ockham seems aware of this objection, because he spends a good deal of time trying to show that the immanent realist has no reason to think a universal is "one thing" in a different way than non-universal items.[31]

Suppose we drill down to the simplest metaphysical parts or constituents that go into an individual—i.e., to the parts or constituents that have no further parts or constituents themselves. And suppose that leaves us with, say, simple universals, haecceities, and the like.[32]

Now take one of the simple universals and one of the non-universal items (a haecceity, for instance). Why think one of these should be more "one thing" than the other? (Or, to employ (27) again, why think one of them could, while the other could not, exist in more than one place simultaneously?) At this level of granularity, Ockham can see no obvious reason to think this.[33] It seems to be an arbitrary stipulation.

Of course, the immanent realist might respond by saying, "it is because the universal is common to other individuals, whereas the haecceity is not." But Ockham could say that begs the question. If the query is "why is it common?" the answer cannot be "because it is common."[34]

I am not sure this argument succeeds, but it may be the strongest argument Ockham makes against the immanent realist. He does provide other arguments, but they seem weaker.

For example, Ockham claims: if natures were immanent universals, God would not be able wholly to create another member of a species after the first, since the universal would already exist in the first.[35] Likewise, God would not be able wholly to annihilate any member of a species except the last, for the universal would continue to exist in the survivors.[36] Ockham finds this absurd.[37]

Furthermore, Ockham claims that universals would be able to exist without any individuals. Consider the fact that any member of a species can die, thereby severing its connection with the universal. If this can happen with each member of the species taken separately, then surely it could happen with all of them taken collectively. The universal could (at least by God's power) exist without any individuals at all. Ockham finds this absurd too.[38]

Whatever the merit of these arguments, it is unclear why the immanent realist would not simply just accept their conclusions. Why not accept that God could sustain a universal all by itself without any individuals? If it really is a distinct constituent in things, why couldn't God separate it off?

Similarly, why not accept that God could only wholly create the first member of a species or wholly annihilate the last (unless he created or annihilated all of them at once)? Why not reserve the labels "creation" and "annihilation" for these special cases of *total* creation and annihilation?[39]

Another argument Ockham offers runs as follows. Since particular accidents inhere in particular individuals, it follows that universal accidents would inhere in those individuals' universal natures:[40]

(28) For any universal accident *F*
and any universal nature *N*,
F inheres in *N* if
F is found to inhere in an individual with *N*.

Now suppose two incompatible accidents exist in different individuals with the same nature. For example, imagine that one stone is bleached white while another remains black. According to (28), it would follow that the universals of white and black would then inhere in the universal nature of stones. But that seems impossible, since black and white are incompatible (nothing can be fully both at the same time).[41]

This is perplexing, since (28) seems dubious. It would only follow if "to inhere in" means something like "to stick in," as a pin sticks in a cushion. But why think that? Why not hold instead that, say, "to inhere in" means "to happen to occupy the same region of space"? Then one could say "this stone is white and that stone is black" because a stone universal and a white universal both happen to be here in this spot, while a stone universal and a black universal both happen to be over there in that spot.

None of Ockham's arguments against immanent realism seem particularly persuasive. At best, they identify certain edge cases that the immanent realist may not typically consider (like God creating the first member of a species). But Ockham does not seem to present anything insuperable.

3.2 Ockham Against Scotus

Ockham attacks Scotus's theory of universals on two fronts. First, as mentioned already he rejects the formal distinction. According to Ockham, no *A* and *B* can be "formally distinct" in the way Scotus defines it.[42]

To establish this, Ockham assumes (rightly) that Scotus must admit that contradictory things are true of natures and haecceities. For instance, Scotus holds that natures are repeatable (in some sense), while haecceities are not.[43] Hence:

(29) For any nature *N* and haecceity *H*,
(i) something *F* is true of *N*, and
(ii) something not- *F* is true of *H*.

Ockham next claims that contradictory things can be true of any *A* and *B* in only three cases. First, if *A* and *B* are really distinct things in reality (outside the mind). For example, since Socrates and Plato really are different people, Socrates can be in the market even while Plato is not.

Second, contradictory things can be true of *A* and *B* if they are distinct concepts. I can imagine Socrates as prone to anti-social behavior, even while I imagine Plato as being the opposite, because my concepts of Socrates and Plato are distinct.

Third, if *A* is a concept and *B* is a real thing in the world, then something can be true of one but not the other. I might believe Socrates is still alive, whereas the real Socrates has long since died, because my concept of Socrates is different from the real Socrates.[44]

(30) For any A and B,
F and not- *F* can be true of *A* and *B* only if

(i) *A* and *B* are really distinct things in the world,
(ii) *A* and *B* are really distinct concepts, or
(iii) *A* is a real thing in the world and *B* is a concept.

Ockham next claims that Scotus denies (i) and (ii), which leaves (iii), and he concludes that any difference we might detect between a nature and the individual it belongs to arises from the fact that the "nature" is just a *concept* we have of the individual.[45]

It seems to me Ockham could formulate a better argument from (30). Natures and haecceities are not just represented by concepts for Scotus. They are real parts or constituents of individuals.

(31) For any real nature *N* and real haecceity *H*,

(i) *N* is not a concept, and
(ii) *H* is not a concept.

That rules out (ii) and (iii) in (30), and the only option left is (i), which says contradictory things can be true of *A* and *B* only if they are really distinct things in the world. Hence, Ockham could point out that, by (30), Scotus's theory entails:

(32) For any real nature *N* and real haecceity *H*,
N and *H* must be really distinct.

As mentioned earlier though, Scotus denies this, insisting instead that the nature and haecceity are only *formally* distinct, not *really* distinct:

(33) For any individual *x*
that has a real nature *N* and real haecceity *H*,
N and *H* are not really distinct.

And (33) contradicts (32). So Ockham could argue that, given (30), Scotus's claim that *A* and *B* can be really the same and yet have contradictory characteristics is itself a contradiction.

Still, even that is not very convincing, for notice that (30) is built around only two types of entities: real things and concepts. But Scotus might believe in a third type of entity—those shadowy natures that count as neither extant particulars nor universal concepts. If that is right, Ockham's (30) begs the question, because it does not take into account Scotus's alleged shadowy natures.

Alternatively, if Scotus believes natures and haecceities are tropes, Ockham could reformulate (30) like this:

(34) For any *A* and *B*,
F and not- *F* can be true of *A* and *B* only if

(i) *A* and *B* are really distinct tropes in the world,
(ii) *A* and *B* are really distinct concepts, or
(iii) *A* is a real trope in the world and *B* is a concept.

This might seem better, for if Scotus believes natures are just tropes, then (34) would not omit any special type of entity that Scotus countenances. Nevertheless, (34) fares no better than (30), for Scotus could simply say that (i)–(iii) in either (34) or (30) is not a complete list: there should also be a fourth option, namely cases where *A* and *B* are formally distinct:

(35) For any *A* and *B*,
F and not- *F* can be true of *A* and *B* only if

(i) *A* and *B* are really distinct tropes in the world,
(ii) *A* and *B* are really distinct concepts,
(iii) *A* is a real trope in the world and *B* is a concept, or
(iv) *A* and *B* are formally distinct tropes in the world.

Another reason Ockham rejects Scotus's formal distinction is that he thinks it leaves no way to distinguish between (a) *really* distinct things, and (b) *formally* distinct things. To make this case, Ockham claims that the primary way we tell if two items are really distinct is if contradictory things are true of them.[46]

(36) For any *A* and *B*,
A and *B* are really distinct if

(i) something *F* is true of *A*, and
(ii) something not- *F* is true of *B*.

But, Ockham points out that, according to Scotus, contradictory things can be true of formally distinct things too (see (29) above). And if contradictory things can be true of both really distinct things and formally distinct things, then there is no way to distinguish between the two cases.[47]

This too is unpersuasive, for (36) begs the question as well. Scotus would outright deny it, insisting instead that on his theory, formally distinct items can and do have contradictory things true of them too.

There is one other iteration here. Ockham's (30), (34), and (36) assume that formally distinct items can bear different properties (in particular, they can bear contradictory properties). But suppose Scotus changed his mind later in his life, so as to think not that formally distinct items bear different properties, but rather that the distinction between them is diminished.[48] In that case, (30), (34), and (36) might not apply.

But that does not seem right, for Scotus was happy to admit even late in his life that a nature and haecceity have different definitions (or would have, if they could be defined). And Ockham would no doubt reply that if some *A* and *B* really *are* just one and the same thing, then surely they cannot have different definitions:

(37) For any *A* and *B*, and
for the definition D_1 of *A* and
the definition D_2 of *B*,
D_1 and D_2 cannot be different if
A and *B* are one and the same thing.

Unfortunately, this too begs the question, for Scotus could simply reject (37), and say that his theory claims precisely that natures and haecceities *can* have different definitions. Ockham cannot stipulate the contrary and call that an "argument."

In the end, Ockham's attempts to reject Scotus's formal distinction fail. At best, he offers a series of theses that stipulate the contrary of what Scotus claims. This is useful for understanding what Ockham thinks, but it is not so useful as a critique of Scotus.

3.3 Ockham Against Scotus Again

The other major criticism Ockham levels against Scotus is that Scotus seems to make inconsistent claims about natures. On the one hand, Scotus likes to say natures are common, but on the other hand, he likes to say they are particular. To be common and particular are, so far as Ockham is concerned, entirely opposite and contradictory. Nothing could be both at the same time.

However, this depends on the assumption that "to be common" means "to be numerically the same in many things":

(38) For any x, y, and F,
F is common to x and y if and only if
F is numerically the same in x and y

and that "to be particular in many things" means "to be numerically distinct in many things":

(39) For any x and y,

(i) there is no F that is numerically identical in x and y,
(ii) there is an F_1 in x,
(iii) there is an F_2 in y, and
(iv) F_1 and F_2 are numerically distinct.

If Scotus really thought natures are both "common" and "particular" in these ways, then his theory would indeed collapse into contradiction, for (38) and (39) are contradictory.[49]

But Scotus may not make this mistake, since he denies (38). As mentioned earlier, Scotus rejects immanent universals because, at least in the physical world, no one thing could be numerically the same in different individuals (recall Scotus's rejection of (7) above).

Furthermore, one needn't interpret "to be common" as "to be numerically the same" (as (38) does). It could just mean that a number of individuals have exactly similar copies of something. Lollipops have a variety of features in common, one of which is that they all have sticks. But that does not mean they have the numerically same stick, and that is perfectly compatible with (39).

On this front too, Ockham's critique seems somewhat lackluster, for it would only hold good if Scotus really thought natures were both "common" and "particular" in the sense of (38) and (39). But there is no reason to think Scotus would defend (38). On the contrary, he seems to outright deny it.

3.4 *Ockham's Own Theory*

As for his own view, Ockham believes that every extant entity is particular. Nothing in the world (outside our minds) can be a universal. Rather, everything must be individual.[50]

(40) For any extant x,
x is individual.

This, however, is ambiguous. On the one hand, it could mean simply that every extant entity is *not* a universal. Or, to use the modern label, every extant entity is a trope:

(41) For any extant *x*,
x is a non-universal particular.

On the other hand, (40) could mean that every entity is entirely unique and unrepeatable—there can be no others like it:

(42) For any extant *x*,
x cannot be repeated or copied.

These are very different propositions. Individual entities as defined by (41) can be repeated: there can be many copies of tropes, for example, each of which is exactly similar. But individual entities as defined by (42) cannot be repeated, since each is entirely singular and unique.

The scholarship rarely attends to this distinction, but it has a significant bearing on how we interpret Ockham's theory of universals. If he maintains (41), Ockham would just be a trope theorist, in which case he could say different individuals are members of the same species because they have exactly similar nature-tropes.[51]

But if he maintains (42), individuals would have nothing in common. In that case, Ockham would have to admit that our grouping of individuals into species is based not on some copied feature, but rather that it is an artifact of our language or our conceptual schemas. And that would make him more of a predicate or concept nominalist.

Ockham does try to explain how we conceive of different individuals as belonging to the same kind. In the *Ordinatio*, he entertains six different theories, each of which tries to explain how concepts (or at least our acts of understanding) represent or apply to different individuals.[52]

On this issue, though, Ockham is somewhat non-commital: he feels that any of those theories are preferable to the realist or Scotistic theories he has already rejected.[53] In later writings, Ockham seems to argue for one particular theory over the others, but it is difficult to tell if he really does prefer that theory, since the later writings may just be an exercise in debate.

But that is an issue that cannot be settled here. What is clear, and relevant for our purposes, is that Ockham thinks concepts (or at least acts of understanding) *can* and *do* represent or apply to many individuals.

Still, what is the basis for this? Why can different individuals be represented by the *same* concept (or act of understanding) in the mind? If Ockham were a trope theorist in line with (41), he could say it is because each member of the species has an exactly similar nature-trope, and our concept represents that nature-trope.

But if he held every extant entity were entirely unique (as (42) says), he would not be able to say our concepts are based on any real similarities. Rather, he would have to say our concepts are artifacts of our language or conceptual schemas.

So Ockham's own view is just as ambiguous as Scotus's. He could be a trope theorist, but he could also be a conceptualist who identifies sameness and similarity with linguistic or mental functions.

4. Conclusion

Scotus and Ockham on universals is a topic that suffers from ambiguities and confusions. Scotus and Ockham are clearly very sophisticated thinkers, and the scholars who write about them are too. But the problems are difficult, and they are technical.

Scotus believes individuals comprise a common nature and a unique haecceity, and that the nature and haecceity are really the same but formally distinct. Yet the sense in which the nature is "common" and the sense in which the nature and haecceity are "formally distinct" are far from clear. Ockham, for his part, rejects immanent realism, and he rejects Scotus's theory too. But at best, his arguments seem unpersuasive, or they beg the question, and it is unclear if Ockham should best be construed as a trope theorist, or a concept nominalist.

It seems to me that whether or not Scotus and Ockham made an important contribution to the problem of universals remains an open question. Answering it, I think, requires resolving at least some of the ambiguities and confusions detailed here, with definitive analysis to back it up. That is a task for future research.

Notes

1. E.g. Mertz (1996).
2. Scotus seems to deny Platonic realism outright. See, for instance, Lect., 2.3.1.1, n. 38 (Vat. 18: 239.11–14, 239.19).
3. For example, Anthony Kenny writes: "To solve this enigma, Scotus introduces a new complication. Any created essence, he says, has two features: replicability and individuality. My essence as a human being is replicable: there can be, and are, other human beings, essentially the same as myself. But it is also individual: it is *my* essence" (Kenny 2007, 206). I am not sure if Kenny means to suggest that Scotus is a trope theorist here, but it is easy enough to see how he could be read that way.
4. See, for instance, Lahey (1998).
5. Scotus also believes in immaterial substances (like angels and God), but to keep things simple, I will concentrate only on physical substances.
6. Ord., 2.3.1.1 (Vat. 7: 391.9-10; Spade, 57).
7. Ord., 2.3.1.1, n. 1 (Vat. 7: 391.14-392.2; Spade, 57).
8. Ord., 2.3.1.1, n. 23 (Vat. 7: 400.21-401-2; Spade, 62).
9. See Ord., 2.3.1.1., nn. 11–15 (Vat. 7: 396–397; Spade, 59–60); Lect. 2.3.1.1, nn. 13–17 (Vat. 18: 232.16-233.18), and Ord., 2.3.1.1, n. 18 (Vat. 7: 398.13-17; Spade, 61).
10. Some specialists might shy away from the label "trope" because they think it has too much philosophical baggage. I do not share these fears, and I see no reason why the modern label "trope" isn't perfectly good in this context. At the most basic level a trope is just a particular bit or item in the world that is not a universal, and that is exactly what we mean here.

11. Ord., 2.3.1.1, n. 37 (Vat. 7: 406.11, 12–13, 407.2-3; Spade, 65).
12. Ord., 2.3.1.1, n. 37 (Vat. 7: 406.15-407.1, 5–9; Spade, 65–66). Scotus maintains that the divine essence can be present in all three divine persons, but nothing else can be universal except for concepts. See Lect., 2.3.1.1, n. 36 (Vat. 18: 238.22-239.4).
13. Ord., 2.3.1.5-6, n. 161 (Vat. 7: 470.16-471.1, 471.3-4; Spade, 99).
14. Ord., 2.3.1.1, nn. 31–32 (Vat. 7: 403.2-7; Spade, 63). Some have argued Scotus's claim that natures "of themselves" are neutral to universality and particularity puts Scotus in the "Aphrodisian tradition." See Tweedale (1993).
15. For instance, Ord., 2.3.1.1, n. 30 (Vat. 7: 402.11-12; Spade, 63).
16. And as is well known, Scotus maintains that natures are naturally prior to haecceities. See, for instance, Ord., 2.3.1.5-6, n. 187 (Vat. 7: 483.9-12; Spade, 106–107).
17. Lect., 2.3.1.1, n. 66 (Vat. 18: 247.13-14). As Scotus explains in Ord., 2.3.1.4, n. 72 (Vat. 7: 424.3-5, 9–10, 14; Spade, 75):

    > Singularity belongs to that to which being divisible into parts of the same kind belongs primarily and per se. Quantity is of this sort, because of itself [any quantity] is capable of being divided [into smaller pieces] . . . To be divisible into parts of the same kind belongs to a thing in virtue of its quantity . . . [so] the division of something into individuals takes place through [its] quantity.

18. Ord., 2.3.1.4, n. 73 (Vat. 7: 425.3, 4–6; Spade, 75).
19. Ord., 2.3.1.4, n. 78 (Vat. 7: 427.18-428.3; Spade, 77) and Lect., 2.3.1.4, n. 78 (Vat. 18: 251.21-23, 251.23-252.1, 3–4).
20. For instance, Ord., 2.3.1.5, nn. 129, 132 (Vat. 7: 458, 459) and Lect., 2.3.1.5-6, n. 128 (Vat. 18: 9–12).
21. Ord., 2.3.1.5-6, n. 140 (Vat. 7: 463.7-8; Spade, 95) and Lect., 2.3.1.5-6, n. 135 (Vat. 18: 272.17-19).
22. Ord., 2.3.1.5-6, n. 177 (Vat. 7: 478.12-13; Spade, 103-104); ibid., nn. 183, 186 (Vat. 7: 481.19-20, 483.1-3; Spade, 105, 106); Lect., 2.3.1.5-6, n. 170 (Vat. 18: 282.12-14); ibid., n. 172 (Vat. 18: 283.25-26).
23. Ord., 2.3.1.5-6, n. 177 (Vat. 7: 478.13-14; Spade, 104).
24. As Scotus himself suggests, he is interested not in a generic kind of individuality, but rather in the unique singularity of each particular individual. See Ord., 2.3.1.4, n. 76 (Vat. 7: 426.18-427.1, 427.5-7; Spade, 76).
25. Scotus does use the word *contrahere,* and the literature often simply anglicizes this to "contract." E.g. see Adams (1982, 413). For an example of this terminology in Scotus, see Lect., 2.3.1.5-6, n. 166 (Vat. 18: 280.24-25). Note, though, that *contrahere* can translate as "to be bound to," which would seem more appropriate if Scotus thinks natures are tropes.
26. Ord., 2.3.1.5-6, n. 188 (Vat. 7: 484.1-5, 7-9; Spade, 107).
27. Ord., 2.1.4-5, n. 200 (Vat. 7: 101.8-9).
28. Ord., 1.2.2.1-4, n. 403 (Vat. 2: 356.16-357.1); ibid., 1.8.1.4, n. 193 (Vat. 4: 261.14-262.1).
29. Lect., 2.3.1.5-6, n. 178 (Vat. 18: 285.17-20).
30. Ockham, Ord., 1.2.4 (OTh: 2: 108; Spade, 119, n. 35).
31. See Ord., 1.2.4 (OTh 2: 108-114; Spade, 119-123, nn. 36–63).
32. Some universals might be complex—i.e., composed of simpler universals. But Ockham thinks we can still ask the same question about the simplest parts of those universals: why think any one of *them* could be more "one thing" than any of the others? Ord., 1.2.4 (OTh 2: 109; Spade, 120, n. 38-39).
33. Ord., 1.2.4 (OTh 2: 108; Spade, 119, n. 36).
34. As Ockham explains in Ord., 1.2.4 (OTh 2: 110; Spade, 121, nn. 45-47), if the realist responds by claiming the universal is shared by many, Ockham asks: "How is it sharable by many, and how is it in many? Either by identity with many and by a real multiplication of itself . . . or without being multiplied or varied in itself it is shared by many and is in them." The former option establishes Ockham's point, and the latter option begs the question.

35. Ord., 1.2.4 (OTh 2: 115; Spade, 124, n. 67).
36. Ord., 1.2.4 (OTh 2: 116; Spade, 124, n. 68).
37. Alternatively, of course, God could wholly create or annihilate all members of a species at once.
38. Ord., 1.2.4 (OTh 2: 115; Spade, 124, n. 65). Adams, however, has argued that this is a bad inference (Adams 1987, 32–33).
39. Ockham attempts to argue against this in Ord., 1.2.4 (OTh 2: 116-117; Spade, 125, nn. 69–72), but his arguments rest on his assumption that creatures can be created and annihilated even if there are other members of the species in existence. That is precisely what the immanent realist could deny.
40. Ord., 1.2.4 (OTh 2: 121-122; Spade, 128, nn. 93–94).
41. Ord., 1.2.4 (OTh 2: 119; Spade, 127, n. 84).
42. The proviso "in the way Scotus defines it" is important, because Ockham uses the phrase "formal distinction" in certain theological contexts (the Trinity, for example). Some have taken this to imply that Ockham begrudgingly accepts Scotus's formal distinction, though only in a few (theological) cases. But this does not seem right, for Ockham is clear that he uses the label "formal distinction" with a different meaning. See Ord., 1.2.1 (OTh 2: 19.3-18), where Ockham explains that when he uses the label "formal distinction," he means nothing more than cases where he has to reject the transitivity of identity.
43. Ord., 1.2.6 (OTh 2: 173 and 177; Spade, 156 and 159, nn. 27 and 39).
44. Ord., 1.2.6 (OTh 2: 173; Spade, 156, n. 25).
45. Ord., 1.2.6 (OTh 2: 173; Spade, 156, n. 26): "The first is denied by him, and the second too, so the third must be given. Therefore, a nature which is distinguished in any way from the individual is just a being of thought." This seems an invalid conclusion, for the distinction that falls in the scope of (30) is not between a nature and the *individual*, it is a distinction between the nature and the *haecceity*, as Ockham himself says just a few sentences before: "if a nature is distinguished in some way from the contracting difference . . ." ibid. (OTh 2: 173; Spade, 156, n. 25). And the formal distinction is not necessarily transitive.
46. Ord., 1.2.6 (OTh 2: 174; Spade, 156, nn. 27 and 28).
47. Ord., 1.2.6 (OTh 2: 174; Spade, 156, n. 27).
48. On the debate over whether Scotus changed his mind about the formal distinction, see Gelber (1974, 71–102); Adams (1976); and Cross (2004). It is difficult to grasp the details of this debate, for it is hard to see how formally distinct entities *wouldn't* be distinct property bearers. If they really do have different defining characteristics, then surely they have different properties (namely, their defining characteristics).
49. Ord., 1.2.6 (OTh 2: 177; Spade, 158–159, n. 39).
50. For instance, Ord., 1.2.4 (OTh 20: 122; Spade, 128–129, n. 95); ibid., 1.2.6 (OTh 2: 196; Spade, 171, n. 105); ibid., (OTh 2: 196; Spade, 171, n. 108).
51. See Lahey (1998, 113–14).
52. Ord., 1.2.8 (OTh 2: 267–270, 271–291; Spade, 215, n. 7; 216, n. 11; 216–217, n. 15; 217, nn. 17-19; 218–231, nn. 22–93).
53. Ord., 1.2.8 (OTh 2: 267; Spade, 215, n. 6).

Bibliography

Post-1800 Works

Adams, Marilyn McCord. 1970. "Intuitive Cognition, Certainty, and Scepticism in William Ockham." *Traditio* 26: 389–98.

——. 1976. "Ockham on Identity and Distinction." *Franciscan Studies* 36: 5–74.

——. 1982. "Universals in the Early Fourteenth Century." In *The Cambridge History of Later Medieval Philosophy*, eds. Norman Kretzmann, Anthony Kenny, and Jan Pinborg. Cambridge: Cambridge University Press.

——. 1987. *William Ockham*. Notre Dame: University of Notre Dame Press.

——. 1995. Introduction. In Abelard (1995).

Adamson, Peter. 2002. *The Arabic Plotinus: A Philosophical Study of the "Theology of Aristotle."* London: Duckworth.

——. 2004. "Non-Discursive Thought in Avicenna's Commentary on the *Theology of Aristotle*." In *Interpreting Avicenna: Science and Philosophy in Medieval Islam. Proceedings of the Second Conference of the Avicenna Study Group*, eds. Jon McGinnis and David Reisman. Leiden: Brill.

Allard, Guy H. "Le 'Contra Gentiles' et le modèle rhétorique." *Laval Théologique et Philosophique* 30: 237–250.

Alston, William P. 1960. "The Ontological Argument Revisited." *The Philosophical Review* 69: 452–74.

——. 1993. "Aquinas on Theological Predication: A Look Backward and a Look Forward." In *Reasoned Faith: Essays in Philosophical Theology in Honor of Norman Kretzmann*, ed. Eleonore Stump. Ithaca and London: Cornell University Press.

Altmann, A. ed. 1967a. *Jewish Medieval and Renaissance Studies*. Cambridge, MA: Harvard University Press.

——. 1967b. Moses Narboni's "Epistle on Shi'ur Qomā." In Altmann (1967a).

——. 1974. "The Religion of the Thinkers." In *Religion in a Religious Age*, ed. S.D. Goitein. Cambridge, MA: Association for Jewish Studies.

d'Alverny, Marie-Thérèse. 1947–1948. "Deux traductions latines du coran au moyen âge." *Archives d'histoire doctrinale et littéraire du moyen âge* 16: 69–131.

Anscombe, G. E. M. 1965. "The Intentionality of Sensation." In *Analytic Philosophy, Second Series*, ed. R. J. Butler. New York: Barnes and Noble.

Arnzen, Rüdiger. 1997. *Aristoteles' De anima: eine verlorene spätantike Paraphrase in arabischer und persischer Überlieferung.* Leiden: E. J. Brill.

Ashworth, E. Jennifer. 1991. "Signification and Modes of Signifying in Thirteenth-Century Logic: A Preface to Aquinas on Analogy." *Medieval Philosophy and Theology* 1: 39–67.

——. 1992. "Analogy and Equivocation in Thirteenth-Century Logic: Aquinas in Context." *Mediaeval Studies* 54: 94–135.

——. 2008. *Les théories de l'analogie du XIIe au XVIe siècle.* Paris: Vrin.

Asín y Palacio, Miguel. 1904. "El Averroismo teológico de Santo Tomás de Aquino." In *Homenaje a don Francisco Codera*, ed. Eduardo Saavedra. Saragossa: M. Escar.

Aubenque, Pierre, Theo Kobusch, Ludger Oeing-Hanhoff et al. 1971. "Abstraktion." In *Historisches Wörterbuch der Philosophie*, vol. 1. Basel: Schwabe and Co.

Balthasar, N. and A. Simonet. 1930. "Le plan de la *Somme contre les Gentils* de saint Thomas d'Aquin." *Revue néo-scolastique de philosophie* 32: 183–214.

Benson, Joshua C. 2004. "Structure and Meaning in St. Bonaventure's *Quaestiones Disputatae De Scientia Christi*." *Franciscan Studies* 62: 67–90.

Berten, M. 1928. "A propos de la *Summa Contra Gentiles*." *Criterion* [Barcelona] 4: 175–83.

Berthier, André. "Un maître orientaliste du XIIIe siècle: Raymond Martin, O. P." *Archivum Fratrum Praedicatorum* 6: 267–311.

Berubé, Camille. 1964. *La Connaissance de l'individuel au Moyen Age.* Montreal: Presse Universtaire de Montréal.

Black, Deborah L. 1997. "Avicenna on the Ontological and Epistemic Status of Fictional Beings." *Documenti e studi sulla tradizione filosofica medievale* 8: 425–53.

——. 1999. "Mental Existence in Thomas Aquinas and Avicenna." *Mediaeval Studies* 61: 45–79.

——. 2010. "Intentionality in Medieval Arabic Philosophy." *Quaestio* 10: 65–81.

——. 2012. "Avicenna's 'Vague Individual' and its Impact on Medieval Latin Philosophy." In *Vehicles of Transmission, Translation, and Transformation in Medieval Cultures*, eds. C. Fraenkel, R. Wisnovsky, F. Wallis, and J. Fumo. Turnhout: Brepols.

Blanche, M. 1924. "Note." *Revue de Philosophie* 24: 444–9.

Blohm, Michelle. 2011. "The Feminine and Masculine as Principles of Ascent in the *Itinerarium mentis in Deum*." *American Catholic Philosophical Quarterly* 85: 25–42.

Blomme, Robert. 1958. *La doctrine du péché dans les écoles théologiques de la première moitié du XIIe siècle.* Louvain: Publications universitaires de Louvain.

Boehner, Philotheus. 1943. "The *notitia intuitiva* of non-existents according to William of Ockham." *Traditio* 1: 223–75.

Boler, John F. 1965. "Scotus and Intuition: Some Remarks." *The Monist* 49: 551–70.

——. 1982. "Intuitive and Abstractive Cognition." In *The Cambridge History of Later Medieval Philosophy*, eds. Norman Kretzmann, Anthony Kenny, and Jan Pinborg. Cambridge: Cambridge University Press.

Bouyges, Maurice. 1925. "Le plan du *Contra gentiles* de S. Thomas." *Archives de Philosophie* 3: 320–41 (or 176–97 in the separate pagination of this special volume).

Bradley, D. J. M. 1997. *Aquinas on the Twofold Human Good.* Washington, D.C.: Catholic University of America Press.

Brentano, Franz. 1867. *Die Psychologie des Aristoteles.* Mainz: Kirchheim.

Brower, Jeffrey. 2004. "Anselm on Ethics." In *The Cambridge Companion to Anselm*, ed. Brian Davies and Brian Leftow. Cambridge: Cambridge University Press.

Brower-Toland, Susan. 2007. "Intuition, Externalism, and Direct Reference in Ockham." *History of Philosophy Quarterly* 24: 317–35.

Burns, Robert I. 1971. "Christian-Islamic Confrontation in the West: The Thirteenth-Century Dream of Conversion," *American Historical Review* 76: 1,386–434.

Cameron, Margaret. 2007. "Abelard (and Heloise?) on Intention." *American Catholic Philosophical Quarterly* 81: 323–38.

Casciaro, José María. 1969. *El diálogo teológico de Santo Tomás con musulmanes y judios, el tema de la profecía y la revelación.* Madrid: CSIC, Instituto Francisco Suarez.
Castagnoli, Pietro. 1928. "La data di composizione della *Summa c. Gentiles* di S. Tommaso." *Divus Thomas* [Piacenza] 31: 489–92.
Cator, Gerald. 1934. "*Itinerarium mentis in Deum.*" *Philosophy* 9: 182–94.
Chazan, Robert. 1974. "Confrontation in the Synagogue at Narbonne: A Christian Sermon and a Jewish Reply." *Harvard Theological Review* 67: 437–57.
——. 1977. "The Barcelona 'Disputation' of 1263: Christian Missionizing and Jewish Response." *Speculum* 52: 824–42.
Chenu, Marie-Dominique. 1974. *Introduction à l'étude de saint Thomas d'Aquin.* Montreal-Paris: Institut d'études médiévales-Vrin. (Original work published 1950.)
Cleary, John. 1985. "On the Terminology of 'Abstraction' in Aristotle." *Phronesis* 31: 13–45.
Colie, Rosalie. 1973. *The Resources of Kind: Genre-Theory in the Renaissance*, ed. Barbara K. Lewalski. Berkeley: University of California Press.
Corbin, Michel. 1974. *Le chemin de la théologie chez Thomas d'Aquin.* Paris: Beauchesne.
Courcelle, Pierre. 1968. *Recherches sur les "Confessions" de saint Augustin.* Paris: E. de Boccard.
Cousins, Ewert. 1978. *Bonaventure and the Coincidence of Opposites.* Chicago: Franciscan Herald Press.
Cross, Richard. 1999. *Duns Scotus.* New York: Oxford University Press.
——. 2004. "Scotus's Parisian Teaching on Divine Simplicity." In *Duns Scot à Paris: Actes du colloque de Paris, 2–4 Septembre 2002*, eds. Olivier Boulnois, Elizabeth Karger, Jean-Luc Solère, and Gérard Sondag. Textes et études du Moyen Age, 26. Turnhout: Brepols.
Cullen, Christopher M. 2006. *Bonaventure.* Oxford: Oxford University Press.
Curtius, Ernst Robert. *European Literature and the Latin Middle Ages*, tr. Willard R. Trask. Princeton: Princeton University Press.
D'Ancona, Cristina. 2008. "Degrees of Abstraction in Avicenna: How to Combine Aristotle's *De Anima* and the *Enneads.*" In *Theories of Perception in Medieval and Early Modern Philosophy*, eds. Simo Knuuttila and Pekka Kärkkäinen. Dordrecht: Springer.
Davidson, Herbert A. 1979. "Maimonides' Secret Position on Creation." In Twersky (1979).
——. 1992. *Alfarabi, Avicenna, and Averroes on Intellect.* New York, Oxford: Oxford University Press.
Davis, H. 1946. *Moral and Pastoral Theology*, 5th edn. 4 vols. London: Sheed and Ward.
Day, Sebastian J. 1947. *Intuitive Cognition: A Key to the Later Scholastics.* St. Bonaventure, NY: The Franciscan Institute.
de Broglie, Guy. 1924–25. "De la place du surnaturel dans la philosophie de saint Thomas." *Recherches de science religieuse* 14 (1924): 193–224 and 481–96, 15 (1925): 5–53.
De Libera, Alain. 1994. "Introduction." In Thomas d'Aquin, *Contre Averroès* tr. Alain de Libera. Paris: GF Flammarion, 9–73.
——. 1999. *L'art des généralités: Théories de l'abstraction.* Paris: Aubier.
Delio, Ilia. 2001. *Simply Bonaventure.* Hyde Park, NY: New City Press.
Denifle, Heinrich and Emile Chatelain. 1889–97. *Chartularium Universitatis Parisiensis.* Paris: Delalain.
De Rijk, L.M. 1952. *The Place of the Categories in Aristotle.* Assen: Van Gorcum.
Dondaine, Hyacinthe F. 1952. "L'objet et le medium de la vision béatifique chez les théologiens du XIIIe siècle." *Recherches de théologie ancienne et médiévale* 19: 60–130.
Doris, John M. 2002. *Lack of Character: Personality and Moral Behavior.* Cambridge: Cambridge University Press.
Dumont, Richard E. 1968. "Scotus' Intuition Viewed in the Light of the Intellect's Present State." In *De doctrina Ioannis Duns Scoti. Acta Congressus Scotistici Internationalis, Oxonii et Edinburgi 11–17 sept. 1966 celebrati*, vol. 2, ed. Commissio Scotistica. Rome: Commissio Scotistica.
Dumont, Stephen D. 1989. "The Scientific Character of Theology and the Origin of Duns Scotus' Distinction between Intuitive and Abstractive Cognition." *Speculum* 64: 579–99.

Ebbesen, Sten. 1988. "Concrete Accidental Terms: Late Thirteenth-Century Debates about Problems Relating to Such Terms as '*Album*'." In *Meaning and Inference in Medieval Philosophy: Studies in Memory of Jan Pinborg*, ed. Norman Kretzmann, 107–74. Synthese Historical Library, 32. Dordrecht, Boston, and London: Kluwer Academic Publishers.

Feinberg, Joel. 2003. *Problems at the Roots of Law*. New York: Oxford University Press.

Feldman, S. 1971. "Creation and Cosmogony." In *Encyclopaedia Judaica* vol. 5, col. 1067–9. Jerusalem: Keter Publishing House, Ltd.

——. 1980. "The Theory of Eternal Creation in Hasdai Crescas and Some of His Predecessors." *Viator* 11: 289–320.

Féret, H.-M. 1930–3. Review of A. Berten, "A propos de la *Summa Contra Gentiles*" and N. Balthasar and A. Simonet, "Le plan de la *Somme contre les Gentils de S. Thomas d'Aquin*." *Bulletin Thomiste* 3: 105–12.

Ferrari, Leo C. 1970. "The Pear-Theft in Augustine's *Confessions*." *Revue des Études Augustiniennes* 16: 233–41.

——. 1971. "Symbols of Sinfulness in Book II of Augustine's *Confessions*." *Augustinian Studies* 2: 93–104.

Fischer, John M., ed. 1986. *Moral Responsibility*. Ithaca: Cornell University Press.

Foot, Philippa. 1978. "Virtues and Vices," in *Virtues and Vices*. Berkeley: University of California Press.

Frankfurt, Harry. 1971. "Freedom of the Will and the Concept of a Person." *Journal of Philosophy* 68: 5–20.

Fuerst, Adrian, O. S. B. 1951. "An Historical Study of the Doctrine of the Omnipresence of God in Selected Writings between 1220 to 1270." *The Catholic University of America Studies in Sacred Theology*, second series, no. 62. Washington, D.C.: The Catholic University of America Press.

Gallagher, David. 1990. "Aquinas on Moral Action: Interior and Exterior Act." *Proceedings of the American Catholic Philosophical Association* 64: 118–29.

——. 1995. Will and deed in Abelard and Aquinas. In *Moral and Political Philosophies in the Middle Age*, eds. B. Carlos Bazán, Eduardo Andújar, and Léonard G. Sbrocchi. Proceedings of the Ninth International Congress of Medieval Philosophy, Ottawa, 17–22 August 1992. New York, Ottawa, and Toronto: Legas.

Garber, Daniel. 2001. *Descartes Embodied: Reading Cartesian Philosophy through Cartesian Science*. Cambridge: Cambridge University Press.

Garcia, F. M. 1974. *Lexicon Scholasticum Philosophico-theologicum*. New York: Georg Olms Verlag.

Gardet, L. 1951. *La Pensée religieuse d'Avicenne*. Paris: J. Vrin.

——. 1976. "La connaissance que Thomas d'Aquin put avoir du monde islamique." In *Aquinas and the Problems of his Time*, eds. G. Verbeke and D. Verhelst. Leuven and The Hague: Leuven University Press and Martinus Nijhoff.

Gauthier, René-Antoine. 1961. "Introduction historique" to vol. 1 of the *Summa contra Gentiles*. Paris: P. Lethielleux.

——. 1993. "Introduction" to *Somme contre les Gentils*, tr. R. Bernier et al. Paris: Editions universitaires.

Gelber, Hester Goodenough. 1974. Logic and the Trinity: A Clash of Values in Scholastic Thought, 1300–1335. Ph.D. dissertation, University of Wisconsin.

Getino, Luis G. 1905. *La "Summa contra gentes" y el Pugio fidei*. Vergara: El Santísimo Rosario.

Gilson, Étienne. 1929–1930. "Les sources gréco-arabes de l'augustinisme avicennisant." *Archives d'histoire doctrinale et litterarie du moyen âge* 4: 5–149.

——. 1940. *The Philosophy of St. Bonaventure*, tr. Dom Illtyd Trethowan and F. J. Sheed. London: Sheed & Ward.

——. 1952. *Jean Duns Scot: Introduction à ses Positions Fondamentales*. Paris: J. Vrin.

Goichon, A.-M. 1937. *La Distinction de l'essence et de l'existence d'après Ibn Sīnā*. Paris: Desclée de Brouwer.

Gohlman, W. E. 1974. *The Life of Ibn Sina.* Albany, NY: State University of New York Press.
Goldman, Eliezar. 1970. "Maimonides' View of Prophecy" (in Hebrew). In *Samuel K. Mirsky Memorial Volume.* New York: Yeshiva University.
Goodman, L. E. 1992. *Avicenna.* London and New York: Routledge.
Gorce, M. M. 1930a. "La lutte 'contre Gentiles' à Paris." In *Mélanges Mandonnet,* vol. 1. Paris: J. Vrin.
——. 1930b. (Remarks on [1930a]). *Bulletin Thomiste* 3: 179–87.
Goris, Wouter. 2011. "Two-Staged Doctrines of God as First Known and the Transformation of the Concept of Reality in Bonaventure and Henry of Ghent." *American Catholic Philosophical Quarterly* 85: 77–97.
Grabmann, Martin. 1957. *Geschichte der scholastischen Methode.* Graz: Akademische Druck- u. Verlaganstalt. (Original work published 1909–11.)
Graf, T. 1934. *De subiecto psychico gratiae et virtutum,* pars prima: de subiecto virtutum cardinalium. Rome: Herder.
Green, T. H. 1883. *Prolegomena to Ethics.* Oxford: Oxford University Press.
Green, William M. 1949. "'Initium omnis peccati superbia': Augustine on Pride as the First Sin." *University of California Publications in Classical Philology* 13: 407–31.
Gutas, D. 1988. *Avicenna and the Aristotelian Tradition.* Leiden: E. J. Brill.
——. 2001. "Intuition and Thinking: The Evolving Structure of Avicenna's Epistemology." In *Aspects of Avicenna,* ed. Robert Wisnovsky. Princeton: Markus Wiener.
Hadot, Pierre. 2002. *What Is Ancient Philosophy?* Cambridge, MA: Harvard University Press.
Hammond, Jay M. 2001. "Order in the *Itinerarium mentis in Deum.*" In J. A. Wayne Hellmann, *Divine and Created Order in Bonaventure's Theology,* tr. Jay M. Hammond. St. Bonaventure, NY: Franciscan Institute Press, 191–271.
——. 2002. "Bonaventure." In *New Catholic Encyclopedia,* 2nd ed., vol. 2. Detroit: Thompson Gale.
——. 2009. "Bonaventure's *Itinerarium*: A Respondeo." *Franciscan Studies* 67: 301–21.
Hartman, David. 1976. *Maimonides: Torah and Philosophic Quest.* Philadelphia: Jewish Publication Society.
Harvey, Warren Zev. 1979. "Review of Hartman (1976)." *Journal of the History of Philosophy* 17: 86–8.
——. 1980. "Political Philosophy and Halakhah in Maimonides" [in Hebrew]. *Iyyun* 29: 198–212.
——. 1981a. "The Question of the Incorporeality of God in Maimonides, Rabad, Crescas, and Spinoza" (in Hebrew). In *Tĕpisat ha- Elohut bĕ-Maḥăšaba ha-Yĕhudit,* eds. S. Heller Wilensky et al. Haifa: University of Haifa.
——. 1981b. "A Third Approach to Maimonides' Cosmology Prophetology Puzzle." *Harvard Theological Review* 74: 287–301.
Hasse, Dag N. 1999. "Das Lehrstück von den vier Intellekten in der Scholastik: von den arabischen Quellen bis zu Albertus Magnus." *Recherches de Théologie et Philosophie médiévales* 66: 21–77.
——. 2000. *Avicenna's* De anima *in the Latin West.* London and Turin: Warburg Institute and Nino Aragno Editore.
——. 2001. "Avicenna on Abstraction." In *Aspects of Avicenna,* ed. Robert Wisnovsky, 39–82. Princeton: Markus Wiener.
Hause, Jeffrey. 2007. Abelard on Degrees of Sinfulness. *American Catholic Philosophical Quarterly* 81: 251–70.
Hayes, Zachary. 1994. "Bonaventure: Mystery of the Triune God." In *The History of Franciscan Theology,* ed. Kenan B. Osborne. St. Bonaventure, NY: The Franciscan Institute.
Herman, Barbara. 1993. *The Practice of Moral Judgment.* Cambridge, MA: Harvard University Press.
Hibbs, Thomas. 1995. *Dialectic and Narrative in Aquinas: A Reinterpretation of the* Summa contra Gentiles. Notre Dame: University of Notre Dame Press.

Hoffmann, Tobias. 2003. Moral Action as Human Action: End and Object in Aquinas in Comparison with Abelard, Lombard, Albert, and Duns Scotus. *The Thomist* 67: 73–94.

Hoffmann, Tobias, Jörn Müller, and Matthias Perkams, eds. 2013. *Aquinas and the Nicomachean Ethics*. Cambridge: Cambridge University Press.

Hoping, Helmut. 1997. *Weisheit als Wissen des Ursprungs: Philosophie und Theologie in der "Summa contra gentiles" des Thomas von Aquin*. Freiburg: Herder.

Huerga, Alvaro. 1974. "Hipótesis sobre la génesis de la 'Summa contra gentiles' y del 'Pugio fidei.'" *Angelicum* 51: 33–57.

Hyman, Arthur. 1967. "Maimonides' Thirteen Principles." In Altmann (1967a).

——. 1976. "Interpreting Maimonides." *Gesher* 6: 46–59.

Idel, Moshe. 1975. "A Fragment of Asher ben Meshulam of Lunel's Philosophical Writings" (in Hebrew). *Kiryat Sefer* 50: 149–53.

Inglis, John. 1999. "Aquinas's Replication of the Acquired Moral Virtues: Rethinking the Standard Philosophical Interpretation of Moral Virtue in Aquinas." *Journal of Religious Ethics* 27 (1): 3–27.

Irwin, Terence H. 1999. "Splendid Vices? Augustine For and Against Pagan Virtues." *Medieval Philosophy and Theology* 8: 105–27.

——. 2007. *The Development of Ethics: A Historical and Critical Study*, vol. 1: *From Socrates to the Reformation*. Oxford and New York: Oxford University Press.

Jaeger, Werner. 1948. *Aristotle*. 2nd ed. Oxford: Clarendon Press.

Jonsen, A. R. and S. E. Toulmin. 1988. *The Abuse of Casuistry: A History of Moral Reasoning*. Berkeley: University of California Press.

Jordan, Mark D. 1999. "Ideals of Scientia moralis and the Invention of the *Summa theologiae*." In *Aquinas's Moral Theory: Essays in Honor of Norman Kretzmann*, eds. Scott MacDonald and Eleonore Stump. Ithaca: Cornell University Press.

——. 2006. *Rewritten Theology: Aquinas after His Readers*. Malden, MA: Blackwell.

Kane, Robert. 1996. *The Significance of Free Will*. Oxford: Oxford University Press.

Kane, Stanley G. 1981. *Anselm's Doctrine of Freedom and the Will*. Lewiston, NY: Edwin Mellen Press.

Kaeppeli, Thomas. 1947. "Une Somme contre les hérétiques de s. Pierre Martyr (?)." *Archivum Fratrum Praedicatorum* 17: 295–335.

Kaplan, Lawrence. 1977. "Maimonides on the Miraculous Element in Prophecy." *Harvard Theological Review* 70:233–56.

Karger, Elisabeth. 1999. "Ockham's Misunderstood Theory of Intuitive and Abstractive Cognition." In *The Cambridge Companion to Ockham*, ed. Paul V. Spade. Cambridge: Cambridge University Press.

Kenny, Anthony. 2007. *Medieval Philosophy: A New History of Western Philosophy* vol.2. Oxford: Oxford University Press.

Kent, Bonnie. 2010. "Virtue Theory." In *The Cambridge History of Medieval Philosophy*, eds. Robert Pasnau and Christina Van Dyke, vol. 1, 493–505. Cambridge: Cambridge University Press.

King, Peter. 1995. "Abelard's Intentionalist Ethics." *The Modern Schoolman* 77: 213–31.

——. 2007. "Rethinking Representation in the Middle Ages: A Vade-Mecum to Medieval Theories of Mental Representation." In *Representation and Objects of Thought in Medieval Philosophy*, ed. Henrik Lagerlund. Farnham, UK: Ashgate Publishing.

Klein-Braslavy, Sara. 1978. *Peruš ha-Rambam lĕ-Sippur Bĕri'at ha-'Olam*. Jerusalem: Israel Society for Biblical Research.

Kluxen, Wolfgang. 1954. "Literargeschichtliches zum lateinischen Moses Maimonides." *Recherches de théologie ancienne et médiévale* 21: 32–50.

——. 1955. "Maimonides und die Hochscholastik." *Philosophisches Jahrbuch* 63: 151–65.

——. 1966. "Die Geschichte des Maimonides im lateinischen Abendland als Beispiel einer christlich-jüdischen Begegnung." In *Judentum im Mittelalter*, ed. Paul Wilpert. Berlin: de Gruyter.

Knuuttila, Simo and Lilli Alanen. 1988. "The Foundations of Modality and Conceivability in Descartes and His Predecessors." In *Modern Modalities*, ed. Simo Knuuttila. Dordrecht: Kluwer Academic Publishers.

Kreisel, Howard. 2001. *Prophecy: The History of an Idea in Medieval Jewish Philosophy.* Dordrecht: Kluwer Academic Press.

Kretzmann, Norman. 1982. "Introduction." In *The Cambridge History of Later Medieval Philosophy*, eds. Norman Kretzmann, Anthony Kenny, and Jan Pinborg. Cambridge: Cambridge University Press.

——. 1997. *The Metaphysics of Theism, Aquinas's Natural Theology in* Summa contra Gentiles I. Oxford: The Clarendon Press.

——. 1999. *The Metaphysics of Creation: Aquinas's Natural Theology in* Summa contra Gentiles II. Oxford: Clarendon Press.

Lahey, Stephen. 1998. "Ockham and Trope Nominalism." *Franciscan Studies* 55:105–20.

LaNave, Gregory. 2005. *Through Holiness to Wisdom: The Nature of Theology according to St. Bonaventure.* Rome: Istituto storico dei cappuccini.

——. 2009. "Knowing God through and in All Things." *Franciscan Studies* 67: 267–99.

Landauer, Samuel. 1875. "Die Psychologie des Ibn Sīnā." *Zeitschrift der deutschen morgenländischen Gesellschaft* 29: 335–418.

Lang, Helen S. 1986. "Bonaventure's Delight in Sensation." *The New Scholasticism* 60: 72–90.

Langston, Douglas C. 1979. "Scotus and Ockham on the Univocal Concept of Being." *Franciscan Studies* 39: 105–29.

——. 1986. *God's Willing Knowledge: The Influence of Scotus' Analysis of Omniscience.* University Park: Pennsylvania State University Press.

——. 1993. "Scotus's Doctrine of Intuitive Cognition." *Synthese* 96: 3–24.

Levering, Matthew. 2000. "Wisdom and the Viability of Thomistic Trinitarian Theology." *The Thomist* 64: 593–618.

Lonfat, Joël. 2004. "Archéologie de la notion d'analogie d'Aristote à saint Thomas d'Aquin." *Archives d'histoire doctrinale et littéraire du moyen âge* 71: 35–107.

Lottin, Odon. 1942–1960. *Psychologie et morale aux XIIe et XIIIe siècles*, 6 vols. Louvain and Gembloux: Duclot.

MacDonald, Scott. 1994. "Primal Sin." In Matthews (1994).

——. 2003. "Petit Larceny, the Beginning of All Sin: Augustine's *Theft of the Pears.*" *Faith and Philosophy* 20: 393–414.

Machamer, Peter and J. E. McGuire. 2009. *Descartes' Changing Mind.* Princeton and Oxford: Princeton University Press.

MacIntyre, Alasdair. 1966. *A Short History of Ethics.* New York: MacMillan.

——. 1981. *After Virtue.* London: Duckworth.

——. 1988. *Whose Justice? Which Rationality?* London: Duckworth.

——. 1990. *Three Rival Versions of Moral Enquiry.* Notre Dame, IN: University of Notre Dame Press.

——. 1999. Dependent Rational Animals. Chicago: Open Court Press.

Mann, William E. 1978. "The Theft of the Pears." *Apeiron* 12: 51–9.

——. 1994. "Inner-Life Ethics." In Matthews (1994).

——. 2004. "Ethics." In *The Cambridge Companion to Abelard*, eds. Jeffrey E. Brower and Kevin Guilfoy. Cambridge: Cambridge University Press.

Marenbon, John. 1997. *The Philosophy of Peter Abelard.* Cambridge: Cambridge University Press.

Marmura, M. E. 1963. "Avicenna's Psychological Proof of Prophecy." *Journal of Near Eastern Studies* 22: 49–56.

——. 1964. "Avicenna's Theory of Prophecy in the Light of Ash'arite Theology." In *The Seed of Wisdom: Essays in Honour of T. J. Meek*, ed. W. S. McCullough. Toronto: University of Toronto Press.

——. 1979. "Avicenna's Chapter on Universals in the *Isagoge* of his *Shifā'*." In *Islam: Past*

Influence and Present Challenge, eds. A. T. Welch and P. Cachia. Edinburgh: Edinburgh University Press.
—— 1984a. "Avicenna on Primary Concepts in the *Metaphysics* of His *Al-Shifā'*." In *Logos Islamikos: Studia Islamica in Honorem Georgii Michaelis Wickens*, eds. R. M. Savory and D. Agius. Toronto: Pontifical Institute of Mediaeval Studies.
—— 1984b. "The Metaphysics of Efficient Causality in Avicenna (Ibn Sina)." In *Islamic Theology and Philosophy: Studies in Honor of George F. Hourani*, ed. M. E. Marmura. Albany: State University of New York Press.
——. 1991. "Plotting the Course of Avicenna's Thought." *Journal of the American Oriental Society* 111: 333–42.
——. 1992. "Quiddity and Universality in Avicenna." In *Neoplatonism and Islamic Thought*, ed. Parviz Morewedge. Albany: State University of New York Press.
——. 2006. "Avicenna's Critique of Platonists in Book VII, Chapter 2 of the *Metaphysics* of his *Healing*." In *Arabic Theology, Arabic Philosophy: Essays in Celebration of Richard M. Frank*, ed. J. Montgomery. Leuven: Peeters.
Marras, Ausonio. 1976. "Scholastic Roots of Brentano's Conception of Intentionality." In *The Philosophy of Brentano*, ed. L. L. McAlister. London: Duckworth.
Matthews, Gareth B., ed. 1994. *The Augustinian Tradition*. Berkeley: University of California Press.
——. 2005. Augustine. Oxford and Malden, MA: Blackwell.
Matthys, M. 1936. "Quid ratio naturalis doceat de possibilitate visionis beatae secundum S. Thomam in Summa contra Gentiles." *Divus Thomas* [Piacenza] 39: 201–28.
McGinnis, Jon. 2006. "Making Abstraction Less Abstract: The Logical, Psychological, and Metaphysical Dimensions of Avicenna's Theory of Abstraction." *Proceedings of the American Catholic Philosophical Association* 80: 169–83.
McInerny, Ralph. 1982. *Ethica Thomistica: The Moral Philosophy of Thomas Aquinas*. Washington, D.C.: Catholic University of America Press.
——. 1996. *Aquinas and Analogy*. Washington D.C.: Catholic University of America Press.
—— and John O'Callaghan. 2010. "Saint Thomas Aquinas". In *The Stanford Encyclopedia of Philosophy*, ed. Edward N. Zalta. Available at: http://plato.stanford.edu/archives/win2010/entries/aquinas/.
Mele, Alfred. 1995. *Autonomous Agents*. Oxford: Oxford University Press.
Mertz, Donald. 1996. *Moderate Realism and Its Logic*. New Haven: Yale University Press.
Metselaar, Suzanne. 2009. "The Structural Similarity between the *Itinerarium mentis in Deum* and the *Collationes in Hexaemeron* with regard to Bonaventure's Doctrine of God as First Known." *American Catholic Philosophical Quarterly* 85: 43–76.
Mews, Constant J. 1985. "The Lists of Heresies Imputed to Peter Abelard." *Revue bénédictine* 94: 73–110.
Michelitsch, Anton. 1913. *Thomasschriften* 1. Graz and Vienna: Styria.
Michot, J. 1986. *La destinée de l'homme selon Avicenne*. Louvain: Peeters.
——. 1997. "La Réponse d'Avicenne à Bahmanyār et al-Kirmānī." *Le Muséon* 110: 143–221.
Montagnes, Bernard. 1963. *La doctrine de l'analogie de l'être d'après Saint Thomas d'Aquin*. Philosophes médiévaux 6. Louvain and Paris: Publications Universitaires and Béatrice-Nauwelaerts.
Mulard, R. 1925. "Désir naturel de connaître et vision béatifique." *Revue des sciences philosophiques et théologiques* 14: 192–5.
Murphy, Thomas. 1969. "The Date and Purpose of the Contra Gentiles." *Heythrop Journal* 10: 405–15.
Narcisse, Gilbert. 1997. *Les raisons de Dieu: Argument de convenance et ésthétique théologique selon saint Thomas d'Aquin et Hans Urs von Balthasar*. Fribourg: Editions Universitaires.
Nelson, Mark T. 2001. "On the Lack of 'True Philosophic Spirit' in Aquinas: Commitment v. Tracking in Philosophic Method." *Philosophy* 76: 283–96.
Noone, T. 2006. "Universals and Individuation." In *The Cambridge Companion to Duns Scotus*, ed. Thomas Williams. Cambridge: Cambridge University Press.

——. 2010. "Divine Illumination." In the *Cambridge History of Medieval Philosophy*, vol. 1, ed. R. Pasnau and C. Van Dyke. Cambridge: Cambridge University Press.
——. and R. E. Houser. 2005. "Saint Bonaventure", *The Stanford Encyclopedia of Philosophy* (Winter 2005 Edition), ed. Edward N. Zalta. Available at: http://plato.stanford.edu/archives/win2005/entries/bonaventure/.
Normore, Calvin. 1990. "Ockham on Mental Language." In *Historical Foundations of Cognitive Science*, ed. J.-C. Smith. Dordrecht: Kluwer Academic Publishers.
——. 2003. "Burge, Descartes, and Us." In *Reflections and Replies: Essays on the Philosophy of Tyler Burge*, eds. Martin Hahn and Bjørn Bamberg, 1–14. Cambridge, MA: The MIT Press.
Nuriel, Abraham. 1964. "The Question of a Primordial or Created World in the Philosophy of Maimonides" (in Hebrew). *Tarinz* 33: 372–87.
O'Connell, Robert J. 1989. *St. Augustine's Confessions: The Odyssey of the Soul*, 2nd ed. New York: Fordham University Press.
O'Donnell, James J., ed. 1992. *Augustine: Confessions*, 3 vols. Oxford: Clarendon Press.
Oppy, Graham. 2001. "On the Lack of True Philosophic Spirit in Aquinas." *Philosophy* 76: 615–24.
Osborne, Thomas M., Jr. 2003. "The Augustinianism of Thomas Aquinas's Moral Theory." *The Thomist* 67: 279–305.
——. 2007. "The Separation of the Interior and Exterior Acts in Scotus and Ockham." *Medieval Studies* 69: 111–39.
Owens, Joseph. 1978. *The Doctrine of Being in the Aristotelian Metaphysics*, 3rd Edition. Toronto: Pontifical Institute of Medieval Studies.
Panaccio, Claude. 2004. *Ockham on Concepts*. Aldershot: Ashgate.
——. 2010. "Intuition and Causality: Ockham's Externalism Revisited." *Quaestio* 10: 241–53.
——. Forthcoming. "Ockham's Externalism." In *Intentionality, Cognition, and Representation in the Middle Ages*, ed. Gyula Klima. New York: Fordham University Press.
—— and David Piché. 2010. "Ockham's Reliabilism and the Intuition of Non-Existents." In *Rethinking the History of Skepticism: The Missing Medieval Background*, ed. Henrik Lagerlund. Leiden and Boston: Brill.
Papineau, David. 2009. "Naturalism." In *The Stanford Encyclopedia of Philosophy (Spring 2009 Edition)*, ed. Edward N. Zalta. Available at: http://plato.stanford.edu/archives/spr2009/entries/naturalism/.
Pasnau, Robert. 2003. "Cognition." In *The Cambridge Companion to Duns Scotus*, ed. Thomas Williams. Cambridge: Cambridge University Press.
Patfoort, Albert. 1992. "La place de l'analogie dans la pensée de S. Thomas d'Aquin. Analogie, noms divins et 'perfections'." *Revue des sciences philosophiques et théologiques* 76: 235–54.
Pegis, A. C. 1934. *St. Thomas and the Problem of the Soul in the Thirteenth Century*. Toronto: Pontifical Institute of Medieval Studies.
——. 1964. "Qu'est-ce que la *Summa contra Gentiles*." In *L'Homme devant Dieu: Mélanges offerts au Père Henri de Lubac*. Paris: Aubier.
Perdrix, Sébastien. 2007. "Les *Questions disputées sur le mystère de la Trinité:* Le *De Deo uno* de saint Bonaventure?" *Revue Thomiste* 107: 591–624.
Petersen-Boring, Wendy. 2010. "St. Bonaventure's 'Doctrine of Illumination': An Artifact of Modernity." In *Dreams and Visions: An Interdisciplinary Enquiry*, ed. Nancy van Deusen. London: Brill.
Piché, David, tr. and ed. 2005. *Guillaume d'Ockham: Intuition et abstraction*. Paris: J. Vrin.
Pilsner, Joseph. 2006. *The Specification of Human Actions in St. Thomas Aquinas*. Oxford: Oxford University Press.
Pines, Schlomo. 1960. "Notes on Maimonides' Views concerning Human Will." *Scripta Hierosolymitana* 6: 195–8.
——. 1979. "The Limitations of Human Knowledge according to Al-Farabi, ibn Bajja, and Maimonides." In Twersky (1979).
Pini, Giorgio. 2004. "Scotus on Assertion and the Copula: A Comparison with Aquinas." In *Medieval Theories on Assertive and Non-Assertive Language*, eds. Alfonso Maierù and Luisa Valente. Florence, Italy: Leo S. Olschki Editore.

——. 2008. "Scotus on the Objects of Cognitive Acts." *Franciscan Studies* 66: 281–315.
——. 2011. "Can God Create My Thoughts? Scotus's Case against the Causal Account of Intentionality." *Journal of the History of Philosophy* 49: 39–63.
——. Forthcoming. "The *Questions on the Metaphysics* by John Duns Scotus: A Vindication of Pure Intellect." In *A Companion to Medieval Metaphysics Commentaries*, eds. Fabrizio Amerini and Gabriele Galluzzo. Leiden: Brill.
Pinsent, Andrew. 2012. *The Second Person Perspective in Aquinas's Ethics: Virtues and Gifts.* London: Routledge.
Rahman, Fazlur. 1952. *Avicenna's Psychology.* Oxford: Oxford University Press.
——. 1958. *Prophecy in Islam: Philosophy and Orthodoxy.* Chicago and London: University of Chicago Press.
——. 1963. "Ibn Sīna." In *A History of Muslim Philosophy*, ed. M. M. Sharif. Wiesbaden: Harrassowitz.
Ravitsky, Aviezer. 1977. The Thought of R. Zerahia b. Isaac b. Shealtiel Hen and the Maimonidean-Tibbonian Philosophy in the 13th Century (in Hebrew). Doctoral diss., The Hebrew University of Jerusalem.
Ravitsky, I. 1966. "The Question of a Primordial or Created World in the Philosophy of Maimonides" (in Hebrew), *Tarinz* 35: 333–48
Reines, Alvin. 1970. *Maimonides and Abrabanel on Prophecy.* Cincinnati: Hebrew Union College.
Review of Calogero Allegro, *Il metodo e il pensiero di san Tommaso d'Aquino.* 1981. *Rassegna di letteratura tomistica* 14: 48–50.
Richardson, Kara. 2008. The Metaphysics of Agency: Avicenna and his Legacy. PhD Diss. University of Toronto. Available at: https://tspace.library.utoronto.ca/bitstream/1807/17289/1/Richardson_Kara_J_200811_PhD_thesis.pdf.
——. Forthcoming. "Avicenna's Conception of the Efficient Cause." *British Journal for the History of Philosophy.*
Rogers, Katherin A. 1997. *The Neoplatonic Metaphysics and Epistemology of Anselm of Canterbury.* Lewiston, NY: The Edwin Mellen Press.
——. 2005. "Anselm on Eudaemonism and the Hierarchical Structure of Moral Choice." *Religious Studies* 41: 249–68.
——. 2008. *Anselm on Freedom.* Oxford: Oxford University Press.
Rohmer, J. 1928. "La Théorie de l'abstraction dans l'école franciscaine d'Alexandre de Halès à Jean Peckham." *Archives d'Histoire Doctrinale et Littéraire du Moyen Age* 3: 105–84.
Rosenzweig, Franz. 1971. *Star of Redemption*, tr. William W. Hallo. New York: Holt, Rinehart and Winston.
Rosier, Irène. 1995. "*Res significata* et *modus significandi*: Les implications d'une distinction médiévale." In *Sprachtheorien in Spätantike und Mittelalter*, ed. Sten Ebbesen. Tübingen: Gunter Narr Verlag.
Rouse, Mary A. and Richard H. Rouse. 1982. "Florilegia of Patristic Texts." In *Les genres littéraires dans les sources théologiques et philosophiques médiévales: Définition, critique, exploitation.* Louvain-la-Neuve: Université catholique de Louvain.
Rowe, William. 1985. "The Ontological Argument." In *Reason and Responsibility*, ed. Joel Feinberg. Belmont, CA: Wadsworth.
Rudavsky, T. M. (2010). *Maimonides.* Hoboken, NJ: Wiley-Blackwell.
Russell, Bertrand. 1945. *A History of Western Philosophy.* New York: Simon and Schuster.
Salman, David. 1937. "Sur la lutte *contra Gentiles* de S. Thomas." *Divus Thomas* [Piacenza] 40: 488–509.
Sanjek, François. 1974. "Raynerius Sacconi O.P., *Summa de Catharis.*" *Archivimi Fratrum Praedicatorum* 44: 31–60.
Saranyana, J. I. 1973. "La creación 'ab aeterno': Controversia de Santo Tomás y Raimundo Martí con San Bonaventura." *Scripta Theologica* [Pamplona] 5: 147–55.
Schenkeveld, Dirk M. 1997. "Philosophical Prose." In *Handbook of Classical Rhetoric in the Hellenistic Period (330 B.C. – A.D. 400)*, ed. Stanley E. Porter. Leiden: E. J. Brill.

Schneewind, Jerome. 1997. *The Invention of Autonomy*. Cambridge: Cambridge University Press.
Schönberger, Rolf. 2001. *Thomas von Aquins "Summa contra gentiles."* Darmstadt: Wissenschaftliche Buchgesellschaft.
Shumacher, Lydia. 2011. *Divine Illumination: The History and Future of Augustine's Theory of Knowledge*. Oxford: Wiley-Blackwell.
Sidgwick, Henry. 1892. *Outlines of the History of Ethics*, 3rd edn. London: Macmillan.
——. 1902. *The Ethics of Green, Spencer, and Martineau*. London: Macmillan.
Sokolowski, Robert. 1985. *Moral action: a phenomenological study*. Bloomington: Indiana University Press.
Solignac, August. 1998. *Les Confessions, Bibliothèque Augustinienne* vol. 13. Paris: Institut d'Études Augustiniennes.
South, J. B. 2002. "Scotus and the Knowledge of the Singular Revisited." *History of Philosophy Quarterly* 19: 125–47.
Spade, Paul Vincent. 1994. *Five Texts on the Mediaeval Problem of Universals: Porphyry, Boethius, Abelard, Duns Scotus, Ockham*. Indianapolis: Hackett.
——. "Medieval Philosophy." In *The Stanford Encyclopedia of Philosophy* (Spring 2013 Edition), ed. Edward N. Zalta. Available at: http://plato.stanford.edu/archives/spr2013/entries/medieval-philosophy/.
Speer, Andreas. 1993. "The Certainty and Scope of Knowledge: Bonaventure's *Disputed Questions on the Knowledge of Christ*." *Medieval Philosophy and Theology* 3: 35–61.
Starnes, Colin. 1990. *Augustine's Conversion: A Guide to the Argument of Confessions I–IX*. Waterloo, Ontario: W. Laurier University Press.
Strauss, Leo. 1952. *Persecution and the Art of Writing*. Glencoe, IL: Free Press.
——. 1967. "Notes on Maimonides' Book of Knowledge." In *Studies in Mysticism and Religion presented to Gershom G. Scholem*. Jerusalem: Magnes Press.
Striker, Gisela. 1999. "Why Study the History of Philosophy?" *The Harvard Review of Philosophy* 7: 15–18.
Stump, Eleonore. 2011. "The Non-Aristotelian Character of Aquinas's Ethics: Aquinas on the Passions." *Faith and Philosophy* 28 (1): 29–43.
Swinburne, Richard. 1977. *The Coherence of Theism*. Oxford: Clarendon Press.
Synave, P. 1930. "La révélation des vérités divines naturelles d'après saint Thomas d'Aquin." In *Mélanges Mandonnet*, vol. 1. Paris: J. Vrin.
Taylor, Richard C. 2006. "Abstraction in al-Fārābī." *Proceedings of the American Catholic Philosophical Association* 80 (2006): 151–68.
te Velde, Rudi A. 1994. "Natural Reason in the *Summa contra Gentiles*." *Medieval Philosophy and Theology* 4: 42–70.
Torrell, Jean-Pierre. 1993. *Initiation à saint Thomas d'Aquin, sa personne et son oeuvre*. Paris-Fribourg: Editions Universitaires-Editions du Cerf.
——. 1997. "La vision de Dieu *per essentiam* selon Thomas d'Aquin." *Micrologus* 5: 43–68.
——. 2005. *St. Thomas Aquinas: The Person and His Work* tr. Robert Royal. [Trslation of Torrell (1993)]. Washington, D.C.: Catholic University of America Press.
Turiel, Quintín. 1974. "La intención de santo Tomás en la 'Summa contra Gentiles.'" *Studium* [Madrid] 14: 371–401.
Tweedale, Martin M. 1993. "Duns Scotus's Doctrine on Universals in the Aphrodisian Tradition." *American Catholic Philosophical Quarterly* 67: 77–93.
Twersky, Isadore. 1967. "Some Non-Halakic Aspects of the Mishneh Torah." In Altmann (1967a).
——. ed. 1979. *Studies in Medieval Jewish History and Literature*. 2 vols. Cambridge, MA: Harvard University Press.
——. 1980. *Introduction to the Code of Maimonides*. New Haven: Yale University Press.
Tyvoll, Stan R. 2006. "Anselm's Definition of Free Will: A Hierarchical Interpretation." *American Catholic Philosophical Quarterly* 80: 155–71.

Vadja, G. 1962. *Recherches sur la philosophie et la kabbale dans la pensée juive du Moyen Age.* Paris: Mouton.
Valente, Luisa. 2008. *Logique et théologie. Les écoles parisiennes entre 1150 et 1220.* Paris: Vrin.
Van Riet, Simone. 1974. "*La Somme contre les Gentils* et la polémique islamo-chrétienne." In *Aquinas and Problems of His Time*, eds. G. Verbeke and R. Verhelst. Louvain: Publications Universitaires.
Vansteenkiste, Clemens. 1959. "Cicerone nell'opera di S. Tommaso." *Angelicum* 36: 343–82.
——. 1968. Review of Thomas Aquinas (1961–1967). *Angelicum* 45: 353–5.
——. 1970. Review of Thomas Aquinas (1961–1967). *Rassegna di letteratura tomistica* 2: 51–6.
Visser, Sandra and Thomas Williams. 2001. "Anselm's Account of Freedom." *Canadian Journal of Philosophy* 31: 221–44.
Watson, Gary. 1984. "Virtues in Excess." *Philosophical Studies* 46 (1): 57–74.
Wawrykow, Joseph. 1994. "The *Summa contra Gentiles* Reconsidered: On the Contribution of the *De Trinitate* of Hilary of Poitiers." *The Thomist* 58: 617–34.
Weisheipl, J. A. 1974. *Friar Thomas D'Aquino: His Life, Thought, and Work.* Garden City, NY: Doubleday.
——. 1982. "Aristotle's Concept of Nature: Avicenna and Aquinas." In *Approaches to Nature in the Middle Ages*, ed. L. D. Rogers. Binghamton, N.Y.: Center for Medieval and Early Renaissance Studies.
Weiss, Roslyn. 2007. "Natural Order or Divine Will: Maimonides on Cosmogony and Prophecy." *Journal of Jewish Thought and Philosophy.* 15: 1–25.
Wetzel, James. 2010. *Augustine: A Guide for the Perplexed.* London: Continuum.
Wiggins, David. 1975–1976. "Deliberation and Practical Reason." *Proceedings of the Aristotelian Society* 76: 29–51.
Williams, Thomas. 2003. "From Metaethics to Action Theory." In *The Cambridge Companion to Duns Scotus*, ed. Thomas Williams. Cambridge: Cambridge University Press.
——. (2009). Review of Katherin Rogers, *Anselm on Freedom. Notre Dame Philosophical Reviews.* Available at: http://ndpr.nd.edu/news/23911/?id=15226.
Wills, Gary. 1999. *Saint Augustine, Penguin Lives Series.* New York: Lipper/Viking Book.
Wippel, John. 1984. *Metaphysical Themes in Thomas Aquinas.* Washington, D.C.: The Catholic University of America Press.
Wolf, Susan. 1990. *Freedom Within Reason.* Oxford: Oxford University Press.
——. 2007. "Moral Psychology and the Unity of the Virtues." *Ratio* 20 (2): 145–67.
Wolfson, Harry A. 1929. *Crescas's Critique of Aristotle.* Cambridge, MA: Harvard University Press.
——. 1938. "The Amphibolous Terms in Aristotle, Arabic Philosophy and Maimonides." *Harvard Theological Review* 31: 151–73. Reprinted in Wolfson (1977).
——. 1942/3. "Hallevi and Maimonides on Prophecy." *Jewish Quarterly Review* 32: 345–70 and 33: 49–82. Reprinted in Wolfson (1977).
——. 1976. *The Philosophy of the Kalam.* Cambridge, MA: Harvard University Press.
——. 1977. *Studies in the History of Philosophy and Religion*, eds. I. Twersky and G. H. Williams. Cambridge, MA: Harvard University Press.
——. 1979. *Repercussions of the Kalam in Jewish Philosophy.* Cambridge, MA: Harvard University Press.
Wohlman, Avital. 1988. *Thomas d'Aquin et Maïmonide. Un dialogue exemplaire.* Paris: Cerf.
——. 1995. *Thomas d'Aquin et Maïmonide. Un dialogue impossible.* Fribourg: Editions Universitaires.
Wolter, Allan B. 1946. *The Trancendentals and Their Function in the Metaphysics of Duns Scotus.* St. Bonaventure, NY: The Franciscan Institute.
——. 1982. "Duns Scotus on Intuition, Memory and Our Knowledge of Individuals." In *History of Philosophy in the Making: A Symposium of Essays to Honor Professor James D. Collins on his 65th Birthday*, ed. Linus J. Thro. Washington, D.C.: University Press of America.
——. 1990. "Duns Scotus on Intuition, Memory, and Our Knowledge of Individuals." In A. B.

Wolter, *The Philosophical Theology of John Duns Scotus*, ed. Marilyn M. Adams. Ithaca and London: Cornell University Press.
—— and Marilyn M. Adams. 1993. "Memory and Intuition: A Focal Debate in Fourteenth-Century Cognitive Psychology: Introduction, Edition, and Translation of Scotus's *Ordinatio* IV, d. 45, q. 3." *Franciscan Studies* 53: 175–230.
Wood, Rega. 1987. "Intuitive Cognition and Divine Omnipotence: Ockham in Fourteenth-Century Perspective." In *From Ockham to Wycliff*, eds. Anne Hudson and Michael Wilks. Oxford: Basil Blackwell.
Zagzebski, Linda Trinkaus. 1996. *Virtues of the Mind: An Inquiry into the Nature of Virtue and the Ethical Foundations of Knowledge*. Cambridge: Cambridge University Press.

Pre-1800 Works

Abelard. 1971. *Peter Abelard's Ethics*, ed. and tr. D.E. Luscombe, D.E. Oxford: Clarendon Press.
——. 1995. *Ethical Writings*, tr. Paul Vincent Spade. Indianapolis: Hackett.
Aegidius Romanus (*See* Giles of Rome.)
Albert the Great. 1890. *Liber de praedicamentis*. In *Opera omnia*, ed. A. Borgnet. Paris: Vivès.
Ambrose. 2001. *De Officiis*, ed. I. J. Davidson. Oxford: Oxford University Press.
Anonymous. 1936. *Compendium philosophiae*, ed. Michel de Douard. Paris: Broccard.
Anselm. 1962. *Saint Anselm: Basic Writings*, tr. S. N. Deane. LaSalle, IL: Open Court.
——. 1967. *Truth, Freedom and Evil: Three Philosophical Dialogues*, eds. and trs. Jasper Hopkins and Herbert Richardson. New York: Harper.
——. 1968. *S. Anselmi Cantuariensis Archiepiscopi Opera Omnia*, ed. Schmitt, Franciscus Salesius, 6 vols. Stuttgart-Bad Cannstatt: Friedrich Fromann Verlag.
——. 1998. *Anselm of Canterbury: The Major Works*, eds. Brian Davies and G. R. Evans. Oxford: Oxford University Press.
Aquinas (*See* Thomas Aquinas.)
Aristotle. 1928. *Categories*, tr. E. M. Edghill. In *The Works of Aristotle*, vol. 1, ed. W. D. Ross. Oxford: Clarendon Press.
——. 1963. *Categories* and *De Interpretatione*, tr. J. L. Ackrill. Oxford: Clarendon Press.
Augustine. 1927. *The Confessions*, 2d ed., *Cambridge Patristic Texts*, eds. John Gibb and William Montgomery. Cambridge: University Press.
——. 1997. *The Confessions*, tr. Maria Boulding. Hyde Park, NY: New City Press.
Averroes. 1962. Long commentary on Aristotle's *Metaphysics* in *Aristotelis Opera cum Averrois Commentariis*, vol. 8. Frankfurt: Minerva. (Original work published 1562–74.)
Avicenna. 1906. *A Compendium on the Soul*, tr. E. A. van Dyck. Verona: Nicola Paderno.
——. 1938. *al-Najāt* [*The Salvation*]. Cairo. (Original work published 1357.)
——. 1947. *Arisṭū 'inda l-'Arab*, ed. A. Badawī. Cairo: Maktabat al-Nahḍa al-Miṣriyya.
——. 1951. *Avicenne: Livre des Directives et Remarques, traduction avec introduction et notes*, tr. A.-M. Goichon. Beirut and Paris: J. Vrin.
——. 1952a. *al-Shifā', al-Manṭiq, al-Madkhal* [Eisagoge], eds. G. C. Anawatt et al. Cairo: Imprimerie nationale.
——. 1952b. *Aḥwāl al-nafs* [*Compendium on the Soul*], ed. A. F. al-Ahwānī. Cairo: el-Halaby and Co.
——. 1956. *Demonstration*, eds. A. E. Affifi and I. Madkour, *Al-Shifā': Al-Burhān*. Cairo: General Egyptian Book Organization.
——. 1959. *Psychology* [*De Anima*], ed. F. Rahman, *Avicenna's De anima, Being the Psychological Part of Kitāb al-Shifā'*. London: Oxford University Press.
——. 1960–1968. *al-Ishārāt wa al-tanbīhāt*, ed. S. Dunyā. 4 vols. Cairo: Dār *al* -Ma'ārif.
——. 1960. *al-Shifā': al-Ilāhtyyāt*, eds. G. C. Anawati and S. Zayed. Cairo: Imprimeries gouvernementales.
——. 1968a. *Avicenna Latinus: Liber de anima seu sextus de naturalibus IV-V*, ed. S. Van Riet. Louvain: Éditions orientalistes / Leiden: E. J. Brill.

——. 1968b. *Fī ithbāt al-nubuwwāt* [*Proof of Prophecies*], ed. M. E. Marmura. Beirut: Dār Al-Nahār.
——. 1969. *Compendium de anima*, ed. and trs. Andrea Alpago. Farnborough: Gregg International. (Original work published 1546.)
——. 1974. *Dāneshnāmeh*, ed. S. M. Meshkāt. Tehran.
——. 1977–1983. *Liber De Philosophia prima sive Scientia divina*, ed. S. Van Riet. 3 vols. Louvain: E. Peeters / Leiden: E. J. Brill.
——. 1986. *Avicenne: Le Livre de science*, trs. M. Achena and H. Massé. 2nd edition. Paris: Les belles lettres/Unesco.
——. 2005. *Metaphysics*, ed. and trs. M. E. Marmura, *The Metaphysics of the Healing.* Provo, UT: Brigham Young University Press.
——. 2009. *Physics*, ed. and trs. Jon McGinnis, *The Physics of the Healing.* 2 vols. Provo, UT: Brigham Young University Press.
Bartholomaeus Anglicus. 1979. *On the Properties of Souls and Bodies (De proprietatibus rerum libri III and IV)*, ed. R. James Long. Toronto: Pontifical Institute of Medieval Studies.
Bonaventure. 1882–1902. *Opera Omnia.* Quaracchi: Collegii S. Bonaventurae.
——. 1956 *Itinerarium mentis in Deum*, tr. and comm. Philotheus Boehner. St. Bonaventure, NY: The Franciscan Institute.
——. 1979. *Disputed Questions on the Mystery of the Trinity*, tr. Zachary Hayes, vol. 3 of *Works of Saint Bonaventure.* St. Bonaventure, NY: The Franciscan Institute.
——. 1993. *The Journey of the Mind to God*, tr. Philotheus Boehner, ed. Stephen F. Brown. Indianapolis: Hackett.
——. 2002. *Itinerarium mentis in Deum*, tr. Zachary Hayes, vol. 2 of *Works of Saint Bonaventure.* St. Bonaventure, NY: The Franciscan Institute.
——. 2005. *Breviloquium*, tr. Dominic V. Monti, vol. 9 of *Works of St. Bonaventure.* St. Bonaventure, NY: Franciscan Institute Publications.
Cajetan, Thomas de Vio. 1939. *Scripta Philosophica: Commentaria in praedicamenta Aristotelis*, ed. M. H. Laurent. Rome: Angelicum.
Capitula haeresum Petri Abaelardi. 1969. In *Petri Abaelardi opera theologica*, ed. E. M. Buytaert and C. J. Mews. 3 vols. Turnhout: Brepols.
Crescas. 1555. *Or Adonay.* Ferrara: Abraham Usque.
Delmedigo, Joseph Solomon. 1631. *Noblot Ḥokma.* Basel: Samuel Ashkenazi.
Duns Scotus. 1891–1895. *Opera Omnia.* Paris: Vivès.
——. 1894. *Ordinatio* IV, d. 43–49. In *Opera omnia* XX and XXI. Paris: L. Vivès.
——. 1895. *Quodlibet.* In *Opera omnia* XXV and XXVI. Paris: L. Vivès.
——. 1950–. *Opera omnia.* Vatican City: Typis Polyglottis Vaticanis.
——. 1950–2011. *Ordinatio* I–IV, distinctio 42. In *Opera omnia* I–XIII. Vatican City: Typis Polyglottis Vaticanis.
——. 1966. *De primo principio.* In John Duns Scotus. *A Treatise on God as First Principle*, tr., ed. and comm. Allan B. Wolter. Chicago: Franciscan Herald Press.
——. 1975. *God and Creatures: The Quodlibetal Questions*, eds. and trs. Allan B. Wolter and Felix Alluntis. Princeton: Princeton University Press.
——. 1982–2004. *Lectura* II and III. In *Opera omnia* XVIII–XXI. Vatican City: Typis Polyglottis Vaticanis.
——. 1986. *Duns Scotus on the Will and Morality*, trs. Allan B. Wolter. Washington, D.C.: Catholic University of America Press.
——. 1993. *Ordinatio* IV, d. 45, q. 3. In Wolter and Adams (1993).
——. 1997. *Quaestiones in Metaphysicam* (= *QMet.*). In *Opera Philosophica* III and IV. St. Bonaventure, NY: The Franciscan Institute.
——. 2005. *Reportatio* I–A. Prologus. In Klaus Rodler. *Die Prologe der Reportata Parisiensia des Johannes Duns Scotus: Untersuchungen zur Textüberlieferung und kritische Edition.* Innsbruck: Studia.
al-Farabi. 1938. *Risāla Fī al-ʿaql* [*Letter on the Intellect*], ed. M. Bouyges, Bibliotheca Arabica Scholasticorum. Série arabe 8.1. Beirut: Imprimerie catholique.

——. 1985. *Mabādi' arā' ahl al-madīna al-fāḍila* [*On the Perfect State*] ed. and tr. R. Walzer. Oxford: Clarendon Press.
al-Ghazālī: Lohr, Charles H. 1965. "*Logica Algazelis*: Introduction and Critical Text." *Traditio* 21: 223–90.
Giles of Rome. 1966. *Quodlibeta*, ed. Petrus Damasius de Coninck. Frankfurt a. M.: Minerva. (Original work published 1646.)
Guillelmus Ockham (*See* Ockham, William.)
Gundissalinus, Dominicus. 1903. *De divisione philosophiae*, ed. Ludwig Baur. Beiträge zur *Geschichte der Philosophie des Mittelalters* 4. Munster: Aschendorff.
Hilary of Poitiers. 1979. *De Trinitate* 1, ed. P. Smulders. Corpus Christianorum Series Latina 62. Turnhout: Brepols.
——. 1999. *Hilaire de Poitiers: La Trinité*, eds. Michael Figura et al. Sources Chrétiennes no. 443. Paris: Editions du Cerf.
Hugh of St Victor. 1939. *Didascalicon*, ed. C. H. Buttimer. Washington, D.C.: Catholic University of America Press.
Isaac Albalag. 1973. *Tiqqun ha-De'ot*, ed. G. Vajda. Jerusalem: Israel Academy of Sciences and Humanities.
John of St. Thomas. 1933. *Cursus Philosophicus*, vol. 1, ed. B. Reiser. O. S. B. Turin: Marietti.
Kilwardby, Robert. 1976. *De ortu scientiarum*, ed. Judy G. Albert. London and Toronto: British Academy-Pontifical Institute of Medieval Studies.
McGinnis, Jon and David C. Reisman, eds. and trs. 2007. *Classical Arabic Philosophy: An Anthology of Sources*. Indianapolis: Hackett.
Maimonides, Moses. 1872. *More Nĕbukim* [Hebrew trslation of the *Guide of the Perplexed*] with Commentaries of Ephodi, Shem Tob ben Joseph ibn Shem Tob, Asher Crescas, and Isaac Abrabanel. Warsaw: Goldman.
——. 1912. *The Eight Chapters of Maimonides on Ethics*, ed. and tr. Joseph Gorfinkle. New York: Columbia University Press.
——. 1962. *The Book of Knowledge*, ed. and tr. M. Hyamson. Jerusalem: Boys Town.
——. 1963. *Guide of the Perplexed*, trstr. Shlomo Pines. Chicago: University of Chicago Press.
——. 1964. *Dux seu director dubitantium aut perplexorum*, ed. A. Giustiani. Frankfurt: Minerva. (Original work published 1520.)
——. 1975. *Ethical Writings of Maimonides*, eds. R. L. Weiss and C. Butterworth. New York: New York University Press.
Migne, Jacques-Paul, ed. 1844–1855; 1862–65. *Patrologia Latina*. 221 vols. Paris: Imprimerie Catholique.
Moses of Narboni. 1852. *Commentary on the Guide of the Perplexed*, ed. J. Goldenthal. Vienna: K. K. Hof- und Staatsdrukerei.
Neusner, Jacob. 1985. *Genesis Rabbah: The Judaic Commentary to the Book of Genesis*. Volume I Chico, CA: Scholars Press, 33
Ockham, William. 1967–1988. *Opera philosophica et theologica*, ed. Gedeon Gál *et al.* 17 vols. St. Bonaventure, NY: The Franciscan Institute.
——. 1967–1979. *Scriptum in primum librum Sententiarum*. In *Opera Theologica* I–IV. St. Bonaventure, NY: The Franciscan Institute.
——. 1980. *Quodlibeta*. In *Opera Theologica* IX. St. Bonaventure, NY: The Franciscan Institute.
——. 1981. *Quaestiones in secundum librum Sententiarum*. In *Opera Theologica* V. St. Bonaventure, NY: The Franciscan Institute.
Pascal, Blaise. 1961. *Pensées*, tr. J. M. Cohen. Hammondsworth: Penguin.
Priscian. 1981. *Institutionum grammaticarum libri XVIII*, ed. Martin Hertz. In *Grammatici Latini*, volumes 2 and 3, ed. Heinrich Keil. Hildesheim and New York: Georg Olms. (Original work published 1855.)
Raymundus Martinus. 1967. *Pugio Fidei adversus Mauros et Judaeos*, ed. Joseph de Voisin. Farnborough: Gregg. (Original work published 1587).
Richard of St. Victor. 1958. *De Trinitate*, ed. Jean Ribaillier. Textes Philosophique du Moyen Age. Paris: Vrin.

Spinoza, Baruch. 1951. *A Theologico-Political Treatise*, tr. R. H. M. Elwes. New York: Dover.
Thomas Aquinas. 1852–1873. *Opera omnia*. Parma: Petrus Fiaccodorus.
——. 1882–. *Opera omnia*. Rome: Commissio Leonina.
——. 1964. *In Decem Libros Ethicorum Aristotelis ad Nicomachum Expositio*, ed. R. M. Spiazzi. Turin: Marietti.
——. 1961–1967. *Liber de Veritate Catholicae Fidei contra Errores Infidelium seu Summa contra Gentiles*, ed. Ceslao Pera, Pierre Marc, and Pietro Carmello. Turin-Paris: Marietti-Lethielleux.
——. 1999. *Somme contre les Gentils*, trs. Vincent Aubin, Cyrille Michon, and Denis Moreau. 4 vols. Paris: GF Flammarion.
——. 2001. *The* De malo *of Thomas Aquinas*, ed. Brian Davies, tr. Richard Regan. Oxford: Oxford University Press.
William of Auvergne. 1963. *Opera omnia*. Frankfurt: Minerva. (Original work published 1674.)

Index